Reference Work in the University Library

Reference Work
in the University Library

Rolland E. Stevens
Professor Emeritus
Graduate School of Library and Information Science
University of Illinois

Linda C. Smith
Associate Professor
Graduate School of Library and Information Science
University of Illinois

1986

Libraries Unlimited   Littleton, Colorado

LIBRARIES UNLIMITED, INC.
P.O. Box 263
Littleton, Colorado 80160-0263

Library of Congress Cataloging-in-Publication Data

Stevens, Rolland Elwell, 1915-
    Reference work in the university library.

    Includes index.
    1. Libraries, University and college--Reference
services. 2. Reference services (Libraries) I. Smith,
Linda C. II. Title.
Z675.U5S75 1986   025.5'2777   86-173
ISBN 0-87287-449-4

Libraries Unlimited books are bound with Type II nonwoven material that meets and exceeds
National Association of State Textbook Administrators' Type II nonwoven material
specifications Class A through E.

CONTENTS

Preface xv

Section 1
Reference Strategies

1 — Reference Service in the University Library 3

2 — Bibliographic Questions 9
  Current Publications 12
    United States 13
    Other Countries 14
  Earlier Publications 14
    United States 15
  Society Publications 16
  Conference Proceedings 17
  Dissertations 18
  Journal Articles 19
  Government Publications 21
    United States 22
    State Government 24
    Local Government 24
    Foreign Countries 24
    United Nations 25
    League of Nations 26
  Other Strategies for Bibliographic Identification 26

3 — Directory Information...28
    Government 29
    Associations 31
    Research Grants..32
    Libraries and Information Centers..............................33
    Publishers 34
    Guides to Directories..35
    Telephone Directories..35

4 — Biographical Information..36
    Current Biography..37
    Retrospective Biography..40
    Credibility and Selectivity....................................43

5 — Statistical Questions..45
    Compilations of Statistics.....................................46
    Indexes to Statistics..48

6 — Book Reviews...49

7 — Bibliographic Instruction......................................52
    Methods and Materials of Bibliographic Instruction.............52
    Planning, Implementing, and Evaluating
            Bibliographic Instruction Programs.....................54
    Bibliographies, Periodicals....................................55
    Handbooks, Textbooks...55

8 — Online Searching...57
    Reference Applications of Online Searching.....................58
    Reference Interview in Online Searching........................58
    Databases as Information Resources.............................58
        Search Strategies..59
    Management Aspects of Online Searching.........................60
    Bibliographies, Periodicals....................................60
    Handbooks, Textbooks...62

Section 2
Reference Sources

Introduction 67

9 – The Humanities 69
    Guides, Bibliographies, Indexes 69
    Conference Proceedings 71
    Grants 72
    Biography 72

10 – Philosophy, Religion, Mythology 73
    PHILOSOPHY 75
        Guides, Bibliographies, Indexes 75
        Dictionaries, Encyclopedias 77
        Directories 78
        Handbooks 78
        Reference Histories 79
    RELIGION 79
        Guides, Bibliographies, Indexes 79
        Dictionaries, Encyclopedias 81
            Christianity 81
            Judaism 83
            Other Religions 83
        Directories 84
        Handbooks 85
        Biography 86
        Religion in the United States and Canada 87
        The Bible 87
            Dictionaries 88
            Concordances 88
            Commentaries 89
            Atlases 90
    MYTHOLOGY 90

11 – Literature 92
    Guides, Bibliographies, Indexes 93
        Special Periods 96
        Special Genres 97
        Anonymous and Pseudonymous Publications 97
        Review of Research 98
        Literary Manuscripts 98
    Dictionaries, Encyclopedias 99
    Directories 101
    Handbooks 101
    Reference Histories 103
    Biography 104

11 — Literature (*continued*)

    Summaries of Literary Works..106

    Literary Criticism...107

    Foreign Literature in English...110

12 — Music 112

    Guides, Bibliographies, Indexes...114

    Dictionaries, Encyclopedias...116

    Directories 117

    Handbooks 117

    Reference Histories..118

    Biography 118

    Guides to Performance Music...120

    Thematic Dictionaries..120

    Opera 121

    Recordings 122

    Popular Music and Songs..123

13 — Fine and Applied Arts...127

    Guides, Bibliographies, Indexes...128

    Dictionaries, Encyclopedias...131

    Directories 133

    Handbooks 134

    Reference Histories..134

    Biography 135

    Art Reproductions...137

14 — Performing Arts..139

    Guides, Bibliographies, Indexes...141

    Dictionaries, Encyclopedias...144

    Directories 146

    Handbooks 146

    Reference Histories..150

    Biography 151

    Films, Plays, Radio and Television Programs.............................153

        Films 153

        Plays 155

        Radio and Television Programs.....................................157

    Reviews of Films, Plays, and Television Programs........................158

15 — Social Sciences..161

    Guides, Bibliographies, Indexes...161

    Dictionaries, Encyclopedias...163

    Conference Proceedings...164

    Biography 164

16 — Education, Psychology..165

   EDUCATION..166

      Guides, Bibliographies, Indexes......................................166

      Dictionaries, Encyclopedias...167

      Education Directories...168

      Guides to Schools and Colleges....................................170

      Statistics...172

      Research...173

      Biography..173

      Ratings of Colleges and College Programs...........................174

      Tests..175

      Scholarships, Fellowships..176

      Certification..176

      Occupation and Career Guidance...................................176

      Study Abroad...177

   PSYCHOLOGY...178

      Guides, Bibliographies, Indexes......................................178

      Dictionaries, Encyclopedias...179

      Handbooks, Reviews..180

      Biography..181

17 — Sociology, Social Work...182

      Guides, Bibliographies, Indexes......................................183

      Dictionaries, Encyclopedias...186

      Directories...187

      Statistical and Other Data..190

      Biography..193

18 — Anthropology..194

      Guides, Bibliographies, Indexes......................................194

      Dictionaries, Encyclopedias...198

      Directories...201

      Handbooks...201

      Research...203

      Biography..204

19 — Business, Economics...205

      Guides, Bibliographies, Indexes......................................206

      Dictionaries, Encyclopedias...209

      Directories...211

      Handbooks...213

      Statistics...214

      Atlases..216

      Biography..217

      Sources on Industries and Companies...............................217

19 – Business, Economics (*continued*)

    Investment Guides 219

    Government Finance and Taxes 220

20 – Political Science, Law 222

    POLITICAL SCIENCE 222

        Guides, Bibliographies, Indexes 222

        Dictionaries, Encyclopedias 224

        Biography 225

        United States Government 226

            Congress 226

            Executive Branch 227

            Supreme Court 228

        State Government 229

        Local Government 229

        Women in Government 230

        Political Behavior and Public Opinion 230

        International Affairs and Comparative Government 232

        Governments of Other Countries 234

    LAW 236

        Guides, Bibliographies, Indexes 236

        Dictionaries, Encyclopedias 237

        Directories 238

        Official Texts 238

        Biography 240

21 – History, Geography 241

    HISTORY 242

        Guides, Bibliographies, Indexes 242

        Dictionaries, Encyclopedias 244

        Directories 247

        Handbooks 247

        Atlases 249

        Statistics 249

        Reference Histories 250

        Biography 250

        United States 251

            Guides, Bibliographies, Indexes 251

            Dictionaries, Encyclopedias 252

            Handbooks 253

            Atlases 254

            Statistics 254

        Other Countries 255

21 — History, Geography (*continued*)
GEOGRAPHY 255
    Guides, Bibliographies, Indexes 255
    Dictionaries, Encyclopedias 256
    Directories 258
    Handbooks 258
    Atlases, Gazetteers 258
    Biography 259

22 — The Sciences 261
    Guides, Bibliographies, Indexes 263
        Guides 263
        Indexes 266
        Bibliographies 268
    Conferences and Conference Proceedings 268
    Translations 270
    Dictionaries, Encyclopedias 271
    Directories 274
    Handbooks 275
    Biography 276

23 — Mathematics 280
    Guides, Bibliographies, Indexes 280
    Dictionaries, Encyclopedias 282
    Handbooks, Tables 284
    Biography 285

24 — Astronomy, Physics 286
    ASTRONOMY 287
    Guides, Bibliographies, Indexes 287
    Dictionaries, Encyclopedias 288
    Handbooks 289
    Atlases 290
    PHYSICS 290
    Guides, Bibliographies, Indexes 290
    Dictionaries, Encyclopedias 292
    Directories 293
    Handbooks 294
    Biography 294

25 — Chemistry 295
    Guides, Bibliographies, Indexes 296
    Dictionaries, Encyclopedias 299
    Directories 302
    Handbooks 302
    Biography 304

26 — **Earth Sciences** 306
    Guides, Bibliographies, Indexes 307
    Dictionaries, Encyclopedias 308
    Directories 312
    Handbooks 312
    Atlases 314
    Biography 314

27 — **Environmental Sciences, Energy** 316
  ENVIRONMENTAL SCIENCES 317
    Guides, Bibliographies, Indexes 317
    Dictionaries, Encyclopedias 319
    Directories 320
    Handbooks 321
  ENERGY 321
    Guides, Bibliographies, Indexes 321
    Dictionaries, Encyclopedias 324
    Directories 324
    Handbooks 325
    Atlases 326
    Biography 326

28 — **Biological Sciences, Agriculture** 327
  BIOLOGICAL SCIENCES 328
    Guides, Bibliographies, Indexes 328
    Dictionaries, Encyclopedias 331
    Directories 335
    Handbooks 335
    Biography 337
  AGRICULTURE 337
    Guides, Bibliographies, Indexes 337
    Dictionaries, Encyclopedias 339
    Directories 341
    Handbooks 341
    Biography 342

29 — **Medical Sciences** 343
    Guides, Bibliographies, Indexes 344
    Dictionaries, Encyclopedias 350
    Directories 352
    Handbooks 353
    Biography 354

30 — Computer Science. 355
    Guides, Bibliographies, Indexes. 356
    Dictionaries, Encyclopedias. 358
    Directories 360
    Handbooks 361

31 — Engineering 362
    Guides, Bibliographies, Indexes. 363
    Dictionaries, Encyclopedias. 366
    Directories 367
    Handbooks. 367
    Biographies 369

    Author/Title Index. 371
    Subject Index. 431

PREFACE

Our purpose in writing this book is similar to that which inspired Rolland E. Stevens and Joan M. Walton in writing a companion book, *Reference Work in the Public Library* (Libraries Unlimited, 1983): to provide practical instruction to library school students and others in the type of reference work typically done in the university library. As in the case of the companion work, no other book has been published that treats reference work in the university library so specifically and that contrasts such reference work with that done in libraries of other types.

The several major classes of users of the university library are described here, as are the types of reference needs most associated with each class. It will be evident throughout this book that most reference needs by far in the university library are associated either with curricular interests of students and faculty or with research interests of faculty, graduate students, and others, and it is these needs to which we pay particular attention in the following chapters.

It is not our intent to give introductory instruction in reference work but, rather, to assume that the student or librarian is already familiar with the use of standard bibliographies, periodical indexes, and other basic reference works. Furthermore, some reference needs of students, faculty, and administrators have no connection with either course work, research, or administrative needs, and these, relatively few, are adequately covered in *Reference Work in the Public Library*.

The several chapters in section 1, "Reference Strategies," describe some of the most common reference needs of the different user groups and how these can be handled, depending on the amount of information provided by the questioner. Strategies are discussed, beginning, usually, with those offering the best chance of success and followed by other methods that can be tried if the initial trials are not successful. General reference sources found useful for these different types of reference questions are also described in these chapters. Some of these titles are repeated under a different entry number in a later chapter, if they are useful for reference work in a specific discipline. In these instances, the value of the work in the discipline is described, instead of its use illustrating a particular type of question, as in the earlier listing in section 1. Several chapters in section 1 describe reference work in the university library in its general aspects.

Section 2, "Reference Sources," describes the major reference tools associated with specific disciplines and their use. In each of these chapters, the most common types of reference questions asked by the several user groups are discussed. Within these chapters, reference sources are grouped under standard types, such as "Guides, Bibliographies, Indexes," "Dictionaries, Encyclopedias," "Directories," "Handbooks." Each reference tool has been classified by the content and the use ordinarily made of it rather than by the presence in its title of a word like *"guide," "dictionary,"* or *"handbook."* Within type, we have not followed an alphabetical arrangement of titles, but, rather, an order based on usefulness: the most general and frequently consulted works followed by more specialized, less-often-used tools. Besides standard types of reference works, there are also subdivisions in the chapters on topics peculiar to a discipline, such as "Literary Criticism," "The Bible," "Scholarships, Fellowships," or "Governments of Other Countries," when these have been deemed important enough to warrant a special subdivision.

In trying to write a book of practical use to students and librarians, we have been selective with respect both to subjects and reference needs within subjects and to reference sources described. We have concentrated on those subjects and types of questions that are treated most often in university reference work. Limiting our discussion to the works we consider to be most important in reference work has been difficult, but we felt that to be less selective would detract from the usefulness of the book. Where special needs call for reference sources not included here, the reader can consult specialized guides that are more comprehensive such as A. Robert Rogers's *The Humanities* (2d ed., Libraries Unlimited, 1979), Carl M. White's *Sources of Information in the Social Sciences* (2d ed., American Library Association, 1973), Margaret C. Patterson's *Literary Research Guide* (2d ed., Modern Language Association of America, 1983) or H. Robert Malinowsky and Jeanne M. Richardson's *Science and Engineering Literature* (3d ed., Libraries Unlimited, 1980).

Our description of sources is based on personal examination and evaluation rather than on the opinions of reviewers, which can be uneven and of doubtful reliability. We have occasionally cited an old reference work which needs revision, where nothing has been published to replace it; if such a source is used with caution, it can provide information not found elsewhere. Even a "vanity" who's who may furnish data on a person who is not listed in the more selective biographical sources. Citations are as complete as possible. For open entries, beginning date and frequency of publication are given; for single volume monographs, pagination is given.

Acknowledging the help of the many librarians who have assisted us in writing this book is like making an acceptance speech upon receiving an Academy Award: no matter how many individuals are singled out for special mention, some who may have been of equal help are certain to be omitted. Understanding this risk, we nevertheless want to name the following persons, all at the University of Illinois, who have assisted us by reading chapters and giving specific advice: Lori Arp, Karen Bingham, Karen Chapman, Constance Fairchild, Frank Itzin, Martha Landis, Linda Main, Nancy O'Brien, Gene Rinkel, and Sharon Van der Laan. Many other librarians at the University of Illinois have also been of help, and to them, too, we are grateful.

Section 1
REFERENCE STRATEGIES

1

REFERENCE SERVICE IN THE UNIVERSITY LIBRARY

The nature of the reference service needed in and provided by a library depends on the type of library, its general purposes, users, geographical location, relationship to other libraries in its region, and similar factors. The four main types of libraries—public, academic, school, and special—present different mixtures of these factors and therefore have different kinds of reference service, although the similarities among them are more apparent than their differences. The public library is the most general of the four types, serving a user population of widely disparate ages, educational backgrounds, and interests. Its collection and the questions it typically receives reflect the broad, popular, practical reference needs of this heterogeneous population. The special library serves the smallest and most homogeneous user population, whether this population consists of engineers, insurance agents, lawyers, theologians, or some other industrial or professional group. Its collection and reference service are, therefore, directed to a limited subject field and a relatively narrow range in the educational background of its users. Because of these limits and the fact that it is usually well staffed compared to the number of users, the special library is able to offer much more service than other types of libraries can, notably maintaining special files of data useful to its users, abstracting books and articles in the collection, and routing journals to users with articles marked of particular interest to them. The reference service in the special library is almost wholly related to the research or professional interests of its users.

Between the extremes of the public and the special library lie both the school library and the academic library. The user population of the former includes elementary and secondary level students and faculty, and its reference service reflects curricular interests, kindergarten through 12th grade. The latter type includes libraries of community colleges, four-year colleges, and universities. The community college follows closely on the secondary school, but, in addition to recent high school graduates, who may or may not intend to continue on to a four-year college, it also serves those students seeking vocational training and adult learners returning to continue their education or to pursue only one or two courses in a practical or academic field of interest. Besides the academic subjects taught in a secondary school or four-year college, the community college offers many vocational subjects not available in other types of institutions. In its breadth of interest and variety of users, it is closer to a public library than is either the school library or the university library. University libraries and research libraries, most of which are attached to universities, not only support curricular needs, which other academic libraries share, but also support research needs of faculty, graduate students, and others. This greatly increases the size and depth of the collection needed and makes demands on the reference staff, which are not present in the other types of libraries. The reference service provided in the university/research library is almost wholly related either to the academic curriculum or to the professional research needs of the users with relatively little attention to practical, non-curricular interests of either students or faculty.

These differences in the reference service provided in the different types of libraries also effect differences in the training and skills needed in the reference staff. In the university/research library and in the special library, the reference staff will need more advanced education; many university/research libraries give preference to applicants who have a subject master's degree in addition to a master's degree in library science. In the ideal case, expertise in a range of subjects would be divided among the staff: at least one person should have scientific/technical background to balance the humanities/arts and the social science interests of other staff members, at least one should have extensive knowledge of U.S. government publications and their reference use, and at least one should have facility in online searching. If more than one member has these uncommon strengths, so much the better. The ability to handle foreign languages, especially German and French, is needed, if only to read bibliographic data and make some sense out of an encyclopedia article. Although these are the requirements in university/research libraries and, to a limited degree, in many special libraries, they are not required in the public, school, or community college library, where support of research is not the main role.

The differences in the nature of reference service in the several types of libraries also dictate differences in the reference collection. More than public or school libraries, the university library will need many scholarly works, bibliographies and large library catalogs, abstract indexes, bibliographies of conference proceedings, specialized encyclopedias and dictionaries, statistical compilations, parliamentary and congressional debates and other government publications, and various other reference works to support research. Many of these works will be in languages other than English. Some of the best and most learned encyclopedias and bibliographies continue to be produced by German scholars and scientists. And, while German and French were traditionally considered to be, along with English, the languages of learning, Russian is now equally important, especially in the sciences. The largest universities support area studies and research, notably for Eastern Europe, the Far East, Southeast Asia, the Middle East, Africa, and Latin America. Each of these departments has its own reference collection and staff capable of reading and using reference materials in the appropriate languages.

The user population of the university library may be divided into several groups, chiefly undergraduate students, graduate students, and faculty. The predominant reference needs of these three groups show clear differences, but for all three groups the needs are related to curricular or research interests. The differences are thus dependent on the educational level of the groups, not on differences in subject interests. The types of reference needs described below are not limited to one or another group, but they are identifiable with one group.

Most of the reference needs of undergraduates are related to class assignments, reports, and term papers. These will include using the library catalog and the periodical indexes to collect references for a paper or report, finding a particular book, article, or book review, and finding a statistic, date, formula, or other specific detail. Bibliographic instruction and help in using reference sources are needed for this group more than for the other groups. Since undergraduates are likely to be reticent about asking the librarian for help, it is important to anticipate their reference needs and to be perceptive about the individual appearing to encounter difficulty using the reference collection or the catalog.

The predominant reference needs of graduate students are similar to those of undergraduates but usually on a more advanced level. Graduates also have class assignments, reports, and papers to prepare. Although they often need help in finding the data they require or need bibliographic instruction, especially in the indexes in their field of specialization, they are often reluctant about seeking help from the librarian because they think they are expected to know the literature of their field. Even some faculty members are hesitant about asking for help, either from misplaced pride or embarrassment at not knowing the literature better. Tact and sensitivity to these feelings are needed to put users at ease while helping them. A fundamental rule of reference service is that all questions deserve serious treatment, none are trivial, and the librarian never feels superior to the questioner. Part of the requirement for an advanced degree is usually some original research and a thesis or dissertation. At this stage, the reference needs of graduate students more closely resemble those of the faculty.

Faculty members usually do not need help in their own subject field. Their most common reference needs are of the bibliographic and directory types. When a member of the faculty comes to the reference desk, it is most often for help in identifying and completing a bibliographic reference found as an incorrect or incomplete footnote or a partially remembered reference from a conference, earlier reading, or other source. Some bibliographic questions involve government publications, unpublished papers, or articles from fugitive publications, which the faculty member could not find by looking in standard bibliographies. The staff may be asked to find a specific title in the library catalog, which the faculty member knows of and believes to be in the library but cannot locate in the catalog. Cataloging and filing rules are often complicated and not according to "normal" usage and expectations, despite the contrary claims of many catalogers. This may present a problem to the user, especially in a very large university library. Even a knowledgeable and persistent scholar may not be able to find an entry in the catalog for a work she or he is sure the library owns. The introduction in many universities of the online catalog to replace or supplement the card catalog solves many of these problems but introduces others. In dealing with online problems, the librarian has recognized expertise, even from faculty members who have extensive bibliographic knowledge and experience in their own field. Another type of question most frequently asked by faculty members is the directory question. Most often, the address or telephone number of a publisher is needed. Directory questions also frequently involve government offices, universities, and learned societies. Statistical information is a third type of reference need of the faculty group. International comparative statistics, as well as those concerning the United States, are often wanted. The address, and sometimes biographical data, about other scholars are also frequently requested.

Beyond these predominant types of reference questions, all three user groups have a wide variety of reference needs related to either curricular or research interests. These include such things as a plot summary of a book, the release date or the cast of a film of some earlier year, the composition of a foreign legislative body, or identification of a musical theme.

Two smaller groups of university library users may be identified, but these overlap partially with the three principal groups just described. The administrators of the university constitute one group: the president, chancellors, assistant chancellors, deans, department heads, registrar, and others. Although administrators are often also members of the faculty, their duties usually leave them little or no time for teaching and research. Nevertheless, they have many reference needs related to their administrative work. Most of these are of the directory and statistical types and for government regulations. Directory needs are typically for the address or telephone number of an administrator or faculty member of another university, an educational association, foundation, government agency, or publisher. Statistical needs are various: educational, demographic, financial, economic, etc. The other user group may, for want of another label, be called "the public." This group includes persons in the community who are not directly associated with the university, business firms, government and private agencies, and libraries, which use the university library because of its special and research collections. This group also includes students, faculty members, and administrators of the university when they have reference needs not related to their study, teaching, research, or administrative work: questions that have arisen from their reading, discussion, hobby, travel, or general interest.

In contrast to the reference questions normally asked in the university library, those typically reaching the public library have to do with practical, day-to-day matters: a culinary recipe, specifications and diagrams for the disassembly and re-assembly of an automobile transmission, the current and recent dividends and sale price of a particular stock issue, identification and value of a cut glass pitcher of a particular pattern, or instructions for playing an outdoor game.

In the organization and location of any reference service, these factors must be considered: easy and inviting access to the service by the user (including members of the library staff other than the reference librarians), easy access to the library catalog, the circulating collection, and the documents collection by the reference librarians, and the expertise of members of the reference staff. Unfortunately, these factors do not complement one another in pointing to a single location.

In the average university library, reference service is not handicapped by inadequate information sources or by inadequate knowledge and skill of the librarians so much as by lack of awareness by potential users of what the library can provide. Better awareness can be promoted, in part, by locating the reference service in an open, inviting part of the library, close to the main entrance. It is also desirable that the reference desk be close to the library catalog, not only because it is often necessary to check the library catalog for a book that seems to be a possible source of needed information, but also because a user will frequently call to ask if a library has a particular book. This problem of proximity has been almost eliminated in libraries that have gone online with the catalog and have provided computer terminals at the reference desk. A related problem is the provision of staff to help bewildered students and other users of the catalog, whether this is a card catalog or an online catalog. Such staff members are often part of the reference department and give service from an "information desk" situated at the catalog.

Some librarians are of the opinion that the reference department should also be close to the circulating collection since it is sometimes necessary to find a book in the collection in order to answer a question. For example, a quotation from Robert Burns that has not been found in one of the general quotation dictionaries will be found in a Robert Burns concordance. In some libraries, this problem is solved by dividing reference service into subject groups and having the question involving modern languages or political science answered in a modern language reading room or a political science reading room where reference books as well as circulating books are in the care of a librarian with background in the subject. But this solution has the obvious disadvantage for the occasional user, who may not know where to take a reference problem. A library can maintain a general reference room in a central location in addition to the departmental reference/reading rooms. Many ready reference or simple questions in modern languages, political science, or other subjects could be answered in the general reference room, and more difficult questions referred to the appropriate departmental reference/reading room.

Another popular organization of reference service is to have a separate undergraduate library with its own reference section separate from the general reference department. Undergraduates, however, can be served in the general reference department, and graduate students, faculty, and others in the undergraduate library, insofar as the reference resources permit, when these users find themselves in libraries other than their own.

One aspect of reference service that creates an organizational problem in the university library is the disposition of government publications, mainly those of the federal government but also, to a lesser degree, those of the United Nations and its agencies and those of the states. Government publications are needed much more in the university library than in the public library, where the problem of where to house them is not so great. Desirable as it is to catalog and classify government publications and integrate them into the rest of the collection, the quantity of federal documents and the fact that they are already cataloged and classified by the Superintendent of Documents cause most university libraries to utilize the Superintendent of Documents classification (SuDocs) and to maintain a separate documents collection. The importance of government publications in reference work supports the argument for locating the documents collection, or at least the catalogs, codes of regulations, and other reference sources, near the reference department and providing the collection with its own reference staff.

The growing importance in university reference work of machine searching of specialized databases and bibliographic collections suggests the locating of computer terminals in or adjacent to the central reference department with staff trained to interview the user and to conduct online searches. This aspect of reference service is further elaborated in chapter 8.

In the reference room itself are kept as many bibliographies, encyclopedias, directories, handbooks, and other frequently needed reference tools as shelf space will permit. Next to the reference desk itself are kept a few (to a few hundred) of the most used books, such as *Statistical Abstract of the United States* and *Encyclopedia of Associations*, where they are accessible for answering telephone or in-person questions. What to keep in this prime location, culled from the rest of the collection, must be based on local need and will change from time to time as new reference books are acquired and as the local need changes. The whole reference collection, as well as the ready reference collection, needs to be weeded at regular intervals. New reference books and sets are acquired, and some of the less often used works must be retired from time to time to the circulating collection or to a storage area. For the usually overworked staff, weeding the collection is not a high priority task and tends to be put off. But keeping the collection to a moderate size is necessary, not only because the space is limited, but also because a collection containing only those works that are consulted, say, no less than once in two years is more efficient to use. Examination of the whole collection and retiring works and sets that are never used should be undertaken every other year or oftener. If a set is retired to a lower priority area and later found to be needed, it can be brought back to the reference collection.

Differences in reference service in the typical university library and the typical public library have already been noted. These differences result mainly from their different missions and from the different clienteles they serve. Since education is a primary mission of the university, it may be expected that instruction in the use of periodical indexes and other reference tools will be emphasized much more in the university library than in other types of libraries. Bibliographic instruction is discussed in chapter 7. Reference service in the university library is further differentiated from that in the public and school library by the sophistication and bibliographic knowledge of a large segment of its users: graduate students, faculty, and administrators. The first two groups prefer to do much of their own reference work. Administrators do not because of lack of time and because most of their reference needs (directory, statistical, and biographical questions) are straightforward and easy to communicate by telephone. In contrast, many of the reference problems of the faculty and graduate students have to do with technical aspects of their research, things which they can look up for themselves more easily than explaining the background of the problem to the librarian. These would include, for example, rather complicated and extensive economic or sociological statistics, congressional actions, historical or biographical background, technical or philosophical definitions, sometimes a lengthy article in German or other language. It is not so much a lack of confidence in the ability of the librarian, but rather a preference to do one's own searching because the parameters of the search change as new discoveries are made during the search. This preference by users to do their own reference work is not so common in the public library.

When assistance is required of the reference librarian, it may frequently be in a field in which the librarian has little background. The interview with the user about his or her reference need may fill in background about the subject for the librarian, while clarifying what the user's need actually is. In answering the reference question, the search will sometimes lead to a bibliography, encyclopedia, or other work in a foreign language. The reference collection of a university library will include a number of such books for which there is no equal in English. *Allgemeines Lexikon der bildenden Künstler*, by Thieme and Becker (entry 554), *Theologische Realenzyklopädie in Gemeinschaft* (entry 275), and *Enciclopedia dello Spettacolo* (entry 595) are examples of excellent works for which there is no counterpart in English. Among the skills and training recommended above for librarians who seek reference positions in the university was a knowledge of foreign languages, particularly German and French. If the librarian has even a beginning grasp of these languages, it is possible to make some sense out of an encyclopedia, or biographical, article not only in German or French, but even one in Dutch, Swedish, Norwegian, Italian, Spanish, or another Germanic or Romance language. A background in Latin is also helpful when guessing the meaning of a passage written in a Romance language. If the questioner being helped knows the language of the article or of a related Germanic or Romance language, he or she may be able to translate the article or at least assist. But even without any training in the language in question or without the help of the questioner, the librarian should scan the article and get what is possible from it. The words or abbreviations before dates in a biographical article can be deduced to be "born" or "died." The word or words for the biographee's profession or nationality can usually be guessed (e.g., Poeta romanziere, librettista, autore dramm. russo, Scenografo francese, Sculpteur, Peintre et architecte, Landschaftsmaler, Silberarbeiter, Filosofo greco, Historiker, Missionar). Statistics can easily be noted and their significance guessed. Many words, especially in French, Italian, and Spanish, are similar to the equivalent English word or to the Latin cognate. German is not so easy for one who has had no previous acquaintance with it. But a person with a basic knowledge of German can guess at much in Dutch, Swedish, Norwegian, or Danish. The main point is to try. If the librarian approaches an article with confidence, high motivation, and a desire to get as much as possible from it, the results will usually be of some value.

This brings us to a final point about reference service. It is a challenge, not a chore, not an eight-to-five job. Every question is interesting; every questioner needs the best help we can give. A reference librarian gets tired and maybe a little grouchy at the end of an active period of desk duty. Schedules for work at the desk are usually two hours, not more than three during the evening, because one does get tired in that time if the traffic is heavy. But it is important that the librarian always gives the most sincerely interested attention to each reference question and a serious and competent effort to its solution. Our attitude should invite and encourage use of the reference service by students and faculty. Our biggest problem is getting people to know and remember how much and how often the reference librarian can help with information needs.

2

BIBLIOGRAPHIC QUESTIONS

The basic technique of answering reference questions – conducting the initial interview with the user, making preliminary guesses, modifying and restricting the search, and clarifying what the user really needs as one proceeds – is already so thoroughly written up in the literature and should be so well understood by the library school student and the practicing librarian that there is no need to expand on it here. We have already noted that most of the reference questions reaching the university library are related either to the research needs of the faculty and the advanced students or to the preparation of course material, the completion of class assignments, the creation of reports and term papers, and other curricular needs. Certain types of reference problems, which may not be very common in the public library, predominate in the average university library: effecting bibliographic verification and completion of bibliographic references, locating directory information of certain kinds, finding certain statistical data, locating federal government reports and data, and assisting in finding appropriate material for term papers. To a lesser extent, there are needs for biographical information, background and general information on a topic, book reviews, and plot summaries, as well as other more or less standard reference needs. It is these issues that are most common in the university library to which we give attention in this section, discussing reference strategies, methods of handling, and sources of needed information that do not pertain specifically to a single discipline or subject field. Sources identified include those available online through either commercial search systems (e.g., BRS and DIALOG) or bibliographic utilities (e.g., OCLC and RLIN). Characteristics of these systems and techniques for searching them are described in more detail in chapter 8, "Online Searching."

Bibliographic questions have two goals: (1) the identification of a footnote or reference found in an article or book but not located in the library catalog or in a bibliography, (2) the completion of the imprint or other part of an incomplete reference. Such questions most often come from members of the faculty and from graduate students working on their dissertations or other research. Clues like the nature of the work (monograph, periodical article, ephemeral pamphlet, unpublished dissertation, etc.), the language, and the known or presumed country and date of publication will direct the librarian to appropriate bibliographies for the initial search. Different bibliographies are used for works in different formats, published in different countries and at different dates. Here is a sampling of partial references to illustrate how the effort to complete a bibliographic citation can be restricted and speeded up by judicial guessing about the publication format, country, and date:

Heilprin, Max. *Thistle as Winter Feed.* Aberdeen Stock Association, 1974.

Possibly a pamphlet of restricted circulation. The question is, where is the Association located, Aberdeen, S.D., or Aberdeen, Scotland? Identification of the association is a first step.

Danton, L. "Thoracolysis Procedures." VII, 318-34.

Seems to be an article in a volume of a medical or surgical work, of which neither title nor editor is given. Best bet would be to identify the author and get further data on place and date, possibly a reference to the work in which this article is found.

Darlan, Thomas. "Effect of Interrupted Rest on Students' Examination Scores."

Could be an article in an educational journal, a research report, or possibly an unpublished dissertation. Best bet might be to search indexes of articles and reports of educational research.

"An Investigation into Charges of Irregularities during the Chicago Mayoral Contest of 1928."

Lack of an author's name might indicate a newspaper article or possibly an official government report, but the date and place give a start for searching newspaper files.

Nygren, Anton. "A Note on the genus Pyrrhuloxia."

Seems to be an article or minor contribution in a scientific journal or publication. Start by identifying Pyrrhuloxia as to subject field, then looking through appropriate journal indexes.

Animadversions on Mr. Royce's Discourse at St. Albans.

Wording and lack of author's name point to an anonymous tract published in England a century or more ago. First step, check *British Museum Catalogue*; if not there, try to identify Mr. Royce of St. Albans for date, then check appropriate bibliographies of British history.

Thornton, E. M. "Apollo and Terpsichore." *Leeds Arch. Notes.* 1912.

Begin by checking *Union List of Serials* for *Leeds Arch. Notes* for location of a file.

Another aid to deciding where the search should begin is the circumstance in which the reference was located. Was it in a footnote in a work the user was consulting? The date of the work sets a *terminus ante quem* for the footnote, and the subject of the text in which the footnote occurred further limits places to search. An incomplete footnote can usually be completed by referring to an earlier reference in the work or to the full entry in the bibliography; while this would seldom create a problem for the user, it might puzzle an unsophisticated student.

Usually there will be something in the reference that will indicate whether the item being sought is likely to be a book, a pamphlet, an article, or other form of publication, some clue as to the time and country of publication, the subject of the work, or other data that will help in deciding where to begin the search. There are various approaches to a bibliographic search. If an author is named, the search under that name is usually easier than one under title or subject. Studies have shown that scholars and research workers typically prefer an author search, believing that it offers the surest and quickest way of identifying a particular bibliographic item, whether in the library catalog or in a bibliography. Lacking any clues, one might infer that the item is a monograph and begin the search in *National Union Catalog* under author. This will offer the best blind, or shotgun, approach when format, date, place, and publisher are all unknown. Begin with *Pre-1956 Imprints* and work up through the latest five-year cumulation.

1. **National Union Catalog: Pre-1956 Imprints.** 754 vols. London: Mansell, 1968-81.

2. **National Union Catalog: A Cumulative Author List.** Washington, D.C.: Library of Congress, 1956- . Monthly with quarterly, annual, and 5-year cumulations.

The former set lists the cataloged holdings of the Library of Congress, regardless of place and date of publication of the items cataloged, if published before 1956. The cataloged monographic holdings of many other major libraries of the United States are also included either totally or selectively. Periodical titles are included only if cataloged by the Library of Congress. Most other entries are under author only, but there are cross-references from an anonymous title or an incorrect form of the author's name to the entry used. The post-1956 set lists locations of cataloged items in more than 750 libraries in the United States besides the Library of Congress. Together, these make up the most comprehensive bibliography in existence. Except in searching for titles known to have been published in recent months, it is the first place to look for a book from any country. There are also separate catalogs of music scores and recordings and of films and filmstrips and a separate subject catalog, but these are not used as often as the above in bibliographic identification.

After 1982 the *National Union Catalog* for books cataloged by the Library of Congress and other major libraries contributing cataloging copy is no longer published In book form; it is issued monthly on microfiche, cumulating each month for the year from January, and is called the Register. The full bibliographic record is given under register number in the Register. There are four indexes to the Register, which give abbreviated catalog information and the register number: Name Index (authors, joint authors, and others for which an added entry has been made), Title Index, LC Series Index, and LC Subject Index. Also issued on microfiche instead of in book format after 1982 are sections of the *National Union Catalog* for U.S. books, audiovisual materials, and cartographic materials. Each of these sections also has a Register and indexes of names, titles, series, and subjects. *National Union Catalog, Register of Additional Locations* (NUC RAL) is also issued on microfiche. At the present time, *Music, Books on Music, and Sound Recordings* continues to be published in book format, as do *National Union Catalog of Manuscript Collections* and *New Serial Titles.*

The searching of books cataloged by the Library of Congress is greatly simplified in those libraries that have computer terminals at or near the reference desk. LC MARC and REMARC are two databases providing complete bibliographic records of these books which can be machine searched through DIALOG. Although these databases have only books cataloged by the Library of Congress and do not have the many additional books for which cataloging copy is sent to the *National Union Catalog* by other major contributing libraries, it is easy to start a search with them without leaving the reference desk.

If such a preliminary search through *National Union Catalog* has not been successful, it may be advisable to verify the name for correct spelling before thrashing about in less comprehensive bibliographies. If the author's name is not readily found, possible alternate spelling should be tried, or the search may be continued in biographical dictionaries. What is given as *Smith* might actually be *Schmidt, Brown* might be *Braun, Stevens* might be *Stephens* or *Stevenson.* Until the name has been verified and, preferably, associated with the subject field of the reference being sought, continued search under the name is chancy. However, the name may have been found in the search through *National Union Catalog.* If so, or if found in a subsequent search through other sources, there will usually be clues to the person's dates, country, subject field(s), institutional affiliation, and other data that may help restrict and speed up the bibliographic search.

Another preliminary search method available in some large libraries that have computer terminals available at the reference desk is to search through bibliographic utilities like OCLC (Online Computer Library Center), RLIN (Research Libraries Information Network), WLN (Western Library Network), etc. These services, to which many university libraries belong, were designed originally for shared cataloging. But since they offer access to millions of bibliographic records, both from their original database, and from additions over the years they have been operating, they have been found to be valuable in bibliographic ver-ification problems, especially for publications of the past 10 or 15 years. OCLC, which began in 1967 and contains MARC records since 1968, the Minnesota Union List of Serials, the University of Pennsylvania serial record, cataloging records from more than 2,500 participating libraries, and other bibliographic records, now has data on more than nine million books, serials, manuscripts, maps, media materials, scores, sound recordings, etc. These can be accessed by author, other personal or corporate name, title, and author-title. Full data are given in MARC-tagged format. RLIN has over seven million bibliographic records including those in BALLOTS (a program developed by Stanford University in the late 1960s for use in acquisition and cataloging), MARC since 1968, and records from various cooperating member libraries for books, serials, maps, films, scores, recordings, and other formats. It is especially suited to the needs of research libraries and was designed for use by RLG (Research Libraries Group). It offers more different points of access than OCLC, including personal name, title phrase, title word, corporate/conference word or phrase, subject phrase, LC card number, and ISBN.[1]

Machine searching of these utilities may be especially useful when there is no clue as to date, place, or format of publication or no author's name. The databases include records for many formats not often included in printed catalogs and bibliographies: manuscripts, media materials, scores, recordings, maps, and government publications. They also offer many points of access besides the main author entry, which often is the only access point in large catalogs and bibliographies. And, if location of a copy is needed for borrowing, one or more participating libraries which have the item are usually indicated.

It is very unlikely that neither the bibliographic data given nor anything provided by the user about the source of the data nor anything discovered during the preliminary search suggested above will help in determining the next steps to take. If the unlikely does occur one would select one of the procedures described below for special kinds of search. Our predilection, lacking any kind of restricting clue, would be to first continue the search through current volumes and issues of *National Union Catalog* and the other bibliographies and lists of current and forthcoming publications, and then continue to look for information about the author, or, if no name is provided, change to a subject approach.

CURRENT PUBLICATIONS

The bibliographic data at hand might include a publication date of a recent year or the current year. Or the person who has brought the question to the library may have information suggesting that the item is a recent or new publication. Even lacking such strong clues of recency, the search should be continued in bibliographies of books published recently or books announced but not yet published if the author is still living. Unless there is information suggesting a place of publication other than the United States, the first place to check would be the volumes and issues of the *National Union Catalog* since the last five-year cumulation (entries 1 and 2) and the various bibliographies listed below under "United States." If a country other than the United States is indicated, the search following the checking of recent volumes and issues of *National Union Catalog* would be in the bibliographies of current publications of that country. If the indication of another country is merely the name of the author (e.g., Giuseppi Sabatini or Klaus von Schade) or the language of the title, the search would lead to bibliographies of the several countries using that language (e.g., for French or a French sounding author's name: France, Belgium, Switzerland, some former colonies of France in Africa or Asia).

---

[1]Julia E. Miller, "OCLC and RLIN as Reference Tools," *Journal of Academic Librarianship* 8 (November 1982): 270-77; Judith B. Droessler and Julia M. Rholes, "Online Services at the Reference Desk: DIALOG, RLIN, and OCLC," *Online* 7, No. 6 (November 1983): 79-86.

United States

3. **Cumulative Book Index.** New York: Wilson, 1898- . Monthly, with quarterly, annual, and 5-year cumulations.

4. **Weekly Record.** New York: Bowker, 1974- . Weekly.

5. **American Book Publishing Record.** New York: Bowker, 1961- . Monthly, with annual cumulations.

6. **Books in Print.** New York: Bowker, 1948- . Annual.

7. **Subject Guide to Books in Print.** New York: Bowker, 1957- . Annual.

8. **Paperbound Books in Print.** New York: Bowker, 1955- . Semiannual.

9. **Forthcoming Books.** New York: Bowker, 1966- . Bimonthly.

10. **Subject Guide to Forthcoming Books.** New York: Bowker, 1967- . Bimonthly.

11. **Publishers' Trade List Annual.** New York: Bowker, 1873- . Annual.

Cumulative Book Index attempts to record all books (of 50 pages or more) in the English language, regardless of their place of publication. Many titles, however, especially revised editions and ephemeral publications, are not picked up, and new titles may not be listed until several months after publication. Nevertheless, it remains the most complete bibliography of current English-language publications and is the one used most frequently, except for publications of the last several months. Approach may be by author, title, or subject. The recent volumes of *Cumulative Book Index* can now be machine searched through Wilsonline. *Weekly Record* and *Forthcoming Books* are less complete but are needed for new and expected publications that have not yet been listed in *Cumulative Book Index*. Generally they will list only trade publications in the United States and foreign publications distributed by U.S. publishers. Approach in *Weekly Record* is by author only. The two series for *Forthcoming Books* offer author, title, and subject approach. *American Book Publishing Record* cumulates titles from *Weekly Record* (formerly from the weekly lists in *Publishers Weekly*) and gives them in Dewey classification order. It is not used for bibliographic identification or verification, but will show what titles have been issued by U.S. trade publishers over a selected period in a given subject. *Books in Print, Subject Guide to Books in Print*, and *Paperbound Books in Print* are not restricted to new books, but list all books reported by U.S. trade publishers and distributors of foreign publications as being "in print," i.e., available from their stock. Although these are favorite bibliographic tools in public libraries and community college libraries, they are not generally used in bibliographic verification problems; they are used for determining if an older publication is still in print and its current price. They are compiled from listings sent in by publishers and contain many errors. New printings are often listed without distinguishing them from new editions, and new books of publishers who do not report to *Books in Print* are not indexed. Despite these shortcomings, *Books in Print* is so much faster to consult than *Cumulative Book Index* that it may be tried first. Approach is by author, title, or subject. *Books in Print* can be machine searched through BRS and DIALOG. The online version includes data from *Forthcoming Books* and *Paperbound Books in Print* as well as *Books in Print*. *Publishers' Trade List Annual* is a collection of the catalogs and lists of certain publishers. It is occasionally needed for the current list of a publisher.

Other Countries

For the bibliographies of current publications of countries other than the United States, consult Eugene Sheehy's *Guide to Reference Books* (9th ed., 1976, and supplements) and Walford's *Guide to Reference Material* (3d ed., Vol. 3. 1977). Both guides have excellent explanatory notes about the scope, arrangement, and use of the standard bibliographies of major publishing countries.

EARLIER PUBLICATIONS

When an older publication is being sought, one normally checks the *National Union Catalog: Pre-1956 Imprints* and the succeeding five-year cumulations of the *National Union Catalog* (see entries 1 and 2). Another useful printed catalog for earlier publications is

12. **Dictionary Catalog of the Research Libraries of the New York Public Library, 1911-1971.** 800 vols. New York: The New York Public Library, Astor, Lenox, and Tilden Foundations; printed and distributed by G. K. Hall, 1979.

Or, one might search OCLC, RLIN, or one of the other bibliographic utilities discussed above. If these steps have not been successful and if there is knowledge or suspicion that the book was published in Great Britain or in another European country, one or both of the following national library catalogs should be checked, especially if the date and country of publication are unknown.

13. British Museum. **General Catalogue of Printed Books.** 263 vols. London: The Trustees of the British Museum, 1965-66. Supplements, 1956-65; 1966-70; 1971-75; and 1976-82.

This edition and its supplements are being replaced by

14. The British Library. **General Catalogue of Printed Books to 1975.** London: Bingley, 1979- . In progress.

15. Paris. Bibliothèque Nationale. **Catalogue générale des livres imprimés. Auteurs.** 231 vols. Paris: Imprimerie Nationale, 1879-1981.

This catalog was so long in progress that a cut-off date of 1960 was adopted for the final volumes. A supplement listing books printed 1960-1969 is now nearly complete.

Like the *National Union Catalog* and the *Dictionary Catalog of the Research Libraries of the New York Public Library, 1911-1971*, these three resources include cataloged books in the library, regardless of when or where they were published and are valuable sources for bibliographic identification when these data are not known. Except for the *Dictionary Catalog of the Research Libraries of the New York Public Library*, however, they list items only under their cataloged entry.

Searching these mammoth catalogs and bibliographic utilities like OCLC and RLIN are shortcuts when the date, place, or format are not known. Certain publications, however, may not have been included in these catalogs or utilities because of their ephemeral character, their lack of importance, the failure of a copy to survive, or other cause. All major publishing countries have various national, trade, or other bibliographies that list all books known to have been published in the country from the earliest time. Some of these also include books about the country or books in the language of the country published elsewhere. Those for the United States are listed here. Since the search for a bibliographic entry not yet found and lacking a date of publication would normally proceed backwards, these bibliographies are listed by period covered from recent to earlier years. Those for other countries can be found in the guides to reference books by Sheehy and Walford. Many of these offer approaches other than, or in addition to, the main entry approach.

United States

16. **Cumulative Book Index.** New York: Wilson, 1898- . Monthly with quarterly, annual, and 5-year cumulations.

Author-title-subject dictionary approach.

17. **American Catalogue.** New York: Publishers' Weekly, 1880-1911.

Lists books published between 1876 and 1910. Author-title approach. Subject index.

18. **American Book Publishing Record, Cumulative 1876-1949.** 15 vols. New York: Bowker, 1980.

Classified approach by Dewey Decimal System. Separate indexes, vols. 13-15, for authors, titles, and subjects.

19. **American Book Publishing Record, Cumulative 1950-1977.** 15 vols. New York: Bowker, 1978.

Classified approach by Dewey Decimal System. Separate indexes, vols. 13-15, for authors, titles, and subjects.

20. Kelly, James. **American Catalogue of Books ... January 1861 to January 1871 ...** 2 vols. New York: Wiley, 1866-71.

This is especially good for pamphlets and ephemera published during the Civil War period. Author-title approach.

21. Roorbach, Orville. **Bibliotheca Americana.** 4 vols. New York: Roorbach, 1852-61.

Covers 1820 up to the date of publication. Author-title approach.

22. Shoemaker, Richard A., and others. **A Checklist of American Imprints, 1820- .** Metuchen, N.J.: Scarecrow, 1964- .

These volumes, each covering one year, are much more complete than the preceding title. Main entry approach in each volume; cumulative indexes of authors and titles, 1820-1829.

23. Shaw, Ralph, and Richard Shoemaker. **American Bibliography: A Preliminary Checklist.** 22 vols. Metuchen, N.J.: Scarecrow, 1958-65.

This set covers the period 1801-1819, the time between Evans's *American Bibliography* and Roorbach's *Bibliotheca Americana*. Each volume covers one year. Main entry approach.

24. Evans, Charles. **American Bibliography ... 1639 Down to and Including the Year 1800.** 14 vols. Chicago: Printed for the Author by the Columbia Press, 1903-36. Vol. 13 (1799-1800) edited by Clifford Shipton. Vol. 14 (author-title index) by Roger Bristol. Vols. 13-14, Worcester, Mass.: American Antiquarian Society, 1955-56. Reprint. New York: Peter Smith, 1941-67.

Chronological approach. Author-title index.

25. Shipton, Clifford. **National Index of American Imprints through 1800: The Short Title Evans.** 2 vols. Worcester, Mass.: American Antiquarian Society, 1969.

This work revises the preceding bibliography, eliminates "ghosts" (titles which were never published, although taken by Evans from announcements and advertisements), and adds many titles which Evans had missed. Main entry approach.

26. Sabin, Joseph. **Dictionary of Books Relating to America from Its Discovery to the Present Time.** 29 vols. New York: Sabin, 1868-92; Bibliographical Society of America, 1928-36. Reprint (29 vols. in 2). Metuchen, N.J.: Scarecrow, 1966.

27. **Author-Title Index to Joseph Sabin's Dictionary of Books Relating to America.** Compiled by John E. Molnar. 3 vols. Metuchen, N.J.: Scarecrow, 1974.

28. Thompson, Lawrence S. **The New Sabin: Books Described by Joseph Sabin and His Successors, Now Described Again on the Basis of Examination of the Originals and Fully Indexed by Title, Subject, Joint Authors, and Institutions and Agencies.** Troy, N.Y.: Whitston, 1974- . In progress.

SOCIETY PUBLICATIONS

A type of bibliographic reference that is difficult to identify but that occurs often enough to be treated here is the citation to a minor publication of an association or society or to some similar item of restricted circulation. These are published as separates, but are too small and of too limited interest to be included in the trade or national bibliography. An example of this type of publication is the note on some local historical event or discovery appearing in a historical/archaeological county society of Great Britain. Another example would be a political or religious tract of eighteenth or nineteenth century Great Britain or America. Yet another would be a technical or instructional pamphlet issued by an industrial firm, an agricultural society, a naturalist group, etc. Those that are believed to have been published some years ago can sometimes be identified in the *National Union Catalog*, the *General Catalogue* of the British Museum, the *Catalogue generale* of the Bibliotheque Nationale, or the early trade and national bibliographies. If not found in one of these general sources, they might be found in a special bibliography of the following type.

Catalogue of the Pamphlets, Books, Newspapers, and Manuscripts Relating to the Civil War ... Collected by George Thomason, 1640-1661. 2 vols. London: Trustees of the British Museum, 1908. (Usually referred to as the Thomason Tracts.)

Bibliotheca Cisorientalia: An Annotated Checklist of Early English Travel Books on the Near and Middle East. Compiled by R. Bevis. Boston: G. K. Hall, 1973.

LeGrand, Leon. *Les Sources de l'histoire religieuse de la révolution.* Paris: Champion, 1914.

Such special bibliographies, of which these are only examples, can sometimes be located by consulting Sheehy's *Guide to Reference Books* or Walford's *Guide to Reference Material.* Another good lead to such special bibliographies is

29. Besterman, Theodore. **A World Bibliography of Bibliographies.** 4th ed. 5 vols. Lausanne: Societas Bibliographica, 1965-66. Supplement, 1964-74 compiled by Alice F. Toomey. 2 vols. Totowa, N.J.: Rowman & Littlefield, 1977.

The printed catalog of a library or collection on a specialized subject also offers hope of identifying a minor or ephemeral publication that has so far eluded identification. Many such special library catalogs have been published in recent years and can be found through

30. Nelson, Bonnie R. **A Guide to Published Library Catalogs.** Metuchen, N.J.: Scarecrow, 1982. 342p.

If the publication is a recent one, the following series is useful.

31. **Associations' Publications in Print.** 2 vols. New York: Bowker, 1981- . Annual.

The first volume each year is a subject index to the publications of some 3,600 national, state, regional, local, and trade associations of the United States and Canada. Volume 2 has indexes to the publications by title, publisher/title, associations, acronyms of associations, and publisher/distributor. It can be machine searched through BRS.

CONFERENCE PROCEEDINGS

Another type of bibliographic reference that may be difficult to track down is the paper given as part of a scientific or other scholarly conference. These also turn up frequently as footnotes and references found in faculty research or as a note (often only partly correct) passed on orally from one research worker to another. The currency of such papers, at the cutting edge of new research, makes them particularly valuable to the scientist and, at the same time, difficult to identify. If the conference at which the paper was given is known, the published proceedings of that conference can be identified through one of the following series.

32. **Bibliographic Guide to Conference Publications.** 2 vols. Boston: G. K. Hall, 1976- . Annual.

33. **Directory of Published Proceedings.** Harrison, N.Y.: InterDok. **Series SEMT** (Science, engineering, medicine, technology), 1965- . Monthly Sept.-June with annual cumulation. **Series SSH** (Social sciences, humanities), 1968- . Quarterly with annual cumulation.

The *Directory of Published Proceedings* is often called InterDok after its publisher. (Included in chapter 9 as entry 225, in chapter 15 as entry 704, and in chapter 22 as entry 1235.)

34. **Proceedings in Print.** Arlington, Mass.: Proceedings in Print, 1964- . Bimonthly with annual cumulation.

These bibliographies list only the conferences with place, date, and their published proceedings. They do not detail the individual papers. The following series do, however, index the individual papers given at the conferences.

35. **Conference Papers Index: Life Sciences, Physical Sciences, Engineering.** Bethesda, Md.: Cambridge Scientific Abstracts, 1978- . Vol. 6- . Monthly with annual cumulation.

Earlier title, *Current Programs.* (Included in chapter 22 as entry 1234.)

36. **Index to Scientific and Technical Proceedings.** Philadelphia: Institute for Scientific Information, 1978- . Monthly with annual cumulation. (Included in chapter 22 as entry 1236.)

37. **Index to Social Sciences and Humanities Proceedings.** Philadelphia: Institute for Scientific Information, 1979- . Quarterly with annual cumulation.

(Included in chapter 9 as entry 226 and in chapter 15 as entry 705.)

38. **BLL Conference Index, 1964-1973.** Boston Spa, England: British Library Lending Division, 1974. 1220p. **BLL Conference Index, 1974-1978.** Boston Spa, England: British Library Lending Division, 1980. Continued by **Index of Conference Proceedings Received.** Boston Spa, England: British Library Lending Division, 1966- . Monthly with annual and 5-year cumulations.

Conference Papers Index, which can be machine searched through DIALOG, includes conference papers which were not published, as well as those in published proceedings. The other indexes include only the papers in published proceedings. Besides their use in bibliographic identification of the papers indexed, they are sometimes consulted merely to establish the date and place in which a conference was held. Although they duplicate one another to a large degree, several of them should be in a good university collection. Most questions about conference papers involve those of current or recent conferences. If a problem about an older conference arises, the following bibliography may be consulted.

39. Gregory, Winifred, ed. **International Congresses and Conferences, 1840-1937: A Union List of Their Publications Available in Libraries of the United States and Canada.** New York: Wilson, 1938. 2290p.

This compilation of an estimated 7,500 congresses and conferences was prepared under the auspices of the Bibliographical Society of America. International congresses and conferences are listed by title under the Library of Congress catalog entry with the place and year and the title of any published proceedings. There is a subject index to the congresses and conferences, but individual papers are not indexed.

DISSERTATIONS

Since doctoral dissertations represent original research, they are often wanted by faculty members and others engaged in research, and, since they are usually not published, they are not included in the types of bibliographies described above. Most often, dissertations of American universities are needed, especially by doctoral students preparing their own dissertations. Both Germany and France have long issued excellent annual lists of dissertations and theses accepted by their universities, and these, too, are sometimes needed in tracking down an elusive footnote or bibliographic reference.

40. **Comprehensive Dissertation Index, 1861-1972.** 37 vols. Ann Arbor, Mich.: Xerox University Microfilms, 1973.

41. **Dissertation Abstracts International.** Ann Arbor, Mich.: University Microfilms, 1938- . Monthly.

These are the indexes used most often. The first has the time-saving advantage of bringing together all dissertations accepted by universities in the United States for the earned doctorate since 1861. Under broad discipline groupings (e.g., chemistry, mathematics and statistics, education, business and economics), dissertations are listed alphabetically by all significant keywords of their title, thus providing a subject index. After 1972 the basic set is updated by annual supplements. Both the basic set and the annual supplements also have a combined author index for dissertations in all subject fields. *Dissertation Abstracts International* (earlier titles: *Dissertation Abstracts, Microfilm Abstracts*) is slower to search unless the year of the dissertation is known. It does include dissertations accepted at a number of foreign universities and abstracts the dissertations. DISSERTATION ABSTRACTS ONLINE, which can be machine searched through BRS and DIALOG, has all of the keyword titles in *Comprehensive Dissertation Index* going back to 1861, plus the abstracts in *Dissertation Abstracts International* since 1980.

42. France. Direction des Bibliothèques de France. **Catalogue des thèses de doctorat soutenue devant les universités françaises, 1884/85- .** Paris, 1885- . Annual.

43. **Jahresverzeichnis der deutschen Hochschulschriften, 1885- .** Leipzig: VEB Verlag für Buch- und Bibliothekswesen, 1887- . Annual.

44. **Deutsche Bibliographie: Hochschulschriften-Verzeichnis.** Frankfurt am Main: Buchhändler-Vereinigung GMBH, 1972- . Monthly.

45. Aslib. **Index to Theses Accepted for Higher Degrees in the Universities of Great Britain and Ireland.** London: Aslib, 1953- .

If a citation is known or believed to refer to a dissertation or thesis but cannot be found in the indexes listed above, you may be able to try a more specific list by consulting the following book.

46. Reynolds, Michael M. **A Guide to Theses and Dissertations: An Annotated International Bibliography of Bibliographies.** Detroit: Gale, 1975. 599p.

This includes an estimated 2,000 lists of dissertations and theses. The lists, which are annotated, are grouped by nation and by individual subject field. Masters' theses are seldom cited in research publications but, if the citation may refer to a thesis, an appropriate list of masters' theses included in the preceding guide can be checked.

JOURNAL ARTICLES

The incomplete footnote that needs identification is often a citation to an article in a journal, newspaper, or other serial. The citation may include the abbreviated journal or newspaper title, which the user has been unable to identify. The first part of the reference search for such a citation, then, is to identify the journal or other publication in order to see if the article has indeed appeared there. For such identification, the following sources are most often used.

47. **Periodical Title Abbreviations.** 4th ed. Compiled and edited by Leland G. Alkire, Jr. 3 vols. Detroit: Gale, 1983.

If the citation gives only initials or other abbreviation of the journal title, making it not readily identifiable, one might try this directory, which lists more than 55,000 periodicals, journals, and other serials under the abbreviations commonly used for them. Volume 2 lists the same items under title and gives the abbreviation(s) by which they are known. By and large, these are periodicals and journals that are currently published, and no data about them are given except title and abbreviation. If the journal cannot be identified through this work or if additional data are wanted, check the following.

48. **Union List of Serials in Libraries of the United States and Canada.** 3d ed. Edited by Edna Brown Titus. 5 vols. New York: Wilson, 1965.

For identification of a periodical published in any country any time before 1950, the *Union List of Serials* is the most complete source. It excludes government documents, newspapers, conference proceedings, almanacs, law reports, house organs, and other types of serials that are ephemeral or of limited circulation.

49. **New Serial Titles.** Washington, D.C.: Library of Congress, 1953- . Monthly with quarterly and annual cumulations; cumulations for 1950-1970, 1971-1975, and 1976-1980.

Serials that began publication after 1950, except newspapers, looseleafs, municipal government documents, and certain other categories, are listed in this bibliography. At the end of the 1950-1970 and later cumulations, a section, "Changes in Serials," lists title changes, cessations, suspensions, and similar changes, but neither changes in frequency of publication nor of price. Both *Union List of Serials* and *New Serial Titles* give locations in more than 900 libraries of the United States and Canada, making them useful for interlibrary loan as well as for bibliographic checking. These two sources are the most comprehensive bibliographies of serials published before or after 1950, respectively. But the following are easier for currently published serials and, although more selective, might be checked first.

50.   **Standard Periodical Directory.** 9th ed., 1985-1986. New York: Oxbridge, 1985. 1452p.

51.   **Ulrich's International Periodicals Directory: A Classified Guide to Current Periodicals, Foreign and Domestic.** New York: Bowker, 1932- . Annual.

52.   **Irregular Serials and Annuals: An International Directory.** New York: Bowker, 1967- . Biennial.

More than 60,000 periodicals currently published in the United States or Canada are listed under small subject categories in *Standard Periodical Directory. Ulrich's International Periodicals Directory* is similar, but includes many periodicals published in countries other than the United States and Canada; it currently lists under broad subject about 65,000 periodicals published regularly twice a year or more frequently. For the United States and Canada however *Standard Periodical Directory* has more entries. *Irregular Serials and Annuals* (currently listing about 35,000 titles) does the same thing for serials that appear at irregular intervals or less than twice a year. All three of these directories give various data about the periodicals listed, such as beginning date, frequency, cost, etc., and have an alphabetical index of titles. As noted above, these are too selective to make them ideal for bibliographic identification, particularly for obscure and ephemeral serials, but they can be checked quickly and are almost always kept close to the reference desk in the ready reference collection. The data from *Ulrich's International Periodicals Directory* and *Irregular Serials and Annuals* are combined in the ULRICH'S INTERNATIONAL PERIODICALS DIRECTORY database, which can be machine searched through BRS and DIALOG.

None of the sources described above includes newspapers. Sleuthing for the title or bibliographic data about a newspaper occurs much less frequently than searching other formats for information. Below are the standard sources for bibliographic data on newspapers.

53.   Gregory, Winifred, ed. **American Newspapers, 1821-1935: A Union List of Files Available in the United States and Canada.** New York: Wilson, 1937. Reprint. New York: Kraus, 1967. 791p.

This standard bibliography serves a function for newspapers similar to that which the *Union List of Serials* does for serials. Arrangement, as in Ayer's directory (see entry 56) and in the following lists, is by state and city. Data include dates of beginning, suspension, and cessation, title changes, frequency, and location of files.

54.   Brigham, Clarence S. **History and Bibliography of American Newspapers, 1690-1820.** 2 vols. Worcester, Mass.: American Antiquarian Society, 1947. Reprint. Hamden, Conn.: Archon, 1962; Westport, Conn.: Greenwood, 1976.

Files are also located in this work for 2,120 older newspapers, arranged by state and city.

55.   **Newspapers in Microform, 1948-1972.** 2 vols. Washington, D.C.: Library of Congress, 1973. Annual supplements, 1975- .

Most United States newspapers and many of those published in other countries have by now been microfilmed. This register of microform copies of 34,289 U.S. newspapers and 8,620 foreign papers, therefore, serves as a very complete bibliography. Dates and title changes are given. Since the other newspaper lists described above include only newspapers of the United States and Canada, this is useful for the major papers of other countries, microform copies of which are held by libraries in this country. Supplements register microform copies made since publication of the basic list.

56. **IMS/Ayer Directory of Publications.** Fort Washington, Penn.: IMS Press, 1869- . Annual.

Currently published newspapers and periodicals published in the United States, Canada, Puerto Rico, Virgin Islands, Bahamas, Bermuda, and the Philippines are listed under state and city. The directory is aimed at the potential advertiser, and the data given for each publication include circulation, format, and similar information of interest for advertisers. It is less useful for bibliographic verification than other directories described in this section.

If the journal has been successfully identified, but the article is not in the volume on the pages given in the citation, it would be worthwhile to try other volumes and pages of the journal before starting on the more difficult task of identifying the article itself. Or, is there another journal with a similar title that might be the journal in which the article was published? If these attempts are not successful, or if no reference was given to a journal or newspaper title, it will be necessary to search for the article itself in a periodical or abstract index. The broad subject area of the article will indicate the appropriate indexes in which to begin such a search. If the subject field is not readily identifiable from the title of the article, the librarian should begin by establishing it, rather than blindly searching through one periodical index after another. If the author has been identified, the subject field in which he or she has previously written will offer a good clue. The periodical and abstract indexes in various subject fields found to be most useful in reference work are described in the chapters on individual disciplines in the second section of this book. Most of these indexes offer author and subject approaches that will be useful when the bibliographic data at hand are incomplete or suspect. The main obstacle in this type of search is the great number of volumes of any given index that must be searched if the date of publication is not known. In several disciplines (history, sociology, political science), there is now available a computer-produced "combined retrospective index set" (C.R.I.S.) that simplifies the search for an older periodical article. Because databases often cover many years of an index and can be searched using keywords from the title as well as by subject and author, it may be more efficient to search online rather than going through volumes of the printed counterpart year by year. However, few databases go back earlier than 1970, so printed indexes must still be used for older articles.

GOVERNMENT PUBLICATIONS

Something in the wording of a title may suggest that the item is an official government publication. Or, the search for information about the author may have revealed that he or she was long associated with a government department. Government documents are often not included in the standard national and trade bibliographies, special subject bibliographies, or library catalogs. Special lists and bibliographies of these official publications must be used.

In this chapter, we are addressing ourselves only to the problem of identifying or completing a reference to a government document, which might have been found in a footnote, bibliography, or other printed source or might have been obtained verbally from another person or partially remembered from a previous use. The problem of locating government publications pertinent to a particular subject or need (e.g., for a report or term paper) can be satisfied through a guide like Ellen Jackson's *Subject Guide to Major United States Government Publications* (Chicago: American Library Association, 1968), or W. Philip Leidy's *A Popular Guide to Government Publications* (4th ed. New York: Columbia University Press, 1976), or by using the subject index to *Monthly Catalog of United States Government Publications* (entry 58).

The best discussion and bibliography of bibliographies and lists of official publications of the United States, other countries, and intergovernmental organizations is

57. Palic, Vladimir M. **Government Publications: A Guide to Bibliographic Tools.** 4th ed. Washington, D.C.: Library of Congress, 1975. 441p.

The reader is referred to this work for bibliographies of the publications of the United States federal, state, or local governments, the United Nations, the League of Nations, foreign governments, and other governmental bodies not treated here.

In the bibliographic identification of a public, or government, document or of a publication that is suspected to be a public document, the first order of business is to establish the country, the level of government, and the department, agency, commission, or other issuing body. Determining the country or narrowing the possibilities to several countries is the easiest of these initial decisions. If the country is not named, the language of the title and possibly the wording of the title will furnish clues. If the level of government (national, state or province, county, municipality, etc.) and the department or agency are not named, there may be a suggestion in the title that will at least narrow the possibilities. If the name of the author, compiler, or other person having some responsibility for the document is given, trace this person through such sources as government directories (see entries 85-90), *Who's Who in Government* (entry 1014), *Who's Who in American Politics* (entry 1013), etc. If no personal name is available, the subject matter indicated in the title may offer clues about the department of government (e.g., agriculture, commerce, weather bureau). It is helpful to know the date or approximate date. Is the publication current or recent? If not, approximately how long ago was it issued? Current government publications are frequently wanted by scientists, engineers, economists, political scientists, and sociologists. References to older documents are usually brought in by faculty and graduate students doing research in history.

United States

Official publications of the United States government are asked for most often. This is fortunate, since the coverage, at least of current publications, is more complete than that for any other country.

58. U.S. Superintendent of Documents. **Monthly Catalog of United States Government Publications.** Washington, D.C.: Government Printing Office, 1895- . Monthly.

Arranged by SuDocs number; indexes by personal/corporate author, title, subject, series/report, contract number, stock number, and title keyword.

59. **CIS/Index.** Washington, D.C.: Congressional Information Service, 1970- . Monthly with quarterly and annual cumulations.

Arranged by accession number of document; indexed by personal name, report number, and subject.

The *Monthly Catalog* is the official list of United States publications cataloged by the Superintendent of Documents or other government agencies. It can be machine searched back to 1976 through BRS and DIALOG. All publications of Congress (reports, documents, hearings, committee prints) are listed and abstracted in the excellent *CIS/Index*. It can be machine searched through DIALOG and SDC back to 1970.

60. U.S. Superintendent of Documents. **Catalog of the Public Documents of Congress and of All Departments of the Government of the United States, Mar. 4, 1893/June 30, 1895-Jan. 1, 1939/Dec. 31, 1940.** Washington, D.C.: Government Printing Office, 1896-1945. Biennial.

Dictionary arrangement by author, subject. Usually called *Document Catalog* after its binding title. For older publications (1893-1940), one may fall back on the *Document Catalog*, which is less time-consuming to check than the annual volumes of the *Monthly Catalog* for those years.

61. **Cumulative Subject Index to the Monthly Catalog of U.S. Government Publications, 1900-1971.** Compiled by William W. Buchanan and Edna M. Kanely. 15 vols. Washington, D.C.: Carrollton, 1973-75.

If the search permits or requires a subject approach, this cumulative index is also a time-saver.

62. U.S. Department of the Interior. Division of Documents. **Comprehensive Index to the Publications of the United States Government, 1881-1893.** Compiled by John G. Ames. 2 vols. Washington, D.C.: Government Printing Office, 1905. Reprint. Ann Arbor, Mich.: Edwards, 1953.

Approach by catchword subject; index of personal names.

63. Poore, Benjamin P. **A Descriptive Catalogue of the Government Publications of the United States, Sept. 5, 1774-March 4, 1881.** Washington, D.C.: Government Printing Office, 1885. 1392p. Reprint. Ann Arbor, Mich.: Edwards, 1953; New York: Johnson Reprint, 1962.

Chronological approach; author, subject index. Entries 62 and 63 are the most comprehensive lists of earlier documents. The former (usually referred to simply as *Ames*) is alphabetically arranged under catchword subject with an index of personal names. Poore's catalog is arranged chronologically with an index of personal or corporate authors and subjects.

64. **Popular Names of U.S. Government Reports: A Catalog.** 3d ed. Compiled by Bernard A. Bernier, Jr., Katherine F. Gould, and Porter Humphrey. Washington, D.C.: Library of Congress, 1976. 263p.

Many important government reports become better known by the name of their personal or corporate author or sponsor than by their official name. This valuable list identifies 1,322 government reports under the personal or other name by which they are popularly known. For each report, the official title, a brief description, the departmental or commission source, and the SuDocs number are given.

65. **CIS: U.S. Serial Set Index.** 36 vols. Washington, D.C.: Congressional Information Service, 1975-79.

66. **CIS: U.S. Congressional Committee Hearings Index.** Washington, D.C.: Congressional Information Service, 1981- .

67. **CIS: U.S. Congressional Committee Prints Index from the Earliest Publications through 1969.** 5 vols. Washington, D.C.: Congressional Information Service, 1980.

The Congressional Information Service, a private firm, has greatly improved the chance of finding an older Congressional document with these three cumulated indexes of documents up through 1969. The *Serial Set* is the set of bound volumes containing all reports and documents of the House and Senate. The indexes to hearings in the following set include approach by subject, organization, personal names, including both witnesses and persons about whom the testimony is given, Congressional bill number, SuDocs number, and report or document number. Committee hearings are especially important in research since they include the testimony of witnesses called before various Congressional committees preparatory to the drafting of legislation. Indexed in the third set are congressional prints, papers prepared for Committee hearings; they are also important in research and are often difficult to track down. Neither hearings nor committee prints are included in the *Serial Set.*

68. **Checklist of United States Public Documents, 1789-1975.** Washington, D.C.: United States Historical Documents Institute, 1976. Microfilm.

Another non-official set which makes it easier to identify an older U.S. document is this checklist of all documents that can be found up to 1975 and its 21 volumes of indexes in printed form. The indexes are by title, SuDocs classification number, personal or corporate author, departmental keyword, serial titles, and keyword of issuing office.

State Government

The need for help in identifying a state document is much less frequent than requests to verify federal documents. The best source covering publications of all the states is the following monthly list of state documents received in the Library of Congress.

69.   U.S. Library of Congress. Exchange and Gift Division. **Monthly Checklist of State Publications.** Washington, D.C.: Government Printing Office, 1910- . Monthly.

This lists about 30,000 documents, monograph and serial, per year, estimated to be only a small part of the state documents published. Arrangement is by state, which is usually known. If not, there is an annual subject index, but It is not completed until sometime during the following year. Palic's *Government Publications* (entry 57) gives references to the serial lists which each state issues of its own documents. State documents that are considered to be of social or political interest are included in the following index.

70.   Public Affairs Information Service. **Bulletin.** New York: Public Affairs Information Service, 1915- . Twice per month, with quarterly and annual cumulations.

The *Bulletin*, which is usually called simply *PAIS*, has a subject approach and annual index of authors since 1977. It is part of the *PAIS* INTERNATIONAL database and can be machine searched back to 1976 through BRS and DIALOG. All state documents indexed in *PAIS* are likely to be listed in the *Monthly Checklist of State Publications* prepared in the Library of Congress, but probably several months later. Older state documents might be found in the following bibliography.

71.   Bowker, Richard R., comp. **State Publications: A Provisional List of the Official Publications of the Several States of the United States from Their Organization.** 4 vols. New York: Publishers' Weekly, 1908.

An alternative source for old state and federal documents is the cumulative volumes of *The American Catalogue*, 1884-90 and 1890-95 (entry 17), which list state documents, as well as federal documents, in an appendix.

Local Government

Although the reference librarian is expected to try to solve a reference problem no matter how bleak the outlook, the publication of a local government is almost impossible to locate, especially if it is more than a few years old. Palic does suggest a few sources that can be tried (entry 57, pp. 142-149).

Foreign Countries

Again, the best place to check for the bibliographies and lists of the documents of a foreign government is Palic's *Government Publications* (entry 57, p. 193ff.). The following reference tool is very useful for older serial documents of foreign countries, which are the series most often consulted because they include legislative papers.

72.   **List of the Serial Publications of Foreign Governments, 1815-1931.** Edited by Winifred Gregory for the American Council of Learned Societies, American Library Association, National Research Council. New York: Wilson, 1932. Reprint. New York: Kraus Reprint, 1966. 720p.

This list is modeled on the *Union List of Serials*, giving locations of files of the serial publications in American libraries as well as bibliographic information on changes of title, dates, etc.

73. Public Affairs Information Service. **Foreign Language Index.** New York: Public Affairs Information Service, 1972- . Quarterly with annual cumulation.

The *Foreign Language Index* is also part of the *PAIS* INTERNATIONAL database and can be machine searched back to 1972 through BRS and DIALOG. It is a selection of current foreign documents of social or political interest written in French, German, Italian, Portuguese, or Spanish.

United Nations

Documents of the United Nations and its various specialized organizations, such as UNESCO, UNICEF, and WHO, are sought in frequency second only to those of the United States. There are several indexes of the complex body of these documents. These are listed below, beginning with the current series and continued by the earlier series, since requests for current documents are most common. As in the other parts of this chapter, we are concerned only with the identification of particular documents. Many requests for United Nations documents are not of this type but are for any United Nations material on a particular subject, such as economic conditions in third world countries or human rights.

74. **UNDOC: Current Index. United Nations Documents Index, 1979-** . Monthly except July and August with annual cumulation.

All documents and publications of the United Nations, its several bodies, and specialized agencies are listed by series symbol. The ten monthly lists are cumulated in the annual edition with indexes of subjects, authors (personal, country, and United Nations agency), and title.

75. **UNDEX: United Nations Documents Index.** New York: United Nations, 1970-80. Monthly except July and August.

There are three series of this index. Series A is a subject index, cumulating annually. It gives under each subject heading the classification numbers of pertinent documents. From this number, full bibliographic data can be found in series C, which is a classified checklist of the documents and publications issued during the year. (Series B is an index of member countries, listing under each country the numbers of documents containing information on that country's debating or voting or on other activity in the United Nations; it has no pertinence to the bibliographic problems treated here.) Series A Is cumulated annually. Series C is cumulated for 1974-78 by the following.

76. **UNDEX Series C. Cumulated ed., 1974-1977.** 3 vols. White Plains, N.Y.: UNIFO, 1979.

77. **UNDEX Series C. Cumulated ed., 1978.** White Plains, N.Y.: UNIFO, 1980.

78. **United Nations Documents Index.** New York: United Nations, 1950-73. Monthly.

This index, called *UNDI*, was issued in two parts. Part 1, a subject index to the documents issued each month, cumulated into an annual index. Part 2, the checklist of documents issued during the month, did not have annual cumulations until vol. 14, 1963.

79. **United Nations Documents Index. United Nations and Specialized Agencies Documents and Publications. Cumulated Index, Volumes 1-13, 1950-1962.** 4 vols. New York: Kraus-Thomson, 1974.

The availability of this cumulated index saves the user from searching through the first part of this series, year by year. It is a dictionary (author-title-subject) index. Whether the plan to issue a similar cumulated index for volumes 14-24 will be fulfilled is not known.

80.   **Checklist of United Nations Documents, 1946-49.** New York: United Nations, 1949-53.

This was the initial listing of documents of the United Nations and its agencies. Separate parts of the checklist were issued for the documents of the different bodies and agencies. It has no subject or title index.

League of Nations

The League existed from 1920 until 1947. Its documents are seldom needed today, except by a few faculty members and graduate students in the fields of history or political science. The principal finding lists for its publications are the following.

81.   Aufricht, Hans. **Guide to League of Nations Publications: A Bibliographical Survey of the Work of the League, 1920-1947.** New York: Columbia University Press, 1951. 682p.

For the bibliographic identification of a League document, this one-volume work is the first place to check, although it is selective. It follows a general description of the League and its publication activities with a description and list of its principal documents (its constitution, documents and papers of the Assembly, the Council, and its committees) and its important publications relating to its activities, such as health organization, social and humanitarian problems, economic and financial questions, etc. Publications of the Permanent Court of International Justice, the International Labor Organization, the International Institute of Intellectual Cooperation, and the other autonomous organs are also included. There is an index of subjects but not one of titles.

82.   World Peace Foundation. **Key to League of Nations Documents Placed on Public Sale, 1920-29.** Compiled by Marie J. Carroll. Boston: World Peace Foundation, 1930. Supplements, 1930-36. Boston: World Peace Foundation; New York: Columbia University Press, 1931-38.

If the desired document was not found in Aufricht, this series may be tried since it is more complete. The lists of periodicals and documents of the policy-making bodies of the League are followed by a list of publications in the 13 categories of the classification scheme used by the League, e.g., minorities; health; social questions; legal questions. The subject index for the 1920-29 volume is at the end of the first supplement; it and the other supplements have their own subject indexes.

83.   Reno, Edward A. **League of Nations Documents, 1919-1946: A Descriptive Guide and Key to the Microfilm Collection.** 3 vols. New Haven, Conn.: Research Publications, 1973-75.

The organization of this work is similar to that of the key compiled by Carroll (entry 82). It serves as the printed index to the microfilm collection of League documents made by Research Publications, which is thought to be the most complete collection in the world.

OTHER STRATEGIES FOR
BIBLIOGRAPHIC IDENTIFICATION

There are times when none of the "standard" reference strategies will effect a satisfactory solution. Of course, the librarian should learn to admit that some reference questions are so marred or defective that a solution is not possible. But a good reference librarian will entertain the hope for years that an answer can be found for the unsolved question and will rarely be able to forego trying for an answer whenever a newly discovered reference book or other possible source is at hand.

If all of the previously described methods have failed to turn up the answer to a bibliographic problem, and if a verified author's name is available, there are several more things that can be tried.

84. Arnim, Max. **Internationale Personalbibliographie.** 2. Auflage. Vol. 1- . Leipzig, Stuttgart: Hiersemann, 1944- . In progress.

This work lists bibliographies of the writings of some 90,000 persons of all countries (although the emphasis is on Germany) who lived after 1800. The volumes 1 and 2 include persons who lived up to 1943; volume 3 brings the compilation to 1959, adding some writers before 1943 who were missed in the first volumes. It includes bibliographies or lists of a person's writings which form part of a book or article as well as those published separately. One of these bibliographies may include the title being sought.

Another device is to check any of the author's books that are available. Authors can seldom resist the chance to cite their own writings in their footnotes and bibliographies. Another possibility is that the title being sought is the title of a chapter or separate paper in one of the author's books.

3

DIRECTORY INFORMATION

Another type of reference question that compares in frequency with bibliographic questions in the academic library is the request for directory information. In many libraries, in fact, this will be the type of questions most often asked. Usually these questions do not present any difficulty, and most can be answered within a few minutes. The request for help in identifying or completing a bibliographic reference is normally made to the reference librarian only after the user has tried unsuccessfully to find the title in the library catalog, a bibliography, a journal, or other place indicated. The user with this need is most often an advanced student or a faculty member engaged in a research project: a dissertation, a paper or book, a report, etc. Thus, the bibliographic question reaching the reference librarian is likely to be one that eluded normal, easy searching. The directory question, on the other hand, more often reaches the librarian by telephone from the office of an administrator or faculty member who needs the information urgently. Help is sought on this type of question not because of the difficulty of finding the needed information but because the directory source of the information is not available in the user's office. The information is often wanted in a hurry in order to address a letter or to telephone the person in question.

The directory information required most often in the academic setting is the address or telephone number of a publisher, association, firm, committee, government department or official, scientist, scholar, or faculty member. Less often it is the name of the person holding a particular position or office. Still less often it may be a fact other than the address, telephone number, or name of a person: e.g., the special fields of a publisher, the broadcasting frequency of a radio or television station, the date of establishment of an association or government commission, the special products of a manufacturer. What ties together these miscellaneous types of questions is that they can be solved easily in a directory.

A large number of directory questions can be answered readily in one of a small number of directories, which the library has within easy reach of the telephone. Most important are the *Encyclopedia of Associations, Literary Market Place*, directories of the federal government, and telephone directories of all major cities in the United States and smaller cities in the library's area, all of which are discussed in this chapter. The directories to be kept most convenient to the telephone will vary from one library to another. Besides the usual urgency of providing directory information noted above, another prime requirement (not always needed for reference questions of other types) is the currency of information. This need is aided not only by the frequent revision of most directories (annually or more often) but also by the library's having standing orders for major directories and telephone directories, so that new editions are received automatically.

Online searching can be used in two ways as a source of directory information. The current address of an individual scholar can often be located by doing an online search for the person as an author in a database which includes author address as part of the bibliographic information for publications indexed and abstracted. Selection of the appropriate database(s) to search depends on the person's field of specialization, where known. The second type of directory information is derived from databases which are directories. Some (e.g., *ENCYCLOPEDIA OF ASSOCIATIONS*) correspond to directories available in printed form, while others exist only in machine-readable form. Many are business directories, such as the ELECTRONIC YELLOW PAGES, a family of databases available on DIALOG. The ELECTRONIC YELLOW PAGES include a construction directory, financial services directory, manufacturers directory, professionals directory, retailers directory, services directory, and wholesalers directory which have been compiled from 4,800 telephone books and specialized directories in the United States. Such directory databases may offer a currency and comprehensiveness not available in printed directories.

Besides the directory sources listed in this chapter, which are the types most often needed by users of a university library, other more specialized directories are included in other chapters. Most of the sources described in this chapter are used to obtain directory data about specific agencies, associations, firms, or persons. Some are approached by subject or need; they indicate the appropriate agencies, associations, and other sources that furnish the required information or help.

GOVERNMENT

The address, telephone number, name of director, or function of a particular government agency, or the name of the person representing a congressional district is often needed, not only by social scientists but also by other members of the academic community in the conduct of their political, social, or other interests. Less often, this kind of information is needed for a state or local government or for a foreign country.

85. U.S. General Services Administration. National Archives and Records Service. Office of the Federal Register. **United States Government Manual.** Washington, D.C.: Government Printing Office, 1935- . Annual. (Included in chapter 20 as entry 1027.)

For data on agencies, committees, and commissions of the three branches of the federal government, the *United States Government Manual* is the first source to check. It is easily available from the Government Printing Office, is found in all libraries, is well organized and indexed, and is used so often that it is usually kept near the telephone. For each agency, an organization chart, names of the key personnel, a brief history, and description of its functions are given. Similar data are given for committees, commissions, and other government bodies. There are complete indexes of personal names, subjects, and agencies.

86. U.S. Congress. **Official Congressional Directory.** Washington, D.C.: Government Printing Office, 1865- . Annual.

87. **Congressional Staff Directory.** Edited by Charles W. Brownson. Mt. Vernon, N.Y.: Congressional Staff Directory, 1959- . Annual.

Unlike the *United States Government Manual*, which is organized by the agencies, committees, and other bodies of the three branches of government, these two directories are centered on data about government personnel. The *Official Congressional Directory* has information on the personnel of all three branches: short biographical sketches of present members of Congress and the names of their administrative assistants and secretaries, names of the personnel of all Senate and House committees, biographical sketches of cabinet members, names of key officials in each department of the executive branch, biographies of members of the Supreme Court, foreign diplomatic personnel, and similar information. The *Congressional Staff Directory* is compiled privately, not by Congress. It is confined to information about members of congress and their staff, but within this branch, it offers more detail than the *Official Congressional Directory.* Either of these directories can supply the legislative district number for a particular city and the name of the representative of that district, a question frequently asked.

88. **Washington Information Directory.** Washington, D.C.: Congressional Quarterly, 1975- . Annual.

This directory is one that is based on subject. It directs the user to those agencies, departments, commissions, and committees of all three branches of the federal government from which information can be obtained on such matters as home economics, energy conservation, migrant farm workers, child protection and support, etc.

89. **Federal Executive Directory.** Washington, D.C.: Carroll, 1979- . Every two months.

This is the most up-to-date of the federal government directories, being revised every two months. Only the telephone number and the department or office are given, but the approach can be by name of the person, the department or office, or the official title. Because of its frequent and careful revision, the directory is often used to be sure of the current incumbent in a government position, when the address and telephone number are not needed.

90. **Federal Regulatory Directory.** Washington, D.C.: Congressional Quarterly, 1979- . Annual. (Included in chapter 20 as entry 1028.)

Many of the names listed in this directory can be found in the *United States Government Manual*, except those of some of the minor officials of federal regulatory agencies which are not listed elsewhere.

91. **State blue book.**

Although requests for addresses and telephone numbers of state legislators, officials, and agencies are not as frequent in the library as requests for information about departments and personnel of the federal government, some state directories are needed. The state blue book (sometimes called the "red book" after the traditional binding color or "official register") is the standard source for such data. It is usually obtainable free from the Secretary of State. Typical contents of the state blue book are a description of each state department and its operation, a roster of its top personnel, biographies of all current legislators, rosters of legislative committees, etc. These official handbooks of each state are revised each year or two.

92. **Other state government directories.**

Since the blue book does not list all of the state employees, but only the top officials of each department, there is usually also a more complete directory of state and county officials. Any such material is available from either the secretary of state or the legislature.

93. **State Administrative Officials Classified by Function.** Lexington, Ky.: Council of State Governments, 1935- . Biennial.

94. **State Elective Officials and the Legislatures.** Lexington, Ky.: Council of State Governments, 1935- . Biennial.

For directory information on officials and legislators of states whose blue books are not in the library, these two supplements to the *Book of the States* (entry 1035) are useful. *State Administrative Officials Classified by Function* is also very good for learning the name of the person whose office is responsible for a function or service in any state, such as aging, aeronautics, agriculture, etc.

95. **Local telephone directory.**

Directory questions about one's own local government or that of another community are not common in the academic library. For one's own city, such questions are best answered by using the telephone directory or by calling the mayor's office or other local government office.

96. **Municipal Yearbook.** Washington, D.C.: International City Management Association, 1934- . Annual.

97. **The County Yearbook.** Washington, D.C.: National Association of Counties and International City Management Association, 1974- . Annual.

For questions on officials of cities and counties of other states, the directory portions of these yearbooks may be helpful. The telephone directories of other cities, if in the library collection, are also useful for these questions.

98. **The Europa Year Book: A World Survey.** London: Europa, 1926- . Annual. (Included in chapter 20 as entry 1071.)

99. **The Statesman's Year-Book.** Edited by John Paxton. New York: St. Martin's, 1864- . Annual. (Included in chapter 20 as entry 1072.)

Names and titles of heads of state and cabinet officers of other countries are readily found in one of these sources.

A final word of caution is needed in the use of these directories. There is always a significant chance that the person named in the most recent edition as the incumbent in a particular office has been replaced by some other person. This possibility also exists when directories of U.S. government officials and other directories are used, but it is more likely that the user and the librarian will be aware of such changes in this country than in other countries. The librarian should always be aware of such risks and should ask the inquirer if there is reason to suspect a change of the incumbent since the directory was published or if checking of more recent sources, although more time-consuming, is wanted by the user. A recent change of a head of state will be reported in *Facts on File* or *Keesing's Contemporary Archives* (London: Keesing's Ltd. Weekly.). For other officials one should look for a recent article on an election or a change of government in the country involved. But let the inquirer decide whether such an extended search is necessary. Librarians cannot be expected to read everything and to be informed on all recent news, but regular perusal of a news magazine like *Time, Newsweek,* or *U.S. News and World Report* will often save the librarian from inadvertently giving an out-of-date answer to one of these directory questions.

ASSOCIATIONS

100. **Encyclopedia of Associations.** 5 vols. Detroit: Gale, 1956- . Annual.

Almost any national association in the United States can be identified readily here with brief information such as address, telephone number, date of founding, number of members, general purpose, principal activities, date and place of the next annual conventions, and publications. This directory can be machine searched through DIALOG. Local associations can usually be identified through the appropriate telephone directory.

101. **Directory of British Associations and Associations in Ireland.** 7th ed. Edited by G. P. Henderson and S. P. A. Henderson. Beckenham, Kent, England: CBD Research, 1982. 473p.

Data on approximately 3,500 national, regional, and local associations and societies in the British Isles, plus some British organizations headquartered abroad are listed in this directory by title with brief data. There are indexes of acronyms/abbreviations and of subjects.

102. **Directory of European Associations.** 3d ed. Edited by I. G. Anderson. 2 vols. Beckenham, Kent, England: CBD Research; Detroit: Gale, 1981-84.

Similarly, European associations can be identified through this directory. Although more selective than *Encyclopedia of Associations* and the *Directory of British Associations and Associations in Ireland*, it includes all the major associations of Europe.

103. **Yearbook of International Organizations.** Brussels: Union of International Associations, 1948- . Annual.

In addition to United Nations, European Economic Community, and other governmental international organizations, this directory lists more than 1,000 non-governmental international organizations in religion, politics, sports, education, and other fields. The Federation of French Language Societies of Gynecology and Obstetrics and the Federation of International Furniture Movers are examples of the organizations, which can be found under title, catchwords, initials, or geographical area.

104. **The World of Learning.** London: Europa, 1947- . Annual. (Included in chapter 16 as entry 720.)

For each country of the world, this book lists learned societies, research institutes, libraries and archives, museums, and universities and colleges and gives names of personnel and other directory information. Only major institutions are listed for some countries where there are too many for a complete roster.

105. **Professional associations.**

Most professional associations, such as the American Economics Association, the American Sociological Association, and the American Library Association, issue a directory of their members that is revised annually or frequently. Many of these directories are listed in the appropriate chapters of section 2.

RESEARCH GRANTS

106. **Annual Register of Grant Support.** Chicago: Marquis Academic Media, 1967- . Annual.

107. **DRG: Directory of Research Grants.** Edited by William K. Wilson and Betty L. Wilson. Phoenix: Oryx Press, 1975- . Annual.

Since grants are usually sought and awarded for support of research projects, the needs for this information come from faculty and graduate students rather than from undergraduates. Grants are described in these two sources, between which there is surprisingly little duplication. Listing is under subject, facilitating the user's search for appropriate sources of financial support. Data include the purpose of the grant program, the amount and duration of grants, due dates for applications, and sponsor. *DRG* is updated by the looseleaf service, *Grant Information System Quarterly*, compiled by Betty L. Wilson and William K. Wilson (Phoenix: Oryx Press, 1974- , quarterly, with *Faculty Alert Bulletins* in the intervening months). *DRG* and its updates can be machine searched using the GRANTS database through DIALOG and SDC.

108. **The Foundation Directory.** 9th ed. Edited by Loren Renz, Kevin Baker, and Patricia Read. New York: The Foundation Center, 1983. 761p.

Important private grantmaking foundations in the United States (more than 4,000) are listed by state, giving address, purpose, financial data (including the amount of grants), and grant application information. There are separate indexes for foundation names, geographic locations, donors and officers, and fields of interest. This is the standard source of information on grantmaking foundations. It can be machine searched through DIALOG.

109. **Awards, Honors, and Prizes.** 5th ed. Edited by Paul Wasserman and Gita Siegman. 2 vols. Detroit: Gale, 1982.

110. **World Dictionary of Awards and Prizes.** London: Europa, 1979. 386p.

More than 11,000 awards and prizes are listed in the first of these books. Volume 1 lists those given by organizations in the United States and Canada; volume 2 has international awards and those given by organizations in countries other than the United States and Canada. Many of these carry no monetary grant but simply a plaque, certificate, medal, or trophy. Each volume has a subject index and an alphabetic index of the awards it lists. *World Dictionary of Awards and Prizes* serves a similar function, listing somewhat more than 2,000 scholarly lectureships, grants and fellowships, prizes and awards for intellectual achievement. Besides data on the sponsor of the award or prize, its purpose, amount, and the method of applying, this book names several of the latest recipients.

LIBRARIES AND INFORMATION CENTERS

111. **American Library Directory.** Edited by Jaques Cattell Press. New York: Bowker, 1908- . Annual.

112. **Directory of Special Libraries and Information Centers.** 9th ed. Edited by Brigitte T. Darnay. 2 vols. Detroit: Gale, 1985.

113. **Subject Directory of Special Libraries and Information Centers.** 8th ed. Edited by Brigitte T. Darnay. 5 vols. Detroit: Gale, 1983.

Directory data on libraries, special collections, and databases are also important to the research worker. These are the standard directories of libraries in the United States and Canada. The *American Library Directory* lists academic, public, and special libraries by state (or province) and city. Branches of a public library and department libraries in universities and public libraries are grouped under the parent library. The directory data provided include address and telephone number, names of directors and division librarians, fiscal and holdings statistics, subjects of special strengths, and automation information. Currently, *American Library Directory* lists more than 32,000 libraries. The *Directory of Special Libraries and Information Centers* is limited to special libraries but includes departmental and divisional libraries devoted to particular subjects within universities and large public libraries, as well as libraries in government agencies, businesses and industries, professional associations, and other institutions in the United States and Canada. Libraries are listed alphabetically in volume 1 by institution, agency, or company. Over 16,000 special libraries are currently listed, giving data similar to that in *American Library Directory*. Volume 2 has a geographic index of libraries and a personnel index. The *Subject Directory of Special Libraries and Information Centers* is divided into volumes for special libraries of different types, such as business libraries, law libraries, health sciences libraries, and social sciences and humanities libraries. Data provided here for each library are the same as those provided in the descriptive listings. These directories of special libraries are very useful, but the cost of the two sets has caused many libraries to continue to use a superseded edition.

114.   Ash, Lee, comp. **Subject Collections: A Guide to Special Book Collections and Subject Emphases as Reported by University, College, Public, and Special Libraries and Museums in the United States and Canada.** 6th ed. 2 vols. New York: Bowker, 1984.

If the scholar/researcher needs to know what libraries in the United States and Canada have exceptionally strong holdings on Robert Frost, fruit culture, fundamentalism, funeral music, or another subject, this guide provides the information. Special collections in United States and Canadian libraries are listed with data on the size of holdings and strengths under small subjects. The user should be aware, however, that information has been provided by the libraries and lacks uniform standards of strength, except insofar as these can be judged from the holdings data.

115.   **Directory of Online Databases.** Santa Monica, Calif.: Cuadra Associates, 1979- . Quarterly. Paper.

116.   **Encyclopedia of Information Systems and Services.** 6th ed. Edited by John Schmittroth, Jr., and others. 2 vols. Detroit: Gale, 1985.

The *Directory of Online Databases* is one of the most used sources of information for machine searching because of its currency, being updated each quarter. Besides the main description of online databases, there are addresses of producers and online services, separate indexes of subjects, producers, online services, and telecommunication networks for each database, and a Master Index of databases, producers, and online services. The latter is especially good when a user wants identification of a name associated with the information field and does not know whether it is a producer, a service, or a database. The *Encyclopedia of Information Systems and Services* is an alphabetically arranged international directory of over 2,500 "organizations, systems, and services using computer and related new technologies to produce and/or provide access to bibliographic, full-text, directory, numeric, and other types of information and data in all subject areas," according to the preface.

117.   **Information Market Place, 1984-1985: The Directory of Information Products and Services.** New York: Bowker, 1984. 280p.

As in the several "market place" directories described in this and other chapters (see entries 118, 375, 542), this furnishes addresses, products, services, and other information on various firms, agencies, and publications in the information field. Its seven major sections are Information Production, Information Distribution, Information Retailing, Support Services and Suppliers (terminal manufacturers, consultants, etc.), Associations and Government Agencies, Conferences and Courses, and Sources of Information. There is a geographic index as well as a names and number index, which provides addresses and telephone numbers for the various companies listed in the United States and abroad.

PUBLISHERS

118.   **Literary Market Place (LMP) with Names and Numbers: The Directory of American Book Publishing.** New York: Bowker, 1940- . Annual.

Members of the university faculty or administration frequently need the address, telephone number, or name of key personnel of a publishing firm. Many non-trade publishers, as well as trade publishers, in the United States are also included in this directory. In some university libraries it is so often used that it is kept at the telephone. There is also the less often needed *International Literary Market Place*, giving information about publishers in other countries.

GUIDES TO DIRECTORIES

119. **The Directory of Directories: An Annotated Guide to Business and Industrial Directories, Professional and Scientific Rosters, and Other Lists and Guides of All Kinds.** Edited by James M. Ethridge. Detroit: Information Enterprises, dist. by Gale, 1980- . Biennial.

More than 5,000 directories of the United States are listed under 15 broad headings: e.g., business, industry, and labor; banking, finance, insurance, and real estate; education; health and medicine. There are indexes of titles and subjects. The three-times-a-year *Directory Information Service* keeps it up to date.

In this chapter, we have described only some of the types of directories used most often for the needs of faculty members, administrators, students, and others in the university but which are not identified with any particular discipline. Many other directories that for the most part pertain to a particular discipline are described in the appropriate chapter in section 2.

TELEPHONE DIRECTORIES

A series of telephone directories should be at hand, including those for towns in the library's own region and major cities throughout the United States and some European cities. These are useful for addresses and telephone numbers of businesses, agencies, and associations, when the city is known.

4

BIOGRAPHICAL INFORMATION

Requests for biographical information come from all user groups in the university library. Most requests are for fairly brief identification rather than for an extended biography, and most are for information on a living person. The extent and nature of a person's publications and research are the data most often wanted. The person in question might be the author of a recent book, and the faculty member or other person who is asked to review the book may want to know the author's credentials in the subject of the book. Students are often given an assignment to learn about the author of a book on which they are to give a class report and to evaluate the book partially on the basis of the author's credentials. Another frequent origin of a biographical question in the university is the need of an administrator or a faculty member to introduce a guest speaker. Or the person about whom the information is sought may be someone nominated for an honorary degree at the university. In all of these examples, the data sought are the publications, research, awards and honors, teaching experience, and such indicators of the person's academic and scholarly achievement; the person about whom information is wanted is a contemporary person of the United States, less often of another country; and the person wanting the information is a faculty member or an administrator, less often a student. But another type of biographical question on a contemporary person that is becoming more frequent is the request from a student for information about a new entertainer, often a rock-and-roll performer, on whom they are writing a term paper or about whom they have an interest.

Identification of and biographical information about a historical person may be wanted by a student for a term paper or a class assignment more often than by other user groups in the university. Such questions will often be about a person who is not well known and about whom information is not readily available in a book, an encyclopedia, or other standard source about which the student already knows. Less frequent than the request for a full biography for a term paper or other class assignment is the inquiry about some little known fact of a person's life that is not reported in the standard biographical sources. A recent example of this was a question about an accident suffered in early life by a famous author, an incident not reported in the known biographical record. This latter type of question will come from an advanced student or a faculty member more often than from an undergraduate or member of the general public, and may be wanted for a dissertation or other intensive study of the person. Almost all questions about persons of the past, whether for a student report or for an intensive study, usually present more difficulty to the librarian than the more usual questions about contemporary writers and scholars. This is either because the biographee is a relatively unknown person or because the fact being sought about a well-known person is not reported in standard sources. Some of the questions of the first type, information, for example, on the author of a book being reviewed by a faculty member, can also be difficult where the author has not written or had any notable achievements earlier. There are many authors of serious, scholarly books who are not listed in any who's who or biographical record. Also the needed information about a rock-and-roll performer, fairly new on the scene, can present some problem.

CURRENT BIOGRAPHY

For the most commonly sought information — biographical data about an author or scholar living in the United States — consult a who's who. If the person is prominent, for example an administrator or established scholar at another university, the easiest source is

120. **Who's Who in America.** Chicago: Marquis Who's Who, 1899- . Biennial.

If the person's name is not found there, look next in

121. **Biography and Genealogy Master Index.** 2d ed. Edited by Miranda C. Herbert and Barbara McNeil. 8 vols. Detroit: Gale, 1980. Annual supplements.

This book consolidates into one alphabet the names included in some 350 who's whos, dictionaries of current biography, and some collections of retrospective biography, e.g., *The Almanac of American Politics, American Men and Women of Science, Authors in the News, A Biographical Dictionary of Film, Contemporary Authors, Directory of American Scholars, Modern German Literature.* These biographical sources are all in English, although some list persons in non-English speaking countries. The index is a good time saver, eliminating the need to search through many different who's whos and biographical dictionaries. The names are listed as given in the different sources and may, therefore, appear in several different forms (e.g., Lancaster, F. Wilfrid, and Lancaster, Frederick Wilfrid). But the year of birth is usually given after the name, which helps to identify the person whose name is sought. Both *Who's Who in America* and *Biography and Genealogy Master Index* can be machine searched through DIALOG. *Who's Who in America* is part of the MARQUIS WHO'S WHO database and *Biography and Genealogy Master Index* is part of the BIOGRAPHY MASTER INDEX database. If the person's name is not listed in *Biography and Genealogy Master Index*, indicating that the person is not included in any of the 350 biographical sources indexed, several other sources can be tried. One usually selects the first sources to be checked according to a combination of several factors: appropriateness to the question, ease of using the book, proximity of the book, and inclusion of much information in a single source. This selectivity increases the likelihood of finding the needed information on one pass. Since the person whose biographical data are sought is believed or known to be an author or a scholar living in the United States, good possibilities for checking next are

122. **National Union Catalog: A Cumulative Author List.** Washington, D.C.: Library of Congress, 1956- . Monthly with quarterly, annual, and 5-year cumulations.

123. **National Union Catalog: Pre-1956 Imprints.** 754 vols. London: Mansell, 1968-81.

124. **Current Contents Address Directory: Science and Technology. Current Contents Address Directory: Social Sciences and Humanities.** Philadelphia: Institute for Scientific Information, 1978- . Annual.

125. **The National Faculty Directory.** Detroit: Gale, 1970- . Annual.

The *National Union Catalog* has been treated fully in chapter 2, "Bibliographic Questions" (entries 1 and 2). If the name is found there, it will probably be accompanied by the person's birth date and the title of one or more publications. The two editions each year of *Current Contents Address Directory* list all of the authors who have published in a journal or book covered that year by the *Arts and Humanities Citation Index* (entry 223), the *Social Sciences Citation Index* (entry 699), the *Science Citation Index* (entry 1223), or one of the other indexes of the Institute for Scientific Information. If the name being searched for is found in this directory, it will be accompanied by the titles of journals in which the person has published that year and the address (usually a university or other professional address) given with the person's article or book. The titles of any books or articles will usually offer a clue about the subject field in which the person works. The *National Faculty Directory* lists all faculty members of all colleges and universities in the United States and Canada: community and junior colleges; business, trade, and technical colleges; Bible colleges; and other institutions of higher education. The faculty member's name is followed by the instructional department, the institution, and the address. These sources do not furnish much biographical data, but one will now possibly have the person's institutional affiliation and the titles of one or more publications, and will know that the name is correctly spelled. In biographical questions, as in bibliographic verification, when the name cannot be found in any of the likely sources, there is always the possibility that the name, as given to the reference librarian, is misspelled. It is a relief and a step ahead, therefore, merely to establish a correct spelling. Furthermore, when a biographical search is beginning to look hopeless (which does not yet apply to this search), one is grateful for any little clue like the person's position and institutional affiliation because these open up additional possibilities for further search. For example, the catalog of the college or university will list courses taught by the faculty member and will sometimes give brief career information. More data might also be found in a professional association directory or a who's who of the profession with which the person is associated (music, finance, health, history, or other).

An author or a person associated with a university will probably be listed in one or more of the sources mentioned above. These are the fastest and easiest places to check. If the name is not found in any of them, suspect a misspelling (see p. 11). The subject of a book or article written by a person, as noted above, may suggest a specialized who's who or directory to be checked. As in bibliographical questions, the source from which the questioner heard or saw the name will probably furnish some clue to be followed up in a further search. Another possibility that can be considered is that the subject of the search has only recently been in the news for some achievement or event, indicating a check of newspaper and periodical indexes such as the *New York Times Index, Facts on File, Readers' Guide to Periodical Literature*, or a periodical index in a subject field.

126. **Biography Index: A Cumulative Index to Biographical Materials in Books and Magazines.** New York: Wilson, 1946- . Quarterly with annual and 3-year cumulations.

Biography Index is also a good source to check when a name has not turned up in any of the sources already described because it indexes more than 1,000 general and specialized periodicals, some in foreign languages, and a number of recent books of individual and collective biography for biographies and biographical notices. The latter include short sketches on the occasion of a person's promotion, accepting a new position, retirement, obituaries, and other brief notices that might escape attention. This index can now be machine searched through Wilsonline.

Thus far, we have primarily considered contemporary persons in the United States. If the subject is a national of another country, there are who's whos of major countries and regions and international who's whos. A sample list of these follows.

127. **Who's Who.** New York: St. Martin's, 1849- . Biennial.

128. **Who's Who in France, qui est qui en France: dictionnaire biographique de personnalités françaises vivant en France, dans les territoires d'Outre-Mer ou à l'étranger et de personnalités étrangeres résidant en France.** Paris: La Fitte, 1952- . Biennial.

129. **Wer ist wer? Das deutsche Who's Who.** Hrsg. von Walter Habel. 23. Ausgabe. Lübeck: Schmidt Römhild, 1984. 1429p.

130. **Who's Who in Germany: A Biographical Encyclopedia of the International Red Series.** 8th ed., 1982-1983. Edited by Karl Strute and Dr. Theodor Doelken. Worthsee near Munich: Who's Who, the International Red Series, Verlag GmbH., 1983.

131. **Who's Who in Italy.** 3d ed. Edited by Otto J. Groeg. Milan: Who's Who in Italy, 1980. 697p.

132. **Who's Who in the Arab World.** 6th ed., 1981-1982. Beirut, Lebanon: Publitec, 1981. 1367p.

133. **Who's Who in Europe.** 4th ed., 1980-1981. Brussels: Servi-Tech, 1980. 2515p.

134. **Dictionary of International Biography: A Biographical Record of Contemporary Achievement.** Vol. 18. Cambridge, England: International Biographical Centre, 1984. 893p.

135. **International Scholars Directory.** Edited by J. W. Montgomery. Strasbourg: International Scholarly Publishers, 1973. 288p.

136. **The International Who's Who.** London: Europa, 1935- . Annual.

137. **Who's Who in the World.** Chicago: Marquis Who's Who, 1971- . Biennial.

If the nationality of the biographee is known and the appropriate who's who is readily at hand, this national who's who would be checked first. If the country is not known or its who's who is not available or the name not found in it, the international who's whos can be checked, but these volumes must be more selective and, therefore, offer poorer prospects than the who's whos of a given country. The who's whos and dictionaries listed here and others we have not listed vary in their selectivity. A discussion of evaluating biographical works for their credibility and selectivity is included at the end of this chapter. If a work is considered of doubtful worth, the library may not have added it to the collection. But the librarian checks those appropriate who's whos and biographical dictionaries that are in the collection both those suspected of having a questionable policy on selecting persons to be included as well as those with a reputation for high standards of selectivity since the former will include many names not to be found in the latter. The data of both types of who's whos are furnished by the biographees and, therefore, have the same credibility. The difference between them lies in the distinction of the persons included and the basis for selecting them, and this is usually not a matter of concern either to the questioner or to the librarian. More who's whos of countries and regions are listed and described in Sheehy's *Guide to Reference Books* (9th ed., 1976, and supplements) and Walford's *Guide to Reference Material* (4th ed. Vol. 2. 1982). If the name is not found in any of the appropriate who's whos available, the librarian can follow the same alternate procedures described above for researching persons in the United States but here the continued search will be more difficult and will often lead to material in languages other than English.

RETROSPECTIVE BIOGRAPHY

The request for biographical information for persons no longer living is not as frequent as that for contemporary persons. Students probably have needs for retrospective biographies for their term papers and in connection with other kinds of class assignments, but they are able to find what they want most of the time through encyclopedias and books in the library. What are requested from the librarian, then, are biographical data about less well-known persons or the more elusive facts about well-known persons. Quick places to check first, if the name is not found in standard encyclopedias, are:

138.   **Webster's Biographical Dictionary: A Dictionary of Names of Noteworthy Persons with Pronunciations and Concise Biographies.** Springfield, Mass.: Merriam, 1976. 1697p.

139.   **Chambers's Biographical Dictionary.** Rev. ed. Edited by J. O. Thorne and T. C. Collocott. New York: Hippocrene Books, 1974. 1432p.

140.   Falk, Byron A., and Valerie R. Falk, comps. **Personal Name Index to "The New York Times Index," 1851-1974.** 22 vols. Verdi, Nev.: Roxbury Data Interface, 1976-83. Supplement, 1975-1979, 1984.

141.   Hyamson, Albert M. **A Dictionary of Universal Biography of All Ages and All People.** 2d ed. London: Routledge, 1951. Reprint. Detroit: Gale, 1981. 680p.

142.   Riches, Phyllis M., comp. **An Analytical Bibliography of Universal Collected Biography, Comprising Books Published in the English Tongue in Great Britain and Ireland, America, and the British Dominions.** London: Library Association, 1934. Reprint. Detroit: Gale, 1980. 709p.

Webster's Biographical Dictionary is the best known and the most widely held of these sources. It lists about 40,000 names of prominent persons of the past with brief biographical data, achievements, major publications, compositions, and other works. *Chamber's Biographical Dictionary* is similar; it has a little more information on approximately 15,000 persons, but British and Irish subjects are favored. A recently published source that should prove very useful for biographical information on a person for whom nothing has yet been found is the index by Byron and Valerie Falk. It lists some 3,000,000 names culled from the *New York Times Index*, 1851-1974, into one alphabet, obviating much tedious searching through the index volumes. The only information provided is a reference to the *New York Times Index* year and page. The main disadvantage of this index is that it involves a three-step search before the needed biographical data are found. Similarly, the indexes by Hyamson and Riches give only minimal data about the thousands of persons listed, but refer to biographical collections where more can be found.

143.   **The McGraw-Hill Encyclopedia of World Biography.** 12 vols. New York: McGraw-Hill, 1973.

A good source for undergraduate needs, this gives biographical articles averaging one-half page in length on a selected 5,000 people from Moses to Richard Nixon, notable for various kinds of achievement in areas of government, conquest, exploration, the arts, philosophy, literature, etc. In the index volume are "study guides," which list biographees under broad subject field. There is also a general index of names and subjects, including titles of novels, paintings, operas, and other works by the biographees. The set is also heavily illustrated.

For fuller biographical information than provided in these quick sources, every major country has a standard or official biographical set on its deceased noteworthy nationals:

persons in government, religion, the military, education, science, the arts, and other recognized areas of achievement. A sampling of these includes:

144. **Dictionary of American Biography.** Edited by Allen Johnson. 20 vols. New York: Scribner's, 1928-37. Reprints. 21 vols. Scribner's, 1943; 11 vols., Scribner's, 1946. Supplements 1-7, 1944-81.

145. **National Cyclopedia of American Biography.** New York: James T. White, 1892-1984. **Current Volumes,** New York: James T. White, 1930-1984. **Index.** Clifton, N.J.: James T. White, 1984. 576p. (Index covers vols. 1-62 of the permanent series and vols. A-M of the current series, plus vol. N-63, completing both permanent and current series by the present publisher.) The permanent series (numbered volumes) have biographies of deceased persons; the current series (lettered volumes) is limited to living persons. Both series are now complete.

146. **Who Was Who in America, with World Notables.** Chicago: Marquis Who's Who, 1950- .

147. **The Dictionary of National Biography.** Edited by Sir Leslie Stephen and Sir Sidney Lee. 22 vols. London: Oxford University Press, 1885-1901. Reprint. Oxford: Oxford University Press, 1936-38. Supplements, 1920- .

148. **Who Was Who.** New York: St. Martin's, 1849- . Biennial.

149. **Dictionnaire de biographie française.** Paris: Letouzey, 1933- . In progress.

150. **Allgemeine deutsche Biographie.** Hrsg. durch die Historische Commission bei der K. Akademie der Wissenschaften. 56 vols. Leipzig: Duncker & Humblot, 1875-1912. Reprint. Duncker & Humblot, 1967-71.

151. **Neue deutsche Biographie.** Hrsg. von der Historische Kommission bei der Bayerischen Akademie der Wissenschaften. Berlin: Duncker & Humblot, 1953- . In progress.

152. **Dizionario Biografico degli Italiani.** Edited by Alberto M. Ghisalberti. Rome: Instituto della Enciclopedia Italiana, 1960- . In progress.

Most of these exclude living persons; some are in progress, now covering only the first portion of the alphabet. All give lengthy biographical sketches except *Who Was Who in America* and *Who Was Who*, which reprint the brief sketches of persons who were formerly in *Who's Who in America* and *Who's Who*, respectively, and were removed from those works by death or inactivity. Further description of these and other biographical dictionaries not listed here are obtained in the guides by Walford and Sheehy. A strong reference collection will have standing orders for all of these definitive biographical sets and for one or more of the who's whos of each major country.

If the name being sought does not turn up in any of these sources, some of the "desperation" steps described above for locating scraps of data on living people can be followed. These include asking the user about the source of his or her information about the person in the hope of finding some clue for further search, checking possible alternate spelling of the name, checking the *National Union Catalog*, checking older directories of professional societies, and checking biographical collections in subject fields (e.g., *Baker's Biographical Dictionary of Musicians*, entry 460 and *Allgemeines Lexikon der bildenden Künstler*, entry 554). In many cases, these subject biographical dictionaries would have been checked first. A good source for finding citations of biographical dictionaries of different countries and regions and for different subjects and vocations follows:

153.   Slocum, Robert B. **Biographical Dictionaries and Related Works: An International Bibliography.** Detroit: Gale, 1967. 1056p. Supplement 1, 1972. Supplement 2, 1978.

With its two supplements, this work lists and annotates more than 12,000 biographical dictionaries, collections of biographies, dictionaries of anonyms and pseudonyms, catalogs of portraits, and related biographical reference tools. In two separate lists, these are arranged by geography and by vocation.

154.   Lobies, Jean-Pierre. **IBN: Index bio-bibliographicus notorum hominum.** Osnabrück: Biblio Verlag, 1972- . In progress.

Pars B of this set is a similar bibliography of 5,145 biographical reference works arranged geographically by subject. *Pars C*, which is in progress and has now reached to *Camelli*, will include all the names in these biographical works.

For persons of the recent past, if a full biography has not been found anywhere, one can look for the obituary. Several general indexes of obituaries are

155.   **The New York Times Obituaries Index, 1858-1968.** New York: New York Times, 1970. 1136p. Supplement, 1969-1978. 1980. 341p.

156.   **Obituaries on File.** Compiled by Felice Levy. 2 vols. New York: Facts on File, 1979.

157.   Roberts, Frank C., comp. **Obituaries from The Times, 1951-1975.** 3 vols. Reading, England: Newspaper Archive Developments, 1975-79.

Files of these two newspapers and *Facts on File* are found in all large libraries, and these obituaries can be looked up easily. The data in obituaries are brief but will normally include family data, education, career experience, and clubs.

158.   Arnim, Max. **Internationale Personalbibliographie.** 2. Auflage. Vol. 1- . Stuttgart: Hiersemann, 1944- . In progress.

If the user wants only a list of a person's publications, this is a good source since it lists personal bibliographies of some 90,000 individuals, with an emphasis on German writers who lived after 1800. Both separately published bibliographies and those that formed part of a book or periodical article are included. This work was recommended in chapter 2 (entry 84) as an alternate method of locating an elusive bibliographic entry.

159.   **Biographie universelle, ancienne et moderne.** Rev. ed. Edited by Joseph Francois Michaud. 45 vols. Paris: Desplaces, 1843-65.

160.   **Nouvelle biographie générale depuis les temps les plus reculés jusqu'à nos jours ...** Edited by J. Ch. Ferdinand Hoefer. 46 vols. Paris: Didot, 1852-66. Reprint. Copenhagen: Rosenkilde & Bagger, 1963-69.

These are two older universal biographical dictionaries which are not used often, but which are kept in the reference collection of all large libraries for occasional use. Both include names not to be found elsewhere. The first set (commonly referred to as "Michaud") is the more carefully researched and has a high reputation for accuracy. It is especially valuable for French nationals, although it covers people of all countries, because the only other work covering retrospective French biography, *Dictionnaire de biographie francaise*, reaches at the present time only to the letter *G*. The other work listed above (commonly called "Hoefer") is not as carefully done but is more popular because it has 52,420 names, compared to an estimated 33,000 in Michaud. With either work, and with the work described next, it must be remembered that the French spelling of the name is used: e.g., Aaron (Haroun al Rashid), Guillaume le Conquerant (William the Conqueror), Haquin (Haakon), Pompée (Pompey).

161.   Chevalier, Cyr Ulysse Joseph. **Répertoire des sources historiques du moyen âge. Bio-bibliographie.** Rev. ed. 2 vols. Paris: Picard, 1905-07. Reprint. New York: Kraus, 1960.

For names in the Middle Ages (ca. 300-1500), this old French set is invaluable. Only very brief identification and dates are furnished for an estimated 60,000 to 75,000 monks, nuns, bishops, kings and nobles, artists, lawyers, and others of those centuries, but references are given to sources for further information. Remember to look for the French form of the name: e.g., Abailard (Abelard), Arnoud (Arnold), Beatrix (Beatrice), or Hilaire (Hilary). The Arab and Byzantine worlds, as well as Europe, are represented.

162.   **The New Century Cyclopedia of Names.** Edited by C. L. Barnhart, with the assistance of William D. Halsey and others. 3 vols. New York: Appleton, 1954.

163.   **Pseudonyms and Nicknames Dictionary.** 2d ed. Edited by Jennifer Mossman. Detroit: Gale, 1982. 955p.

164.   Sharp, Harold S., comp. **Handbook of Pseudonyms and Personal Nicknames.** 2 vols. Metuchen, N.J.: Scarecrow, 1972. 1st Supplement. 2 vols. 1975. 2nd Supplement. 1982.

There is always the possibility that the name being sought will not be found in a biographical dictionary because it is not a person's name but a character in a novel or play, the name of a ship, a place, a work of art, a literary work, or other name. Or, it could be the nickname or pseudonym of a person. The latter are often given in biographical dictionaries with a cross-reference to the person's name. But names of literary characters, places, ships, operas, etc., are not listed in biographical dictionaries. The *New Century Cyclopedia of Names* has over 100,000 proper names of all kinds with a short identification. The other works listed above are useful for finding the real name of persons using a pseudonym or known by a nickname. Sharp, in the basic set and two supplements, lists some 35,000 persons of all eras and countries and about 60,000 nicknames and pseudonyms they have used. Mossman's dictionary has names of more than 90,000 authors, sports figures, entertainers, politicians, military leaders, underworld figures, religious leaders, and others of the past and present. For each name she gives dates, reference to sources for further information, nationality, occupation, and nicknames and pseudonyms. The entry under the latter refers to the real name.

CREDIBILITY AND SELECTIVITY

In consulting biographical dictionaries and who's whos, the librarian should be aware of two qualities of the works: their credibility and their policy of selection of biographees. Credibility, which applies to other types of reference works as well as to the types discussed in this chapter, refers to the accuracy and the authenticity of the facts and figures contained in the work. In general, the librarian learns to base confidence in a reference book at least partially on who publishes it. Oxford, Harvard, and other university presses, Knopf, Bowker, Wilson, Prentice-Hall, and McGraw-Hill are a few of the many publishers one has learned to trust because their publications of past years have indicated careful editing and selection of authors and material following criteria other than marketability. Subsidy publishers like Vantage Press or Exposition Press will publish anything legal and moral for which the author will underwrite the publishing cost. Certain trade publishers are more concerned with potential sales than with high standards of accuracy, and this soon becomes apparent to the reference librarian. Biographical data in who's whos, however, are usually supplied by the biographee, so the accuracy of these data are not dependent on the publisher, except for typographical errors. The definitive national retrospective sets described above are usually carefully researched and edited and can be relied on for accuracy. Some older biographical sets, however, were renowned for their poor editing. *Appleton's Cyclopedia of American*

Biography has some fictitious biographies of persons who never existed, supplied by one or more of their compilers, who were paid by the number of articles submitted. (See the note in Sheehy's *Guide to Reference Books*, 9th ed., #AJ40.) The first edition of the work by Hoefer lifted a number of articles unchanged from *Michaud* (entry 159), but the practice was later forbidden by the French court. (See Sheehy, #AJ17.) A number of county and local biographical collections published in the United States in the nineteenth and early twentieth centuries must be used cautiously since their content, both as to selectivity and accuracy, is more a function of who and what families of the community supported the project financially than of careful and objective research and editing.

Selectivity, the second quality of biographical works with which we are concerned, is the set of criteria by which persons are included in the work and the professions or vocations to which it is restricted. These are usually, or should be, set out in a preface. Some who's whos take pains to explain that no fee is charged to the biographee to be included nor must the biographee purchase a copy of the work. Inspection of the qualifications of persons included, however, and noting the omission of prominent and highly qualified persons will sometimes reveal that the criteria for selection must have been something other than notable achievement or distinction. But, as noted above, selectivity in a who's who or biographical dictionary is usually not important to either the questioner or the librarian. What both want is dependable biographical information about a given individual. Some biographical works that include information on persons who have not had a distinguished career or made outstanding contributions in their field are welcome in the library because information on these people may be especially hard to find. The biographical section of the reference collection, then, should include not just the best works, but as many as possible that are believed to be accurate and are about people in the professions and subject fields in which reference questions are likely to be asked. A book like *Outstanding Teenagers of America* would not be acquired, but one that aimed to include data on every librarian or anthropologist in the United States who submitted a completed form would be.

5

STATISTICAL QUESTIONS

Many questions asked in university and research libraries are for statistics on a certain subject. This type of question is associated mostly with research and therefore is not as common in the public library, high school library, or community college library, where research is not such an important part of the program. Usually statistics are wanted by social scientists and their graduate students, but university and college administrators also need statistics to support a budget request, to prepare a report to the board of trustees, or for some other purpose related to administration. The statistics needed are most often internal data about the administrator's own institution; those for which the administrator uses the library may be comparative statistics about other universities or some economic or social data about the United States.

The more numerous statistical questions asked by faculty members and their students in sociology, social work, economics, commerce, political science, and education are related most often to the national picture in the United States. "What are the comparative figures over the past fifty years, state by state, on the percent of eligible voters who have registered and voted?" "What is the percent of college students in vocational training programs?" "How many nursing homes are there in each state?" "How does the number of bankruptcies in 1982 compare with the number in other selected years?" Statistics on one's own state and international comparative statistics are also often needed. "How does the crime rate in one's own state compare with the national average?" "What countries have the best health record, as indicated by figures on infant mortality, life expectancy, and the incidence of certain diseases?"

Reference sources of statistical data may be divided into two groups: those that have statistical tables (primary sources) and those that index compilations of statistics (secondary sources). Most often the inquirers want the needed statistical data themselves, not a reference to where the data can be found (except in the case of an extended and time-consuming project, where the inquirer would prefer to select the needed data from the sources). Primary sources, therefore, are tried first. General compilations, such as *Statistical Abstract of the United States, World Almanac*, or *Information Please Almanac* for statistics on the United States, and *United Nations Statistical Yearbook, Europa,* and other international statistical compilations for other countries not only offer the best chance of finding the needed data because of the wide range of their content, but also are usually most convenient to the reference desk because of their frequent use. When these fail to provide the needed data, one may consult the more specialized and detailed collections, such as *Survey of Current Business, Economic Indicators, Historical Statistics of the United States*, or indexes to printed sources of statistics, such as *American Statistics Index, Statistical Reference Index*, or *Statistics Sources.* Only those sources of general statistics are treated in this chapter; sources of statistics in specific fields are included in the chapters in section 2.

In answering all reference questions, it is important to learn exactly what it is that the user wants, but this is especially essential for questions on statistics. The users themselves are often not sure of this, but the librarian can help by suggesting several appropriate possibilities, either in the pre-search interview or during the search. Does a user want to know, for example, how many high school graduates in the United States proceed the next year to college, how many sooner or later go to college, what percent of high school graduates start college, what percent of 18-year-olds attend college, or some other similar statistic? The precise form of the statistic acceptable to the user may be affected by what can be found and by how much time the user has available.

The librarian should also note carefully the unit of measurement employed in a statistical table. For large numbers, the unit may be thousands or millions. It may be a percent, a rate per capita or per thousand capita, or an index number. Index numbers give only the value of a statistic compared to an earlier time or compared to an average figure. An index number shows the amount of rise or fall of a statistic like population or consumer prices from a base year, often selected as being a typical year. If the user wants to compare the cost of living in different countries, these index numbers cannot be used to answer the question asked; they can only show the amount that the cost has increased or decreased in each country from a stated base year. The only way that cost of living could be compared between several countries (or between several cities) would be to base the costs on a standard medium of purchase such as dollars or, even better, on a day's wages in each country. But in any case, the librarian must note what the unit of measurement is and what it tells. If a percent is given, it is important to note what the percent represents. The unit of measurement might be a value not familiar to the average American, such as piasters or hectares, and may need to be interpreted. Because of the difficulty of this type of question, it will frequently be necessary to help the user find a needed statistic instead of simply furnishing an appropriate source and expecting the user to do the searching, as is often done with periodical indexes.

COMPILATIONS OF STATISTICS

165.   U.S. Department of Commerce. Bureau of the Census. **Statistical Abstract of the United States.** Washington, D.C.: Government Printing Office, 1879- . Annual.

166.   U.S. Department of Commerce. Bureau of the Census. **County and City Data Book, 1983.** Washington, D.C.: Government Printing Office, 1983. 996p.

167.   U.S. Department of Commerce. Bureau of the Census. **State and Metropolitan Area Data Book, 1982.** Washington, D.C.: Government Printing Office, 1982. 611p. Paper.

168.   U.S. Department of Commerce. Bureau of the Census. **Historical Statistics of the United States, Colonial Times to 1970.** 2 vols. Washington, D.C.: Government Printing Office, 1976.

Statistical Abstract of the United States has so many up-to-date statistics on various subjects that it is usually the first source to check. It has summary statistics on social, political, and economic characteristics of the United States under 34 broad sections such as population, vital statistics, education, public lands, and prices. If more detail is needed, the source of the summary data is given at the foot of each table. *County and City Data Book*, irregularly revised, provides statistics on population, housing, retail and wholesale trade, finance, schools, hospitals, climate, and other measurable aspects of geographical units smaller than those covered in *Statistical Abstract.* Primary arrangement is by geographical-political unit: states, counties, cities with 25,000 or more inhabitants, and places with 2,500 or more inhabitants. The last unit includes incorporated towns and cities and census designated places. The *State and Metropolitan Area Data Book* has similar social and economic data for SMSAs, core cities, and regions/divisions/states. SMSAs (Standard Metropolitan Statistical Areas) are areas, designated by the U.S. Office of Management and Budget, that contain a large population nucleus with surrounding communities having a high degree of social and economic integration with the core city. *County and City Data Book* and *State and Metropolitan Area Data Book* supplement the *Statistical Abstract*, which does not analyze statistics by geographical/political units other than states and selected major cities. *Historical Statistics of the United States* gives figures on the social, economic, political, and geographical development of the country from the time of the earliest data available to the present.

169.   U.S. Department of Commerce. Bureau of the Census. **Census.** Washington, D.C.: Government Printing Office, 1790- . Decennial.

The statistics presented in the 1980 decennial *Census* are heavily used, especially by faculty and students in the areas of sociology, urban planning, and commerce. Characteristics of the family in the United States, such as the number of one-parent families, family size, income, housing, and number of wage earners in the family, are wanted by sociologists. Students and faculty in urban planning are interested in population changes and migration. Commerce students want marketing data, family income, and population concentration. The decennial census consists of series on population and housing. The *Census of Population: Characteristics of the Population* is the most used set. It has separate issues for each state, territory, and dependency; each of these has detailed statistics on the number of inhabitants, general population characteristics, general social and economic characteristics, and detailed population characteristics. Besides this set, there are the *Census of Housing: Characteristics of Housing Units*, the *Census of Population and Housing: Census Tract Reports*, and other detailed parts. The amount of data and their various analyses are overwhelming, and it would be helpful to spend some free time studying the census reports to learn what is available.

170.   United Nations. Statistical Office. **Statistical Yearbook.** New York, 1949- . Annual.

This compilation is similar to *Statistical Abstract of the United States.* It gives comparative statistics for all countries of the world on population, manpower, education, agriculture, trade, wages and prices, and other social and economic statistical data. These are provided by each country to the Statistical Office of the United Nations, and if a country fails to send updated figures, the *Yearbook* uses the latest available data.

171.   **Monthly Bulletin of Statistics. Bulletin mensuel de statistique.** New York: United Nations, Statistical Office, 1947- . Monthly.

Most needs for statistics are for the most recent data available. The *Monthly Bulletin of Statistics* is an effort to meet such needs for international statistics. Data from more than 200 countries are given on population, employment, production, trade, wages, finance, etc. Each issue also has detailed figures on some special subject. This bulletin serves much the same function for the statistics on foreign countries as *Survey of Current Business* and *Economic Indicators* do for those of the United States.

172.   Mitchell, B. R., ed. **European Historical Statistics, 1750-1975.** 2d rev. ed. New York: Facts on File, 1980. 868p.

Statistics are arranged under 11 broad areasa such as climate, population and vital statistics, labor force, and agriculture. These are reproduced from official publications of the various countries. The research for this book has been done carefully, but the figures between countries are not always comparable and must be used with caution. Data on some subjects are lacking here and must be sought in other compilations, such as Michael Alderson's *International Mortality Statistics* (New York: Facts on File, 1981).

173. **Annuaire de statistique internationale des grandes villes. International Statistical Yearbook of Large Towns.** Vol. 6, 1972. The Hague: Institut International de Statistique, 1976. 488p. Paper.

Population and vital statistics, housing and building statistics, and statistical data on economy, public utilities and transport, culture, and sports are given for European cities of 100,000 population or larger, for cities of other countries of 750,000 or more inhabitants, and for important capitals, if smaller than 750,000 population.

INDEXES TO STATISTICS

174. **American Statistics Index: A Comprehensive Guide and Index to the Statistical Publications of the U.S. Government** (ASI). Washington, D.C.: Congressional Information Service, 1973- . Monthly with annual cumulations.

175. **Statistical Reference Index: A Selective Guide to American Statistical Publications from Sources Other Than the U.S. Government** (SRI). Washington, D.C.: Congressional Information Service, 1980- . Monthly with annual cumulations.

176. **Index to International Statistics: A Guide to Statistical Publications of International Intergovernmental Organizations** (IIS). Bethesda, Md.: Congressional Information Service, 1983- . Monthly with quarterly and annual cumulations.

177. Wasserman, Paul, and Jacqueline O'Brien, eds. **Statistics Sources.** 8th ed. 2 vols. Detroit: Gale, 1983.

178. **SISCIS: Subject Index to Sources of Comparative International Statistics.** Compiled by F. C. Pieper. Beckenham, Kent, England: CBD Research, 1978. 745p.

Finding statistics in just the form and recency required by the user taxes both the ingenuity of the most experienced reference librarian and the resources of the most complete reference collection. Indexes like these, which refer to compilations of statistics, are of great value. *American Statistics Index* is a detailed listing of current statistical publications of the United States government with abstracts and a subject index. The two-volume annual cumulation, issued in July, lists all statistical publications available as of the preceding January 1st. It is in two parts: the *Index* volume, arranged by detailed subject and referring to the *Abstract* volume, where each document is abstracted. Monthly supplements are also divided into index and abstract sections, cumulating with number 6 in mid-year. *American Statistics Index* can be machine searched back to 1973 through DIALOG and SDC. *Statistical Reference Index* provides similar indexing to the statistical publications of trade, professional, and other nonprofit associations, business organizations, university research centers, state government agencies, and other American sources. The third of the publications by Congressional Information Service listed above indexes the English language publications of 80 to 90 major organizations, such as the United Nations and its satellite bodies, the Organization for Economic Cooperation and Development, the European Community, and the Organization of American States. Each issue consists of abstracts and various indexes. The following indexes are provided: subject, names and geographic areas; categories (e.g., age, commodity, country, industry); issuing sources; titles; and publication numbers. *Statistics Sources* covers statistics of the United States and many other countries, arranged by subject. Examples: educational advertising; education-veterans, Egypt-books translated, gasoline-taxes, Germany-chemical production. *SISCIS* indexes a number of statistical compilations covering the world or several countries. Under each subject, the area or countries for which statistics are available and a code symbol referring to the statistical compilation are indicated. A list of the compilations indexed is in the back of the volume.

6

BOOK REVIEWS

In most university libraries there will be many requests for help in finding book reviews. One large source of such requests is the student who has been asked to evaluate the authority and reliability of books cited in a term paper. This can be done by checking the credentials of the authors in who's whos and biographical dictionaries and by looking up reviews of the books. Another reason students want book reviews is to learn about the subject of a book and its scope, which are usually summarized in a review. In literature courses, where critical study of literary classics is emphasized, the student is sometimes asked to look up critical reviews of the work contemporary with its publication, as well as more modern criticism. In all of these cases, reviews are wanted primarily for older books rather than for recently published ones. In this respect, book review needs in the university library differ from those common in the public library. There will also be some requests for reviews of new books in the university library, but these will usually be for reference books and other scholarly, nonfiction books, rather than for novels, which are often wanted in the public library. Such requests for reviews of new books may come from all user groups: students, faculty, administrators, librarians, or the general public. In the public library and the school library, book selection commonly waits on several favorable reviews before a purchase is made. In large university libraries, however, this is seldom done. If the title of a new book fits the collection interests of the university and the book is being brought out by a respected publisher, it is acquired without waiting for reviews. Some universities have standing orders for the entire output of certain publishers. At least, this has been the past general practice of large university libraries, where book budgets were fairly generous. If budgets continue to be restricted, as they have been in recent years, university libraries may begin to depend more on reviews before ordering expensive works.

The first reviews to appear on a new book, usually in *Library Journal* and *Kirkus Reviews*, tend to be adequate for book selection purposes but do not go into the critical depth that students need. *Library Journal* reviews are very short; *Kirkus* reviews are longer but describe the content of the book more than its strong and weak points. The best informed and most critical reviews of nonfiction books are in the scholarly journals. These are written usually by specialists (many of whom have themselves written on the subject), are long (one to several pages), and are valuable for their critical comment. They often do not appear for a year or more after the book was published; but these are the reviews that best answer student needs.

Finding suitable reviews, like answering directory questions, seldom presents a problem to the librarian. Excellent indexes to book reviews are now available that simplify finding even the older reviews in scholarly and foreign language journals. We devote this separate chapter to them, however, because of their importance in the university library.

179. **Book Review Digest.** New York: Wilson, 1905- . Monthly except February and July with annual cumulation.

180. **Current Book Review Citations.** New York: Wilson, 1976- . Monthly except August with annual cumulation.

181. **Book Review Index.** Edited by Gary C. Tarbert and others. Detroit: Gale, 1965- . Bimonthly with issues 2, 4, and 6 cumulating the previous issue and annual cumulation. Cumulated edition, 1965-1984. Edited by Gary C. Tarbert and Barbara Beach. 10 vols. 1985.

These are the three most general indexes to book reviews. *Book Review Digest* is heavily used in the public library but is not as useful in the university library as the other sources described in this chapter. It is the most selective of these three, citing only books published or distributed in the United States or Canada and which have received at least two reviews in the English language periodicals it indexes (four reviews for fiction books) within 18 months after publication of the book. Government publications, textbooks, and technical books in the sciences and law are excluded. Only about 5,200 books per year are included in this service, and these are late, waiting until the required two to four reviews have appeared. An advantage *Book Review Digest* has over the other indexes to book reviews is that it reprints excerpts from the reviews and indicates whether or not they are favorable, making it often unnecessary to find the complete reviews. It can now be machine searched through Wilsonline. *Current Book Review Citations* collects citations to the book reviews in the more than 1,200 journals indexed by the various Wilson services. It does not reprint excerpts, but it cites reviews to more than 50,000 titles per year, fiction and nonfiction, covering all subjects, some foreign language titles, and books for children and young adults. Citations also are more up-to-date than in *Book Review Digest* since they are included as soon as each appears without waiting for a required number. *Book Review Index* is a similar index, citing reviews of approximately 56,000 books per year in 420 journals and major newspapers. Some science book reviews are included, but it is mostly reviews of books in the humanities and social sciences. *Book Review Index* can be machine searched back to 1969 through DIALOG.

182. **An Index to Book Reviews in the Humanities.** Williamston, Mich.: Phillip Thomson, 1960- . Annual.

References to book reviews in the fields of art, architecture, biography, theater, folklore, history, language, literature (even mystery stories), music, philosophy, travel, and adventure are indexed from about 450 journals in English, German, French, Spanish, and other languages. Reviews of about 75,000 books per year are cited, some in consecutive years, as reviews of a book continue to appear.

183. **Technical Book Review Index.** Pittsburgh: JAAD Publishing, 1935- . Monthly except July and August with cumulative index for the year.

Reviews of about 3,000 books per year are compiled in cooperation with the Science and Technology Department, Carnegie Library of Pittsburgh, and the Maurice and Laura Falk Library of the Health Professions, University of Pittsburgh. Until 1977 this index was published by the Special Libraries Association. Arrangement is by author within five broad subject categories: pure sciences, life sciences, medicine, agriculture, technology. Entries begin with complete bibliographic information for the book reviewed and include excerpts from the review as well as a citation. Due to time lag, this index is not useful for selection of current materials in science and technology, but it can be used by students, faculty, and librarians to locate reviews of older titles which have appeared in a wide range of scientific, technical, medical, and trade journals. The inclusion of excerpts in this index may eliminate the need to locate the original source in which the review appeared.

184. **National Library Service Cumulative Book Review Index, 1905-1974.** 6 vols. Princeton, N.J.: National Library Service, 1975.

185. **Combined Retrospective Index to Book Reviews in Scholarly Journals, 1886-1974.** Edited by Evan Farber and others. 15 vols. Arlington, Va.: Carrollton Press, 1979.

186. **Combined Retrospective Index to Book Reviews in Humanities Journals, 1802-1974.** Edited by Evan Farber, Susan Hannah, and Stanley Schindler. 10 vols. Woodbridge, Conn.: Research Publications, 1982-84.

The need for reviews of books published in earlier years and the effort to make easier the task of searching back files of hundreds of journals has spawned these three time-saving indexes. The first indexes the titles in *Book Review Digest*, 1905-1974, and the book reviews in *Library Journal*, 1907-1974, *Saturday Review*, 1924-1974, and *Choice*, 1964-1974. The *Combined Retrospective Index to Book Reviews in Scholarly Journals* offers author and title access to the book reviews in 459 scholarly journals from their beginning in the fields of history, political science, and sociology: e.g., *British Journal of Political Science* (1971-), *Canadian Welfare* (1924-), *Colorado Magazine* (1923-), *Economic History Review* (1927-), *Foreign Affairs* (1922-). Its companion work, the *Combined Retrospective Index to Book Reviews in Humanities Journals*, has author and title access to book reviews from more than 150 humanities journals from their beginning: e.g., *Classical Journal* (1905-), *Comparative Literature* (1949-), *Folklore* (1890-), *Mind* (1876-), *North American Review* (1815-). These retrospective book review indexes are especially suitable to university students' needs.

187. **Internationale Bibliographie der Rezensionen wissenschaftlicher Literatur (IBR).** Hrsg. von Otto und Wolfram Zeller. Osnabrück: Dietrich, 1971- . Semiannual.

A strong reference collection will also have this continuing set [*International Bibliography of Book Reviews of Scholarly Literature*] and the *Internationale Bibliographie der Zeitschriften-literatur* [*International Bibliography of Periodical Literature*], of which it forms part C. The bibliography of book reviews will probably not be used as often as the other indexes in this chapter, but it will be a valuable supplementary set to them. It indexes the book reviews in some 4,000 scholarly journals in English, German, French, Slavic, Italian, and other languages. Access is by subject, author of the book, and author of the review. This bibliography supplements the older set, *Bibliographie der Rezensionen*, vol. 1-77, 1900-1943 (Leipzig: Dietrich, 1901-44).

188. Gray, Richard A. **A Guide to Book Review Citations: A Bibliography of Sources.** Columbus, Ohio: Ohio State University Press, 1969. 221p. (Ohio State University Libraries, Publications, no. 2).

Lastly, we include this excellent work in which Gray cites, with annotations, 512 sources that index book reviews exclusively or along with other articles and features. These range from *Wellesley Index to Victorian Periodicals* to Greenway's *Bibliography of the Australian Aborigines and the Native Peoples of Torres Strait to 1959*. Items are arranged under subject in classified order and include serial publications, separately published bibliographies, and bibliographies published regularly in a journal. All subjects are covered, but sources which index only critical studies of literature are excluded. Each entry specifies the scope of the index or bibliography and its arrangement. There are indexes by subject, personal name, title, chronology ("Sources that cite reviews of books published 1800-1900"; "Sources that cite reviews of books published before 1800"), and country.

7

BIBLIOGRAPHIC INSTRUCTION

The one-on-one encounter between the reference librarian and the library user in the university may involve some instruction specific to the question which brought the user to the reference desk. Many reference librarians in university libraries have recognized the need for additional forms of instruction, particularly to aid students in making more effective use of the library's varied resources. As a result, bibliographic instruction programs have been developed as part of the information services provided by the reference department. This chapter provides an overview of the elements of these programs and identifies sources useful in their development.

In its most general sense, bibliographic instruction encompasses all activities designed to teach the user about library resources and research techniques. It is sometimes distinguished from library orientation, the activities that introduce users to the facilities, organization, services, and policies of a particular library. Terms such as *library instruction, library user education, bibliographic instruction,* and *bibliographic education* are then used interchangeably to denote teaching the efficient and effective use of the library and its resources. Activities can be designed to meet the needs of specific user groups such as freshmen, upperclassmen, and/or graduate students, while other activities serve the user community as a whole. Well-developed bibliographic instruction programs may increase the amount of work at the reference desk and the complexity of users' questions as users become more aware of the resources available and of the reference librarians' knowledge and skills. Although responsibility for bibliographic instruction often lies within the reference department, other organizational arrangements, such as a separate department for instruction, are possible. Subject specialists or bibliographers may be involved in instruction in their areas of expertise and audiovisual staff may assist in the development of instructional programs using nonprint media. In a decentralized library system with many departmental libraries, some effort may be required to coordinate instructional programs provided by the various service units.

METHODS AND MATERIALS OF BIBLIOGRAPHIC INSTRUCTION

A number of different methods of providing instruction can be employed. When orientation is the objective, tours are usually provided. Although tours conducted by a reference librarian are probably the most common, self-guided tours using either an audiotape or printed guide are an alternative which can be scheduled at the convenience of the user. A slide/tape presentation is another alternative, with pictures on slides replacing movement around the library.

Reference librarians often have opportunities to provide instruction through lectures in conjunction with courses in which a student is enrolled. A distinction is sometimes made between course-related instruction and course-integrated instruction. The former usually involves a single lecture given by the librarian, with instruction centering on the specific needs of the students in a particular class. Course-integrated instruction includes library instruction as an essential part of the course and requires cooperation between faculty and librarians in course design. At some universities, such instruction has become formally recognized as a separate, credit-bearing course in the curriculum. Content of such a course could include discussion of library resources, research methodology, and information retrieval. Where user needs can be identified, seminars and workshops may also be planned independent of any particular course. Examples include workshops on using special collections such as government documents or automated resources such as a library's online catalog.

One-on-one instruction is used for situations where the lecture method is inappropriate. Many libraries staff term paper clinics with librarians serving as term paper counselors, helping students to locate materials on a specific topic. More in-depth tutorials may be arranged for students working on theses or dissertations. For complex reference tools to be used effectively, point-of-use instruction may be employed. Information in either a print or nonprint format is prepared and located near the tool being explained. Programmed instruction, in either printed workbook or computer-assisted form, is also suitable for the individual user. Although computer-assisted instruction (CAI) has not yet been widely used because of the expense of equipment and program development, the growing availability of microcomputers is likely to lead to an increase in CAI for bibliographic instruction when the content is best conveyed through an interactive program.

Each instructional method may make use of one or more forms of instructional materials. Although many of these are prepared inhouse, it is also possible to purchase published sources or to borrow materials developed at other libraries and made available through a clearinghouse. The major clearinghouse operating at the national level in the United States is LOEX (Library Orientation-Instruction Exchange) at Eastern Michigan University, established in 1972 to collect, organize, and disseminate library instructional materials.[1]

Many materials in printed form, such as library handbooks and individual sheets describing library policies or services, are intended for all users of the library. Others, such as workbooks and exercises, are distributed to users attending lectures, courses, or workshops. Guides to particular tools are prepared as part of point-of-use instruction or for distribution to groups likely to make use of these tools. When topics of interest to library users are identified, the reference staff may compile subject guides for distribution. These can take the form of either bibliographies or pathfinders, structured guides that arrange the basic resources available in search strategy order.

Although the preparation and display of nonprint materials requires special equipment, they are often used as an alternative or supplement to print materials. For example, transparencies can accompany lecture presentations, audiocassettes can support point-of-use instruction, and slide/tapes can be used for orientation to the library or explanation of particular tools. Other possible formats include videotapes, films, and filmstrips. The floppy disk with instructional software is likely to become a more popular medium as microcomputers become more available.

---

[1]Carolyn A. Kirkendall, "Library Use Education: Current Practices and Trends," *Library Trends* 29 (1980): 29-37.

PLANNING, IMPLEMENTING, AND EVALUATING BIBLIOGRAPHIC INSTRUCTION PROGRAMS

No single method of instruction or type of instructional material is appropriate to every situation. Given the wide variety of instructional methods and materials which could be used as part of a bibliographic instruction program, the program must be designed to exploit each to best advantage. The "Guidelines for Bibliographic Instruction in Academic Libraries" prepared by the Bibliographic Instruction Task Force of the Association of College and Research Libraries identifies a number of factors to consider in planning, implementing, and evaluating bibliographic instruction programs.[2]

Planning should begin with an assessment to identify user needs for orientation to the library's facilities and services and for instruction in the use of the library's collection and bibliographic structure. Methods of assessing needs include study of the curriculum, analysis of available campus data, collection of opinions from students and faculty through interviews and questionnaires, and review of the types of questions already handled at the reference desk. The needs of each institution will be somewhat different depending on the institutional setting (size of the university and types of programs offered), library facilities (degree of decentralization, arrangement of the collection, level of automation), and student population (level, background). The needs assessment is followed by preparation of a written profile of the user community's information needs, which serves as the basis for the development of a written statement of objectives for bibliographic instruction. The content of the program will be the knowledge, skills, processes, and attitudes to be learned or developed, as suggested by the needs assessment.

Plans for the bibliographic instruction program must specify what is to be taught, the methods to be used, the sequence of activities, the audience for each activity, and the instructors, resources and facilities required. Some activities will be the responsibility of reference librarians alone while others will involve cooperation with other people on campus, such as faculty members teaching courses for which course-integrated instruction is suitable. Where plans are made for instruction of students in a particular discipline or department, it is necessary to take into account the unique information needs and use patterns of that subject area. Each instructional activity will demand certain resources: staff time for preparation, presentation and updating; equipment and space for preparation and presentations; and the instructional materials themselves. Depending on the content which is to be covered, it may be possible to purchase or borrow materials developed elsewhere instead of developing materials inhouse. If a library is to be involved in bibliographic instruction, continuing financial support is required to provide the staff, equipment, materials, and facilities necessary to attain the delineated objectives. An evaluation component should be included in the instruction program to monitor its effectiveness and to suggest areas for further development and improvement.

Several publications suitable for use by librarians involved in planning or further developing bibliographic instruction programs are now available. Selected publications of particular interest to the academic librarian are described in the next two sections of this chapter. The emphasis here is on publications for the librarian involved in bibliographic instruction rather than for the library user.

---

[2]"Guidelines for Bibliographic Instruction in Academic Libraries," *College & Research Libraries News* 38 (1977): 92.

BIBLIOGRAPHIES, PERIODICALS

189.   Lockwood, Deborah L., comp. **Library Instruction: A Bibliography.** Westport, Conn.:
       Greenwood, 1979. 166p.

This annotated bibliography arranges 934 items in three broad categories: general philosophy, types of libraries, and teaching methods and formats. Sources listed are either published or available through ERIC and are intended to be of use to the librarian developing an instructional program. Most materials were published in the 1970s, with selective coverage before then. An author index is provided.

190.   Rader, Hannelore B. "Library Orientation and Instruction — [year]." **Reference Services Review.** Ann Arbor, Mich.: Pierian Press, 1974- . Annual.

This regularly updated annotated bibliography covers publications for a given year which deal with some aspect of orienting library users to the library or instructing them in the use of library resources. All types of libraries are included, but discussions of programs in academic libraries are the most numerous. The growth of literature in bibliographic instruction is evident in the corresponding growth of this bibliography, from three pages with 29 entries for the literature of 1973 to thirteen pages with 161 entries for the literature of 1983.

191.   **Research Strategies: A Journal of Library Concepts and Instruction.** Ann Arbor, Mich.:
       Mountainside Publishing, 1983- . Quarterly.

Articles appearing in this journal discuss instructional content and techniques, controversies in bibliographic instruction, and problems of bibliographic instruction organization, administration, and evaluation. There are regular columns and book and article reviews.

192.   **LOEX News: The Quarterly Newsletter of the Library Orientation-Instruction Exchange, The National Clearinghouse for Library Use Instruction.** Ypsilanti, Mich.:
       Center of Educational Resources, Eastern Michigan University, 1973- . Quarterly.

Designed as a medium for current awareness, this newsletter regularly lists items available for borrowing through the LOEX clearinghouse. New commercially available instructional materials that can be purchased are also listed. Regular sections include news, letters, a calendar of conferences, and bibliographies of articles and ERIC documents related to bibliographic instruction.

HANDBOOKS, TEXTBOOKS

193.   Renford, Beverly, and Linnea Hendrickson. **Bibliographic Instruction: A Handbook.**
       New York: Neal-Schuman, 1980. 192p.

194.   Freedman, Janet L., and Harold A. Bantly. **Information Searching: A Handbook for Designing & Creating Instructional Programs.** Rev. ed. Metuchen, N.J.: Scarecrow, 1982. 198p.

Bibliographic Instruction: A Handbook provides a practical guide for those involved in developing and improving bibliographic instruction programs and activities. Separate chapters consider the major instructional methods and materials: orientation, printed materials (handbooks, bibliographies, topical guides, and signs), course-related instruction, library skills workbooks, credit instruction, computer-assisted instruction, and audiovisual materials. A brief glossary defines basic bibliographic instruction terminology. *Information Searching* provides step-by-step guidelines for designing programs to assist users in gaining access to information resources. Separate chapters cover purposes, needs assessment, program development, and program evaluation. In addition, the chapter on approaches and methods includes specific examples of pathfinder-type guides, slide-tape programs, subject-related units, and a course in information searching.

195.   American Library Association. Association of College and Research Libraries. Bibliographic Instruction Section. Research Committee Subcommittee on Evaluation. **Evaluating Bibliographic Instruction: A Handbook.** Chicago: American Library Association, 1983. 122p.

For the librarian unfamiliar with evaluation techniques, this handbook offers an introduction to the basics of evaluation together with guides to additional sources of information. Chapters trace the evaluation process through a logical sequence: describe the purpose of the evaluation, describe the program in terms of goals and objectives, determine criteria to be used for evaluation, develop evaluation procedures and overall design of the study, develop instruments and collect data, analyze data and report results. The handbook includes both a glossary and a bibliography of related works.

196.   Beaubien, Anne K., Sharon A. Hogan, and Mary W. George. **Learning the Library: Concepts and Methods for Effective Bibliographic Instruction.** New York: Bowker, 1982. 269p.

197.   Breivik, Patricia Senn. **Planning the Library Instruction Program.** Chicago: American Library Association, 1982. 146p.

Learning the Library examines the concepts, techniques, and applications of bibliographic instruction in the academic library and is intended as a how-to guide for successful program development. The focus of instruction emphasized is the research process, as presented in either a single lecture or full course. Aspects of planning and implementation are also discussed. *Planning the Library Instruction Program* surveys all aspects of planning and implementing programs rather than exploring particular instructional methods in depth.

198.   Rice, James, Jr. **Teaching Library Use: A Guide for Library Instruction.** Westport, Conn.: Greenwood, 1981. 169p.

199.   Roberts, Anne F. **Library Instruction for Librarians.** Littleton, Colo.: Libraries Unlimited, 1982. 159p.

Although not restricted to academic libraries, *Teaching Library Use* provides practical information on designing library instruction programs suitable for university libraries. Discussion of instructional methods is in three parts: library orientation, library instruction, and bibliographic instruction, used here to denote formal courses in bibliography. Several useful appendixes follow the main text, including lists of sources for commercially available audiovisual materials, sources to assist with local production of audiovisual materials, selected textbooks for use in library instruction, and sources to assist with local construction of tests. *Library Instruction for Librarians* is another text covering all aspects of planning and implementing bibliographic instruction programs. Its appendixes reprint a number of key documents, including a model statement of objectives for academic bibliographic instruction and a series of checklists for organizing and managing a library instruction program. Discussion of instructional methods highlights advantages and disadvantages, and some chapters conclude with exercises in addition to suggested lists of readings.

8

ONLINE SEARCHING

The availability of machine-readable databases accessible through online search systems has extended the range of information sources which university reference librarians regularly use in their work. Many databases are the byproducts of the process used to create printed reference tools and thus are similar or identical in content to sources already available in the university library's reference collection. However, the fact that the contents are machine-readable means that different approaches to searching those contents are possible. In addition, a growing number of databases are available only in machine-readable form. Use of online search systems thus allows access to information sources and provision of services not possible otherwise. This chapter provides an overview of the capabilities of online search systems and databases, and suggests how they can be integrated into reference work. In addition, sources useful to the librarian involved in online searching are described.

It is helpful to begin discussion of online searching by identifying the types of organizations contributing to the availability of databases online. The database producer is the organization which collects or generates information and produces it in machine-readable form. Many database producers also publish a print product equivalent to or derived from the machine-readable database. Many publishers of reference tools, such as Marquis Who's Who and The H. W. Wilson Company, are now also database producers. The organization which makes one or more machine-readable databases available for searching online is referred to as an *online vendor* or *search service*. In some cases the database producer may also be an online vendor, as in the case of the Wilsonline service provided by The H. W. Wilson Company. In other cases the database producer arranges to make the database available through one of the major online vendors who provide access to databases created by many different producers. The three major vendors of this type in the United States are Bibliographic Retrieval Services (BRS), DIALOG Information Services (DIALOG), and SDC Information Services (SDC). Although the words *BRS* and *DIALOG* are also used to refer to the online search system provided by the search service, in the case of SDC the search system is called *ORBIT*. The third type of organization involved in accessing databases online is the telecommunications network which provides the communication links between the online vendor's computer system and user terminals. Although ordinary telephone lines can be used for this purpose, it is more common to use a network dedicated to data communications, such as TYMNET, TELENET, or UNINET. Another category of online systems used in reference work is the bibliographic utility, such as OCLC and RLIN. These systems provide access to machine-readable catalog records for many types of materials which have been contributed by member libraries.

REFERENCE APPLICATIONS OF ONLINE SEARCHING

For several years after the introduction of online search systems, they were used primarily for comprehensive retrospective searching of the literature. Because many databases are updated on a regular basis and search strategies can be stored online, selective dissemination of information (SDI) is also possible, with periodic printouts of references related to a particular topic. As reference librarians have become more familiar with online searching and as the number and variety of databases available online have increased, the use of online searching for ready reference has become much more common. Examples of the types of questions which can be handled quickly online include verification of partial or garbled citations, identification of appropriate subject headings under which to search for a topic, identification of current addresses for authors who have recently published an article indexed in one of the databases, and location of articles which discuss new terms for which entries have not yet been added to dictionaries. The bibliographic utilities such as OCLC are also used for verification and can identify holding libraries for materials sought by library users but unavailable locally.

REFERENCE INTERVIEW IN ONLINE SEARCHING

When online search systems are used for ready reference, the reference interview is not likely to differ from that in traditional reference work. When the objective is retrospective searching of the literature, an extended interview may be required so that the librarian fully understands the user's request before undertaking a search on the user's behalf. Many libraries make use of search request forms to give the librarian a written, rather than merely a verbal, statement of the information needed. The search request form asks the user to provide a narrative description of the need. In addition, search limitations may be specified if the user is interested in only some languages, document types, or a limited time period. Other elements of the request form can ask the user to specify the purpose of the search and to note references already known. The latter can be helpful to the librarian in preparing a search strategy or in checking its correctness.

With the completed search request form in hand, the librarian will focus the interview on clarifying concepts that are not understood and expanding upon those that are not adequately described. The librarian may conclude at this point that the request is better handled by available printed tools. When the decision is made to carry out an online search, the interview must include some discussion of what computer searching can and cannot do, so that the user has realistic expectations of the outcome of the search. In addition, if the user will be charged a fee for the service, the interview should include some explanation of the basis for determining the cost of the search. Given the information gained through the interview, the librarian can select databases most likely to contain relevant references and devise a search strategy. In many libraries the user is encouraged to be present when the online search is conducted so that the output can be judged for relevance, and revisions — if required — can be made in the search strategy as the online search progresses.

DATABASES AS INFORMATION RESOURCES

A taxonomy of databases can be used to categorize the resources available online. The most common distinction is between bibliographic and nonbibliographic databases. In a bibliographic database, the records contain information about a document (title, author, source, subject) rather than the document itself. Bibliographic databases correspond to indexes, abstracts, and bibliographies. Nonbibliographic databases are of several types: numeric, directory, and full text. Numeric databases include numbers and associated descriptive data. Census data, stock market quotations, and property data for chemical substances are all examples of numeric (or textual-numeric) databases. As noted in chapter 3, a number of directory databases, such as the ELECTRONIC YELLOW PAGES, are now online. With the availability of inexpensive mass storage devices for machine-readable data, full text databases have emerged as an important category. A number of periodicals, newsletters, and newspapers now have their full texts online. In addition some publishers of reference books, such as encyclopedias, have made the full text, but not illustrations, available online. Although the use of bibliographic databases in reference work is well established, possible uses for the many forms of nonbibliographic databases are still being explored.

Search Strategies

Search strategy development begins with selection of the database(s) to be searched. Factors to be considered in selecting a database include subject content, type of source material cited, contents of a database record available for searching, time period covered, and cost of the database. Search strategy formulation may be thought of as a translation process, taking the user's information request and creating a strategy in a language and format acceptable to the online system. This process begins with an identification of all the separate concepts that make up the search request. Each of these concepts is then expressed by one or more terms. Depending on the database to be searched, these terms may be selected from a thesaurus or subject heading list or they may be "free text" terms likely to occur in document titles and abstracts. For free text terms, truncation can be used, matching on any term that begins with the specified word stem. Once terms have been selected, logical operators are applied to the concept groups. Terms within the same group are connected by OR, meaning that any of the terms in that group may occur in a retrieved document. The AND operator is used to combine groups, specifying that at least one term from each group must occur in order for a document to be retrieved. Terms may be excluded from retrieved documents by using NOT. Some search systems have additional logical operators for searching the text of title and abstract. For example, the searcher may be able to specify that two terms occur in the same sentence or immediately adjacent to each other. If the user has expressed a desire to limit by language, document type, or time period, these restrictions can also be incorporated into the search strategy.

To take full advantage of the capabilities of online search systems when developing search strategies, the librarian must be thoroughly familiar with the features of both the search systems and the databases to which they provide access. Several advantages can be identified when online searching is compared to manual searching of printed tools. Where databases represent cumulations of many years of coverage or a merging of the contents of several printed tools, it is possible to search the complete contents at one time, thus reducing considerably the time required to conduct a search. There are more access points for subject searching online because words from title and abstract are searchable in addition to assigned subject headings. Using logical operators, the librarian can search several terms in the required logical combinations at one time. The search can be narrowed or broadened as needed by using limiting features or making the strategy less restrictive. A strategy can be saved and processed quickly on several databases in succession. Finally, the printout from databases is more convenient than the citations copied from printed sources.

In spite of the numerous advantages of online searching, certain disadvantages should also be recognized. Subject and time period coverage do not yet match what is available in printed indexes and abstracts. Browsing is difficult and a search is most successful if the topic can be precisely specified. The computer is matching terms rather than concepts, and so relevant items will be missed unless all possible ways of expressing a concept can be anticipated. In addition, some users may be reluctant to delegate the literature searching activity to another person or they may not be able to afford the fees charged for the service.

MANAGEMENT ASPECTS OF ONLINE SEARCHING

Introduction of online searching as a service of the reference department raises a number of management issues that can only be mentioned here. Provision of the service necessitates adequate facilities and equipment. Terminals or microcomputers with communications capability must be purchased and convenient locations readied for them. Search services to be used must be selected, based on such factors as databases offered, training required, and fees charged. Documentation supporting the databases and search systems to be used must be purchased and regularly updated. Staffing patterns must be determined and staff selected to provide the service must be trained. If online searching is to be used in ready reference, then all reference staff should develop at least basic search skills. For the more comprehensive retrospective searching, staff may develop areas of specialization, becoming expert in the use of particular databases and/or search systems. Sufficient opportunities to do online searching must be available if searching skills are to be retained. In addition, some consideration should be given to continuing education so that skills can be further developed. Methods for evaluating performance of the service should be implemented.

Because there is a charge each time an online system is used, costs and methods for cost recovery must be considered. Charges reflected on the bills for using online systems have several components: telecommunications, connect time, database royalties, and print charges for citations printed online or offline at the vendor's site. A number of cost recovery options exist: the library covers all costs, costs are divided between the library and the user, or the user pays all costs. The most common arrangement is for the user to pay some of the costs, such as those billed by the online vendor, with the library absorbing all other costs associated with providing the service including staff time.

The final two sections of this chapter include a number of sources which discuss the basics of online searching and management considerations in establishing online searching as one of the services of the reference department. In addition, several sources for keeping up with changes in available search services and databases are identified. No effort has been made to list documentation available from database producers or online vendors, but selected database and search service directories are described in chapter 3 (entries 115-117). In addition, whenever a database corresponding to one of the reference sources described in this book is available through one of the major online vendors, this is noted in the annotation for that source.

BIBLIOGRAPHIES, PERIODICALS

The literature of potential relevance to the online searcher is large, scattered, and rapidly growing. Fortunately a number of bibliographies are available to assist in locating older material. Periodicals devoted to new developments in online searching and databases help the librarian stay abreast as the technology changes and databases proliferate.

200.   Hall, J. L., and A. Dewe. **Online Information Retrieval, 1976-1979.** London: Aslib, 1980. 230p. (Aslib Bibliography 10).

201.   Hawkins, Donald T. **Online Information Retrieval Bibliography, 1964-1979.** Marlton, N.J.: Learned Information, 1980. 175p.

The bibliography compiled by Hall and Dewe covers journal articles, reports, conference proceedings, and monographs, emphasizing subject-oriented information retrieval from bibliographic files rather than numeric data retrieval or computerized catalog access. It includes 890 annotated items in the main section and almost 170 unannotated items in the supplement. Both sections are in first author order. In addition, entries in the main section are accessible through a personal author index, report number index, and subject index. In contrast, Hawkins's bibliography is unannotated and specific subject access is provided through a keyword-in-context index based on article titles. The main body of the bibliography includes 1,784 items arranged by author within seven broad subject sections. There is also an author index. Sources covered include journal articles, conference papers, ERIC documents, and books. The bibliography is a merging of bibliographies which appeared annually in volumes 1-4 of *Online Review* (entry 204).

202.   Byerly, Greg. **Online Searching: A Dictionary and Bibliographic Guide.** Littleton, Colo.: Libraries Unlimited, 1983. 288p.

This source performs two functions: a dictionary of more than 1,200 entries gives brief but clear definitions for terms commonly found in the online literature and a bibliographic guide presents a topically arranged annotated bibliography of 722 journal articles. In addition, there is a short guide to sources of additional information and three indexes: periodicals cited, author, and subject. Terms included in the dictionary include words, acronyms, database names, and online commands for the three major search systems (BRS, DIALOG, and ORBIT). The bibliographic guide includes two major sections of articles: a general overview of online searching and specialized subject areas and databases of online searching. The latter section is intended for the experienced searcher since the articles cited provide details of how to perform searches in specific subject areas.

203.   **Library Hi Tech.** Ann Arbor, Mich.: Pierian Press, 1983- . Quarterly.

Two regular features of this periodical are of particular value to the online searcher. The Database Review Index (beginning in vol. 1, no. 2) is an annotated bibliography of articles on specific databases and changes in databases that have appeared in selected journals, monographs, or conference proceedings. Each bibliography is followed by an index of databases cited in the articles listed in the bibliography. The Search Strategy Index (beginning in vol. 2, no. 1) is an annotated bibliography of articles containing useful hints on search procedures, record structures and contents, and new database developments. Cited articles are drawn from the newsletters of database producers and online vendors, as well as selected journals and trade publications. The bibliography is accompanied by an index listing the names of databases and vendors cited in the articles listed in the bibliography.

204.   **Online Review: The International Journal of Online Information Systems.** Medford, N.J.: Learned Information, 1977- . Bimonthly.

205.   **Online: The Magazine of Online Information Systems.** Weston, Conn.: Online, 1977- . Bimonthly.

206.   **Database: The Magazine of Database Reference and Review.** Weston, Conn.: Online, 1978- . Bimonthly.

All three of these periodicals are devoted in their entirety to developments in online searching and databases, and they have similar features. All include news sections, feature articles, and book reviews. *Online Review* also includes a calendar of meetings and an annual update of Hawkins's bibliography (entry 201). Both *Online* and *Database* have regular columns covering such topics as document delivery, management of online services, and techniques for searching the chemical literature. *Online Review* has a more international perspective. *Online* and *Database* are complementary, with the former carrying articles on new technology in relation to online searching and the latter covering specific databases or groups of related databases. All three periodicals are valuable tools for the continuing education of the librarian involved in online searching.

HANDBOOKS, TEXTBOOKS

The books described in this section all introduce the reader to concepts and techniques of online searching. None can substitute for access to documentation provided by database producers and online vendors, however. Available documentation for the databases and search services to be used by the reference department must be acquired and studied as well, so that details specific to each source and service to be searched can be mastered. In addition, documentation is essential to provide current information, since features of databases and search systems may change over time, and books such as those in this section cannot keep pace with these changes.

207.   Fenichel, Carol H., and Thomas H. Hogan. **Online Searching: A Primer.** 2d ed. Medford, N.J.: Learned Information, 1984. 188p.

208.   Borgman, Christine L., Dineh Moghdam, and Patti K. Corbett. **Effective Online Searching: A Basic Text.** New York: Marcel Dekker, 1984. 201p.

As the titles of these books indicate, both are basic texts concerned with the concepts and skills necessary to search online systems effectively. Although there is considerable overlap in topics covered, each has unique features. *Online Searching* includes a discussion of the management aspects of offering the service and has a series of appendixes providing names and addresses of organizations in the online business as well as a glossary of online terminology. *Effective Online Searching* includes step-by-step instruction in search techniques and has a series of exercises, each using the same search topics, to illustrate search strategy construction, basic search steps, database selection, and term selection.

209.   Meadow, Charles T., and Pauline Atherton Cochrane. **Basics of Online Searching.** New York: Wiley, 1981. 245p.

210.   Chen, Ching-chih, and Susanna Schweizer. **Online Bibliographic Searching: A Learning Manual.** New York: Neal-Schuman, 1981. 227p.

Both of these texts are intended to teach the principles of online bibliographic searching. While *Basics of Online Searching* gives equal emphasis to commands used in three major search systems (BRS, DIALOG, ORBIT), *Online Bibliographic Searching* emphasizes DIALOG and devotes one chapter to comparisons among systems. *Basics of Online Searching* provides thorough discussions of the presearch interview and search strategy, while *Online Bibliographic Searching* includes discussion of online search service management. It also has a glossary and answers to online exercises in the *DIALOG Lab Workbook.*

211.   Palmer, Roger C. **Online Reference and Information Retrieval.** Littleton, Colo.: Libraries Unlimited, 1983. 149p.

212.   Klingensmith, Patricia J., and Elizabeth E. Duncan. **Easy Access to DIALOG, ORBIT, and BRS.** New York: Marcel Dekker, 1984. 220p.

Online Reference and Information Retrieval, a text intended for use as a workbook, is organized into three parts. The first provides an overview of the role of database producers, vendor systems, and the searcher. The second provides a practical orientation to searching on the ORBIT, DIALOG, and BRS systems. The final part includes analysis of the interview process and a discussion of trends and issues in online searching. Assignments accompany the text. *Easy Access to DIALOG, ORBIT, and BRS* is more advanced since it is directed at searchers who are already familiar with one of the three systems and want to be able to search the others. Throughout the text the similarities among the three systems are noted first, followed by the differences in the way each search function is performed. Problems are given at the end of each section, with answers at the end of the volume.

213. Gilreath, Charles L. **Computerized Literature Searching: Research Strategies and Databases.** Boulder, Colo.: Westview Press, 1984. 177p.

214. **Online Search Strategies.** Edited by Ryan E. Hoover. White Plains, N.Y.: Knowledge Industry Publications, 1982. 345p.

Search strategy is the focus of both books, but they differ in their intended audience. While *Computerized Literature Searching* is addressed to the scientist or advanced student unfamiliar with the development of search strategies for using computerized literature searching systems, *Online Search Strategies* offers online searchers practical tips and hints on the effective use of bibliographic databases and search systems in various disciplines. *Computerized Literature Searching* has a series of six chapters discussing research strategies for broad subject areas: agricultural and life sciences; social sciences and education; physical sciences and engineering; business; law; and humanities, the arts, and architecture. Each discipline-oriented chapter has three parts: a discussion of the characteristics and terminology of that field, a discussion of available aids for search strategy development, and a list of commonly available databases for that field. In contrast, *Online Search Strategies* begins with a discussion of the primary databases in a particular subject area. Sample searches are then used to illustrate database and search system features. Topics covered include U.S. government information, chemical information, biosciences, energy and the environment, social and behavioral sciences, patents, legal research, health sciences, news databases, and business and economics.

Section 2
REFERENCE SOURCES

INTRODUCTION

Many valuable reference works are described in section 1, "Reference Strategies." These are mostly general bibliographies, directories, encyclopedias, and other tools not related to specific disciplines or subject fields, and they are discussed in connection with reference needs of certain types, such as bibliographic verification, statistical questions, help with term papers and class reports, machine searching, etc. Section 2 is organized by academic discipline in the traditional grouping of humanities, social sciences, and basic and applied sciences. Many additional reference sources to aid in the study of particular subject fields are described in the following chapters. We have grouped these in each chapter by type: guides, bibliographies, indexes; dictionaries, encyclopedias; directories; and biography. Other divisions apply to sub-fields or to reference needs peculiar to the subject, such as "Religion in the United States and Canada," "Literary Criticism," "Tests."

In most major disciplines, one or more guides to the literature are available. These are always described, if available and recommended, at the beginning of the discussion of the particular subject. Such a guide is distinguished from a bibliography of the subject by its introductory instruction (selecting a term paper topic, finding pertinent information on the topic, using the library catalog and periodical indexes), by its selection of the best reference books for the beginning student, and by its evaluative annotations. All of these distinguishing features are not found in every guide to the literature. The bibliography (although sometimes titled "A Guide to ...") is either unannotated or has descriptive, rather than evaluative, annotations, and does not have instructions for the beginning student. We do not separate abstract indexes from periodical indexes that lack abstracts since their use by the student or research worker is essentially the same. Under the heading "Directories" we include only those directories of agencies, organizations, societies, or institutions. Membership directories of professional associations and others that simply list persons with their professional position are included under "Biography." Their use in reference work is often to obtain minimum information about a person for whom no other source of biographical information is available. "Handbooks" is a rubric for which a distinctive definition cannot easily be offered. A handbook is generally a compilation of useful directory, statistical, and other information for answering a miscellany of questions about a subject. We have included under this heading yearbooks, almanacs, companions, scientific tables, and other reference tools of a miscellaneous nature. Many of these are kept in the ready-reference collection. Other sub-divisions in the chapters of section 2 are self-explanatory and do not require comment here.

9

THE HUMANITIES

We begin this second section with the humanities because they antedate the sciences and social sciences as distinct studies or disciplines. The term *humanities* to designate those studies that are "concerned with human values and expressions of the spirit of man" (*New Encyclopedia Britannica*) goes back to the Renaissance term *studia humanitatis.* The English term *humanities* to designate studies concerned with human culture was not used until after 1700. The humanities are sometimes identified with liberal arts or the studies appropriate for the education of a free man (as opposed, in ancient Greece, to those for a slave or a barbarian). But today, liberal arts include the humanities, social sciences, and natural sciences and constitute those studies pursued for their own sake, not (necessarily) as preparation for a vocation. In this book we follow the usual division of academic disciplines into three groups: humanities, social sciences, and basic and applied sciences.

GUIDES, BIBLIOGRAPHIES, INDEXES

215. Rogers, A. Robert. **The Humanities: A Selective Guide to Information Sources.** 2d ed. Littleton, Colo.: Libraries Unlimited, 1979. 355p.

Rogers annotates 1,200 reference books and periodicals in the fields of philosophy, religion and mythology, the visual arts (painting, architecture, sculpture, and the applied arts), the performing arts (music, dance, and theater), language and literature. Even though there are special guides to the literature of most of these disciplines, this guide is an essential tool in the reference collection. It also has excellent introductory essays on accessing information in the several subjects, including a survey of the field and its divisions, subject headings under which a search of the literature may be made, and a description of associations, information centers, and special collections in the field.

216. Besterman, Theodore. **A World Bibliography of Bibliographies.** 4th ed. 5 vols. Lausanne: Societas Bibliographica, 1965-66. Supplement, 1964-74. Compiled by Alice F. Toomey. 2 vols. Totowa, N.J.: Rowman & Littlefield, 1977.

217. **Bibliographic Index.** New York: Wilson, 1938- . Semiannual.

218. Gray, Richard A. **Serial Bibliographies in the Humanities and Social Sciences.** Ann Arbor, Mich.: Pierian Press, 1969. 345p.

Often a bibliography on a specific small subject such as athletics in ancient Greece, the art of champlevé enamel in the Middle Ages, or Walt Whitman and his poetry is needed as a starting point for a term paper or to identify a bibliographic reference for which an author is not known. The first source to check for such a bibliography, after the library's own catalog, is *A World Bibliography of Bibliographies.* It lists more than 117,000 separately printed bibliographies from the sixteenth century to date. Toomey's supplement adds another 18,000 titles. Library catalogs, exhibit catalogs, and other lists of books on special subjects are included, but only those which have been issued with their own pagination. Bibliographies are listed without annotations under small subjects, many of which are proper names: e.g., military arts; mineralogy and mining; Minerva Press; Minet, Jean; miniature books; Minneapolis. The index volume lists bibliographies under author or, failing an author, under title. *Bibliographic Index* lists bibliographies published during the previous year whether issued separately or as part of a journal article or book. Subject headings are much more specific than in the Besterman work and many smaller bibliographies (approximately 10,000 per year) are included. This index will be consulted for a bibliography on any subject of recent interest, as well as for bibliographies supplementing those in Besterman's work. Recent volumes can now be machine searched through Wilsonline. Gray's book lists bibliographies which are published as a serial and those published regularly as part of a journal or yearbook. The latter, which Gray calls "concealed bibliographies," appear in one or more issues each year of such journals as *Walt Whitman Review, Ethnomusicology, PMLA,* or *Bulletin Thomiste.*

219.   **Humanities Index.** New York: Wilson, 1974- . Quarterly with annual cumulation.

As the information explosion makes a literature search in any specific subject more and more complicated, periodical indexes tend to become more specialized. *Humanities Index* and *Social Sciences Index* (entry 698) have succeeded *Social Sciences and Humanities Index* (1965-74), which in turn grew out of Wilson's *International Index* (1916-65). *Humanities Index* is usually the first place to start a search for periodical literature in any of the humanities, especially for undergraduate needs. It covers about 250 English language periodicals which are more specialized than those indexed in *Readers' Guide to Periodical Literature,* e.g., *Classical Review, Dance Magazine, Film Quarterly, Keats-Shelley Journal.* It is machine searchable through Wilsonline.

220.   **American Humanities Index.** Troy, N.Y.: Whitson, 1975- . Quarterly with annual cumulation.

Supplementing *Humanities Index* is this more specialized service which covers those "creative, critical, and scholarly serials in the arts and humanities that either are not indexed at all elsewhere or that are available only in indexing services not universally available." It indexes between 230 and 250 English language journals and little magazines, mostly in literature, e.g., *Menckeniana, Milton Quarterly, Mundus Artium, New Orleans Review, Pequod.*

221.   **British Humanities Index.** London: The Library Association, 1962- . Quarterly with annual cumulation.

Also supplementing the preceding indexes is *British Humanities Index,* which covers about 400 periodicals in the humanities, many of which are not widely held in this country: e.g., *Bedfordshire Archaeological Journal, Dorset Yearbook, German Life and Letters, Hermathena, Oriental Ceramic Society Transactions.* This index continues part of the earlier *Subject Index to Periodicals* (1915-61).

222.   Harzfeld, Lois A. **Periodical Indexes in the Social Sciences and Humanities: A Subject Guide.** Metuchen, N.J.: Scarecrow, 1978. 174p.

Periodical indexes covering special subjects are listed in this guide. More than 250 indexes are grouped under subject headings such as African studies; anthropology; archaeology; architecture; history of science; humanities; or Jewish studies. Most are in English, a few in French, German, or other Western language.

223.   **Arts & Humanities Citation Index.** Philadelphia: Institute for Scientific Information, 1976- . Three times per year with annual cumulation.

Modeled on the earlier *Science Citation Index* (entry 1223) and *Social Sciences Citation Index* (entry 699), this, too, is a valuable addition to the collection. It has several related uses. Its primary function is to indicate who has cited any previously published article, book, or other writing and in what journal article or book. The assumption is that a useful bibliography on a subject can be made by linking together the body of writings that are used and cited in further research on the subject. Besides its use for compiling a list of writings on a subject, it is a good tool for identifying a bibliographic reference that could not be found elsewhere, since it cites writings from so many sources over so many years. It is also often used to judge the importance of an individual's published work by the frequency with which it is cited by later writers. The three citation indexes published by the Institute for Scientific Information are made up of a Source Index, a Permuterm Subject Index, and a Citation Index. Some 6,400 journals and 120 books (numbers which increase each year) are checked for their citations in *Arts & Humanities Citation Index.* Of the journals, 1,200 are fully covered: articles, editorials, letters, notices, etc.; another 5,200 journals in sciences and social sciences are selectively covered for any articles that fall within the broad areas of arts and humanities. The books that are checked each year are multi-author biographical works, thematic collections of essays, and collections of critical essays. All articles and essays from these journals and books are cited under author in the Source Index. The Permuterm Subject Index lists all of these articles and essays under permuted words of their titles, rather than under subject headings applied to them. This index may be used to find articles of the previous year on a given subject or to identify an article by its title, even when the title is not correctly remembered. The Citation Index, which is the main index of the set, lists under author and title every writing cited in the articles of the Source Index, whether it be a book, article, report, or unpublished communication and regardless of its date. *Arts & Humanities Index* can now be machine searched through BRS.

224.   **Chicorel Index to Abstracting and Indexing Services: Periodicals in Humanities and the Social Sciences.** 2d ed. Edited by Marietta Chicorel. 2 vols. New York: Chicorel, 1978.

A library user sometimes wants to know if a particular journal is indexed or abstracted by any service and, if so, by which one. For example, a reader recalls seeing an article, the title and author of which may not be remembered, in a particular journal but cannot recall how many years ago. It is easier to check an indexing service under subject (or under author or title, if remembered) than to check volumes of the journal, especially if the volumes do not include annual indexes. Many of the indexing and abstracting services have multi-year cumulations, making the search easier. This Chicorel tool lists approximately 50,000 periodicals and serials in the humanities and social sciences and indicates the services which index or abstract each one.

CONFERENCE PROCEEDINGS

225.   **Directory of Published Proceedings.** Series SSH (Social sciences, humanities). Harrison, N.Y.: InterDok, 1968- . Quarterly with annual cumulation.

226.   **Index to Social Sciences and Humanities Proceedings.** Philadelphia: Institute for Scientific Information, 1979- . Quarterly with annual cumulation.

Conferences and conference papers are extremely important to the scholarly community because they represent the cutting edge of research. These two indexes, which focus on conferences in the humanities and social sciences, have been described above (entries 33, 37). The first lists only the conferences, with place, date, and their published proceedings. It does not detail the individual papers. The second indexes the individual papers given at the conferences as well.

GRANTS

227. Coleman, William E. **Grants in the Humanities: A Scholar's Guide to Funding Sources.** 2d ed. New York: Neal-Schuman, 1984. 175p.

Directories of sources of grants, awards, and other funds for support of research were described above in chapter 3, entries 106-110. This guide lists 136 funding sources for research projects in the humanities, with information on application deadlines and similar data needed by the applicant.

BIOGRAPHY

228. **Directory of American Scholars: A Biographical Directory.** 8th ed. 4 vols. New York: Bowker, 1982.

More than 37,500 living scholars of the United States and Canada are included in this edition with brief biographical data. Names are listed under broad field: volume 1, history; volume 2, English, speech, and drama; volume 3, foreign language, linguistics, and philology; volume 4, philosophy, religion, and law. Volume 4 also has an alphabetical index of names in all four volumes.

10

PHILOSOPHY, RELIGION, MYTHOLOGY

Philosophy, the pursuit of knowledge for its own sake (rather than a means to the practical control of one's environment), is the oldest of the academic disciplines. Western philosophy was a creation of the ancient Greeks, for whom it embraced all subjects. Aristotle speculated and lectured on the physical and biological sciences, politics, psychology, and literature as well as on logic, ethics, cosmology, and other subjects with which philosophy later became identified. In all subjects, his interest and that of the other philosophers was to get beyond popularly accepted notions and mythology and to discover the origins and fundamental reality of the world, to draw general conclusions and to formulate principles that would explain man and the world. Gradually, one after another of the modern academic disciplines separated itself from philosophy and redefined its fields of interest. The sciences, for example, were called "natural philosophy" as recently as the nineteenth century. The main branches of philosophy that developed through its history are cosmology (the nature of the universe), ontology (the essence of being), epistemology (the nature of knowledge), logic (the principles of proof), ethics (the nature of the moral), and aesthetics (the nature of the beautiful).

As more and more of the academic disciplines have established separate areas of research (sometimes including a branch of the subject such as "philosophy of history" or "philosophy of education"), philosophy as a separate discipline has tended to reserve for itself the role of explaining what lies behind and governs all other disciplines. In a general sense, philosophy, like mathematics, differs from other disciplines in being highly contemplative and based on reason rather than on observation. Philosophy seeks answers about the ultimate nature of things. An early question of the first Greek philosophers was, what is the fundamental stuff of which the universe is composed? A major project of two modern British philosophers was to specify with mathematical certainty the laws by which further truths can be deduced from universally accepted axioms in any science.[1] The contribution of another contemporary philosopher was a theory about how basic concepts of science and the questions scientists seek to answer change over a period of time.[2]

---

[1]Whitehead, Alfred North, and Bertrand Russell. *Principia Mathematica*, 2d ed., 3 vols. (Cambridge, England: The University Press, 1963).

[2]Kuhn, Thomas S. *The Structure of Scientific Revolutions* (Chicago: University of Chicago Press, 1963).

The reference literature of philosophy is smaller than that of most of the other traditional disciplines, as can be noted by checking Sheehy's *Guide to Reference Books*, Walford's *Guide to Reference Material*, or any other general guide to reference books. The boundaries of philosophy and its area of interest are much more defined than those of other disciplines. Except for the subject of the history of philosophy, research is in large part introspective and does not have the need to search out facts, statistics, references to literature, and other data for which reference books are used. If such a need does occur, it is likely to be in the investigation of some other discipline or disciplines and in the use of their literature. Much of the reference literature of philosophy is highly technical and difficult for the non-philosopher. This is particularly true of some of the dictionaries, since terms like *being, causation, matter,* or *truth* may be used in a very special sense. Such technical dictionaries will be familiar to the faculty members or graduate students in philosophy, who will do their own reference searching rather than try to initiate the reference librarian into the mysteries of their language. A representation of these technical works is included here, but our emphasis is on reference books needed for the undergraduate or the layman interested in philosophy.

Religion and mythology are included — perhaps unjustly — with philosophy in this chapter, but they lie closest to that discipline in their content. They, too, are concerned with ultimate causes, explanation of the beginning and end of the universe and man, and underlying bases of things. But where philosophy aims at detached and non-judgmental examination of fundamental questions, religion is strongly attached to, and supportive of, a particular body of doctrine and liturgy. Although religion is not one of the traditional academic disciplines, questions on religion are not infrequent in the university library, even in those universities that do not have a department or school of religious studies. All campuses have churches for one or more of the major Christian denominations and often for other major religions. Also, college students have more than an average amount of interest in religion, in cults, and other religious movements. Term papers in beginning English or rhetoric courses often include titles like "Religion in Dostoevski and Kazantsakis," "Brainwashing in Cults," or "The Shroud of Turin." Most university libraries, therefore, maintain at least a modest collection of the bibliographies, handbooks and yearbooks, encyclopedias, and sacred books of the major religions and Christian denominations. In addition, there is need for a handbook or other reference tool that identifies and explains sects and religious bodies that are not part of an established church. The religious questions most often encountered in a university (except in those universities that support a strong school of theology) are definitions of a term, identification of a person or a religious body, or directory or statistical questions. If a preponderance of the reference tools cited in this chapter concern Christianity and the Bible, it is because most questions, by far, relate to these. Other religions and religious bodies are represented, however, in the following pages.

Questions on mythology, usually questions of definition, arise from courses in literature or mythology. A few standard dictionaries of mythology are sufficient for such questions. Folklore is sometimes confused with mythology, but should not be. Mythology is a body of tales about the gods and the universe, intended to explain origins and observed phenomena. Folklore comprises the body of tales, beliefs, and superstitions that grew up in past years among illiterate people of a region and which still persists among some, especially those in an isolated rural area. Neither one is to be confused with interest in the occult. We do not include material on the occult in this book. Folklore studies have attracted increased attention in recent decades. We group folklore with anthropology, and reference sources on folklore are included in chapter 18.

PHILOSOPHY

GUIDES, BIBLIOGRAPHIES, INDEXES

229. DeGeorge, Richard T. **The Philosopher's Guide to Sources, Research Tools, Professional Life, and Related Fields.** Lawrence, Kans.: The Regents Press of Kansas, 1980. 261p.

A useful guide, listing from 2,500 to 3,000 books and articles, briefly annotated, but also including a section describing philosophical associations and other information on professional activity in philosophy. Besides philosophy as a separate discipline, the philosophy of education, philosophy of history, and philosophy of other disciplines are covered. Selected reference sources of other fields that may be useful to the philosopher in research are added. Most items are in English, but important references in French, German, Italian, Spanish, Russian, and Latin are included.

230. Tice, Terence N., and Thomas P. Slavens. **Research Guide to Philosophy.** Chicago: American Library Association, 1983. 608p. (Sources of Information in the Humanities, no. 3).

This is a type of guide different from the work by DeGeorge. Most of *Research Guide to Philosophy* is a historical survey of the whole field to the present time with references to bibliographies on each period and on its principal philosophers. Another large section surveys the major subdivisions of philosophy and the philosophy subdivisions of religion, history, education, and other disciplines. A small final section covers reference works in philosophy. Its value, then, lies more in helping the reader see the various aspects of the field and its development through centuries than in its introduction to the reference sources, where DeGeorge is stronger.

231. Guerry, Herbert. **A Bibliography of Philosophical Bibliographies.** Westport, Conn.: Greenwood, 1977. 332p.

Philosophy, like other fields, has a large number of specialized bibliographies, and these are often unknown to the reader or difficult to find. Guerry's work lists 2,353 bibliographies published either as monographs or as contributions to journals. A few bibliographies published as an appendix to a scholarly monograph on philosophy are included.

232. Totok, W., and others. **Handbuch der Geschichte der Philosophie.** 6 vols. Frankfurt am Main: Klosterman, 1964- . In progress.

233. Varet, Gilbert. **Manuel de bibliographie philosophique.** 2 vols. Paris: Presses Universitaires de France, 1956.

The best general bibliography of philosophy is the *Handbuch der Geschichte der Philosophie*, by W. Totok and others. But, like many monumental works undertaken by German scholars, it is slow in being finished. When complete, it will be in six volumes. As of this writing, it is through volume 4 (1981), *Frühe Neuzeit: 17. Jahrhundert* (*Early Modern Time: 17th Century*). The older French work by Varet is much smaller, but it is completed and will probably satisfy most undergraduate needs.

234. Bechtle, Thomas C., and Mary F. Riley. **Dissertations in Philosophy Accepted at American Universities, 1861-1975.** New York: Garland, 1978. 537p.

Ph.D. dissertations in the field of philosophy accepted at an American or Canadian university are listed by author, with an index by subject.

235. **Bibliography of Philosophy. Bibliographie de la philosophie.** Paris: Vrin, 1954- .
     Quarterly.

Only books are listed, with abstracts, but the bibliography is very complete. It attempts to
include every important book on the subject in English or other European language,
currently about 1,700 per year. Abstracts are in English, French, or German, depending on
the source of the abstract, and are arranged under broad divisions, e.g., logic, semantics,
philosophy of science, aesthetics. The annual index includes authors, titles, and subjects.

236. **Répertoire bibliographique de la philosophie.** Louvain: Éditions de l'Institut Supérieur
     de Philosophie, 1949- . Quarterly.

This is acknowledged as the most complete bibliography of the current literature, but it is
not annotated and is less well indexed than the other serial bibliographies described here.
From 11,000 to 12,000 items are listed each year in the first three issues: all articles from
more than 400 regularly screened journals, all books in Western languages, and selected
articles from additional journals. Arrangement is under broad subject. A list of the book
reviews and the annual indexes make up the fourth issue of each volume.

237. **Bulletin signalétique. 519: Philosophie.** Paris: Centre de Documentation Science
     Humaines, 1947- . Quarterly.

The French serial bibliography, *Bulletin signalétique*, is one of the best general periodical
indexes in the western world. Its different series cover many different disciplines; 519 lists
some 5,000 journal articles per year, selected from over 850 journals. The extremely wide
range of source journals includes many minor publications, titles in Japanese and Hebrew,
and journals on sociology, psychology, history, and other fields related to philosophy, as
well as many Western world journals on philosophy. Items with brief annotations are
arranged under broad subject. Author and subject indexes of each issue cumulate annually.

238. **The Philosopher's Index: An International Index to Philosophical Periodicals.** Bowling
     Green, Ohio: Philosophy Documentation Center, Bowling Green State University,
     1967- . Quarterly with annual cumulation.

Philosopher's Index would probably be the choice of the library that can afford only limited
coverage of the field. Articles and book reviews from all major philosophical journals in
English, French, German, Spanish, and Italian, plus selected journals in other languages are
indexed, currently about 1,200 items from about 260 journals per year. Each issue has three
parts: an index under small subject, giving only author-title information; an author index,
giving full bibliographic data and an abstract; and a book review index. *Philosopher's Index*
can be machine searched back to 1940 through DIALOG.

239. **The Philosopher's Index: A Retrospective Index to U.S. Publications from 1940.** 3 vols.
     Bowling Green, Ohio: Philosophy Documentation Center, Bowling Green State
     University, 1978.

240. **The Philosopher's Index: A Retrospective Index to Non-U.S. English Language
     Publications from 1940.** 3 vols. Bowling Green, Ohio: Philosophy Documentation
     Center, Bowling Green State University, 1980.

To aid in the search of the literature of philosophy since 1940, these two indexes,
supplementing the current *Philosopher's Index*, have been compiled. Books published
1940-76 and articles published 1940-66 are indexed. About 25 percent of both books and
articles have abstracts in the author section, volume 3. Articles published after 1966 are
found through the quarterly issues and annual cumulations of *Philosopher's Index.* Only
English language articles and books are included in these two sets, but publications in other
languages are indexed in the quarterly issues. Volumes 1 and 2 of each set are the subject
index without annotations; volume 3 is the author index with annotations.

DICTIONARIES, ENCYCLOPEDIAS

241.   Lacey, A. R. **A Dictionary of Philosophy.** New York: Scribner's, 1976. 239p. Paper.

242.   Flew, Anthony, ed. **A Dictionary of Philosophy.** New York: St. Martin's, 1979. 351p.

Often the user needs simply the identification of a person or a term associated with philosophy rather than a longer account. Either of these dictionaries is very good for such a need. The definitions in Lacey's dictionary are fuller, but the dictionary edited by Flew has about three times more entries (about 1,000 exclusive of cross-references compared to about 300 in Lacey).

243.   Brugger, Walter. **Philosophical Dictionary.** American ed. Translated and edited by Kenneth Baker. Spokane: Gonzaga University Press, 1972. 460p.

If possible, this dictionary should also be added to a collection. It is translated and adapted from a scholarly German dictionary that has long and authoritative, but clearly written, articles on terms, concepts, and philosophical schools (e.g., German idealism, good, guilt, historical certitude, hylemorphism, impossibility, individual). It does not include articles on proper names.

244.   Ritter, Joachim, ed. **Historisches Wörterbuch der Philosophie.** Rev. ed. 8 vols. Basel: Schwabe, 1971- .

The large collection on philosophy will also have this scholarly German work. It fills the same need as Brugger's *Philosophical Dictionary* — a discussion of the technical meanings of philosophical terms and concepts — but it goes much further. The original meaning of a term or concept and its subsequent changes and evolution as used by different writers are discussed in the long articles. Each article ends with a short bibliography of critical writings that discuss the concept further. When completed, it will be in eight volumes; as of this writing, it has reached volume 5, through the letters *Mn.* This work is a complete revision of Rudolf Eisler's *Wörterbuch der philosophischen Begriffe* (4th ed. 4 vols. Berlin: Mittler, 1927-30). Another older dictionary that discusses terms and concepts technically and cites their use by different philosophers is Andre Lalande's *Vocabulaire technique et critique de la philosophie* (Paris: Presses Universitaires de France, 1972).

245.   **The Encyclopedia of Philosophy.** Edited by Paul Edwards. 8 vols. New York: Macmillan & Free Press; London: Collier-Macmillan, 1967.

246.   Urmson, J. O., ed. **Concise Encyclopedia of Western Philosophy and Philosophers.** 2d ed. London: Hutchinson, 1975. 319p.

The *Encyclopedia of Philosophy* is another clear choice for the small reference collection that has only the most essential works in philosophy. Its articles tend to be heavy and technical, but it is the most authoritative and comprehensive encyclopedia in the subject. Bibliographies at the end of articles are useful if further information is needed. Philosophers, schools and movements in philosophy, and philosophical concepts are represented in the articles: e.g., cabala; Caird; Calvin; Cambridge Platonists; categories; causation; certainty. For minor subjects within articles, the index should be consulted, as should a subject index in any encyclopedia. This multi-volume encyclopedia is probably the single most used reference work in philosophy. An excellent one-volume encyclopedia of Western philosophers and philosophical thought is Urmson's book. Its discussions of philosophical systems and the thought of individual philosophers are better written and clearer than in most other works, although some philosophers take issue with certain of the comments expressed here.

247.   **Enciclopedia filosofica.** 2d ed. 6 vols. Florence: Sansoni, 1968-69.

If another encyclopedia is wanted in the strong reference collection, this is a desirable addition. Its articles are somewhat shorter than those of the *Encyclopedia of Philosophy*, but it covers many more terms and proper names. Even though neither the librarian nor the user may know Italian, a knowledge of Latin or one of the other Romance languages combined with a little imagination can enable one to pick the needed information from an article.

DIRECTORIES

248.   **Directory of American Philosophers, 1962-63-** . Edited by Archie Bahm. Bowling Green, Ohio: Philosophy Documentation Center, Bowling Green State University, 1962- . Biennial.

249.   **International Directory of Philosophy and Philosophers, 1965-** . Edited by Ramona Cormier and others. Bowling Green, Ohio: Philosophy Documentation Center, Bowling Green State University, 1965- .

These are companion volumes. Both list universities under a geographical arrangement. In the former work, names of faculty members in university departments of philosophy and summary statistics for each state (number of institutions offering philosophy, number of degrees awarded, and number of faculty members) are given. The international directory lists universities, journals, and publishers in the field.

HANDBOOKS

250.   Magill, Frank N., and Ian P. McGreal, eds. **World Philosophy: Essay-Reviews of 225 Major Works.** 5 vols. Englewood Cliffs, N.J.: Salem, 1982.

In any library, this set will get use by philosophy students and others who have not made this their principal study. The classics of philosophy are described in chronological order, beginning with the *Fragments* of Anaximander (6th century B.C.) and continuing to Wittgenstein (mid-twentieth century). For each work, there are introductory data (author, type of work, date, and principal ideas in the work); this is followed by a summary/critical essay of the work and abstracts of a few further critical sources. A glossary of about 200 terms is in the front of volume 1; an alphabetical list of the authors of the 225 classics and a bibliography of the further critical readings cited are at the end of the set. This is an expanded version of Magill's *Masterpieces of World Philosophy in Summary Form.* It is useful not only for students who have not completed assigned reading but also for students and others who need further understanding of a book they have attempted to read.

251.   Burr, John R., ed. **Handbook of World Philosophy: Contemporary Developments since 1945.** Westport, Conn.: Greenwood, 1980. 641p.

Recent developments in each country or region of the world are outlined in a series of chapters by scholars in those countries: prominent writers and teachers of philosophy, their major works, and their views. Philosophical associations, congresses, and meetings in the different countries are listed in appendixes, and there are two indexes, one for names of philosophers and teachers referred to, and another for subjects.

REFERENCE HISTORIES

252. Brehier, Emile. **The History of Philosophy.** Translated by Joseph Thomas and Wade Baskin. 7 vols. Chicago: University of Chicago Press, 1963-69.

253. Copleston, F. C. **A History of Philosophy.** 8 vols. Westminster, Md.: Neewman, 1963-66.

Questions such as "What school of philosophical thought in Japan was contemporaneous with Descartes?" or "What political origins, if any, were there for the rise and popularity of Neo-Platonism?" can sometimes be answered more satisfactorily with a good history of philosophy than with an encyclopedia or other type of reference source. The two widely available works listed above are among the best histories of philosophy available.

RELIGION

GUIDES, BIBLIOGRAPHIES, INDEXES

254. Adams, Charles J., ed. **A Reader's Guide to the Great Religions.** Rev. ed. New York: Free Press, 1977. 521p.

This guide is well suited to the needs of students, both graduate and undergraduate, who are curious about the religions of other countries and who want a good introduction to their history and their principal tenets. In a series of chapters by specialists, the best books and articles for an elementary study and understanding of Buddhism, Hinduism, and the other major living religions, as well as primitive and ancient religion, are described. Emphasis throughout is on books in English, but major sources in other languages and important articles are also included.

255. Wilson, John F., and Thomas P. Slavens. **Research Guide to Religious Studies.** Chicago: American Library Association, 1982. 192p. (Sources of Information in the Humanities, no. 1).

The first part of this book is a discussion of religious scholarship, citing hundreds of major studies. The second part is an annotated list of more than 200 major atlases, bibliographies, dictionaries, encyclopedias, and other reference works on religion. The emphasis here is more on research studies of the history and development of religion and of particular religions than on introduction to the religions. *A Reader's Guide to the Great Religions* cites five or more times more references to an individual religion than this work does.

256. Sandeen, Ernest R., and Frederick Hale. **American Religion and Philosophy: A Guide to Information Sources.** Detroit: Gale, 1978. 377p. (American Studies Information Guide Series, vol. 5).

It is a truism that the more restricted the subject of a bibliography, dictionary, or other reference source, the more intensely that subject is likely to be treated. Hence, this guide, as expected, has much more on the religions practiced in America than will be found in more general bibliographies. The authors aim to supplement Burr's *A Critical Bibliography of Religion in America*, citing books, dissertations, and articles published after 1961. Its 1,639 annotated references are arranged in chapters by chronological development of religion in America and by subject division within broad periods from the American Indian to the emergence of the counterculture movements of the 1960s.

257. Reynolds, Frank E., John Holt, and John Strong. **Guide to Buddhist Religion.** Boston: G. K. Hall, 1981. 415p. (Asian Philosophies and Religions Resource Guide).

258. Dell, David J., and others. **Guide to Hindu Religion.** Boston: G. K. Hall, 1981. (Asian Philosophies and Religions Resource Guide). 461p.

259. Ede, David, and others. **Guide to Islam.** Boston: G. K. Hall, 1983. (Asian Philosophies and Religions Resource Guide). 261p.

The series, which will also include a volume on Chinese religion and philosophy, is in answer to recent student interest in these subjects. Each guide is organized into chapters on the historical development, religious thought, authoritative and sacred texts, popular beliefs, the arts, social life and politics, ritual and practice, ideal beings (gods, demi-gods, saints), mythology, sacred locations, soteriology, and research aids. The references (mostly in English) are annotated.

260. **Religion Index One: Periodicals (RIO).** Edited by Paul D. Petersen. Chicago: American Theological Library Association, 1967- . Quarterly with semiannual and biennial cumulations.

261. **Religion Index Two: Multi-author Works.** Edited by Albert E. Hurd. Chicago: American Theological Library Association, 1976- . Annual.

The first of these indexes was formerly *Index to Religious Periodical Literature* (1953-76); it indexes more than 300 journals in English and other Western languages. Ancient and living religions of the world are covered in both of these journals. Entries in the subject index refer to the author index, where abstracts of the articles are included. There is also a book review index. *Religion Index Two* indexes monographs. It is supplemented by two special editions that extend its coverage: *Religion Index Two: Festschriften, 1960-1969*, edited by Betty A. O'Brien and Elmer J. O'Brien (1980); and *Religion Index Two: Multi-author Works, 1970-1975*, edited by G. Fay Dickerson and Ernest Rubinstein (2 vols., 1982). These indexes have been merged to form a single database which can be machine searched through BRS and DIALOG.

262. **The Catholic Periodical and Literature Index.** Haverford, Pa.: Catholic Library Association, 1969- . Bi-monthly. Cumulates every two years.

This index succeeds *Catholic Periodical Index* (1939-68) and *Guide to Catholic Literature* (1940-1968), continuing the volume numbering of the former. More than 200 Catholic periodicals, most in English, are now indexed, and selected books by Catholic authors or of interest to Catholic readers are included. Papal documents are indexed under the name of the appropriate pope. Many reviews are indexed under the headings Book Reviews and Moving Picture Reviews. Nontheological articles in Catholic periodicals on such subjects as counseling, creation, credit, crime, etc., are indexed. In this respect, the index resembles the *New Catholic Encyclopedia*, which is a general encyclopedia for the Catholic reader and has many articles on nontheological subjects.

263. **Bulletin signalétique.** 527: **Sciences religieuses.** Paris: Centre de Documentation Science Humaines, 1947- . Quarterly.

Although published in France and not available in every library, this is the most comprehensive bibliography of current periodical literature on religion. Some 1,200 journals on religion, philosophy, sociology, archeology, and related fields are now indexed. Most of these are in a major Western language.

264. **International Bibliography of the History of Religions.** Leiden: Brill, 1954- . Annual.

Nearly 500 journals on religion, archaeology, and antiquities are indexed; the content of these journals concerns primitive, prehistoric, and classical religion, as well as historical articles on living religions. But the editors have a struggle to get this index out; only one volume per year is issued, and it appears some six or seven years after the articles it indexes.

DICTIONARIES, ENCYCLOPEDIAS

265. **Abingdon Dictionary of Living Religions.** Edited by Keith Crim. Nashville: Abingdon, 1981. 830p.

266. **A Dictionary of Comparative Religion.** Edited by S. G. F. Brandon. New York: Scribner's, 1970. 704p.

Both of these dictionaries are very good for terms and names associated with the world's religions. The articles in *Abingdon Dictionary of Living Religions* are written by specialists and are scholarly, often ending with a short bibliography. But it is restricted to living religions, particularly to Christianity. A sampling of its articles' topics include: calendar, Christian; calendar, Jewish; caliph; Calvin, John; Campbell, Alexander; candlemas; canon law; canonization; Canterbury. Terms and names associated with the world's religions, whether living or dead, are in *A Dictionary of Comparative Religion.* Since its aim is to offer a comparative view of religions, the beliefs or practices of different religions are included in articles such as those on apostasy; apotheosis; arcana discipline; architecture (religious); art, sacred; asceticism; or astral religion.

267. **Encyclopaedia of Religion and Ethics.** Edited by James Hastings. 13 vols. New York: Scribner's, 1908-1927.

Although old, this work has never been adequately replaced by anything in English, and it must be in any good collection on religion. Its articles are long and scholarly, emphasizing the sociological and anthropological background of religion. Its best use is for primitive and ancient religion and religious practices, and, like *A Dictionary of Comparative Religion*, it offers much contrast among different religions. The index volume (Vol. 13) will lead to information on a given topic in many articles other than the main article. A more up-to-date encyclopedia that is also known for its research and scholarly articles is the German work (usually referred to simply as *RGG*), *Die Religion in Geschichte und Gegenwart: Handwörterbuch für Theologie und Religionswissenschaft* (3d ed. Edited by Kurt Galling. 7 vols. Tübingen: Mohr, 1957-1965). But, although it represents religions of different parts of the world and different eras, its emphasis is very heavily on Christianity.

Christianity

268. **The Oxford Dictionary of the Christian Church.** 2d ed. Edited by F. L. Cross and E. A. Livingstone. London: Oxford University Press, 1974. 1518p.

269. **The New International Dictionary of the Christian Church.** Rev. ed. Edited by J. D. Douglas. Grand Rapids, Mich.: Zondervan, 1978. 1074p.

When brief information is wanted on a topic, event, theological or liturgical term, person, group, or anything else associated with Christianity and its development, either of these dictionaries may be a good place to try first. *The Oxford Dictionary of the Christian Church* has more entries but is not quite as up-to-date as *The New International Dictionary of the Christian Church.*

270. **Encyclopedic Dictionary of Religion.** Edited by Paul K. Meagher, Thomas C. O'Brien, and Sister Consuelo Maria Aherne. 3 vols. Washington, D.C.: Corpus, 1979.

Although ostensibly covering all religions, this work is predominantly about the Christian religion and specifically about the Catholic religion. Many entries refer to non-Christian religions, groups, persons, and terms primarily as they have had an impact on Christianity. The Catholic orientation of the dictionary is reflected in the number of articles on Catholic persons and topics and in the treatment of theological and ethical topics.

271. Hardon, John A. **Modern Catholic Dictionary.** Garden City, N.Y.: Doubleday, 1980. 635p.

Although there are other dictionaries and encyclopedias devoted to Catholic interests and persons, the value of this one lies in its recent date, allowing it to reflect in its definitions the many changes in Catholic thought since the Second Vatican Council (1962), as well as in its coverage of older terms, events, and persons important in the Catholic Church. Its useful appendixes include a list of popes with their birthplace and the dates of their papacy; the Roman calendar, as revised after the Second Vatican Council; the Byzantine calendar; and a list of abbreviations for religious communities and secular institutes in the United States and Canada.

272. **The Maryknoll Catholic Dictionary.** Compiled and edited by Albert J. Nevins. Wilkes-Barre, Pa.: Dimension Books, 1965. 710p.

273. Richardson, Alan, ed. **A Dictionary of Christian Theology.** Philadelphia: Westminster, 1969. 364p.

The emphasis of these two dictionaries is theological and doctrinal. *The Maryknoll Catholic Dictionary* defines terms, concepts, and theological doctrines; places and proper names are included, but not personal names. Sample entries: pope, deposition of a; population control; portable altar; portiuncula indulgence; pragmatic sanction. Appendixes list patron saints; Catholic forms of address; biographies of deceased Catholics in the United States; and international Catholic organizations. *A Dictionary of Christian Theology* is written from the non-Catholic viewpoint but does not ignore Catholic doctrine. A number of professors of theology have contributed definitions. Among its approximately 1,500 entries are Apostolic Fathers; apotheosis; appropriation; ascension of Christ; monism; monolatry; and personal names Hume, Huss, Husserl, Marcellus of Ancyra, and Melanchthon. Names of psychiatrists and philosophers occur, as well as those of theologians.

274. **New Catholic Encyclopedia.** Prepared by an Editorial Staff at The Catholic University of America. 17 vols. New York: McGraw-Hill, 1967-1981. Reprint. Palatine, Ill.: Publishers Guild, 1981.

As a general encyclopedia for the Catholic reader rather than a strictly religious encyclopedia, its articles cover all aspects of knowledge and not only religious terms and names. A sampling of the articles includes abstract art; academic freedom; academies, literary; agricultural economics. Volumes 16 (1964) and 17 (1979) are supplements to the main set, covering "teachings, history, organization, and activities of the Catholic Church since the close of Vatican Council II."

275. **New Schaff-Herzog Encyclopedia of Religious Knowledge.** Edited by S. M. Jackson. 13 vols. New York: Funk & Wagnalls, 1908-1912. Index by George W. Gilmore. New York: Funk & Wagnalls, 1914. Reprint. 13 vols. Grand Rapids, Mich.: Baker, 1949-1950.

A new edition of this full, scholarly encyclopedia in English, written from the Protestant point of view, is sorely needed. This seventy-year-old work has definitive articles on Protestant denominations, liturgical and theological terms defined from a Protestant viewpoint, and persons who were important in the Protestant movement, as well as articles on persons and subjects associated with the Catholic Church before the Reformation. *Twentieth Century Encyclopedia of Religious Knowledge*, edited by L. A. Loetscher (2 vols., Grand Rapids, Mich.: Baker, 1955) supplements and updates articles in *New Schaff-Herzog Encyclopedia of Religious Knowledge* but cannot adequately replace the larger work. The scholarly German Protestant encyclopedia, *Theologische Realenzyklopädie*, edited by Gerhard Krause and Gerhard Müller (Berlin: De Gruyter, 1977-) is in progress, having at this time reached the letter *G*. It succeeds *Realencyklopädie für protestantische Theologie und Kirche* (24 vols., 1896-1913), on which *New Schaff-Herzog Encyclopedia of Religious Knowledge* was based.

Judaism

276. **Encyclopaedia Judaica.** 16 vols. New York: Macmillan, 1971-1972.

This is the best and most authoritative encyclopedia of the Jewish religion and culture in English. It is an international, scholarly project with long articles, which may be more than some readers want or need. An excellent one-volume encyclopedia is *Standard Jewish Encyclopedia*, edited by Cecil Roth (New York: Doubleday, 1959). Both include many articles relating to Jewish culture and history, as well as articles on theology, liturgy, and practices.

277. Klein, Isaac. **A Guide to Jewish Religious Practice.** New York: The Jewish Theological Seminary of America, 1979. 588p. (Moreshet series, Studies in Jewish History, Literature and Thought, v. 6).

A detailed, but easy-to-read, explanation and description of Jewish religious practice is given in this guide, which is certain to be used by students. Included are articles on general worship, special holy days, and observance of the law on different occasions: laws of mourning, dietary laws, marriage, dissolution of marriage, etc.

Other Religions

278. Parrinder, Edward G. **Dictionary of Non-Christian Religions.** Philadelphia: Westminster, 1973. 320p.

Non-Christian religions and mythologies are covered briefly in this dictionary. So much is attempted here, in fact, that it is seldom a first choice in answering a question but might be consulted if other sources fail. A few sample entries indicate the variety of articles: Harun-al-Rashid; haruspex; Harut and Marut; Hasidism; Heimskringla; hekaloth; Heket; Helen; Helios; henotheism; Heracles; Heracleitus.

279. Rice, Edward. **Eastern Definitions: A Short Encyclopedia of Religions of the Orient.** Garden City, N.Y.: Doubleday, 1978. 433p.

The author has tried to include those words from Eastern philosophy and religion which one might find in reading popular or scholarly books in English. Definitions vary from brief identification to lengthy articles. Entries are labeled by the religion with which they are related. There are also articles on topics, describing the practice in the different Eastern religions, e.g., caste, fire, food, human sacrifice. Articles on individual religions give their basic beliefs.

280.   **The Encyclopedia of Islam.** New ed. Edited by H. A. R. Gibb and others. Leiden: Brill, 1954- . In progress.

This is a comprehensive, scholarly encyclopedia, written for the specialist or advanced student. Such a user will not be hindered by the paucity of entries under English forms of names and subjects. Most articles are under the Arabic term or name, but in Roman type. Dates are given in both Moslem and Christian eras. Since this edition has not yet reached the middle of the Roman alphabet, it will be necessary to refer to the older edition (Brill, 1911-1938) for some time. Readers for whom this encyclopedia is too technical might use *Abingdon Dictionary of Living Religions, A Dictionary of Comparative Religion, Dictionary of Non-Christian Religions,* or *Encyclopedia of Religion and Ethics.* None of these, however, give the full treatment of Islamic culture that *The Encyclopedia of Islam* does.

281.   Stutley, Margaret, and James Stutley. **Harper's Dictionary of Hinduism: Its Mythology, Folklore, Philosophy, Literature, and History.** New York: Harper & Row, 1977. 372p.

282.   Walker, Benjamin. **The Hindu World: An Encyclopedic Survey of Hinduism.** 2 vols. New York: Praeger, 1968.

Explanation of terms, rituals, taboos, customs, and other aspects of Hindu religion and culture and identification of mythological and real persons are covered adequately in both of these works. Both are well written and authoritative, and both give full detail.

DIRECTORIES

283.   **The Directory of Religious Organizations in the United States.** 2d ed. Falls Church, Va.: McGrath, 1982. 518p.

General religious organizations, but not religious bodies, churches, or orders, are included in this directory. The 1,628 organizations are headquarters of national churches, professional associations, volunteer groups, government agencies, religious publishers, suppliers, and other businesses, foundations, fraternal societies, etc. For each one, the religious affiliation (if any), the name of the director, the address, and a brief explanation of its nature or purpose are given.

284.   Melton, J. Gordon. **A Directory of Religious Bodies in the United States, Compiled from the Files of The Institute for the Study of American Religion.** New York: Garland, 1977. 305p.

All of the 1,275 primary religious groups currently existing in the United States are listed alphabetically here, giving only the address and the title of their publication, if any. The directory also has an extended explanation of "primary religious groups" and of their classification by type. Also given in the back of the volume is a description of 18 families into which religious groups have been classified with a list of the particular groups belonging to each family.

285.   **Directories of individual denominations.**

Major Christian denominations have their own directories, usually published annually. Noteworthy examples are *The Official Catholic Directory,* the *Lutheran Church in America Yearbook,* the *Episcopal Clerical Directory,* and the *Directory of the American Baptist Churches in the U.S.A.* Typically, these list their churches and affiliated organizations throughout the United States, often have membership and other statistics, and a register of clergy and church officials. The *Episcopal Clerical Directory* is only a register of clergy. *The Yearbook of American and Canadian Churches* (entry 286) also has a good directory section.

HANDBOOKS

286. **Yearbook of American and Canadian Churches.** Edited by Constant H. Jacquet, Jr. Nashville: Abingdon, 1916- . Annual. Paper.

There are three parts to the yearbook, which is not limited to Christian churches but includes all organized religions in the United States and Canada. These are a "calendar for church use," which shows for the current year and three following years the major days of religious observance for Christians, Jews, and Muslims; directories of national religious organizations, religious bodies, ecumenical agencies, theological seminaries, church-related colleges and universities, religious periodicals, and service agencies; and a statistical and historical section, which gives statistics of church membership, number of churches, and number of clergy for each religious body, financial statistics on religion, a summary of findings of national surveys on religion in America, and a list of depositories of church archives in the United States and Canada. Only the national headquarters of each religious body, not local churches, is included in the directory. Users should be made aware that statistics of church membership are supplied by each denomination and are necessarily subject to different interpretations of some terms.

287. **Catholic Almanac.** Edited by Felician A. Foy and Rose M. Avato. Huntington, Ind.: Our Sunday Visitor, 1904- . Annual.

Like general information almanacs, this includes a variety of historical and current data, such as dates and events of church history, ecumenical councils, church calendar, apparitions of Mary, addresses of cathedral and chancery offices in the United States, patron saints and intercessors, and other information of interest to Catholics.

288. **American Jewish Yearbook.** Edited by Milton Himmelfarb and David Singer. New York: The American Jewish Committee; Philadelphia: The Jewish Publication Society of America, 1899- . Annual.

In each yearbook are articles about the current state of Judaism in America and abroad, directories of interest to Jews (organizations, federations, community councils, periodicals, and others), and a necrology of prominent Jews in the United States who died the previous year. In the back of each issue is an index of the articles that have been published since volume 51 of the yearbook.

289. Magill, Frank N., and Ian P. McGreal, eds. **Masterpieces of Christian Literature in Summary Form.** New York: Harper & Row, 1963. 1193p.

290. Magill, Frank N., A. R. Caponigri, and Thomas P. Neill, eds. **Masterpieces of Catholic Literature in Summary Form.** New York: Harper & Row, 1965. 1134p.

The familiar Magill format is followed in both of these books. Summaries of works and documents that have been important in the development of Christianity are arranged according to the date of their writing. At the beginning of each summary are a list of "Principal Ideas Advanced," the author, date, and genre (apologetic, allegory, autobiography, or other). In the front of the book there is an alphabetical list of titles and in the back a list of authors. *Masterpieces of Christian Literature in Summary Form* has writings from the Apostolic Fathers to the present, including many that figured prominently in the Reformation. The other work emphasizes those writings, again from the early fathers to recent times, that reflect Catholic doctrine; some are important papal encyclicals. It also has some writings (e.g., Galileo's *Dialogue Concerning the Two Chief World Systems*) that were not supported by the Church but were written by Catholics.

BIOGRAPHY

291. **Who's Who in Religion.** 2d ed. Chicago: Marquis Who's Who, 1977. 736p.

292. **American Catholic Who's Who.** Edited by Joy Anderson. Washington, D.C.: National Catholic News Service, 1911- . Biennial.

293. **Who's Who in World Jewry: A Biographical Dictionary of Outstanding Jews.** Edited by I. J. Carmin Karpman. Tel-Aviv: Olive Books of Israel, 1978. 974p.

The first who's who listed above has brief biographical data on more than 18,000 religious leaders in the United States and Canada. These include clergy and church officials, educators, directors of religious organizations and foundations, among others. *American Catholic Who's Who* has data on more than 6,000 prominent Catholics in the United States. Most of these persons are noteworthy for their contribution to Catholicism and Catholic service organizations, but some are included because of their achievement in their own profession. *Who's Who in World Jewry* has brief data on some 12,000 prominent Jewish men and women in science, the arts, religion, economics, Jewish service, and other fields. Most of these are in the United States or Israel, but other countries are also represented.

294. Bowden, Henry W. **Dictionary of American Religious Biography.** Westport, Conn.: Greenwood, 1977. 572p.

This and the following work differ from the previously listed who's whos in giving biographical data on persons of the past. In this work are biographies of 425 men and women who were prominent in American religious history, regardless of their theological orientation. A list of the person's writings and major sources of further biographical data are given at the end of each article. About 75 percent of these biographees are also in *Dictionary of American Biography*, but here the data on these religious leaders are brought together in one volume.

295. Delaney, John J., and James E. Tobin. **Dictionary of Catholic Biography.** Garden City, N.Y.: Doubleday, 1961. 1245p.

This dictionary has short biographies of about 15,000 important Catholic men and women from apostolic times to the present day. These include martyrs, saints, religious leaders, authors, artists, and others who have made a major contribution to the history and development of the Church. For saints, the feast day is indicated. The book has some very useful appendixes: a list of saints as patrons; a list of symbols used in art for the different saints; a chronological chart of popes and world rulers.

296. Butler, Alban. **Lives of the Saints.** Rev. ed. Edited by Herbert Thurston and Donald Attwater. 4 vols. New York: Kenedy, 1963.

297. Farmer, David H. **The Oxford Dictionary of Saints.** Oxford: Oxford University Press, 1978. 440p.

Interest in biographies of saints is not nearly so widespread as it was in past centuries. Queries about saints reaching the university library are likely to be of more depth and to require more research than most of those coming to the public library. Butler's *Lives of the Saints*, which has been noted since its first edition in 1759 for its detail and critical handling of resources, is more suitable for the university library than shorter versions. The traditional arrangement by the Christian calendar, listing for each day the saints who are commemorated on that day, is followed here. Each volume, covering three months of the calendar, has its alphabetical index of saints' names; volume 4 has a general index of saints' names for the entire set. *The Oxford Dictionary of Saints* includes about 1,300 saints, or about half the number in the larger work: all of the saints who have had general worship or a notable cult in England and representative saints of Ireland, Scotland, and Wales. It has briefer information than *Lives of the Saints.* But it has two useful appendixes: an index of places in Great Britain and Ireland associated with particular saints and a calendar of the feast days of the saints according to the reformed Roman calendar (1969), which eliminated some saints included in the old calendar and changed the feast days of others.

RELIGION IN THE UNITED STATES AND CANADA

298. Melton, J. Gordon, ed. **The Encyclopedia of American Religions.** 2 vols. Wilmington, N.C.: McGrath, 1978.

299. Piepkorn, Arthur C. **Profiles in Belief: The Religious Bodies of the United States and Canada.** 7 vols. New York: Harper & Row, 1977- . In progress.

Melton's *Directory of Religious Bodies in the United States* (entry 284) classifies and lists the 1,275 primary religious groups currently active in the United States, giving only their address. *The Encyclopedia of American Religions* goes beyond this, giving a short history and the fundamental or distinguishing beliefs of the primary denominations and sects in the United States. The primary denominations are described in the first volume, grouped by religious families: Lutheran family, Pentecostal family, Liturgical family (western), etc. Volume 2 describes sects and cults, also grouped by type: e.g., Psychic and New Age family; Flying saucer groups. Each volume has its own index. Both volumes are invaluable in university library reference work, but information on cults is so hard to find that this part of Melton's work is especially useful. See also Ellwood's *Religious and Spiritual Groups in Modern America*, described below. The multi-volume *Profiles in Belief*, begun by Piepkorn and continued by John A. Tietjen of Christ Seminary-Seminex (St. Louis) after Piepkorn's death, is very detailed and scholarly and will be needed only for those doing exhaustive study of the history and role of religious bodies in the United States. Its four volumes published thus far cover Roman Catholic and Eastern Orthodox (Vol. 1), Protestant denominations (Vol. 2), and Holiness and Pentecostal churches (Vols. 3-4).

300. Ellwood, Robert S. **Religious and Spiritual Groups in Modern America.** Englewood Cliffs, N.J.: Prentice-Hall, 1973. 334p.

There is probably more religious experimentation today than ever before in the United States. Information about some of the new, unorthodox groups that have arisen recently may be found in this book, which groups them roughly by type: those revising ancient lore (Rosicrucians and others); UFO groups; Western groups following a *sadhana*, or spiritual path; neo-Pagan groups; Hindu movements; and others.

THE BIBLE

There are a number of reference books devoted entirely to the Bible and its study. A large collection of these will not usually be needed, unless the university has a department or school of theology and students who are preparing for a career in the ministry. But all university libraries need a representation of four different types of Bible reference books: dictionaries, concordances, commentaries, and atlases. A sampling of these is given below. Such Bible reference books are needed to satisfy the questions that arise from literature and other non-religion courses and from students' curiosity and interest in the Bible.

The reference librarian should be aware of the principal versions of the Bible in English. These are the King James or Authorized Version (1611), the Revised Version (1881-1885), the Revised Standard Version or "RSV" (1946-1952), the New English Bible (1961-1970), the New

International Version (1978), the Douay Version (1582-1610), and the New American Bible (1970). The last two are translations approved for Roman Catholics. Many persons still prefer the King James Version because of its poetic, although archaic, language. Later versions are retranslations, often based on more recently discovered manuscripts. In using a Bible concordance, it is especially important that the English language version on which the concordance was based be recognized. The Apocrypha, or books of the Bible whose authorship and authority are questioned by many scholars, are included in some versions (the Douay, the Revised Standard, the New English Bible) but not in others.

Dictionaries

301. Gehman, Henry S., ed. **The New Westminster Dictionary of the Bible.** Rev. ed. Philadelphia: Westminster, 1970. 1027p., 16 maps.

302. Hastings, James, ed. **Dictionary of the Bible.** Rev. ed. Edited by Frederick C. Grant and H. H. Rowley. New York: Scribner's, 1963. 1059p.

303. **The Interpreter's Dictionary of the Bible.** 4 vols. and supplement. Nashville: Abingdon, 1962-76.

304. **The International Standard Bible Encyclopedia.** Rev. ed. Edited by Geoffrey W. Bromiley and others. 4 vols. Grand Rapids, Mich.: Eerdmans, 1979- . In progress.

305. McKenzie, J. L. **Dictionary of the Bible.** Milwaukee: Bruce, 1965. 954p., 14 maps.

306. Miller, Madeleine S., and J. Lane Miller. **Harper's Bible Dictionary.** 8th ed. New York: Harper & Row, 1973. 853p., 18 maps.

The Bible dictionary is the most used of the four types of reference tools about the Bible. The listing of six representative dictionaries here (only a sampling) shows its importance. Articles vary from short definitions to fuller treatment. All persons, places, and other proper names mentioned in the Bible are identified, usually giving the book, chapter, and verse in which mention is made, if citations are not numerous. Many articles are on general topics or subjects: e.g., bank, barley, basket, beard, fondling, food, foot. These discuss the use or custom relating to the topic in Biblical time. Each book of the Bible has an article telling when and by whom the book is believed to have been written, its content, and its role in the larger Scripture. The Bible dictionary is not to be confused with the dictionaries on Christianity, a Christian denomination, or Judaism described above (entries 268-69, 274-76). These also have many articles on major places and persons or on parts of the Bible but relate more to the veneration or interpretation in that denomination or religion. The information given in the Bible dictionary is mostly factual and identifying rather than interpretive; therefore, denominational differences are not so important in the use of these books.

Concordances

307. Ellison, J. W. **Nelson's Complete Concordance of the Revised Standard Version Bible.** New York: Nelson, 1957. 2157p.

308. **A Concordance to the Apocrypha/Deuterocanonical Books of the Revised Standard Version.** Grand Rapids, Mich.: Eerdmans, 1983. 479p.

309. Strong, James. **Exhaustive Concordance of the Bible.** Nashville: Abingdon, 1964. 1340, 262, 126, 79p. 4 parts in 1.

310. Thompson, N. W., and Raymond Stock. **Complete Concordance to the Bible (Douay Version).** St. Louis: Herder, 1947. 1914p.

The concordance is simply an alphabetical list of all words used in a particular literary or other text, identifying where the word occurs in the particular edition or version of the text used in compiling the concordance. The four titles listed above are concordances to different English versions of the Bible. No definition or explanation of the name or word is given but only a reference to the Bible passage in which it is used. All uses of a word (omitting certain common words like *the, a, an, as, for*) are arranged according to the order of books and chapters in the Old and New Testaments, with the line of text in which the word occurs given for easy identification of the passage. The most frequent use of a concordance is to identify a passage which a person is trying to recall. The best way to use a concordance is to check one or more words that are relatively uncommon in the text. It would not be efficient to check a Bible concordance under such words as *children, Christ, come,* or *do,* if some less common words are used in the passage. If the passage being sought is not readily found, it is possible that the passage is being misquoted; that the passage, as remembered, is from an English language version of the Bible different from the version used in compiling the concordance being checked; or that the passage is from one of the books of the Apocrypha, which are not included in the concordance being checked.

311. Morrison, Clinton. **An Analytical Concordance to the Revised Standard Version of the New Testament.** Philadelphia: Westminster, 1979. 770p.

This book differs from other Bible concordances in being compiled for the member of the clergy or other person interested in intensive study of the New Testament and its interpretation. It is compiled for those who want to know what Greek word lies behind the English translation of the Revised Standard Version and to compare its meaning with other Greek words that can be translated by the same English word. Robert Young's *Analytical Concordance to the Bible* (Grand Rapids, Mich.: Eerdmans, 1955) serves a similar purpose for Hebrew and Greek words in the Old and New Testaments.

312. Stevenson, Burton E. **The Home Book of Bible Quotations.** New York: Harper & Row, 1949. 645p.

This work differs from a concordance, although it may be pressed into use as one. Its purpose is to aid in finding one or more passages in the Bible which express a particular thought or subject and may be used by someone preparing a speech or an article. It fails as a concordance in that many Bible passages are not included if they are not particularly quotable. (It is difficult to work "And Asa begat Jehosaphat, and Jehosaphat begat Joram" into a speech or conversation.) Quotations are listed under the subject, whether or not that word actually occurs in the passage, e.g., ant, antiquity, cloud, coals. The index, which is by individual word in the quoted passage, may be used as a concordance, if it is remembered that the compilation is selective.

Commentaries

313. **The Interpreter's Bible.** 12 vols. New York and Nashville: Abingdon-Cokesbury, 1951-1957.

314. **The Jerome Biblical Commentary.** Edited by Raymond E. Brown, Joseph A. Fitzmyer, and Roland E. Murphy. 2 vols. in 1. Englewood Cliffs, N.J.: Prentice-Hall, 1968.

315. **The New Bible Commentary.** Rev. ed. Edited by D. Guthrie and J. A. Motyer. Grand Rapids, Mich.: Eerdmans, 1970. 1310p.

The Bible commentary is an exegesis or explanation of the Bible, its books, and individual passages. It differs from the Bible dictionary in that it follows the order of the books of the Bible rather than an alphabetical arrangement of subjects. Also, it stresses the spiritual interpretation, although the history and authoritativeness of the different books are also discussed. Unlike the Bible dictionary, the denominational background of the commentary is important. The three titles listed above are only a few of the many commentaries that are available. The multi-volume *Interpreter's Bible* is found in most libraries. *The Jerome Biblical Commentary* and *The New Bible Commentary* are one-volume works representing the Catholic and Protestant points of view, respectively.

Atlases

316. Aharoni, Yohanan, and Michael Avi-Yonah. **The Macmillan Bible Atlas.** Rev. ed. New York: Macmillan, 1977. 184p.

317. May, Herbert G., ed. **Oxford Bible Atlas.** 2d ed. London: Oxford University Press, 1974. 144p.

318. **Reader's Digest Atlas of the Bible: An Illustrated Guide to the Holy Land.** Pleasantville, N.Y.: Reader's Digest, 1981. 256p.

Most Bible dictionaries have several maps showing the areas mentioned in the Bible and locating Biblical countries, cities, and natural features. The separate Bible atlas is not, therefore, an essential work in the small collection. But it does have, with accompanying text and illustrations, many specialized maps showing the topography and climate of the area, details of small areas, wanderings and exiles of the Jews, battle campaigns, plans of important cities or the Temple, routes of missionary activity, and other Bible-related maps.

MYTHOLOGY

319. Cotterell, Arthur. **A Dictionary of World Mythology.** New York: Putnam, 1980. 256p.

320. Carlyon, Richard, comp. **A Guide to the Gods.** New York: Morrow, 1982. 402p.

321. Sykes, Egerton, comp. **Everyman's Dictionary of Non-Classical Mythology.** New York: Dutton, 1965. 280p.

322. Tripp, Edward. **Crowell's Handbook of Classical Mythology.** New York: Crowell, 1970. 631p.

Most questions on mythology ask for simple identification of a god or other mythological person, place, event, or subject. The first three of these listed above are useful for mythology other than that of Greece and Rome or when the particular mythology has not been identified. The first two are arranged by part of the world, treating different mythologies separately, but both have a general index, combining beings and subjects from all mythologies. *A Dictionary of World Mythology* has introductory sections beginning each chapter, explaining the mythology prevalent in a particular part of the world; this is followed by an alphabetical list of the major gods and heroes, briefly identified. *A Guide to the Gods* is limited to gods, omitting heroes, who are born of a union of a god and a mortal being. But it includes a large number of gods from all parts of the world which are not in *A Dictionary of World Mythology.* Its chief value lies in the amount of attention it gives to the less familiar mythologies. *Everyman's Dictionary of Non-Classical Mythology* has several thousand entries for gods, heroes, and places, briefly identified and all in a single alphabet. *Crowell's Handbook of Classical Mythology* tries to combine the dictionary arrangement with a retelling of the principal myths by having both a long article under the name of a major figure in the myth (Odysseus, Heracles) and references to these names from those of minor figures.

323. Bell, Robert E. **Dictionary of Classical Mythology: Symbols, Attributes and Associations.** Santa Barbara, Calif.: ABC-Clio, 1982. 390p.

This dictionary gives a different approach to Greek and Roman mythology by listing those persons to whom a given characteristic or attribute, arranged alphabetically, applies. Under *Abandonment* are listed Ariadne, Dido, and Oenone, all of whom were abandoned by their lover; under *Abduction* are listed 45 persons, mostly women, who were abducted; under *Artist* are four mythological persons known as artists, including Epeius, who fashioned the Trojan horse; under *Asphodel* is named Dionysus, to whom the plant was sacred. As appendixes, there are Surnames, Epithets, and Patronymics and Heroic Expeditions. There is also an index of names with reference to the several attributes under which the person is listed.

324. **The Mythology of All Races.** Edited by Louis H. Gray. 13 vols. Boston: Marshall Jones, 1916-1932. Reprint. New York: Cooper Square, 1964.

325. **Larousse Encyclopedia of Mythology.** New York: Prometheus, 1959. 500p.

Several of the dictionaries listed above (e.g., those by Cotterell and Tripp) try to give some account of the major myths along with identification of persons and places. Where this is not sufficient, one can try more extended and organized accounts of the myths such as the two listed above. *Larousse Encyclopedia of Mythology* usually will be detailed enough without referring to the older but excellent volumes, each by a specialist on a particular mythology, of *Mythology of All Races.*

11

LITERATURE

In this chapter, questions and reference sources relating to the study and research in the field of literature are discussed. This means mostly English and American literature, just as the previous chapter emphasized Christianity and the Bible since questions on these subdivisions of the discipline far outnumber, in most university libraries, questions on other religions or literatures. Where questions relating to the literatures of other countries are considered in this chapter, they are usually the questions of users who do not read the language involved. Questions of advanced students and faculty members who are competent in classical and modern languages other than English are not treated here, as the reference sources required in these literatures are too specialized for our inclusion and are already known to such users.

Most frequent of the types of literary questions are those dealing with a particular writer or a particular work, as contrasted with those on a broader literary topic. If only a brief identification of a writer or a work is wanted, the appropriate Oxford companion is the first source to check. For a writer or a work in a literature for which no Oxford companion is available, there are Benet's *Reader's Encyclopedia, Cassell's Encyclopedia of World Literature*, and the *Encyclopedia of World Literature in the 20th Century*.

Undergraduates often want a plot summary of a literary work, once they learn that plot summaries are available. Graduate students preparing for their doctoral examination are also users of plot summaries. Several popular sources of plot summaries are described below. Although these books include summaries of several thousand literary works between them, the book for which a student has a need may not be one of the summaries. In such a case, a review of the book will often give a short account of its content. See chapter 6, "Book Reviews," for appropriate indexes.

Another frequent need in this field, especially for undergraduates who are taking a literature course, is for critical analysis of a particular work. The Magill series described below (entries 373-74, 405-8) have short critical essay-reviews on the literary works they cover. Where these are not sufficiently detailed, the student can be introduced to the indexes to literary criticism described below (entries 419-31), which require the further step of locating the books and articles which contain the critical comments, but which give more and better treatment of the work in question. Criticism of a newer work covered neither in the Magill series nor in the indexes to literary criticism may be found in a book review, although these, being written soon after the first appearance of the book, often will not offer as much critical insight as the more studied analysis prepared by a specialist after more mature consideration of the work.

Besides the questions regarding individual writers and particular works, undergraduates sometimes want a definition of a literary term, especially a figure of speech, a literary device, a genre, a metrical device, or other technical term. These, again, are easily answered in an appropriate Oxford companion or one of the dictionaries described below. A more extended definition or discussion may be found in one of the specialized encyclopedias of literature.

GUIDES, BIBLIOGRAPHIES, INDEXES

326. Patterson, Margaret C. **Literary Research Guide.** 2d ed. New York: Modern Language Association of America, 1983. 559p.

The guide to the literature of a subject field is intended to help the beginning student (and others who are more familiar with the bibliographies and reference sources in the subject) to find and use tools pertinent to their study or research. Patterson's new edition is a model of what such a guide should ideally be. It is based on a thorough knowledge of the best reference sources in literature. About 1,650 items are described and evaluated. The emphasis is on English and American literature, but other world literatures, classical, and comparative literature are also included. The introduction on refining and conducting research in the field is helpful. Besides the great amount of useful information presented, the guide is written in a clear and witty style.

327. Fenster, Valmai K. **Guide to American Literature.** Littleton, Colo.: Libraries Unlimited, 1983. 243p.

For the student of American literature, this guide will be found useful for its second section, in which bibliographies, critical analyses, and biographical studies are listed for some 100 major writers.

328. Thompson, George A., Jr. **Key Sources in Comparative and World Literature: An Annotated Guide to Reference Materials.** New York: Ungar, 1982. 383p.

Patterson's *Literary Research Guide* (entry 326) lists selected reference tools in English on French, German, and a few other literatures. This guide, however, lists many more of the principal bibliographies and guides to the literatures of other countries in their own languages. It is useful for these references, which Patterson does not include. Many of the citations are briefly annotated. For the study of comparative literature, as distinct from the study of the literature of a particular country, the bibliography by Baldensperger and Friederich (entry 334) is still indispensable.

329. **The New Cambridge Bibliography of English Literature.** Edited by George Watson. 5 vols. Cambridge, England: Cambridge University Press, 1969-77. Vol. 1, 600-1660; Vol. 2, 1660-1800; Vol. 3, 1800-1900; Vol. 4, 1900-1950, edited by I. R. Willison; Vol. 5, Index compiled by J. D. Pickles.

330. **Literary History of the United States.** 4th rev. ed. Edited by Robert E. Spiller and others. New York: Macmillan, 1974. Vol. 2, Bibliography.

For English and American literature, respectively, these are the standard bibliographies and should be familiar to all students in these departments. *The New Cambridge Bibliography of English Literature (NCBEL)*, organized by broad periods, lists all separately published works by major literary writers of Great Britain from 600 to 1950 and selected books and articles about these writers. "Literary" is broadly interpreted here, at least up to the nineteenth century, and includes those who wrote extensively in history, philosophy, economics, and other areas. Selected references are also given in *NCBEL* on the literature of various periods and on literary topics and related fields: e.g., the English Bible, travel, book production and distribution, education. Volume 5 is an index to the entire work. The *Shorter New Cambridge Bibliography of English Literature* (Cambridge University Press, 1981) is a one-volume abridgment, listing all writings by the major authors and many minor ones, but fewer of the writings about them. It will quickly answer many questions, however, where the need is simply to verify the date or authorship of a particular work. *Literary History of the United States* is still considered definitive, and its bibliography may be considered the best comprehensive bibliography of the subject. Unfortunately, this edition of the bibliography is merely a reprint of the 1948 bibliography and its two supplements of 1959 and 1972, printed side-by-side but now with continuous paging and combined contents page and index. Thus it is necessary to consult all three of these bibliographies on most persons and topics.

331. Blanck, J. N. **Bibliography of American Literature.** 8 vols. Compiled for the Bibliographical Society of America. New Haven, Conn.: Yale University Press, 1955- . In progress.

Jacob N. Blanck, considered the dean of American literary bibliography, died in 1974. Volume 7 of his monumental undertaking was completed by Virginia L. Smyers and Michael Winship and published in 1983. Volume 8, under the editorship of Earle E. Coleman will complete the set. *The Bibliography of American Literature* has a very specialized use and will not be consulted nearly as often as the bibliography of *Literary History of the United States*. It lists, with excruciating bibliographical detail, all separately published books by some 300 major American authors up to 1930. It has no references about these authors nor about American literature and its history. Its value lies principally in identifying definitively the first and later editions of each work published during the author's lifetime. Editions published after the author's death are not listed, as they could not show any revisions or changes made by the author.

332. Howard-Hill, T. H. **Index to British Literary Bibliographies.** New York: Oxford University Press, 1969- .

   I   **Bibliography of British Literary Bibliographies.** 1969. 570p.

   II   **Shakespearian Bibliography and Textual Criticism.** 1971. 322p.

   III   **British Bibliography to 1890.** In preparation.

   IV-V   **Bibliography of British Bibliography and Textual Criticism.** 2 vols. 1979.

   VI   **British Literary Bibliography and Textual Criticism, 1890-1969: An Index.** 1980. 864p.

   VII   **British Literary Bibliography, 1970-1979: A Bibliography.** In preparation.

333. Nilon, Charles H. **A Bibliography of Bibliographies in American Literature.** New York: Bowker, 1970. 483p.

Thousands of bibliographies on special aspects of British and American literature and on individual writers are available. All of these cannot be included in the general bibliographies of these two literatures described above (entries 329-30). The works listed here can often supply references to specialized bibliographies needed for a term paper, dissertation, or other study.

334. Baldensperger, Fernand, and W. P. Friederich. **Bibliography of Comparative Literature.** Chapel Hill, N.C.: University of North Carolina Press, 1950. Reprint. New York: Russell, 1960. 705p.

Despite its age, this work has never been superseded, although the study of comparative literature continues to attract many students and researchers. Books, periodical articles, and some significant dissertations on the influence of the literature of one country on that of another, the influence of a country's literature on an individual writer, or the influence of a writer on the literature of another country are noted. Unfortunately, the book has no index, but the table of contents is very detailed.

335. Modern Language Association of America. **MLA International Bibliography of Books and Articles on the Modern Languages and Literatures.** 2 vols. New York: Modern Language Association of America, 1921- . Annual.

For literature as a whole, this is the single most important bibliography. Numerous books and articles from some 1,200 journals published in the previous year or two produce annually about 35,000 to 40,000 references in this bibliography. These are listed in the Classified Volume under national literatures, subdivided by century and individual writer; linguistics; general literature and related topics; and folklore. Each item is listed only once in the Classified Volume, where it seems to fit best. But in the Index Volume, it may appear under as many subjects as are appropriate. This volume also has an index of authors. *MLA International Bibliography* can be machine searched back to 1970 through DIALOG.

336. **MLA Directory of Periodicals: A Guide to Journals and Series in Languages and Literatures.** Compiled by Eileen M. Mackesy, Karen Mateyak, and Diane Siegel. New York: Modern Language Association of America, 1979- . Biennial.

A companion to the preceding bibliography, this gives full bibliographic description, subscription information, editorial description, and requirements for submission of papers for nearly 3,000 journals and series indexed for the bibliography.

337. Modern Humanities Research Association. **Annual Bibliography of English Language and Literature.** Cambridge, England: Modern Humanities Research Association, 1920- . Annual.

Although limited to the year's scholarly production on the English language and the literatures of Great Britain, the United States, and other English-speaking countries, this bibliography cites more books, articles, and reviews in these fields (some 13,000 per year) than the *MLA International Bibliography* does. The sections on literature are organized by century, subdivided by genre (drama, fiction, literary history and criticism) and by individual writers prominent in that century.

338. Leary, Lewis G., comp. **Articles on American Literature, 1900-1950.** Durham, N.C.: Duke University Press, 1954. 437p.

339. Leary, Lewis G., comp. **Articles on American Literature, 1950-1967.** Durham, N.C.: Duke University Press, 1970. 751p.

340. Leary, Lewis G., and John Auchard, comps. **Articles on American Literature, 1968-1975.** Durham, N.C.: Duke University Press, 1979. 745p.

Current awareness of scholarly writing on American literature is best managed with the quarterly issues of *American Literature*. Each issue has a bibliography arranged by broad period (1607-1800; 1800-1870; 1870-1920; and 1920-present), under which are the writers prominent in that period and general studies of the period. These three cumulations have greatly eased the tedious searching of the quarterly bibliographies before 1975.

341. Wortman, William A. **A Guide to Serial Bibliographies for Modern Literatures.** New York: Modern Language Association of America, 1982. 124p. (Selected Bibliographies in Language and Literature, 3).

Bibliographies on the literatures of various countries which are published at regular intervals either as separates or as part of a scholarly journal are listed here. This updates the literature sections of *Serial Bibliographies in the Humanities and Social Sciences*, by Richard Gray (entry 218). Following sections on the literatures of various countries is a section of bibliographies on special subjects, such as biography, Black studies, book reviews, book trade, and children's literature.

342. McNamee, Lawrence F. D. **Dissertations in English and American Literature: Theses Accepted by American, British, and German Universities, 1865-1964.** New York: Bowker, 1968. 1124p. Supplement for 1964-1968 (1969) 450p.; supplement for 1969-1973 (1974) 690p.

343. Woodress, James L. **Dissertations in American Literature, 1891-1966.** 3d ed. Durham, N.C.: Duke University Press, 1968. 185p.

The complete search will include unpublished doctoral dissertations, even though many of these are not as significant as the published literature. Both of these compilations have included dissertations accepted at European and American universities.

Special Periods

344. Greenfield, Stanley B., and Fred C. Robinson. **A Bibliography of Publications on Old English Literature to the End of 1972.** Toronto: University of Toronto Press, 1980. 437p.

345. Severs, Jonathan Burke, and Albert E. Hartung, eds. **A Manual of the Writings in Middle English, 1050-1500.** 6 vols. New Haven, Conn.: The Connecticut Academy of Arts and Sciences, 1967- . In progress.

346. **The Eighteenth Century: A Current Bibliography, n.s. 1975- .** Edited by Robert R. Allen. New York: AMS Press for the American Society for Eighteenth-Century Studies, 1978- . Annual.

These sources are examples of the bibliographies that intensively cover a limited period of English or other literature. Because of their limited field, they turn up minor studies and studies in related fields not included in bibliographies of wider scope and are able to give more detail about them. *A Manual of the Writings in Middle English, 1050-1500*, for example, describes every writing known from that period and lists extant manuscripts, printed editions, and major critical writings about it. When completed, it will replace John E. Wells's *A Manual of the Writings in Middle English, 1050-1400.* These specialized bibliographies and those in the following sections are used by faculty and graduate students who need to know about everything that has appeared about their subject. The needs of undergraduates and others not pursuing a research project are better met by the *New Cambridge Bibliography of English Literature, Literary History of the United States* bibliography, the library catalog, and general periodical indexes.

347. **American Literature, English Literature, and World Literature in English Information Guide Series.** Edited by Theodore Grieder. Detroit: Gale.

Volumes in this series, which began in 1974, are similar to the works listed above. Examples of these presently available are *American Fiction to 1900; English Drama, 1600-1800;* and *Irish Literature, 1800-1875.*

Special Genres

348. Brogan, Terry V. F. **English Versification, 1570-1980: A Reference Guide with a Global Appendix.** Baltimore: Johns Hopkins University Press, 1981. 794p.

349. Davis, Lloyd, and Robert Irwin. **Contemporary American Poetry: A Checklist.** Metuchen, N.J.: Scarecrow, 1975. 179p.

350. Congdon, Kirby. **Contemporary Poets in American Anthologies, 1960-1977.** Metuchen, N.J.: Scarecrow, 1978. 228p.

351. **Granger's Index to Poetry.** 6th ed. Edited by William James Smith. New York: Columbia University Press, 1973. 2223p.

Indexes 514 anthologies published through 1970.

352. **Granger's Index to Poetry.** 7th ed. Edited by William James Smith and William F. Bernhardt. New York: Columbia University Press, 1982. 1329p.

Indexes 248 anthologies published 1970-1981.

353. Chicorel, Marietta, ed. **Chicorel Index to Short Stories in Anthologies and Collections.** 4 vols. New York: Chicorel, 1974.

354. **Short Story Index: An Index to Stories in Collections and Periodicals.** New York: Wilson, 1953- . Annual with 5-year cumulations.

355. Messerli, Douglas, and Howard N. Fox, comps. and eds. **Index to Periodical Fiction in English, 1965-1969.** Metuchen, N.J.: Scarecrow, 1977. 764p.

356. Reginald, R. **Science Fiction and Fantasy Literature: A Checklist, 1700-1974, with Contemporary Science Fiction Authors II.** 2 vols. Detroit: Gale, 1979. Supplement, 1975-1982. 2 vols. 1985.

Another way of limiting the field of a literature bibliography is by genre or genre and period. Entries 348-56 are a few examples of works that achieve special usefulness by discovering and listing literature of a specific kind, published, perhaps, in an ephemeral or otherwise elusive medium. These and similar bibliographies and indexes are needed in the complete literature collection.

Anonymous and Pseudonymous Publications

357. Halkett, Samuel, and John Laing. **Dictionary of Anonymous and Pseudonymous English Literature.** New & enl. ed. Edited by James Kennedy, W. A. Smith, and A. F. Johnson. 9 vols. Edinburgh: Oliver & Boyd, 1926-62.

The standard source for learning the name of the known or supposed author of a book published anonymously or under a pseudonym. The two final volumes, edited by Dennis E. Rhodes and Anna E. C. Simoni, brought the coverage up to 1950. A third edition, under the direction of John Holden, will coordinate the entries of the second edition and its several supplements, revise them, and provide full documentation for the attribution of authorship. Instead of a single alphabet of anonymous and pseudonymous publications up to the present time, it will be published in volumes covering chronological periods to match the several parts of the *Short Title Catalogue.* Volume 1, covering the period 1475-1640, has appeared (Harlow, England: Longman Group, 1980).

Review of Research

Most of the bibliographies described above list scholarly studies about literature and individual writers rather than the literary writings themselves. Only the *New Cambridge Bibliography of English Literature*, the bibliography volume of *Literary History of the United States, A Manual of the Writings in Middle English, 1050-1500*, and *Dictionary of Anonymous and Pseudonymous English Literature* include the primary works as well as studies of the literature and individual writers. Sources in this section differ from the bibliographies described above in being more critical and evaluative of recent literary scholarship and in comparing various analyses, theories, and conclusions.

358. Somer, John, and Barbara E. Cooper. **American and British Literature, 1945-1975: An Annotated Bibliography of Contemporary Scholarship.** Lawrence, Kans.: Regents Press, 1980. 326p.

The 1,528 studies in this bibliography are organized under general studies, drama, fiction and prose, poetry, critical theory, studies published after 1975, and study guides. References in the first five sections are annotated; those in the last two sections are not. The book has an author-subject index.

359. English Association. **The Year's Work in English Studies, 1920-** . London: Oxford University Press, 1921- . Annual.

A critical review of papers and research findings of the past year is given in a series of review-essays by specialists: e.g., Old English literature; the later sixteenth century, excluding drama; Milton. There are two final chapters on the year's research in American literature. The index of "critics" includes the authors of the research papers cited; the subject index includes the names of English and American writers studied.

360. **American Literary Scholarship, 1963-** . Edited by J. Albert Robbins and Warren G. French. Durham, N.C.: Duke University Press, 1965- . Annual.

Studies of the previous year are summarized and discussed by specialists in chapters on the major writers (e.g., Emerson, Twain, Hemingway) or on periods (e.g., Fiction: 1900 to the 1930s) and genres (e.g., Black literature). The author index includes the names of those whose research studies are cited; the subject index, the names of the writers studied. Until the 1982 volume, the series was edited by James Woodress.

361. **The Year's Work in Modern Language Studies.** London: Modern Humanities Research Association, 1930- . Annual.

Articles are written on the different literatures of Europe by scholars reporting on research, conference notes, and publications of the past year.

Literary Manuscripts

362. Modern Language Association of America. American Literature Section. **American Literary Manuscripts: A Checklist of Holdings in Academic, Historical, and Public Libraries, Museums, and Authors' Homes in the United States.** 2d ed. Compiled by J. A. Robbins and others. Athens, Ga.: University of Georgia Press, 1977. 387p.

363. **Index of English Literary Manuscripts.** Compiled by Peter Beal and others. 5 vols. London: Mansell; New York: Bowker, 1980- . In progress.

Doctoral students and faculty occasionally need to locate all extant manuscripts of a writer whom they are studying. *American Literary Manuscripts* checks the location of manuscripts of some 2,800 American writers in over 600 libraries and other repositories. Unfortunately, it does not describe the manuscript, except in listing the type (letters, journals or diaries, literary manuscripts, etc.) nor does it name the title of the poem, novel, or other creative work. Under the name of the writer are listed (by symbol) those libraries reporting holdings and the number of manuscripts of the different types they hold. If the researcher is interested only in particular titles, he or she can write or call the library for further detail. The *Index of English Literary Manuscripts* reports much more detail about the individual manuscripts of selected English writers, namely all literary writers in *The Concise Cambridge Bibliography of English Literature* (2d ed. Edited by George Watson. Cambridge, England: Cambridge University Press, 1965). Some researchers complain that this policy is too selective, but, given the long period covered and the number of writers active during that time, a less selective policy might inordinately delay the completion of the work. As it is, only the first volume, covering the years 1450-1625, and part one of Volume 4, 1800-1900, of the planned five volumes have yet appeared.

DICTIONARIES, ENCYCLOPEDIAS

364.　Beckson, Karl, and Arthur Ganz. **Literary Terms: A Dictionary.** New York: Farrar, Straus & Giroux, 1975. 275p.

365.　Cuddon, J. A. **A Dictionary of Literary Terms.** Rev. ed. Harmondsworth, Middlesex, England: Penguin, 1982. 761p. Paper.

366.　Holman, Clarence H. **A Handbook to Literature.** 4th ed. Indianapolis: Bobbs-Merrill, 1980. 537p.

The three most widely used dictionaries of literary terms. The first two define many terms related to literature other than English and American literature (e.g., cantar de pandeiro, cantica de serrana, canzone, chastushka, edda, haiku, hubris, Pleiade). *A Handbook to Literature* is written principally for students of English and American literature, although it too includes terms from other literatures. One appendix is a chronological outline of English and American literary history with contemporary historical events. Another appendix lists the winners of the Nobel and Pulitzer Prizes from their beginnings in 1901 and 1918, respectively. (See entries 384-85, 389 for more detailed chronologies of English literature and lists of winners of literary prizes.)

367.　Abrams, M. H. **A Glossary of Literary Terms.** 4th ed. New York: Holt, Rinehart & Winston, 1981. 220p.

More than seven hundred literary terms are defined and discussed in about three hundred essay-articles; this style has the advantage of bringing like terms together in one place. Under *meter* are defined the various metrical feet, lines, and devices; under *Neoclassic and Romantic* is given a full discussion of these literary periods, emphasizing English literature. The Index of Terms identifies the essay-article in which the term is discussed. Many articles end with references to books that give more information on the subject.

368.　**Cassell's Encyclopedia of World Literature.** Rev. and enl. Edited by John Buchanan-Brown. 3 vols. New York: Morrow, 1973.

Part one (volume 1) of this encyclopedia has articles on national and regional literatures, literary terms and topics, and some major literary classics: e.g., dactyl; Dance of Death; Danish literature; David of Sasun; Dedekorkut stories; detective stories; devil in literature; Devotio Moderna. Part two (volumes 2-3) has short biographies of authors with a list of their writings and selected books about them. For Irish and Italian literature, respectively, the following give greater depth: Robert Hogan, ed., *Dictionary of Irish Literature* (Westport,

Conn.: Greenwood, 1979), and Peter Bondanella and Julia Bondanella, eds., *Dictionary of Italian Literature* (Westport, Conn.: Greenwood, 1979). Both have articles on writers, literary movements and other topics, and literary terms of their literature.

369. **Columbia Dictionary of Modern European Literature.** 2d ed. Edited by Jean-Albert Bédé and William B. Edgerton. New York: Columbia University Press, 1980. 895p.

"Modern European literature" here encompasses the end of the nineteenth century to the present. The dictionary has articles on writers, which are critical as well as biographical, and on national literatures.

370. **Encyclopedia of World Literature in the 20th Century.** Rev. ed. Edited by Leonard S. Klein. 4 vols. New York: Ungar, 1983-84.

This work has profusely illustrated articles and recent writers, which are longer than those in the shorter work described above (entry 369). Most of the articles in volumes 1-3 are on individuals, but there are a few on national literatures and on literary movements. Volume 4 is a supplement, adding new names but not revising the articles of the first volumes.

371. Gassner, John, and Edward Quinn, eds. **The Reader's Encyclopedia of World Drama.** New York: Crowell, 1969. 1030p.

This encyclopedia is a one-volume work with articles on playwrights, schools of dramatic writing, dramatic terms, and major plays, but none on actors and actresses. The appendix, "Basic Documents in Dramatic Theory," reprints notable selections from Aristotle's *Poetics* to Friedrich Dürrenmatt's preface to *Four Plays*.

372. **Princeton Encyclopedia of Poetry and Poetics.** Enl. ed. Edited by Alex Preminger and others. Princeton, N.J.: Princeton University Press, 1974. 992p.

Articles in this work range from a brief definition of a metrical term to a long discussion of a movement or school of poetry or the poetry of a country. Obviously, this encyclopedia will give more information on a term or topic related to poetry than will the literary dictionaries described above (entries 364-67).

373. **Critical Survey of Short Fiction.** Edited by Frank N. Magill and Walter Beacham. 7 vols. Englewood Cliffs, N.J.: Salem, 1981.

374. **Critical Survey of Long Fiction.** Edited by Frank N. Magill. 8 vols. Englewood Cliffs, N.J.: Salem, 1983.

These two sets could have been included with the other Magill-inspired collections of summaries and essay-reviews of literary works (entries 405-8) or in the biography section (entries 392-404). But they are placed here with encyclopedias because of the variety of material they include on these two literary genres, short and long fiction. The main part of each set is a series of articles on major writers of the United States and other countries, arranged alphabetically by name. These articles give biographical data, an analysis of the writer's work, principal writings, and a selection of comments about the person. Added to these articles on writers are essays on the genre: techniques, development and history, and special categories and types of short and long fiction.

DIRECTORIES

375.   **Literary Market Place (LMP) with Names and Numbers: The Directory of American Book Publishing.** New York: Bowker, 1940- . Annual.

376.   **Writer's Market.** Edited by John Brady and P. J. Schemenaur. Cincinnati: Writer's Digest Books, 1934- . Annual.

Literary Market Place is a directory of literary agents, publishers, editorial services, book illustrators, translators, book manufacturers, and other services for writers. It is among the most used books in a university library, where the faculty is active in publishing and frequently needs the address, telephone number, or other information about publishers. Among the other useful lists in this directory are writers' conferences, literary magazines, literary awards, and reference books about the publishing industry. *Writer's Market* is directed toward helping a writer sell his or her work. Most of this directory is a listing of book and magazine publishers, with a thumbnail description of the kind of material in which they are interested and the way to contact them (direct interview, by mail, through an agent, etc.).

HANDBOOKS

We have used this heading to cover a miscellany of one-volume companions, handbooks, chronologies, gazetteers, and other works useful for ready reference questions on literature, even though their title may include the word *dictionary* or *encyclopedia*, qualifying them for inclusion in another section of this chapter.

377.   Benet, William R. **The Reader's Encyclopedia.** 2d ed. New York: Crowell, 1965. 1118p.

378.   Hart, James D. **The Oxford Companion to American Literature.** 5th ed. New York: Oxford University Press, 1983. 896p.

379.   Harvey, Sir Paul. **The Oxford Companion to English Literature.** 4th rev. ed. Edited by Dorothy Eagle. New York: Oxford University Press, 1967. 961p.

380.   Stapleton, Michael. **The Cambridge Guide to English Literature.** Cambridge, England: Cambridge University Press; Middlesex, England: Newnes, 1983. 992p.

These and other Oxford companions to literature (Classical, French, German, Spanish) are among the most useful sources for a quick answer to a question such as a definition of a literary term, identification of a writer or the date of a literary work, etc. The use of the word *companion* or *guide* in the title (what used to be called a vade mecum, literally a "go with me") implies that these are valuable to have at hand because they can quickly furnish such needed information. If the needed information is not found in the companion, the search can be continued in one of the more specialized dictionaries or encyclopedias described above. *The Cambridge Guide to English Literature* supplements *The Oxford Companion to English Literature* in several ways. It covers literatures of the English-speaking world, including the younger literatures of South Africa and the West Indies, as well as British and American literature. It briefly summarizes many more early and recent novels, plays, and major poems and identifies more fictional characters but has fewer definitions of literary terms, schools, and movements than does *The Oxford Companion to English Literature*; it also has less information on persons, mythological beings, places, and events serving as literary allusions.

381.   McMurtry, Jo. **Victorian Life and Victorian Fiction: A Companion for the American Reader.** Hamden, Conn.: Archon, 1979. 315p.

Although this does not compare in general usefulness to the books described in the previous paragraph, it is included here as an illustration of some of the more specialized handbooks available and because it is fun. It has short notes about the social, economic, and political life of the Victorian period, arranged under broad topics. "Titles and Social Rank" has notes on addressing peers and social classes in fiction; "The Army" has a military glossary; "Servants" tells where servants, nurses, and nannies came from; "Courtship, Marriage, and Sex" has notes on courtship ethics, elopements, and contraceptive techniques. There is an index of subjects.

382.   Magill, Frank N., ed. **Cyclopedia of Literary Characters.** New York: Harper & Row, 1963. 1280, 14, 50p.

383.   Freeman, William. **Dictionary of Fictional Characters.** Rev. ed. Edited by Fred Urquhart. Boston: The Writer, 1974. 579p.

These two works identify characters from novels, plays, poems, and short stories. The Oxford companions and Benet's *The Reader's Encyclopedia* (entries 377-79) include many fictional characters but not nearly as many as are identified in these works, which specialize in this kind of information. The *Cyclopedia of Literary Characters* lists and identifies about 16,000 characters from 1,300 literary works of all countries and periods. Arrangement is under the title of the work, listing characters in order of their importance. A brief summary of the plot and the role played by each character is given in the article. If the title of the work is not known, the alphabetical index of characters may be used. This is also published as *Masterplots: Cyclopedia of Literary Characters* (2 vols. Englewood Cliffs, N.J.: Salem Press, 1963). The *Dictionary of Fictional Characters* is limited to novels, plays, poems, and short stories of the United States, Great Britain, and Commonwealth countries, but, within these limits, it is more complete and easier to use than *Cyclopedia of Literary Characters*. Its approximately 22,000 characters from some 2,300 sources are listed alphabetically and identified. Its index includes the author and title of the literary works analyzed.

384.   Rogal, Samuel J. **A Chronological Outline of British Literature.** Westport, Conn.: Greenwood, 1980. 341p.

385.   Harbage, Alfred. **Annals of English Drama, 975-1700: An Analytical Record of All Plays, Extant or Lost, Chronologically Arranged and Indexed by Authors, Titles, Dramatic Companies, etc.** Rev. ed. Edited by S. Schoenbaum. London: Methuen, 1964. 321p. Supplements, 1966, 1970. Evanston, Ill.: Northwestern University.

Occasionally, a chronological view of literature or history gives a needed perspective that is not furnished by an alphabetical presentation. These handbooks (like the chronological tables described earlier, entry 366) offer such a view that is quicker to comprehend than the chronological perspective given in a literary history (see entries 390-91). The first work above lists births, deaths, literary events, and major publications by year from the beginning of British literature to 1979. *Annals of English Literature, 1475-1950* (2d ed. Oxford: Clarendon Press, 1961) performs a like function, actually listing more events per year than does Rogal, but over a shorter period. *Annals of English Drama, 975-1700* gives a tabular presentation by year, showing also the auspices under which each play was produced and the date of the earliest text and of the latest edition. Appendixes list editions other than the first and latest, and list plays that were submitted in typescript as dissertations but not published. There are indexes of playwrights, plays, and dramatic companies.

386. Eagle, Dorothy, and Hilary Carnell, eds. **The Oxford Illustrated Literary Guide to Great Britain and Ireland.** 2d ed. Oxford, England: Oxford University Press, 1981. 312p., 13 maps.

387. Fisher, Lois H. **A Literary Gazetteer of England.** New York: McGraw-Hill, 1980. 740p.

Both of these books list and identify towns, villages, houses, and natural features which have a literary association: where a writer was born, lived, or died. Neither book lists fictional places.

388. Mangual, Albert, and Gianni Guadalupi. **The Dictionary of Imaginary Places.** New York: Macmillan, 1980. 438p.

Unlike the two gazetteers in the preceding description, this text includes fictional places from the world's literature, but excludes those names used in fiction to disguise actual places (e.g., Proust's Balbec, Hardy's Wessex, Faulkner's Yoknapatawpha). Places are located and described, when possible, based on information in the literary source from which it comes. There are many illustrations and maps and an index of authors and titles of the literary works from which imaginary places are taken.

389. **Literary and Library Prizes.** 10th ed. Revised and edited by Olga S. Weber and Stephen J. Calvert. New York: Bowker, 1980. 651p.

This edition lists 454 awards, divided into four sections: International Prizes, American Prizes, British Prizes, and Canadian Prizes. The dominant section, American Prizes (making up some 80 percent of the book), is further subdivided by type. Each prize is described, followed by a list in chronological order of all winners from its establishment. The index lists all awards included in this and previous editions, whether still offered or not, and all recipients listed in the present edition.

REFERENCE HISTORIES

390. **The Oxford History of English Literature.** Edited by F. P. Wilson and B. Dobrée. 13 vols. Oxford, England: Clarendon Press, 1945- . In progress.

391. **Literary History of the United States.** 4th rev. ed. Edited by Robert E. Spiller and others. 2 vols. New York: Macmillan, 1974.

Occasionally, one must use a historical account of literature when the needed information is not obtainable from an encyclopedia or handbook. This happens, for example, when a question involves the background of a literary movement or style, contemporary events, or causes and effects. The two histories named above are considered to be the definitive histories of English and American literature, respectively. *The Oxford History of English Literature*, unfortunately, has still not been completed, lacking, as of the date of writing, the volumes on English literature before the Norman Conquest, Middle English literature, the mid-nineteenth century, and the most recent period to be covered, 1890-1945. For these periods, one must consult the excellent history by Albert C. Baugh, *A Literary History of England* (2d ed., 4 vols. New York: Appleton, 1967) or the older *Cambridge History of English Literature* (15 vols. Cambridge, England: Cambridge University Press, 1907-27). *Literary History of the United States* has been mentioned above (entry 330) for its bibliography volume. The text of this history is a reprint of the 1948 edition with two later chapters bringing the account to the 1950s.

BIOGRAPHY

Biographical questions are much less frequently asked in the university library than questions involving the critical evaluation of a writer or of an individual work. Many questions of simple identification of a well-known writer (dates, place of birth or death, major works) can be answered in one of the handbooks, companions, or encyclopedias described above. Further biographical information can be sought in the following sources, which take up far more room in the reference collection than their use warrants but which, nevertheless, must be there.

392.   **Author Biographies Master Index.** 2d ed. Edited by Barbara McNeil and Miranda C. Herbert. 2 vols. Detroit: Gale, 1984.

393.   Havlice, Patricia P. **Index to Literary Biography.** 2 vols. Metuchen, N.J.: Scarecrow, 1975. First supplement, 2 vols. 1983.

Indexes of this type serve a timesaving function similar to that provided by *Biography and Genealogy Master Index.* They index the names in many who's whos and biographical collections of writers, both past and current, e.g., *Catholic Authors, The Female Poets of America, Indiana Authors and Their Books, Écrivains d'aujourd'hui, 1940-1960, Living Black American Authors.* They do not themselves provide any biographical data but direct the reader to one or more sources where such information can be found. Even if the library does not own the who's who or other books referred to, the information can be obtained by a call or visit to a neighboring library that does own the source.

394.   **Wilson Authors Series.** New York: Wilson.

The volumes of this series are usually limited to those writers who are best known and for whom biographical data are most often sought. They are directed to high school, college, and popular use. Articles are one-half page to two pages in length and include a picture of the writer, a bibliography of major writings, and a list of biographical sources about the person. Volumes in the series are:

> **Twentieth Century Authors.** Edited by Stanley S. Kunitz and Howard Haycraft. 1942. 1577p. First supplement, edited by Kunitz and Vineta Colby. 1955. 1123p.

> **World Authors, 1950-1970.** Edited by John Wakeman. 1975. 1594p.

> **World Authors, 1970-1975.** Edited by John Wakeman. 1980. 894p.

> **British Authors of the Nineteenth Century.** Edited by Stanley S. Kunitz and Howard Haycraft. 1936. 677p.

> **British Authors before 1800.** Edited by Stanley S. Kunitz and Howard Haycraft. 1952. 584p.

> **American Authors, 1600-1900.** 8th ed. Edited by Stanley S. Kunitz and Howard Haycraft. 1977. 846p.

> **European Authors, 1000-1900.** Edited by Stanley S. Kunitz and Vineta Colby. 1967. 1016p.

> **Greek and Latin Authors, 800 B.C.-A.D. 1000.** Edited by Michael Grant. 1980. 492p.

Since their articles include evaluative, as well as factual, information, the following works are more scholarly and better adapted to the research needs of university students and faculty.

395. **Dictionary of Literary Biography.** Edited by Matthew J. Bruccoli. Detroit: Gale, 1978- . In progress.

396. **Dictionary of Literary Biography Yearbook, 1980-** . Detroit: Gale, 1981- . Annual.

397. **Dictionary of Literary Biography: Documentary Series: An Illustrated Chronicle.** Edited by Margaret A. Van Antwerp. Detroit: Gale, 1982- . In progress.

The original plan of this monumental set was to provide biographies of American and British writers, then to continue on with European writers. Thus far, it has run beyond the 20 volumes initially planned without proceeding beyond American and British writers. The volumes are prepared by scholars on writers of different genres and eras, e.g., "American Novelists since World War II"; "British Poets, 1914-1945"; "Twentieth Century American Science Fiction Writers"; "American Newspaper Journalists, 1873-1900"; "British Dramatists since World War II." Biographical material centers mostly on the development of the writer's style, the effect of personal experiences on the artist's work, the public reception of major writings, etc. Many photographs and illustrations are included. Each volume has a cumulative index of all writers included in earlier volumes of these three sets. The *Yearbooks* add biographical material on new writers, update biographies of writers included in earlier volumes (particularly on the occasion of the writer's death), and give some literary news of the year, such as winners of literary prizes. The *Documentary Series* reprint many photographs, letters, excerpts of diaries, and other personal documents of selected American writers.

398. **British Writers.** Edited under the Auspices of the British Council by Ian Scott-Kilvert. New York: Scribner's, 1979- . In progress.

399. **American Writers.** Edited by Leonard Unger and George T. Wright. 4 vols. New York: Scribner's, 1974. Supplement, 2 vols. 1979. Supplement, 2 vols. 1981.

Both sets are collections of articles that were published originally as pamphlets on individual writers or groups of writers. They are adapted to undergraduate needs but are more detailed and critical than articles in the Wilson series. *American Writers* includes some articles on lesser known new writers for whom biographical and critical material may be difficult to find.

400. Burke, W. J., and W. D. Howe. **American Authors and Books, 1640 to the Present Day.** 3d ed. Revised by Irving Weiss and Ann Weiss. New York: Crown, 1972. 719p.

Brief identification of minor authors, bibliographers, librarians, booksellers, and others related to the American literary scene which may not be available elsewhere can be found in this book. The third edition includes approximately 14,000 names. Other information about American literature is also included, but this is usually available elsewhere.

401. Kirkpatrick, D. L., ed. **Twentieth Century Children's Writers.** New York: St. Martin's, 1978. 1507p.

Since writers of children's books often do not receive as much notice as other writers do, this book is a good addition to the other biographical sources listed above. Biographies are given for more than six hundred authors of English-language books for children and young adults. Articles list their books, both those written for children and young adults and those written for other reader groups. The appendix has a list of writers of children's books of the late nineteenth century and a section on outstanding children's books written in other languages but translated into English.

402.   **Writers for Young Adults Biography Master Index.** Edited by Adele Sarkissian. Detroit: Gale, 1979. 199p. (Gale Biographical Index Series, 6).

403.   **Children's Authors and Illustrators: An Index to Biographical Dictionaries.** 3d ed. Edited by Adele Sarkissian. Detroit: Gale, 1981. 667p. (Gale Biographical Index Series, 2).

For authors and illustrators of books for young adults and children, these fill a function similar to the one *Author Biographies Master Index* and *Index to Literary Biography* fill for other writers. Several hundred who's whos and biographical dictionaries are indexed by each work, many of which do not limit their entries to only writers and illustrators, e.g., *ASCAP Biographical Dictionary, Atlantic Brief Lives, Dictionary of Film Makers, Who's Who in World Jewry.*

404.   Atkinson, Frank. **Dictionary of Literary Pseudonyms: A Selection of Popular Modern Writers in English.** 3d ed. London: Bingley, 1982. 305p.

The Dictionary of Anonymous and Pseudonymous English Literature (entry 357) has indexes of pseudonyms and of the known or supposed authors of anonymous and pseudonymous publications. This edition of Atkinson's work lists approximately four thousand twentieth century authors with the pseudonyms they have used, followed by a list of some six thousand pseudonyms and the writer's real name.

SUMMARIES OF LITERARY WORKS

For undergraduates, the two most common types of reference needs arising from literature courses are summaries of novels, plays, and poems, especially when accompanied by some critical evaluation, and literary criticism of individual works. Brief summaries of major literary works are often found in Benet's *The Reader's Encyclopedia*, the Oxford companions, and other handbooks and encyclopedias described above. But so many good sources answering such needs in more detail are available that this section is devoted to them.

405.   Magill, Frank N., ed. **Masterplots: 2010 Plot Stories and Essay Reviews from the World's Fine Literature.** Rev. ed. 12 vols. New York: Salem, 1976.

Long familiar to librarians for summaries of well-known literary works is the name of Frank Magill, who began publishing *Masterplots* in 1950. Magill was not the originator of this type of reference book, which goes back to Helen Keller's *Reader's Digest of Books* (1929) and earlier. But Magill carried the form to the fullest extent, as witnessed by the many series under his editorship. *Masterplots* has summaries of the most famous novels, plays, stories, poems, and epics of the world from Homer to modern times. Most of these summaries are accompanied by one- or two-page critical essays. These are helpful, not only for the student who has not read an assigned novel or other work, but also for the person who did read it but would like a memory refresher, especially for a difficult work like Joyce's *Finnegan's Wake.*

406.   Magill, Frank N., ed. **Survey of Contemporary Literature.** Rev. ed. 12 vols. Englewood Cliffs, N.J.: Salem, 1977.

Each year, beginning in 1954, the Magill series, *Masterplots Annual*, provided summaries of one hundred major works, literary and non-literary, published in the United States the previous year. These 2,300 essay-reviews through 1976 are brought together as *Survey of Contemporary Literature.*

407. **Magill's Literary Annual, 1977- .** Englewood Cliffs, N.J.: Salem, 1978- .

Each year about two hundred outstanding literary and other works published in the United States the previous year are summarized in this series, which was formerly *Masterplots Annual.* Each annual has a cumulative index of all titles included from the 1977 volume to the present.

408. **Survey of Science Fiction Literature: Five Hundred 2,000-Word Essay-Reviews of World-Famous Science Fiction Novels.** Edited by Frank N. Magill. 5 vols. Englewood Cliffs, N.J.: Salem, 1979.

Besides the summary and critique of each of the 513 science fiction books included in this series, the date of its initial publication, the time and locale of the story, a one-sentence outline, a list of the characters, sources for further study of the novel, and citations to reviews are given.

409. Weiss, Irving, and Ann de la Vergne Weiss, comps. and eds. **Thesaurus of Book Digests, 1950-1980.** New York: Crown, 1981. 531p.

An older *Thesaurus of Book Digests* by Hiram Haydn and Edmund Fuller (1949) is supplemented by this work, which has approximately 1,700 entries and cross-references for novels, plays, poetry collections, and non-fiction books.

410. **Plots and Characters Series.** Hamden, Conn.: Archon.

The volumes in this series summarize the plots and identify the characters in the novels of selected authors. Most volumes are on the novels of an individual, usually British or American (e.g., Jane Austen, James Fenimore Cooper, Theodore Dreiser), but volumes have been published on eighteenth century English authors, classic French fiction, and major Russian fiction.

411. **Magill Books Index: All Authorized Editions, 1949-1980, by Title and Author.** Compiled by The Salem Press Staff. Englewood Cliffs, N.J.: Salem, 1980. 799p.

412. Kolar, Carol K., comp. **Plot Summary Index.** 2d ed., rev. & enl. Metuchen, N.J.: Scarecrow, 1981. 526p.

Since there are now so many different series of plot summaries, use of these indexes greatly simplifies locating the summary of a particular novel, play, poem, or other work. The index compiled by Kolar covers 111 collections of plot summaries, of which 21 are under the Magill editorship.

LITERARY CRITICISM

The most frequent need in the field is for articles and books explaining, interpreting, and analyzing individual literary works or discussing critically the work of an individual writer. Undergraduates, especially, ask for this type of material in completing class assignments or preparing term papers. Such help, if properly used, is not considered dishonest but, rather, suggestive to the student of qualities to look for in a literary work and conducive to teaching the student certain standards. Many libraries maintain a collection of books and indexes to books on literary criticism in a readily accessible location, where users can find what they need. Different types of these books and indexes are described in this section.

413. Tucker, Martin, ed. **The Critical Temper: A Survey of Modern Criticism on English and American Literature from the Beginnings to the Twentieth Century.** 3 vols. New York: Ungar, 1969. Supplement, vol. 4. 1980. 550p. (A Library of Literary Criticism).

414. Temple, Ruth Z., and Martin Tucker, eds. **Modern British Literature.** 3 vols. New York: Ungar, 1966. Supplement, edited by Martin Tucker and Rita Stein, vol. 4. 1975. 650p. (A Library of Literary Criticism).

415. Temple, Ruth Z., and Martin Tucker, eds. **Twentieth Century British Literature: A Reference Guide and Bibliography.** New York: Ungar, 1968. 261p.

416. Curley, Dorothy Nyren, Maurice Kramer, and Elaine F. Kramer, eds. **Modern American Literature.** 3 vols. New York: Ungar, 1973. Supplement, vol. 4. 1976. 605p. (A Library of Literary Criticism).

417. Ferres, John H., and Martin Tucker, comps. and eds. **Modern Commonwealth Literature.** New York: Ungar, 1977. 561p. (A Library of Literary Criticism).

418. Curley, Dorothy Nyren, and Arthur Curley, eds. **Modern Romance Literatures.** New York: Ungar, 1967. 510p. (A Library of Literary Criticism).

In general, there are two types of reference books of literary criticism. Some, exemplified by these works, reprint excerpts from articles and books about individual novels, plays, long poems, etc. The arrangement is by writer and the major literary works of that writer. Articles which are simply descriptive or biographical are usually not included. Other volumes in this series reprint criticism of Slavic, Latin American, and French literature. The advantage of this type of book is that the reader is provided with examples of critical writing and does not have to track down call numbers and look for the periodicals and books from which the examples were extracted. The disadvantage is that only a selection of critical writing can be provided.

419. Bell, I. F., and Donald Baird. **The English Novel, 1578-1956: A Checklist of Twentieth Century Criticism.** Chicago: Swallow, 1958. Reprint. Hamden, Conn.: Shoe String, 1974. 168p.

420. Palmer, Helen H., and Anne J. Dyson, comps. **English Novel Explication: Criticism to 1972.** Hamden, Conn.: Shoe String, 1973. Supplement 1, compiled by Peter L. Abernethy, Christian J. W. Kloesel, and Jeffrey R. Smitten. 1976. 305p. Supplement 2, compiled by Kloesel and Smitten. 1981. 326p.

421. **The English Novel: Twentieth Century Criticism.** Vol. 1, **Defoe through Hardy.** Edited by Richard J. Dunn. Chicago: Swallow, 1976; Vol. 2, **Twentieth Century Novelists.** Edited by Paul Schlueter and June Schlueter. Athens, Ohio: Ohio University Press/Swallow, 1982.

422. Cassis, A. F. **The Twentieth Century English Novel: An Annotated Bibliography of General Criticism.** New York: Garland, 1977. 413p.

423. Gerstenberger, Donna, and George Hendrick. **The American Novel since 1789: A Checklist of Twentieth Century Criticism.** 2 vols. Chicago: Swallow, 1961-70.

424. Kearney, Elizabeth I., and Louise S. Fitzgerald, eds. **The Continental Novel: A Checklist of Criticism in English, 1900-1966.** Metuchen, N.J.: Scarecrow, 1968. 460p.

425. Fitzgerald, Louise S., and Elizabeth I. Kearney, eds. **The Continental Novel: A Checklist of Criticism in English, 1967-1980.** Metuchen, N.J.: Scarecrow, 1983. 496p.

426. Coleman, Arthur, and G. R. Tyler. **Drama Criticism.** Vol. 1, **A Checklist of Interpretation since 1940 of English and American Plays.** Denver: Swallow, 1966. 457p. Vol. 2, **A Checklist of Interpretation since 1940 of Classical and Continental Plays.** Chicago: Swallow, 1971. 446p.

427. Breed, Paul F., and Florence M. Sniderman. **Dramatic Criticism Index: A Bibliography of Commentaries on Playwrights from Ibsen to the Avant-Garde.** Detroit: Gale, 1972. 1022p.

428. Eddleman, Floyd E., ed. **American Drama Criticism: Interpretations, 1890-1977.** 2d ed. Hamden, Conn.: Shoe String, 1979. 488p.

429. Palmer, Helen H. **European Drama Criticism, 1900-1975.** 2d ed. Hamden, Conn.: Shoe String, 1977. 653p.

430. Walker, Warren S., comp. **Twentieth Century Short Story Explication: Interpretations, 1900-1975, of Short Fiction since 1800.** 3d ed. Hamden, Conn.: Shoe String, 1977. 880p. Supplement 1, 1980. 257p. Supplement 2, 1984. 346p.

431. Kuntz, Joseph M., and Nancy C. Martinez. **Poetry Explication: A Checklist of Interpretation since 1925 of British and American Poems, Past and Present.** 3d ed. Boston: G. K. Hall, 1980. 570p.

If further critical notes are needed beyond what was provided by the excerpts in the first type of books, the search will proceed to indexes of this type. These, a sampling of an ever-growing genre, are arranged like the collections of critical excerpts—by writer and work—but they give only references to books, periodical articles, and sections of critical books. Again, references are limited to those books and articles which offer critical comment and omit those which are simply descriptive or laudatory. Using these indexes is more time-consuming than using the collections of excerpts since the articles and books cited must still be found, but the student or other reader preparing a paper or report on a writer or a single work will find much more critical material through this search.

432. **Gale Literary Criticism Series.** Detroit: Gale.

The collections of excerpts and the indexes of critical writing cited above are supplemented by these continuing series. Each volume reprints excerpts from critical writings about a selection of writers from the period covered by the particular series:

Contemporary Literary Criticism. Edited by Jean C. Stine. 1973- .

Twentieth Century Literary Criticism. Edited by Dennis Poupard. 1978- .

Nineteenth Century Literature Criticism. Edited by Laurie L. Harris and Sheila Fitzgerald. 1981- .

Literary Criticism from 1400 to 1800 (excluding Shakespeare). Edited by Dennis Poupard. 1983- .

Shakespearean Criticism. Edited by Laurie L. Harris. 1983- .

Editors of the series have changed from year to year but currently are as indicated. The extracts reprinted are from critical writings contemporary with the literary work and up to the present, arranged chronologically. In the front of each volume are lists of the writers in the current volume and those selected for the next several volumes. At the end of each volume is a cumulative index of all writers included in previous volumes and a cumulative index of the critics whose articles were excerpted in all previous volumes. The period covered in each volume is evident from the title except for *Twentieth Century Literary Criticism*, which concludes with 1959, and *Contemporary Literary Criticism*, which begins with 1960.

433.   Magill, Frank N., ed. **Magill's Bibliography of Literary Criticism.** 4 vols. Englewood Cliffs, N.J.: Salem, 1979.

Still another set under the general editorship of the indefatigable Frank Magill. This covers 2,546 literary works of 613 writers from various countries and from the beginnings of western literature to the present. References (not excerpts) are to books, parts of books, and articles. This is a handy source to try if the writer or literary work being studied is not covered in one of the collections or indexes described above, or if the library does not have many of the collections and indexes of literary criticism.

434.   **Series on literary criticism.**

Since the demand is so large for works of literary criticism, the large library will probably acquire volumes in some of the series like the following, which excerpt critical writings on individual writers. If space can be provided, the library may want to keep these together in an accessible location, as suggested above.

> **Casebook Series.** London: Macmillan, 1968- .

> **Critical Heritage Series.** London: Routledge, 1980- .

> **Studies in English Literature.** London: Edward Arnold, 1961- .

> **Twentieth Century Interpretations.** Englewood Cliffs, N.J.: Prentice-Hall, 1967- .

> **Twentieth Century Views.** Englewood Cliffs, N.J.: Prentice-Hall, 1961- .

More detail on these and similar series and the volumes available in each series as of 1982 can be found in Patterson's *Literary Research Guide* (see entry 326, pp. 107, 401-403).

FOREIGN LITERATURE IN ENGLISH

435.   **The Literatures of the World in English Translation.** New York: Ungar, 1967- .

436.   O'Neill, Patrick. **German Literature in English Translation: A Select Bibliography.** Toronto: University of Toronto Press, 1981. 242p.

437.   Columbia University. Columbia College. **A Guide to Oriental Classics.** Prepared by the Staff of the Oriental Studies Program, Columbia College. 2d ed. Edited by W. T. DeBary and A. T. Embree. New York: Columbia University Press, 1975. 257p.

Bibliographies of the classics of other literatures which are available in English are useful for those readers who do not have command of the foreign language in which they were written. Many colleges offer courses on world literature in English translation. Bibliographies by specialists are available in the series, *The Literatures of the World in*

English Translation: Richard C. Lewanski's *The Slavic Literatures* (1967. 630p.), George B. Parks's *The Greek and Latin Literatures* (1968. 442p.), and George B. Parks's *The Romance Literatures* (2 vols., 1970). Volumes on the Celtic, Germanic, and other literatures of Europe and on the literatures of Asia and Africa are projected.

12

MUSIC

Most universities do not have as many faculty and students in music as they do in literature. Therefore, there usually is not as much emphasis on reference work in music as there is in literature and some other fields. Three types of user can be identified in the university that has a school or department of music: the musicologist, the performer, and the listener or non-musician. A user may belong to two or all three of these groups, but at a given time his or her reference question will reflect one type of interest. Students and faculty of the school of music are predominantly musicologists or performers. Most of the questions of the third type come from students, faculty, and other persons outside the school of music. Reference work in the university library will differ from reference work in the public library because in the university library there will be a greater number of questions about — and a stronger collection in — musicology and performance than there will be in the public library where questions and resources tend to center on the needs of the listener. The latter — dates of musical compositions and popular songs, biographical questions, definitions of music terms, members of a particular rock, country, or other musical group, history of music and musical instruments, words of popular songs and hymns, etc. — are predominant in public libraries but frequent also in the university library. The past few decades have seen a rise in serious study of popular, folk, country, western, and rock music as well as classical music, and this has changed the nature of reference work and, consequently, the collection in the university library. Many new dictionaries and encyclopedias, handbooks, who's whos, and other reference tools on popular, jazz, rock, country, and other non-classical forms of music are now available and needed in the university library.

The types of reference questions most often encountered in the university library will be dependent upon the presence and strength of a school of music in the institution, the surrounding community, and the relationship with other neighboring libraries. Music interests in the community and the dependence of other libraries on the university library will increase the proportion of questions of a popular nature. But, since many of these will be referred from the local public library, which could not answer them from its limited resources, they may be more difficult than the usual question of this type.

Faculty and graduate students in musicology do most of their own reference work. The various reference books supporting musicology are needed in the library, but the services of the reference librarian are usually called for only when a needed book cannot be found or is not held by the library. Undergraduates in the school of music, like undergraduates in other parts of the university, often need instruction in the use of the library catalog, periodical indexes, and other bibliographical tools. Students and faculty specializing in music performance, the second group of users, do not have many reference needs. For the most part, they want access to music scores but can usually locate these for themselves, if they are available. Questions of the third group, non-musicians from within or outside the university, are generally easy to answer. As in the field of literature, these are often about a particular person (composer, lyricist, or performer) or a particular composition or song. A piece's composer or lyricist or its date, the date and public reception of an opera, some biographical fact about a composer or performer (who belonged to a musical group at a particular date and where they are at present), the words and music of a popular or art song—these are all typical examples of questions of the third group. The following sample of questions asked in the Music Library of a large university may be considered as representative of questions from all three of these groups:

> Someone from the National Council of Teachers of English (in Urbana, Illinois) would like to know, "Do you have the lyrics to 'Lullaby of Birdland'?"

> In a telephone inquiry, the caller states, "I need the composer and title to a circus tune that goes ya-da, da-da-da, ya-da, dum-dum."

> A staff member from the Assembly Hall (the University of Illinois hall for major events) inquires frantically: "We need a recording of the South Korean national anthem for this evening. Can you supply one?"

> At the information desk, a client asks, "Do you have a recording of Taco Bell's Canon?"

> A graduate student in music inquires, "Where can I find English translations of the Latin texts *Super flumina Babylonis* and *Vox in Roma*?"

> Another inquirer seeks a photograph or a facsimile of Stephen Foster's signature.

> An undergraduate student wants to know, "Who has the largest private or institutional collection of Glenn Miller recordings?"

> Another student asks, "Who was the original Sergeant Pepper model for the Beatles' album, *Sergeant Pepper's Lonely Hearts Club Band*?"

> From the University Library's Research and Reference Center comes the request, "Please supply information about the eighteenth-century Parisian harp maker, Sebastian Erard."

> An employee of the local music publisher, Mark Foster Music Co., needs to know the current holder of the copyright for Paul Hindemith's book, *Traditional Harmony*.

> A television crew, on location near Springfield, Illinois, for a major network production, needs to get the words and music to the drinking song of which the first line is "That night I came a-ridin' home, as drunk as drunk could be." A key line from the chorus is "But a mustache on a cabbage head I've never seen before."

> A graphics designer is trying to locate a picture of an eighteenth-century ornate music stand.

> A staff member from the University's News Bureau needs to know the source and/or the original statement for the quotation, "Vivaldi didn't write 400 concertos, he wrote the same concerto 400 times."[1]

---

[1]William M. McClellan, "A Sampling of American Music in the Music Library," *Non Solus* 8 (1981): 19-20.

Finding the words and music of an obscure song or a very new song or learning the present whereabouts of a performer who was popular some years ago may present difficulties, but most questions of this type are fairly simple to answer.

If the library has a large number of questions about current popular music, a special section of reference tools and periodicals containing data and information on recent popular music might be maintained, along with a staff member who is expert in this field. Another special collection that is found in the music division of the library is a collection of recordings and record players with headphones. Local policy will determine what proportion of the record collection will be classical music and what proportion, if any, will be popular recordings. In the Music Library, the collection will probably be wholly or mostly classical music in support of classes on music history and appreciation, theory and composition, performance, etc. In the main library, a record collection may have a large proportion of popular music, folk music, readings from Shakespeare and other literary classics, cassettes for learning foreign languages, etc., as well as classical music. The trend is away from supporting recreational listening, however, partly because of reduced library budgets and partly because students prefer to use the more portable stereo headsets while they are studying.

In the following paragraphs, we describe the reference books on music likely to be of most use in the typical university library, reflecting the needs of the three types of users and the interest in serious study of popular, folk, and other music forms. Books on the musical theater and musical films are included in chapter 14, "Performing Arts."

GUIDES, BIBLIOGRAPHIES, INDEXES

438.   Duckles, Vincent. **Music Reference and Research Materials.** 3d ed. New York: Free Press, 1974. 526p.

439.   Marco, Guy, and others. **Information on Music: A Handbook of Reference Sources in European Languages.** Littleton, Colo.: Libraries Unlimited, 1975- . In progress.

Since some of the reference sources most important in musicology are in German, French, and other European languages, help from a guide to the reference literature is useful even to the advanced student. Both of the guides listed here are very valuable. *Music Reference and Research Materials* has almost 2,000 carefully annotated entries organized under broad categories, e.g., dictionaries and encyclopedias; histories and chronologies; guides to systematic and historical musicology; bibliographies of music literature. There are separate indexes for authors/editors/reviewers; subjects; titles. *Information on Music* is even more critical and evaluative of the information sources for music. Unfortunately, it is slow in being completed. Three of the proposed eight volumes have now been published. The first covers basic and universal sources; the second is on sources pertaining to music in the Americas; the third on the European countries. The second and third volumes include sections updating the earlier volumes, and the editors promise supplements to these three volumes in the form of either separates or journal articles. If the initial plan is adhered to, future volumes will cover the music of Africa, Asia, and Oceania, special topics in music, individual musicians, and a guide to musical editions.

440.   Horn, David. **The Literature of American Music in Books and Folk Music Collections: A Fully Annotated Bibliography.** Metuchen, N.J.: Scarecrow, 1977. 556p.

All types of music in North America are covered in the 1,700 entries of this bibliography: music of the American Indian, folk song of many kinds, religious music, black, jazz, rock-and-roll, etc. Annotations of these items are thorough, and there is an author-subject index.

441.   New York Public Library. The Research Libraries. **Dictionary Catalog of the Music Collection.** 2d ed. 45 vols., 45 reels. Boston: G. K. Hall, 1982.

442.   Boston Public Library. **Dictionary Catalog of the Music Collection.** 20 vols. Boston: G. K. Hall, 1972. Supplement, 4 vols. 1977.

The publisher is known for reprinting in book form the dictionary catalogs of library collections that are outstanding in their special field. Although these catalogs are expensive and require a large shelf space, they are so valuable in bibliographic identification that the library having both the budget and the room should acquire G. K. Hall catalogs for subject areas in which it does a substantial amount of reference work. The New York collection is outstanding for its book material, and its catalog includes analyzed titles from Festschriften. It is now available on 35mm microfilm. The catalog of the Boston Public Library music collection is superior for its scores.

443.   U.S. Library of Congress. **Music, Books on Music, and Sound Recordings.** Washington, D.C.: 1973- . Semiannual with annual and 5-year cumulations.

This section of the Library of Congress Catalog series is also important in bibliographic identification. Recordings, scores, sheet music, libretti, and books about music and musicians cataloged by the Library of Congress and nine cooperating libraries in the United States and Canada are included. As of 1986, this part of the Library of Congress Catalog series continues to be published in book form.

444.   **Music Index: A Subject-Author Guide to Current Music Periodical Literature.** Detroit: Information Coordinators, 1949- . Monthly with annual cumulation.

Although students may complain about the number of monthly issues of this index they must search because of the late appearance (five to six years) of the yearly bound cumulation, this is the only periodical index covering all types of music: folk, religious, jazz, rock, and international, as well as classical. Monthly issues are also nearly a year late. Some three hundred or more journals and periodicals, many in languages other than English, are indexed in dictionary arrangement. Books are also indexed under author and subject. Book reviews are listed under the heading "Book Reviews," with a cross-reference from the author's name and the title.

445.   **RILM: Abstracts of Music Literature.** New York: Répertoire Internationale de la Littérature Musicale, 1967- . Quarterly.

Although it is also late in appearing (five years), this is *the* scholarly index for music. It was established in 1966 by the International Musicological Society and the International Association of Music Libraries to help correct the deficiencies in the bibliography of serious music and musicology. The attempt is to include all significant music literature in whatever form: books, articles, essays, dissertations, catalogs, etc. Arrangement is under broad heading, e.g., reference and research materials; history, Western art music; ethnomusicology and non-Western art music; instruments and voice. The fourth issue is the cumulative author-subject index for the year. *RILM* can be machine searched back to 1971 through DIALOG.

446.   Diamond, Harold J. **Music Criticism: An Annotated Guide to the Literature.** Metuchen, N.J.: Scarecrow, 1979. 316p.

Arranged under type of musical composition (solo works, operas, vocal music, orchestral music, etc.), then under composer, this guide lists the books and articles containing criticism and evaluation of individual compositions. Books and articles in languages other than English and dissertations are excluded.

447.   Heyer, A. H. **Historical Sets, Collected Editions, and Monuments of Music: A Guide to Their Contents.** 3d ed. 2 vols. Chicago: American Library Association, 1981.

This is a completely revised edition of an important bibliography, listing alphabetically more than 1,300 collections of the music of several or a number of composers and complete editions of the works of major composers. Emphasis is on older classics. The work is helpful in learning the contents of such monumental collections as *Denkmäler deutscher Tonkunst* or *Plainsong and Medieval Society Publications*; also for identifying minor pieces in a composer's collected works. The index volume refers from the name of a composer or a particular composition to the sets or editions which include it. A less comprehensive bibliography serving a similar purpose is Sidney R. Charles's *Handbook of Music and Music Literature in Sets and Series* (New York: Free Press, 1972). It has separate sections for "Sets and Series Containing Music of Several Composers and Sets and Series Containing Both Music and Music Literature"; "Sets and Series Devoted to One Composer"; "Music Literature Monograph and Facsimile Series"; and "Music Periodicals and Yearbooks" besides a master index.

448.   Krummel, D. W., and others. **Resources of American Music History: A Directory of Source Materials from Colonial Times to World War II.** Urbana, Ill.: University of Illinois Press, 1981. 463p. (Music in American Life).

The holdings of 1,689 repositories of material useful for the study of American music history are described briefly in this work. The holdings generally include recordings, sheet music, manuscripts, personal papers, etc. Most of these repositories in libraries, music societies, historical societies, private collections, and publishers are, as would be expected, in the United States; a few are in Canada and other countries. There is a single index of personal names, repositories, and subjects.

DICTIONARIES, ENCYCLOPEDIAS

449.   Apel, Willi. **Harvard Dictionary of Music.** 2d ed. Cambridge, Mass.: Harvard University Press, 1969. 935p.

This is acknowledged to be the best dictionary of music terms in English. It does not include biographical articles, but does list names of well-known operas, songs, and dances. German, French, and Italian terms are included as well as those in English, and the English term is followed by the equivalents in other languages. Many of the long articles have bibliographies. Valuable lists are given under such articles as "Libraries," "Dictionaries of Music," and "Editions, Historical." The latter article lists contents of 52 most widely known sets, serving as a mini-Heyer (see entry 447).

450.   **The New Grove Dictionary of Music and Musicians.** Edited by Stanley Sadie. 20 vols. London: Macmillan, 1980.

Few people would question that the *New Grove Dictionary of Music and Musicians* is the single most valuable reference source in the field for university libraries. The emphasis is on classical music, but there is also much on ethnic music, folk music and dances, and other subjects that would not be considered classical music in the strict sense. It has articles of varying length on composers and other persons associated with music, terms, names of instruments, well-known operas and compositions, musical styles and movements, and other subjects pertaining to music. Articles on composers give a list of their compositions. Articles on collections of music and songs list their contents. There have been five previous editions, all highly valued by scholars and students. This edition, however, has been so completely revised and changed that the decision was to name it *The New Grove Dictionary* instead of a sixth edition. It is greatly expanded, contains more lists of compositions and bibliographies, even on some little-known composers, and has about twice as many words as the fifth edition.

451. Thompson, Oscar. **The International Cyclopedia of Music and Musicians.** 10th ed. Edited by Bruce Bohle. New York: Dodd, Mead, 1975. 2511p.

Although it is not equal to *Grove*, Duckles considers this "the best one-volume general dictionary of music in English." It covers composers, instrumentalists, singers, and others associated with classical music, well-known compositions and operas, musical terms, associations, and topics. The length of articles varies considerably, not always consonant with the importance of the subject. Articles on major composers list their compositions and printed editions. Some readers will prefer *The New Oxford Companion to Music* (see entry 455).

452. **Die Musik in Geschichte und Gegenwart.** Edited by Friedrich Blume. Kassell, Germany: Barenreiter, 1949- .

This is the definitive encyclopedia of music, which, even though in German, is preferred by scholars because of its depth and the extensive research that went into its writing by many specialists. Usually it is called simply *MGG*. The alphabetic portion in 14 volumes and the 2-volume supplement, bringing the main set up to date as of 1976, are now complete, leaving only the index still to be published.

453. Vinton, John, ed. **Dictionary of Contemporary Music.** New York: E. P. Dutton, 1974. 834p.

The emphasis here is on concert music of the twentieth century, with excellent articles of varying length on composers, developments and experiments in contemporary music, and trends in different countries. Some articles are on the late nineteenth century.

DIRECTORIES

454. **The Musician's Guide: The Directory of the World of Music.** 6th ed. Chicago: Marquis Academic Media, 1980. 943p.

As the standard directory in the field of American music, this is found in all libraries. It has sections listing music associations, schools, scholarships, music libraries, national music centers, recent publications In the field, periodicals, festivals, agents, unions, etc. There are also separate discographies recommended for classical, jazz, and rock collections.

HANDBOOKS

455. **The New Oxford Companion to Music.** Edited by Denis Arnold. 2 vols. Oxford, England: Oxford University Press, 1983.

Consistent with the treatment of Oxford companions in other chapters, this is listed under "Handbooks," although it is of the dictionary/encyclopedia type. Like *The New Grove Dictionary of Music and Musicians*, this has been greatly expanded and rewritten and is retitled rather than being called an 11th edition. It has more on the music of Asia, covers more subjects in music, has longer articles and less whimsy and fewer anecdotes than the previous edition. It still favors British composers and music over American ones but may, nevertheless, be preferred as a short encyclopedia to the older *International Cyclopedia of Music and Musicians* (entry 451).

456. Downes, Edward. **Guide to Symphonic Music.** New York: Walker & Co., 1981. 1058p.

A work of this kind, which describes well-known symphonic works, is wanted for the non-specialist. This edition describes the important works of 108 composers, giving the background of each composition, its music (with themes, counterthemes, and the dominance at certain times of different instruments, movement by movement), public reception at its first performance, and similar interesting information. An earlier edition was titled *The New York Philharmonic Guide to the Symphony.* For the average listener, whether at home or at the concert, such an introduction to the great music of the past is a great help in music appreciation. A similar guide to the great operas is described below (entry 473).

REFERENCE HISTORIES

457. **New Oxford History of Music.** 11 vols. New York: Oxford University Press, 1954- . In progress.

When background is needed on a major movement in music or on the music of a given country and century, this is often obtained better from the more extended account in a history of music than from an encyclopedia or dictionary. *New Oxford History of Music*, the definitive history in English, is now approaching completion, with the following volumes still to be published: volume 6, *The Growth of Instrumental Music (1630-1970)*, volume 9, *Romanticism (1830-1890)*, and volume 11, chronological tables and general index. The volumes of the *Norton History of Music* are also highly respected. Although these have never been offered as a set, examples are *The Rise of Music in the Ancient World, East and West*, by Curt Sachs (New York: Norton, 1943); *Music in the Renaissance*, by Gustave Reese (Rev. ed., New York: Norton, 1959); and *Music in the 20th Century from Debussy through Stravinsky*, by William W. Austen (New York: Norton, 1966). A good one-volume history is *A History of Western Music* by Donald J. Grout (3d ed. New York: Norton, 1980).

458. Eisler, Paul E., Neal Hatch, and Edith Eisler, comps. and eds. **World Chronology of Music History.** Dobbs Ferry, N.Y.: Oceana, 1972- . In progress.

A detailed chronology of musical events, most in the Western world, from prehistoric time to the present day. At the time of writing, published work had reached the end of 1796 (volume 6). When complete, an alphabetical index to the entire set will be compiled. This chronological approach is sometimes useful when one wishes to compare what was happening in different countries in the musical world in a given year or span of years.

459. Slonimsky, Nicholas. **Music since 1900.** 4th ed. New York: Scribner's, 1971. 1595p.

For the twentieth century up to 1969, a similar chronology is given in this work. The chronology is followed by a reprint of letters and documents that had a particular impact during this 70-year period. There is a dictionary of musical terms and an index of names and subjects.

BIOGRAPHY

460. Baker, Theodore. **Baker's Biographical Dictionary of Musicians.** 6th ed. Revised by Nicholas Slonimsky. New York: Schirmer, 1978. 1955p.

Biographical questions do not compare in frequency with questions about individual compositions. For simple facts about a person, their dates, what they have composed or other achievements, the appropriate entry in the *New Grove Dictionary of Music and Musicians*, the *International Cyclopedia of Music and Musicians*, the *New Oxford Companion to Music*, or a work of this kind will probably suffice. When there is no entry in one of these encyclopedias for the person sought, refer to the above work, which has brief data in its approximately 8,000 entries on many lesser-known musicologists, performers, writers, teachers, and others in the field. *The New Grove Dictionary* has almost as many biographical articles as Baker, but each of these works has many that are lacking in the other. *Grove* leans toward classical musicians, authors, educators, and others associated with musicology and classical music; Baker has recent and living musicians not in *Grove* and has many associated with popular music.

461. Claghorn, Charles E. **Biographical Dictionary of American Music.** West Nyack, N.Y.: Parker, 1973. 491p.

Since this work is limited to American musicians of the past and present, it possibly has data on minor figures for whom there is no entry in any of the more general encyclopedias or *Baker's Biographical Dictionary of Musicians.* More than 5,200 composers and musicians who were born in the Colonies or the United States or who lived and worked here for an extensive period are included. There are figures from classical, jazz, popular, and other music. Some names of groups and bands are included.

462. **ASCAP Biographical Dictionary.** 4th ed. Compiled by Jaques Cattell Press. New York: Bowker, 1980. 589p.

It sometimes happens that no entry can be found for a particular person in any of the standard biographical sources, especially for someone who has only recently become active in his field. The membership directory of the person's professional association may furnish some needed data when nothing else can be found. This directory has brief data, including a list of compositions or songs, of some 8,000 members of ASCAP (the American Society of Composers, Authors, and Publishers). Former members, now deceased, are included.

463. Bull, Storm. **Index to Biographies of Contemporary Composers.** 3 vols. Metuchen, N.J.: Scarecrow, 1964-74.

Composers of the twentieth century, about whom information is not as easy to find as it is for earlier composers, are covered in these two volumes. Vinton's *Dictionary of Contemporary Music* (see entry 453), the *The New Grove Dictionary of Music and Musicians* (see entry 450), and *Baker's Biographical Dictionary of Musicians* (see entry 460) should be checked first, since they provide biographical data directly. If the composer's name cannot be found in one of these sources, it will probably be found in this index, but then there will be the additional step of locating the book or collection containing the biographical information.

464. Ewen, David. **Composers since 1900.** New York: Wilson, 1969. 639p.

465. Ewen, David. **Composers of Tomorrow's Music.** New York: Dodd, Mead, 1971. Reprint. Westport, Conn.: Greenwood, 1980. 176p.

466. Ewen, David. **Musicians since 1900: Performers in Concert and Opera.** New York: Wilson, 1978. 974p.

David Ewen has written a number of biographical collections about musicians. These are popularly written and better suited to the public library or high school library than to the needs of music school students and faculty. But they will serve as additional sources for term papers or for users from other parts of the university. These three titles are examples of the many works by Ewen.

GUIDES TO PERFORMANCE MUSIC

467.   Espina, Noni. **Repertoire for the Solo Voice.** 2 vols. Metuchen, N.J.: Scarecrow, 1977.

468.   Farish, Margaret, ed. **String Music in Print.** 2d ed. Philadelphia: Musicdata, 1980. 464p. (Music in Print Series, vol. 6).

469.   Hinson, Maurice. **Guide to the Pianist's Repertoire.** Bloomington, Ind.: Indiana University Press, 1975. 832p. Supplement, 1980.

A school of music with students and faculty who are primarily performers has need of guides like these, which list printed sources containing music of a certain needed kind. They are usually arranged in a form suited to the performer's needs, grouping music by performance characteristics or level of difficulty. A number of guides to performance music are available for orchestra, organ, and various individual instruments.

THEMATIC DICTIONARIES

470.   Barlow, Harold, and Sam Morgenstern. **A Dictionary of Musical Themes.** Rev. ed. New York: Crown, 1975. 642p.

471.   Barlow, Harold, and Sam Morgenstern. **A Dictionary of Opera and Song Themes.** New York: Crown, 1976. 547p.

Thematic dictionaries like these resemble quotation dictionaries. They enable one to find the composition in which a particular musical theme is prominent. The two volumes by Barlow and Morgenstern are arranged by composer, beneath whose name are listed the musical notation for a number of prominent themes (in the vocal music dictionary, music and words). At the back of each volume is an alphabetical index of themes, converted to the key of C. The toreador theme from Bizet's *Carmen*, for example, is GAGEEED in the key of C. The user or librarian must be able to convert the phrase, as remembered, into the key of C. For a phrase hummed over the telephone, this may present some difficulty, even for an accomplished musician. Each of the Barlow/Morgenstern dictionaries lists about 10,000 themes. The "revised edition" of *A Dictionary of Musical Themes* has little or no change from the 1948 edition of the work. *A Dictionary of Opera and Song* has themes from operas, oratorios, Lieder, art songs, and other forms. It is a reprint, without apparent change, of the 1950 edition, titled *A Dictionary of Vocal Themes*. Other thematic catalogs list themes in musical notation under the composer's name, but do not have an alphabetical index of themes. *Concerto Themes* (New York: Simon and Schuster, 1951) and *Symphony Themes* (New York: Simon and Schuster, 1942) by Raymond M. Burrows and Bessie C. Redmond are examples of books in which it is necessary to know (or suspect) who composed a work in order to check the theme. Another type of thematic catalog is used primarily in musicology: the thematic catalog of the complete works of a single composer, e.g., *Das Werk Beethovens: thematisch-bibliographisches Verzeichnis seine sämtlichen vollendeten Kompositionen*, by G. Kinsky (Munich-Duisburg: Henle, 1955). This type serves to bring together all of the compositions of one person, but in a classified order rather than by opus number or by title.

472. Brook, Barry S. **Thematic Catalogues in Music: An Annotated Bibliography.** Hillsdale, N.Y.: Pendragon Press, 1972. 347p.

Under the name of composers, alphabetically arranged, are 1,444 thematic catalogs. There is an index of authors, composers, and subjects.

OPERA

473. Kobbé, Gustave. **The New Kobbé's Opera Book.** Edited and revised by the Earl of Harewood. New York: Putnam, 1976. 1694p.

There are so many people interested in opera, from the occasional opera fan to the accomplished musician or musicologist, that a separate section is justified. This handbook is probably the best-known general book on opera and is found in nearly all libraries. Some 350 operas, arranged under century-country-composer, are described: circumstances of composition, first presentation to the public and early history, summary of plot, and description of some favorite arias. The index has names of operas, composers, and singers.

474. Rosenthal, Harold, and John Warrack. **The Concise Oxford Dictionary of Opera.** 2d ed. London: Oxford University Press, 1979. 561p.

475. Orrey, Leslie, ed. **The Encyclopedia of the Opera.** New York: Scribner's, 1976. 376p.

These dictionaries have brief entries defining terms from opera and identifying composers, librettists, conductors, designers, producers, singers, operas, arias, and theaters. The first has about 5,000 entries but no illustrations; *The Encyclopedia of the Opera* is illustrated and has about 3,000 entries.

476. Martin, George. **The Opera Companion to Twentieth-Century Opera.** New York: Dodd, Mead, 1979. 653p.

Since little has been written on recent operas compared to what is available on older ones, this book is very much needed. Following several essay-chapters about opera in the twentieth century are synopses of 78 operas from Janavek's 1904 opera, *Her Step-Daughter*, to Benjamin Britten's 1976 *Death in Venice*. Some background information about the composing of the opera and its first presentation is given. A final section of the book lists the repertory year by year and attendance statistics by opera and date at 23 of the world's leading opera houses.

477. Loewenberg, Alfred. **Annals of Opera, 1597-1940.** 3d ed. Totowa, N.J.: Rowman & Littlefield, 1978. 1756 col.

478. Seltsam, William H. **Metropolitan Opera Annals: A Chronicle of Artists and Performances.** New York: Wilson, 1947. 751p. Supplement, 1947-1957 (1957); Supplement, 1957-1966 (1968); Supplement, 1966-1976 (1978).

Annals of Opera, a reference book for the musicologist or other person who has a scholarly interest in opera history, is a chronological list of operas, giving the names of the composer and the librettist, the date and place of first performance, the date of first performance in other cities, the date of first performance in translation, and variant titles. There is often a brief note about the opera's initial success but nothing on the plot, cast, or other facts of its production. Although selective, it includes between 3,000 and 4,000 titles, more than are listed in any other single work in English. Indexes of operas, composers and librettists, and a general index are provided. *Metropolitan Opera Annals* lists all of its productions, season by season, since the first in 1883, giving cast and excerpts from critical notices for each production. The main volume and each supplement have indexes of operas and performers.

479. Drone, Jeanette M. **Index to Opera, Operetta, and Musical Comedy Synopses in Collections and Periodicals.** Metuchen, N.J.: Scarecrow, 1978. 171p.

Synopses of 1,605 operas and other musical works in 74 collections and 4 periodicals can be found through this index.

RECORDINGS

480. **The New Schwann Record and Tape Guide.** Boston: Schwann, 1983- . Monthly.

This guide attempts to do for records and tapes what *Books in Print* does for books: to list all records and tapes, U.S.-made and foreign, that would be currently available in a well-stocked music store. Until December 1983, the guide was issued monthly as *Schwann-1 Record and Tape Guide*, listing classical and popular records and tapes in separate categories. This was supplemented by quarterly issues of *Schwann-2*, listing items in such low-demand categories as classical and jazz monos, spoken records (bird songs, railroad sounds, readings from literature, etc.), international pop and folk records, and others. These two parts are now combined in *The New Schwann Record and Tape Guide.* Each issue lists all records and tapes of classical music currently available, including many major European labels. Prices are not given for each listing, but in front of each issue is a price list for all record and tape labels. Also in the front of each issue is a section, "New Listings," giving data on new releases of classical, popular, jazz, spoken, and other records and tapes. The new releases of non-classical and spoken records or tapes, however, are not listed in succeeding issues, as are the new releases of classical music. They are, however, cumulated from the January issue in the April and August issues. The December issue of the *New Schwann Record and Tape Guide* does list all categories of records and tapes available, classical, popular, spoken, and other. It also lists children's records and Christmas music.

481. **Phonolog.** Los Angeles: Trade Service Publications, 1948- . Looseleaf, three times each week.

482. **List-O-Tapes "All in One" Tape Catalog.** Los Angeles: Trade Service Publications, 1964- . Looseleaf, weekly.

If the library has a great many questions about records and tapes, it might be worth the subscription price to have these two looseleaf services. *Phonolog* currently costs $296 per year, *List-O-Tapes*, $133 per year, with a slight reduction for a combination order. *Phonolog* lists all U.S.-made records: 78, 45, and 33⅓ rpm; singles and albums; popular, classical, spoken, and miscellaneous. Listings offer various approaches: by record or album title, by performer, by composer (for classical records), by type (children's, Christmas, Hawaiian, band, etc.). Individual song titles are indexed, referring to the different artists and recordings of that song. *List-O-Tapes* offers similar reference approaches to music on tapes but does not index the individual songs, only the title song on the tape. All currently available tapes are included: popular and classical, reels, cassettes, cartridges, 2-track, 4-track, 8-track, and quadraphonic, U.S. and foreign. The currency of information by frequent updating is an important value of these services.

483. Rodgers and Hammerstein Archives of Recorded Sound. New York Public Library. Performing Arts Research Center. **Dictionary Catalog.** 15 vols. Boston: G. K. Hall, 1981.

484.   Sibley Music Library. University of Rochester. **Catalog of Sound Recordings.** 14 vols. Boston: G. K. Hall, 1977.

The large university will have these G. K. Hall catalogs in its Music Library. The Rodgers and Hammerstein Archives has many more records and tapes in its collection (approximately 75,000) than the Sibley Music Library and more of the non-classical types. Sibley Library recordings are mostly of classical music. But there is surprisingly little duplication in the holdings of the two libraries. The Library of Congress *Music, Books on Music, and Sound Recordings* also lists cataloged recordings.

485.   **Notes.** Washington, D.C.: Music Library Association, 1934- . Quarterly.

486.   Myers, Kurtz, comp. & ed. **Index to Record Reviews.** 5 vols. Boston: G. K. Hall, 1978.

487.   **Records in Review.** Compiled and edited by Edith Carter. Great Barrington, Mass.: Wyeth Press, 1955- . Annual.

488.   **Annual Index to Popular Music Record Reviews, 1972-** . Compiled by Dean Tudor and Linda Biesenthal. Metuchen, N.J.: Scarecrow, 1973- . Annual.

489.   **Index to Record and Tape Reviews, 1982-** . Compiled by Antoinette Maleady. San Anselmo, Calif.: Chulainn Press, 1983- . Annual.

Record collectors often want to know what reviewers have said about a new recording since it is usually not possible to listen to a record before buying it in the way it is possible to examine a book. The sources listed here make it easier to locate reviews of a particular recording. Each issue of the quarterly journal, *Notes,* has an "Index to Record Reviews," compiled and edited by Kurtz Myers. Reviews of recordings of classical music in 21 periodicals are indexed in this source. For the years 1949-1977, it is cumulated in his *Index to Record Reviews. Records in Review* reprints reviews of classical records from issues of *High Fidelity* magazine. *Annual Index to Popular Music Record Reviews* covers reviews appearing in 71 popular music periodicals. Reviews are organized by type of music: rock, mood-pop, country, old time music and blue grass, folk and ethnic, jazz, and others. Both of these indexes, however, are some years behind in appearing. *Index to Record and Tape Reviews* indexes the reviews of classical music recordings from 43 periodicals, 14 of which are also indexed by Myers.

POPULAR MUSIC AND SONGS

490.   Kinkle, Roger D. **The Complete Encyclopedia of Popular Music and Jazz, 1900-1950.** 4 vols. New Rochelle, N.Y.: Arlington, 1974.

This is the most general of the many books on popular music in the United States. It includes an index to popular songs, recordings, and musical films and shows of the years 1900-1950 and biographies of song writers, singers, and instrumentalists. The first volume is a chronological record of the popular music, records, and shows each year. Volumes 2 and 3 have short biographies of about 2,000 writers and performers with lists of their recordings. Most are popular music and jazz figures, but some are from classical, blues, country, and western music. The final volume has lists of poll and award winners, numerical lists of record labels (mostly from mid-1920s to early 1940s), and separate indexes of personal names, Broadway and movie musicals, and popular songs.

491.   Craig, Warren. **Sweet and Lowdown: America's Popular Song Writers.** Metuchen, N.J.: Scarecrow, 1978. 645p.

Writers of popular music are listed with their songs in three historical periods: "Before Tin Pan Alley"; "Tin Pan Alley" (i.e., about 1895-1930); and "After Tin Pan Alley." In an appendix, they are rated by the number of hit songs they wrote. Separate indexes list song titles, musical productions, and names. Rock, country, and western music is omitted.

492.   Feather, Leonard. **The Encyclopedia of Jazz.** New ed. New York: Horizon, 1960. 527p.

493.   Feather, Leonard. **The Encyclopedia of Jazz in the Sixties.** New York: Horizon, 1966. 312p.

494.   Feather, Leonard, and Ira Gitler. **The Encyclopedia of Jazz in the Seventies.** New York: Horizon, 1976. 393p.

The usefulness of these three books is reduced by the biographical entries in Kinkle's *Complete Encyclopedia of Popular Music and Jazz, 1900-1950*, and in Claghorn's *Biographical Dictionary of Jazz.* But the Feather books have many good photographs of jazz musicians not found in the other books. Information about jazz musicians is sometimes difficult to find, since jazz has acquired respectability in the formal musical world only in the past few decades. Feather and the staff of *Downbeat* magazine were pioneers in digging out such information and making jazz a respected musical form. The last of the three books listed above includes brief mention of persons in the earlier volumes, but fuller biographies of pre-1966 performers and their photographs are in the first two volumes.

495.   Claghorn, Charles E. **Biographical Dictionary of Jazz.** Englewood Cliffs, N.J.: Prentice-Hall, 1982. 377p.

About 2,500 individuals and 500 jazz groups are identified in this more recent book on jazz artists.

496.   Stambler, Irwin, and Grelun Landon. **Encyclopedia of Folk, Country, and Western Music.** 2d ed. New York: St. Martin's, 1983. 902p.

497.   Stambler, Irwin. **Encyclopedia of Pop, Rock, and Soul.** New York: St. Martin's, 1977. 609p.

Out of jazz have come a variety of other styles of popular music, some based on older roots. These two general encyclopedias will cover most of these popular forms, although not in the same depth as some books devoted to only one style. Most of the articles in both encyclopedias are on individual performers and groups in the several styles, with a few articles on terms (acid rock, bubble-gum, Appalachian dulcimer, dobro, Grand Ole Opry, etc.). Lists of award winners in the several categories are also included.

498.   Hoffmann, Frank. **The Literature of Rock, 1954-1978.** Metuchen, N.J.: Scarecrow, 1981. 337p.

The bibliography of 4,400 books, articles, and parts of books is arranged by period, showing the development of rock-and-roll from its antecedents (rhythm and blues, rockabilly) to late forms (powerpop). Articles on topics related to the rock-and-roll movement (drugs, festivals, and concerts; historical studies) are also included.

499.   Miller, Jim, ed. **The Rolling Stone Illustrated History of Rock & Roll.** Rev. ed. New York: Random House, 1980. 474p.

500.   Nite, Norm N. **Rock On: The Illustrated Encyclopedia of Rock n' Roll.** 2 vols. Vol. 1, **The Solid Gold Years.** Updated ed. New York: Harper & Row, 1982. Vol. 2, **The Years of Change, 1964-1978.** Updated ed. New York: Harper & Row, 1984.

The history and the performers associated with rock-and-roll music are outlined in these two books. The history, edited by Jim Miller, is a series of 81 essays by various authors, chronologically describing the development of the form from its beginnings in the early 1950s and listing the many individual performers and groups most identified with its several styles. A discography is given for the individual and group performers. Norm Nite's two-volume encyclopedia is an alphabetical presentation of the individual stars and groups with photographs and lists of hit records and albums. Each volume has an index of song titles. Volume 3, covering 1978-83, is in preparation.

501.   York, William. **Who's Who in Rock Music.** New York: Scribner's, 1982. 413p.

If information about some rock performer cannot be found in either of the works described in the previous paragraph, it should be among the 13,000 entries in this who's who, which attempts to identify every individual and every group that has recorded a rock album or has performed on one. For each of the individuals, the instrument, group performed with, and albums are listed; for each group, the names of members and their instruments and albums.

502.   Lawless, Ray M. **Folksingers and Folksongs of America: A Handbook of Biography, Bibliography, and Discography.** 2d ed. New York: Duell, Sloan, and Pearce, 1965. Reprint. Westport, Conn.: Greenwood, 1981. 750p.

Where Stambler and Landon's *Encyclopedia of Folk, Country, and Western Music* is almost entirely on the individual performers and groups associated with these forms, the present handbook has separate chapters about folksong and major printed collections, instruments, folklore societies, and festivals. The handbook has an index of names and subjects and a separate index of titles of published collections and albums.

503.   Shapiro, Nat. **Popular Music: An Annotated Index of American Popular Songs.** Vols. 1-6, New York: Adrian, 1964-73; Vols. 7-8, Edited by Bruce Pollock. Detroit: Gale, 1984.

504.   Mattfeld, Julius. **Variety Music Cavalcade, 1620-1961: A Chronology of Vocal and Instrumental Music Popular in the United States.** Rev. ed. Englewood Cliffs, N.J.: Prentice-Hall, 1962. 713p.

Very often a library user will want to know what year a particular popular song was introduced, what singer or what musical film or show introduced it, or who wrote the words and music. This type of question is most easily answered by consulting the popular song index in volume 4 of *The Complete Encyclopedia of Popular Music and Jazz, 1900-1950* (entry 490), rather than consulting the chronological section of volume 1 under the year indicated. Or one may try Shapiro's *Popular Music*, which lists thousands of songs by year of introduction or revival. Each volume covers a decade or a five-year period, but volumes are not in chronological order: vol. 1, 1950-1959; vol. 2, 1940-1949; vol. 3, 1960-1964; vol. 4, 1930-1939; vol. 5, 1920-1929; vol. 6, 1965-1969; vol. 7, 1970-1974; vol. 8, 1975-1979. Songs are listed under year of original copyright, but cross-reference is given from another year in which the song first became popular or had a revival. For each song, the composer, lyricist, and person or occasion responsible for its popularity (vocalist, musical comedy, award, etc.) are given. Many foreign songs that were translated into English and became popular in the United States are included. Each volume has an index of song titles, but there is not yet a master index covering all volumes. *Variety Music Cavalcade, 1620-1961*, covers a much longer period and has a single title index but, except for pre-1920 songs, is less likely to produce the needed information than Shapiro's work.

505.   Havlice, Patricia. **Popular Song Index.** Metuchen, N.J.: Scarecrow, 1975. 933p. Supplement 1, 1978. Supplement 2, 1984.

506.   DeCharms, Desiree, and P. F. Breed. **Songs in Collections.** Detroit: Information Service, 1966. 588p.

507.   Brunnings, Florence E. **Folk Song Index: A Comprehensive Guide to the Florence E. Brunnings Collection.** New York: Garland, 1981. 357p. (Garland Reference Library of the Humanities, no. 252).

Another type of frequent reference request is to find the words and music of a popular song of the past. These works will be of help with such questions. *Popular Song Index* lists the songs contained in 301 song books published 1940-1972; the first supplement indexes another 72 books published up to 1975. Scores and lyrics of individual songs can be found in these books. Various types of songs are included here: folk songs, popular tunes, spirituals and hymns, children's songs, sea chanties, and blues. Songs are listed in a single alphabet by title, first line, and first line of chorus. The song books indexed are all in English, but a number of songs originally written in other languages are included. Cross-references from alternate song titles are numerous. The book is useful, as are the others listed above, for identifying a song, even if the words and music are not needed. A composer/lyricist index is given in the back of the book. *Songs in Collections* is similar, indexing more than four hundred collections, some in languages other than English, so that this, too, is useful for identifying a foreign song. *Folk Song Index* does the same thing for some 50,000 traditional ballads, cowboy songs, work songs, sea chanties, love songs, nursery rhymes, and others in the folk song tradition, some in foreign languages. It indexes more than 1,000 books and 695 recordings. An older work of this type, which is in nearly all libraries and is still consulted, is *Song Index*, by Minnie Sears, assisted by Phyllis Crawford (New York: Wilson, 1926. Supplement, 1934. Reprint. Hamden, Conn.: Shoe String, 1966).

508.   **Folio-Dex: (V)oice, (P)iano, (O)rgan, (G)uitar.** Loomis, Calif.: Folio-Dex, 1970- . Looseleaf. Irregular.

This looseleaf index has proved to be very useful in identifying a source of words and score for songs and individual compositions of various types: classical, popular, sacred, folk, and other. It indexes thousands of music folios and published collections, and its regular updating by looseleaf sheets makes it useful for presently popular songs as well as for old classics. In addition to identifying the singer or artist and the folio, it indicates by a symbol whether the music is written for voice, piano, organ, or guitar. If the library does not own one of the folios indexed, it can possibly be located through interlibrary loan. The subscription price (currently $140 per year) may be a factor against its acquisition in some libraries.

509.   British Broadcasting Corporation. Central Music Library. **Song Catalogue.** 4 vols. London: BBC, 1966.

For older songs, this catalog of some 60,000 songs by 8,500 composers is a very good identifying source. Volumes 1 and 2 list the songs by composer; volumes 3 and 4, by song title. The only information given besides the composer and title is the publisher and publisher's number, so that the catalog is useful primarily for identifying a song.

13

FINE AND APPLIED ARTS

In this chapter are covered the major reference works and their use in answering reference questions on the fine arts: drawing and painting, sculpture, and architecture. Decorative arts are also represented but not crafts or antiques, as the university library has less to do with these subjects than the public library. Finding reproductions of works of art is covered but locating illustrations of objects and scenes is not. As in other subjects, reference work in the fine arts in the university library is more likely to follow study and research within the formal discipline. Three major types of users, similar to the three user groups in music, have reference needs in fine arts: the student or researcher in the history and criticism of art; the student or faculty member who is principally interested, as an artist, in drawing, painting, sculpture, or other art form, or in architecture; and, finally, the person who is primarily neither an artist nor engaged in the study or teaching of art but who has a nonprofessional interest in art. Students and faculty members in the first two groups satisfy many of their own reference needs and frequently do their own searching because of their familiarity with the reference sources in their fields. The art historian will most often be looking for some fact or detail about an artist, work of art, art trend or movement that is not well known and may, therefore, require an extended search. The artist usually does not have as many reference needs as the other two groups. Reference needs of the architect are also minimal, but may include information about building materials, structural requirements, and other technical matters, and about specific buildings and floor plans. The nonprofessional group, whether in the university or not, has mostly ready reference questions about an artist or work of art, an art technique or term, a school of art or design, a detail of art history, an explanation about a movement or style, and similar questions that are readily answered. A need to see a reproduction of a painting or a photograph of a sculpture or a building is common. Sometimes the user wants to know where a particular painting or sculpture is presently located. Most questions of these types are easily answered in an art dictionary or encyclopedia or one of the reproduction indexes. But another type of question about a specific painting or drawing is not so easily answered: the request for an evaluation of an art work in the questioner's possession. Since the university is known to have knowledgeable people on its art faculty, members of the community sometimes expect to get a free appraisal of a work of art they own. Usually the person with such a question, whether it is about a work of art, an antique, or a book or manuscript, should be referred to a professional appraiser, whose name can be found in the yellow pages of the telephone directory. Appraisal questions are too difficult and risky to be attempted by the librarian; even questions on the value of a book or manuscript, although within the competence of the librarian, are best referred to an outside appraiser. Another type of question that comes up frequently is common to all three user groups: the directory question on the address of a person, a school, a dealer, an architectural or design firm, or an association.

As in the other subject areas, the number and kinds of reference questions in the fine arts in a particular university will depend not only on the size and strength of its fine arts department but also on individuals, interest groups, and other libraries in the community. A selection of the standard reference books that are most useful in answering the types of reference questions described above follows.

GUIDES, BIBLIOGRAPHIES, INDEXES

510.   Arntzen, Etta, and Robert Rainwater. **Guide to the Literature of Art History.** Chicago: American Library Association, 1981. 616p.

511.   Ehresmann, Donald L. **Fine Arts: A Bibliographic Guide to Basic Reference Works, Histories, and Handbooks.** 2d ed. Littleton, Colo.: Libraries Unlimited, 1979. 349p.

Both of these are superior guides to the literature of fine arts. The first was intended to revise and update Mary Chamberlin's *Guide to Art Reference Books* (1959) but has gone much beyond that. Its first section, "General Reference Sources," has over 530 items, arranged by type of reference tool; section 2, "General Primary and Secondary Sources," lists nearly 900 titles, and section 3, "The Particular Arts," has more than 2,700 books and serials. This third part includes photography and decorative arts as well as the traditional fine arts. Many exhibition catalogs are among the monographic works, but not books on individual artists. Most libraries retain Mary W. Chamberlin's *Guide to Art Reference Books* (Chicago: American Library Association, 1959) for information on reference tools that has not been included in this new work. Ehresmann's *Fine Arts* lists over five hundred bibliographies, library catalogs, indexes, directories, and other reference works and, in a separate section, some 1,100 histories and handbooks on fine arts. This section is arranged by period and country. Both guides describe many works in French, German, Italian, and other languages, which are important in reference work in fine arts.

512.   Lucas, Edna. **Art Books: A Basic Bibliography on the Fine Arts.** Greenwich, Conn.: New York Graphic Society, 1968. 245p.

A basic general bibliography on world art for all periods, *Art Books* has about 4,000 unannotated entries. Its special strength is its selected monographs on individual artists, a category omitted from the two guides listed in the previous paragraph. Most items are in English, making the book a good guide for undergraduate needs.

513.   **Arts in America: A Bibliography.** Edited by Bernard Karpel. 4 vols. Washington, D.C.: Smithsonian Institution, 1979.

A number of contributors have made this a monumental bibliography, intended to correct older notions that the significant achievements in Western art have been made in Europe. More than 20,000 monographs, exhibition and museum catalogs, reference sources, and serials on the arts in America are described. Arts include music and the performing arts as well as the fine arts. Volume 4 is an index of authors, artists, subjects, and selected titles.

514.   Bell, Doris L. **Contemporary Art Trends, 1960-1980: A Guide to Sources.** Metuchen, N.J.: Scarecrow, 1981. 171p.

Information on the many styles, theories, and movements in painting, sculpture, and the other fine arts during this period is not as easy to find as material on older styles. Bell discusses the books and exhibition catalogs that best define and explain these trends.

Monographs on individual artists are not included. (See entry 534, for a dictionary of these many trends and experiments.)

515.   Ehresmann, Donald L. **Architecture: A Bibliographic Guide to Basic Reference Works, Histories, and Handbooks.** Littleton, Colo.: Libraries Unlimited, 1984. 338p.

More than 1,300 books on the architecture of all time periods and countries are listed with excellent, informative annotations. The literature in French, German, and Italian, as well as that in English, is well covered. Future bibliographies by Ehresmann on sculpture, painting, and the graphic arts are awaited.

516.   Ehresmann, Donald L. **Applied and Decorative Arts: A Bibliographic Guide to Basic Reference Works, Histories, and Handbooks.** Littleton, Colo.: Libraries Unlimited, 1977. 232p.

A variety of so-called minor arts are included in this bibliography, e.g., arms and armor; ceramics; clocks, watches, and automata; costume; enamels; furniture. Thorough annotations are given for the 1,240 items.

517.   **ARTbibliographies Modern.** Oxford, England, and Santa Barbara, Calif.: Clio, 1969- . Semiannual.

Books, exhibition catalogs, dissertations, and periodical articles on the fine arts and design after 1800 are listed by subject, including names of artists, artists' groups, collectors, and critics. Some 300 periodicals in English and other languages are indexed. The author/editor/ interviewer index cumulates for the year in the second issue. There is also an index of museums and galleries. *ARTbibliographies Modern* can be machine searched back to 1974 through DIALOG.

518.   **Art Index.** New York: Wilson, 1929- . Quarterly with annual cumulation.

This index of some 250 periodicals in English and other Western languages is essential for any university library. All of the fine and applied arts are covered, plus archaeology, photography, film, landscape architecture, city planning, and other related fields. Indexing is by author and subject. Reproductions of paintings are indexed under the name of the artist, and book reviews, in a separate section at the end of the issue, are indexed under the author of the book reviewed. *Art Index* is machine-searchable through Wilsonline.

519.   Columbia University. Avery Architectural Library. **Catalog.** 2d ed., enl. 19 vols. Boston: G. K. Hall, 1968. Supplement 1, 4 vols. 1972. Supplement 2, 4 vols., 8 reels. 1976. Supplement 3, 3 vols., 6 reels. 1977. Supplement 4, 6 reels. 1980.

520.   Freer Gallery of Art, Washington, D.C. Library. **Dictionary Catalog of the Library of the Freer Gallery of Art, Smithsonian Institution, Washington, D.C.** 6 vols. Boston: G. K. Hall, 1967.

521.   Harvard University. Fine Arts Library. **Catalogue of the Harvard University Fine Arts Library, The Fogg Art Museum.** 15 vols. Boston: G. K. Hall, 1971. Supplement 1, 3 vols. 1976.

522.   New York. Metropolitan Museum of Art. Library. **Library Catalog of the Metropolitan Museum of Art.** 2d rev. ed., 48 vols. Boston: G. K. Hall, 1980. Supplement 1, 1981.

523.   New York. Museum of Modern Art. **Catalog of the Library of the Museum of Modern Art.** 14 vols., 28 reels. Boston: G. K. Hall, 1976.

524. New York Public Library. Research Libraries. **Dictionary Catalog of the Art and Architecture Division.** 30 vols. Boston: G. K. Hall, 1975. 1974 Supplement, 1976. **Bibliographic Guide to Art and Architecture,** 1975- . Annual.

525. Henry Francis du Pont Winterthur Museum. Libraries. **The Winterthur Museum Libraries Collection of Printed Books and Periodicals.** 9 vols. Wilmington, Del.: Scholarly Resources, 1974.

The importance of bibliographic identification in university library reference work is the justification for having these budget- and space-consuming sets. They are also useful for locating scarce items which may be requested on interlibrary loan. If the library cannot get all of these, the most important sets are the catalogs of the Metropolitan Museum, Harvard, New York Public, and Museum of Modern Art libraries. *Bibliographic Guide to Art and Architecture* serves as an annual supplement to the dictionary catalog of the Art and Architecture Division of the New York Public Library Research Libraries, reprinting the entries for books and other materials cataloged during the year by that library and the Library of Congress. The Freer Gallery is noted for its collections of the art of Asia and the Near East. The Winterthur Museum is strong in the decorative arts. The catalogs of the Freer Gallery and the New York Museum of Modern Art and the second, third, and fourth supplements to the catalog of the Avery Architectural Library are available on 35mm microfilm.

526. **RILA: International Repertory of the Literature of Art.** Williamstown, Mass.: RILA, 1975- . Semiannual.

527. **Répertoire d'art et d'archéologie.** Paris: Centre National de la Recherche Scientifique, Centre de Documentation Sciences Humaines, 1910- . Quarterly.

For any scholarly research, these are the essential bibliographies, covering recent books, exhibition catalogs, journal articles, and other literature. *RILA* is patterned after *RILM* (entry 445) in attempting to abstract the current literature of the field that is important for scholarly work. It covers the art of the Western world from the fourth century to the present, indexing about three hundred English and foreign-language journals. Each issue has an index of authors and an index of subjects. There is also a cumulative index for volumes 1-5, 1975-1980. *Répertoire d'art et d'archéologie* indexes more than one thousand journals and lists more than one hundred monographs per year. Exhibition catalogs, Festschriften, and other more or less elusive publications are included among the monographs.

528. Chicago Art Institute. Ryerson Library. **Index to Art Periodicals.** 11 vols., 22 reels. Boston: G. K. Hall, 1962. Supplement, 1 reel. 1975.

529. Columbia University. Avery Architectural Library. **Avery Index to Architectural Periodicals.** 2d ed., rev. & enl. 15 vols., 30 reels. Boston: G. K. Hall, 1973. Supplement 1, 1 vol., 2 reels. 1975. Supplement 2, 1 vol., 2 reels. 1977. Supplement 3, 1 vol., 2 reels. 1979.

When the older periodical literature is needed, these two sets are invaluable. *Index to Art Periodicals* is the book form of the card file of articles in art periodicals assembled in the Ryerson Library since 1907. After 1929, when *Art Index* was begun, cards were inserted in this file for articles in the museum bulletins and less well known foreign journals which were not indexed in *Art Index*. About 350 art periodicals in French, German, Italian, and English are indexed under subject. A similar card file of articles from architecture periodicals has been kept by the Avery Architectural Library of Columbia University since the 1930s. Some five hundred architectural journals in English and other languages are indexed by author and subject, going back in some files to the nineteenth century. Supplements are issued about every two years. The index is very good for identifying many architects on whom information may not be easily found, since a special effort was made at Avery to include a reference card under the name of any architect mentioned in an article. The Avery Library also published an index of obituaries of thousands of architects taken from journals and the *New York Times* (see entry 566). Both of the indexes listed above are available on 35mm microfilm.

530.   Archives of American Art. **The Card Catalog of the Manuscript Collection of the Archives of American Art.** 10 vols. Wilmington, Del.: Scholarly Resources, 1980.

In its use this catalog differs somewhat from the other catalogs of library collections listed above (entries 519-25) in that it is a file of manuscripts and manuscript collections. These are the letters, diaries, notes, and other papers of American artists. This catalog would not be used for bibliographic identification of a footnote or other reference, as the other catalogs of printed items often are. Rather, its principal value is in learning what manuscripts of a particular artist are held by the Archives before visiting it. The Archives is a part of the Smithsonian Institution in Washington, D.C., but it has several regional centers in different parts of the country which maintain microfilm copies of most of the manuscripts. These microfilms can be used in the regional center or borrowed by researchers on interlibrary loan.

DICTIONARIES, ENCYCLOPEDIAS

531.   **McGraw-Hill Dictionary of Art.** 5 vols. Edited by Bernard S. Myers. New York: McGraw-Hill, 1969.

As in the other humanities, a large number of reference questions can be answered easily with a good dictionary or encyclopedia. The *McGraw-Hill Dictionary of Art* serves in this way. It actually resembles an encyclopedia in its comprehensiveness, having some 15,000 articles with numerous black-and-white and color illustrations. Articles, some of which are lengthy, are on artists, famous paintings, sculptures, monuments, buildings, art terms, materials, techniques, schools, movements, associations, countries, etc.

532.   **Encyclopedia of World Art.** 15 vols. New York: McGraw-Hill, 1959-68. Vol. 16, supplement. **World Art in Our Time.** New York: McGraw-Hill; Palatine, Ill.: Publishers Guild, 1983.

Both this and the preceding work belong in every university library; neither work can replace the other. Where the dictionary has thousands of articles of varying length but mostly brief definitions, identifications, explanations of terms, topics, and names of artists and works of art, the *Encyclopedia of World Art* has no more than one thousand long, comprehensive articles on broad subjects, countries, schools of arts, and major artists: e.g., cinematography; classic art; Clodian; coins and medals; games and toys; Garnier, Charles; Gaudi y Cornet, Antonio; Gauguin, Paul; gems and glyptics. The index volume can be consulted for smaller terms, topics, and names not represented by an article in the encyclopedia. Many terms and proper names found in the *McGraw-Hill Dictionary of Art*, however, are not found in this work, which is better for a broad overview of a subject. Articles are full, scholarly, and have long bibliographies. Each volume is very well illustrated. The final volume is a supplement to the work, edited by Bernard S. Myers.

533.   **The Britannica Encyclopedia of American Art.** Chicago: Encyclopaedia Britannica Educational Corp., 1973. 669p.

The long artistic tradition of Europe with its many artists and achievements is apt to overshadow the shorter period of development of art in America in books like the *Encyclopedia of World Art* and the *McGraw-Hill Dictionary of Art*. The *Britannica Encyclopedia of American Art*, with its articles by specialist contributors on painting, sculpture, architecture, folk art, photography, ceramics, and other arts in America, helps to restore balance. This one-volume encyclopedia is well illustrated and, following the alphabetically arranged articles on the arts and artists, terms, materials, and movements, has a list of the articles classified by art form and a guide to museums and public collections.

534.   Walker, John A. **A Glossary of Art, Architecture, and Design since 1945.** 2d ed. London: Bingley; Hamden, Conn.: Linnet, 1977. 352p.

So many new styles, techniques, trends, and movements have been introduced in recent decades that this glossary is of considerable help in reference work. Some five hundred articles define these terms and styles, often quoting from art critics and writers. A sampling of the entries includes contextualism, cool art, co-realism, critical realism, cultural art, emballages, endless architecture, environmental art, eventstructure.

535.   Pevsner, Nikolaus, John Fleming, and Hugh Honour. **A Dictionary of Architecture.** Rev. & enl. ed. Woodstock, N.Y.: Overlook Press, 1976. 554p.

536.   Hunt, William D., Jr. **Encyclopedia of American Architecture.** New York: McGraw-Hill, 1980. 612p.

537.   **Encyclopedia of Modern Architecture.** Edited by W. Pehnt. New York: Abrams, 1964. 336p.

538.   Harris, Cyril M. **Dictionary of Architecture and Construction.** New York: McGraw-Hill, 1975. 553p.

The best general dictionary of architectural terms, styles, movements, associations, and names of famous architects is the first of these books, *A Dictionary of Architecture.* Earlier editions were issued as *The Penguin Dictionary of Architecture* by John Fleming and others. Since it is a British dictionary, although covering architecture worldwide, Hunt's dictionary, which emphasizes American architecture, is useful for balance. It is well illustrated and has articles on architects and other persons associated with architecture, types of buildings and sites (airport, dam, factory), parts of buildings (column, dome, door, fireplace), styles, topics related to architecture (building codes, energy, esthetics), and materials (aluminum, brick, concrete). *Encyclopedia of Modern Architecture* stresses movements and styles from the late nineteenth century, persons identified with modern architecture, and trends in different countries. (See entry 553 for a historical, rather than alphabetical, treatment of modern architecture.) *Dictionary of Architecture and Construction* has very brief definitions or identification of about 17,000 terms, with many line drawings. It is technical and intended for the architect and the builder.

539.   **Studio Dictionary of Design and Decoration.** New York: Viking, 1973. 538p.

The nature of this dictionary can be guessed from the following sample entries: Halfpenny, Willam; half-timbering; hall; hall chair; Hallett, William; hammer beam; hanging shelves. It defines hundreds of terms in architecture and the decorative arts and has brief biographical information on persons noted in their fields.

540.   Hall, James. **Dictionary of Subjects and Symbols in Art.** Rev. ed. New York: Harper & Row, 1979. 349p.

The purpose of this dictionary is to explain paintings and other art on Christian and mythological themes. Entries are of three types: persons, mythological or real, who were frequent subjects of paintings (Diana, Dido, Don Quixote); traditional titles or themes in art (descent of the Holy Ghost, dispute with the doctors); and symbols and objects identified with Christian saints, mythological beings, and others (dice, dog, dolphin). Entries of these three types are mingled in alphabetical order.

DIRECTORIES

541.   **American Art Directory.** Edited by Jaques Cattell Press. New York: Bowker, 1898- . Biennial.

542.   **Fine Arts Market Place.** Edited by Paul Cummings. New York: Bowker, 1973- . Biennial. Paper.

American Art Directory is the general directory of the field, useful for students, faculty, and general public. Among its lists are art schools, art departments of colleges and universities, societies and associations, art magazines, newspaper art critics, scholarships and fellowships in art, and art museums of the United States and Canada. Major museums of other countries are also included. The second directory is more for the artist and dealer. Its lists include dealers, services (photographers, packers and movers, advertising agencies, etc.), sources of art materials, organizations, and exhibitions.

543.   **The Official Museum Directory.** Washington, D.C.: The American Association of Museums; Wilmette, Ill.: National Register, 1961- . Annual.

544.   Hudson, Kenneth, and Ann Nichols. **The Directory of World Museums.** 2d ed. New York: Facts on File, 1981. 681p.

The Official Museum Directory gives facts on more than 6,000 museums, historical societies, court houses, and other repositories of museum collections in the United States. Data include the type of collection, activities, hours of opening, and personnel. Its appendix lists the directors and department heads of museums and lists institutions by category, e.g., art museums and galleries, children's and junior museums, college and university museums, general museums. *The Directory of World Museums* lists, under country and city, some 25,000 museums of all kinds, giving address, brief description of the type of collection, and hours. In the back is a classified index of museums by type of collection under 45 headings, e.g., fine art, coins, medical sciences, fishing/hunting, crime/police, music. *World of Learning* (entry 720) also lists major museums of all countries but gives only address, founding date, nature of collection and special strength, number of volumes in its library, and name of its director.

545.   **Money Business: Grants and Awards for Creative Artists.** Boston: The Artists Foundation, 1982. Paper.

A directory of approximately 400 grants and other opportunities from 279 organizations, foundations, and government agencies for "creative artists," i.e., poets, film makers, composers, choreographers, painters, photographers, and others. Opportunities include awards, grants, retreats, and state programs.

546.   **ProFile: The Official Directory of the American Institute of Architects.** Edited by Henry W. Schirmer. Topeka, Kans.: Archimedia, 1978- . Annual.

Architectural firms are listed under state and city, with the type of work they do, specialties, and size of staff. Some 14,000 firms are listed. Following this is an alphabetical list of more than 40,000 members and associate members of the AIA with their current address.

HANDBOOKS

547. **The Oxford Companion to Art.** Edited by Harold Osborne. New York: Oxford University Press, 1970. 1277p.

548. **The Oxford Companion to Twentieth Century Art.** Edited by Harold Osborne. New York: Oxford University Press, 1981. 656p.

These two companions by Harold Osborne have thousands of entries on artists, terms, styles, techniques and materials, artists' associations, movements or schools, and other topics related to art. The second work treats the subject worldwide since 1900, with information on artists and innovators, trends, and developments in different countries. These, because of their wealth of information in a compact form, will usually be the first source to try when a fact or identification is all that is needed. But they do not have the richness of illustration that *McGraw-Hill Dictionary of Art* has.

549. **The Oxford Companion to the Decorative Arts.** Edited by Harold Osborne. Oxford: Clarendon Press, 1975. 865p.

Supplementing the two companions described above, which take the fine arts as their field, this book has entries for terms, objects, craftsmen and artists in such areas as leather working, ceramics, textiles, costume, woodworking, metal working, glass making, etc. A few sample entries are: cutlery, damascening, diagrams, diamond, doves press, dragon.

REFERENCE HISTORIES

550. Gardner, Helen. **Art through the Ages.** 7th ed. Revised by Horst de la Croix and Richard G. Tansey. New York: Harcourt Brace Jovanovich, 1980. 922p.

551. Janson, H. W., and D. J. Janson. **History of Art: A Survey of the Major Visual Arts from the Dawn of History to the Present Day.** 2d ed. New York: Abrams, 1977. 767p.

For standard histories of art, comparable to those described in previous chapters for literature and music, these are probably the best known and most widely used in college courses. The graphic arts, sculpture, and architecture from earliest time to the present are very well developed in both books, but *Art through the Ages* has much about art on continents other than Europe, which is not in *History of Art* except for a brief postscript. Both histories are copiously illustrated.

552. Fletcher, Sir Banister Flight. **A History of Architecture.** 18th ed. Revised by J. C. Palmes. New York: Scribner's, 1975. 1390p.

553. Giedion, Siegfried. **Space, Time and Architecture: The Growth of a New Tradition.** 5th ed., rev. & enl. Cambridge, Mass.: Harvard University Press, 1967. 897p.

Architecture through the ages is included in both previously described histories, but is more developed and described with more detail and illustrations in these two works. Both are considered classics and have gone through a number of revisions since their first edition. Sir Banister Fletcher's work has always been a favorite in teaching the history of architecture, since it tries to compare each style and period to others, showing similarities, borrowings, and innovations, and placing each in the context of its time. It is especially valuable for its numerous photographs, drawings, and floor plans. *Space, Time and Architecture* has much on newer concepts in architecture introduced in the past hundred years: city planning, space-time in art and architecture, etc. It, too, is excellently illustrated.

BIOGRAPHY

554.   Thieme, Ulrich, and Felix Becker. **Allgemeines Lexikon der bildenden Künstler von der Antike bis zur Gegenwart.** 37 vols. Leipzig: Seeman, 1907-1950.

555.   Vollmer, Hans. **Allgemeines Lexikon der bildenden Künstler des XX. Jahrhunderts.** 6 vols. Leipzig: Seeman, 1953-1962.

556.   Benezit, Emmanuel. **Dictionnaire critique et documentaire des peintres, sculpteurs, dessinateurs, et graveurs de tous les temps et tous les pays.** New ed. 10 vols. Paris: Grund, 1976.

Thieme and Becker [*Universal Dictionary of the Formative (or Plastic) Artists from Antiquity to the Present*] is the most complete dictionary of artists of all periods and all countries in any language. It attempts to identify all known painters, sculptors, engravers, architects, and minor artists (such as miniaturists, wood engravers, painters of glass). *Bildenden* means *form* or *plastic* arts, as distinct from performing arts, but includes architects. Approximately 225,000 persons are identified in articles varying from a paragraph to several pages and including a bibliography and a list of major works; sometimes, present locations of paintings are indicated. The final volume, *Meister mit Notnamen und Monogrammisten*, identifies artists not known by name but known only by stylistic relationship to an extant work or by initials used in signing works, e.g., Master of the High Altar at Heilsbron; Master of the Visitation (Bamburg); the Cerberus painter (Athenian vase painter). These artists are listed alphabetically by the attribution, with an explanation of the attribution, dates, and other works they are believed to have painted. Artists identified only by a year during which they were especially productive are also listed in the final volume, e.g., Master of 1445; anything that is known about them and paintings attributed to them are included. Lastly in this volume are artists known only by the monogram with which they signed their work, listed alphabetically by the first letter of the monogram, e.g., Monogrammist AW. Vollmer [*Universal Dictionary of the Formative Artists of the Twentieth Century*] continues this work by the identification of another 50,000 artists. Benezit [*Critical and Documentary Dictionary of Painters, Sculptors, Draughtsmen, and Engravers*] is the second most complete dictionary of artists of all countries from the fifth century B.C. to the present, but does not include architects. More than 150,000 artists are identified, although for some only the country and dates are given. Representation of Oriental artists is especially good. Artists known only through the monogram with which they signed their work are listed at the close of each letter.

557.   **Larousse Dictionary of Painters.** New York: Larousse, 1981. 467p.

Probably all of the names found in this work will be found also in *McGraw-Hill Dictionary of Art*, but the articles in this dictionary give more detail on the person's artistic style and usually have a representative reproduction different from that shown in *McGraw-Hill*. About six hundred painters are included.

558.   Havlice, Patricia P. **Index to Artistic Biography.** 2 vols. Metuchen, N.J.: Scarecrow, 1973. Supplement, 1981.

Biographies are not included in this work, but 134 biographical collections on artists are indexed in the main set and the supplement. Since it is necessary to locate the book indexed either in the local library or another library before the needed information can be found, this set would be consulted only if sufficient biographical information could not be found directly in an encyclopedia or another work. Names can be found here, however, that are not included in the other works described above, despite their completeness. Havlice does not include architects, but does index names of many minor American artists not in Thieme/Becker, Vollmer, or Benezit.

559. Cummings, Paul. **A Dictionary of Contemporary American Artists.** 4th ed. New York: St. Martin's, 1982. 653p.

For information on an American artist who has been prominent during all or part of the past 25-30 years, this is the best source. It has brief biographical data on the training, experience, awards, and exhibitions of more than nine hundred artists and a selection of black-and-white reproductions of their work. Information about them in sources like the *Dictionary of Contemporary Artists* (entry 560) and *Who's Who in American Art* (entry 561) will be more brief and factual and without illustrations, while their listing in *Index to Artistic Biography* (entry 558) will only lead to other sources of biographical data.

560. **Dictionary of Contemporary Artists.** Edited by V. Babington Smith. Oxford, England, and Santa Barbara, Calif.: Clio, 1981. 451p.

Very brief sketches are given for about four thousand living artists of the United States and other countries who had an exhibition of their work during the year preceding publication. Architects are not included, but photographers and others in the graphic and applied arts are. A list of the artists included, classified by art field and country, is in the back of the dictionary. This was intended to become an annually revised publication, but thus far only the first volume has appeared.

561. **Who's Who in American Art.** Edited by Jaques Cattell Press. New York: Bowker, 1936- . Biennial.

562. **Who's Who in Art.** Havant, Hants, England: Art Trade Press, 1927- . Biennial.

More than 10,000 living persons in the United States, Canada, and Mexico associated in some way with the visual arts (artists, architects, educators, critics, dealers, administrators) are in the latest edition of *Who's Who in American Art.* In the back of the volume is a geographical index and a professional classifications index. The other who's who listed above has data mostly on British artists.

563. **Contemporary Artists.** 2d ed. Edited by Muriel Emanuel and others. New York: St. Martin's, 1983. 1041p.

Biographical data and lists of individual and group exhibitions and publications of approximately 1,000 living or recently deceased outstanding artists of the world are given in this work.

564. **American Architects Directory.** 3d ed. Edited by John F. Gane. Published under the sponsorship of American Institute of Architects. New York: Bowker, 1970. 1119p.

565. **Contemporary Architects.** Edited by Muriel Emanuel. New York: St. Martin's, 1980. 933p.

The first title has brief sketches of about 23,000 living American architects, many of whom are AIA members. Members and associate members of AIA are listed in *ProFile* (entry 546), but only a current address is given. *Contemporary Architects* is limited to about 575 outstanding architects living in the United States and other countries with full data on their achievements.

566. Columbia University. Avery Architectural Library. **Avery Obituary Index of Architects.** 2d ed. Boston: G. K. Hall, 1980. 530p.

Although biographical data are not included, this index is very important in leading to information on architects no longer alive in 1980, and for some of whom perhaps nothing else can be found. The index reproduces file cards from the Avery Library obituary file, giving reference to obituaries in architectural journals, the *New York Times*, and other sources. More than 17,000 architects, art historians, archaeologists, and city planners are included. The first edition (G. K. Hall, 1963) included artists as well, but file cards on artists have not been carried over to this second edition.

567. Colvin, Howard M. **A Biographical Dictionary of British Architects, 1600-1840.** Rev. & enl. ed. New York: Facts on File, 1980. 1080p.

One of the lesser-used reference books on architecture, this, nevertheless, will have a place in the collection. Biographies of these architects (more than 2,000) are carefully researched, many with a list of their buildings, parts of buildings, and restorations. Some of these architects will be in *The Dictionary of National Biography* (entry 147) but not with as much detail about their architectural achievement.

ART REPRODUCTIONS

568. New York Graphic Society. **Fine Art Reproductions of Old and Modern Masters.** Greenwich, Conn.: The Society, 1980. 576p.

One of the college students' most frequent reference needs in the fine arts is to find a reproduction of a painting or other work of art for study. Usually this need is for a class assignment or in preparation for an examination. But faculty members in fine arts and students, faculty, and public outside the department also have this type of need, whether in preparation for a lecture or class assignment or simply from general interest. Suitable reproductions can frequently be found in *McGraw-Hill Dictionary of Art, Encyclopedia of World Art*, or one of the other encyclopedias or handbooks described above. *Fine Art Reproductions of Old and Modern Masters* has good color illustrations of reproductions the Society offers for sale. An index in the front of the book lists some of these reproductions under subject, e.g., barns; birds; Black art and artists; bridges and rivers; bullfight and bulls. UNESCO also publishes two catalogs of art reproductions, mostly paintings, which can be purchased from museums: *Catalogue of Reproductions of Paintings Prior to 1860* (10th ed., Paris: UNESCO, 1978) and *Catalogue of Reproductions of Paintings, 1860-1979* (11th ed., Paris: UNESCO, 1981). These have small illustrations of the paintings, but they are seldom suitable for study. These catalogs must be useful, however, for persons who want to know where a reproduction may be purchased, its size, cost, etc.

The works described below do not themselves have illustrations but are indexes to books which do have art reproductions. We do not include here indexes to pictures of miscellaneous objects and scenes, such as windmills, thatch-roofed cottages, spinning wheels, sailboats, etc.

569. Havlice, Patricia P. **World Painting Index.** 2 vols. Metuchen, N.J.: Scarecrow, 1977. Supplement 1, 1973-1980. 2 vols. 1982.

570. Korwin, Yale H. **Index to Two-dimensional Art Works.** 2 vols. Metuchen, N.J.: Scarecrow, 1981.

Nearly 1,800 books published since 1940 which contain reproductions of paintings are indexed by Havlice. In one section, paintings by unknown artists are listed by title. Another section lists paintings under the name of the artist, followed by a title index. Korwin indexes books published 1960-1977, listing reproductions under the name of the artist. A title-subject index follows. Overlap in the books indexed in these two competitive works is about 20-25 percent.

571. Smith, Lyn W., and Nancy D. W. Moure. **Index to Reproductions of American Paintings Appearing in More Than 400 Books, Mostly Published since 1960.** Metuchen, N.J.: Scarecrow, 1977. 931p.

The title explains the scope of this index, most of which is arranged by artist or by title for paintings by unknown artists. The final one-third of the book is a list by type of subject, e.g., allegorical; animals; architectural subjects; illustrations from literature; Indians of North America.

572. Monro, Isabel S., and Kate M. Monro. **Index to Reproductions of American Paintings.** New York: Wilson, 1948. 731p. Supplement, 1964. 480p.

573. Monro, Isabel S., and Kate M. Monro. **Index to Reproductions of European Paintings.** New York: Wilson, 1956. 668p.

Two older indexes to reproductions which are occasionally used. Havlice and Smith do not index books included in these older works. Both of these list reproductions under subject (e.g., fairs and festivals; fishermen and fishing; foxes; games and sports), painters, and titles of paintings in a single index.

574. Parry, Pamela J., comp. **Contemporary Art and Artists: An Index to Reproductions.** Westport, Conn.: Greenwood, 1978. 327p.

More than 60 books and exhibition catalogs are indexed for reproductions of paintings, sculptures, drawings, happenings, and other art forms (but not architecture, craft objects, and decorative art) since 1940. Reproductions are listed under artist and, selectively, under title, but there is an extensive subject and title index.

575. Clapp, Jane. **Sculpture Index.** 2 vols. in 3. Metuchen, N.J.: Scarecrow, 1970.

This work indexes reproductions of sculptures from 950 books, museum catalogs, and exhibition catalogs, most in English. Sculpture is widely defined to include decorative objects (weathervanes), architectural features (arches), medals, cameos, and church accessories (altars). The sculptures indexed were made in various countries in various centuries, although most emphasis is on post-1900 Europe. There are three types of entries: sculptor; distinctive title of a sculpture (Le Baiser), and subject (dancers, jugs, shepherds). Information provided for each listing also includes present location, material, and dimension, as well as the work or catalog containing a reproduction.

14

PERFORMING ARTS

In this chapter we discuss reference questions and sources of information on film, theater, radio, and television, and, to a much lesser extent, on circus, magic shows, street performances, and other performances. As in other chapters, the basic arrangement is by type of reference book, followed by certain areas of reference needs that frequently arise in dealing with the performing arts. Of the four major performing arts, questions about film clearly predominate in the university library. This emphasis follows from the emergence in the past 20 or 30 years of curricular interest in the film as an art form. Not only do a number of students enroll in courses on the film, but they are much more critical and informed an audience, have questions about particular films and film personnel, both domestic and foreign, and choose topics about film for freshmen rhetoric term papers. The second most popular performance medium among undergraduates is television, generating many reference questions, whether for term papers or from general interest. Radio is not as important to students since they did not know it as a principal entertainment medium. Questions on theater and plays, as distinguished from drama as literature, are relatively infrequent, coming either from students in theater or from students, faculty, and the public interested in a play appearing locally.

Questions on film or television for term papers are mostly of four kinds: on types of films or television programs (spy, western, sitcom, crime); history of the film or television industry; the films of a particular director, screen writer, performer, or other person; or topics (the impact of television on reading or violence, comparison of the Japanese and American film industry, the economics of the movie or television industry). Term paper topics will often cluster around a particular director or type of film that is currently popular or enjoying a renaissance.

But film questions from students and others arising from a general interest, an argument or discussion, or from seeing or remembering a film are more likely to be of the ready reference type: about a specific film, director, actor, award, or other specific detail. Questions on television not related to a term paper are also typically about a certain program, its cast, date, or other specific fact. Another frequent need is for a review of a film or play. Fortunately, reviews of television programs, which are harder to find, are not requested as often, but, unfortunately, it is most often a new film or play for which a review is wanted. Local showing of a film or play will generate requests from various library user groups for reviews. These are sought so often that we have devoted a section in this chapter to finding them. Scripts of plays are often wanted and, less often, scripts of television programs.

Questions from faculty or graduate students in connection with a research project, far fewer than term paper and other questions from students and the general public cited above, are typically for statistics, costs, technical matters, government regulations, and such background about the movie, radio, or television industry. Depending on the strength and reputation of the university library and its collection, some questions may come from the business community relating to the radio or television industry. These will be technical questions about costs and finances, the local market for radio/television programs of a certain kind, and similar needs related to a business interest.

A few sample requests, typical of those received in a large university library, follow; they are without designation of the user group or need from which they originate:

Statistics on minority ownership of the media.

Statistics on advertising expenditures and costs in the different media.

A list of radio programs for women.

A list of Oscar (or Emmy) winners.

The address of the CBS station in New Orleans.

The name of the actor playing Rhoda's father.

The name of James Caan's agent.

The name of the distributor for *National Velvet.*

How can I get a radio broadcast license?

How is a TV script written?

How can I legally videotape a PBS series?

Biographical information on Dan Rather (or on Dianne Keaton, or on Federico Fellini).

What films has the cameraman, Bill Butler, made?

What other films did the screenwriter of *Chinatown* write?

Find reviews of *Superman III.*

Find reviews of the book on which *Red* was based.[1]

---

[1]Nancy H. Allen, "Mass Media Sources," *Collection Building: Studies in the Development and Effective Use of Library Resources* 4, no. 3: 48-49. 1982.

Our arrangement of reference sources continues to be, as in other chapters, from the most used and first consulted in reference work to the less used. Normally, this is from the most general sources and those of widest scope to those of more specific scope. In this chapter, however, which treats four major performance media, books only about film are arbitrarily described first, followed by those about theater, and radio and television. Rather than trying to give equal space and attention to each medium, we have also given the most consideration to film since that is where most study and reference work usually is.

GUIDES, BIBLIOGRAPHIES, INDEXES

576.   Whalon, Marion K. **Performing Arts Research: A Guide to Information Sources.** Detroit: Gale, 1976. 280p. (Performing Arts Information Guide Series, vol. 1).

Film, theater, and dance are covered by this guide, with some references to radio, television, music, fine art, costume, and other subjects related to the theater. Reference sources with short annotations are grouped by type, such as guides, dictionaries, encyclopedias, directories, and indexes. Patterson's *Literary Research Guide* (entry 326) also has short sections on film (W1229-1268) and performing arts (W1468-1472). Although these sections include only a small number of reference sources, the annotations are so informative that they should be checked.

577.   **Performing Arts Books, 1876-1981.** New York: Bowker, 1981. 1656p.

Approximately 50,000 books on all aspects of the performing arts which were published or distributed in the United States since 1876 are listed by subject. Full bibliographic description is given but not annotations. Separate indexes by author and title are provided. There is also a subject list, giving full bibliographic description, of some 3,000 performing arts periodicals from various countries. This list also has its title index.

578.   **Performing Arts Information Guide Series.** Detroit: Gale.

A series of bibliographies on the performing arts being published by Gale. Sample titles that have been published or are anticipated indicate the scope of the series: *American Actors and Acting* (Stephen M. Archer, ed., 1983); *The American Stage from World War I to the 1970's* (Don B. Wilmeth, ed., 1978); *Business of the Theatre, Films, and Broadcasting* (J. Kline Hobbs, ed., not yet published); *Guide to Dance in Film* (Esther Siegel and David Parker, eds., 1978); *American and English Popular Entertainment* (Don B. Wilmeth, ed., 1980); *Law of the Theatre, Film, and Broadcasting* (Daniel J. Strehl, ed., not yet published); *Stage Scenery, Machinery, and Lighting* (Richard Stoddard, ed., 1977); *Theatre and Cinema Architecture* (Richard Stoddard, ed., 1978); *Theatrical Costume* (Jackson Kesler, ed., 1979). *Performing Arts Research* (cited above, entry 576) is volume one in this series.

579.   Armour, Robert A. **Film: A Reference Guide.** Westport, Conn.: Greenwood, 1980. 251p.

580.   Sheahan, Eileen. **Moving Pictures: An Annotated Guide to Selected Film Literature with Suggestions for the Study of Film.** South Brunswick, N.J.: Barnes, 1979. 146p.

The student preparing a term paper or other person beginning study and research on the film is the focus of both of these guides. The first has essays discussing the best sources on the history of film, film production, film criticism, film and society, major actors and directors, major films, and other aspects of the subject on which a student may be writing a term paper. Each chapter ends with a bibliography of the books discussed. The subject index lists topics, film titles, and persons working in films. The book also has an index of authors, editors, and interviewees. *Moving Pictures* annotates about four hundred selected books, excluding screenplays, monographs on individual films or persons, and books of collected criticism. Items are arranged by type, as guides and handbooks, dictionaries and encyclopedias, bibliographies and catalogs, film lists and sources, film histories, or biography.

581.   Rehrauer, George. **The Macmillan Film Bibliography.** 2 vols. New York: Macmillan, 1982.

582.   Ellis, Jack C., Charles Derry, and Sharon Kern. **The Film Book Bibliography, 1940-1975.** Metuchen, N.J.: Scarecrow, 1979. 764p.

The *Macmillan Film Bibliography* is the most recent and, although selective, most comprehensive of the bibliographies on all aspects of the film: technical books about film making, books on the industry, critical works, biographies, film scripts, and many others. Novelizations of films are not included. Some seven thousand books are listed by title with annotations both descriptive and critical. Volume 2 of the work has indexes by subject, author, and script title. The *Film Book Bibliography* lists more than five thousand books organized in chapters by broad subject, e.g., reference; film technique and technology; film industry; film history (in different countries); documentaries and genres (comedy, westerns, thrillers, etc.); biography; and film history and criticism. It does not have annotations but often has a brief contents note. Items within subject sections are listed chronologically by date of publication to help the student find the more recent information. The book has a title index of books and films and a name index. This book is better for the student or researcher collecting material for a paper since books on the same subject have been brought together. The subject index of the *Macmillan Film Bibliography*, however, offers subject access.

583.   **Film Literature Index.** Albany, N.Y.: Film and Television Documentation Center, 1973- . Quarterly with annual bound cumulation.

584.   **International Index to Film Periodicals.** Edited by Michael Moulds. London: International Federation of Film Archives (FIAF), 1972- . Annual.

Current periodical articles about films and the movie industry are found through these two indexes. But also see indexes described (entries 685-89) under "Reviews." *Film Literature Index* covers about 235 periodicals in English and other Western languages. Arrangement is by author and subject in a single alphabet. *International Index to Film Periodicals* also covers nearly 100 film periodicals in English and other languages. Most of these are also indexed by *Film Literature Index*, but *International Index to Film Periodicals* may be easier to use for some projects since it is organized by classification. Typical of these classes are: institutions, festivals, conferences; film industry; distribution, exhibition; and society and cinema. Each volume has separate indexes by director, author, and subject.

585.   Batty, Linda, ed. **Retrospective Index to Film Periodicals, 1930-1971.** New York: Bowker, 1975. 425p.

586.   Gerlach, John, and Lana Gerlach. **The Critical Index: A Bibliography of Articles on Film in English, 1946-1973, Arranged by Names and Topics.** New York: Teacher's College Press, 1974. 726p.

587.   MacCann, Richard D., and Edward S. Perry, eds. **New Film Index: A Bibliography of Magazine Articles in English, 1930-1970.** New York: E. P. Dutton, 1975. 522p.

For periodical articles of earlier years, these three can be checked. *Retrospective Index to Film Periodicals, 1930-1971* indexes 14 film periodicals, which are among the 92 indexed by *International Index to Film Periodicals* and, therefore, complements that index. Only two of these periodicals, however, go back before 1950. A list of reviews to individual films by film title comprises the first section of this index. The rest is an alphabetical arrangement of small subjects; personal names of actors, actresses, directors, and others are included in the subject section. The *Critical Index* covers 22 British, American, and Canadian film periodicals (12 of which are also indexed in *New Film Index*) and more than 60 general periodicals. Part 1 is an alphabetical list of names of actors, actresses, directors, cinematographers, and others, with articles about them. Part 2 indexes articles under about 140 small topics, arranged under several broad headings, such as economics, film history, theory, film and society, technique, and education and scholarship. It has an index of authors and one of film titles. The latter gives neither a page nor item number but the name of the film's director, under which an article about the film can be found. *New Film Index* is organized by broad subjects, e.g., motion picture arts and crafts; film theory and criticism; biography; motion picture industry. It indexes 35 film periodicals, 21 of which are indexed by the Gerlachs, plus hundreds of other general and specialized periodicals, selectively indexed. Although a large amount of duplication will result from checking a given topic or name through all three of these retrospective indexes, a full and careful study will warrant it.

588.   Baker, Blanch M. **Theatre and Allied Arts: A Guide to Books Dealing with the History, Criticism, and Technic of the Drama and Theatre and Related Arts and Crafts.** New York: Wilson, 1952. Reprint. New York: Blom, 1967. 536p.

589.   **Chicorel Theater Index to Drama Literature.** Edited by Marietta Chicorel. New York: Chicorel, 1975. 474p. (Chicorel Index Series, vol. 21).

Theatre and Allied Arts is still considered a standard work on theater, even though it is now a quarter of a century old. Books and parts of books on theater, dance, music, and costume are listed with annotations. Only English language books are included. *Chicorel Theater Index to Drama Literature* lists periodical articles and books on theater, vaudeville, burlesque, minstrels, magic shows, circus, and other theatrical shows. The approximately 7,500 entries, which are representative of different countries and eras, are arranged under small subjects, but there is no index.

590.   **Cumulated Dramatic Index, 1909-1949.** 2 vols. Boston: G. K. Hall, 1965.

Some 150 periodicals on theater and related subjects are indexed in this cumulated set, covering 40 years of the annual *Dramatic Index*. Dictionary arrangement of authors, titles, and subjects is used. Synopses of individual plays are found under title in the main alphabet. An appendix lists texts of plays in books and periodicals.

591.   Stratman, Carl J. **Bibliography of the American Theatre, Excluding New York City.** Chicago: Loyola University Press, 1965. 397p.

This specialized bibliography lists almost four thousand references to books, articles, and dissertations on the theater of the United States outside of New York City. Arrangement is by state. There are some very brief, explanatory notes and a name and subject index.

592.   Young, William C. **American Theatrical Arts: A Guide to Manuscripts and Special Collections in the United States and Canada.** Chicago: American Library Association, 1971. 166p.

Manuscript materials and special collections in North American libraries and repositories about people associated with the theater in the United States and Canada are located under state and province. The index includes entries for professional roles (e.g., actors and actresses, authors, choreographers, columnists, comedians) under which are listed the names of those persons whose manuscripts and special collections are located in the guide.

593.   McCavitt, William E., comp. **Radio and Television: A Selected Annotated Bibliography.**
       Metuchen, N.J.: Scarecrow, 1978. 229p. Supplement 1, 1977-1981. 1982.

Books and periodicals, but not periodical articles, on all aspects of broadcasting and the
radio and television industries are listed under broad fields, such as surveys, history,
regulation, organization, programming, society, cable television. The 1,100 items are briefly
annotated.

594.   Poteet, G. Howard. **Published Radio, Television, and Film Scripts: A Bibliography.**
       Troy, N.Y.: Whitston, 1975. 245p.

Students and others frequently want to read the script of a film or a radio or television
program. More than 2,300 published scripts are listed here in separate sections for radio,
television, and film. Both separate shows and episodes of series are among the radio and
television scripts.

DICTIONARIES, ENCYCLOPEDIAS

595.   **Enciclopedia dello Spettacolo.** 9 vols. Rome: Maschere, 1954-1962. Supplement
       (Aggiornamento), 1955-1965. 1966. Index. Rome: Unione Editoriale, 1968.

Sorry that this superb encyclopedia is in Italian, but reread pages 7-8 and take heart.
There is no English-language encyclopedia of the subject to approach this in
comprehensiveness and thoroughness of treatment. All aspects of theatrical entertainment
from the circus to the opera of all countries and eras are treated in full articles with long
bibliographies and many illustrations, most of which are black-and-white. An index of some
145,000 titles of plays, operas, and other dramatic forms covers those mentioned in the main
set and the supplement.

596.   Wilmeth, Don B. **The Language of American Popular Entertainment: A Glossary of
       Argot, Slang, and Terminology.** Westport, Conn.: Greenwood, 1981. 305p.

Popular entertainment is defined here to include circus, carnivals, fairs, vaudeville,
burlesque, and minstrels. Some 3,200 terms and phrases used by the entertainers in these
shows are defined. Most of these words and phrases are not found in other slang
dictionaries.

597.   Katz, Ephraim. **The Film Encyclopedia.** New York: Crowell, 1979. 1266p.

598.   **The International Encyclopedia of Film.** New York: Crown, 1972. 574p.

These two books have brief information about directors, actors and actresses, and others in
films in this country and abroad, plus definitions of film terms and techniques, associations,
the film industry in different countries, and other film-related topics. *The Film Encyclopedia*
has about seven thousand entries, including cross-references, and identifies many persons
whose film connection may have been minimal, while *The International Encyclopedia of Film*
has only about one thousand articles. Neither encyclopedia has entries for individual films,
for which Halliwell's *Filmgoer's Companion* (entry 613) or *The Oxford Companion to Film*
(entry 612) may be used. These latter and other books described below under "Handbooks"
are useful for ready reference on the film.

599.   Green, Stanley. **Encyclopedia of the Musical Film.** New York: Oxford University Press,
       1981. 344p.

Films in which a number of songs are sung by leading cast members or in which musical
background is a prominent part of the production are the subject of this encyclopedia. Its
approximately two thousand entries are for titles of such films and for actors, actresses,

directors, dancers, choreographers, designers, and others prominent in one or more musical films. Articles on these people list the films in which they played or on which they worked. Articles on the individual films list the cast, director, producer, and others involved, and principal songs.

600.   **The Encyclopedia of World Theater.** Edited by Martin Esslin. New York: Scribner's, 1977. 320p.

Based on *Friedrichs Theaterlexikon*, by Karl Gröning and Werner Kliess and edited by Henning Rischbieter, this work has short articles on actors and actresses, directors, playwrights, set designers, and others in the theater, and on terms, plays, theaters, associations, movements, and other matters connected with the theater. It covers theater from Aeschylus to Broadway and has many illustrations. See Phyllis Hartnoll's *The Oxford Companion to the Theatre* (entry 619) for similar information.

601.   **McGraw-Hill Encyclopedia of World Drama.** 2d ed. Edited by Stanley Hochman. 5 vols. New York: McGraw-Hill, 1983.

Biographies of dramatists comprise most of this encyclopedia, but it also has articles on movements and styles in playwriting, dramatic terms, and the drama in different countries. It does not have articles on individual plays (see entries 600, 619-21 for this), but does have an index of play titles, referring to the author under whose article the play is listed. In this index, foreign titles beginning with an article (Der, La, Une) are alphabetized under that article.

602.   Koegler, Horst. **The Concise Oxford Dictionary of Ballet.** 2d ed. New York: Oxford University Press, 1982. 459p. Paper.

603.   Chujoy, Anatole, and P. W. Manchester. **The Dance Encyclopedia.** Rev. and enl. ed. New York: Simon & Schuster, 1967. 992p.

604.   **The Encyclopedia of Dance and Ballet.** Edited by Mary Clarke and David Vaughan. New York: Putnam, 1977. 376p.

Questions about dance and ballet are relatively infrequent, compared with questions on the other major performing arts. *The Concise Oxford Dictionary of Ballet* has several thousand entries including personal names, individual ballets, terms, and ballet companies, schools, and theaters, but articles are very brief, and the book has few illustrations. The two encyclopedias cover folk and popular dance to a degree, but ballet is their main content. Articles cover famous dancers, choreographers, and set designers, terms, well-known individual ballets, types of dance (sarabande, saltaretto, minuet), dance trends, and dance in different countries. Both works are richly illustrated.

605.   Green, Stanley. **Encyclopedia of the Musical Theatre.** New York: Dodd, Mead, 1976. 488p.

The musical has become recognized, in the United States, at least, as a separate performing art. This basic book on the musical in New York and London has some two thousand entries connected with the musical theater: composers, lyricists, librettists, actors and actresses, choreographers, directors, producers, individual musical plays, and songs. Articles on persons give a list of the productions with which they are associated. Appendixes list winners of awards and prizes (e.g., Pulitzer Prize for Drama; Tony; New York Drama Critics Circle Award for a Musical) to 1975, long runs on- and off-Broadway and in London, a bibliography, and a discography.

606.   Brown, Les. **Les Brown's Encyclopedia of Television.** New York: New York Zoetrope, 1982. 496p.

A variety of terms, committees and commissions, government agencies and regulations, television programs and series, actors, actresses, producers, newscasters, and others in television make up the content of the 3,000 brief articles in this encyclopedia, whose first edition (1977) was called *The New York Times Encyclopedia of Television.*

DIRECTORIES

607.   **The National Directory for the Performing Arts and Civic Centers.** 3d ed. Edited by Beatrice Handel. New York: Wiley, 1978. 1049p.

608.   **The National Directory for the Performing Arts/Educational.** 3d ed. Edited by Beatrice Handel. New York: Wiley, 1978. 669p.

The first of these companion directories lists, by state and city, auditoriums and civic centers which can be rented for a touring group or show. Listings of these give the type of facility, date built, manager, architect, acoustical consultant, seating capacity, stage dimensions, type of stage, and whom to contact for rental. The directory also lists performing groups (theater, instrumental music, dance, etc.) resident in the city, giving address, management and officers, purpose, budget, season, and where they perform. A categorical index lists facilities and performing groups under type (auditoriums, civic centers, ethnic/folk dance groups, chamber music groups). There is also an alphabetical index. The second directory lists major schools and institutions by state and city that offer training in the performing arts, giving address, head, number of faculty and students, degrees offered, financial assistance available for students, and similar data. This directory also has a categorical index and an alphabetical index.

609.   Merin, Jennifer, and Elizabeth B. Burdick. **International Directory of Theatre, Dance, and Folklore Festivals.** Westport, Conn.: Greenwood, 1979. 480p.

Under country, then city, various types of regularly held festivals are listed and briefly described. The estimated 1,300 festivals (excluding the United States, for which other sources are available[1]) include various types — national and international, local, regional, amateur and professional.

HANDBOOKS

610.   **Variety: International Showbusiness Reference.** New York: Garland, 1981. 1135p.

Data on show biz from the files of *Variety* are assembled under several categories. With nearly 6,000 short biographies of living entertainers, choreographers, cinematographers, composers, dancers, set designers, and others, it is claimed to be the largest single such compilation. The biographies give birth date and place, brief summary of experience, and principally, films, plays, and programs in which the person worked. The handbook also gives the credits for films, television programs, and plays, domestic and foreign, produced from 1976 to 1980; Oscar, Emmy, Tony, and Grammy awards; the top 50 Nielsen-rated television shows; Pulitzer Prize plays; long-running Broadway plays; Platinum records; and other entertainment world achievements and data.

---

[1]*Chase's Calendar of Annual Events, Special Days, Weeks and Months in the Year.* Flint, Mich.: Apple Tree Press, 1958- . Annual. (Title varies).

611.	Sharp, Harold S., and Marjorie Z. Sharp, comps. **Index to Characters in the Performing Arts.** 4 vols. in 6. Metuchen, N.J.: Scarecrow, 1966-73. Vol. 1 (2 parts): **Characters in Non-Musical Plays.** 1966. Vol. 2 (2 parts): **Operas and Musical Productions.** 1969. Vol. 3: **Ballets.** 1972. Vol. 4: **Radio, Television.** 1973.

Among the handbooks must be included *Index to Characters in the Performing Arts.* Volume 1 lists about 30,000 characters from some 3,600 plays written in English or translated into English, giving a brief identification of the character, the name, author, and date of the play. The other volumes briefly identify the character and refer to the full citation of the production, ballet, or program at the end of the volume through a five-letter code. Volume 2 lists about 20,000 characters from 2,542 operas and musicals; volume 3, 3,000 characters from 818 ballets; and volume 4, some 20,000 characters from about 2,500 programs (radio programs to 1955; TV programs to 1972).

612.	**The Oxford Companion to Film.** Edited by Liz-Anne Bawden. New York: Oxford University Press, 1976. 700p.

The content of this useful companion includes articles on various people (actors, actresses, directors, producers, and others) associated with the film in the United States, England, and on the Continent, schools, terminology, filmmaking in different countries, etc. There are also articles on well-known films of past years, giving date, credits, length, brief description, and critical comment.

613.	Halliwell, Leslie. **The Filmgoer's Companion.** 7th ed. New York: Scribner's, 1980. 745p.

Generally acknowledged (except by competitors) to be the most useful ready-reference book on the film, this guide has about 9,000 to 10,000 brief entries on film personalities, major films, filmmaking terms, and topics (e.g., dance bands, deaf mutes, death, desert islands, devil), telling the treatment in films of the topic. Biographical articles give filmographies, some complete, as of 1978. Especially useful is its examples of films with a certain setting (desert, hospital) or theme (deaf mute, homosexuality). In the back is an index of the films mentioned in the text. Not illustrated, this book chooses to give information rather than pictures.

614.	Michael, Paul. **The American Movies Reference Book: The Sound Era.** Englewood Cliffs, N.J.: Prentice-Hall, 1969. 629p.

The variety of data here is similar to that of the preceding guide, but this book is much more selective, very fully illustrated, and arranged by chapters: history, players, films, directors, producers, awards. Data for actors and actresses, directors and producers include a list of their films; data on films include the cast, credits, date, studio, and other vital facts, but no summary. Black-and-white pictures accompany almost every article on a film or a person.

615.	**The New York Times Directory of the Film.** New York: Arno/Random, 1971. 1243p.

Although the major part of this book is a reprint of *New York Times* reviews of award-winning films, other features of the directory cause us to include it with the handbooks. A list of films selected for the "*New York Times* 'Ten Best' " from 1924 to 1970, the New York Film Critics Circle Awards from 1935 to 1970, and Academy Awards from 1927 to 1970, is followed by reviews of these films, arranged by year, from the *New York Times.* In the back, a "Portrait Gallery" includes portraits of some 2,000 actors and actresses. A "Personal Name Index," listing all persons in the production or cast of films reviewed in the *New York Times* from 1913 to 1968, not only those award-winning films listed in the front of the volume, and a "Corporation Index" of the film companies involved in the production and distribution of these films conclude the directory.

616.   **International Motion Picture Almanac.** New York: Quigley, 1929- . Annual.

Like other almanacs, this has a great variety of facts, data, and information about the film industry. Early sections of the almanac have statistics, "The Great Hundred" (best films of all times), awards and polls, and a directory of international film festivals. A large section of the almanac is a who's who of film personalities living in the United States or abroad. Another large section lists the credits for feature films of the previous year. A directory (studio, date, leads, and length) of features from 1955 to the present follows. Other information about the film industry, mostly in the United States, but some information about the industry of other countries, is also given.

617.   **Screen World.** New York: Crown, 1950- . Annual.

This, and its two companion annuals, *Theatre World* (entry 623), and *Dance World* (entry 624) are summaries of the previous year's activities in their respective arts. Domestic and foreign films released in the United States during the year are listed with credits, cast, and black-and-white stills, but neither plot summaries nor critical comment. Other sections include portraits of promising new actors and actresses, Academy Awards of past years, brief data (birth date and place and real name) of hundreds of living actors and actresses, and obituaries of screen personalities who died during the year.

618.   Steinberg, Cobbett S. **Film Facts.** New York: Facts on File, 1980. 476p.

Many miscellaneous data, often good for ready reference, are assembled in chapters. In "The Marketplace," for example, are the top two hundred money-making films and the average price of a movie ticket in previous years; "The Stars" gives salaries of some leading stars; "The Studios" has annual profits of major studios; "The 'Ten Best' List" offers such lists as the best films about women, best of the Sixties, and ten best directorial achievements. Other chapters are "The Festivals," "The Awards," and "The Codes and Regulations." The index has personal names and film titles. But, as in the *McGraw-Hill Encyclopedia of World Drama*, foreign film titles beginning with an article (Der, La, or Une) are alphabetized under the article.

619.   **The Oxford Companion to the Theatre.** 4th ed. Edited by Phyllis Hartnoll. New York: Oxford University Press, 1983. 945p.

All forms of theater from ancient Greece to the present time are included in this companion: minstrels, Punch-and-Judy shows, street performances, and circus, as well as legitimate theater. There are entries for persons in the theatrical arts, past and present, terms and topics (e.g., Absurd, Theatre of the; acoustics and sound; act; after piece; amateur theatre), famous theaters, actors' associations, and other proper names associated with the theater.

620.   **The Oxford Companion to American Theatre.** Edited by Gerald Bordman. New York: Oxford University Press, 1984. 734p.

Concentrating on the theater in America, this companion has short articles on playwrights, actors, actresses, directors, and others connected with the American theater, well-known plays, famous theaters, and theater organizations.

621.   **Notable Names in the American Theatre.** Edited by Raymond D. McGill. Clifton, N.J.: James T. White, 1976. 1250p.

Notwithstanding the title of this book, which would lead one to look for it under "Biography," it is included with handbooks because of the variety of lists and data it includes about the theater. For example, a section, "New York Productions," lists alphabetically all plays, musicals, and reviews staged in New York from 1900 to 1975 with the date of opening, type of production, theater, and number of performances. "Premieres in America" lists premieres anywhere in the United States since 1968, with brief data. "Premieres of American Plays

Abroad" lists these chronologically from December 1948, to April 1974. Other short sections identify theatrical groups and companies in the United States, describe theater buildings opened since 1964 in the United States, list theater awards with past winners, list biographies and other books about notable persons in the theater, and give a necrology of theater personalities who have died since publication of the previous edition (*The Biographical Encyclopedia and Who's Who of the American Theatre*, edited by Walter Rigdon, New York: Heineman, 1966). The main part lists some 2,500 notable living persons in the American theater (directors, performers, producers, playwrights, stage and costume designers, composers, choreographers) with theater and screen credits and books.

622.   **The New York Times Directory of the Theater.** New York: Arno/Quadrangle, 1973. 1009p.

This directory closely resembles the directory on the film (entry 615). Award-winning plays (Pulitzer Prize, New York Drama Critics Circle, Tony, and Obie) are followed by *New York Times* reviews of these plays. This directory does not have portraits, but does have a title index of all plays reviewed in the *New York Times* from 1920 to 1970 (approximately 21,000) and a personal name index of all persons, both cast and production crew, mentioned in the reviews.

623.   **Theatre World.** New York: Crown, 1945- . Annual.

624.   **John Willis' Dance World.** New York: Crown, 1966- . Annual.

These are similar to *Screen World*, described above (entry 617) in having information, with numerous photographs, of the past year's activity in the United States in the theater and dance, respectively. Much of the value of these two annuals lies in their information on touring and regional companies and on festivals around the country. *American Theatre Annual*, edited by Catherine Hughes (Detroit: Gale, 1980-) also covers the year's productions on- and off-Broadway and those by touring companies and regional theaters. It, too, has many still photographs of plays but does not give as much detail as does *Theatre World*. Volumes of *American Theatre Annual* earlier than 1980 were titled *New York Theatre Annual* and covered only New York.

625.   **Best Plays of [year].** Edited by Otis L. Guernsey, Jr. New York: Dodd, Mead, 1899- . Annual.

The New York theater season has been covered annually in this publication for many years. It has undergone title changes and editor changes a number of times. Ten selected plays have abridged text, hence the title of the annual. It has also playbills of theaters on- and off-Broadway, awards, long runs, a necrology, and other information about the past season. An alphabetical list of the plays whose abridged script has been published in previous annuals is in the back of each volume. There is also a name and play title index to the current volume.

626.   Leonard, William T. **Broadway Bound: A Guide to Shows That Died Aborning.** Metuchen, N.J.: Scarecrow, 1983. 618p.

More than 400 plays and shows that were intended for Broadway runs but were never opened there are described in this unusual compilation, which may be exactly what is needed for identifying an obscure show. The credits, history, and reason for failure are given for each production. Numerous indexes (chronological, actor, playwright, producer, director, and others) are included.

627.   Hummel, David. **The Collector's Guide to the American Musical Theatre.** 2 vols. Metuchen, N.J.: Scarecrow, 1984.

A very valuable and useful addition to musical show literature, this work attempts to list every musical comedy, musical drama, operetta, revue, burlesque, and other show with musical background or featuring music as a prominent part that was presented on stage somewhere in the United States, even if only for a single performance. Arranged alphabetically by show title, it gives the composer, lyricist, author, book or play on which based, city, date, theater, number of performances, list of songs, cast, variant versions, and records and tapes of the music. Volume 2 is an index of all personal names cited in the first volume.

628.   **International Television Almanac.** New York: Quigley, 1956- . Annual.

Except for a few pages in the front of this almanac on statistics and awards in the television industry, its first two-thirds are an exact reprint of the companion *International Motion Picture Almanac* (entry 616) with its lengthy who's who of film personalities and list of feature films since 1955. The last portion of the book has directories of television networks and major companies, cable television companies, television stations and their network affiliations listed by state and city, and others.

629.   Steinberg, Cobbett S. **TV Facts.** Rev. ed. New York: Facts on File, 1984. 640p.

630.   Norback, Craig T., Peter G. Norback, and the Editors of *TV Guide* magazine. **TV Guide Almanac.** New York: Ballantine, 1980. 680p. Paper.

The first book above resembles the author's *Film Facts.* Its chapters, with numerous statistics, tables, and lists, are "The Programs," "The Viewers," "The Ratings," "The Advertisers," "The Awards, Polls, and Surveys," and "The Networks and Stations." *TV Guide Almanac* is similar to *TV Facts*, but is more complete, better arranged, and better indexed. Reminiscent of *The World Almanac and Book of Facts*, it is organized under 34 major topics, e.g., college television stations; Emmy awards; how to apply for a broadcast station; major TV production stations; politics and TV; satellite communications. Ratings and other data that show frequent change go through the 1978/1979 season. (Those in *TV Facts* go through 1977). The index is detailed, listing names, programs and shows, and topics.

REFERENCE HISTORIES

631.   Freedley, George, and John A. Reeves. **A History of the Theatre.** 3d rev. ed. New York: Crown, 1968. 1008p.

Reference work in the performing arts does not necessitate use of a chronological survey of the subject as is required in literature, music, and fine arts. The needs in performing arts are more concerned with specific facts and data and with current matters than with the history and development. When the need for a history of theater does arise, this work by Freedley and Reeves offers the most detail and the most information on the achievements and innovations of individual playwrights and directors. Two other histories of the theater, which are briefer but are good for an overall picture of theatrical change and development through the centuries, are Sheldon Cheney's *The Theatre: Three Thousand Years of Drama, Acting, and Stagecraft* (4th rev. ed. New York: McKay, 1972) and Marion Geisinger's *Plays, Players, and Playwrights: An Illustrated History of the Theatre* (Rev. ed. Updated by Peggy Marks. New York: Hart, 1975).

632.   Martin, John. **Book of the Dance.** New York: Tudor, 1963. 192p.

633.   Sachs, Curt. **World History of the Dance.** Translated by Bessie Schonberg. New York: Norton, 1963. 469p.

Book of the Dance concerns only ballet and is brief for a history but is very well illustrated. *World History of the Dance* is a more detailed, scholarly account, but mainly treats the development of the art form from primitive dance to the eighteenth century, with very little on the immediate past and present centuries.

BIOGRAPHY

634.   **Performing Arts Biography Master Index.** 2d ed. Edited by Barbara McNeil and Miranda C. Herbert. Detroit: Gale, 1981. 701p.

Similar timesavers, which index a large number of who's whos and biographical dictionaries in a subject, have been discussed earlier (entries 121, 392, 402-3). Typical of the 39 collections indexed in this are *A Biographical Dictionary of Film, McGraw-Hill Encyclopedia of World Drama, National Playwrights Directory, Twenty Years of Silents,* and *Women Who Made Movies.*

635.   Perry, Jeb H. **Variety Obits: An Index to Obituaries in Variety, 1905-1978.** Metuchen, N.J.: Scarecrow, 1980. 309p.

In addition to the reference to the date and page of the obituary in *Variety,* the person's age at death, date of death, and theatrical occupation (actor, actress, assistant director, animation artist, announcer) are given. If such information is all that is needed, the obituary does not have to be looked up. The names of those who were engaged only in the business aspect of film, theater, radio, television, or another performance medium and those who were active only in night clubs, cabarets, burlesque, the circus, and music (outside the theater) are generally omitted.

636.   **The Illustrated Who's Who of the Cinema.** Edited by Ann Lloyd and Graham Fuller. New York: Macmillan, 1983. 480p.

637.   Quinlan, David. **The Illustrated Directory of Film Stars.** New York: Hippocrene Books, 1981. 497p.

When a photograph is wanted of an actor or actress or other person in films, one of these books may supply the need. The first has almost twice as many entries as the latter and includes directors and others in the film industry as well as actors and actresses. It also has more persons in the film in other countries. Biographical data are brief, but photographs, usually in color, accompany most of the three thousand articles. Quinlan's work has a photograph, brief data, a characterization of type of roles and individual acting style, and full film credits for about 1,600 British and American actors and actresses and a few major stars of other countries. But directors, producers, and other industry personnel are not included. The duplication of names between these works is more than 50 percent, but each has articles on persons not in the other work. Pictures are better in *The Illustrated Who's Who of the Cinema,* but film credits are more complete in the other book.

638.   **The World Encyclopedia of the Film.** Edited by John M. Smith and Tim Cawkwell. New York: World, 1972. 444p.

Biographies of approximately 2,200 directors, producers, and performers are in this encyclopedia. Articles list the films in which the biographees acted, directed, or were otherwise active. The index of film titles refers to the person under whose name it is listed.

639.   Truitt, Evelyn M. **Who Was Who on the Screen.** 3d ed. New York: Bowker, 1983.
       788p.

Included in this directory are only actors, actresses, and bit players who were no longer living when the book was compiled, but not directors, screenwriters, or others unless they appeared on the screen. More than 13,000 performers are represented, chiefly American, British, French, and German, including many who had minor roles and are not usually mentioned in film biographies. Biographical data are brief, but include the cause of death and screen credits.

640.   Stewart, John, comp. **Filmarama.** Metuchen, N.J.: Scarecrow, 1975- . In progress.

This multi-volume work serves a function similar to that of the preceding book except that living, as well as deceased, actors and actresses are included, and film credits are more complete. For each person, dates are given, the real name (if different from the movie name), and a list of all films and representative stage, radio, and television work. The index of film titles also gives the release date and the entry numbers of actors and actresses in it. The disadvantage of this work is the need to consult several volumes, if the date of the performer's main activity is not known. At this time, only volume 1, *The Formidable Years, 1893-1919*, and volume 2, *The Flaming Years, 1920-1929*, have appeared. Further volumes covering later decades are expected. Complete film credits from 1949 through 1974 can also be found by consulting the index of *An Actor Guide to the Talkies* (entries 655-56).

641.   **Variety Who's Who in Show Business.** Edited by Mike Kaplan. New York: Garland,
       1983. 330p. Paper.

Short biographies with credits are given for about 6,500 performers in theater, film, television, music (classical and popular), sports, and other performing arts.

642.   **Who's Who in the Theatre: A Biographical Record of the Contemporary Stage.** 17th ed.
       Edited by Ian Herbert with Christine Baxter and Robert E. Finley. 2 vols. Detroit: Gale,
       1981.

643.   **Who Was Who in the Theatre, 1912-1976.** 4 vols. Detroit: Gale, 1978.

Those whose career is principally on the stage or who appear on the stage as well as in films and television are included in *Who's Who in the Theatre.* Living actors, actresses, directors, playwrights, and others from the New York and London stage (approximately 2,400) have short biographies here. In volume 2 are reprinted all playbills of the major New York and London theaters and those of Stratford-upon-Avon and the Stratford festival of Ontario from 1976 to 1979 inclusive. Long runs in the New York and London theaters are also listed. *Who Was Who in the Theatre* is a collection of the biographical entries that were dropped from earlier volumes of *Who's Who in the Theatre* because of death or inactivity in the field.

644.   Wearing, J. P. **American and British Theatrical Biography: A Directory.** Metuchen, N.J.:
       Scarecrow, 1979. 1007p.

This work indexes 47 biographical collections and annuals for more than 45,000 names of persons who have at some time been connected with the British and/or the American stage, some as early as the sixteenth century. Years of birth and death are given (when known), nationality, theatrical occupation, and sources for further information.

645.   Young, William C. **Famous Actors and Actresses on the American Stage.** 2 vols. New
       York: Bowker, 1975.

Articles of several pages in length are given here about approximately one hundred American actors and actresses of the past and present. These consist mostly of excerpts of critical writings about their achievements and acting.

646.   Cohen-Stratyner, Barbara N. **Biographical Dictionary of Dance.** New York: Schirmer, 1982. 980p.

This is the best source for identification of dancers and dance groups, choreographers, composers and designers for the ballet. Groups and persons of various countries who have performed in the United States or Europe are included in the nearly three thousand biographical articles. Ballet, tap, and other performance dance forms are represented. The book is not illustrated.

FILMS, PLAYS, RADIO AND TELEVISION PROGRAMS

Although the distinction cannot always be made clearly between the indexes and other works described here and those described under "Dictionaries, Encyclopedias" or under "Handbooks," we have intended this section to include those catalogs and works that primarily list or index films, plays, or programs. Also included here are selections of "best" films or plays, sometimes with texts, sometimes with plot summaries or critical notes. But reviews of films and plays and indexes to reviews are gathered together under the next heading, "Reviews."

Films

647.   **American Film Institute Catalog of Motion Pictures Produced in the United States.** New York: Bowker, 1972- . In progress.

When this monumental catalog has been completed, it will answer most questions about films produced in this country, not only Hollywood films, but also those made by firms, associations and societies, government agencies, and others. As of this writing, the only parts of the catalog available are *Feature Films, 1921-1930* (2 vols., 1971) and *Feature Films, 1961-1970* (2 vols., 1976). Partly due to lack of funding from the American Film Institute, publication of this work was suspended for a time but has now resumed. *Feature Films, 1911-1920* was expected in 1985. "Feature film" is defined as a film of four thousand feet or more. The arrangement of each portion of the catalog is alphabetical by film title; data for each film include date, length, color, sound, and other identifying features, production credits, cast credits, a description of the contents, and the subject headings used in the index. The index volume has a credit index, listing "all personal, group, institutional, and corporate names credited in the *Catalog* with any aspect of film production and distribution or with the performance of film roles." There are also literary and dramatic source indexes, crediting by author any play, opera, ballet, novel, or other source of the screenplay, and a subject index, listing films in the *Catalog* under a number of applicable subjects. Eventually, the *Catalog* will cover all films before 1911, feature films and short films from 1911 to the present, and newsreels from 1908 to the present.

648.   Halliwell, Leslie. **Halliwell's Film Guide.** 4th ed. New York: Scribner's, 1983. 936p.

In his *Filmgoer's Companion*, Halliwell was able to include fewer than eight hundred selected films, but in this companion book, which is limited to films, he describes some 14,000 English-language talking films, plus another estimated 3,000 silent and foreign-language films. For each, he gives the country and date, studio, length, color, brief description, rating, credits, major cast, and awards.

649.   **Magill's Survey of Cinema: English Language Films, First Series.** Edited by Frank N.
       Magill, Stephen L. Hanson, and Patricia K. Hanson. 4 vols. Englewood Cliffs, N.J.:
       Salem, 1980.

650.   **Magill's Survey of Cinema: English Language Films, Second Series.** Edited by Frank
       N. Magill, Stephen L. Hanson, and Patricia K. Hanson. 6 vols. Englewood Cliffs, N.J.:
       Salem, 1981.

651.   **Magill's Survey of Cinema: Silent Films.** Edited by Frank N. Magill, Patricia K. Hanson,
       and Stephen L. Hanson. 3 vols. Englewood Cliffs, N.J.: Salem, 1982.

652.   **Magill's Cinema Annual.** Englewood Cliffs, N.J.: Salem, 1982- . Annual.

The two series of English-language talking films have descriptive and critical articles on 515
and 751 films, respectively, produced in the United States, Great Britain, Canada, or another
English-speaking country from 1927 to the present. The article on each film gives the date,
producer, director, and other production staff, cast, running time, plot, and critical review.
Series 2 has several indexes (titles, directors, screenwriters, cinematographers, editors,
performers, and a chronological list of titles) that cover the contents of both series. The third
series has a glossary of terms used in the production of silent films, a roster of the major
studios of those years, several essays on the silent film and on some of the prominent stars,
and sketches similar to those on the talking films of more than three hundred silent films
made in the United States and abroad from 1902 through Chaplin's *Modern Times* (1936). The
various indexes of series 2 are also included in this set. There is to be a further series on
foreign language films shown in the United States. *Magill's Cinema Annual* selects about
one hundred films of the past year (with an occasional film of an earlier year not selected for
one of the first two series), giving production data and essay-reviews as in the series on
English language films. The annual also includes interview essays, cinema news and
awards of the year, and indexes of titles, directors, screenwriters, and others.

653.   Dimmitt, Richard B. **A Title Guide to the Talkies: A Comprehensive Listing of 16,000
       Feature-Length Films from October, 1927, until December, 1963.** 2 vols. New York:
       Scarecrow, 1965.

654.   Aros, Andrew A. **A Title Guide to the Talkies, 1964 through 1974.** Metuchen, N.J.:
       Scarecrow, 1977. 336p.

655.   Dimmitt, Richard B. **An Actor Guide to the Talkies: A Comprehensive Listing of 8,000
       Feature-Length Films from January, 1949, until December, 1964.** 2 vols. Metuchen,
       N.J.: Scarecrow, 1967-68.

656.   Aros, Andrew A. **An Actor Guide to the Talkies, 1965 through 1974.** Metuchen, N.J.:
       Scarecrow, 1977. 771p.

Valuable reference books tend to be of two general types: those that cover a great variety of
data on a given subject, like the Oxford companions, and are useful as a first source to
check in ready reference, and those that treat a very limited aspect of a subject, but treat it
exhaustively. These guides are of the second type, as is Stewart's *Filmarama* (entry 640). The
single purpose of *A Title Guide to the Talkies* and its continuation by Andrew Aros is to
identify a novel, short story, poem, or other work on which a talking movie has been based.
Aros adds another 3,400 movies for the decade 1965-1974 to the 16,000 listed by Dimmitt.
United States-produced films and foreign films exhibited in the United States are included.
An Actor Guide to the Talkies and its supplement by Aros list members of the cast of some
11,400 feature-length films produced since 1948 under the name of the film. Films produced
by minor studios in the United States and some foreign films are included. The index lists

the actors and actresses with page numbers or entry numbers indicating the films in which they acted.

657.   Parish, James R., and Michael R. Pitts. **The Great Spy Pictures.** Metuchen, N.J.: Scarecrow, 1974. 585p.

658.   Willis, Donald C. **Horror and Science Fiction Films III.** Metuchen, N.J.: Scarecrow, 1984. 349p.

These are examples of books on films of a certain genre. Parish and Pitts have written several books of this type, e.g., science fiction, westerns, gangster films. They describe films of the type, often including films from other countries and sometimes listing radio or television shows on the same theme.

659.   Emmens, Carol A. **Famous People on Film.** Metuchen, N.J.: Scarecrow, 1977. 355p.

The main idea of this book is to list all of the non-theatrical films on famous persons that are currently available in the United States from major distributors. This means educational, promotional, and other non-Hollywood films. A selection of feature films on famous people (Anne of a Thousand Days, Becket) is added in an appendix.

Plays

660.   Bronner, Edwin. **The Encyclopedia of the American Theatre, 1900-1975.** New York: Barnes, 1980. 659p.

Vital facts on some 3,000 plays produced on- and off-Broadway, 1900-1975, are given. These include opening, theater, number of performances, brief summary, leading cast, author, producer, costume and set designers, choreographer, screen version with the studio, date, and movie cast. Appendixes include a theatre calendar (notable premieres, by month), debuts of actors and actresses, debuts of playwrights, longest runs, and awards.

661.   Ewen, David. **New Complete Book of the American Musical Theater.** New York: Holt, Rinehart & Winston, 1970. 800p.

662.   Bordman, Gerald. **American Musical Theatre: A Chronicle.** New York: Oxford University Press, 1978. 749p.

Ewen summarizes musical shows by American composers produced in New York since 1866 with a brief history of each. Following the descriptions of shows, which are arranged by title, are short biographical sketches of librettists, lyricists, and composers. A chronology of America's musical shows and a list of outstanding songs are in appendixes. Bordman's work is more a history of the musical theater in America from the eighteenth century to 1978. But its three indexes (shows and sources, songs, and people) make it also useful for ready reference.

663.   **The London Stage, 1660-1800: A Calendar of Plays, Entertainments and Afterpieces, together with Casts, Box Receipts and Contemporary Comment ...** 5 parts in 11 vols. Carbondale, Ill.: Southern Illinois University Press, 1960-1968.

664.   Schneider, Ben Ross, comp. **Index to "The London Stage, 1660-1800."** Edited by William Van Lennep and others. Carbondale, Ill.: Southern Illinois University Press, 1979. 939p.

665.   Wearing, J. P., comp. **The London Stage, 1890-1899: A Calendar of Plays and Players.** 2 vols. Metuchen, N.J.: Scarecrow, 1976.

666.   Wearing, J. P., comp. **The London Stage, 1900-1909: A Calendar of Plays and Players.** 2 vols. Metuchen, N.J.: Scarecrow, 1981.

667.   Wearing, J. P., comp. **The London Stage, 1910-1919: A Calendar of Plays and Players.** 2 vols. Metuchen, N.J.: Scarecrow, 1982.

667a.   Wearing, J. P., comp. **The London Stage, 1920-1929: A Calendar of Plays and Players.** 3 vols. Metuchen, N.J.: Scarecrow, 1984.

668.   Odell, George C. D. **Annals of the New York Stage.** 15 vols. New York: Columbia University Press, 1927-1949.

A different kind of reference need – the scholarly study of the London or New York theater in past years – may call for these works. Undergraduates will rarely need the kind of detail provided in these books. *The London Stage, 1660-1800* reprints playbills of the major London theaters year by year according to the date on which a play opened. Information about each play includes the cast and production personnel, comment on the performance, box receipts, and other information that could be found in theater records and contemporary sources like Pepys's *Diary.* Each volume has an index of dramatists, composers, actors, and other persons mentioned in the playbills, titles of plays, operas, pantomimes, and other performances. Schneider's master index to the set covers the same entries and includes even names of prominent members of the audience and important businessmen of contemporary London. Wearing has compiled a similar work on the London stage from 1890 to 1929, reprinting playbills in chronological order. The index volume of each of these four parts also gives full access to the plays and persons acting in them and staging them. Odell's work does not follow this pattern but is a detailed, day-by-day history, rather than a reprint of playbills. The *Annals* run from about 1750 to 1894; Odell planned to take the book to 1900, but his death left it unfinished. Each volume has a detailed index of actors, actresses, producers, and others associated with the New York theater, many of whom are relatively obscure. A master index covering the entire work has never been compiled. The many portraits in the work have, however, been indexed in *Index to the Portraits in Odell's "Annals of the New York Stage"* (New York: American Society for Theatre Research, 1963).

669.   Shipley, Joseph T. **Guide to Great Plays.** Washington, D.C.: Public Affairs Press, 1956. 867p.

Some seven hundred of the world's greatest plays since Aeschylus (d. 456 B.C.) are summarized with a brief account of the circumstances of their writing, their early production, and reception by the public. The plays are arranged under the author, but there is an alphabetical title index of plays. About one-third of the plays can also be found summarized in the Magill series of literary plot summaries (see entries 405-8). For recent Broadway productions, see the volumes of *Best Plays of [year]* (entry 625), which give an abridged text of 10 selected plays of each season.

670.   Leonard, William T. **Theatre: Stage to Screen to Television.** 2 vols. Metuchen, N.J.: Scarecrow, 1981.

As suggested by the title, the purpose of this work is to trace the subsequent rewriting and production of successful plays as revivals on the stage, in film, and on television. Some three hundred successful plays are described with details on stage productions, and film and television adaptations. Most of these are of the twentieth century with a few first staged in the late nineteenth century, although some are based on earlier novels and other literary sources.

671.   **Chicorel Theater Index to Plays.** Edited by Marietta Chicorel. 5 vols. New York: Chicorel, 1970-77. (Chicorel Index Series, vols. 1-3, 8, 25).

672.   Keller, Dean H. **Index to Plays in Periodicals.** Rev. & expanded ed. Metuchen, N.J.:
        Scarecrow, 1979. 824p.

673.   **Ottemiller's Index to Plays in Collections: An Author and Title Index to Plays
        Appearing in Collections Published between 1900 and Early 1975.** 6th ed., rev. & enl.
        Edited by John M. Connor and Billie M. Connor. Metuchen, N.J.: Scarecrow, 1976.
        523p.

674.   Samples, Gordon. **The Drama Scholar's Index to Plays and Filmstrips: A Guide to
        Plays and Filmstrips in Selected Anthologies, Series, and Periodicals.** 2 vols.
        Metuchen, N.J.: Scarecrow, 1974-80.

As we noted above (entry 594), students and other users often want to read the script of a
play, especially one being produced on campus or locally. The library catalog should be
checked first, in order to learn if the library has a copy of the play, published as a separate. If
the play is not found in the catalog, these indexes aid in finding the text of the play if it is
part of an anthology or collection or if it is published in a periodical. Plays published
separately and in anthologies can also be identified through *Play Index* (entry 675).

675.   **Play Index.** New York: Wilson, 1953- . Cumulative volumes irregularly issued; the
        latest, 1973-1977.

676.   Salem, James M. **Drury's Guide to Best Plays.** 3d ed. Metuchen, N.J.: Scarecrow, 1978.
        421p.

The use of these and older indexes like them (see Eugene P. Sheehy, *Guide to Reference
Books*, 9th ed., American Library Association, 1976, #BD169-178) is different from the use of
the indexes described in the previous paragraph. Here one is likely to look for a play with
certain characteristics that is suitable for performance by a school, church, or other amateur
or professional acting group. These two works index plays, separately published or in a
collection, by number and sex of cast, number and type of sets, music requirements, and
subject (e.g., blacks, labor, marriage, Jesus Christ, courtroom, teenagers). *Drury's Guide to
Best Plays* also has lists of plays which have won national awards and plays which have
been popular with high school and other amateur groups.

Radio and Television Programs

677.   Dunning, John. **Tune in Yesterday: The Ultimate Encyclopedia of Old-Time Radio,
        1925-1976.** Englewood Cliffs, N.J.: Prentice-Hall, 1976. 703p.

The call for this book will not be large among students who did not know the years before
television. But some users will want to know who played the dumb detective in the radio
series, "Broadway Is My Beat," when the series ran, when "Information Please" started, or
some other fact about well-known, or not so well-known radio shows. Articles on some 1,000
shows tell their history, nature, personnel, sponsor, dates, and other facts.

678.   Terrace, Vincent. **The Complete Encyclopedia of Television Programs, 1947-1979.** 2d
        ed. 2 vols. South Brunswick and New York: Barnes, 1981.

679.   McNeil, Alex. **Total Television: A Comprehensive Guide to Programming from 1948 to
        the Present.** New York: Penguin, 1984. 1087p. Paper.

While there is a large amount of duplication between these two books, each has a few
programs not in the other (with McNeil printing more). Terrace's book is more impressive in
format and has some photographs; but essentially the same information on dates, program

time, cast, producer, etc., is in both. McNeil has some lists and tables not in Terrace: a chronological list of 570 notable special programs; a tabular presentation of prime-time schedules of the three networks through that period; Emmy and Peabody Award winners; and top-rated series. Both books have extensive indexes of personnel connected with the shows. *Les Brown's Encyclopedia of Television* (entry 606) has short articles on selected programs, but these are the better-known works.

680.   Gianakos, Larry J. **Television Drama Series Programming: A Comprehensive Chronicle, 1947-1959.** Metuchen, N.J.: Scarecrow, 1980. 565p.

681.   Gianakos, Larry J. **Television Drama Series Programming: A Comprehensive Chronicle, 1959-1975.** Metuchen, N.J.: Scarecrow, 1978. 794p.

682.   Gianakos, Larry J. **Television Drama Series Programming: A Comprehensive Chronicle, 1975-1980.** Metuchen, N.J.: Scarecrow, 1981. 457p.

682a. Gianakos, Larry J. **Television Drama Series Programming: A Comprehensive Chronicle, 1980-1982.** Metuchen, N.J.: Scarecrow, 1983. 686p.

This is another work that intensively treats a specific aspect of television programming. It names the individual episodes of drama series on television chronologically from their start. The cast is named for each episode. Only drama series are included, not sitcoms, variety shows, detective series, or others. The volume covering 1975-1980 has an index of series titles in it and the two previous volumes.

683.   **TV Season.** Compiled and edited by Nina David. Phoenix: Oryx Press, 1976- . Annual.

All national television programs and regularly scheduled shows of the past season are listed with data on the time and date shown, producing and acting personnel, length, and a brief description. There are also lists of the past season's shows by program type (crime drama, documentary series, feature film series), shows captioned for the hearing-impaired, new shows, cancelled shows, and Emmy and Peabody awards. The index lists personnel and organizations. This annual provides a supplement to Terrace's *Complete Encyclopedia of Television Programs, 1947-1979* (entry 678).

REVIEWS OF FILMS, PLAYS, AND TELEVISION PROGRAMS

Reviews are called for so often that we devote a separate section to locating them. Students may want to see reviews on films or plays or on directors or playwrights on whom they are writing. Students and other members of the campus or community may want reviews on a film or, particularly, on a play being shown locally. We have already noted requests for a script or text of a film or play being shown on campus. Besides (or instead of) seeing a script, some users also want to know what critics thought of a film or theatrical production. We distinguish, when possible, critical writings about a theatrical production from those about a playwright or a drama as literature. The latter are included in chapter 11, "Literature."

684.   Samples, Gordon. **How to Locate Reviews of Plays and Films: A Bibliography of Criticism from the Beginnings to the Present.** Metuchen, N.J.: Scarecrow, 1976. 114p.

In separate sections for plays and films, Samples has more than five hundred briefly annotated references to study guides for the theater in different times and countries, indexes to reviews in periodicals and newspapers, checklists of criticism, collected reviews, play synopses, and other critical material on plays and films.

685. Salem, James M. **A Guide to Critical Reviews.** Metuchen, N.J.: Scarecrow.

   Part 1. **American Drama, 1909-1969.** 2d ed. 1973. 591p.

   Part 2. **The Musical from Rodgers-and-Hart to Lerner-and-Loewe.** 1967. 353p.

   Part 3. **British and Continental Drama from Ibsen to Pinter.** 1968. 309p.

   Part 4. **The Screen Play from The Jazz Singer to Dr. Strangelove.** 2 vols. 1971. Supplement 1, 1963-1980. 1982.

The several parts of this multi-volume set index the critical reviews in the *New York Times* and a selection of popular American and Canadian magazines. Brief information is given about the play (opening date, number of performances), musical (opening date, number of performances, production credits), and film (release year), in addition to references to reviews. Tables and lists are also given following the index to reviews, such as birthplace and dates of playwrights, most successful productions (by length of runs), and most popular playwrights (by number of plays produced). The reviews cited in Part 3 are for the New York production of plays by authors of other countries.

686. Heinzkill, Richard. **Film Criticism: An Index to Critics' Anthologies.** Metuchen, N.J.: Scarecrow, 1975. 151p.

687. Bowles, Stephen E., comp. and ed. **Index to Critical Film Reviews in British and American Film Periodicals together with Index to Critical Reviews of Books about Film.** 4 vols. in 3. New York: Franklin, 1974-79.

These two works index anthologies of reviews by individual critics and periodicals for reviews of films. Most of the anthologies indexed by Heinzkill were published in the 1960s and 1970s, the latest being 1973. Bowles indexes 31 periodicals through 1971, when the annual bibliography by International Federation of Film Archives begins. Volumes 1 and 2 of this work list reviews of films under film title; volume 3 has reviews of books about film under book title. There are several indexes: directors, film reviewers, authors, book reviewers, and subjects of books.

688. **The New York Times Film Reviews, 1913-1968.** 6 vols. New York: New York Times, 1970. Biennial supplements, 1969/70- .

689. **Variety Film Reviews, 1907-1980.** 16 vols. New York: Garland, 1983.

All reviews of films, domestic and foreign, are reprinted chronologically by issues of the *New York Times*, 1913-1968, in volumes 1-5 of the first set. Volume 6 has addenda to the first five volumes, lists of film awards, reviews of the award-winning films, the Portrait Gallery of film stars, and indexes of film titles, all persons mentioned in the reviews, actors, actresses, directors, producers, and others, and corporations. These indexes are most useful, often eliminating the need to find a review by providing themselves the answer to a question. Note that the lists of awards, the reviews of award-winning films, the Portrait Gallery, and the indexes are also in the *New York Times Directory of the Film* (entry 615). Film reviews from *Variety*, 1907-1980, are now also available.

690. **The New York Times Theater Reviews, 1920-1970.** 10 vols. New York: New York Times, 1971. Biennial supplements, 1971/72- .

691. **New York Theatre Critics' Reviews.** New York: Critics' Theatre Reviews, 1940- . Weekly. Index, 1940-1960, vols. 1-21. 1961; Index, 1961-1972, vols. 22-33. n.d.

On the same pattern as the *New York Times Film Reviews*, the first set above reprints all reviews of plays, on- and off-Broadway from 1920 to 1970. Volume 9 lists the winners of several prizes and theatre awards during those years: Nobel Prize, Pulitzer Prize, New York Drama Critics Circle Awards, Antoinette Perry (Tony) Awards, and Off-Broadway (Obie) Awards. These lists and the *New York Times* reviews of the awards are followed by statistical summaries of productions and performances each season, 1920-1971. The three indexes in volumes 9 and 10 cover all play titles, production companies, and all personal names credited in the reviews. These award lists, reviews of award-winning plays, and the three indexes are also in the *New York Times Directory of the Theater* (entry 622). Reviews of Broadway plays and some off-Broadway plays from eight New York newspapers and two New York television stations are reprinted in *New York Theatre Critics' Reviews.* An annual index lists the plays reviewed for the year, plays reviewed in past volumes, off-Broadway reviews, and names of actors, actresses, and production personnel in the plays reviewed for the year.

692. **Access: The Supplementary Index to Periodicals.** Edited by John G. Burke and Ned Kehde. Evanston, Ill.: Burke, 1975- . 3 issues per year, annual cumulation.

Reviews of new plays and films are most often wanted. *New York Theatre Critics' Reviews* (entry 691), is good for the recent and current Broadway plays. Several current indexes to film literature, *Film Literature Index* (entry 583) and *International Index to Film Periodicals* (entry 584) are good for recent films, but they are issued only quarterly and annually, respectively. *Access* has been found to be helpful for film and play reviews. It indexes about 140 periodicals not covered by other indexes. Reviews are found by checking the subject index in each issue and in the annual cumulation under the title of the film or play.

693. **Review of the Arts: Film and Television.** New Canaan, Conn.: Newsbank, 1978- . Monthly. Microfiche. Printed index. Monthly, cumulating annually. Looseleaf.

694. **Review of the Arts: Performing Arts.** New Canaan, Conn.: Newsbank, 1977- . Monthly. Microfiche. Printed index. Monthly, cumulating annually. Looseleaf.

These services are even more up-to-date for indexing current reviews. Reviews of films and television programs, stories about the filmmaking and television industries, and interviews with film and television personalities are selected from more than one hundred U.S. newspapers and issued on microfiche each month to subscribers to the first service. The second is similar, covering newspaper articles on music, theater, dance, recordings, and circus. A looseleaf printed index is issued monthly, cumulating annually for each service. Names of persons, titles of films, television programs, plays, and other performances, and subjects are indexed. The current subscription price is $190 per year for each service.

15

SOCIAL SCIENCES

Compared with the disciplines we call the humanities and the natural sciences, the social sciences are late comers, emerging as distinct disciplines only in the nineteenth century. The definition of social sciences and the disciplines to be included among them vary with different writers, but a broad definition of the group would be those fields that are primarily concerned with "the behavior of man in relation to his fellows and to the environment they share."[1] Allowing for minor differences, the following are generally admitted as social sciences: anthropology (social and cultural), economics, psychology, sociology, geography (social and economic), political science, law, and history. Education, social work, and business administration are not considered to be true social sciences, but they can be thought of as applications of social sciences. Law might also be thought of as an applied social science. Some consider history to be properly a humanistic discipline, but here we are grouping it with the social sciences. All of the pure (as contrasted with the applied) social sciences in the twentieth century have seen a movement toward behavioral, statistical, and rigorous research, bringing them closer, methodologically and philosophically, to the natural sciences. But all of the social sciences (with the possible exception of psychology) encounter difficulty in formulating definitions and hypotheses as clear and unambiguous as those it has long been possible for the natural sciences to formulate.

In the rest of this introductory chapter, we describe some of the most important reference works that apply generally to the social sciences, rather than specifically to a single discipline. A few works that cover both the humanities and the social sciences have already been described in chapter 9, and will be mentioned here only briefly.

GUIDES, BIBLIOGRAPHIES, INDEXES

695. White, Carl M., and associates. **Sources of Information in the Social Sciences: A Guide to the Literature.** 2d ed. Chicago: American Library Association, 1973. 702p.

---

[1]Carl M. White, ed., *Sources of Information in the Social Sciences: A Guide to the Literature*, 2d ed. (Chicago: American Library Association, 1973), 1.

696.   McInnis, Raymond G., and James W. Scott. **Social Science Research Handbook.** New York: Barnes & Noble, 1975. 395p. Paper.

697.   Li, Tze-chung. **Social Science Reference Sources: A Practical Guide.** Westport, Conn.: Greenwood, 1980. 315p. (Contributions to Librarianship and Information Science, no. 30).

Sources of Information in the Social Sciences, by Carl White and associates, is unquestionably the best of the several guides to the literature of all of the social sciences. It covers history, geography, economics and business administration, sociology, anthropology, psychology, education, and political science. In each chapter, a survey of the subject and its several aspects, with a list of the introductory and standard works, is given. This is followed by an annotated list of guides to the literature, review journals, abstract journals, bibliographies, dictionaries, and other information sources for the discipline. Each chapter has been written by a specialist. But since the subfields of investigation and the information sources are under continual change, the age of this guide is a disadvantage. *Social Science Research Handbook* is another useful guide to the literature of the social sciences: anthropology, demography, economics, geography, history, political science, and sociology. Following these disciplines are several chapters on area studies, divided into eight areas of the world. Each of the chapters presents first the general reference works of the subject, then special works applying to subfields. A total of more than three thousand information sources are described in very informative bibliographic essays. The best of the more recent guides to the social sciences is Li's *Social Science Reference Sources*, which covers cultural anthropology, economics and business, education, history, law, political science, psychology, and sociology. This is a more selective guide, describing in essay chapters more than eight hundred works, but it is very useful and more up-to-date than the other two guides.

698.   **Social Sciences Index.** New York: Wilson, 1974- . Quarterly with annual cumulation.

Current literature is more important to the social scientist than publications more than a few years old. Social needs change in importance from year to year, and fields of interest to the research worker change more rapidly in the social sciences than in the humanities. Current research and up-to-date statistical data are needed. The social sciences, therefore, are better supplied with periodical indexes and abstract services than with retrospective bibliographies. Covering the social sciences generally is *Social Sciences Index.* Among the 275 periodicals indexed in this Wilson service are *Journal of Abnormal Psychology, Law and Society Review, Nursing Outlook, Review of Economic Studies,* and *Soviet Review.* Such journals are usually held by university libraries and often publish the kind of papers and data needed in student papers and reports. Beginning in late 1984, *Social Sciences Index* can be machine searched through Wilsonline. Earlier titles of this service were *International Index* and *Social Sciences and Humanities Index.* For periodical indexes that cover the individual social sciences, one can consult Harzfeld's *Periodical Indexes in the Social Sciences and Humanities* (entry 222). To learn what periodical index or abstract service covers a particular social science journal, see the *Chicorel Index to Abstracting and Indexing Services* (entry 224).

699.   **Social Sciences Citation Index.** Philadelphia: Institute for Scientific Information, 1973- . Three times per year; the 3d issue is the annual cumulation. Five-year cumulations: 1966-70; 1971-75; 1976-80. A ten-year cumulation, 1956-65, is planned.

The companion *Arts & Humanities Citation Index* has been described above (entry 223). The *Social Sciences Citation Index* has similar uses. One can consult the Source Index as a comprehensive bibliography of articles taken from the current issues of approximately 1,400 journals in all languages in the social sciences, a selection of pertinent articles from more than 3,100 journals on subjects related to the social sciences, and essays from selected monographic series. Or one can learn which of these articles and essay-chapters are on any social science subject by using the Permuterm Subject Index, which lists all of the items in the Source Index under permuted words of its title. The main index, the Citation Index, lists every title cited by any article in the Source Index, regardless of its form (book, periodical article, essay, article in an encyclopedia, unpublished communication, etc.) and regardless of its date. The titles are listed under their author with a list of the articles in the Source Index which cited them. This index can be used to see whether a book or article, of which the author is known, is currently being cited by researchers. Or, since it lists so many writings of different formats and different dates, it might be used for verifying a bibliographic reference that could not be found elsewhere. *Social Sciences Citation Index* can be machine searched back to 1972 through BRS and DIALOG.

DICTIONARIES, ENCYCLOPEDIAS

700. Reading, Hugo F. **A Dictionary of the Social Sciences.** London: Routledge & Kegan Paul, 1977. 231p.

701. Gould, Julius, and W. L. Kolb. **A Dictionary of the Social Sciences.** New York: Free Press, 1964. 761p.

When a definition of a term is needed, one is advised to consult a dictionary of the particular social science, if possible, since it will usually have more terms, more specifically defined, than a dictionary which tries to cover the terminology of all of the social sciences. This is not always possible, either because the particular discipline in which the term is used is not known or because a dictionary of that discipline is not available. In such a situation, Reading's dictionary might be used. It defines approximately 7,500 terms used in the several social sciences except economics and linguistics. Examples are: conduct; configuration, symbolic; conflict, approach-avoidance; contagion, affective; control, secondary; conurbation. As seen from these examples, compound terms are usually inverted. The work by Gould and Kolb is restricted to some 750 concepts, rather than particular terms, e.g., culture complex; culture history; currency reform; custom; cybernetics. Full, authoritative, carefully written discussions of these are provided with reference to sources further elaborating the subject.

702. Miller, P. McC., and M. J. Wilson. **A Dictionary of Social Science Methods.** New York: Wiley, 1983. 124p.

A more specialized dictionary, covering terms used in statistical and other research methods used in the social sciences. Examples are canonical correlation analysis, categorical variable, causal model, causation, cell frequency, Chi square.

703. **International Encyclopedia of the Social Sciences.** Edited by David Sills. 17 vols. New York: Macmillan and Free Press, 1968. Vol. 18, **Biographical Supplement.** New York: Free Press; London: Collier Macmillan, 1979. Reprint ed. 8 vols. New York: Free Press, 1977. **Biographical Supplement.** New York: Free Press, 1979.

Some social sciences do not have a suitable encyclopedia. This general encyclopedia is useful in those fields. But it is also good for supplementing the specialized encyclopedias that are available in fields like psychology and education. Articles are found here that apply to a single science as well as articles covering all of the social sciences. They are written by specialists in each field, are authoritative and scholarly, and have bibliographies of works for further study. Biographies of "eminent social scientists who had been too young in the mid-1960s to qualify for inclusion in the original volumes" are in the biographical supplement.

CONFERENCE PROCEEDINGS

704. **Directory of Published Proceedings.** Series SSH (Social sciences, humanities). Harrison, N.Y.: InterDok, 1968- . Quarterly with annual cumulation.

705. **Index to Social Sciences and Humanities Proceedings.** Philadelphia: Institute for Scientific Information, 1979- . Quarterly with annual cumulation.

The importance of conferences and the papers given at them has been mentioned earlier under "Humanities" (see entries 225 and 226). These bibliographies are frequently used by members of the faculty to learn about conferences of their professional associations and other conferences related to their research interests and about the published proceedings thereof. The first bibliography lists conferences with a note about the date, place, and published proceedings but does not index the individual papers, as the second index does.

BIOGRAPHY

706. **American Men and Women of Science: Social and Behavioral Sciences.** 13th ed. New York: Bowker, 1978. 1545p.

This volume of *American Men and Women of Science* includes noted social scientists in the fields of administration and management, area studies, business, communication and information science, community and urban studies, economics, environmental studies, futuristics, international studies, political science, psychology, and sociology. Scholars in history are included in the *Directory of American Scholars* (entry 228). Approximately 24,000 social scientists are included in the 13th edition with brief biographical data. Separate indexes list the biographees by discipline and by geography. Further editions of this part of *American Men and Women of Science* have been postponed, with consideration being given to include some social and behavioral sciences in the *Directory of American Scholars* or to add data on social and behavioral scientists to the online database for inclusion in future editions of *American Men and Women of Science*. They are not included, however, in the 15th edition of this work (entry 1269).

16

EDUCATION, PSYCHOLOGY

Although education is not one of the traditional social sciences, it is a field that is important in almost all universities and one in which there are many reference needs. Most universities have a college of education with a sizeable faculty and enrollment of undergraduate and graduate students. Undergraduates typically need help in finding suitable material for term papers, mostly journal articles. Sufficient references can usually be located through periodical indexes, but students often need instruction in using indexes. Graduate students and faculty members have more difficult reference problems. They can (or ought to be able to) do their own searching through periodical indexes, bibliographies, and the library catalog, but may need help in more difficult searching, such as machine searching.

Besides literature searching, graduate students and faculty members may want help in finding statistics of a particular kind, such as the ratio of male to female teachers employed in different countries or the number of students enrolled in specific curricula in different states. Another common type of reference question, asked especially by faculty members, is the address of a colleague in another university or in a nonacademic profession. Directory questions about educational programs and about specific schools and administrators are asked by undergraduates considering a transfer of schools or program, by graduating students looking for employment, and by faculty members. Graduating students are also often in need of certification requirements in the different states. Another type of question that is often asked is the rating of a division or department of one's own university in comparison with other universities. Opportunities for study or teaching in a foreign country are of interest to some students and faculty. And information on educational or research grants is also frequently wanted, especially by faculty members.

The most frequently asked reference questions in education will depend on the aspects of the field emphasized at a particular institution. One department or even one member of the faculty may be active in educational testing and assign students research problems in this area. Another may be involved and involve students in international education, causing heavy use of reference books on educational programs in other countries. Questions that attract attention across the country, such as the role of athletic competition in the university, collective bargaining by teachers, or financial rewards based on excellence in teaching will create new areas of reference needs. The reference librarian should be alert to these new areas and anticipate them in finding and acquiring information sources about them. Failing to anticipate these needs, the librarian can at least act in response to the first questions asked in these areas.

The reference literature in education is very large. Specialized bibliographies and directories and guides to colleges and universities are numerous. Selection of the most useful reference sources for this chapter has been difficult. For awareness of the many specialized reference works in this field, check Marda Woodbury's *A Guide to Sources of Educational Information* (entry 707).

Psychology, which is one of the traditional social sciences, is included in this chapter because it is the social discipline most closely related to education. Questions asked by students and faculty in psychology resemble the questions most often asked in education. Undergraduates want references to articles pertinent to a term paper they are writing and need instruction in the use of *Psychological Abstracts.* Graduate students also use *Psychological Abstracts* very much, but do not usually need help using it. They do, however, need help in conducting online searches of the literature and in difficult bibliographic verification. They also want information on tests and testing in support of their dissertation research. Members of the faculty seek help with online searching and with bibliographic verification of some items. They also seek information on specific tests and often need the current address of a colleague in the field.

The literature of psychology is not nearly as large as that of education. One reason for this is that fewer people specialize in psychology than in education. Also, much of the research in the field is laboratory-bound and depends on less literature than does research and study in education. Some reference books in the final section of this chapter cover psychiatry as well as psychology, but books devoted wholly to psychiatry have been included in chapter 29, "Medical Sciences."

EDUCATION

GUIDES, BIBLIOGRAPHIES, INDEXES

707. Woodbury, Marda. **A Guide to Sources of Educational Information.** 2d ed. Washington, D.C.: Information Resources Press, 1982. 430p.

This introductory work is the best guide to the literature of the field, replacing the older *Documentation in Education*, by A. J. Burke and M. A. Burke. Directed to the student and beginning researcher in the field, *A Guide to Sources of Educational Information* has sections on doing research and preparing the report. The most useful parts for reference work are the sections describing more than 1,000 reference sources, printed research tools, and nonprint sources. Another recent, but less comprehensive, guide is Dorothea M. Berry's *A Bibliographic Guide to Educational Research* (2d ed. Metuchen, N.J.: Scarecrow, 1980).

708. **Current Index to Journals in Education.** Phoenix: Oryx Press, 1969- . Monthly with semiannual cumulations.

Faculty members and students at all levels use indexes of journal articles much more often than the selective guides and bibliographies in the previous paragraph. *Current Index to Journals in Education* (*CIJE*) is more comprehensive than *Education Index* (entry 709). *CIJE* indexes some 780 journals in education, psychology, sociology, library science, and other subjects related to education. The National Institute of Education (NIE), an agency of the U.S. Department of Education, maintains 16 Educational Resources Information Centers (ERIC) in universities and professional organizations throughout the country. These 16 clearinghouses acquire and abstract journal and monographic literature on specialized educational areas. Examples of the centers are Reading and Communication Skills (National Council of Teachers of English, Urbana, IL); Educational Management (University of Oregon); Handicapped and Gifted Children (Council for Exceptional Children, Weston, VA); and Tests, Measurement, and Evaluation (Educational Testing Service, Princeton University). *Current Index to Journals in Education* and *Resources in Education* (entry 752) are compiled and published from the abstracted citations furnished regularly by these 16 clearinghouses. Instead of conventional subject headings, *Current Index to Journals in*

Education uses specific descriptors, the same as those used in *Resources in Education.* For an intelligent search of either of these indexes, the user should consult the *Thesaurus of ERIC Descriptors* (10th ed. Phoenix: Oryx Press, 1984). The main section of *CIJE* offers brief abstracts of articles arranged by document accession number under the 16 broad areas that are the specializations of the ERIC clearinghouses. Indexes provide access by subject or author, and a third lists the contents of each journal issue indexed. The complete runs of *CIJE* and *RIE* can also be machine searched through BRS, DIALOG, and SDC, and this convenient service is often used by faculty and graduate students for a complete search of their research topic. *Education Index,* although less comprehensive than *Current Index to Journals in Education,* is still preferred by many users when the requirement for completeness is not so great. It uses conventional subject headings with subdivisions and cross-references, which are more familiar to many users than descriptors. About three hundred English language periodicals are covered, and selected government publications, proceedings, and yearbooks of educational associations are included, although not so many as in earlier years of the index. Items are arranged under author-subject dictionary format so that indexes are not needed. *Education Index* is one of the Wilson indexes that can now be machine searched through Wilsonline.

709. **Education Index.** New York: Wilson, 1932- . Monthly, except July-August, with annual cumulation.

DICTIONARIES, ENCYCLOPEDIAS

710. Good, Carter V., ed. **Dictionary of Education.** 3d ed. New York: McGraw-Hill, 1973. 681p.

711. Page, Terry G., J. B. Thomas, and A. R. Marshall. **International Dictionary of Education.** London: Kogan Page, 1977. 381p.

If only a brief definition of a term or identification of a person or association is needed, one of these compact books will be the quickest source. Good's *Dictionary of Education* has been the standard dictionary since its first edition in 1945. The third edition has approximately 33,000 terms and cross-references but does not include names of persons, associations, or other proper names. Terms used in Canada or Great Britain which differ from the American counterpart are in appendixes. Other foreign terms are not included. *International Dictionary of Education* has more than 10,000 terms, names of persons, associations, tests, publications, other proper names, and abbreviations, including many from countries other than the United States.

712. **The Encyclopedia of Education.** Edited by Leigh C. Deighton. 10 vols. New York: Macmillan & Free Press, 1971.

The Encyclopedia of Education is the first source to check for general information about education, when more than a simple dictionary definition is needed. More than one thousand articles, written by specialists in their field and containing selective bibliographies, give background on educational policies and practices, surveys of special types of education and of teaching methods used for different subjects, biographies, and historical topics. The emphasis is on American education, but there are good surveys of education in other countries. The final volume contains a directory of contributors and their credentials, a list of articles and cross-references, and an index of subjects.

713. **The International Encyclopedia of Higher Education.** Edited by Asa S. Knowles. 10 vols. San Francisco: Jossey-Bass, 1977.

Although the previous encyclopedia has survey articles about the total educational system in other countries, this work offers more up-to-date information about higher education in those countries. Comprehensive articles cover national systems, contemporary topics, fields of study, and educational associations, but there are no articles on persons or on individual universities. A directory of documentation and information organizations in 150 countries is in volume 9 following the final article, and an index of personal names and a subject index are in volume 10.

714.   **Handbook on Contemporary Education.** Compiled and edited by Stevens E. Goodman. New York: Bowker, 1976. 622p.

We have included this handbook with the encyclopedias because it is a good, convenient source of information on many educational topics that were of current interest in 1975, including many that are still controversial. Among the 118 state-of-the-art papers, which average 3 to 4 pages in length, are such topics as records confidentiality, college grading systems, pregnant teachers, Head Start, textbook selection, nutrition and learning in preschool children. The articles review the literature and discuss the several sides of each issue.

EDUCATION DIRECTORIES

High in frequency among ready-reference questions in the university library are directory questions. We have divided education directories into two groups: the true directories that list only the address, telephone number, name of director, and similar brief data, and those guides which give more information about schools and colleges and are intended to help students and their parents select an appropriate school or college to apply to. Those directories in the first group often cover various levels and types of educational institutions, and some give data on foreign universities and institutions.

715.   U.S. Department of Education. National Center for Education Statistics. **Education Directory.** Washington, D.C.: Government Printing Office, 1912- . Annual.

The several parts of this directory, not all of which are revised annually, are Local Education Agencies (formerly Public School Systems); Colleges and Universities; State Education Agency Officials; and Education Associations. Most libraries have this, and it is a convenient place to find the name of a local school superintendent, high school principal, administrator of a college or university, or director of an association.

716.   **Patterson's American Education.** Mount Prospect, Ill.: Educational Directories, 1904- . Annual.

Patterson's American Education is another directory that covers education at several levels and has much information not easily found elsewhere. Different sections give the names of principals of public secondary schools, directories of Roman Catholic, Lutheran, and Seventh Day Adventist schools, and directory of private and public schools for certain specialized studies, e.g., embalming and mortuary science, business, fashion art, graduate schools.

717.   **American Universities and Colleges.** 12th ed. New York, Berlin: De Gruyter, 1983. 2156p.

Since this directory, under the sponsorship of the American Council on Education, restricts itself to universities and colleges, it can give more detail than the two previous sources, which also cover secondary schools, school systems, and educational associations. The data given in this work for each institution include a brief history, governance, term system, scholastic characteristics of entering freshmen, admission and degree requirements, tuition and fees, campus life, etc. Identification of the colors and trappings of American academic costume, degree abbreviations, and statistics of higher education in the United States are in appendices.

718. **Yearbook of Higher Education.** Chicago: Marquis Professional Publications, 1969- . Annual.

This is a directory of those public and private institutions of higher education in the United States and Canada that are listed by one or more of the accrediting agencies belonging to the Council on Postsecondary Accreditation (COPA). Also included are some information on how to apply and who is eligible for college scholarships, a directory of educational associations, and some statistics on enrollment and other higher education data.

719. **Higher Education Exchange 78/79: Directory Marketplace Almanac.** Edited by Janet A. Mitchell. Philadelphia: Peterson's Guides/Lippincott, 1978. 766p.

A great variety of directory information applicable to higher education is provided here. The volume has three parts: "Higher Education Institutions": profiles of 3,200 institutions in the United States and Canada, university presses, radio stations, national student organizations, social fraternities and sororities, etc.; "Marketplace": publishers, mailing list vendors, consultants, food service management, and other services needed by universities; and "Almanac": statistics of interest in higher education.

720. **The World of Learning.** London: Europa, 1947- . Annual.

721. **Commonwealth Universities Yearbook: A Directory to the Universities of the Commonwealth and the Handbook of Their Association.** London: The Association of Commonwealth Universities, 1914- . Annual.

722. **International Handbook of Universities and Other Institutions of Higher Education.** 9th ed. Berlin, New York: De Gruyter, 1983. 1131p.

These and the remaining directories in this section are for countries outside the United States. *The World of Learning* is the most general, listing for each country the leading universities, academies, research institutions, learned societies, libraries, and museums, with brief information: address, principal officers or faculty, number of volumes, etc. The other two directories, which are limited to the universities of the respective countries, give additional information about them: brief history, admission requirements, fees, degrees offered, and rosters of the administrators and faculty. One problem with *International Handbook of Universities and Other Institutions of Higher Education* (which covers all countries except the United States and Commonwealth nations) is that universities are listed in the index only under their full name, not under the name by which they are popularly known: Sorbonne is listed under "Université de Paris-Sorbonne"; Salerno is under "University of Salerno."

723. **World Guide to Higher Education: A Comparative Survey of Systems, Degrees and Qualifications.** 2d ed. New York: Bowker for UNESCO, 1982. 369p.

This book differs from the three previously named directories in that it describes the higher education system as a whole for each country rather than the data for individual universities. Its purpose is to provide opportunity for comparative study of higher education in different countries: requirements for admission, degrees, number of years of study required, etc.

724. **World Guide to Scientific Associations and Learned Societies. (Verbände und Gesellschaften der Wissenschaft: Ein Internationales Verzeichnis.)** Edited by Barbara Verrel and Helmut Optiz. Munich: Saur, 1984. 947p.

More than 11,000 scientific and learned societies are listed by continent and country, but, since the directory is a translation from the German original, countries are alphabetical under their German name. Thus, the English table of contents must be used for the location of a particular country. Similarly, the subject index in German and English is arranged according to the German subject word, but a List of Key Words (in English) refers to the index page.

GUIDES TO SCHOOLS AND COLLEGES

725. **Peterson's Annual Guide to Undergraduate Study.** Edited by Karen C. Hegener and Joan Hunter. Princeton, N.J.: Peterson's Guides, 1964- . Annual. Paper.

726. Cass, James, and Max Birnbaum. **Comparative Guide to American Colleges for Students, Parents, and Counselors.** 11th ed. New York: Harper & Row, 1983. 706p.

727. Fiske, Edward B. **Selective Guide to Colleges, 1984-85.** New York: Times Books, 1983. 483p. Paper.

728. **Lovejoy's College Guide.** 16th ed. Edited by Charles T. Straughn and Barbarasue Lovejoy Straughn. New York: Monarch, 1983. 549p.

729. **The College Blue Book.** 19th ed. 3 vols. New York: Macmillan, 1983.

730. **Barron's Profiles of American Colleges.** 13th ed. 2 vols. Woodbury, N.Y.: Barron, 1982. Paper.

Although not always clearly distinguishable from some of the directories in the previous section, these guides have been prepared, in general, as aids to parents and students in selecting a suitable college or preparatory school. Some of the better-known and more popular guides are listed above. Besides information on admission requirements, tuition, degrees offered, term system, financial aid available, size of faculty and student body, and subjects or curricula offered, they also give such information as the difficulty of being admitted (by giving the average achievement test scores or rank in high school graduating class of entering freshmen), housing available, religious orientation, athletics, social activities, and other aspects of college life. *Comparative Guide to American Colleges for Students, Parents, and Counselors* is especially good at listing colleges according to the difficulty of being accepted. Fiske's *Selective Guide to Colleges* is also a good first choice for the prospective student since it concentrates on the 265 colleges in the United States considered by the authors to be "the best and most interesting four-year institutions in the country," instead of burdening the reader with details on the approximately three thousand colleges that could be considered. In addition to data on the number of applicants, the number accepted, and the median SAT (or ACT) scores of accepted students, it rates each college on academics, social life, and "quality of life" (i.e., lack of undue pressure, "is it a pleasant place in which to live?"). *Peterson's Annual Guide to Undergraduate Study* can be machine searched as the PETERSON'S COLLEGE DATABANK through BRS.

731. **National College Data-bank: The College Book of Lists.** 3d ed. Edited by Karen C. Hegener. Princeton, N.J.: Peterson's Guides, 1984. 750p. Paper.

732. **Barron's Guide to the Best, Most Popular, and Most Exciting Colleges.** Woodbury, N.Y.: Barron, 1982. 437p.

733. **Barron's Guide to the Most Prestigious Colleges.** Woodbury, N.Y.: Barron, 1982. 359p.

These three guides single out colleges that have certain characteristics: women's colleges, colleges with less than 10 percent black enrollment, those with more than 50 percent of graduates going on to graduate and professional schools, colleges with coed housing, those with the best facilities and faculties, those with unconventional philosophies, programs, or teaching methods, and many others.

734. Halterman, William J. **The Complete Guide to Nontraditional Education.** New York: Facts on File, 1983. 172p. Paper.

"Nontraditional" education is many things: correspondence classes, self-paced instruction, credits gained by examinations or for experiential learning, independent study, and similar non-curricular education. Most of this book is detailed description of approximately 125 educational institutions, arranged under states, that offer nontraditional programs. Costs, time required, admission requirements, and degrees offered are among the data given in each case.

735. **Who Offers Part-Time Degree Programs? A National Survey of Post-Secondary Institutions Offering Daytime, Evening, Weekend, Summer, and External Degree Programs.** Princeton, N.J.: Peterson's Guides, 1981. 349p.

For the student who can attend classes only a certain part of the week, the term, the year, or who must study off campus, this guide points out the colleges that offer such programs.

736. **Peterson's Annual Guide to Graduate Study.** Princeton, N.J.: Peterson's Guides, 1966- . Annual. Paper.

Concentrating on opportunities and facilities for graduate study, this annually revised guide goes into great depth, describing programs and degrees offered, cost, facilities, faculty, enrollment in graduate programs, and number of degrees granted in past years in each department. The guide is published in five volumes, divided according to subject area.

737. **Barron's Guide to the Two-Year Colleges.** 7th ed. 2 vols. Woodbury, N.Y.: Barron, 1981.

Some students in two-year colleges are preparing to transfer to a four-year college, but many are preparing for a vocation or trade that does not require a college education. Thus, the present guide has one part on profiles of some 1,200 two-year colleges, and a second part, an "Occupational Program Selector." The latter is a tabular presentation showing whether credits earned in a two-year college may be transferred to a four-year college for continued study.

738. **Lovejoy's Career and Vocational School Guide.** 5th ed. Edited by Charles T. Straughn and Barbarasue Lovejoy Straughn. New York: Simon & Schuster, 1978. 142p.

Another vocation-centered guide to schools. More than three hundred careers and vocations are listed with capsule descriptions of schools offering training. To indicate the breadth of this guide, a sampling of the careers and vocations listed includes: fashion design, flight engineer, illustration, insurance, massage, and meat cutting.

739. **The Handbook of Private Schools: An Annual Descriptive Survey of Independent Education.** Boston: Porter Sargent, 1914- . Annual.

740. **Lovejoy's Prep and Private School Guide.** 5th ed. Edited by Charles T. Straughn and Barbarasue Lovejoy Straughn. New York: Simon & Schuster, 1980. 218p.

741. **Peterson's Annual Guide to Independent Secondary Schools.** Edited by Rebecca A. Shepherd, Joan Hunter, and P. Susanne Mast. Princeton, N.J.: Peterson's Guides, 1980- . Annual. Paper.

742. **Private Independent Schools.** Wallingford, Conn.: Bunting & Lyon, 1939- . Annual.

Lastly, these guides to private secondary and preparatory schools are listed. They include information about the setting, facilities, costs, faculty, housing, special offerings (such as study abroad or programs for the gifted), and special types (such as girls' schools or boys' schools).

STATISTICS

743. National Center for Educational Statistics. **Digest of Educational Statistics.** Washington, D.C.: Government Printing Office, 1962- . Annual.

For enrollment, financial, and other statistics about education in the United States, this compilation is the first choice, providing the most detailed and widest data. Statistics are taken from various sources, including some prepared by the Center. They are presented in groups covering different levels of education: elementary/secondary, college and university, adult and vocational, federal programs, etc. There is an index of subjects.

744. National Center for Education Statistics. **The Condition of Education: Statistical Report.** Washington, D.C.: Government Printing Office, 1975- . Annual.

This report consists of graphs, tables, and articles on issues and conditions in society that affect education in the United States. It is arranged by educational level and topic: "Elementary/Secondary Education," "Higher Education," "Higher Education Finance," "Adult and Occupational Education," "Preprimary Education." On its limited subject, it is more analytical and explanatory than *Digest of Educational Statistics.*

745. National Center for Education Statistics. **Projections of Educational Statistics.** Washington, D.C.: Government Printing Office, 1974- . Biennial.

Statistics on enrollment, graduates, teachers, and expenditures for elementary schools through universities are projected eight to nine years beyond the date of publication. These are based on statistics of past years and assume continuation of present trends. At the time of this writing, the latest edition, published in 1982, projected statistics to 1990-91.

746. **Standard Education Almanac.** Chicago: Marquis Professional Publications, 1968- . Annual.

Standard Education Almanac is a convenient one-volume source of statistics and articles covering aspects and issues on education in this country. The statistics are taken from various publications, such as *The Condition of Education, Projections of Educational Statistics,* and *The Chronicle of Higher Education*, and are presented in chapters by level of education and topic.

747. **UNESCO Statistical Yearbook.** Paris: United Nations Educational, Scientific and Cultural Organization, 1963- . Annual.

Cultural and educational statistics supplied by some two hundred member countries and territories are revised annually. Tables include literacy, education, libraries and museums, publishing, paper consumption, film, radio, and television. Since the presentation and comparison of international statistics is so complex, each section of the yearbook is introduced with an explanation of its tables, definition of terms, sources of data, and other background. Use of the book is hampered by the lack of an index, but the table of contents, which is very detailed, takes the place of an index. The table of contents and explanatory notes are given in English, French, and Spanish.

RESEARCH

748. **Encyclopedia of Educational Research.** 5th ed. Edited by Harold E. Mitzel. 4 vols. New York: Free Press, 1982.

Greatly expanded and revised from the fourth edition, this standard source has 256 signed articles on areas of study, teaching methods, research methodology, special education, and other topics on which research is currently being done. Lists of the articles, classified and alphabetical, are in the front of the first volume, a subject index in the final volume.

749. **Review of Research in Education.** Itasca, Ill.: F. E. Peacock, 1973- . Annual.

750. **Review of Educational Research.** Washington, D.C.: American Educational Research Association, 1931- . Quarterly.

Review essays on various subjects which differ from year to year are published in *Review of Research in Education.* Sample topics in recent volumes are "Economics of Education," "Language and Schooling," "Policy Research," and "Research and Evaluation." Articles in the quarterly *Review of Educational Research* cover various educational topics. This journal is indexed in *Education Index* (entry 709) and *Current Index to Journals in Education* (entry 708).

751. Travers, Robert M., ed. **Second Handbook of Research on Teaching: A Project of American Educational Research Association.** Chicago: Rand McNally, 1973. 1400p.

Research on various topics on teaching and teaching method is surveyed in 42 articles in this handbook. Sample papers include "Theory Construction for Research on Teaching," "The Social Psychology of Teaching," "Teaching the Emotionally Disturbed," and "Research on Teaching Foreign Languages."

752. **Resources in Education.** Phoenix: Oryx Press, 1966- . Monthly.

The published and unpublished reports collected and organized in the 16 Educational Resources Information Centers (ERIC) are abstracted and published in this index. The centers have been described above (entry 708). The abstracted reports are arranged by document accession number under the special areas of the centers. *Resources in Education* (*RIE*) can be machine searched as part of ERIC through BRS, DIALOG, and SDC.

BIOGRAPHY

753. **The National Faculty Directory.** 2 vols. Detroit: Gale, 1970- . Annual.

754. **Who's Who Biographical Record: School District Officials.** Chicago: Marquis Who's Who, 1976. 666p.

755.   **Who's Who Biographical Record: Child Development Professionals.** Chicago: Marquis Who's Who, 1976. 515p.

756.   **Who's Who in Library and Information Services.** Edited by Joel M. Lee. Chicago: American Library Association, 1982. 559p.

Questions about persons in the educational professions come mostly from members of the faculty and administration. Usually only directory information is needed: position title and address. Since the personal data given in the sources listed above are brief and their titles are descriptive of the professions included, sources are not described individually. The listing is from general to specific. *The National Faculty Directory* gives only the title, institution, and address, but it is used most often because it lists persons in higher education and is nonselective, attempting to list all faculty members in junior colleges, colleges, and universities in the United States and those in selected institutions in Canada. Data are taken from college and university catalogs. Additional information about selected faculty members is in *American Men and Women of Science* (entry 706) and *Directory of American Scholars* (entry 228).

757.   **Biographical Dictionary of American Educators.** Edited by John F. Ohles. 3 vols. Westport, Conn.: Greenwood, 1978.

758.   **Dictionary of American Library Biography.** Edited by Bohdan S. Wynar. Littleton, Colo.: Libraries Unlimited, 1978. 596p.

Less often than the directory information on living educators, for which the directories and who's whos described in the previous paragraph are used, biographical information is wanted on an educator of the past. Such questions may come from students for term papers, from graduate students for dissertations, or from faculty and administrators for a speech or article. Biographies of prominent educators from colonial times to 1976 are found in *Biographical Dictionary of American Educators.* Personal and career data include a list of the person's publications and references to further biographical information. Appendixes list the educators by place of birth, state of major service, field of work, and year of birth. A final appendix gives important dates in American education. Biographies of persons who made important contributions in the development of education in other countries are in the *Encyclopedia of Education. Dictionary of American Library Biography* has short sketches of those who have contributed to library development in this country in past years.

RATINGS OF COLLEGES AND COLLEGE PROGRAMS

759.   Gourman, Jack. **The Gourman Report: A Rating of Undergraduate Programs in American and International Universities.** 4th ed., rev. Los Angeles: National Education Standards, 1983. 124p.

760.   Gourman, Jack. **The Gourman Report: A Rating of Graduate and Professional Programs in American and International Universities.** 2d ed., rev. Los Angeles: National Education Standards, 1982. 163p.

761.   Conference Board of Associated Research Councils. **An Assessment of Research-Doctorate Programs in the United States.** 5 vols. Washington, D.C.: National Academy Press, 1982.

Most students and faculty members are interested in how their department compares with others in their field in terms of academic excellence. A number of attempts have been made to survey the leading universities and to rate the best of them. The pioneer surveys were Allan M. Cartter's *An Assessment of Quality in Graduate Education* and Kenneth D. Roose and Charles J. Andersen's *A Rating of Graduate Programs.* There have also been ratings of individual disciplines and professions. Most of the earlier surveys were peer ratings by faculty and professional workers around the country. Such ratings presented obvious problems of reliability. The three surveys listed above combine peer rating with certain objective measures, such as size of library, research grants awarded, faculty publications, number of degrees granted, and difficulty of admission. Individual disciplines and programs are rated. Other ratings of individual disciplines and professional schools may be found through *Education Index* (entry 709) under "Colleges and Universities — Accreditation" and "Higher Education — Evaluation" or through *Current Index to Journals in Education* (entry 708) and *Resources in Education* (entry 752) under "Institutional Evaluation," "College Programs," and "Graduate Study." Also check *Comparative Guide to American Colleges for Students, Parents, and Counselors* (entry 726) for the largest colleges and those most difficult to get into.

TESTS

762. **Mental Measurements Yearbook.** Edited by Oscar Buros. 1st-7th eds. Highland Park, N.J.: Gryphon, 1938-72; 8th ed. Lincoln, Nebr.: University of Nebraska Press, 1978.

763. **Tests in Print III: An Index to Tests, Test Reviews, and the Literature on Specific Tests.** Edited by James E. Mitchell, Jr. Lincoln, Nebr.: Buros Institute of Mental Measurements, University of Nebraska-Lincoln, 1983. 714p.

Questions on educational and psychological tests come mainly from graduate students and faculty in connection with their research. The need may be for information about a specific test or, more often, for information on what tests are available to measure for a specific trait or achievement. The eight editions of *Mental Measurements Yearbook* (*MMY*) include critical reviews of educational and psychological tests and bibliographies of writings about them. Early editions are not superseded by later editions. *Mental Measurements Yearbook* can be machine searched back to 1977 through BRS. *Tests in Print III* lists 2,672 tests available (in 1983) from the publisher. Brief data are furnished for each test: age of applicability, and reference to earlier Buros Institute publications and other sources of descriptive and evaluative information. Tests are arranged alphabetically, but there is an index of tests included in this volume and also out-of-print tests described in *Tests in Print II* (1974) and editions of *MMY*. There is also a Classified Subject Index (e.g., achievement batteries; neuropsychological; personality; vocations) to enable the reader to locate tests of a particular type. A further aid for persons interested in tests of particular types are the collections of tests from the various *Mental Measurements Yearbooks* republished in the following books: *English Tests and Reviews; Foreign Language Tests and Reviews; Intelligence Tests and Reviews; Mathematics Tests and Reviews; Personality Tests and Reviews* and *Personality Tests and Reviews II; Reading Tests and Reviews* and *Reading Tests and Reviews II; Science Tests and Reviews* and *Science Tests and Reviews II; Social Studies Tests and Reviews;* and *Vocational Tests and Reviews.*

764. **ETS Test Collection.** Princeton, N.J.: Educational Testing Service. Microfiche.

This is a collection on microfiche of published and unpublished tests. *MMY*, on the other hand, refers to various tests, but does not reproduce the tests themselves. Tests in this collection are indexed by title, subject, and author in the accompanying *Tests in Microfiche, Annotated Index* (Princeton, N.J.: Educational Testing Service, 1975-).

765. Borich, Gary D., and Susan K. Madden. **Evaluating Classroom Instruction: A Sourcebook of Instruments.** Reading, Mass.: Addison-Wesley, 1977. 496p.

766. Chun, Ki-Taek, and others. **Measures for Psychological Assessment: A Guide to 3,000 Original Sources and Their Applications.** Ann Arbor, Mich.: Survey Research Center of the Institute for Social Research, The University of Michigan, 1975. 664p.

There are a number of guides to tests for particular purposes. These are two of the more comprehensive and more general of such guides, which are more selective and more descriptive than *MMY* and *TIP III* (entries 762 and 763).

SCHOLARSHIPS, FELLOWSHIPS

767. Feingold, S. Norman, and Marie Feingold. **Scholarships, Fellowships, and Loans.** Volume 7. Arlington, Mass.: Bellman, 1982. 796p.

768. **Financial Aids for Higher Education.** 1983 Catalog by Oreon Keeslar. Dubuque, Iowa: William C. Brown, 1983.

769. **The College Blue Book. 19th Edition. Scholarships, Fellowships, Grants, and Loans.** New York: Macmillan, 1983. 763p.

With the rising and sometimes prohibitive costs of higher education today, most students and prospective students want to know what financial help is available and what scholarships and loans they might qualify for. These guides not only list thousands of scholarships and other types of financial aid, but for ease of searching also group them by subject field or eligibility requirement. The Feingold volume has a Vocational Goals Index, listing the scholarships, fellowships, and loans by subject field. *Financial Aids for Higher Education* has an opening section in which qualifying questions are asked, e.g., "Are you a member of one of these clubs or organizations?" or "Are you descended from one of these races, nationalities, or ethnic groups?" *The College Blue Book* lists scholarships and other forms of aid under more than one hundred specific subject fields.

CERTIFICATION

770. Burks, Mary P., ed. **Requirements for Certification for Elementary Schools, Secondary Schools, Junior Colleges.** Chicago: University of Chicago Press, 1935- . Annual.

Students about to graduate and looking for a position in elementary-secondary teaching want to know the requirements for certification in the different states. In this book, formerly edited by Elizabeth H. Woellner, are described the certification requirements for all school levels in every state, including the requirements for counselors, school librarians, and administrators.

OCCUPATION AND CAREER GUIDANCE

771. U.S. Department of Labor. Bureau of Labor Statistics. **Occupational Outlook Handbook.** Washington, D.C.: Government Printing Office, 1945- . Biennial.

Material is needed to help many students select a career or occupation. Students leaving college often do not have the same career goals they had when entering as freshmen. For general information on employment opportunities, educational or training requirements, and other aspects of any profession or occupation, this is the first place to look. Although the handbook is updated every two years, data on employment prospects and salaries must be treated with reserve.

772. Goodman, Leonard H. **Current Career and Occupational Literature, 1973-79.** 2 vols. New York: Wilson, 1978-80.

773. Goodman, Leonard H. **Current Career and Occupational Literature, 1982.** New York: Wilson, 1982. 195p.

774. **NVGA Bibliography of Current Career Information.** 1978 ed. Edited by E. Weinstein. Washington, D.C.: National Vocational Guidance Association, 1978. 152p.

775. Schuman, Patricia G., Sue A. Rodriguez, and Denise M. Jacobs, eds. **Materials for Occupational Education: An Annotated Source Guide.** 2d ed. New York: Neal-Schuman, 1983. 384p.

Further information on specific occupations and careers can be found in the pamphlets and leaflets in the bibliographies by Goodman and the National Vocational Guidance Association and by contacting the eight hundred publishers, associations, research centers, and other sources of curriculum and training materials described in detail in *Materials for Occupational Education.*

STUDY ABROAD

776. Garraty, John A., Lily von Klemperer, and Cyril J. H. Taylor. **The New Guide to Study Abroad: Summer and Fall Programs for High School Students, College and University Students, and Teachers.** 1981/82 ed. New York: Harper & Row, 1981. 464p.

777. **Study Abroad: International Scholarships; International Courses.** Paris: UNESCO, 1948- . Biennial.

778. **U.S. College-Sponsored Programs Abroad: Academic Year.** Edited by Gail A. Cohen. New York: Institute of International Education, 1983. 206p. (The Learning Traveler, vol. 1).

779. **Vacation Study Abroad.** Edited by Gail A. Cohen. New York: Institute of International Education, 1983. (The Learning Traveler, vol. 2). 183p.

For those students who would like to supplement or continue their study by attending a college in another country, the information provided in these guides is important. The colleges and universities in each country which have programs for American students are listed with data on courses or programs offered, language of instruction, fees and other costs, and whether credit may be used toward a degree in an American college. *U.S. College-Sponsored Programs Abroad* is limited to those foreign study programs which do carry credit through an American college. Its companion guide, *Vacation Study Abroad*, is limited both to programs giving American college credit and to those offered during the summer term. Data on tuition and living costs are very subject to change and should be read thus.

780. **Teaching Abroad.** Edited by Barbara C. Conotillo. New York: Institute of International Education, 1984. 160p. Paper.

This guide, similar to the ones listed above, offers data on opportunities for teaching abroad at the elementary and higher levels. Organizations, U.S. and foreign, which offer such teaching-abroad opportunities are listed under broad geographic areas. Information includes the type and level of teaching, requirements, language of instruction, salary and other benefits, and how to apply. Some data on teaching abroad are also offered in *The New Guide to Study Abroad* (entry 776).

781. **Directory of Resources for Cultural and Educational Exchanges and International Communication: List of Contacts in U.S. Government Agencies and Non-Profit Organizations.** Washington, D.C.: United States International Communication Agency (USICA), 1979. 103p.

If satisfactory information has not been found in the preceding guides by the person wishing to study, teach, or do research in a foreign country, this directory lists agencies and organizations which offer or have an interest in foreign cultural and educational exchange programs.

782. Eisenberg, Gerson G. **Learning Vacations.** 4th ed. Princeton, N.J.: Peterson's Guides, 1982. 264p.

A variety of opportunities in the United States and abroad combining learning experiences with recreation are described by type: college campus programs, travel programs, archaeological excavations, backpacking, sailing, and wilderness programs, etc. Some of the programs offer college credit. There are two indexes, by sponsor and by location.

783. **ISS Directory of Overseas Schools, 1981/82.** Princeton, N.J.: International Schools Services, 1981- . Annual.

784. **Schools Abroad of Interest to Americans.** 5th ed. Boston: Porter Sargent, 1982. 520p.

The two directories listed here are for families considering a position or extended stay abroad. They list elementary and secondary schools in foreign countries established for educating children of American families living abroad or accepting such students. Schools on military bases are not included. *Schools Abroad of Interest to Americans* has selected post-secondary and specialized educational programs as well as elementary and secondary schools.

PSYCHOLOGY

GUIDES, BIBLIOGRAPHIES, INDEXES

785. McInnis, Raymond G. **Research Guide for Psychology.** Westport, Conn.: Greenwood, 1982. 604p. (Reference Sources for the Social Sciences and Humanities, 1).

Of the several guides to the reference and research material in psychology currently available, this is unquestionably the best. It describes thoroughly more than 1,000 reference works on psychology or on related fields which include psychology. Following a section on general reference sources applying to the whole field, there are chapters on different subfields of the discipline.

786. Reed, Jeffrey G., and Pam M. Baxter. **Library Use: A Handbook for Psychology.** Washington, D.C.: American Psychological Association, 1983. 137p. Paper.

This is a less-ambitious guide to the literature of psychology, but a very useful one for beginning students. It has chapters on selecting a research topic, finding pertinent material in the library catalog, and using abstracting and citation indexes like *Psychological*

Abstracts (788), *Current Index to Journals in Education* (708) and *Resources in Education* (752), *Sociological Abstracts* (814), *Social Sciences Citation Index* (699), *Mental Measurements Yearbook* (762), and others. There is also information on doing a computer search and on getting material through interlibrary loan.

787. **Contemporary Psychology: A Journal of Reviews.** Washington, D.C.: American Psychological Association, 1956- . Monthly.

Reviews of selected new books on psychology and related fields make up the entire contents of this journal. The books selected for review and the reviews themselves represent the scholarly and research side of the discipline, rather than its popular side. Each issue includes full reviews of 50 to 60 titles, plus short notices of others.

788. **Psychological Abstracts.** Arlington, Va.: American Psychological Association, 1927- . Monthly. Cumulated author and subject indexes, quarterly and annually.

Psychology is considered by many to be the "hardest" of the social sciences, that is, the most rigorous and closest to the natural sciences. This characteristic is reflected in the excellence of some of its reference sources, like *Psychological Abstracts* and the handbooks and annual reviews of new and recent research described below (entries 796-98). In *Psychological Abstracts* are published the abstracts of all important books, periodical articles, conference papers, and other writings. These abstracts are full and detailed, written by the authors of the books and articles or by knowledgeable researchers for the PSYCINFO database. Their publication here is usually within six months to a year after the publication of the book or article abstracted. The organization of abstracts is under 16 broad subfields: e.g., experimental psychology, physiological psychology, experimental social psychology. Author and subject indexes in each issue cumulate quarterly and annually. The subject index is very precise and detailed. If *Psychological Abstracts* seems difficult to some users, it is because of the immense amount of material abstracted, but machine searching back to 1967 is possible on the PSYCINFO database through BRS, DIALOG, and SDC.

DICTIONARIES, ENCYCLOPEDIAS

789. Statt, David. **A Dictionary of Human Behavior.** London: Harper & Row, 1981. 132p.

790. English, H. B., and A. C. English. **A Comprehensive Dictionary of Psychological and Psychoanalytical Terms: A Guide to Usage.** New York: McKay, 1958. 594p.

791. **The Encyclopedic Dictionary of Psychology.** Edited by Rom Harré and Roger Lamb. Cambridge, Mass.: MIT Press, 1983. 718p.

792. White, Owen R., comp. and ed. **A Glossary of Behavioral Terminology.** Champaign, Ill.: Research Press, 1971. 220p. Paper.

Here are four good dictionaries of psychology, psychiatry, and behavioral science, serving different needs. The first is best adapted to the needs of beginning students. It defines or identifies about 1,300 terms, concepts, abbreviations, and persons prominent in the development of psychology. Entries are selected from those encountered most often in introductory texts; definitions and explanations are clear and helpful to the novice. *A Comprehensive Dictionary of Psychological and Psychoanalytical Terms* is, despite its age, still a standard dictionary of the discipline. It attempts to include "all terms frequently used in a special or technical sense by psychologists" at the time the dictionary was compiled. *The Encyclopedic Dictionary of Psychology* is midway between a dictionary and an encyclopedia of psychology, with a strong tendency toward the latter. Articles of 100 to 1,500 or more words, signed and with a bibliography, on all aspects of the subject make up the dictionary. It includes the practical applications of psychology and "fringe" psychology outside the academic psychological professions. *A Glossary of Behavioral Terminology*, which is directed to research interests, serves a somewhat different need. It includes only 1,000 or fewer terms (English and English has about 10,000 terms but no proper names), but it furnishes full and technical definitions of these. It has much information on statistical measures and many graphs and drawings.

793. **Encyclopedia of Psychology.** Edited by H. J. Eysenck. 3 vols. New York: Herder & Herder, 1972.

794. Goldenson, Robert M. **The Encyclopedia of Human Behavior: Psychology, Psychiatry, and Mental Health.** 2 vols. Garden City, N.Y.: Doubleday, 1970.

For a fuller treatment of a topic in psychology, one of these encyclopedias can be used. The first emphasizes theoretical and applied psychology (which are the focus of this section), rather than psychiatry, but many of its articles are little more than dictionary definitions. Goldenson's work, on the other hand, is heavy on psychiatry and clinical method and describes illustrative cases of mental and behavioral disorders. It is included in this section because it also has short articles on psychological terms and concepts and on persons who figured in the history of psychology as a discipline, and because it often summarizes research findings on topics of interest.

795. Bugelski, B. Richard, and Anthony M. Graziano. **Handbook of Practical Psychology.** Englewood Cliffs, N.J.: Prentice-Hall, 1980. 296p.

This handbook is included with the encyclopedias because it has short articles, alphabetically arranged, defining, discussing, evaluating, and assessing such psychological topics as "ability and capacity," "accidents and accident proneness," "achievement tests," "adaptation and sensory adjustments," "addiction," and others. It is adapted more to the undergraduate student than to the advanced research worker.

HANDBOOKS, REVIEWS

796. Eysenck, Hans J. **Handbook of Abnormal Psychology.** 2d ed. London: Pitman, 1973. 906p.

797. Lindzey, Gardner, and Elliot Aronson. **The Handbook of Social Psychology.** 2d ed. Reading, Mass.: Addison-Wesley, 1968. 819p.

Here, too, the resemblance of psychology to the hard sciences is seen in the publication of handbooks which summarize current and recent research. These are two such handbooks, each with chapters on specific research areas written by specialists. They are very useful to the student in outlining present knowledge and research conclusions.

798. **Advances in Experimental Social Psychology.** New York: Academic Press, 1964- . Annual.

799. **Annual Review of Psychology.** Stanford, Calif.: Annual Reviews, 1950- . Annual.

The function of this type of publication is similar to that of the handbook, but, because they are published annually, these books can review the recent research on more specific areas of current interest. Examples of the chapters, written by specialists, in recent volumes of these series are "Hormonal Influences on Memory," "Thinking and Concept Formation,"

"Verbal and Nonverbal Communication in Deception," and "Predictability and Human Stress."

BIOGRAPHY

800.   **APA Membership Register.** Washington, D.C.: American Psychological Association, 1967- . Annual.

The latest register (1984) lists over 58,000 fellows, members, and associates with their address and telephone number. Special lists at the end of the volume include rosters by membership in the different divisions of the American Psychological Association, a roster of diplomates in the American Board of Professional Psychology, and the taxonomy of psychological specialties and other fields.

17

SOCIOLOGY, SOCIAL WORK

To attempt to place any of the academic disciplines into a neat compartment with well-defined boundaries is frustrating, if not foolhardy. This is especially true of sociology, the newest of the social sciences, emerging as a separate discipline in the first half of the nineteenth century. It concerns itself with the ways in which social groups are formed, its leaders are identified, its members controlled by rules of the group, changes occur in social structure, social communication is effected, social mobility is possible, and related questions. Demography (the study of population) and vital statistics may be considered a part of sociology. Social work, the professional field closely associated with sociology and with education, addresses itself to correcting social ills and to aiding the poor, the handicapped, alcoholics, drug addicts, criminals, and other classes unable, without help, to sustain themselves as useful members of society. Library of Congress classification schedules significantly call this field "social pathology." Sociology is a scientific discipline that seeks to find out why and how things happen in a society and to formulate laws governing social behavior; social work is a profession with the mission of ameliorating or eliminating substandard social conditions and of helping the socially disadvantaged. Both fields are included in this chapter.

As in all areas of reference service in the academic library, most of the questions connected with sociology and social work arise either from research interests of the faculty and advanced graduate students or from curricular needs of students and the teaching faculty. For members of the faculty, the most recent available statistics on population, poverty, unemployment, housing, and other social indicators are often needed. Recent legislation, congressional committee hearings, government regulations, and court decisions are also very important. Since both statistical and legislative research may present difficulties, it is here that the faculty member may most often want help from the librarian. Questions of bibliographic identification and verification, information about recent books and articles, and directory information are also needed, but for such kinds of information, the experienced faculty member is more likely to do his or her own searching.

For students, the typical information needs involve finding appropriate materials for term papers, locating a specific book or article, and finding a general encyclopedia article on a topic or a definition of a term.

The twentieth century has seen an ever increasing concern with social problems and their correction; this trend is particularly evident in efforts to promote equal opportunities and rights for minority groups. These overdue concerns have resulted in many information needs and in new kinds of reference sources to answer them. The reference librarian must be alert to these developing interests and to new reference books in these areas.

There are few bibliographies and other reference books on the field of sociology as a whole. But, besides the guides to the research literature of sociology and social work described below (entries 801-2), see the guides to the literature of the social sciences in chapter 15.

GUIDES, BIBLIOGRAPHIES, INDEXES

801. Bart, Pauline, and Linda Frankel. **The Student Sociologist's Handbook.** 3d ed. Glenview, Ill.: Scott, Foresman, 1981. 249p. Paper.

Because the intended audience of this book is the beginning student, it may be of less use in reference work than some other books. It lists and annotates about five hundred journals, reference books, government publications, statistical compendia, and other sources for the student writing a paper or doing research in the field. Many of these are general indexes and reference sources, and some introductory information is given on writing the paper and using the library.

802. Conrad, James H. **Reference Sources in Social Work: An Annotated Bibliography.** Metuchen, N.J.: Scarecrow, 1982. 201p.

A number of the 656 citations in this guide are to general sources useful to social workers, such as *Current Index to Journals in Education, Readers' Guide to Periodical Literature*, and Gale's *Directory of Special Libraries and Information Centers.* The largest portion of the guide, however, is on particular areas of the profession, e.g., family planning; mental health; suicide. Appendixes list social work journals, social service agencies, and social work libraries. The latter are listed first by state, later by special area (aging, drug abuse, etc.). Separate indexes are provided for authors, titles, and subjects.

803. **International Bibliography of Sociology.** London: Tavistock, 1951- . Annual.

For current publications on sociology, this is the most comprehensive bibliography. It is one of four annual bibliographies sponsored by UNESCO in order to correct a serious gap, which existed in the early 1950s, in the coverage of the social sciences. The others cover social and cultural anthropology, economics, and political science, and are included in the chapters on those subjects. These annual bibliographies are useful in identifying a book, document, or article from a country having a modest publication program, since these citations are usually elusive. The International Committee on Social Science Information and Documentation, operating under the sponsorship of UNESCO, invites each country to submit a list of its important books, journal articles, reports, and government publications on sociology published during the year. Items are arranged under a classification, which is summarized in the front of the volume. An author index and separate subject indexes in English and French are at the end of the volume. Current volumes list more than 6,000 items annually.

804. **C.R.I.S. The Combined Retrospective Index Set to Journals in Sociology 1895-1974.** Edited by Annadel N. Wile and Arnold Jaffe. 6 vols. Washington, D.C.: Carrollton Press, 1978.

All articles on sociology and anthropology from 531 selected English language journals from their inception to 1974 are brought together in this bibliography. Articles are arranged under broad fields, e.g., anthropology; applied sociology; culture; death and death rates; institutions. Within broad groups, titles are arranged alphabetically under key words. Volume 6 is an index of authors. Other sets in the *C.R.I.S.* series are on history (entry 1114) and political science (entry 1005).

805.   **Contemporary Sociology: A Journal of Reviews.** Washington, D.C.: American
        Sociological Association, 1972- . Six issues per year.

More than four hundred reviews of books on sociology are listed per year in this journal.
There are also critical review articles in each issue, making it a useful source for keeping up
on current monographs. Although not as extensive in its coverage as *International
Bibliography of Sociology* (entry 803), it includes all of the most important current books on
sociology in English.

806.   Schlachter, Gail A., and Donna Belli. **Minorities and Women: A Guide to Reference
        Literature in the Social Sciences.** Los Angeles: Reference Service Press, 1977.
        349p.

Still more restricted is this and the several following bibliographies on subdivisions of
sociology and social work. *Minorities and Women* includes annotated citations for 738
reference books in English on the major ethnic minority groups in America and on women.

807.   Buenker, John D., and Nicholas C. Burckel. **Immigration and Ethnicity: A Guide to
        Information Sources.** Detroit: Gale, 1977. 305p.

808.   Kolm, Richard. **Bibliography of Ethnicity and Ethnic Groups.** Rockville, Md.: National
        Institute of Mental Health, Center for Study of Metropolitan Problems, 1973.
        250p.

809.   Miller, Wayne C. **A Comprehensive Bibliography for the Study of American Minorities.**
        2 vols. New York: New York University Press, 1976.

Minority groups in America and their acculturation and assimilation into society form the
content of these three bibliographies. *Immigration and Ethnicity* does not include material
on blacks and the American Indian, partly because of other bibliographies available about
them and partly because they are not immigrants to the United States. These two large
ethnic groups are included in the other two bibliographies. Kolm's work is the smallest of the
three with approximately 1,700 entries, 450 of which are annotated. *A Comprehensive
Bibliography for the Study of American Minorities* is the largest with nearly 30,000 entries for
books, pamphlets, and articles on minority peoples in America, whether immigrants,
persons brought in as slaves, or native Americans. Primary arrangement is by the part of the
world from which they came to America and by ethnic or national group; secondary
arrangement is by format of publication and subject.

810.   Kline, Paula. **Urban Needs: A Bibliography and Directory for Community Resource
        Centers.** Metuchen, N.J.: Scarecrow, 1978. 257p.

The subtitle of this book is partially misleading since it is not a directory. It is an annotated
bibliography of information sources (including directories) on community and economic
development, employment, housing, laws and legal services, education, etc.

811.   Gilmartin, Kevin J., and others. **Social Indicators: An Annotated Bibliography of
        Current Literature.** New York: Garland, 1979. 123p.

Social indicators research is a relatively young science, starting only in the late 1960s. It
endeavors to identify quantifiable factors to measure the level of social well-being (e.g.,
Gross National Product, employment, income, crime, housing, air pollution, and health) and
to assess the results of social programs. This bibliography of works published after 1972
acts as a supplement to *Social Indicators and Societal Monitoring: An Annotated
Bibliography*, by L. D. Wilcox and others (San Francisco: Jossey-Bass, 1972). Gilmartin's
book is arranged by broad subjects, such as Overviews; Theoretical Approaches;

Methodological Approaches; Examples of Indicators in Use. The six bibliographies that comprise entries 806-11 are examples of the many bibliographies covering a single branch or aspect of one of the social sciences. Others, as needed, may be found by consulting Eugene P. Sheehy and others, comps., *Guide to Reference Books*, 9th ed. and supplements (Chicago: American Library Association).

812. **Annual Review of Sociology.** Palo Alto, Calif.: Annual Reviews, 1975- . Annual.

For a review of recent and contemporary research in sociology and its related fields, this publication, like its counterparts in psychology and many other sciences (see entries 798-99), is authoritative, well known, and much needed. Each volume includes chapters by specialists on different aspects of sociological research. These are presented under several categories (e.g., Institutions; Social Processes; Urban Sociology; The Individual and Society; Demography). At the end of each chapter, there is a bibliography of the recent noteworthy books, reports, and periodical articles on the subject. The topics of the review articles vary from year to year, but each volume includes a cumulative index of titles and authors of chapters in earlier volumes, facilitating the location of a review of research on a specific subject.

813. Abramson, Harold J. **Index to Sociology Readers, 1960-1965.** 2 vols. Metuchen, N.J.: Scarecrow, 1973.

This index (vol. 1, *Authors*; vol. 2, *Subjects*) to all the articles in 227 sociology readers published between 1960 and 1965 is a useful addition to the meager bibliography of the field. Ideally, the editors of these readers selected the outstanding writings on different sociological topics or invited a specialist to contribute an original article to their reader.

814. **Sociological Abstracts.** San Diego, Calif.: Sociological Abstracts, 1952- . Bimonthly.

For most sociologists and graduate students in sociology, this is the most important of the general bibliographic tools. It abstracts each year about 10,000 journal articles, 100 monographs, and 1,000 conference papers from various sociological association meetings in the United States and abroad. Additionally, it indexes without abstracts about 6,000 book reviews. The main part of each issue consists of the abstracts of journal articles, grouped in large subject divisions to facilitate regular reviewing of the literature of a particular branch of sociology (e.g., sociological theory; social structure; industrial sociology; interaction of groups). A separate section of each issue lists book reviews and abstracts books. Most issues are accompanied by a supplement outlining the activities of the International Sociological Association and abstracting the papers of a sociological conference such as the American Sociological Association, the Pacific Sociological Association, or the Society for the Study of Social Problems. The sixth issue contains the cumulated indexes of subjects, authors, and journal issues indexed in the volume. *Sociological Abstracts* can be machine searched back to 1963 through BRS and DIALOG.

815. **Social Work Research and Abstracts.** New York: National Association of Social Workers, 1965- . Quarterly.

Social workers find this service very pertinent to their interests. It abstracts more than 1,700 articles annually and presents them under broad subjects such as Community Organization; Psychology and Social Psychology; Mental Health; Family and Child Welfare; Casework. The fall issue also carries abstracts of doctoral dissertations on social work completed during the year. The final issue has the cumulated author and subject indexes. The title change in 1977 (formerly *Abstracts for Social Workers*) shows more concern for abstracting dissertations and other original research in the field.

816.   **Human Resources Abstracts.** Beverly Hills, Calif.: Sage, 1975- . Quarterly.

This and the three following journals publish abstracts in more limited areas of sociology and social work than the two preceding sources. Books, official publications, and journal articles on the labor market, income distribution, social problems, health services, and other subjects of interest to the social worker and to legislators trying to deal with poverty and unemployment are abstracted in *Human Resources Abstracts.* Approximately one thousand abstracts and about two hundred related citations without abstracts are published per year. *PHRA* and *Poverty and Human Resources* are earlier titles.

817.   **Rehabilitation Literature.** Chicago: National Easter Seal Society, 1940- . Bimonthly.

Each issue has articles on the rehabilitation of handicapped and injured persons plus about one hundred abstracts of articles. In addition to literature on rehabilitation of crippled children and adults, the original scope of this journal, it now includes literature on rehabilitation of the deaf, blind, burn victims, alcoholics, aged persons, and others needing therapy.

818.   **Women Studies Abstracts.** Rush, N.Y.: Rush, 1972- . Quarterly.

All aspects of the women's movement, women's rights, problems of adjustment for the single or divorced woman, and similar topics are covered in this journal. It no longer abstracts but lists about three thousand books and articles and more than four hundred book reviews per year. There is no cumulated index for the year.

819.   **Population Index.** Princeton, N.J.: Office of Population Research, School of Public Affairs, Princeton University, and Population Association of America, 1935- . Quarterly.

Population world-wide, its changes, and vital statistics are the focus of this index. Besides articles in each issue, recent books and articles are listed with brief annotations or contents notes. Most of the listed items are in English or another European language, a few important publications in an Asian language. The index is arranged by broad subject with sections at the end on professional conference proceedings, new periodicals, official statistical publications, and machine-readable data files on population. Author and geographical indexes are cumulated for the year.

DICTIONARIES, ENCYCLOPEDIAS

820.   Hoult, Thomas F. **Dictionary of Modern Sociology.** Totowa, N.J.: Littlefield, Adams, 1969. 408p.

821.   Theodorson, George A., and Achilles G. Theodorson. **A Modern Dictionary of Sociology.** New York: Crowell, 1969. 469p.

If only a short definition of a term is wanted, either of these dictionaries, though old, is useful. Each has several thousand terms used in sociological writing: e.g., deference behavior, deferred gratification pattern, demographic transition, goal attainment, government graphic rating scale, great man theory. Hoult also includes slang terms, coined terms, and others. He also includes short quotations from the literature, illustrating the term's usage.

822.   Mitchell, G. D. **Dictionary of Sociology.** Chicago: Aldine, 1968. 224p.

This is not the usual type of dictionary with brief definitions of many terms. Rather, it resembles *A Dictionary of the Social Sciences* (entry 701) in giving full discussions of a limited number of terms and concepts used in the discipline, e.g., empirical, endogamy, equilibrium, essentialism, ethnocentrism. A number of social scientists have contributed articles. Reference is frequently made to sources that furnish further discussion of these concepts. Short articles on famous sociologists are also included.

823. Williams, Vergil L. **Dictionary of American Penology: An Introductory Guide.** Westport, Conn.: Greenwood, 1979. 530p.

Articles of several pages in length make this work more of a mini-encyclopedia than a dictionary. Articles cover well-known prisons (Alcatraz; California Correctional System), associations (American Correctional Association; National Prisoners Reform Association), persons prominent in penology (David Fogel, John Keith Irwin), and topics (Attica uprising; deinstitutionalism; moral development theory). Appendixes fill much of the volume; these are directories of reform organizations, state planning agencies, and prison systems, and a long section of U.S. government statistics on crime and penology.

824. **Encyclopedia of Social Work.** 17th issue. Edited by John B. Turner. 2 vols. Washington, D.C.: National Association of Social Workers (NASW), 1977.

Except for the *International Encyclopedia of the Social Sciences*, there is no good encyclopedia for sociology. Social workers, however, have this excellent work, which is brought up to date every few years. Many of its articles are several pages in length, e.g., those on crime and delinquency, disability and physical handicap, vocational rehabilitation, family breakdown, halfway houses, migrant farm workers. Interspersed are many shorter biographical articles on prominent social workers, past and present. There are also statistical tables on social work and demography at the end of the second volume.

825. **Encyclopedia of Crime and Justice.** Edited by Sanford H. Kadish. 4 vols. New York: Free Press, 1983.

Professors and other specialists on criminology and law have written the approximately three hundred articles in this encyclopedia. Articles (e.g., Abortion; Accomplices; Actus Reus; Adultery and Fornication; Adversary System; Age and Crime) are replete with legal citations, discuss the past and current legal attitude toward various criminal offenses, and have bibliographies.

826. **Harvard Encyclopedia of American Ethnic Groups.** Edited by Stephen Thernstrom, Ann Orlov, and Oscar Handlin. Cambridge, Mass.: Harvard University Press, 1980. 1076p.

Articles in this encyclopedia on more than one hundred ethnic groups living in the United States summarize their culture, education, and socioeconomic life in America.

DIRECTORIES

827. Kruzas, Anthony T., comp. and ed. **Social Service Organizations and Agencies Directory: A Reference Guide to National and Regional Social Service Organizations Including Advocacy Groups, Voluntary Associations, Professional Societies, Federal and State Agencies, Clearing Houses and Information Centers.** Detroit: Gale, 1982. 525p.

The most comprehensive directory of social service organizations is this work by Anthony Kruzas. Its breadth is indicated in the lengthy subtitle. Some 6,700 organizations and bodies of interest in social work are listed under 47 headings, e.g., child welfare; civil rights; death and dying; family planning; nursing homes; speech defects. In its arrangement and in the data given for each entry, it resembles Gale's other excellent and much-used directory,

Encyclopedia of Associations. The address, telephone number, name of director, date of founding, number of members and staff, and a summary of its mission or purpose, its publications and its other activities are included in the brief description. The name and keyword of title index so useful in *Encyclopedia of Associations* is also provided here.

828. **National Directory of Private Social Agencies.** Compiled and edited by Helga B. Croner. Queens Village, N.Y.: Croner, 1964- . Looseleaf.

About 15,000 private social agencies, organizations, and homes are listed by state. Only the address is given. An index of agencies by type of service (e.g., adoption, alcoholism, elderly persons, homemaker services, legal services, transients, battered persons) is in the front of the volume. A good feature of this directory, since the latest data are usually wanted, is its updating by monthly inserts.

829. National Association of Social Workers. **Directory of Agencies: U.S. Voluntary, International Voluntary, Intergovernmental.** Washington, D.C.: The Association, 1980. 104p.

Information on the programs and purposes of over three hundred agencies offering aid to disadvantaged persons and other services of concern to social workers is given in this directory.

830. **Social Service Organizations.** Edited by Peter Romanovsky and Clarke A. Chambers. 2 vols. Westport, Conn.: Greenwood, 1978. (The Greenwood Encyclopedia of American Institutions, no. 2).

The principal interest in this work, as in other volumes of the series, is in the historical background of the institutions listed, some of which are no longer in existence. Some two hundred organizations are described with information on their founding and subsequent history, their leaders, structure, and important activities. Sources of further information about each organization are also listed. Appendixes group organizations by function, religious affiliation, and date of founding (earliest was the American Seamen's Friend Society, founded in 1825). A fourth appendix gives changes of name, mergers, and dissolutions.

831. Schmidt, Alvin J., and Nicholas Babchuk, eds. **Fraternal Organizations.** Westport, Conn.: Greenwood, 1980. 410p. (The Greenwood Encyclopedia of American Institutions, no. 3).

Some of the more than 450 organizations described in this book are benefit societies such as the Croatian Fraternal Union of America and the Loyal Christian Benefit Society, formed originally to provide life insurance and burial services for members. Others are secret societies, such as Masons and Elks. But service organizations (Kiwanis, Rotary), patriotic organizations (American Legion, Daughters of the American Revolution), and college fraternities are not included.

832. Barkas, J. L. **The Help Book.** New York: Scribner's, 1979. 667p.

The Help Book is a directory of federal, national nongovernmental, and state agencies arranged under 52 sections applying to different social needs and groups, e.g., adoption, aging, alcoholism, animal rights, battered adults, childbearing, consumer affairs. To each of these sections is added a list of important books and magazines for further information.

833. Johnson, Willis L., ed. **Directory of Special Programs for Minority Group Members.** 3d ed. Garrett Park, Md.: Garrett Park, 1980. 612p.

834. Cole, Katherine, ed. **Minority Organizations: A National Directory.** Garrett Park, Md.: Garrett Park, 1982. 814p. Paper.

Directories of services and organizations founded to benefit certain minority groups and other special groups are also important to have in the reference collection. The first work listed above presents the data by type of program available to minority group members: educational and employment assistance, career counseling, college financial aid. The other work gives brief information (address, telephone number, activities) on more than 2,700 organizations that were founded by minority groups or to benefit them. An additional number of such groups are listed by name only. There are indexes by geography and by function or subject.

835. **Women Helping Women: A State-by-State Directory of Services.** New York: Women's Action Alliance, 1981. Distributed by Neal-Schuman. 179p.

Agencies for battered women/rape victims, career counseling, displaced homemakers, planned parenthood, etc., are listed by state and city.

836. Norback, Craig, and Peter Norback. **The Older American's Handbook.** New York: Van Nostrand, Reinhold, 1977. 310p. Paper.

The book lists government and private programs, agencies, and important publications in 34 subject areas of interest to older persons: e.g., legal services, recreation, friendly visiting.

837. American Foundation for the Blind. **Directory of Agencies Serving the Visually Handicapped in the United States.** 22d ed. New York: The Foundation, 1984. 547p. Paper.

838. **International Directory of Services for the Deaf.** Edited by Steve L. Mathis, III. Washington, D.C.: International Center on Deafness, 1980. 231p. Paper.

Directories like these list many national, state, and local services (such as schools, financial agencies, and libraries) helping these handicapped persons.

839. **The Directory for Exceptional Children: A Listing of Educational and Training Facilities.** 10th ed., 1984-85. Boston: Porter Sargent, 1984. 1428p.

About 3,000 schools and other training institutions are grouped by type of disability they serve: learning disabled, emotionally disturbed and socially maladjusted, autistic, mentally retarded, deaf, blind, and others. Information on each facility includes services, size of staff, enrollment, tuition, and other useful data.

840. **Alcoholism and Drug Abuse Treatment Centers Directory.** Santa Monica, Calif.: Ready Reference Press, 1981. 350p.

Data given here are minimal: name of agency, address, and telephone number. Centers are listed by state and city.

841. **Directory of Social and Health Agencies of New York City, 1981-1982.** 63d ed. Edited by Nancy Lecyn and William P. Germano. New York: Published for the Community Council of Greater New York by Columbia University Press, 1981. 614p.

842.   **Social Service Directory, Metropolitan Chicago, 1980.** Chicago: Comprehensive Community Services, 1979. 338p. plus appendixes and indexes, 181p.

843.   **Crisis Bulletin — Emergency After-Hours Facilities.** Los Angeles: Information and Referral Service of Los Angeles County, 1979. 95p.

Large cities have directories of social service agencies in their own area. These are useful, even in libraries not located in these areas. *Crisis Bulletin* lists facilities in Los Angeles County that are open evenings and weekends.

844.   Aptakin, Karen, ed. **Good Works: A Guide to Social Change Careers.** Washington, D.C.: Center for the Study of Responsive Law, 1980. 289p. Paper.

The purpose of this directory is to furnish information for persons interested in working in this field. Short profiles are given of nine individuals in social change careers, detailing what they do, what they like about their work, and how they got into it. The profile section is followed by a directory of 275 organizations with date of founding, purpose, activities, budget, size of staff, hours of work week, and starting salary. Typical of the organizations are American Indian Law Center, Audubon Naturalist Society, Bread for the World, and Campaign for Political Rights.

STATISTICAL AND OTHER DATA

Research in the social sciences makes frequent use of statistical data. The multitude of statistical reports, the difficulty of finding them when they have been issued by relatively unknown governmental agencies, nonprofit groups, and other non-trade publishers, and the problem of finding data that give the specific type of information needed often make research workers, who normally find their own information, seek the help of a librarian. Widely believed sayings like "You can prove anything with statistics" and titles of books like *How to Lie with Statistics* are true only for readers who are careless and unknowledgeable about statistical data, their collection, and their use. The careful researcher and librarian pay very close attention to the methods that were used in compiling statistics, the definition of terms and units of measurement that were used in their presentation, and the limitations of the data. While these precautions are needed in the interpretation and use of any research report, they are especially necessary when using statistical data. Usually the most recent figures are wanted, but the user will often have to be satisfied with data several years or more old and make due allowances for their age. The number and variety of statistical compilations available make it impossible to give more than a small selection here of the most general collections and certain compilations on special subjects that exemplify the different kinds there are and the different types of bodies that issue them. Often the librarian will have to use guides to reference sources, indexes to statistical sources, and other aids to locate data of a particular kind that may be needed. Some of the more general compilations and indexes to statistics have already been described in chapter 5.

845.   United Nations. Statistical Office. **Compendium of Social Statistics.** 2d ed. New York: United Nations, 1980. 1325p.

The several statistical compilations published by the United Nations Statistical Office are very useful for data on foreign countries. *Statistical Yearbook* has been described above (entry 169) and is usually the first place to look for statistical data on a foreign country or for comparative data on several countries. For statistics on basic social indicators not found there, this compendium can be tried. It has detailed tables on population, health conditions, food consumption, housing, education, labor force, etc., for member countries.

846. U.S. Department of Commerce. Bureau of the Census. **Social Indicators III: Selected Data on Social Conditions and Trends in the United States.** Washington, D.C.: Government Printing Office, 1980. 585p. Paper.

This is a similar publication on social indicators in the United States. Its statistics cover population, health and nutrition, housing, social security and welfare, and other indicators of the social well-being of the nation.

847. United Nations. Statistical Office. **Demographic Yearbook.** New York: United Nations, 1948- . Annual.

Population and vital statistics are among those most often wanted by sociologists. Summary figures on population and vital statistics of foreign countries are in *Compendium of Social Statistics* (entry 845), but much more detail and more current data are found in this yearbook. Each volume since 1948 makes intense study of a single aspect (e.g., census, mortality, natality, population trends, marriage and divorce) while giving summary statistics of the other aspects. The half title lists the special subjects of previous yearbooks, while the cumulative subject index in the back of each volume covers the tables of earlier volumes. Explanatory material, as in other United Nations publications, is in both French and English.

848. U.S. Department of Commerce. Bureau of the Census. **Demographic Estimates for Countries with Population of 10 Million or More: 1981.** Washington, D.C.: Government Printing Office, 1981. 169p. Paper.

This work presents the most recent data available for 56 countries on their population in 1950 and each five-year period since then, supplemented by projected estimates to 1981. The source of data and the method used to derive estimates are given in footnotes for each country.

849. Nortman, Dorothy L., and Joanne Fisher. **Population and Family Planning Programs: A Compendium of Data through 1983.** 12th ed. New York: Population Council, 1984. Paper.

International data on population and family planning are given in this booklet. Demographic, social, and economic data are presented for different countries and a description of their efforts and activities toward population control and family planning.

850. McEvedy, Colin, and Richard Jones. **Atlas of World Population History.** London: Penguin, 1978. 368p.

For each country a graph is given showing population from 400 B.C. to 1975 and projected to the year 2000. Where hard data are not available (and that is often), estimates are used. Rounded population figures are given for separate points in time 200 years apart up to 1000 A.D., 100 years apart until 1500, then 50 years apart. Each graph is accompanied by explanatory text. This is a good source for showing the overall trend of population in a given country.

851. United Nations. Statistical Office. **Compendium of Housing Statistics.** 3d issue. New York: United Nations, 1980. 354p.

Data on housing conditions in various countries are given in this useful compilation. Tables are by country, displaying such information as population, number of households, number of dwellings, size of dwellings, number of persons per dwelling, availability of water, electricity, and toilets in dwellings. If available, comparative data are given for a country in approximately 10-year periods since 1960 to show how much improvement in housing conditions has been made, if any, over that period.

852. National Criminal Justice Information and Statistics Service. **Sourcebook of Criminal Justice Statistics.** Washington, D.C.: U.S. Law Enforcement Assistance Administration, 1973- . Annual.

The primary goal of this sourcebook is to collect and publish nationwide statistical data on criminal justice. There are many statistics here that are not found anywhere else, including estimates of unreported crimes, the attitude of people toward crime (analyzed by demographic characteristics of respondents), and characteristics of persons arrested for crime. Many tables give comparative data by state, some by major city.

853. **Uniform Crime Reports.** Washington, D.C.: Federal Bureau of Investigation, 1930- . Annual.

Statistical analyses are given on crimes reported during the past year. Breakdowns are by state, city, and type of crime. Among the useful tables is one giving the number of crimes of different types reported on university and college campuses. Since information is obtained by questionnaire from local enforcement agencies, there may be some discrepancy in what is reported, despite efforts for standardized reporting. Many states offer detailed statistics of crime in the state, compiled by their law enforcement department. Such publications may be obtained for the library's own state.

854. **Sourcebook on Aging.** 2d ed. Chicago: Marquis Academic Media, 1979. 539p.

This work is prepared in four parts. The first and second parts are state-of-the-art descriptions of selected readings and legislation on aging. The other two parts are more useful in reference work. Part 3 is statistical data: population and vital statistics of the elderly population with special emphasis on the black elderly. The final section, "Resources," has lists of books, periodicals, and organizations pertaining to study of the elderly.

855. Converse, Philip E., and others. **American Social Attitude Data Sourcebook, 1947-1978.** Cambridge, Mass.: Harvard University Press, 1980. 441p. Paper. Spiral binding.

856. Gallup, George H. **The Gallup Poll: Public Opinion, 1935-1971.** 3 vols. New York: Random House, 1972. Reprint. Wilmington, Del.: Scholarly Resources, 1978.

857. Gallup, George H. **The Gallup Poll: Public Opinion, 1972-1977.** 2 vols. Wilmington, Del.: Scholarly Resources, 1978.

858. Gallup, George H. **The Gallup Poll: Public Opinion, 1978-** . Wilmington, Del.: Scholarly Resources, 1979- . Annual.

859. Gallup, George H. **The Gallup International Public Opinion Polls: Great Britain, 1937-1975.** 2 vols. New York: Random House, 1976.

860. Gallup, George H. **The Gallup International Public Opinion Polls: France, 1939, 1944-1975.** 2 vols. New York: Random House, 1976.

861. Hastings, Elizabeth H., and Philip K. Hastings, eds. **Index to International Public Opinion, 1978/79-** . Prepared by Survey Research Consultants International. Westport, Conn.: Greenwood, 1980- . Annual.

Although public opinion polls and surveys are neither as sophisticated nor as reliable as carefully gathered statistics, there is a great amount of interest in their results. Here are seven collections of survey result data. The first book is the most restricted in content, but it covers attitudes on the national economic outlook and on government spending as well as on social issues. The other works have much on political, economic, and social issues.

BIOGRAPHY

Information about people in sociological research or in the social work profession is not needed nearly as often as bibliographic, directory, or statistical data. Sociologists who have made some notable contribution are the subjects of articles in *The International Encyclopedia of the Social Sciences* (see entry 703) and its predecessor, *Encyclopedia of the Social Sciences.* Notable social workers, past and present, are included in *Encyclopedia of Social Work* (see entry 824). Living sociologists who have made important contributions in the field are included in *American Men and Women of Science: Social and Behavioral Sciences* (entry 706). Brief data can be found for living sociologists and social workers who are not included in those more selective sources in the following membership directories. The membership directory of a professional society is a good source to try for minimal data when a name cannot be found elsewhere. If nothing else can be found, it is a help to verify the correct spelling of the name and the person's current professional affiliation. Membership directories are often updated annually.

862.   American Sociological Association. **Directory.** New York: The Association, 1950- . Annual.

The current edition of this directory lists about 14,000 members. Only the address, current position, education, and area of specialization are given for each member. The list is alphabetical, but at the end of the directory there is a geographical list of members and a list by area of specialization.

863.   National Association of Social Workers. **NASW Directory of Professional Social Workers.** Washington, D.C.: The Association, 1978. 1733p.

Similar professional data are given for the 78,000 members listed alphabetically here. No geographical list nor list by area of specialization is given, however. Approximately 9,000 members who are in clinical social work are also listed in *NASW Register of Clinical Social Workers* (3d ed., 1982), as well as being included in this larger membership directory.

18

ANTHROPOLOGY

Anthropology has two major divisions: physical anthropology, allied to biology and geology, and social anthropology, related to the social sciences. Physical anthropology is not part of this chapter. Within the discipline of social, or cultural, anthropology, scholars are not in agreement on the precise division and definition of subject fields, but in general it consists of ethnography, the description of individual cultures or ethnic groups; ethnology, the comparative and theoretical study of cultures; archaeology; and linguistics, the science of language, man's supreme cultural achievement. Folklore is a closely allied field, encompassing knowledge transmitted orally, before the adoption of a written tradition, and arts (folk dance, music, games, etc.) learned by imitation.

Anthropology does not elicit a large number of reference questions in the average university library. Most of the interest in the field is from a small number of faculty members and their students. It is seldom a large department. What anthropologists lack in numbers, however, they are apt to make up in interest. Undergraduate term papers are done only occasionally in anthropology. The most popular subfields are archaeology and folklore. Interest in classical archaeology will be shown by faculty and graduate students in the Classics Department, itself not a large department. As is true in most subjects, this relatively small number of reference questions in anthropology is reflected in fewer reference tools than are available in other fields. There is, for example, no adequate guide to anthropological literature as a whole. There is no who's who or other biographical dictionary for anthropologists, and they are no longer represented in *American Men and Women of Science: Social and Behavioral Sciences.* If this chapter appears to be thin compared to other chapters, it is not because of lack of interest by the authors but rather because of a relative lack of good reference tools.

In listing and describing reference books under the various divisions by type, the following order is observed: anthropology in general, ethnic groups, archaeology, linguistics, and folklore. Material on minority groups in the United States and their social problems is included in chapter 17, "Sociology, Social Work." Ethnographic studies of peoples and tribes are represented in this chapter.

GUIDES, BIBLIOGRAPHIES, INDEXES

There is no satisfactory guide to the literature of anthropology as a whole. The best general sources of the reference literature of the subject are found in White's *Sources of Information in the Social Sciences* (entry 695), approximately 350 items, and the more recent and more selective *Social Science Reference Sources*, by Li (entry 697), 30 books and 10 periodicals.

864. Harvard University. Peabody Museum of Archaeology and Ethnology. Library. **Catalogue.** 53 vols., 51 reels. Boston: G. K. Hall, 1963. Supplement 1, 12 vols., 24 reels. 1970. Supplement 2, 5 vols., 8 reels. 1971. Supplement 3, 7 vols., 14 reels. Supplement 4, 7 vols. 1979.

The catalog of this library, now named the Tozzer Library, is the best general bibliography of anthropology. The main strength of the library is in American archaeology and ethnology, but all subfields of contemporary anthropology are covered. The staff of Tozzer Library indexes some 1,200 journals currently received, and these cards, as well as those for books and pamphlets in the library, are included. The catalog is kept up-to-date regularly by supplements, the latest in 1979. With the fourth supplement, the entire catalog includes more than 430,000 entries. This is an excellent source for bibliographic verification of an older reference or for finding references under a subject.

865. **International Bibliography of Social and Cultural Anthropology.** London: Tavistock; Chicago: Aldine, 1958- . Annual.

Similar to the *International Bibliography of Sociology* (entry 803), this includes material from most countries of the world. Physical anthropology and archaeology are covered selectively, but the emphasis is on social and cultural anthropology. About 6,500 selected items per year are listed in classified arrangement. All formats are represented, but most are books and articles from an estimated six hundred journals.

866. **Anthropological Literature: An Index to Periodical Articles and Essays.** Compiled by Tozzer Library, Peabody Museum of Archaeology and Ethnology, Harvard University. South Salem, N.Y.: Redgrave, 1979- . Quarterly.

867. Museum of Mankind Library. **Anthropological Index to Current Periodicals.** London: Museum of Mankind Library, 1963- . Quarterly.

868. **Abstracts in Anthropology.** Farmingdale, N.Y.: Baywood, 1970- . Quarterly.

Current anthropological literature is very thoroughly covered by the preceding annual bibliography and these three quarterly indexes. The best is *Anthropological Literature*, listing more than 10,000 journal articles and papers from Festschriften and other scholarly collections each year. It has annual cumulated indexes by author, archaeological site and culture, ethnic and linguistic group, and geography. *Anthropological Index to Current Periodicals*, compiled by the Museum of Mankind Library of London (formerly the Royal Anthropological Institute of Great Britain and Ireland Library), has about 9,000 references per year drawn from some 900 journals. Items are arranged by world region. There is an annual author index. It would be expected that there is a considerable overlap in the journals indexed by these two sources, but each covers a surprising number of journals not in the other. *Anthropological Index to Current Periodicals* is more prompt in indexing than *Anthropological Literature*. Approximately 4,000 abstracts from some 165 journals in *Abstracts in Anthropology* are arranged in four major divisions: cultural anthropology, linguistics, archaeology, and physical anthropology. Most entries are journal articles, bulletins, and reports of local societies and nearly all are in English. One value of this quarterly is in indexing of sources that are not widely available and which might go unnoticed but for their being abstracted here.

869. **Reviews in Anthropology.** South Salem, N.Y.: Redgrave, 1974- . Quarterly.

Scholarly book reviews of four or five pages or more form the only contents of this quarterly. About 50 books on anthropological subjects are reviewed in a year, and there is an annual author-title-reviewer index.

870. Fürer-Haimendorf, Elizabeth von, comp. **An Anthropological Bibliography of South Asia.** 3 vols. Paris: Mouton, 1958-70.

871. Murdock, George P., and Timothy J. O'Leary. **Ethnographic Bibliography of North America.** 4th ed. 5 vols. New Haven, Conn.: Human Relations Area Files, 1975.

872. O'Leary, Timothy J. **Ethnographic Bibliography of South America.** New Haven, Conn.: Human Relations Area Files, 1978. 414p. Paper.

873. Theodoratus, Robert J. **Europe: A Selected Ethnographic Bibliography.** New Haven, Conn.: Human Relations Area Files, 1969. 544p.

These works are typical of the scholarly bibliographies on the tribes of different continents or regions. Such bibliographies, which are usually not annotated, cover cultural, social, and other aspects of life in the tribe.

874. Hirschfelder, Arlene B., Mary G. Byler, and Michael A. Dorris. **A Guide to Research on North American Indians.** Chicago: American Library Association, 1983. 330p.

875. Haas, Marilyn L. **Indians of North America: Methods and Sources for Library Research.** Hamden, Conn.: Library Professional Publications, 1983. 163p.

876. Hodge, William. **A Bibliography of Contemporary North American Indians.** New York: Interland, 1976. 310p.

A number of bibliographies about the American Indian have been published in recent years. *A Guide to Research on North American Indians* lists approximately 1,100 books, articles, government documents, and other English language publications, with extensive annotations. Entries are arranged under broad fields, e.g., archaeology and prehistory; land tenure and resources; federal and state Indian relations; economic aspects; warfare patterns. This useful bibliography has an author-title index and an index of small subjects. *Indians of North America* is prepared for the beginning student-researcher and has a long introductory section on the use of the library and of general indexes, handbooks, dictionaries, government documents, and other reference tools. A second section lists about one hundred books under broad subjects, such as agriculture, alcohol, archaeology, art, and artifacts. These books have lengthy annotations. The final section lists some two hundred books, without annotations, under the names of individual tribes. Hodge's book studies the contemporary Indian in general terms and arranges its 2,600 entries (books, pamphlets, bulletins, periodical articles) under subjects without separation by tribe. Examples of the subject divisions are history, material culture, social organization, migration patterns, city living, and economics.

877. Heizer, Robert F., Thomas R. Hester, and Carol Graves. **Archaeology: A Bibliographical Guide to the Basic Literature.** New York: Garland, 1980. 434p.

This guide was prepared for professional archaeologists and their students. More than 4,800 books, periodicals, and chapters and papers in collected works on archaeology are included; they cover the background, field work, analysis of finds, dating methods, and other aspects of archaeological research.

878. Rice, Frank A., and Allene Guss. **Information Sources in Linguistics: A Bibliographical Handbook.** Washington, D.C.: Center for Applied Linguistics, 1965. 42p.

Rice and Guss have prepared a guide similar to entry 877 on archaeology for those entering the field of linguistics and language behavior. More than five hundred information sources are listed; these have only very brief annotations or no annotation.

879. Permanent International Committee of Linguists. **Bibliographie linguistique de l'année ... et complément des années précédentes. Linguistic Bibliography for the Year ... and Supplement for Previous Years, 1939/1947- .** The Hague: Nijhoff, 1948- . Annual.

880. **LLBA: Language and Language Behavior Abstracts.** San Diego, Calif.: Sociological Abstracts, 1967- . Quarterly.

The current literature of linguistics is well covered in these two indexes. More than 12,000 items per year (books, periodical articles, Festschriften, etc.) are included in the first index. Besides references on linguistics and its subfields, there are items on the many individual languages of the world, such as dictionaries, word frequency counts, grammars, and other language-related books and articles. But this bibliography is slow in appearing, about five to six years after the literature it covers. *LLBA* is another aid for linguistic researchers, with an approximate seven thousand abstracts per year of articles in the 1,500 journals covered. Annual indexes of authors and of subjects are provided. *LLBA* can be machine searched back to 1973 through BRS and DIALOG.

881. Brunvand, Jan H. **Folklore: A Study and Research Guide.** New York: St. Martin's, 1976. 144p.

This excellent guide to the study of folklore has sections on the composition and subdivisions of folklore, its reference works, and preparation of the research paper. The middle section is a bibliographic essay evaluating the reference works, journals, histories, surveys, and other materials needed by the folklorist.

882. Flanagan, Cathleen C., and John T. Flanagan. **American Folklore: A Bibliography, 1950-1974.** Metuchen, N.J.: Scarecrow, 1977. 406p.

This is the best and most recent bibliography on American folklore available. It brings more than 3,600 books and articles together under broad classification by type: "Festschriften, Symposia, Collections," "Bibliography, Dictionaries, Archives," "Folklore: Study and Teaching," "General Folklore," "Ballads and Songs," "Tales and Narrative Material," etc.

883. Haywood, Charles. **A Bibliography of North American Folklore and Folksong.** 2d rev. ed. 2 vols. New York: Dover, 1961.

Although it is now quite out of date, this bibliography still has usefulness because of the great wealth of items (earlier than 1951) on the folklore and folksongs of North America. Recordings and collections of songs are listed as well as books and periodical articles. Volume 1, which is about non-Indian settlers north of Mexico, has sections on regional bibliography, ethnic bibliography, and occupational bibliography (cowboy, lumberjack, hobo, and railroad songs and folklore). Volume 2 is about the folklore and folksongs of the American Indian. No new material has been added to the original (1951) edition, but errors of that edition have been corrected, and an index of composers, arrangers, and performers of the folksongs was added.

884. Cleveland Public Library. John G. White Department. **Catalog of Folklore and Folk Songs.** 2 vols. Boston: G. K. Hall, 1964.

The private library of John G. White, a Cleveland attorney, was bequeathed in 1928 to the Cleveland Public Library. The total collection covers the fields of folklore, Orientalia, and chess. This catalog is limited to the 25,000 titles pertaining to folklore and folksong of all lands, which are listed under one or more of 150 subject headings.

885.   Thompson, Stith. **Motif-Index of Folk Literature: A Classification of Narrative Elements in Folk-Tales, Ballads, Myths, Fables, Mediaeval Romances, Exempla, Fabliaux, Jest Books, and Local Legends.** Rev. and enl. ed. 6 vols. Bloomington, Ind.: Indiana University Press, 1955-58.

886.   Baughman, Ernest W. **Type and Motif-Index of the Folktales of England and North America.** The Hague: Mouton, 1966. 606p. (Indiana University Folklore Series, no. 20).

Motifs (or themes) found in folktales of various lands are indexed by Thompson in an elaborate classification: mythological motifs, animals, tabu, the dead, ogres, etc. Examples of individual motifs are "Culture hero tames sea monster," "Sight of mermaid bathing makes man immortal," "Tabu — eating certain parts of animals," and "Parrot unable to tell husband details as to wife's infidelity." Collections of folk tales which are indexed in this work are listed in the front of volume 1. If a particular motif is being searched, it will usually be easier to locate it through the synopsis of the classification at the beginning of volume 1; a more detailed synopsis precedes each section. Some might prefer to seek a particular motif in the alphabetical index at the end of volume 6. Baughman's work, modeled on the preceding one, is limited to folktales of England and North America. See also *A Dictionary of British Folk-Tales in the English Language* (entry 899).

887.   Hand, Wayland D., Anna Cassetta, and Sondra Thiederman, eds. **Popular Beliefs and Superstitions: Folklore from the Ohio Collection of Newbell Niles Puckett.** 3 vols. Boston: G. K. Hall, 1981.

This work has a use similar to that of a motif-index. It is a reprint of a card collection of more than 70,000 folk beliefs compiled by Puckett, Professor of Sociology at Western Reserve University until 1965, from field interviews which he made throughout Ohio and from oral and printed sources. The folk sayings and beliefs are arranged in a classified order, e.g., "Birth, Infancy, Childhood: Birthmarks: The mother's preoccupation with food and drink;" "Physical Characteristics: Bodily Attributes: The Life Span, Longevity: Body traits as indicators of a long life"; "Domestic Economy: Household Activities: Eating Utensils: Beliefs about forks and spoons." The classification is laid out in detail in the contents. Volume 3 has an alphabetical subject index and an ethnic finding list of beliefs by ethnic source: Acadian French, African, Albanian, American Indian.

DICTIONARIES, ENCYCLOPEDIAS

888.   Winick, Charles. **Dictionary of Anthropology.** New York: Philosophical Library, 1956. Reprint. Westport, Conn.: Greenwood, 1970. 579p.

There are few reference works that cover the whole field of anthropology. This work, despite its age, is the most comprehensive dictionary with brief definitions of an estimated 7,500 to 8,000 technical and common terms, e.g., marriage-beena; maschalismos; mating; mermaid; mesological; labial click; cliffhouse; ground, happy hunting; group, blood.

889.   **Encyclopedia of Anthropology.** Edited by David E. Hunter and Phillip Whitten. New York: Harper & Row, 1976. 411p.

Articles varying in length from a brief definition to a four-page discussion are presented in this work. Terms, customs, artifacts, concepts, and persons well known in anthropology make up the estimated 1,400 articles. The encyclopedia has many illustrations, diagrams, and maps. There is little here on archaeology, but below (entries 892-96) we describe several dictionaries and encyclopedias of archaeology. *The International Encyclopedia of the Social*

Sciences (entry 703) has 151 articles on anthropology and anthropologists, another 14 on archaeology and archaeologists, 12 on linguistics, and 11 on societies.

890.   Leitch, Barbara A. **A Concise Dictionary of Indian Tribes of North America.** Algonac, Mich.: Reference Publications, 1979. 646p.

891.   Weekes, Richard V., ed. **Muslim Peoples: A World Ethnographic Survey.** Westport, Conn.: Greenwood, 1978. 546p.

There are several sources for easy identification of American Indian tribes. The best is Hodge's *Handbook of American Indians North of Mexico* (entry 907), not only because it identifies more tribes than any other source, but also because of its "Synonymy" at the back of volume 2, which lists the tribes under many variant names. For present day tribes living in the United States and Canada, *A Concise Dictionary of Indian Tribes of North America* is the best source since it gives up-to-date information on population, location, and bibliography and gives more information on the tribe than Hodge gives. About three hundred tribes are listed alphabetically, giving population in early years and in 1970, location, language, culture, life, fate, and a short bibliography. There are maps of regions, language groups, culture groups, and Indian reservations, lands, and communities. *Muslim Peoples* similarly describes Muslim groups of 100,000 population or larger around the world. Articles and their statistics are prepared by specialists who have studied the group.

892.   Champion, Sara. **A Dictionary of Terms and Techniques in Archaeology.** New York: Facts on File, 1980. 144p.

Several very adequate dictionaries and encyclopedias of archaeology are described immediately below, and these include articles on techniques, analyses, and methods used in the science. Champion's dictionary is also up-to-date, reflects the many recent changes and innovations (e.g., false color infra-red photography, fishbone analysis, fission track dating, flot, flotation, fluorine test), and has clear explanations with diagrams and illustrations. Names of cultures and artifacts are not included in the more than 3,000 entries.

893.   Whitehouse, Ruth D., ed. **The Facts on File Dictionary of Archaeology.** New York: Facts on File, 1983. 597p.

894.   **The Illustrated Encyclopedia of Archaeology.** Edited by Glyn Daniel. New York: Crowell, 1977. 224p.

The Facts on File Dictionary of Archaeology (English edition, *The Macmillan Dictionary of Archaeology*) includes some 3,500 terms, sites, techniques and methods, and personal names associated with archaeology. Definitions are clear and useful to both the amateur and the professional archaeologist. It has some line drawings and diagrams. *The Illustrated Encyclopedia of Archaeology* has many more black-and-white illustrations, but only about half as many (approximately 1,700) articles. Both works are very useful in the university library.

895.   **The Cambridge Encyclopedia of Archaeology.** Edited by Andrew S. Sherratt. New York: Crown, 1980. 495p.

896.   **Larousse Encyclopedia of Archaeology.** Edited by Gilbert Charles-Picard. Translated from the French by Anne Ward. New York: Putnam, 1972. 432p.

For certain kinds of information, these encyclopedias are better because they are organized in chapters rather than alphabetically by term, name, or topic. Chapters are on the science and methods used in archaeology, and on archaeology in different parts of the world and different ages of man, from the Ice Age to recent centuries. Both encyclopedias are very well illustrated, but *The Cambridge Encyclopedia of Archaeology* has more on continents other than Europe, has more diagrams, plans, and maps, and is more up-to-date in this rapidly changing field. Both encyclopedias have bibliographies for further study and detailed indexes.

897. Stillwell, Richard, William L. McDonald, and Marian H. McAllister, eds. **The Princeton Encyclopedia of Classical Sites.** Princeton, N.J.: Princeton University Press, 1976. 1019p.

For a recent description of an archaeological site of the classical world, this encyclopedia provides brief information on the location of the site, the present status, who is conducting the research, important finds, and a brief bibliography about the dig. Approximately three thousand sites are described, representing cultures from the mid-eighth century B.C. to about 600 A.D. and in extent from Alexander's farthest penetration into India to the northern and western boundaries of the Roman Empire. There are no illustrations, but 15 regional maps locate the sites.

898. **Funk & Wagnalls Standard Dictionary of Folklore, Mythology, and Legend.** Rev. ed. Edited by Maria Leach and Jerome Fried. New York: Funk & Wagnalls, 1972. 1236p.

For the fascinating, but diverse and loosely organized, field of folklore, this dictionary is indispensable and should be in every reference librarian's repertoire. Its estimated five thousand alphabetically arranged articles cover gods, heroes, mythological beings, folk songs, folk dances, folk games, objects figuring in magic, superstition, and folklore, and important scholars in folklore. Sample entries are: glass mountain, Glusgabe, gnome, goat, goat dance, goat that flagged the train, gobadan, goblin, shoes, shmoo, turmeric, turquoise, twins. The table of contents lists 55 longer survey articles. This one-volume edition differs little from the two-volume edition of 1949-50. A new feature of this edition is the key at the end of the volume to the 2,405 countries, regions, cultures, cultural areas, peoples, tribes, ethnic groups, and major world religions presented or discussed in the articles.

899. Briggs, Katharine M. **A Dictionary of British Folk-Tales in the English Language.** 2 vols. in 4. Bloomington, Ind.: Indiana University Press, 1970-71.

Although concerned with British folktales, this definitive collection has a wider use than that implies, since many of these tales have migrated from the Continent or farther. Tales are arranged by type (e.g., fairy tales, jocular tales, nursery tales, tales about black dogs, Beauty and the beast, the man from the gallows) within two large divisions: folk narratives, which were told for entertainment but not actually believed, and folk legends, which were believed to be true. This is a scholarly achievement, giving data on the source and variants of the tales as well as summaries. There are indexes of tale types and of story titles. Thompson (entry 885) does not give summaries of tales, but does index collections.

900. **The Oxford Dictionary of English Proverbs.** 3d ed. Revised by F. P. Wilson. Oxford, England: Clarendon Press, 1970. 930p.

901. Taylor, Archer, and Bartlett J. Whiting. **A Dictionary of American Proverbs and Proverbial Phrases, 1820-1880.** Cambridge, Mass.: The Belknap Press of Harvard University Press, 1967. 418p.

Proverbs are part of folk wisdom, and these are two of the many dictionaries of these sayings, complete with references to printed sources. In the Oxford dictionary, as in the *Oxford English Dictionary*, printed sources of the proverbs are listed in chronological order.

DIRECTORIES

902. **Fifth International Directory of Anthropologists.** Chicago: University of Chicago Press, 1975. 496p.

Anthropologists from all countries which cooperated by returning the requested data (China and the U.S.S.R. did not) and from various subfields of anthropology are represented among the approximately five thousand entries in this directory. Brief biographical notes accompany most names. In a separate list are the names of 369 anthropologists who did not return information to the editor. The several interesting divisions of the names include a geographical index, a chronological index (denoting the era of anthropological interest, not the age, of each person), and an index of subject interest. The American Anthropological Association also publishes directories of anthropologists and of anthropological institutions irregularly in its journal, *Current Anthropology.*

903. American Anthropological Association. **Guide to Departments of Anthropology.** Washington, D.C.: The Association, 1962- . Annual.

Institutions having a department of anthropology are listed alphabetically under "Academic Departments," "Museum Departments," or "Research Departments." For each academic department are listed members of the faculty and staff, degrees offered, number of students, special programs and activities, requirements for the degree(s), and graduate student financial support available. Similar information is given for museum and research departments. At the end of the directory are additional lists of the number of degrees held by faculty and staff members and their source, the number of students enrolled, Ph.D. degrees granted, topics of dissertations completed in the previous year, and an index of individuals.

HANDBOOKS

904. Murdock, George P. **Ethnographic Atlas.** Pittsburgh: University of Pittsburgh Press, 1967. 128p.

This is not an atlas in the usual sense of a collection of maps; *atlas* also means a collection of charts or tables that systematically display a given subject. This atlas presents tables of such ethnographic characteristics as mode of marriage, family organizations, marital residence, types of kin groups, size of communities, sex taboos, and games. In each table, the practices and beliefs of 862 tribes from various parts of the world are listed for comparative study.

905. **Rand McNally Atlas of Mankind.** Chicago: Rand McNally, 1982. 191p. plus glossary and indexes.

With many maps, diagrams, and illustrations, this book describes the culture, rituals, and art of different peoples of the world. This is a very useful manual for undergraduates and the nonspecialist.

906. **Human Relations Area Files (HRAF).** New Haven, Conn.: Yale University, 1949- . In progress.

The *Human Relations Area Files* were developed at Yale University and later made available to a number of participating major universities. They are a collection of primary source materials (mostly books and articles, but also some unpublished manuscripts) on some three hundred cultures of the world. Pages from these source materials are copied and sent to subscribing libraries to be filed under culture (e.g., Kikuyu, Hottentot, Bedouin, Ute) and under aspect of cultural information as applicable (e.g., language, food quest, exchange, territorial organization, kin groups, religious beliefs). University libraries that do not have the

HRAF Paper Files can subscribe to *HRAF-Microfiles.* Beginning in 1984, all but one of the 17 sponsoring university libraries have gone to *HRAF-Microfiles* instead of *Paper Files.* Use of *HRAF* can be for the study of a particular culture (e.g., the Tuareg culture of the Middle East in all its aspects), for cross-cultural study of a particular aspect (the use of alcoholic beverage among several Middle Eastern cultures), for testing a cultural hypothesis across different cultures (to test the hypothesis that use of alcoholic beverages is more prevalent among peoples in cold climates than among those living in warm climates), and similar studies. Typical experience in large universities which have *HRAF* is that they are used intensively by a small number of faculty members and graduate students in anthropological or related research; they are not typically used by undergraduates and other groups in the university community.

907.   Hodge, Frederick W. **Handbook of American Indians North of Mexico.** 2 vols. Washington, D.C.: Government Printing Office, 1907-1910. (U.S. Bureau of American Ethnology. Bulletin 30). Reprint. New York: Pageant, 1959; Grosse Pointe, Mich.: Scholarly Press, 1968; New York: Greenwood, 1969; Totowa, N.J.: Rowman & Littlefield, 1975.

908.   **Handbook of North American Indians.** Edited by William C. Sturtevant. 20 vols. Washington, D.C.: Smithsonian Institution, 1978- . In progress.

909.   **Handbook of Middle American Indians.** Edited by Robert Wauchope. 16 vols. Austin: University of Texas Press, 1964-76.

910.   Steward, Julian H. **Handbook of South American Indians.** 7 vols. Washington, D.C.: Government Printing Office, 1946-59. (U.S. Bureau of American Ethnology. Bulletin 143). Reprint. New York: Cooper Square, 1963.

Despite the amount of research and publication now in progress on Indians of North America, Hodge's handbook continues to be an essential reference tool. Thousands of Indian villages, pueblos, tribes, chiefs, and other leaders are identified, and other articles discuss artifacts, implements, foods, customs, and other subjects in Indian life. Many articles have bibliographies and, although these are now old, they can still point to needed sources of information. The other three sets listed above are scholarly works covering the ethnology of the various tribes, linguistics, archaeology, and physical anthropology. Volumes 12-15 of the *Handbook of Middle American Indians* constitute a *Guide to Ethnohistorical Sources,* and volume 16, edited by Margaret A. L. Harrison, is an index of *Sources Cited and Artifacts Illustrated* in volumes 1-11. As volumes of the *Handbook of North American Indians* become available, the information in them will be much preferred, because of its recency, to information on the same place or tribe found in Hodge. The latter may be useful, however, for quick identification, when a large amount of information is not needed.

911.   **The Black American Reference Book.** Edited by Mabel M. Smythe. Sponsored by the Phelps-Stokes Fund. Englewood Cliffs, N.J.: Prentice-Hall, 1976. 1026p.

912.   Ploski, Harry A., and James Williams, comps. and eds. **The Negro Almanac: A Reference Work on the Afro-American.** 4th ed. New York: Wiley, 1983. 1550p.

Both are useful works, bringing together much information on blacks, their history, and contributions in the United States: a chronology of the civil rights movement; the black American worker and labor relations; the black family; blacks in art, literature, the professions, entertainment, and sport, etc. *The Black American Reference Book* is a scholarly project by a number of well-known authors. *The Negro Almanac* is the more popular work and is richly illustrated.

913. **Handbook of American Popular Culture.** Edited by M. Thomas Inge. 3 vols. Westport, Conn.: Greenwood, 1978- . In progress.

Although ethnologists formerly studied primitive societies because they were thought to be simple and to exhibit an uncomplicated cultural pattern, attention has been turned in recent decades to groups in modern urban life. This handbook of popular culture in America is a series of chapters by specialists on the culture of the automobile, comic art, detective and mystery novels, sports, film, the supernatural and occult, etc. Besides a thumbnail history of study in each area, each chapter includes discussion of the principal reference sources and periodicals, research centers, and collections.

914. Whitehouse, David, and Ruth Whitehouse. **Archaeological Atlas of the World.** London: Thames & Hudson; San Francisco: W. H. Freeman, 1975. 272p.

915. Hawkes, Jacquetta, ed. **Atlas of Ancient Archaeology.** New York: McGraw-Hill, 1974. 272p.

916. Finley, M. I., ed. **Atlas of Classical Archaeology.** New York: McGraw-Hill, 1977. 256p.

Articles on some three thousand archaeological sites of the classical world are found in *The Princeton Encyclopedia of Classical Sites*, described above (entry 897). These atlases are similar to it in use, but present information on the sites through maps and plans rather than in descriptive articles. The *Archaeological Atlas of the World* has more than one hundred maps, each locating archaeological sites of a particular type or culture or noted for some special discovery: e.g., "Neandertal Fossils," "Post-glacial Hunters and Gatherers in Europe," "Pre-dynastic Egypt," "Rock-cut Tombs in Europe," "Neolithic Sites in China," "The Maya and Their Predecessors." There is an alphabetical index of individual sites. *Atlas of Ancient Archaeology* describes sites occupied by earliest man up to later civilizations in Central and South America, but not including the classical world. Sites for the study of classical civilization in Asia Minor, Greece, and the Roman Empire are similarly described in Finley's *Atlas of Classical Archaeology*. In these two works, each site is illustrated with a map or ground plan accompanied by a brief description of the site and what has been found. There is no duplication of sites in these two atlases.

917. Wilson, Josleen. **The Passionate Amateur's Guide to Archaeology in the United States.** New York: Collier Books, 1980. 464p.

The introductory part of this book describes early man in the United States and his migrations. There is also information on archaeology and on visiting archaeological sites. The main part of the book is a state-by-state survey of excavation sites, their particular finds and importance, how to get there, hours, and admission.

RESEARCH

918. **Annual Review of Anthropology.** Palo Alto, Calif.: Stanford University Press, 1972- . Annual.

Like the other review series of this publisher, this annual is excellent for keeping up with the latest research and theories. Review articles, written by specialists in the field, change from year to year. Sample chapters in recent volumes include "The Anthropologies of Illness and Sickness," "Ethnographies as Texts," "Forensic Anthropology," "Slavery," and "Sociobiology: Primate Field Studies." Essays conclude with a bibliography of important publications on the subject. This series succeeds *Biennial Review of Anthropology* (Stanford, Calif.: Stanford University Press, 1959-1971).

BIOGRAPHY

There is no who's who or biographical dictionary devoted to anthropologists. Brief biographical data are given for most of the persons listed in the *Fifth International Directory of Anthropologists* (entry 902): birth date, position, institution, research interests, selected publications, and language competence. Some anthropologists are now included in the Physical-Biological Sciences volumes of *American Men and Women of Science* (entry 1269); in editions earlier than the 13th (1978), they were in the Social-Behavioral Sciences volume (entry 706). Biographical articles for 73 persons prominent in the development of anthropology are in the *International Encyclopedia of the Social Sciences* (entry 703): Franz Boas, James G. Frazer, Earnest Hooten, Bronislaw Malinowski, Edward Westermarck, etc.

19

BUSINESS, ECONOMICS

Modern economics, the study of the production, distribution, and consumption of material goods and services, is generally considered to have begun, as a social science, with the publication in 1776 of *The Wealth of Nations* by the Scottish economist, Adam Smith. Economics is the social science most closely related to business, and so the latter is included in this chapter. Business is a more popular course of study than economics, but students in each of the disciplines usually take one or more courses in the other.

In many universities the volume of questions in the joint fields of economics and business may equal that in the fields of literature, film, and education because of the large number of students working on class assignments in economics and business. In the business field, the type of assignment may be to learn as much as possible about a particular company: its history, organization, financial data, stock record, prospects for the future, etc. Questions relating to individual companies certainly rank high in the commerce division of the average university library. Another source of such questions is the interest in a company shown by investors. Some of these may be persons not on the campus. As in other subject areas, the less adequate the local public library, the more members of the community will turn to the university library and its superior resources. A second frequent reference need is for economic and social statistics. A common exercise for undergraduates in economics courses is to select several seemingly related statistical variables, to note the degree of their correlation, and to determine their relationship, if any. When a large class gets an assignment of this kind, you can expect many calls for help in finding statistical series of a certain type. Of all social scientists, economists have developed the most statistical measures and ratios, which are intended to be fair barometers of the nation's economic health and forecasters of what will happen in the near future. Just as they seek information about particular companies, investors will want these statistical measures and ratios, believed to be forecasters of the future of a company or an industry. Investors, however, will usually be already familiar with the sources of such data and will not require assistance from the librarian, unless it is to learn where such sources are shelved. Still a third popular type of question is on goverment finances and taxes. These come mostly from accounting students, especially any who are preparing for CPA examinations.

Beyond these main types of reference needs in business and economics, there are others that come up less frequently. The identification of a federal or international agency, known sometimes only by its initials, the precise meaning of a term or concept used in economics, the equivalent of an economic term in Spanish or another language are examples of these occasional needs. Not all reference questions concern the present or future of a business or of the economy. A lawyer or accountant may want to know the value of a particular stock at some earlier date, a fact needed in figuring the tax due on the estate of a deceased client. Generally, biographical and historical questions are infrequent. But identification of a living person is frequently needed. Directory questions, where all that is needed is the address, telephone number, or name of the head of a company or an agency, are not uncommon. For the faculty, who can generally find their way through the economics and business literature, the most frequent need, as we have noted repeatedly in the other disciplines, is for help in identifying a bibliographic reference. Reports, newsletters, and other forms of what are sometimes called "fugitive" publications are often wanted in the study of a company, and these are not always readily identified or found.

Fortunately, there is no shortage of bibliographies, directories, and other reference aids in the field of business. One format that is more prevalent here than in other subject areas is the looseleaf service. These are needed to inform the subscriber of statistical, legal, regulatory, legislative, or other data and changes, where the most up-to-date information possible is wanted. They are usually issued in looseleaf form on a daily or weekly basis and are understandably expensive. Many services in the investment, tax, and business fields are published by Bureau of National Affairs and Commerce Clearing House.[1] Because of the large number of reference sources available in the business field, only a selection of the most useful are included in this chapter. Although sources in business and those in economics are often similar and wanted by persons in either field, we have followed the general pattern of describing business sources first and then comparable sources in economics.

GUIDES, BIBLIOGRAPHIES, INDEXES

919. Daniells, Lorna M. **Business Information Sources.** Rev. ed. Berkeley, Calif.: University of California Press, 1985. 673p.

920. **Encyclopedia of Business Information Sources.** 5th ed. Edited by Paul Wasserman, Charlotte Georgi, and James Woy. Detroit: Gale, 1983. 728p.

Business Information Sources is an excellent guide to reference sources in accounting, management, investment, insurance, marketing, and the other subdivisions of the field. Annotations are informative and evaluative. They are arranged in broad topics, such as a type of reference need (information about companies, statistical information) or a subdivision of business (accounting, marketing). This guide is the first choice if one wants to know what a particular business reference tool or service covers or what is a good reference tool for a particular need. *Encyclopedia of Business Information Sources* would be used where information or data are needed on a specific, rather than a broad, topic. Under hundreds of specific subjects (e.g., bicycle industry, biography, boat industry, bonds, book catalogs, and business statistics) are listed information sources of different formats: encyclopedias and dictionaries, handbooks and manuals, trade associations and professional societies, periodicals, directories, statistics sources, online databases. A most useful and frequently updated guide.

921. Melnyk, Peter. **Economics: Bibliographic Guide to Reference Books and Information Sources.** Littleton, Colo.: Libraries Unlimited, 1971. 263p.

---

[1]See *Directory of Business and Financial Services*, edited by Mary M. Grant and Riva Berleant-Schiller, 8th ed. (New York: Special Libraries Association, 1984) and David M. Brownstone and Gorton Carruth's *Where to Find Business Information*, 2d ed. (New York: Wiley, 1979).

A guide to the literature of economics and its various divisions: theory, private and public finance, commerce and marketing, international economics, agricultural and land economics, and population and statistics. It annotates nearly 1,300 books and lists 170 periodicals. This guide is old but useful for pre-1970 references.

922. Harvard University. Graduate School of Business Administration. Baker Library. **Business Reference Sources: An Annotated Guide for Harvard Business School Students.** Rev. ed. Compiled by Lorna M. Daniells. Boston: Baker Library, Graduate School of Business Administration, Harvard University, 1979. 133p. (Reference List, no. 30).

Although meant for Harvard students, this is an excellent selective bibliography for anyone interested in the subject. It describes about seven hundred reference books, journals, and bulletins by type of source and type of information sought, e.g., bibliographies, indexes and abstracts, dictionaries, directories, financial sources, statistical sources, and market research sources.

923. **International Bibliography of Economics.** London: Tavistock, 1952- . Annual.

This resembles the three other parts of the *International Bibliography of the Social Sciences*, those for sociology (entry 803), social and cultural anthropology (entry 865), and political science (entry 1002). Its best feature is its worldwide coverage of economics literature, not its promptness.

924. **Directory of Industry Data Sources: The United States and Canada.** 2d ed. 3 vols. Cambridge, Mass.: Ballinger, 1982.

The purpose of this large set is to identify and describe sources of marketing and financial information for key industries in the United States and Canada. An introductory section of volume 1 covers over 2,200 general reference sources. Following this, the main part of the set describes data sources on different major industries, e.g., advertising, apparel, beverages, electric utilities, and food processing. Volume 3 has detailed indexes by SIC number, small subject, and title. The Standard Industrial Classification (SIC) was developed by the U.S. Department of Commerce and the Bureau of the Budget for use in their own statistics and publications, and is widely used by the business community and by publishers of business services. Data sources include market research reports, investment banking reports, industry statistical reports, financial/economics studies, forecasts, directories, and handbooks, among others.

925. **Business Periodicals Index.** New York: Wilson, 1958- . Monthly except August with quarterly and annual cumulation.

The principal periodical index covering business. More than three hundred English language periodicals on accounting, advertising, banking, economics, finance, marketing, and other aspects of the business field are indexed by subject. This index is easy to use and familiar to students because of their use of other Wilson periodical indexes. Book reviews, arranged by author of the book reviewed, are indexed in a separate section at the end of each issue and cumulation. This is included in the Wilsonline databases.

926. **Business Index.** Belmont, Calif.: Information Access, 1979- . Microfilm.

Many libraries have this convenient index on microfilm. More than five hundred business-related journals are indexed. Subscribers receive each month an updated cumulation of the index on a microfilm reel covering the current year and four previous years. The film is scanned in a motorized transport reader furnished with the subscription. Entries are under subject, author, company, and product in a single alphabet. If the user needs references farther back than four years, these have been transferred to microfiche, accessible in a separate reader. The same publisher issues *Magazine Index*, which covers more than 350 general periodicals on a microfilm updated monthly. Current subscription price of *Business Index* is $2,100 per year.

927. **Predicasts F & S Index: United States.** Cleveland: Predicasts, 1979- . Weekly with monthly, quarterly, and annual cumulation.

928. **Predicasts F & S Index: Europe.** Cleveland: Predicasts, 1978- . Monthly with quarterly and annual cumulation.

929. **Predicasts F & S Index: International.** Cleveland: Predicasts, 1977- . Monthly with quarterly and annual cumulation.

The former *F & S Index of Corporations and Industries* has now expanded into these three series. Since industry and company information is so important in the university library, these indexes are as important as *Business Periodicals Index* (entry 925). Each of the series has two parts: "Industries and Products," arranged by major industry groups according to SIC number, and "Companies," arranged alphabetically by the name of the company. The Europe and International series also have a section, "Countries," which lists the articles in the other two sections under country. The value of this service lies partly in its more frequent publication (for the United States series), but even more in the many financial newspapers, industry newsletters, and other special serials in this field, some in German and French, which it indexes. The three indexes are combined to form the PTS F & S INDEXES database which can be machine searched back to 1972 through BRS and DIALOG.

930. **Business Publications Index and Abstracts.** Detroit: Gale, 1983- . Monthly with quarterly and annual cumulation.

More than 650 periodicals, proceedings, and transactions in the business field are indexed. Each monthly issue is in two parts: subject and author citations, and abstracts. The citations are cumulated quarterly and annually; the abstracts, which are arranged numerically, do not require cumulation. This is a printed version of the MANAGEMENT CONTENTS database, which goes back to 1980. A retrospective cumulation of *Business Publications Index and Abstracts* back to January, 1980, is being prepared.

931. **Journal of Economic Literature.** Edited by Moses Abramovitz and others. Nashville, Tenn.: American Economic Association, 1969- . Quarterly.

This official journal of the American Economic Association is useful not only for its articles, but also for keeping current on economic literature: each issue carries reviews of approximately 40 new books, annotations on another 400 new books, a listing of the contents of some 150 new issues of journals, a classified subject listing of these articles, and abstracts of selected articles. There is an author index for the articles listed in the issue, but there is no cumulative author index or subject index for the year, making the journal difficult to use for a subject search over many volumes.

932. **Index of Economic Articles in Journals and Collective Volumes.** Prepared under the auspices of the *Journal of Economic Literature* of the American Economic Association. Edited by Naomi Perlman and Drucilla Ekwurzel. Homewood, Ill.: Irwin, 1961- . Annual.

If there is a need for searching the older literature of economics, this index will be more useful than the *Journal of Economic Literature.* Its volumes 1-7 (1961-69) cover the literature from 1886 to 1965. Since then, each volume indexes the literature of about one year, but is published about five years behind. Currently, 244 journals considered most useful to researchers and teachers of economics are indexed, plus Festschriften, conference publications, proceedings, and other collected papers. Only articles in English are indexed. Arrangement is by subject classification, followed by an alphabetical list of the articles by author. Both the index section of the *Journal of Economic Literature* (entry 931) and the *Index of Economic Articles* are included in the ECONOMIC LITERATURE INDEX database, which can be machine searched back to 1969 through DIALOG.

DICTIONARIES, ENCYCLOPEDIAS

The number of dictionaries, glossaries, and encyclopedias available for business and economics far outstrips the need. Relative to directories, indexes, and collections of statistics, these are little used. They are acquired and shelved in the reference collection, however, for their occasional need. (Also, compared to the other, more frequently used reference tools just mentioned, they are inexpensive and require little shelf space). Following our usual order of items, sources of wider scope are listed before more specialized ones, and dictionaries and encyclopedias on economics follow those on business.

933.   Rosenberg, Jerry M. **Dictionary of Business and Management.** 2d ed. New York: Wiley, 1983. 631p.

934.   Heyel, Carl, ed. **The Encyclopedia of Management.** 3d ed. New York: Van Nostrand, Reinhold, 1982. 1371p.

These cover business and management generally: accounting, advertising, marketing research, personnel management, etc. The encyclopedia (as would be expected) has lengthier discussions of topics by specialists. Although its articles are arranged alphabetically, it has lists of articles in the front of the volume grouped under broad aspects of management. The dictionary defines or identifies briefly some nine thousand terms, including names and acronyms of agencies. Its definitions are clear and specific.

935.   Shafritz, Jay M. **Dictionary of Personnel Management and Labor Relations.** Oak Park, Ill.: Moore, 1980. 429p.

Among the 2,500 entries on this aspect of management are terms, organizations, court cases, federal legislation, journals, tests, and names of persons associated with the labor movement or personnel management. Some articles ("Labor Organizations," "Test Publishers," "Tests and Testing") are actually small directories. This is a good dictionary for this subject and has many graphs and tables.

936.   Rosenberg, Jerry M. **Dictionary of Banking and Finance.** New York: Wiley, 1982. 690p.

937.   Munn, G. G. **Encyclopedia of Banking and Finance.** 8th ed., rev. & enl. Edited by F. L. Garcia. Boston: Bankers Publishing Co., 1983. 1024p.

The *Dictionary of Banking and Finance* has about 10,000 terms, names of agencies, and acronyms covering accounting, capitalization, computer systems, credit, government regulations, import-export, and other financial subjects. These are briefly, but clearly, defined or identified. The *Encyclopedia of Banking and Finance* has only one-third as many entries and, while many of these are simply brief definitions, others are lengthy articles. Its tone is practical and instructive, rather than theoretical.

938.   **Kohler's Dictionary for Accountants.** 6th ed. Edited by W. W. Cooper and Yuji Ijiri. Englewood Cliffs, N.J.: Prentice-Hall, 1983. 574p.

Terms and names of agencies that commonly occur in accounting literature are included in the entries (about 3,500) of this dictionary. Some articles are full discussions of a topic, others are brief definitions or identifications. A more elementary dictionary for those beginning in accounting is Ralph Estes's *Dictionary of Accounting* (Cambridge, Mass.: M.I.T. Press, 1981) with approximately nine thousand terms, names of agencies, and acronyms.

939.   Ross, Martin J., and Jeffrey S. Ross. **New Encyclopedic Dictionary of Business Law –
with Forms.** 2d ed. Englewood Cliffs, N.J.: Prentice-Hall, 1981. 349p.

Legal terms that are likely to be encountered in business are defined and, in some cases (e.g., "Commercial paper," "Contract," "Corporation"), discussed at length. Definitions are written for readers without legal training. Many legal forms are reprinted along with the definitions.

940.   **Trade Names Dictionary.** 3d ed. Edited by Donna Wood. 3 vols. Detroit: Gale, 1982.

Trade names and brand names are listed selectively in *Thomas's Register of American Manufacturers* (entry 951) and other reference books along with other directory information, but this dictionary, with approximately 130,000 trade names and brand names, is the most comprehensive. Trade names and company names are interfiled in volumes 1 and 2; volume 3 lists companies and the various brands they make.

941.   Greenwald, Douglas. **McGraw-Hill Dictionary of Modern Economics.** 3d ed. New York: McGraw-Hill, 1983. 632p.

942.   Moffat, Donald W. **Economics Dictionary.** 2d ed. New York: Elsevier, 1983. 331p.

943.   Nemmers, Erwin E. **Dictionary of Economics and Business.** 4th ed. Totowa, N.J.: Rowman & Littlefield, 1978. 523p.

944.   Pearce, David W. **The Dictionary of Modern Economics.** Rev. ed. Cambridge, Mass.: MIT Press, 1983. 481p. Paper.

All of these dictionaries of economics are good. A strong collection will have several of them, not only because words in some one of them are not always in the others, but also because the definition of a term or concept found in one is sometimes clearer and more satisfying than those in the others. This will be a particular asset in a field like economics, where terms and concepts are not as precisely understood as are the terms in most other business subjects. The *McGraw-Hill Dictionary of Modern Economics*, which was first published in 1965, has a good reputation among economists; although it includes only about 1,400 terms and concepts, these are the ones most frequently needing a clear definition. Reference is frequently given to other, fuller discussions of the term. Descriptions of 235 private, public, and nonprofit agencies, associations, and research organizations are in a separate section. The three other dictionaries listed above include more terms, agencies, and names of persons, but define and identify them more briefly.

945.   **Encyclopedia of Economics.** Edited by Douglas Greenwald. New York: McGraw-Hill, 1982. 1070p.

Specialists, on the invitation of editor Greenwald, have contributed articles on some three hundred subjects from "Acceleration Principle" and "Accuracy of Economic Forecasts" to "Zero Population Growth." These are fuller discussions than are found in the dictionaries and include references to books and articles about the concept. An appendix groups the articles under the different subfields of economics.

DIRECTORIES

946. **Standard and Poor's Register of Corporations, Directors, and Executives.** 3 vols. New York: Standard & Poor, 1928- . Annual.

947. **Million Dollar Directory.** 3 vols. Parsippany, N.J.: Dun & Bradstreet, 1959- . Annual.

The leading corporations in the United States, Canada, and other countries are listed in volume 1 of *Standard and Poor's Register*, with address and telephone number, names of officers and directors, principal banks and accounting and law firms, products and services, annual sales, number of employees, and divisions of the company. Subsidiary firms are listed under their own names with reference to the parent firm. In the current edition, approximately 40,000 corporations are listed. Some of these are major foreign firms. Volume 2 lists executives and directors of the corporations with minimum biographical data. The indexes in volume 3 are by SIC number and by state (or province) and major city. There is also an index of corporate families, first listing subsidiaries, divisions, and affiliates with reference to their parent company, then listing parent companies with all of their divisions, subsidiaries, and affiliates. *Million Dollar Directory* has similar data on more than 115,000 corporations in the United States having net assets of more than $500,000. They are divided among the three volumes by net worth, with those having the largest assets in the first volume. Each volume lists the companies in three ways: alphabetically, geographically by state and city, and by SIC number. The *Million Dollar Directory* can also be machine searched through DIALOG. These two directories are among the most used books in the business library because of the amount of data they include about so many companies.

948. **America's Corporate Families: The Billion Dollar Directory.** Parsippany, N.J.: Dun & Bradstreet, 1981- . Annual.

949. **America's Corporate Families and International Affiliates.** Parsippany, N.J.: Dun & Bradstreet, 1983- . Annual.

Two more Dun and Bradstreet directories of the largest corporate families. Criteria for listing in the first directory are being a parent company based in the United States or Canada and having annual sales of $50 million or more. Multi-national corporate families based in the United States or Canada and those of other countries having one or more subsidiaries in the United States or Canada are in the second directory. Both of these have data similar to that provided in *Million Dollar Directory* for parent companies, their divisions, and subsidiaries.

950. **Directory of Corporate Affiliations: Who Owns Whom.** Skokie, Ill.: National Register, 1967- . Annual with bi-monthly supplements.

A similar source of information about subsidiaries, affiliates, and their parent companies. Currently, this directory lists over 38,000 divisions, subsidiaries, and affiliates with reference to their parent company. These four thousand parent companies are listed in the first part of the directory with address, telephone number, ticker symbol and stock exchange, assets, liabilities, net worth, volume of sales, number of employees, type of business, and names of officers and directors. There is also a geographical index by state and city of parent companies, subsidiaries, divisions, and affiliates and a separate index by SIC number. Mergers, acquisitions, and name changes between 1976 and 1982 are listed in the front of the directory. The advantage that this directory has over the Dun and Bradstreet directories described above lies in its currency of information supplied through five bi-monthly supplements. Current information on mergers, reorganizations, bankruptcies, name changes, and other company changes is also obtained from the *Predicasts F & S Index* series described above (entries 927-29). Predicasts also brings this information together in its quarterly publication, *Predicasts F & S Index of Corporate Change.*

951. **Thomas's Register of American Manufacturers.** 19 vols. New York: Thomas, 1906- .
      Annual.

952. **Kelly's Manufacturers and Merchants Directory.** East Grinstead, West Sussex,
      England: Kelly's Directories, 1880- . Annual.

The principal use of *Thomas's Register of American Manufacturers* is to learn what
companies make a given product. Unlike the Standard and Poor or Dun and Bradstreet
directories, from which this information could be learned through their SIC indexes, Thomas
lists even small manufacturers. In the main part of the register, products are listed
alphabetically in detail (e.g., dials (elevator), dials (enameled), dials (fluorescent), dials
(gauge), dials (instrument), diamond compounds, diamond dust or powder, diamond powder
reclaiming). Under the product, manufacturers are listed with their address and a refinement
of the product they sell. A separate listing of companies, "Company Profiles," gives the
address, telephone number, asset rating, and names of officials. At the end of the section is
a selective "Trademark Index." But *Trade Names Dictionary* (entry 940) is more inclusive.
Kelly's Manufacturers and Merchants Directory is similar for manufacturers and merchants
of Great Britain. A selection of the exporters of other countries (those requesting to be
listed) is in a separate section.

953. Kruzas, Anthony, and Kay Gill, eds. **Business Organizations and Agencies Directory.**
      2d ed. Detroit: Gale, 1984. 950p.

A very useful directory of various associations, organizations, agencies, services, and
centers related to business and often needed by people in business. Among the 26 groups in
this directory are labor unions, Chambers of Commerce, Better Business Bureaus, U.S.
diplomatic offices in other countries, visitor and convention bureaus, business publishers,
and research centers. The introduction identifies the sources of information for each
chapter.

954. **Directory of National Unions and Employee Associations.** Washington, D.C.:
      Government Printing Office and Bureau of National Affairs, 1972- . Biennial.

Librarians and others can still get this valuable directory, thanks to the Bureau of National
Affairs, a commercial publisher. The information on unions and employee associations and
the data on their membership were formerly collected and compiled by the U.S. Bureau of
Labor Statistics, but the directory was discontinued after the 1979 edition, a victim of the
cuts in the early 1980s in government services. The Bureau of National Affairs published the
1982/83 and the 1984/85 editions and plan to continue the series. Another source of directory
and membership figures on national unions and employee associations is the *Labor
Almanac* (entry 959).

955. **Guide to Graduate Study in Economics and Agricultural Economics in the United
      States of America and Canada.** 6th ed. Edited by Wyn F. Owen and Larry R. Cross.
      Boulder, Colo.: Economics Institute, 1982. 585p.

Detailed description of the graduate programs in economics and agricultural economics at
about 275 U.S. and Canadian universities (admission requirements, faculty, resources, cost,
etc.) is followed by an analysis of the programs. A comparative table reveals different facts
about the programs viewed side by side, and the findings of recent rating studies of the
leading programs are reported.

HANDBOOKS

956. **Accountants' Handbook.** 6th ed. Edited by Lee J. Seidler and D. R. Carmichael. 2 vols. New York: Wiley, 1981.

The basic text for accountants, aiming to answer "every reasonable question on accounting and financial reporting that may be asked by accountants" and others. Specialists have contributed 45 chapters on various topics in accounting.

957. **Financial Handbook.** 5th ed. Edited by Edward I. Altman and Mary Jane McKinney. New York: Wiley, 1981. Various paging.

This is similar to *Accountants' Handbook*, with chapters by specialists on different kinds of investing, banking, overseas money and capital markets, securities and portfolio management, and various other aspects of finance.

958. **The Dow Jones-Irwin Business and Investment Almanac.** Homewood, Ill.: Dow Jones-Irwin, 1977- . Annual.

Statistical data are assembled, showing business conditions during the previous year, performance of the stock market industry by industry, financial data on the largest public and private companies, etc. There is a long introductory chronology reviewing business conditions during the previous 12 months and articles like "Executive Compensation Practices," "Taxes and Tax Sheltered Investments," and "How to Do Business with the Government."

959. Paradis, Adrian A., and Grace D. Paradis. **The Labor Almanac.** Littleton, Colo.: Libraries Unlimited, 1983. 205p.

A summary of labor history highlights, a directory of national labor organizations and statistics of membership, directories of federal and state labor agencies, identification of prominent living and deceased labor leaders, and a summary of principal laws and regulations affecting labor are among the features of this almanac.

960. **The Developing Labor Law: The Board, the Courts, and the National Labor Relations Act.** 2d ed. Edited by Charles J. Morris and others. 2 vols. Washington, D.C.: The Bureau of National Affairs for the Section of Labor and Employment Law, American Bar Association, 1983.

For a complete understanding of the National Labor Relations Act, its history and various provisions and protections as developed through legislation and court actions, this set is the standard work. It will not be used every day, but should be on hand when needed.

961. **Economic Handbook of the World: 1981- .** Edited by Arthur S. Banks and others. Published for the Center for Social Analysis of the State University of New York at Binghamton. New York: McGraw-Hill, 1981- . Annual.

This handbook has articles on the world economy in general, followed by articles on individual countries and on intergovernmental organizations. It is about two years late in appearing.

962. **World Development Report.** Published for the World Bank. New York: Oxford University Press, 1978- . Annual.

This annual also reports on the state of the world economy. It covers special problems of groups of countries (e.g., oil consuming, developing countries; oil exporting countries), but does not have articles on the individual countries. They are included, however, in the tables at the end of the report, "World Development Indicators."

963.   **Commodity Yearbook.** New York: Commodity Research Bureau, 1939- . Annual.

Articles and statistics on the world production, export, import, prices, and consumption of about one hundred commodities are included in this annual. Emphasis is on the United States.

STATISTICS

In the prefatory note at the head of this chapter, we pointed out that statistical series are very important to the economist, and that students in economics courses are assigned to study different series to estimate their relationship to one another. Statistics are also important in business and investment. The use of these economic and business statistics, whether by a student, an economist, an investor, or a government official, is almost always for the purpose of predicting what will happen in the near future. The government official and legislator are also interested in a longer economic future and whether or not it can be changed or modified. Statistics are needed on a large number of financial and economic indicators, reaching back a number of years, brought up to the most recent date possible, and broken down in a number of different analyses. Ways of measuring employment, prices, productivity, and other aspects of business and economic activity are revised from time to time in the hope of presenting more accurate and meaningful figures. Fortunately, there is no shortage of helpful statistics in these fields. *Statistical Abstract of the United States* (entry 165), *County and City Data Book* (entry 166), the decennial *Census* (entry 169), and other statistical compilations that are constantly used are described in chapter 5. Here we describe some of the series that are used primarily in economics and business.

964.   **Editor and Publisher Market Guide.** New York: Editor and Publisher, 1924- . Annual.

965.   **Survey of Buying Power.** New York: Sales and Marketing Management, 1918- . Annual.

Each of these annual surveys has the same purpose: to provide manufacturers and suppliers with an estimate of the buying potential of different communities in the United States and Canada. Each one has tables that rank all Metropolitan Statistical Areas (MSAs), leading counties, and leading cities by population, disposable personal income (personal income after taxes), total retail sales, food sales, and disposable personal income per household. The Metropolitan Statistical Area (there are currently 275 in the United States) is a concept used by the U.S. Office of Management and Budget to designate an area that includes a total metropolitan population of at least 100,000 and an urbanized area of at least 50,000 or a city with a population of at least 50,000. Other tables in these surveys rank MSAs and leading counties and cities by the amount of sales in different categories, such as apparel, food, furniture, etc. *Editor and Publisher Market Guide* also has a large section that gives data on all communities in the United States and Canada that have one or more daily newspapers. These data include location, railroads, bus lines, and airlines that serve it, population, number of households, number of passenger autos, principal industries, average climate, nature of tap water, principal shopping centers, shopping days and hours, major department stores and chain stores, and newspapers. These data are useful not only to sales forces and businesses looking for branch sites, but also to a person considering a move to a new community.

966.   U.S. Department of Commerce. Bureau of Economic Analysis. **Survey of Current Business.** Washington, D.C.: Government Printing Office, 1921- . Monthly.

967.   U.S. Department of Commerce. Bureau of Economic Analysis. **Business Statistics.** Washington, D.C.: Government Printing Office, 1932- . Biennial.

968.   U.S. Department of Commerce. Bureau of Economic Analysis. **Business Conditions Digest (BCD).** Washington, D.C.: Government Printing Office, 1972- . Monthly.

The most-used part of *Survey of Current Business* is the blue pages, "Current Business Statistics." Various statistics that measure the strength and stability of business in the United States are given for each of the previous 14 months and totals for the two previous years. Included are statistics such as personal income for the entire country and how it was used (taxes, purchases of durable and nondurable goods and services, etc.), industrial production, business inventories, sales, commodity prices, construction and real estate, domestic and foreign trade, labor force, employment, and similar data intended to show current business health in the United States. There are also detailed statistics on different industries: production, prices, exports and imports, etc. These same statistics are presented in *Business Statistics* over a longer period — the previous 4 years by month and the previous 22 years by year. *Business Conditions Digest* is a similar production, but its focus is more on long range economic trends. Certain economic time series have been found to lead, coincide with, or lag behind cyclical economic movements. These are called "cyclical indicators" and include such statistical series as employment and unemployment; production and income; consumption, trade, orders, and deliveries; fixed capital investment; inventories; stock and commodity prices; and money and credit. Graphs and tables of these time series over a number of past years are presented in *Business Conditions Digest* as an aid to estimating and predicting the nation's economic health. Individual industries are not covered, as they are in *Survey of Current Business*, but federal, state, and local government expenditures and receipts and production and prices in selected countries with which the United States has a large amount of trade are among the statistics and graphs. There are also various historical series that show a given trend (e.g., "Consumer installment credit outstanding"; "Average weekly overtime"; "Consumer prices, France") over a period of 30 years or longer. These historical series differ in each issue, but the issue index tells when a particular series was last included.

969.   U.S. Council of Economic Advisors. **Economic Indicators.** Prepared for the Joint Economic Committee. Washington, D.C.: Government Printing Office, 1948- . Monthly.

970.   U.S. President. **Economic Report of the President to the Congress.** Washington, D.C.: Government Printing Office, 1949- . Annual.

Basic statistical series (gross national product; income and spending; employment, unemployment, and wages; production and business activity; prices, money and credit, etc.) that measure the nation's economic health are shown over the past 8 to 12 years to provide data for legislators. Similar series are published annually in the *Economic Report of the President to the Congress.* These, however, are more detailed and are given over a much longer period of time, usually 35 years or longer.

971.   U.S. Department of Labor. Bureau of Labor Statistics. **Handbook of Labor Statistics.** Washington, D.C.: Government Printing Office, 1983. 447p. (Bureau of Labor Statistics Bulletin, 2175).

This is a collection of various statistics (most from the earliest available data through 1982) on the labor force and employment, employment by different industries, work absences, wages, consumer and producer prices, and other statistics applying to labor conditions. It was published annually until 1978 but is now irregular. Statistics on union membership are no longer included in the handbook; they are found in the *Directory of National Unions and Employee Associations* (entry 954) and in *The Labor Almanac* (entry 959).

972.   **International Financial Statistics.** Washington, D.C.: International Monetary Fund, 1948- . Monthly with Yearbook.

973. International Bank for Reconstruction and Development. **World Tables.** 2d ed.
      Baltimore, Md.: Published for the World Bank by the Johns Hopkins University Press,
      1980. 474p.

International Financial Statistics has many tables showing for each country the currency
exchange rate over a period of years, international liquidity, fund position in the
International Monetary Fund, banking, assets, commodity prices, and other data that
indicate a country's monetary stability. *World Tables* is published in order to facilitate
comparative study of countries by different economic variables. These are shown for each
country of the world over a period of past years. There are four series of tables. Series 1
covers population, national accounts, and prices, 1950-1977; series 2, balance of payments,
external public debt, foreign trade indexes, and central government finances, 1970-1977;
series 3, comparative economic data over various time periods; and series 4, social
indicators, 1950 and 1960.

974. **Yearbook of International Trade Statistics.** 2 vols. New York: United Nations, 1950- .
      Annual.

Tables in volume 1 show for each country the amount of imports and exports over a period of
past years, the amount of imports and exports to and from other countries, and the amount
of imports and exports by individual commodities. Volume 2 shows trade by commodity: the
amount exported and imported by each country. Other tables, "Commodity Matrix Tables,"
show the amount of each commodity imported by the principal importers from the principal
exporters. These statistics are much more detailed, both as to the variety of commodities
and as to the activity of each country, than the data in *Commodity Yearbook* (entry 963). The
latter is to be preferred for an overview, with emphasis on what happened to a particular
commodity in the previous year.

ATLASES

975. **Rand McNally Commercial Atlas and Marketing Guide.** Chicago: Rand McNally,
      1895- . Annual.

Some questions are answered better with a graphical, rather than a statistical, presentation.
Atlases are useful for this kind of display. The *Rand McNally Commercial Atlas and
Marketing Guide* is well known by librarians, persons in the marketing field, and others. It
has many topical maps of the United States, e.g., mileage and driving time, AMTRAK,
telephone area codes, railroads, colleges and universities, and college population. Maps of
the individual states show counties, cities, towns, Ranally Metro Areas, railroad lines, and
other features of economic interest. Ranally Metro Areas are similar to MSAs but are not
restricted to county lines, as MSAs are. (See p. 214.) There are also detailed maps of such
large metropolitan areas as Chicago, Detroit, Philadelphia, Los Angeles, and San Francisco.
Besides the maps, there are many indexes and directories: sales data for the one hundred
largest metro areas, colleges and universities with enrollment, county population changes,
1970-1980, and others.

976. **Oxford Economic Atlas of the World.** 4th ed. New York: Oxford University Press, 1972.
      248p.

977. Ginsburg, Norton S. **Atlas of Economic Development.** Chicago: University of Chicago
      Press, 1961. 119p. (University of Chicago, Department of Geography. Research Paper,
      68).

Economic atlases show production of agricultural and mineral products, energy, manufactured goods, and other products. The *Oxford Economic Atlas of the World* is a well-known, general atlas of this type. Oxford also has regional economic atlases for the United States and Canada, Africa, and Western Europe, which show resources and products in greater detail. The *Atlas of Economic Development* has world maps showing density and growth of population, infant mortality, agricultural production, railway and road density, energy and resource consumption, international trade, and other maps of economic interest.

BIOGRAPHY

978.   **Who's Who in Finance and Industry.** Chicago: Marquis Who's Who, 1936- . Biennial.

In the current edition, brief sketches are given for approximately 22,600 living executives and others who, by reason of their present position or because of outstanding achievement in accounting, advertising, industry, investment, and various financial and business fields, were invited to submit biographical data. Educators and researchers, labor union leaders, and government officials are also included. While the emphasis is on the United States, important business leaders of other countries are also represented.

979.   **Who's Who in Economics: A Biographical Dictionary of Major Economists, 1700-1981.** Edited by Mark Blaug and Paul Sturges. Cambridge, Mass.: MIT Press, 1983. 435p.

980.   American Economic Association. **Directory of Members.** Appears irregularly as part of an issue of *The American Economic Review.*

Economists, who were formerly in the Social and Behavioral Sciences volume of *American Men and Women of Science*, are among the social scientists whose future inclusion in that work is now in doubt. (See p. 164.) They were listed in the last edition of the Social and Behavioral Sciences section (13th ed., 1978). *Who's Who in Economics* has articles on 1,071 prominent economists of the past and present. Approximately one-half of these did or now live in the United States, and 63 percent (674) of the biographees are living. Data include the year and place of birth, present and recent positions, degrees, career information, major fields of interest, principal contributions in economics, and major publications. The three indexes list the biographees by principal field of interest, by country of residence, if not the United States, and country of birth, if not the United States. The latest membership directory of the American Economic Association (in *The American Economic Review*, December, 1981) lists about 15,000 members with year of birth, office and home address, current position, degrees, past positions, and field of interest and research. Indexes list them by field of specialty and by academic affiliation.

SOURCES ON INDUSTRIES AND COMPANIES

At the beginning of this chapter, we noted that undergraduates are commonly given an assignment to learn all they can about some industry or about some individual company within that industry. About the industry they should learn about the different components and subdivisions, the nature of the market (government contracts, foreign orders, health field, housing), the outlook for the industry in the near future, the record of production and sales over a 10-year or longer period, and other financial data. For an individual company, they want more detailed information: the history of the company, its products or services, its divisions and subsidiaries, assets, liabilities, financial and operating statistics, number of employees, sales, earnings, credit rating, rank within the industry, etc. Much of this statistical and financial information is wanted over a period of some years up to the present in order to observe trends and to predict the future outlook. Investors and others besides students also have interest in particular industries and individual companies. Although their interest stems from needs different from those of the students, they use the same sources of information, some of which are described here.

981.   **Industry Surveys.** New York: Standard & Poor, 1974- . Quarterly.

Overall prospects and statistical data are issued periodically in this publication for some 70 industries, e.g., chemicals, food and beverages, health care, steel and heavy machinery. Surveys consist of "Basic Analysis" and "Current Analysis" for each industry, and these are updated periodically. Within each industry, comparative statistical data are given for leading companies: sales, earnings, capital, assets to liabilities ratio, and similar data. Both types of surveys are issued in pamphlet form and collected in quarterly issues.

982.   U.S. Department of Commerce. Bureau of Industrial Economics. **Industrial Outlook: Prospects for Over 300 Industries.** Washington, D.C.: Government Printing Office, 1960- . Annual.

A publication intended to provide a forecast for the near future and five-year future in various industries. The forecasting methodology and data on which forecasts were made are explained carefully at the beginning of the volume. A brief discussion of the current situation, the outlook for the year ahead, and five-year prospects are given for the economy as a whole and for each industry, accompanied by many statistics.

983.   **Value Line Investment Survey.** New York: Value Line, 1944- . Weekly.

Over the year, ninety-five industries are analyzed. Following the survey of the industry as a whole with a prediction for the year ahead, detailed analysis is given for major companies in the industry with indexes for the safety and expected performance of the stock.

984.   **Dun's Business Rankings.** Parsippany, N.J.: Dun & Bradstreet, 1982- . Annual.

Part of this annual publication ranks the leading companies of each industry by their sales volume. This provides an overview of the industry.

985.   **Moody's Manuals.** New York: Moody, 1929- . Annual.

986.   **Standard Corporation Records.** New York: Standard & Poor, 1925- . Annual.

There are numerous sources of data on individual companies, especially on public companies, which are required by law to file reports about their financial strength in general, any significant changes in the management and operations of the company, and any new securities issue. *Moody's Manuals* are issued in six series: *Bank and Finance Manual, Industrial Manual, Municipal and Government Manual, OTC Industrial Manual, Public Utility Manual,* and *Transportation Manual.* Although the information furnished in the *Municipal and Government Manual* differs in part, the others give the following data: a brief history of the company, its mergers and acquisitions of other companies, subsidiary companies, branches, description of its products and services, names of officers, directors, legal firm, auditor, time of annual meeting, number of stockholders, number of employees, and the address of the central office. In addition, fairly complete data are given on consolidated income accounts and balance sheets, financial and operating data, and long-term debt and stocks; these data are taken from the company's annual reports to stockholders, reports to the Securities and Exchange Commission, and other reliable sources. Much of this financial information is given for the past five years; production activity and other information cover a longer period. Each series is kept up-to-date by its semi-weekly "News Report" and its indexes, which cumulate weekly and monthly. *Standard Corporation Records* give similar, but less extensive, data on companies. Public companies are listed alphabetically in this set, rather than by type. These sets are more useful for background on a company than for current data. Standard and Poor's data are available in the database, STANDARD AND POOR'S CORPORATE DESCRIPTIONS, which can be machine searched through DIALOG.

Information on large private, as well as public, companies is found in the several publications described above under "Directories" (entries 946-50). Data on small privately owned companies are difficult to find, but, fortunately, information on such companies is least often required. Directory and product information on such a company that is a manufacturer can be found in *Thomas's Register of American Manufacturers* (entry 951) and in the appropriate state directory of manufacturers, compiled by the state department of commerce or a similar state agency or by a commercial publisher. Industrial and business directories available for each state are listed in the *Dow Jones-Irwin Business and Investment Almanac* (entry 958). Directory information on incorporated companies, manufacturers as well as non-manufacturers, can be found in the official list of corporations licensed to do business within a state; these are the companies which comply with the state's business corporation act. Finally, if the city where a company is located is known, minimal directory information about it can be found in the local telephone directory. Recent information about a company may be found through the *Predicasts F & S Index* series (entries 927-29). For further reference sources on industries and individual companies, see M. Balachandran's "A Subject Approach to Business Reference Sources."[1]

INVESTMENT GUIDES

A number of statistical services are available to aid the investor in predicting the safety of a security and its performance in the near future, most offered by Moody, Standard and Poor, and Value Line. These are used by investors, both on- and off-campus, and by students who must learn their use and importance for different kinds of information. Instruction and help in using them is seldom requested of the librarian, since investors and students are normally familiar with and knowledgeable about them.

987.   **Value Line Investment Survey.** New York: Value Line, 1944- . Weekly.

988.   **Security Owner's Stock Guide.** New York: Standard & Poor, 1947- . Monthly.

989.   **Moody's Handbook of Common Stocks.** New York: Moody, 1955- . Quarterly.

These three guides, listed in descending order of frequency of publication, are used most often. The number of different stocks covered, the amount, type, and currency of data, and their use differ in the three, all of which are needed in the large library. Of the three, *Value Line* offers the most evaluation and prediction of safety and future performance of individual stocks. During a year, *Value Line* reports on nearly 1,700 stocks. *Moody's Handbook of*

---

[1]University of Illinois, Graduate School of Library Science, *Occasional Papers*, no. 128. June 1977.

Common Stocks gives a very brief summary of the background, recent developments, prospects, and 10-year statistics on revenues, profits, return on equity, net income, earnings and dividends per share and other statistics, time of the annual meeting, number of stockholders, names of officers, and other data on some nine hundred stocks of high investor interest. This is a good source for quick and easy access to information on this small number of stocks. *Security Owner's Stock Guide* offers information updated monthly on nearly six thousand stocks traded on the New York, American, and regional exchanges and over-the-counter. This guide covers more stocks and has more current data than do the other two, but it does not offer any evaluation or assessment of future activity, except for ratings of security and the likelihood of dividends on preferred issues.

990. **Bond Guide.** New York: Standard & Poor, 1938- . Monthly.

Financial data on corporate, municipal, convertible, foreign, and other bonds, similar to the data on stocks in *Security Owner's Stock Guide*, are in this service. The interest dates, cash position, current assets and liabilities, redemption provision, total debt, and Standard & Poor's quality rating (assessment of the firm's credit) are among the data given.

991. **Investment Companies.** New York: Wiesenberger, 1941- . Annual with monthly supplements.

Wiesenberger's *Investment Companies* describes some 780 open-end mutual funds and closed-end investment companies, details their past record of earnings per share, and gives various data on them. These companies select a portfolio of stocks and bonds for maximum earnings for their investors, who do not have to decide on individual stock issues. Mutual funds continually offer and redeem shares; closed-end companies invest a fixed amount of capital and neither offer new shares nor redeem shares, except on their own terms.

GOVERNMENT FINANCE AND TAXES

992. U.S. Executive Office of the President. Office of Management and Budget. **Budget of the United States Government.** Washington, D.C.: Government Printing Office, 1923- . Annual.

993. State budget.

Two primary sources of government financial data needed in all libraries are the current federal budget and the current state budget. The *United States Budget in Brief*, issued annually by the Office of Management and Budget, is a summary account with many tables and graphs to simplify the presentation. For some questions, this will be more useful than the full budget report. For others, the more detailed *Budget of the United States Government — Appendix* will be more suitable. It has the most detail of any publication on the federal budget. For the budget of one's own state, the title, source (usually the governor's office), and the frequency of publication of the budget of each state can be learned by consulting David W. Parish's *State Government Reference Publications* (entry 1036), chapter 4, "State Government Finances."

994. U.S. Department of Commerce. Bureau of the Census. **Census of Governments.** Washington, D.C.: Government Printing Office, 1942- . Published every five years in years ending with 2 or 7.

This is another primary source of much financial data on school districts, special districts, county governments, and local governments.

995. **Facts and Figures on Government Finance.** Washington, D.C.: Tax Foundation, 1939- . Biennial.

The current edition of this valuable handbook has nearly three hundred tables of data on revenues from tax receipts and other sources and on expenditures of the federal, state, and local governments. These data are broken down in various ways. The Tax Foundation is a nonprofit research and public education organization with the mission of monitoring and keeping the public informed on government finance at all levels. Data are collected from official sources such as the *Budget of the United States Government*, and publications of the Treasury Department and of the Bureau of the Census.

996. **Federal Tax Guide.** 5 vols. Chicago: Commerce Clearing House. Looseleaf.

Commerce Clearing House publishes several looseleaf services on taxes. Most questions on federal income tax, excise tax, estate tax, and gift and generation-skipping transfer taxes will be answered here. Volume 1 is the complete Internal Revenue Code; volume 2 describes tax tactics and taking a case before the IRS and the tax court; the remaining volumes have the regulations, rulings, and court decisions that have modified or interpreted sections of the Code. Complete explanations with examples and illustrations give the latest interpretations of these provisions. A topical index at the front of volume 1 makes it easy to turn to the desired section for any subject.

20

POLITICAL SCIENCE, LAW

The study of government, how it works and how it should work, has been a subject of philosophical thought since the time of Plato and Aristotle. The theory of government and descriptions of the ideal form of government have especially interested writers of all eras. As a distinct academic discipline, however, political science is young, belonging essentially to the present century. In the past 50 years, there has been increasing concern with scientific methodology and behaviorism as an appropriate foundation for the study of government. There has also been increasing interest in the study of different forms and styles of government. But interest in the utopian government has faded.

The focus here, as in the other chapters, is on political science and law as studied in the university and on the kind of reference service needed to satisfy the curricular and research needs in the university. Although there is some interest in the local government and in current state legislation, that interest does not dominate reference needs in the academic library as it does in the public library. Questions and information needs about the government of other countries and historical questions about government are also evident in the academic library.

Reference work in the field of law is specialized and technical. Most of it is taken care of in the law library, usually by library staff with legal training. There is no attempt here to go deeply into the corpus of legal materials. Only some of the basic books in law, which belong in any good academic library, are described here.

POLITICAL SCIENCE

GUIDES, BIBLIOGRAPHIES, INDEXES

997. Brock, Clifton. **The Literature of Political Science: A Guide for Students, Librarians, and Teachers.** New York: Bowker, 1969. 232p.

998. Holler, Frederick L. **The Information Sources of Political Science.** 3d ed. Santa Barbara, Calif.: ABC-Clio, 1981. 278p.

The best introduction to the literature of political science is the first title, now unfortunately some 15 years old. It is well organized and readable and is a valuable aid to the beginning student. *The Information Sources of Political Science* has been revised and is a good updating for Brock's guide. It lists some 1,750 reference sources, many of which cover other social sciences, as well as political science. The section on "International Relations and Organizations, Comparative and Area Studies" is especially helpful. Li's *Social Science Reference Sources* (entry 697) is an excellent, though briefer, guide, describing about fifty books and ten journals in political science and forty-seven books and eight journals in law.

999.   Harmon, Robert B. **Political Science: A Bibliographical Guide to the Literature.** New York: Scarecrow, 1965. Supplements, 1968, 1972, 1974.

A more extensive bibliography, but without the instructional text of the guides, is Harmon's *Political Science.* With its three supplements, it lists a total of about 11,000 texts and general writings as well as reference sources, organized in chapters by broad subject. It does not cover the periodical literature.

1000.   **Universal Reference System: Political Science, Government, and Public Policy Series.** 10 vols. Princeton, N.J.: Princeton Research Publishing Co., 1967-69. Supplement (now *Political Science Abstracts*), 1967- . Annual.

For yet a more complete coverage of the general literature of political science, this set can be consulted. Produced by computer, it is not a simple bibliography to use. The basic 10-volume set lists, with abstracts, some 3,500 books and articles, most of which were published after 1950. The index portion of the set has some 725 alphabetically arranged descriptors, under each of which are listed all of the pertinent documents abstracted in part 1. *Political Science Abstracts*, listing about 8,000 documents per year, is arranged in the same manner, and is now indexed under more than 2,000 descriptors. Despite the difficulty of using this set, it has been found to be especially useful in retrieving information on social indicators.

1001.   **United States Political Science Documents (USPSD).** Pittsburgh: NASA Industrial Applications Center, University of Pittsburgh, 1976- . Annual.

1002.   **International Bibliography of Political Science.** London, New York: Tavistock, 1954- . Annual.

1003.   **International Political Science Abstracts.** Paris: International Political Science Association, 1953- . Bimonthly.

Of the three annual bibliographies listed here, *USPSD* will be generally found the most useful since it concentrates on articles published in the United States and is very well indexed. Over three thousand articles from 125 journals are abstracted each year and indexed under author, subject, geographical area, proper name, and journal. A three-year lag in publishing this bibliography is now being caught up. It also can be machine searched through DIALOG back to 1976. The other two indexes both have UNESCO connections and cover the foreign literature most adequately. *International Bibliography of Political Science* (one of the four parts of UNESCO-sponsored *International Bibliography of the Social Sciences*) lists, without annotations, about six thousand books, periodical articles, government documents, and reports per year, including literature from almost every country. It is very good on international relations and comparative government. The publication lag is about three years. Although the citations are not annotated, it does cross-reference to abstracts in *International Political Science Abstracts.* This abstract journal emphasizes the European literature and abstracts about five thousand articles (no books) per year from more than eight hundred journals. Abstracts are in French except those for articles in English.

1004.   **ABC POL SCI: A Bibliography of Contents: Political Science and Government.** Santa Barbara, Calif.: ABC-Clio, 1969- . Bimonthly.

The table of contents of some three hundred journals in political science, government, law, sociology, and economics are reprinted here. The last issue is a cumulated subject and author index for the year. This bibliography is very useful to faculty and others trying to keep abreast of the literature.

1005.   **C.R.I.S. The Combined Retrospective Index Set to Journals in Political Science, 1886-1974.** Edited by Annadel N. Wile and Jeffrey Levi. 8 vols. Arlington, Va.: Carrollton Press, 1977.

Another computer-produced index, this set makes a search of the older political science literature much simpler and faster than was possible with earlier bibliographies. The basic arrangement of the volumes is by broad category, secondarily by key words of the article title. It is similar to *C.R.I.S. The Combined Retrospective Index Set to Journals in Sociology 1895-1974*, which was described above (entry 804).

DICTIONARIES, ENCYCLOPEDIAS

1006.   Lacquer, Walter, ed. **A Dictionary of Politics.** Rev. ed. New York: Free Press, 1974. 565p.

This is a good general dictionary of terms, abbreviations, names of persons, groups, legislation, treaties, and similar entries pertinent to the study of politics. It covers the politics of all countries, where the remaining dictionaries in this section are limited to, or concentrate on, the politics of the United States.

1007.   Smith, Edward C., and Arnold J. Zurcher. **Dictionary of American Politics.** 2d ed. New York: Barnes & Noble, 1968. 434p.

1008.   Plano, Jack, and Milton Greenberg. **The American Political Dictionary.** 6th ed. New York: Holt, Rinehart and Winston, 1982. 472p.

1009.   Plano, Jack C., Robert E. Riggs, and Helenan S. Robin. **The Dictionary of Political Analysis.** 2d ed. Santa Barbara, Calif.: ABC-Clio, 1982. 197p. Paper.

Even though these dictionaries cover the same ground, all three are useful because of their different approach to the subject. *Dictionary of American Politics* is the standard dictionary of the field, with about 4,500 terms, government agencies, and legislation which have had significance in American politics and law. *The American Political Dictionary* is arranged for study and review of the subject, as well as for defining a single term. About 1,200 terms, government agencies, court decisions, and federal statutes are arranged in chapters on broad political subjects: e.g., political ideas, U.S. Constitution, immigration and citizenship, civil liberties. An index lists all terms, agencies, cases, and statutes in a single alphabet so that definition or identification of a particular item may be found readily. But the best use of this dictionary is for review of the whole field or a part of it by a doctoral candidate or other student. *The Dictionary of Political Analysis* excludes proper names and terms of political history that are purely descriptive, and concentrates on a selection of 250 terms and concepts in the discipline with the aim of providing a clear and precise definition of them. Typical of the terms and concepts are: heuristic device, historical approach, holism, homeostasis, and hypothesis. Each definition is followed by a paragraph on the significance of the term, giving examples and applications. Two other dictionaries that have a similar purpose are Geoffrey K. Roberts's *A Dictionary of Political Analysis* (New York: St. Martin's, 1971) and James B. Whisker's *A Dictionary of Concepts on American Politics* (New York: John Wiley, 1980).

1010.   Safire, William. **Safire's Political Dictionary.** 3d ed. New York: Random House, 1978.
        845p.

1011.   Sperber, Hans, and Travis Trittschuh. **American Political Terms: An Historical
        Dictionary.** Detroit: Wayne State University Press, 1962. 516p.

The two dictionaries listed here are nontraditional in that they list phrases and slogans, as
well as terms, that have been significant in political history, e.g., antediluvian, basket
meeting, big stick, feet to the fire, grandpa's pants won't fit Benny, little old ladies in tennis
shoes. *American Political Terms* is the more scholarly of the two. Both dictionaries cite the
first known use of the term or phrase in a newspaper, political speech, or other source.

1012.   **International Encyclopedia of the Social Sciences.** Edited by David L. Sills. 17 vols.
        New York: Macmillan, 1968.

There is no English language encyclopedia of political science. Lacquer's *Dictionary of
Politics* (entry 1006) is the closest to an encyclopedia. The *International Encyclopedia of the
Social Sciences* has numerous articles on terms, concepts, and persons associated with
political science, international relations, and law.

BIOGRAPHY

1013.   **Who's Who in American Politics.** 9th ed., 1983-84. Edited by Jaques Cattell Press.
        New York: Bowker, 1983. 1704p.

Brief biographical data are given in this ninth edition for approximately 23,000 persons who
are active in politics at the national, state, or local level. Lists of biographees by state, state
delegations to the party convention, and state party chairpersons are useful. Professors of
political science, writers, and others whose influence on the political scene may be
important but less direct are likely to be in the *Membership Directory* of the American
Political Science Association (entry 1015) rather than here.

1014.   **Who's Who in Government.** 3d ed., 1977-78. New York: Marquis Who's Who, 1977.
        753p.

Unless a revised edition is published, this book has limited usefulness, although it does
have information, especially on persons in state and local government, not available
elsewhere. The third edition has entries for about 18,000 office holders on the federal, state,
and local levels and in international government. The main arrangement is alphabetical, but
there are lists by level of government. Other sources of biographical information for persons
in government in the United States are described in the next section of this chapter.

1015.   American Political Science Association. **Membership Directory, 1985.** Washington,
        D.C.: The Association, 1985. 387p. Irregular.

All present members of the American Political Science Association are listed with brief
biographies. This directory will list many people in the profession who may not be included
in one of the other who's whos. The 1985 edition includes 9,450 members. Lists by field of
interest and by state and city are in the back of the volume.

1016.   **Directory of European Political Scientists.** 4th ed. Edited by the European
        Consortium for Political Research. New York: Saur, 1984. 560p.

Data for more than two thousand European political scientists include birth date and
nationality, degree, title of doctoral thesis, past and present positions, major publications,
and academic interests and research areas. An index by research area is in the back of the
volume.

UNITED STATES GOVERNMENT

The foregoing parts of this chapter describe some of the important reference tools that cover political science in general. This and following sections cover separate aspects of political science; the section "Governments of Other Countries" is followed by general reference works on law. In most libraries, the majority of reference needs in the field of political science concern the government of the United States or, less often, state and local government.

Congress

1017. U.S. Congress. **Official Congressional Directory.** Washington, D.C.: Government Printing Office, 1865- . Annual.

1018. **Congressional Staff Directory.** Edited by Charles B. Brownson. Mt. Vernon, Va.: Congressional Staff Directory, 1959- . Annual.

These directories have been described in chapter 3, "Directory Information" (entries 86 and 87). Because of their frequent use and the need for the most up-to-date information, the library should keep them convenient to the telephone and should have standing orders for the latest editions.

1019. **CQ Weekly Report.** Washington, D.C.: Congressional Quarterly, 1943- . Weekly.

1020. **Congressional Quarterly Almanac.** Washington, D.C.: Congressional Quarterly, 1945- . Annual.

1021. **Congressional Index.** Chicago: Commerce Clearing House, 1937- . Looseleaf.

Most questions on legislation, committee hearings, and other activities of Congress will be for current or recent events. Congressional Quarterly is a nonpartisan company that gathers and publishes information on the current Congress and its activities. *CQ Weekly Report* is a summary of the week's action and, often, of the background of these actions. Inside the front cover of each issue is a status report on important bills ("House committee," "passed House," "Conference committee," etc.); inside the back cover is a roll call of votes on important bills before the House or Senate. Both of these tables are handy for answering a type of question that is frequently asked. Quarterly and annual indexes are issued. *Congressional Quarterly Almanac* is similar, covering the year's activity in each major legislative area: e.g., agriculture, appropriations, education and welfare, foreign policy. A report on lobbying, voting on major legislation by each senator and representative, bills introduced by each legislator, and similar information is also included. These two publications of Congressional Quarterly cover only the major bills, but it is these that concern the average library user. For a more complete index of bills introduced, voting records on bills, status of pending bills, brief biographies and committee assignments of the members of congress, the personnel of committees, the meetings and hearings scheduled for committees, etc., the more expensive looseleaf service, *Congressional Index* may be used.

1022. **Congressional Quarterly's Guide to the Congress of the United States: Origins, History and Procedure.** 3d ed. Washington, D.C.: Congressional Quarterly, 1982. 1185p.

Unlike the preceding reference services, this guide is for questions on the history, background, and procedures of Congress: its powers, how it works for the electorate, pressures on Congress, ethical questions, etc. All past members of Congress are briefly noted as to party and state, birth and death dates, and dates of service in the Congress. The texts of some documents that have figured importantly and the rules of Congress are also included.

1023.   **Politics in America: Members of Congress in Washington and at Home.** Edited by Alan Ehrenhalt and Michael Glennon. Washington, D.C.: Congressional Quarterly, 1983. 1734p. Biennial.

1024.   **The Almanac of American Politics: The Senators, the Representatives — Their Records, States, Districts.** Compiled by Michael Barone, Brant Ujifusa, and Douglas Matthews. Boston: Gambit, 1972- . Biennial.

A type of question that is also common is for information on a particular member of Congress, particularly a voting record and an overall rating by partisan groups, liberal and conservative. Some information on voting by each member on individual bills can be found in *CQ Weekly Report* and other sources described above. But a better profile of any representative or senator currently serving can be found in one of these books, both of which give summary data on the person's political background, campaign leading to election to current term, voting record on key issues (e.g., draft registration, ban $ to Nicaragua, delay MX missile) and rating by various special interest groups.

1025.   Close, Arthur C., and Craig Colgate, Jr., eds. **Washington Representatives.** Washington, D.C.: Columbia Books, 1977- . Annual.

Although lobbyists have various functions, their activities are directed mostly toward members of Congress. This directory is an alphabetical list of Washington representatives of business firms, labor unions, national associations (such as the American Library Association), foreign governments, and other lobbyists and representatives of special interest groups. Brief data are given for each of these people, including address and telephone number, background, company or other body represented, clients, etc. A second section of the directory lists organizations, subjects, and foreign governments represented.

1026.   U.S. Congress. **Biographical Directory of the American Congress, 1774-1971.** Washington, D.C.: Government Printing Office, 1971. 1972p.

Short biographies (250 to 300 words) of all past members of Congress and the Continental Congress make up the main part of this work. Although most of these biographies can be found elsewhere, it may be convenient to have all of them here in a one-volume work. The initial one-fourth of the book is composed of rosters of all of the administrations and Congresses.

Executive Branch

1027.   U.S. General Services Administration. National Archives and Records Service. Office of the Federal Register. **United States Government Manual.** Washington, D.C.: Government Printing Office, 1935- . Annual.

1028.   **Federal Regulatory Directory.** Washington, D.C.: Congressional Quarterly, 1979- . Annual.

These directories have also been described in chapter 3, "Directory Information" (entries 85 and 90). They are again listed in this chapter because of their great importance and frequent use.

1029.   Kane, Joseph N. **Facts about the Presidents: A Compilation of Biographical and Historical Data.** 4th ed. New York: Wilson, 1981. 464p.

The information given about past U.S. presidents in *World Almanac, Information Please Almanac*, and other general almanacs is sufficient to answer most questions: birth and death dates, dates of presidency, names and dates of office of cabinet members, important acts of presidency, etc. The data given here about each president are more likely to be trivia and less likely to be wanted by faculty or students, e.g., age at marriage, length of time he outlived his wife or was outlived by her, presidents who did not go to college, occupation after presidency.

1030.   Sobel, Robert, ed. **Biographical Directory of the United States Executive Branch, 1774-1977.** 2d ed. Westport, Conn.: Greenwood, 1977. 503p.

Political biographies of the presidents, vice-presidents, and cabinet heads but excluding those acting heads who were not subsequently confirmed in office by the Senate) are included in this directory. It has also many lists of the approximately 550 biographees by the office or other capacity in which they served, military service, education, place of birth, and marital information (wife's name, date of marriage).

1031.   **Political Profiles.** Edited by Nelson Lichtenstein and Eleanora N. Schoenebaum. 6 vols. New York: Facts on File, 1976- .

A more in-depth look at the people who played important roles in the administration of Presidents Truman, Eisenhower, Kennedy, Johnson, Nixon, Ford, and Carter is provided in this work; not only those in government, but also journalists, business executives, labor leaders, and others are included. Their brief profiles, emphasizing the role they played in government affairs, make up the main part of these volumes. A chronology of important events of the administration, a roster of major officials and Congress, a bibliography, a topical index (names indexed under major activity), and a general index are added. Volumes on presidents after Carter will probably appear later.

1032.   **Historic Documents of [year].** Washington, D.C.: Congressional Quarterly, 1972- . Annual.

The text of a speech, report of a government committee, court decision, or other document judged to be significant in the government and politics of the United States may be needed. The documents selected for this annual publication are arranged chronologically, and each volume has a cumulated index of subjects of the documents in the past five volumes.

Supreme Court

1033.   **Congressional Quarterly's Guide to the U.S. Supreme Court.** Washington, D.C.: Congressional Quarterly, 1979. 1022p.

Questions concerned with the decisions of the Supreme Court on the rights of an unwed father toward his illegitimate children, the exclusion of sick pay for women employees who are absent due to pregnancy or childbirth, the legitimacy of certain state taxes, and many other legal questions are easier to answer since the publication of this book. It summarizes Supreme Court action from 1789 to the present on thousands of issues organized by broad areas (e.g., the Court and the states; freedom for ideas; search and seizure; double jeopardy). There is an index of small subjects and a case index.

1034.   Barnes, Catherine. **Men of the Supreme Court: Profiles of the Justices.** New York: Facts on File, 1978. 221p.

The legal background, philosophy of the law, and important cases for which these 26 justices who served the Supreme Court from 1945 to 1976 were noted are included in their biographies in this work. The factual information about these men can be found elsewhere, but the emphasis here is on their contribution to the Supreme Court.

STATE GOVERNMENT

1035.   **The Book of the States.** Lexington, Ky.: Council of State Governments, 1935- . Biennial.

Information about the federal government is relatively easy to find since many reference sources on the national government are available and well known. This is unfortunately not true for information about state government, particularly about a state other than one's own. Many questions about the government of another state can be answered in this book. It is useful for looking up such things as the outstanding debt, taxes, methods of selecting officials, services offered, names of the top officials and names of judges, and new developments and innovations in different areas of state government. The two directories issued biennially as supplements to *The Book of the States, State Administrative Officials Classified by Function* (entry 93) and *State Elective Officials and the Legislatures* (entry 94), have been described in chapter 3, "Directory Information."

1036.   Parish, David W. **State Government Reference Publications: An Annotated Bibliography.** 2d ed. Littleton, Colo.: Libraries Unlimited, 1981. 355p.

This bibliography of 1,756 reference publications is also very useful in learning of other sources of information, when the answer could not be found in *The Book of the States.* Most of the citations are to official publications of the states; some are to state university publications and other books about the state government. Under each state, these are arranged according to the type of data, e.g., official state bibliography, blue book, legislative manuals, tourist guides.

1037.   Glashan, Roy R., comp. **American Governors and Gubernatorial Elections, 1775-1978.** Westport, Conn.: Meckler, 1979. 370p.

1038.   Sobel, Robert, and John Raimo, eds. **Biographical Directory of the Governors of the United States, 1789-1978.** 4 vols. Westport, Conn.: Meckler, 1978.

American Governors and Gubernatorial Elections, 1775-1978, is good for ready reference. For each state, tables list governors from the beginning of statehood to 1979 and executives during the revolutionary period. Birth date and place, date and age on becoming governor, party, major occupation, state residence, date of death and age at death are given for each governor. Gubernatorial election statistics are also given for each state. The larger work listed above has approximately two thousand biographies, averaging one-half to one page in length and arranged by state and chronologically within the state. Many of these biographies are not easily found elsewhere. Each volume has an index of all the governors, indicating the state, volume, and page number where their biography is found.

LOCAL GOVERNMENT

1039.   **Municipal Yearbook.** Washington, D.C.: International City Management Association, 1934- . Annual.

1040.   **The County Yearbook.** Washington, D.C.: National Association of Counties and International City Management Association, 1974- . Annual.

The statistical tables and directories of these two annuals serve a function for information about the governments of various cities and counties similar to that which *The Book of the States* serves for states. Admittedly, the chance of finding what one needs in one of these comparative tables is small, but these are the most convenient and first places to check. Failing here, one can consult the following bibliography for possible leads to other sources.

1041.   Hernon, Peter, and others, eds. **Municipal Government Reference Sources: Publications and Collections.** New York: Bowker, 1978. 341p.

The information sources and libraries which contain special collections about a community are annotated and arranged under state and major city. Indexes of counties and subjects are provided.

WOMEN IN GOVERNMENT

1042.   Center for the American Woman in Politics. **Women in Public Office: A Biographical Directory and Statistical Analysis.** 2d ed. Metuchen, N.J.: Scarecrow, 1978. 510p.

As women achieve a more and more important role in government, this reference source provides information that may be increasingly requested. It has various statistical tables on the number of women in public office at all three levels of government and has brief biographical data on women office holders, arranged by state and position which they hold.

POLITICAL BEHAVIOR AND PUBLIC OPINION

One of the areas which attracts increasing interest among political scientists comprises the behavior of the voter, the factors that contribute to a successful political campaign, methods of predicting the outcome of an election, public opinion and how it can be measured, and similar matters that revolve around the campaign and the election. A few of the reference works that may aid in the study of political behavior and public opinion are described in this section.

1043.   Maurer, David J. **U.S. Politics and Elections: A Guide to Information Sources.** Detroit: Gale, 1978. 213p.

More than one thousand titles on political campaigns and elections from colonial times to the present are listed with brief annotations. Periodical articles are not included. Authors, titles, and subjects are listed in separate indexes.

1044.   Smith, Dwight A., and Lloyd W. Garrison, eds. **The American Political Process: Selected Abstracts of Periodical Literature (1954-1971).** Santa Barbara, Calif.: ABC-Clio, 1972. 630p.

Abstracts of articles from *Historical Abstracts* (entry 1115), and *America: History and Life* (entry 1163) on American politics are reprinted here. Political parties, American elections, political behavior, and political institutions are the four aspects of the subject covered. Although an updating of this bibliography is very much needed, it is still a convenient way to cover the major journal literature on American politics from 1954 to 1971.

1045.   Johnson, Donald B., comp. **National Party Platforms, 1840-1976.** Rev. ed. 2 vols. Urbana, Ill.: University of Illinois Press, 1978. Supplement: **National Party Platforms of 1980.** Urbana, Ill.: University of Illinois Press, 1982. 233p.

Occasionally in political science research, there is need for the full text of the platform adopted by a political party in some past campaign. The platforms of all major parties in the

United States from the first platform in the campaign of 1840 through the campaign of 1980 are reprinted in this work and its latest supplement. The platforms adopted by the major parties in the campaign of 1984 will be issued in a later supplement. Volume 1 of this set covers the campaigns of 1840 through 1956; volume 2, 1960 through 1976. For each campaign year, the parties are represented alphabetically. The earlier editions of this work were compiled by Kirk H. Porter, later by Porter and Johnson.

1046.   Chester, Edward W. **A Guide to Political Platforms.** Hamden, Conn.: Archon, 1977. 373p.

Where Johnson gives the full text of each party platform, Chester gives a narrative account of the campaigns of 1840 through 1976 and the construction and significance of the platforms in these campaigns.

1047.   Schlapsmeier, Edward L., and Frederick H. Schlapsmeier. **Political Parties and Civic Action Groups.** Westport, Conn.: Greenwood, 1981. 554p. (Greenwood Encyclopedia of American Institutions).

Ever since Sons of Liberty was founded in 1765 to protest against the Stamp Act and other obnoxious British restrictions, there have been many organizations whose purpose was to further some political cause and to influence the vote. This volume describes 475 organizations of this type in American history, including — in addition to political parties — the American Library Association, the National Congress of Parents and Teachers, Common Cause, Coxey's Army, the American Vegetarian Party, and Action on Smoking and Health. Appendixes list the organizations by function and by date of founding, and there is an index by title and subject.

1048.   Garling, Marguerite, comp. **The Human Rights Handbook: A Guide to British and American International Human Rights Organizations.** Compiled for The Writers and Scholars Educational Trust. New York: Facts on File, 1979. 299p.

1049.   Wiseberg, Laurie S., and Harry M. Scoble, comps. **North American Human Rights Directory.** Garrett Park, Md.: Garrett Park, 1980. 181p.

1050.   Wiseberg, Laurie S., and Harry M. Scoble, comps. **Human Rights Directory: Latin America, Africa, Asia.** Garrett Park, Md.: Garrett Park, 1980. 243p.

The organizations listed in these directories with a description of their purpose and program are specifically those concerned with achieving and protecting civil and political rights of individuals. *The Human Rights Handbook* stresses British organizations, but similar groups in the United States and a few international organizations in other countries are included. Human Rights Internet, Washington, D.C., has published several directories of human rights organizations in countries other than the United States and Canada.

1051.   Blackey, Robert. **Revolutions and Revolutionists: A Comprehensive Guide to the Literature.** Santa Barbara, Calif.: ABC-Clio, 1982. 488p. (War/Peace Bibliographic Series, no. 17).

Political behavior reaches an extreme in revolution, a form not unknown in this country. Blackey's bibliography lists 6,200 unannotated references to books and articles on revolutions and revolutionists from fourth century B.C. Greece to the present. Indexes of authors/editors and of subjects are included.

1052.   **America Votes: A Handbook of Contemporary American Election Statistics.** Compiled and edited by R. M. Scammon. New York: Macmillan, 1956- . Biennial.

Research in political science today is highly behavioral and statistical. Detailed statistics on past elections are of interest to some political scientists. These in *America Votes* are compiled by the Elections Research Institute of the Governmental Affairs Institute, an unofficial but authoritative body, and issued about one year after each national election. Statistics for each Congressional district analyze the vote by county and by political party for the U.S. president, senators, and governors. Besides the analysis by county, statistics are given for major cities. Votes for representatives to the U.S. House, by state, and other election summaries are also included.

1053.   Mackie, Thomas T., and Richard Rose. **The International Almanac of Electoral History.** New York: Free Press, 1974. 434p.

This almanac is a compilation of election results in 23 major countries of the world since the beginning of their competitive elections. Tables give for each country the names of the political parties and the year they entered elections, the total and percentage of votes in each election, the number of seats won, and other data.

1054.   Gallup, George H. **The Gallup Poll: Public Opinion, 1935-1971.** 3 vols. New York: Random House, 1972. Reprint. Wilmington, Del.: Scholarly Resources, 1978.

1055.   Gallup, George H. **The Gallup Poll: Public Opinion, 1972-1977.** 2 vols. Wilmington, Del.: Scholarly Resources, 1978.

1056.   Gallup, George H. **The Gallup Poll: Public Opinion, 1978- .** Wilmington, Del.: Scholarly Resources, 1979- . Annual.

1057.   Gallup, George H. **The Gallup International Public Opinion Polls: Great Britain, 1937-1975.** 2 vols. New York: Random House, 1976.

1058.   Gallup, George H. **The Gallup International Public Opinion Polls: France, 1939, 1944-1975.** 2 vols. New York: Random House, 1976.

1059.   Hastings, Elizabeth H., and Philip K. Hastings, eds. **Index to International Public Opinion, 1978/79- .** Prepared by Survey Research Consultants International. Westport, Conn.: Greenwood, 1980- . Annual.

Summaries of these polls and their findings have been described in chapter 17 (entries 856-61). Attempts to sample voter attitude before an election, test public opinion on what social, economic, and political issues are most important, measure the success of the president in meeting these issues as based on public opinion, and similar attempts of interest to political scientists have been made by public opinion researchers, and the results of many of these surveys are of value in political science research.

INTERNATIONAL AFFAIRS AND COMPARATIVE GOVERNMENT

1060.   **Guide to American Foreign Relations since 1700.** Edited by Richard Dean Burns for The Society for Historians of American Foreign Relations. Santa Barbara, Calif.: ABC-Clio, 1983. 1311p.

The definitive bibliography on this aspect of political science is this long-awaited work, replacing the excellent but outdated *Guide to the Diplomatic History of the United States, 1775-1921* by Bemis and Griffin. More than one hundred specialists have helped in the selection of references under the editorship of Burns. An estimated 10,000 references (about twice the number in the earlier work) are annotated and arranged in 40 chapters, most of which cover periods of American history in chronological order. The annotations are short but very satisfactory, and the number of cross-references and the detailed indexes (one for authors, another for subjects) make the work easy to use. An appendix gives short biographies of all Secretaries of State from the first (Robert R. Livingston, Head, 1781-83, of the Department of Foreign Affairs, predecessor of the Department of State) to George Schultz.

1061.   **International Relations Information Guide Series.** Detroit: Gale.

Examples of this guide series presently available are Alexine Atherton's *International Organizations* (1976), Helga Hernes's *The Multinational Corporation* (1977), and Ann Schulz's *International and Regional Politics in the Middle East and North Africa* (1977). A number of other volumes are in press or in preparation. These are written, not by theorists, but by practitioners in the field.

1062.   **Foreign Affairs Bibliography: A Selected and Annotated List of Books on International Relations.** New York: Bowker for The Council on Foreign Relations, 1933- . 10-year cumulations.

1063.   **Foreign Affairs 50-Year Bibliography: New Evaluations of Significant Books on International Relations, 1920-1970.** Edited by Byron Dexter. New York: Bowker for The Council on Foreign Relations, 1972. 832p.

The annotated bibliographies printed in quarterly issues of *Foreign Affairs* are the most authoritative source of current publications on foreign governments and political developments abroad. These bibliographies are cumulated into decennial volumes, the most recent covering 1962-1972. Only monographs, most in English, are included. The *Foreign Affairs 50-Year Bibliography* is a selection from the books in these decennial cumulations, based on the perspective gained some years after publication. The selection of the 2,130 titles and the evaluative essays are by more than four hundred specialists in foreign affairs.

1064.   **Bulletin analytique de documentation politique, économique, et sociale contemporaine.** Paris: Fondation Nationale des Sciences Politiques, 1946- . Monthly.

Nearly 2,500 journals in English and other Western languages are indexed. Each issue has two main parts: Problèmes nationaux (arranged by country) and Relations internationales et études comparatives. As this division suggests, this is an excellent index for international affairs and comparative government. There is an annual subject index.

1065.   Findling, John E. **Dictionary of American Diplomatic History.** Westport, Conn.: Greenwood, 1980. 622p.

The subjects of the brief articles in this dictionary are persons, events, treaties, associations, and terms important in American diplomatic history from the American Revolution to 1978. Bibliographic references are included in the articles. Material in the appendixes covers a chronology of American diplomatic history; key diplomatic personnel in each administration; initiation, suspension, and termination of diplomatic relations with different countries; place of birth of key diplomatic personnel; and locations of collections of manuscripts and oral histories important in the study of American diplomatic history. The index includes names and subjects.

1066.   **Encyclopedia of American Foreign Policy: Studies of the Principal Movements and Ideas.** Edited by Alexander De Conde. 3 vols. New York: Scribner's, 1978.

Longer articles by political scholars comprise this encyclopedia. Examples of the articles' topics are balance of power, colonialism, the domino theory, embargoes, national security, and naval diplomacy. Volume 3 has biographical sketches of persons prominent in American foreign policy of the past and present. It also has a detailed index of names and subjects.

1067.   **United States Treaties and Other International Agreements, 1950- .** Washington, D.C.: Government Printing Office, 1952- . Annual.

1068.   U.S. Department of State. **Treaties and Other International Acts Series (TIAS).** Washington, D.C.: Government Printing Office, 1945- . Irregular.

1069.   U.S. Department of State. **Treaties in Force: A List of Treaties and Other International Agreements of the United States in Force.** Washington, D.C.: Government Printing Office, 1929- . Annual.

Before 1950, the official text of treaties between the United States and other countries was published in *Statutes at Large.* The official (or proclamation) form of treaties is now published in the annual, *United States Treaties and Other International Agreements.* They are also published in slip form, as they are signed and ratified, in the *Treaties and Other International Acts Series (TIAS). Treaties in Force* lists all treaties and international agreements of which the United States is a party in force as of January 1; this does not give the text of the treaty or agreement, but cites the source where the official text may be found. There have been several editions of all the treaties of which the United States has been a party. For a discussion of these several editions and their authoritativeness, see Carl M. White and others, *Sources of Information in the Social Sciences,* 2d ed. (Chicago: American Library Association), 556-57, entry 695.

1070.   Israel, Fred L., ed. **Major Peace Treaties of Modern History.** 4 vols. New York: Chelsea House, McGraw-Hill, 1967.

Major treaties of the world from the Treaty of Westphalia (1648) to the Tashkent Declaration (1966) are reprinted here in English translation.

GOVERNMENTS OF OTHER COUNTRIES

1071.   **The Europa Year Book: A World Survey.** London: Europa, 1926- . Annual.

1072.   **The Statesman's Year-Book.** Edited by John Paxton. New York: St. Martin's, 1864- . Annual.

These directories are useful for a quick check on the nature of the government of a foreign country, names of the head of state and leading officials, number of seats in the legislative body held by the different political parties, names of diplomatic representatives to and from other countries, and various other summary information about the constitution (see entries 1074 and 1075 for the full text of constitutions), the monetary system, geography, the press, communication, transportation, industry, trade, etc. Useful as they are, the caution in chapter 3, "Directory Information," about the currency of their information should be reiterated.

1073.   **Countries of the World and Their Leaders Yearbook.** 2 vols. Detroit: Gale, 1974- . Annual.

Principally, this yearbook reprints the latest editions of the series prepared by the U.S. State Department entitled *Background Notes on Countries of the World.* These are up-to-date reports on political, social, and economic conditions in each country. Additional data in the yearbook are lists of chiefs of state and cabinet members of the countries; U.S. embassies, consulates, and foreign service posts; information on passports and visas; foreign travel health information; international treaty organizations; and climates of the world.

1074. Peaslee, Amos J. **Constitutions of Nations.** 3d ed. 4 vols. in 7. The Hague: Nijhoff, 1965-70.

1075. Blaustein, Albert P., and Gisbert H. Flanz. **Constitutions of the Countries of the World: A Series of Updated Texts, Constitutional Chronologies and Annotated Bibliographies.** Dobbs Ferry, N.Y.: Oceana, 1971- . Looseleaf.

Both series have the full texts of the constitutions of all countries, translated into English. The latter work is continuously updated to include revised or new constitutions.

1076. DeLury, George E., ed. **World Encyclopedia of Political Systems and Parties.** 2 vols. New York: Facts on File, 1983.

A description of the system of government (national, regional, and local), its electoral system, and its major parties is given for each country of the world. These are written by specialists, most of whom are American university professors.

1077. Alexander, Robert J., ed. **Political Parties of the Americas: Canada, Latin America, and the West Indies.** 2 vols. Westport, Conn.: Greenwood, 1983. (The Greenwood Historical Encyclopedia of the World's Political Parties).

1078. McHale, Vincent E., and Sharon Skowronski, eds. **Political Parties of Europe.** 2 vols. Westport, Conn.: Greenwood, 1983. (The Greenwood Historical Encyclopedia of the World's Political Parties).

These two sets provide information on all of the political parties in each country, not only the major parties described in *World Encyclopedia of Political Systems and Parties*, which emphasizes the current status of the political system and parties. These two works have more on the history of the parties.

1079. Cook, Chris, and John Paxton, eds. **European Political Facts, 1789-1973.** New ed. 3 vols. New York: Facts on File, 1978-81.

1080. Cook, Chris, and John Paxton, eds. **Commonwealth Political Facts.** New York: Facts on File, 1979. 293p.

For a restricted geographical and time frame, these books offer a variety of political data: heads of state, treaties, chronologies of revolutions and other movements, statistics of mobilization for wars, military losses, population and urbanization, and similar information.

1081. Kurian, George. **Encyclopedia of the Third World.** Rev. ed. 3 vols. New York: Facts on File, 1982.

1082. Thompson, Carol L., Mary M. Anderberg, and Joan B. Antell, eds. **The Current History Encyclopedia of Developing Nations.** New York: McGraw-Hill, 1982. 395p.

Data on the countries which we have grouped under the terms "developing nations" and "Third World" are not as easily available as information on the more highly productive countries. To assemble such data for approximately 125 Third World countries is the aim of each of these encyclopedias.

1083. United Nations. **Yearbook.** New York: United Nations, Department of Public Information, 1946- . Annual.

1084. **Annual Review of United Nations Affairs.** Dobbs Ferry, N.Y.: Oceana, 1949- .
       Annual.

Activities of the United Nations are summarized in these two annual reviews. The first is the
official organ of the United Nations, and it gives a detailed account of actions grouped under
several broad headings: e.g., political and security questions, economic and social
questions, legal questions, administrative and budgetary questions. Directory and
statistical information about the United Nations and its agencies is included. *Annual Review
of United Nations Affairs* is a commercially published review. It gives a briefer summary of
meetings of the General Assembly and of special committees and other groups, actions
taken, votes on resolutions, debates, etc.

LAW

As we said in the headnote to this chapter, our intent here is to describe some of the
basic tools in the field of law which will be found in any strong reference collection in a
college or university. We are not thinking here about the law library with its fairly extensive
collection of court reports and other materials for legal education and research. Legal
research is too complex to introduce here at even an elementary level. An introduction to
legal research and the handling of legal reference tools can be found in one of the guides
described below.

GUIDES, BIBLIOGRAPHIES, INDEXES

1085. Cohen, Morris. **Legal Research in a Nutshell.** 2d ed. St. Paul, Minn.: West, 1971.
       259p.

1086. Coco, Al. **Finding the Law: A Workbook on Legal Research for Lay Persons.**
       Washington, D.C.: Government Printing Office, 1982. 272p.

1087. Cohen, Morris, and Robert C. Berring. **How to Find the Law.** 8th ed. St. Paul, Minn.:
       West, 1983. 790p.

1088. Jacobstein, J. Myron, and Roy M. Mersky. **Fundamentals of Legal Research.** 2d ed.
       Mineola, N.Y.: Foundation Press, 1981. 614p.

1089. Price, Miles O., Harry Bitner, and Shirley R. Bysiewicz. **Effective Legal Research.** 4th
       ed. Boston: Little, Brown, 1979. 643p.

Any of these are suitable for learning about the intricacies of legal research, how statutes
and reports of court decisions are codified and published, and the use of various officially
and privately published reference sources and services. Since this section is especially
intended for librarians and users without legal background, the first two guides listed above
are recommended. The manual by Coco was prepared for workers in the Bureau of Land
Management, but it is suitable for anyone who needs instruction on legal research and is
available from the Government Printing Office.

1090. **Index to Legal Periodicals.** New York: Wilson, 1909- . Monthly, except September,
       with quarterly and annual cumulations.

1091.   **The Current Law Index.** Menlo Park, Calif.: Information Access in cooperation with the American Association of Law Libraries, 1980- . Eight monthly issues with quarterly and annual cumulations.

Most users are familiar and comfortable with the Wilson index, but *The Current Law Index* is more comprehensive and more thoroughly indexed. It covers more than 700 law periodicals, which are selected and reviewed annually by the Committee on Indexing of Periodical Literature of the American Association of Law Libraries. *Index to Legal Periodicals* covers about 450 periodicals. The latter can be machine searched through Wilsonline. Both services index mainly English language journals and stress Anglo-American law. Wilson also publishes *Index to Foreign Legal Periodicals and Collections of Essays.* The microfilm version of *The Current Law Index, Legal Resource Index*, which is searched on a motorized transport reader, is even more comprehensive; it adds to the 700-odd periodicals of the printed service a number of legal and national newspapers, government documents, and other related literature. Each issue and cumulation of *The Current Law Index* has four separate parts: Subject Index, Author/Title Index, Table of Cases, and Table of Statutes. *The Current Law Index* is more expensive than the *Index to Legal Periodicals*, and *Legal Resource Index* is still more expensive, but the library which has a large volume of legal searching to do (usually a law library) would be justified in subscribing to these more comprehensive services. *Legal Resource Index* can be machine searched back to 1980 through DIALOG.

1092.   Foster, Lynn, and Carol Boast. **Subject Compilations of State Laws: Research Guide and Annotated Bibliography.** Westport, Conn.: Greenwood, 1981. 473p.

A type of question that sometimes comes up and that is difficult and time-consuming to search is a list of all state laws on a particular subject (e.g., cigarettes, citizen's arrest, collective bargaining, credit cards) or the laws of a particular state on a subject. This index makes such questions much easier to answer. In part, it gives instructions for compiling a list of all state laws on a subject or for locating an existing compilation. Most of the book, however, is a bibliography of all compilations of state laws on particular subjects that could be located in treatises, reference books, journal articles, state and federal documents, and other sources. These 1,242 compilations are annotated and listed under 403 subjects.

DICTIONARIES, ENCYCLOPEDIAS

1093.   Black, Henry C. **Black's Law Dictionary.** 5th ed. Edited by Joseph R. Nolan and Michael J. Connolly. St. Paul, Minn.: West, 1979. 1511p.

1094.   Ballentine, James A. **Law Dictionary with Pronunciations.** 3d ed. Edited by William S. Anderson. Rochester, N.Y.: Lawyer's Cooperative, 1979. 1429p.

A reference section needs one or more legal dictionaries since many words in common use (e.g., eyewitness, fabric, facilities, property, trespass) take on special meaning in legal context. Legal dictionaries also cite a court decision in which a definition of a term was laid down. Also included are Latin and French terms and maxims occurring in legal writing. Legal maxims are brief statements from early law which are so universally accepted that they require no argument or proof: e.g., "Equity suffers not a right without a remedy"; "Maris et foeminae conjunctio est de jure naturae"; "Soit baile aux commons." Maxims in Latin and French are translated.

1095.   **The Guide to American Law: Everyone's Legal Encyclopedia.** 12 vols. St. Paul, Minn.: West, 1983- . In progress.

This legal encyclopedia for the lay reader has articles of one paragraph to 20 pages or more in length on legal principles and concepts, landmark documents and acts, famous trials, events important in legal history, government departments, organizations, and individuals prominent in the development of the law, especially in Great Britain and the United States. Numerous appendixes in each volume include cases and popular name acts cited in the volume and lists of articles under special topics.

DIRECTORIES

1096. **Martindale-Hubbell Law Directory.** 7 vols. Summit, N.J.: Martindale-Hubbell, 1931- . Annual.

This is the standard directory of law firms and lawyers in the United States and Canada. The main part of the directory is arranged by state (or province) and city. Within each unit, lawyers and law firms are listed separately. Data on firms include directory information and any special competencies of the firm. For lawyers a rating is given based on length of time the individual has been a member of the bar. Brief biographies are also given. Volume 7 digests the law of each state and U.S. copyright, patent, and trademark law.

OFFICIAL TEXTS

1097. **The Constitution of the United States of America: Analysis and Interpretation. Annotations of Cases Decided by the Supreme Court of the United States to June 29, 1972.** Washington, D.C.: Government Printing Office, 1972. 1978 Supplement, 1979; 1980 Supplement, 1982.

A number of questions are asked about the exact interpretation of freedom of the press, the right to bear arms, separation of church and state, and other Constitutional provisions. This edition has copious notes and explanations of each sentence of the Constitution and gives its current interpretation in the light of pertinent Supreme Court decisions. It is revised about every six to eight years, and interim supplements keep it current.

1098. **United States Code. 1982 Edition Containing the General and Permanent Laws of the United States in Force on January 14, 1983.** 25 vols. plus supplements. Washington, D.C.: Government Printing Office, 1983.

All general and public laws of the United States which are still in force are gathered together by subject, and their text printed in the *United States Code.* The subjects or "titles" are broad areas like agriculture, commerce, census, conservation, food and drugs, and highways. The set is indexed by small subject. A new edition is prepared every six years, and supplements are issued for each Congress between editions. Still more current information about new laws and their text can be found in the commercially published service, *United States Code Congressional and Administrative News* (entry 1100).

1099. **United States Statutes at Large, Containing the Laws and Concurrent Resolutions Enacted from the Organization of the Government in 1789.** Boston: Little, Brown, 1845-1873; Washington, D.C.: Government Printing Office, 1875- .

When a session of Congress has been concluded, the acts, resolutions, presidential proclamations, reorganization plans, and acts repealed or amended during that session are published in the *Statutes at Large.* Arrangement is chronological by date of enactment for each type of act: public laws, private laws, proclamations, etc. An index by subject and one by personal name are in each volume. This is the official text of the law, as enacted, and is preferred to the text in the *United States Code* (entry 1098) as court evidence.

1100.   **United States Code Congressional and Administrative News.** St. Paul, Minn.: West, 1941- . Monthly.

The texts of public laws, presidential orders, proclamations, and messages, and reorganization plans are published here long before the volume of the official *United States Statutes at Large* in which they will later appear. Also included are federal court rules and selected administrative rules and regulations. Especially valuable in legal research is the legislative history of each law, reprinting the official committee reports which explain the background of the legislation. In the last volume of the permanent edition and in the back of each monthly issue are tables of public laws, amendments and repeals, federal regulations, etc., keying them to the current volumes of *United States Statutes at Large* (entry 1099), *Code of Federal Regulations* (entry 1103), and other official publications. Other tables give the status of major bills in Congress and popular names of new public laws. The paperbound issues also have summaries of recent legislative debate and action.

1101.   **Federal Register.** Washington, D.C.: Government Printing Office, 1936- . Daily, except Sunday and Monday and days following legal holidays.

1102.   **CIS Federal Register Index.** Bethesda, Md.: Congressional Information Service, 1984- . Weekly.

1103.   **Code of Federal Regulations.** Washington, D.C.: Government Printing Office, 1958- .

1104.   **CFR Index and Finding Aids.** Washington, D.C.: Government Printing Office. Annual.

1105.   **LSA-List of CFR Sections Affected.** Washington, D.C.: Government Printing Office. Monthly.

1106.   **Index to the Code of Federal Regulations.** Washington, D.C.: Capital Services.

There are probably more questions about particular regulations of federal agencies than about particular laws or Constitutional provisions. The *Federal Register* is the official newspaper of the executive branch and carries the official text of presidential proclamations, executive orders, new rules and regulations, and other legal directives of the executive branch. Through use of the *CIS Federal Register Index*, one can quickly locate new and proposed rules, regulations, and other federal directives pertaining to a subject (aid to families with dependent children, air carriers), an agency or department (Bureau of Indian Affairs, Commodity Futures Trading Commission), company or industry (Boeing Commercial Airplane Company, construction industry), an act (Arms Export Control Act, Consumer Product Safety Act), or personal name (Black, Arthur R.; Bradley, James D.). Regulations are codified and printed in the *Code of Federal Regulations* under 50 titles, similar to but not corresponding exactly to the titles of the *United States Code*, so this is the first place to check to learn what regulations are in force on a particular subject. *CFR Index and Finding Aids* and the commercially published Index to the *Code of Federal Regulations* provide an approach by small subject to the Code, referring to title and part. *LSA-List of CFR Sections Affected* can be checked to learn if any amendments have been made to a particular regulation since the pertinent title was last revised (annually). *Federal Register* can be checked for any changes since the last monthly issue of *LSA-List of CFR Sections Affected.* See Joe Morehead's *Introduction to United States Public Documents*, 3d ed. Littleton, Colo.: Libraries Unlimited, 1983, 234-36, or Al Coco's *Finding the Law* (entry 1086, pp. 30-37) for fuller explanation of searching for a federal regulation.

1107.   **State code.**

The codification of the laws of one's own state is another frequently used reference tool. The law codes of all of the states (under slightly various titles) are available from West Publishing Company in St. Paul, Minn. These are similar to the *United States Code*, reprinting the text of all general and permanent laws of the state in force at the time of compilation, grouped under broad titles, e.g., agriculture, aliens, aviation, bail, banks.

1108.   **Shepard's Acts and Cases by Popular Names: Federal and State.** 2d ed. Colorado Springs, Colo.: Shepard's, 1979. 1373p. Supplements.

State and federal acts which are commonly known under a popular name are listed alphabetically with reference to the code or published statutes where the official text can be found. Examples are "Invited Guest Law," "Involuntary Manslaughter Act," "Ipswich Sewerage Loan Act," and "Iron Curtain Act."

BIOGRAPHY

1109.   **Who's Who in American Law.** 3d ed. Chicago: Marquis Who's Who, 1983. 863p.

Approximately 34,000 lawyers, judges, law school professors, and others associated with the legal profession are included in this edition. The brief biographical data emphasize the person's legal training and experience.

21

HISTORY, GEOGRAPHY

Neither of these fields generates the number of questions in the average university library that one encounters from the performing arts, literature, music, religion, education, and some of the other fields written about in previous chapters. History is a vast subject, covering not only an expanse of time from the earliest printed records to the recent past and peoples of all parts of the earth, but also including developments and achievements in politics, government, the arts and sciences, and all other fields.

The most frequent type of reference question on history from members of the faculty is bibliographic verification or completion of a faulty or incomplete reference. This type of question has been treated in chapter 2. Another typical faculty need is for help in locating a known item in the library catalog. Both types of question are commonly asked by faculty members in all subject fields. For undergraduates, the most usual types of questions have to do with the location of appropriate material (books and articles) for a term paper or assignment and for reviews of a particular book they are using for a source. Both of these types of questions have also been discussed in our introductory section.

Beyond these types are various questions of dates, identification of persons, places, battles, and incidents, or origins and background of events. For students, such questions are often connected with a paper they are writing or arise from their reading. But questions of this kind are also received by telephone from the community outside the university. They may be questions from a person's reading, general curiosity, conversation, or a contest. Seldom do such questions go beyond the ready-reference type. The most difficult or time-consuming are questions about a very recent event that has not yet been absorbed into the various history reference books. This type of question, which has to be answered in contemporary sources like *Facts on File*, a recent newspaper index, or recent issues of a newspaper may not be considered as a history question.

Questions related to geography are also relatively infrequent. Most geography questions are gazetteer questions, calling for the identification of a particular place or geographical feature, rather than requests for background information about a country or region. These are usually not course- or research-related and come from students, faculty members, and the general public. Sometimes, however, graduating students who have accepted a position or are considering a position in a city with which they are unfamiliar may want background information about that city. They are interested especially in the economic, cultural, and political climate of the place. Requests for detailed maps of particular areas of the United States or another country or for other types of maps (topographic, geologic, economic, etc.) which are not to be found in standard atlases are next most frequent after gazetteer questions. But these, too, are relatively infrequent. When it becomes known, however, that the university has exceptional map and gazetteer resources, a number of questions may be received on the telephone from the public and the public library. Many of these are to identify a town In Europe or the United States from which a person's ancestor came. This user group will also want a detailed map of a place that cannot be found in the general world atlas. Descriptive material may be wanted of a place a person wishes to visit or a place to which a faculty member has a research grant or a sabbatical leave.

Geography is treated in this chapter as an academic discipline. We have, therefore, not included travel guides. Physical geography is included with other earth sciences in chapter 26.

HISTORY

GUIDES, BIBLIOGRAPHIES, INDEXES

1110.   Poulton, Helen J., and Marguerite S. Howland. **The Historian's Handbook: A Descriptive Guide to Reference Works.** Norman, Okla.: University of Oklahoma Press, 1972. 304p.

Intended for the student and beginning researcher, this guide describes more than 940 bibliographies, national library catalogs, encyclopedias, dictionaries, and other reference sources in history and related areas and their use in historical research. A good introductory work.

1111.   American Historical Association. **Guide to Historical Literature.** New York: Macmillan, 1961. 962p.

Chapters on early periods of history and on later history of different parts of the world prepared by specialists in each field make this standard work a selected bibliography rather than a guide, like *The Historian's Handbook*, for the research worker. In each chapter the major reference works, sets, general histories, special histories, biographies, government publications, academy publications, periodicals, and outstanding library collections are listed. One problem with the work is that the index contains only authors but no titles, not even for works having no author entry.

1112.   International Committee of Historical Sciences. **International Bibliography of Historical Sciences.** Munich: Saur, 1926- . Annual.

In this annual selection of the most important books and articles in the field of history prepared by the International Committee of Historical Sciences and sponsored by UNESCO, all periods and areas of the world are represented. Each year, the bibliography is prepared by a different member country, and prefatory and explanatory matter is given in the language of that country. In the front of each volume, general bibliographies in history which have appeared during the year are listed; specialized bibliographies are listed at the head of each section, marked by an asterisk. This work is good for an overview of the year's literature, but scholars usually prefer more specialized lists on their own subject area. A serious problem with this bibliography is the tardiness of its publication, usually some five to six years after the works it lists. No volumes have appeared for the years 1940-46.

1113.   Roach, John, ed. **A Bibliography of Modern History.** Cambridge, England: Cambridge University Press, 1968. 388p.

The *New Cambridge Modern History* (entry 1158), unlike the other Cambridge history sets, was published without bibliographies at the end of each chapter, on the ground that bibliographies are easily found in more specialized histories. Partly to answer criticism for this lack, *A Bibliography of Modern History* was prepared under the editorship of John Roach. The authors of chapters of the *New Cambridge Modern History* were asked to select major references in their subject area for this bibliography. This bibliography is more selective than the *Guide to Historical Literature* (entry 1111) and has a narrower focus, favoring history of Europe over that of other parts of the world; but is a little more up-to-date than the *Guide* over the same years. Both bibliographies should be checked, however, for history since 1492.

1114. **C.R.I.S. Combined Retrospective Index Set to Journals in History, 1838-1974.** 11 vols. Arlington, Va.: Carrollton Press, 1977.

This set and the other indexes in the C.R.I.S. series (see entries 804, 1005) were produced by computer to meet student needs to examine older files of scholarly journals for suitable references for term papers. *C.R.I.S. Combined Retrospective Index to Journals in History, 1834-1974* indexes 243 English language periodicals from the beginning of their publication through 1974. Volumes 1-9 of the set index articles under subject (volumes 1-4, world history; volumes 5-9, U.S. history). The final two volumes list articles under authors.

1115. **Historical Abstracts.** Santa Barbara, Calif.: ABC-Clio, 1955- . Three issues per year plus annual cumulative author and subject indexes; 5-year cumulative author and subject indexes.

Historical Abstracts includes abstracts of periodical articles and selected Festschriften, proceedings, collections, books, and dissertations on modern history of all parts of the world. Currently, about 13,000 items are included in a year. These are published in two parts of the index: Part A, "Modern History Abstracts, 1450-1914," and Part B, "Twentieth Century Abstracts, 1914-Present." Cumulative annual and cumulative five-year author and subject indexes are issued. But a survey of the favorite methods used by historians for finding appropriate material in their field of research showed that use of abstract indexes and periodical indexes ranked low, and that *Readers' Guide to Periodical Literature* was used more often than *Historical Abstracts* by those in United States history and as often by those in other historical study.[1] *Historical Abstracts* can be machine searched back to 1973 through DIALOG.

1116. Paetow, Louis J. **A Guide to the Study of Medieval History.** Rev. ed. Prepared under the auspices of the Medieval Academy of America. New York: Crofts, 1931. Reprint ed. New York: Kraus, 1980. 643p.

1117. Boyce, Gray C., comp. and ed. **Literature of Medieval History, 1930-1975: A Supplement to Louis John Paetow's A Guide to the Study of Medieval History.** Sponsored by the Medieval Academy of America. 5 vols. Millwood, N.Y.: Kraus, 1981.

With the relative wealth of bibliographical sources recently published or in progress, one may wonder why we continue to include Paetow's 50-year-old work. But it is still very useful, especially for the person beginning work in this field. Following an initial section on general bibliography for medieval studies (reference works, histories, auxiliary sciences, collections of sources) are chapters under "General History of the Middle Ages" and "Medieval Culture." Each chapter has study topics, a list of books recommended for first attention, and additional sources of information. Books, articles, and theses written since 1930 are in the set compiled by Boyce. The definitive bibliography of chronicles and other original sources

[1]Margaret Stieg, "The Information Needs of Historians," *College and Research Libraries* 42 (November 1981): 549-60.

for medieval study is August Potthast's *Bibliotheca Historica Medii Aevi: Wegweiser durch die Geschichtswerke des Europäischer Mittelalters bis 1500*. (2. Aufl., 2 vols. Berlin: Weber, 1896. Reprint. Graz: Akademische Druck- und Verlagsanstalt, 1957). This is being superseded by *Repertorium Fontium Historiae Medii Aevi* (Rome: Instituto storico italiano per il medio evo, 1962- . In progress).

1118.   Crosby, Everett U., C. Julian Bishko, and Robert L. Kellogg. **Medieval Studies: A Bibliographical Guide.** New York: Garland, 1983. 1131p.

This is the latest selective bibliography for medievalists. It is compiled for the student and the general user, not for the experienced medievalist. All aspects of European, Byzantine, Islamic, and Jewish culture during the Middle Ages and all facets of medieval study are represented under 138 topical chapters.

1119.   **International Medieval Bibliography.** Edited by Richard J. Walsh. Leeds, England: University of Leeds, 1967- . Semiannual.

This, the principal index to current literature for medieval studies, currently includes about four thousand references per year drawn from some 1,300 journals and 200 Festschriften and other collections of articles.

1120.   Rouse, Richard H. **Serial Bibliographies for Medieval Studies.** Berkeley, Calif.: University of California Press, 1969. 150p. (Publications of the Center for Medieval and Renaissance Studies, 3).

A specialized but useful list of 283 bibliographies for medieval studies which are regularly included as part of a journal or are published as a serial. Part 1 lists bibliographies that are general and regional, giving for each the scope, forms of literature included, frequency, and publication lag. Part 2 lists bibliographies under special subject: auxiliary sciences (e.g., numismatics, palaeography, diplomatics), art, ecclesiastical history, economic history, etc.

1121.   **L'Année philologique: bibliographie critique et analytique de l'antiquité gréco-latine.** Paris: Société d'Édition "Les Belles-Lettres," 1928- . Annual.

For the current literature about the classical world, this is far the best bibliography. It covers all aspects of Greek and Roman history and culture plus some material on the Byzantine civilization, Judaeo-Christian culture, and medieval Europe. Currently listing approximately 12,000 references per year from about one thousand journals, Festschriften, and other collections, it has two parts. Part 1 lists material on classical authors and their writings; part 2, material on literary history of the period, paleography and papyrology, archaeology, history, science, and other aspects of classical culture. Indexes are many: collective titles of classical writings, names of real and mythological persons of the classical world, a geographic index, names of humanists, and names of the authors of articles listed.

DICTIONARIES, ENCYCLOPEDIAS

1122.   Wetterau, Bruce. **Macmillan Concise Dictionary of World History.** New York: Macmillan, 1983. 867p.

Here one finds brief identification of persons, events, terms, battles, and places of historical importance from earliest times to 1982. Some articles (countries, cities, regimes, wars) give chronologies. This book often gives enough information for ready reference.

1123.   Langer, William L., comp. and ed. **An Encyclopedia of World History: Ancient, Medieval, and Modern, Chronologically Arranged.** 5th ed., rev. & enl. Boston: Houghton Mifflin, 1972. 1569p.

1124.   **Harper Encyclopedia of the Modern World: A Concise Reference History from 1760 to the Present.** Edited by Richard B. Morris and Graham W. Irwin. New York: Harper & Row, 1970. 1271p.

Instead of the alphabetical arrangement of articles usual in an encyclopedia, these works give a condensed chronological account of the major events, movements, and governments of their respective periods. Langer covers the world from prehistory through 1970. This is a very good source for the date of a monarch or event or for the bare bones of history. Especially useful are the genealogical tables of royal houses, from the Maccabees of Jewish history to the emperors of Japan after 1867, and its lists (in the appendix) of Roman, Byzantine, and Holy Roman emperors; popes; kings of England and France; and other leaders whose succession or dates are sometimes wanted. The arrangement is by broad period and by country or region. When the history of a country or region is postponed or resumed, the page on which it is to be continued or from which it is continued is given; the same is done for genealogical tables of continuing royal families. There is also a two-volume edition, *The New Illustrated Encyclopedia of World History*, but it differs from this edition only in adding illustrations to an identical text. The *Harper Encyclopedia of the Modern World* is similar to Langer in arrangement and use, but covers its two centuries in greater detail.

1125.   Dupuy, R. Ernest, and Trevor N. Dupuy. **The Encyclopedia of Military History from 3500 B.C. to the Present.** New York: Harper & Row, 1977. 1464p.

Prior to the twentieth century, history texts concentrated on the political-military aspect of history. Modern writers cover economics, religion, culture, and social and other concerns as well as politics and military events. However, much that is omitted from modern history texts is given in this book, which has details of military organization, strategy, and the conduct of campaigns and individual battles. There are numerous diagrams, maps, and battle plans; arrangement is chronological and geographical to 1975. End material includes a bibliography, general index, index of battles and sieges, and an index of wars.

1126.   Williams, E. N. **The Facts on File Dictionary of European History, 1485-1789.** New York: Facts on File, 1980. 509p.

This book and the rest described in this section are restricted to the events of a particular epoch and a particular part of the world. These limitations of scope allow their editors to include more information about their subject than are given in the general works mentioned above. Williams's book contains articles, some lengthy, on persons, groups, and topics associated with the history of the three centuries ending with the French Revolution. Sample entries are "American Independence, War of"; "Anabaptists"; "Armada, the Spanish"; "Arminians"; "Augsburg Confession"; "Augsburg, Peace of"; "Austrian Succession, War of"; and "Balance of Powers." An index of names and subjects included within the articles is also given.

1127.   **A Concise Encyclopaedia of the Italian Renaissance.** Edited by J. R. Hale. New York: Oxford University Press, 1981. 360p.

1128.   **The New Century Italian Renaissance Encyclopedia.** New York: Appleton-Century-Crofts, 1972. 978p.

Broad coverage of the individuals, leading families, events, life, and customs of the period (which is generally considered to begin in Italy with Petrarch and end with the death of Michelangelo, or about 1325 to 1565) is given in these works. The second encyclopedia has more and longer articles than *A Concise Encyclopaedia of the Italian Renaissance* and covers more of the persons and topics outside Italy, but is limited more to the art and literature of the period. Most of its articles are on individuals, but it includes some articles on subjects (architecture, astrology and magic, humanism), major writings of the period (*Aspramonte, Decameron, Dicts and Sayings of the Philosophers, Divina Commedia*), and characters in literary works (Argalia, Dipsodes). The first encyclopedia has more on the life and society of the period, covering subjects like "Children"; "Chivalry"; "Class, Social"; and "Clergy, Secular."

1129.   **Dictionary of the Middle Ages.** Edited by Joseph R. Strayer. Vol. 1- . New York: Scribner's, 1982- . In progress.

1130.   Grabois, Aryeh. **The Illustrated Encyclopedia of Medieval Civilization.** New York: Mayflower Books, 1980. 751p.

The titles of these two works on the Middle Ages should be reversed because the former has more articles and lengthier treatment of the period, generally taken to be roughly from A.D. 500 to A.D. 1500, than the latter. *The Dictionary of the Middle Ages'* detailed articles, many with bibliographies, are contributed by some two hundred scholars, who are listed in the front of each volume with the articles in that volume which they have written. Topics, persons, art and architecture, literature, science, and other medieval achievements are covered. The project is under the sponsorship of the American Council of Learned Societies. The *Illustrated Encyclopedia of Medieval Civilization* also gives excellent, detailed coverage, despite its being the work of a single author. Both works cover, in addition to European civilization, the Byzantine, Moslem, and Jewish civilization of those centuries, and both have many illustrations.

1131.   **The Encyclopedia of Ancient Civilizations.** Edited by Arthur Cotterell. New York: Mayflower Books, 1980. 367p.

Richard E. Leakey's chapters on prehistory and Colin Renfrew's on the emergence of civilization are followed by chapters by other scholars on ancient civilizations of various parts of the world. These are described in detail with many illustrations. The history, literature, achievements in science and technology, economy and social structure, and government of each civilization are covered. This is a very good source for an overview of a civilization, religion, or topic in ancient history: e.g., evolution of the alphabet, early science and technology in China. Classical Greece and Rome are also included here, but not in Hawkes's *The Atlas of Early Man* (entry 1143).

1132.   **Oxford Classical Dictionary.** 2d ed. Revised and augmented by N. G. L. Hammond and H. H. Scullard. Oxford: Clarendon Press, 1970. 1176p.

This book resembles the other Oxford dictionaries and companions in giving authoritative, compact, and informative articles on a wide variety of topics and names. The *Oxford Classical Dictionary*, although not as complete as the older *Harper's Dictionary of Classical Literature and Antiquities* (Edited by Harry T. Peck. New York: Harper, 1896. Reprint. Cincinnati: American Book Co., 1923; New York: Cooper Square, 1965), identifies Greek and Roman individuals, places, mythological beings, subjects, customs, and terms. Christian persons and terms, except for the most prominent, are omitted, although falling within the time period covered here (into the fourth century), because of their full treatment in other reference books. The definitive, scholarly encyclopedia of classical learning is *Pauly's Realencyclopädie der klassischen Altertumswissenschaft* (usually called simply "Pauly-Wissowa" after its editors or, by German writers, *RE*).

DIRECTORIES

1133.   U.S. General Services Administration. National Archives and Records Service. National Historical Publications and Records Commission. **Directory of Archives and Manuscript Repositories in the United States.** Washington, D.C.: Government Printing Office, 1978. 905p.

Scholars doing historical research frequently need archives and manuscripts. Stieg's survey shows that manuscripts and archives are used next most by historians after books and periodicals.[1] A directory like this one is, therefore, useful in telling where records on a certain person or group or subject (e.g., "immigrants, Swedish"; "India, Trade with U.S."; "Indians") can be located. For each of the 2,675 repositories listed by state and city, the directory gives the opening hours and facilities, types of materials solicited, type and number of holdings, and reference to catalogs and other publications about the repository and its holdings. The general index includes names of repositories, subjects, and names of persons or institutions whose papers are located in one or more of the libraries and archives. There is also a list of repositories by type (federal agencies, local historical societies, museums, or public libraries). This directory revises *A Guide to Archives and Manuscripts in the United States* (Edited by Philip A. Hamer. New Haven, Conn.: Yale University Press, 1961).

1134.   **Directory of Historical Societies and Agencies in the United States and Canada.** 12th ed. Compiled and edited by Tracy L. Craig. Nashville, Tenn.: American Association for State and Local History, 1982. 416p.

The address and telephone number, name of president/director, founding date, number of members, number of staff, major programs, and period covered by the collections are given for each of the 5,865 historical societies and agencies that are listed here by state and city. The institutions are also listed alphabetically and by type (agriculture; archaeology; ethnic heritage, race, religion; genealogy; historic individuals) in separate indexes.

HANDBOOKS

1135.   Collison, Robert, comp. **Dictionary of Dates.** Rev. ed. New York: Transatlantic Arts, 1967. 428p.

1136.   Mirkin, Stanford M. **What Happened When: A Noted Researcher's Almanac of Yesterdays.** New York: Washburn, 1966. 442p.

A common ready-reference question is simply about the date of an event, a person's birth or death, or some other date in history. There are a number of quick sources for such a question, and the choice is often made according to which, of several possible sources, is closest. If it is the birth date or death date of a famous person, the easiest place to try is the section, "Biographical Names," in the back of *Webster's New Collegiate Dictionary* or *Webster's Biographical Dictionary.* If the date of a well-known event (the Battle of Actium, the Sicilian Vespers) is wanted, use Langer's *An Encyclopedia of World History* (entry 1123); and Joseph Kane's *Famous First Facts* (4th ed., expanded and rev. New York: Wilson, 1981) is useful for the date of inventions, discoveries, and innovations in the United States. The two handbooks listed above are compiled partly with such a reference need in mind. The first is an alphabetical list of persons, events, subjects, cities, inventions, institutions, etc., with their dates. It also presents these dates and anniversaries in a calendar arrangement. Mirkin's work is arranged by the calendar, listing events by the day of the year. It has an alphabetical

---

[1]Stieg, "The Information Needs of Historians," *College and Research Libraries* 42 (November 1981): 551.

index, referring events to the day on which they occurred. This is useful for learning what events and anniversaries are observed on any particular day, but it is not as convenient for learning the date on which something happened. It has a strong emphasis on American events, while Collison's *Dictionary of Dates* stresses British events.

1137. Grun, Bernard. **The Timetables of History: A Horizontal Linkage of People and Events.** New, updated ed. New York: Simon & Schuster, 1979. 676p.

1138. Trager, James, ed. **The People's Chronology: A Year-by-Year Record of Human Events from Prehistory to the Present.** New York: Holt, Rinehart & Winston, 1979. 1206p.

1139. Mellersh, H. E. L. **Chronology of the Ancient World, 10,000 B.C. to A.D. 799.** London: Barrie & Jenkins, 1976. 500p.

1140. Storey, Robin L. **Chronology of the Medieval World, 800 to 1491.** London: Barrie & Jenkins; New York: McKay, 1973. 705p.

1141. Williams, Neville. **Chronology of the Expanding World, 1492 to 1762.** London: Barrie & Rockliff, Crescent Press, 1979. 700p.

1142. Williams, Neville. **Chronology of the Modern World, 1763 to 1965.** London: Barrie & Jenkins, 1966; New York: McKay, 1967. 923p.

Books like these are useful for noting what happened and what discoveries and achievements in literature, music, art, science, and technology were made in a given year in different parts of the world. Books on history are frequently limited to a particular subject, such as politics, literature, music, or art. A user sometimes wants to know what scientific discoveries and inventions were made in Shakespeare's time or what oriental artists were contemporary with Michelangelo. If the year in which an event occurred or a person died or an opera was composed is not known, this can be looked up in the index; parallel events then can be checked by looking under the year. Usually, only the year in which something occurred is given, not the day.

1143. Hawkes, Jacquetta. **The Atlas of Early Man.** New York: St. Martin's, 1976. 255p.

1144. Platt, Colin. **The Atlas of Medieval Man.** New York: St. Martin's, 1980. 256p.

These have a use similar to that of the chronologies just described, but present parallel developments in a heavily illustrated, descriptive text as well as in tabular form. Hawkes covers achievements and events around the world from the emergence of Homo sapiens (about 40,000 years ago) to A.D. 500 in eight broad time periods. Platt does the same kind of thing by century from A.D. 1000 to A.D. 1500. Neither book pins occurrences down to precise dates, as the preceding chronologies do, but both atlases are profusely illustrated and very interesting to read.

1145. **Rulers and Governments of the World.** 3 vols. London & New York: Bowker, 1977-78. Vol. 1, **Earliest-1491.** Compiled by Martha Ross; vol. 2, **1492-1929.** Compiled by Bertold Spuler; vol. 3, **1930-1975.** Compiled by Bertold Spuler and others.

As noted earlier, emperors, kings, popes, caliphs, and statesmen of selected empires and countries can be found through Langer's *An Encyclopedia of World History* (entry 1123). But many more governments and dynasties are listed here. This will often be helpful to the student or other user who needs to know where a particular monarch or statesman fits into a succession or to know the inclusive dates of a reign. If the relationship of an emperor or king to his predecessor or other person in the dynasty is wanted, however, the genealogical table in Langer is usually better. A convenient one-volume handbook which, however, is much less complete than the above is *Kings, Rulers, and Statesmen* (Rev. ed. Compiled by Edward W. Egan and others. New York: Sterling, 1976).

ATLASES

1146.   **Muir's Historical Atlas: Ancient, Medieval, and Modern.** 10th ed. Edited by R. F. Treherne and H. Fullard. 2 vols. in 1. London: G. Philip, 1976. (Reprint of *Muir's Historical Atlas: Ancient and Classical*, 6th ed., 1963, and *Muir's Historical Atlas: Medieval and Modern*, 11th ed., 1969).

1147.   **Rand McNally Historical Atlas of the World.** Edited by R. I. Moore and others. Chicago: Rand McNally, 1981. 192p.

1148.   **Shepherd's Historical Atlas.** 9th rev. ed. Edited by William R. Shepherd. New York: Barnes & Noble, 1980. 341p.

1149.   **The Times Concise Atlas of World History.** Edited by Geoffrey Barraclough. Maplewood, N.J.: Hammond, 1982. 192p.

1150.   Vries, Sjoerd de, and others. **An Atlas of World History.** London: Nelson, 1966. 183p.

These examples of well-known historical atlases, or others like them, will answer many questions from students, general readers, and scholars. They are useful for designating political boundaries at various epochs, routes followed by explorers and conquerors, the distribution of monastic centers in medieval Europe or of printing centers during the Reformation, city plans of ancient Rome or London, and for other maps which aid us in understanding history. At least three or four of these should be available, as each offers maps not in others. Specialized historical atlases can go into more depth about their specific area and epoch than these general historical atlases. Examples of specialized historical atlases are John Baines and Jaromir Malek's *Atlas of Ancient Egypt* (New York: Facts on File, 1980), Nicholas Hammond's *Atlas of the Greek and Roman World in Antiquity* (Park Ridge, N.J.: Noyes, 1981), Kenneth T. Jackson's *Atlas of American History* (entry 1176), and Bible atlases (entries 316-18).

STATISTICS

1151.   Mitchell, B. R. **European Historical Statistics, 1750-1975.** 2d ed. New York: Facts on File, 1980. 868p.

1152.   Mitchell, B. R. **International Historical Statistics: Africa and Asia.** New York: New York University Press, 1982. 761p.

1153.   Mitchell, B. R. **International Historical Statistics: The Americas and Australasia.** Detroit: Gale, 1983. 949p.

Statistics are not sought in historical research as often as in research in other social sciences. The three works listed here, however, can be very helpful when statistics of past years are needed. All three draw statistics from official publications of the countries involved. Tables give comparative figures on climate, population and vital statistics, labor force, agriculture, industry, trade, transport and communications, finance, prices, education, and national accounts of the different countries. The dates covered go back, on occasion, to the mid-eighteenth century for countries of Europe and to the mid-nineteenth century for the countries of other continents. Also see *Historical Statistics of the United States, Colonial Times to 1970* (entry 1177).

REFERENCE HISTORIES

1154. **Cambridge Ancient History.** Edited by I. E. S. Edwards and others. 12 vols. of text, 5 vols. of plates. Cambridge, England: Cambridge University Press; New York: Macmillan, 1923-39. Rev. ed., vols. 3-11, 1951-54. 3d ed., vol. 1- . 1944- . In progress.

1155. **Cambridge Medieval History.** Planned by J. B. Bury, edited by H. M. Gwatkin and others. 8 vols. Cambridge, England: Cambridge University Press; New York: Macmillan, 1911-36.

1156. **The Shorter Cambridge Medieval History.** Edited by C. W. Previté-Orton. 2 vols. Cambridge, England: Cambridge University Press, 1952.

1157. **Cambridge Modern History.** Planned by Lord Acton, edited by A. W. Ward and others. 13 vols. and atlas. Cambridge, England: Cambridge University Press, 1902-12.

1158. **New Cambridge Modern History.** Edited by G. R. Potter and others. 14 vols. Cambridge, England: Cambridge University Press, 1957-79.

The Cambridge histories are widely known and respected as authoritative, scholarly works. They are most useful when a fairly extensive and dependable account of a subject is wanted, but one which could be covered in a relatively brief time. Each chapter is written by a scholar specializing in the subject. *Cambridge Ancient History* covers the period from prehistory and the earliest civilizations of Babylonia and Egypt down to the decline and temporary recovery of the Roman Empire in A.D. 324. The third edition adds much new research; it now reaches to the expansion of the Greek world of the eighth to the sixth century B.C. The *Cambridge Medieval History* covers the Eastern Roman Empire as well as medieval Europe and from Constantine (beginning of the fourth century A.D.) through the Renaissance. Its volume 4 was revised and issued as *The Byzantine Empire* (2 vols., 1966-67). These works are scholarly, heavily documented, and have bibliographies for each chapter. The *New Cambridge Modern History* is less well documented and does not have bibliographies. Roach's *A Bibliography of Modern History* (entry 1113) was published to make up for this lack. Nevertheless, and despite the much-needed updating of the new set, most libraries keep the older *Cambridge Modern History* alongside it for its additional information.

BIOGRAPHY

1159. **Historical Biographical Dictionaries Master Index: A Consolidated Index to Biographical Information Covering Historical Personages in Over 35 of the Principal Retrospective Biographical Dictionaries.** Edited by Barbara McNeil and Miranda C. Herbert. Detroit: Gale, 1980. 1003p.

This timesaver resembles Gale's other biographical master indexes, notably *Biography and Genealogy Master Index* (entry 121). More than 304,000 entries have been brought together from collections such as *Appleton's Cyclopedia of American Biography, Biographical Cyclopedia of American Women, Biographical History of Medicine,* and *Twentieth Century Biographical Dictionary of Notable Americans.* Although the emphasis is on Americans, persons from other countries are represented.

Biographical information on historians living in the United States and Canada is found in the *Directory of American Scholars* (entry 228). The first volume of the current edition lists about 11,000 historians, giving career information and major publications. The *International Encyclopedia of the Social Sciences* (entry 703) has biographical articles on thirty prominent historians of the past. Biographies of historically important rulers, warriors, writers, explorers, inventors, and others are usually found easily in a general encyclopedia or in one of the historical dictionaries and encyclopedias described above (entries 1122, 1126-30, 1132). If not found there, try the appropriate national biographical work referred to in chapter 4. Brief identifying data and reference to sources of further information (usually in a language other than English) for a person of the Middle Ages whose name has not been located elsewhere may be found in Chevalier's *Répertoire des sources historiques du moyen âge, Biobibliographie* (entry 161). There are also a number of collections of biographies of a particular period of history, such as Holger H. Herwig and Neil M. Heyman's *Biographical Dictionary of World War I* (Westport, Conn.: Greenwood, 1982); Jon L. Wakelyn's *Biographical Dictionary of the Confederacy* (Westport, Conn.: Greenwood, 1977); Alan Palmer and Veronica Palmer's *Who's Who in Shakespeare's England* (New York: St. Martin's, 1981); John Fines's *Who's Who in the Middle Ages* (New York: Stein & Day, 1970); and Diana Bowder's *Who Was Who in the Greek World* (Ithaca, N.Y.: Cornell University Press, 1982) and *Who Was Who in the Roman World* (Ithaca, N.Y.: Cornell University Press, 1980). Seldom, however, will these add either names or amount of information to what can be found elsewhere.

UNITED STATES

More students will usually have an interest in the history of the United States than in the history of other countries and early periods. Reference works pertaining to the United States have, therefore, been put in this special section.

Guides, Bibliographies, Indexes

1160.   Beers, Henry P. **Bibliographies in American History, 1942-1978: Guide to Materials for Research.** 2 vols. Woodbridge, Conn.: Research Publications, 1982.

A new edition of this famous bibliography of bibliographies makes it again of much value to graduate students, faculty, and others doing research in American history. Nearly 12,000 monographic bibliographies, bibliographies published as articles, bibliographies in progress, and manuscript bibliographies, most published or completed in 1942 or later, are listed. All aspects of American history are covered: general, economic, educational, military and naval, religious, social, regional and state. There is an extensive index, which should also be searched for additional material.

1161.   **Harvard Guide to American History.** Rev. ed. Edited by Frank Freidel and Richard K. Showman. 2 vols. Cambridge, Mass.: Belknap Press of Harvard University Press, 1974.

Unquestionably the best single bibliography on American history. Thousands of references are given to books and periodical articles on Colonial and United States history, arranged by special area (e.g., government, law, politics, education, social ills and reform, and religion) in volume 1 and by chronological period in volume 2. There are also sections on research methods and materials, biographies and personal records, and comprehensive and area histories. To supplement this work, one might check *C.R.I.S. Combined Retrospective Index to Journals in History* (entry 1114), of which volumes 5-9 are on the history of the United States.

1162. **Writings on American History, 1906- .** Washington, D.C.: American Historical Association, 1908- . Annual.

For still more references, this annual bibliography can be checked. Early volumes contained references to material on British North America and Latin America, as well as the United States. Beginning in 1936, it was restricted to material on the history of the United States, and beginning with a new series edited by James J. Dougherty, *Writings on American History, 1962-* , only periodical articles are included.

1163. **America: History and Life.** Santa Barbara, Calif.: ABC-Clio, 1964- .

This, the principal index to articles on past and current life in the United States and Canada, is issued in four parts. Part A, "Article Abstracts and Citations," 3 issues per year, indexes articles from some two thousand serial publications. Abstracts are arranged by classification of chronological period and area. Part B, "Index to Book Reviews," 2 issues per year, cites reviews arranged by author of book reviewed; a title index and a reviewer index are included. Part C, "American History Bibliography," annual, is arranged by the same classification used in Part A. It lists by author the articles from Part A and the book reviews from Part B. It is intended as a basic annual bibliography for United States and Canadian history. Part D is the annual cumulated subject index, author index, book title index, book reviewer index, list of periodicals indexed, and list of abstractors. *America: History and Life* can be machine searched back to 1964 through DIALOG.

1164. Tingley, Donald F. **Social History of the United States: A Guide to Information Sources.** Detroit: Gale, 1979. 260p.

1165. Ireland, Norma. **Index to America: Life and Customs.** 4 vols. New York: Faxon, 1976- . In progress.

Materials for the study of the social history of the United States are presented in *Social History of the United States* by century from the colonial era to the present and by broad subject, e.g., "Black Americans," "Other Ethnic Groups," "Women and Feminism," "Children and Youth," and "Poverty and Its Remedy." A total of approximately 1,200 references are annotated. Separate author, title, and subject indexes are provided. The second work indexes several hundred books on American culture and history by small subject and proper names. Thus far, two volumes have been completed, covering the seventeenth and eighteenth centuries. Two further works, on the nineteenth and twentieth centuries, are in preparation.

Dictionaries, Encyclopedias

1166. **Dictionary of American History.** Rev. ed. 8 vols. New York: Scribner's, 1976.

If a summary article or an identification of an event, place, battle, legislative act, court case, or subject of significance in American history is needed, the *Dictionary of American History* is the source most librarians would check first. Biographical articles on prominent Americans are not included since these are in the companion set, the *Dictionary of American Biography* (entry 144). Sample articles are "Delaware Circle," "Delegation of Powers," "DeLima v. Bidwell (1901)," "Demarcation Line," "Export-Import Banks," "Fair Deal," "Fair-Trade Laws," "Lighthouse Service," "Lighting," and "Ligonier, Fort." The index volume should be used for subjects and names discussed within main articles. Most articles in this work have been rewritten in shorter form for the one-volume *Concise Dictionary of American History* (edited by David W. Voorhees and others. New York: Scribner's, 1983). This shorter work is handy for a quick reference. Also see *The Oxford Companion to American History* (entry 1170).

1167. Hochman, Stanley. **Yesterday and Today: A Dictionary of Recent American History.** New York: McGraw-Hill, 1979. 407p.

Since information on events in fairly recent history is often wanted, this compilation of articles on topical events and subjects in American life since the end of World War II is useful. While much is necessarily on political events and subjects, there is also information on social, economic, educational, and cultural topics. A sampling of nonpolitical entries: action painting, acupuncture, *The Affluent Society*, agribusiness, airmobile, Alaskan pipeline, alienation index, "All in the Family."

1168. Lamar, Howard R., ed. **The Reader's Encyclopedia of the American West.** New York: Crowell, 1977. 1306p.

Approximately one-half of the 2,400 entries of this book are biographical articles for writers, political figures, artists, engineers, trappers, educators, and others prominent in the development of the West from the first expansion of European settlers to recent post-World War II history. Places, events, and subjects constitute the other half. About two hundred contributors have supplied the articles on such topics as dime novels, the Disciples of Christ, diseases, Disneyland, doctors, Dolores, NM, Donelson's Line, and Donner party.

1169. Fogarty, Robert S. **Dictionary of American Communal and Utopian History.** Westport, Conn.: Greenwood, 1980. 271p.

The main part of this specialized dictionary is biographical sketches of some 150 leaders of communal and utopian societies in America during the late eighteenth to the early twentieth centuries, followed by brief articles on about twenty such societies. An appendix is an annotated list of 270 settlements arranged chronologically by date of founding.

Handbooks

1170. Johnson, Thomas H. **The Oxford Companion to American History.** New York: Oxford University Press, 1966. 906p.

Brief articles identifying topics, terms, events, persons, Indian tribes, legislation and court cases, and battles that were significant in American history comprise this companion. Examples of its estimated four thousand entries: "Fitzpatrick, Thomas," "Five civilized tribes," "Five Forks, Battle of," "Flag Day," "Flag of the United States," "Flagler, Henry Morrison," "Flapper," "Flathead Indians," "Fletcher v. Peck," and "Flexner, Abraham."

1171. Morris, Richard B., and Jeffrey B. Morris, eds. **Encyclopedia of American History.** 6th ed. New York: Harper & Row, 1982. 1285p.

1172. **Webster's Guide to American History: A Chronological Survey and Compendium.** Springfield, Mass.: Merriam, 1971. 1428p.

A year-by-year summary of American history, giving major events, is the opening section of each of these handbooks. The *Encyclopedia of American History* also has a "Topical Chronology," which recounts American history by subject: "The Expansion of the Nation," "Population, Immigration, and Ethnic Stock," "The American Economy," "Science, Invention, and Technology," "Thought and Culture." Its final section is a series of biographies, "Five Hundred Notable Americans." *Webster's Guide to American History* has a section of historical maps and various tables. There are, for example, tables of states, with dates and order of admission to the Union, capital cities, area and rank order; presidents and their cabinets; and various historical statistics. This book also has a section of biographies of notable Americans.

1173.   Commager, Henry S., ed. **Documents of American History.** 9th ed. Englewood Cliffs, N.J.: Prentice-Hall, 1973. 815p.

An essential tool in any library, this is a compilation of 695 documents deemed important in American and United States history. The documents (translated into English, if necessary) are reprinted in full or in part and arranged chronologically from "Privileges and Prerogatives Granted to Columbus" by Ferdinand and Isabella of Spain in 1492 to *Miller v. California*, the Supreme Court decision of 21 June 1973, defining obscenity. Speeches, letters, treaties, court decisions, presidential proclamations, and legislative acts are among the documents. A brief headnote often explains the background or the significance of the document. There is an index of documents, personal and corporate names, keywords, and subjects.

1174.   Carruth, Gorton, and others. **The Encyclopedia of American Facts and Dates.** 7th ed. New York: Crowell, 1979. 1015p.

This resembles *The Timetables of History* (entry 1137) in presenting both major and minor events in American history year by year in four parallel columns: "Politics and Government; War; Disasters; Vital Statistics," "Books; Paintings; Drama; Architecture; Sculpture," "Science; Industry; Economics; Education; Religion; Philosophy," and "Sports; Fashions; Popular Entertainment; Folklore; Society." An alphabetical index helps locate the year of an event, invention, or publication; events, innovations, or achievements in other areas of American life in that year and surrounding years can then be found. This edition has simply added a supplement covering the years 1970-1977, with its own index, to the main chronology and its index, which ends with 1969.

Atlases

1175.   **The American Heritage Pictorial Atlas of United States History.** New York: American Heritage, 1966. 424p.

1176.   **Atlas of American History.** Rev. ed. Edited by Kenneth T. Jackson. New York: Scribner's, 1978. 294p.

Maps in these atlases show state and territorial boundaries and the advance of the frontier at different periods of our history, sites of Indian wars, major roads, canals, and railroads, exploration routes, immigration and settlement, population distribution at different times, and other pictorial aids to understanding American history.

Statistics

1177.   U.S. Department of Commerce. Bureau of the Census. **Historical Statistics of the United States, Colonial Times to 1970.** 2 vols. Washington, D.C.: Government Printing Office, 1976.

Statistics on population, causes of death, health and medical care, labor, prices, industry, housing, education, crime, and all other aspects of life in the United States are given from the earliest date for which records are available to 1970. Arrangement is by broad subject groups. Each volume has a "Time Period Index," summarizing the dates covered in each table, and an alphabetical subject index covering both volumes.

OTHER COUNTRIES

In order to limit the length of this chapter, we do not describe the primary aids for studying the history of all countries. A majority of students in history will be interested in the history of the United States and, to a lesser extent, of Great Britain and Commonwealth countries, and we have given reference sources for them in the previous section. In studying these countries, students can avoid a foreign language problem. The faculty member or graduate student doing research in French, German, Italian, or Slavic history or the history of another country will be familiar with the principal bibliographies, encyclopedias, and other reference tools for such study, and will be able to read the appropriate language. Additional references are found in Sheehy's *Guide to Reference Books,* Walford's *Guide to Reference Material*, and White's *Sources of Information in the Social Sciences.* For helping the student or faculty member who has a reference question about the history of another country but does not have the interest, the time, or the language ability to pursue the question deeply, sufficient information might be found in a general encyclopedia like *Encyclopaedia Britannica* or in one of the general works on historical research described above.

GEOGRAPHY

GUIDES, BIBLIOGRAPHIES, INDEXES

1178. Brewer, J. Gordon. **The Literature of Geography: A Guide to Its Organization and Use.** 2d ed. London: Bingley, 1978. 264p.

The best general guide to the literature of geography is this one, directed to the beginning student. All of geography and its subdivisions are covered in bibliographic essay form. Most titles are in English, but a few in German and French are cited. An author-title-subject index is provided.

1179. Harris, Chauncy D. **Bibliography of Geography.** Part 1: **Introduction to General Aids.** Chicago: The University of Chicago, Department of Geography, 1976. 276p. (Research Paper, no. 179).

The standard guide to the field, John K. Wright and Elizabeth T. Platt's *Aids to Geographical Research* (2d ed. New York: Columbia University Press, 1947. Reprint. Westport, Conn.: Greenwood, 1971), was to be superseded by this work, of which only the first part has appeared to date. It discusses almost six hundred bibliographies of geographical material, published as books, serials, government documents, dissertations, and in other forms. It also has a list of 55 atlases, gazetteers, encyclopedias, and handbooks selected for a small geographical reference collection.

1180. Goddard, Stephen, ed. **A Guide to Information Sources in the Geographical Sciences.** Totowa, N.J.: Barnes & Noble, 1983. 273p.

Only selected areas of geography are covered in this work in bibliographical essays by specialists. These are four subdivisions of the discipline (geomorphology, historical geography, agricultural geography, and industrial geography), four regions (Africa, South Asia, United States, and U.S.S.R.), and four kinds of research tools (maps, atlases, gazetteers; aerial photographs and satellite information; statistical materials and the computer; and archival materials). There is no index to the material described.

1181.   American Geographical Society. **Research Catalogue.** 15 vols. Boston: G. K. Hall, 1962. 1st Supplement, 4 vols. 1972. 2d Supplement, 2 vols. 1978.

1182.   **Current Geographical Publications: Additions to the Research Catalogue of the American Geographical Society Collection.** Milwaukee: The University of Wisconsin-Milwaukee, The Golda Meir Library, 1938- . 10 issues per year.

The reprinted catalog of the American Geographical Society is the most complete general English language bibliography of the entire field. More than 300,000 books, pamphlets, periodical articles, atlases, and maps are listed in the basic catalog and its two supplements. Another 8,000 items per year are listed in *Current Geographical Publications*, each issue of which is divided into four parts: "Topical," "Regional," "Selected Maps," and "Selected Books and Monographs." This serial has an annual cumulated index.

1183.   Lewthwaite, Gordon R., and others, eds. **A Geographical Bibliography for American College Libraries.** Washington, D.C.: Association of American Geographers, 1970. 214p. (Commission on College Geography Publication, no. 9).

This selected bibliography of 1,760 items groups them as "General Aids and Sources," "History, Philosophy, and Methods," "Works Grouped by Topic," (e.g., population geography, political geography, medical geography, climatology, economic geography), and "Works Grouped by Region."

1184.   **Geo Abstracts.** Norwich, England: Geo Abstracts, 1966- . 6 issues per year.

There are currently seven series of this abstract index, each published six times per year. Since we defer physical geography to chapter 26, only three series concern us here: C: *Economic Geography,* D: *Social and Historical Geography*, and F: *Regional and Community Planning.* A combined annual index of these three series is issued.

1185.   **Bibliographie géographique internationale. International Geographical Bibliography.** Paris: Laboratoire d'Information et de Documentation en Géographie (Intergéo). Centre National de la Recherche Scientifique, 1891- . Quarterly.

Although non-English literature is also covered in *Current Geographical Publications*, this quarterly bibliography is more extensive, indexing more than five hundred journals plus selected monographs and including some seven thousand citations per year. It has annual indexes of subjects, places, and authors.

1186.   Winch, Kenneth L., ed. **International Maps and Atlases in Print.** 2d ed. London and New York: Bowker, 1976. 866p.

Maps and atlases of all parts of the world that were in print in 1975 are listed here. The arrangement under continent and country is by type of map: road maps, official surveys, relief maps, geology, climate, and others. For each map and atlas, the scale, publisher, size in centimeters, price, and other data are given.

DICTIONARIES, ENCYCLOPEDIAS

1187.   Buchanan, R. Ogilvie, ed. **An Illustrated Dictionary of Geography.** London: Heinemann, 1974. 242p.

1188.   Schmieder, Allen A., and others. **A Dictionary of Basic Geography.** Boston: Allyn & Bacon, 1970. 299p.

Written for the novice in geographical study, both of these dictionaries cover all aspects of the subject: physical, agricultural, economic, political, cultural, and human geography. Buchanan has about 2,500 terms used in geographical study (about twice the number in Schmieder), and has drawings and illustrations.

1189.   Stamp, Laurence D., and Audrey N. Clark, eds. **A Glossary of Geographical Terms.** 3d ed. Based on a List Prepared by a Committee of the British Association for the Advancement of Science. New York: Longman, 1979. 571p.

The most scholarly dictionary of geographical terms, giving origins, current usage, and sometimes illustrative quotations and sources. Geography and all of its subdivisions are covered. The definition and origin, as given in the *Oxford English Dictionary*, is frequently cited.

1190.   **Encyclopedia of World Geography.** London: Octopus Books, 1974. 400p.

1191.   **Larousse Encyclopedia of World Geography.** Edited by Pierre Deffontaines. New York: Odyssey, 1965. 736p.

For questions from students about a country, its topography, climate, flora and fauna, agriculture, industry, economy, and people, these one-volume encyclopedias will probably provide a quick answer. The information is not enough for an in-depth study, but will satisfy general questions. Both books are well illustrated.

1192.   **Worldmark Encyclopedia of the Nations.** 6th ed. Edited by M. Y. Sachs. 5 vols. New York: Wiley, 1984.

If additional information about a country is needed, this encyclopedia with its more detailed treatment may have it. Volume one is about the United Nations, its organization, procedures, and its several affiliated world groups. The remaining four volumes, by continent, have 163 articles on individual countries, giving a description of the country, brief history, people, language, religion, government, economy, industry, health, education, and various other information.

1193.   **Cities of the World.** Edited by Margaret W. Young. 4 vols. Detroit: Gale, 1982. Supplement, 1983.

This set is similar, covering 131 countries and about 2,000 major cities. The information is for American travelers to a foreign country and would-be residents. The type of data furnished includes a description of a country and its people, government, transportation, industry, major cities, schools for English-speaking children, places to visit, recreation and cultural facilities, and notes (such as currency, local customs, etc.) for travelers. The supplement updates information on some countries and cities.

1194.   Gresswell, R. Kay, and Anthony Huxley, eds. **Standard Encyclopedia of the World's Rivers and Lakes.** New York: Putnam, 1965. 384p.

A full description is given for some five hundred major rivers, lakes, reservoirs, and falls. This includes the location, length, source, and outlet for rivers, the area, length, and breadth for lakes and reservoirs, and the height and breadth for falls. Besides the location, map coordinates are given for all features. For two thousand other rivers, lakes, and falls, the location, and length or size are briefly given in a separate gazetteer.

DIRECTORIES

1195.   **Orbis Geographicus. World Directory of Geography.** Compiled and edited by E. Meynen on behalf of the International Geographical Union. Wiesbaden: Steiner, 1974. 798p.

Part 1 of this directory lists member countries of the International Geographical Union and their officers, geographical societies, agencies, and institutes of all countries, giving the address, name of secretary, and date of founding. Important map collections are also listed. Part 2, a list of geographers, is described below (entry 1209).

1196.   Association of American Geographers. **Guide to Graduate Departments of Geography in the United States and Canada.** Washington, D.C.: The Association, 1968- . Annual.

Data are furnished for some 150 graduate departments of geography, including the date founded, degrees offered, degrees awarded the previous year, the number of students, programs and research facilities, admission requirements and financial aid, a list of the faculty and staff members, and titles of doctoral dissertations completed the previous year. At the back of the guide are a consolidated staff directory and a geographic index.

HANDBOOKS

1197.   Sharp, Harold S. **Handbook of Geographic Nicknames.** Metuchen, N.J.: Scarecrow, 1980. 153p.

1198.   Kane, Joseph N., and Gerard L. Alexander. **Nicknames and Sobriquets of U.S. Cities, States, and Counties.** 3d ed. Metuchen, N.J.: Scarecrow, 1979. 429p.

Much less frequent than gazetteer questions, but sometimes arising, are requests to identify a place known only by some popular nickname. Sharp lists a number of nicknames of places and identifies the real place, e.g., "City of Churches" (Toronto), "City of Diamonds" (Golconda, India), "Eternal City" (Rome), "The Holy River" (Ganges), "Pearl of the Mediterranean" (Alexandria, Egypt). The real place names are also listed with the various nicknames by which they are known. He does not include American cities, counties, and states, which are treated in the similar work by Kane and Alexander.

1199.   Kane, Joseph N. **The American Counties: Origins of Names, Dates of Creation and Organization, Area, Population, Historical Data, and Published Sources.** 4th ed. Metuchen, N.J.: Scarecrow, 1983. 546p.

The origin of the name of a county in the United States is the main content of this book, which, however, also gives the date on which it was created, the area, the population as of 1970, 1960, and 1950, and the nickname, if it is known by one. If alternate stories about the origin of a county name are current, they are also given.

ATLASES, GAZETTEERS

Those graduate students and faculty members doing research in geography are capable of doing much of their own reference searching. The most frequent request of other students and faculty will be for identification and location of a particular town or geographic feature or for a map of a particular place. Atlases and gazetteers for answering such questions are described here. Only general world atlases are included in this section. Other types of atlases are described elsewhere: Bible atlases, entries 316-18; economic atlases, entries 975-77; and historical atlases, entries 1146-50, 1175-76. Where the atlas is a collection of maps, the gazetteer is a non-graphic dictionary of places: towns, countries, mountains, rivers, and other physical features. Gazetteers frequently give brief geographical information about a place, in addition to locating it.

1200.   Kister, Kenneth F. **Kister's Atlas Buying Guide: General English-Language World Atlases Available in North America.** Phoenix: Oryx Press, 1984. 236p.

1201.   Walsh, S. Padraig. **General World Atlases in Print, 1972-1973: A Comparative Analysis.** New York: Bowker, 1973. 211p.

Both books are restricted to English-language world atlases available in the United States. Both have a section describing the qualities to look for in selecting an atlas. Although most of the atlases in print in 1972-73 have been replaced by later editions, Walsh rated the major English-language world atlases in a survey.

1202.   **The Times Atlas of the World.** 5 vols. London: The Times, 1955-59.

1203.   **The New International Atlas.** Chicago: Rand McNally, 1981. 568p.

1204.   **The New York Times Atlas of the World.** New York: Times Books, 1980. 276p. (Same as *The Times Concise Atlas of the World*.)

These three atlases were rated highest by Walsh, along with the Britannica and Compton atlases available with two encyclopedias of the same name. For non-English-language atlases, *Atlante internazionale* (Milan: Touring Club Italiano, 1968) and *Atlas Mira* (2d ed., Moscow, 1967) are generally recognized as superior, although in the latter atlas, certain locations within the U.S.S.R. are intentionally misplaced, presumably for security reasons.

1205.   **The Columbia-Lippincott Gazetteer of the World.** Edited by Leon Seltzer. New York: Columbia University Press, 1962. 2170p.

1206.   **Webster's Geographical Dictionary.** Springfield, Mass.: Merriam, 1972. 1370p.

1207.   **The Times Index-Gazetteer of the World.** London: The Times, 1965. 956p.

The first is considered the best all-round gazetteer for identifying the largest number of places and giving information about them. Location, pronunciation, and brief historical and economic notes are given for approximately 130,000 places: towns, cities, countries, rivers, lakes, mountains, and other physical features. Webster gives similar identification and description for about 47,000 places plus 15,000 cross-references. Population is given for inhabited places as of 1970. The *Times Index-Gazetteer of the World* identifies the most places (about 345,000, including physical features) but gives only the location: country, longitude and latitude coordinates, and reference to a map in the *Times Atlas of the World*.

BIOGRAPHY

Biographical articles on a handful of prominent geographers of the past (e.g., Isaiah Bowman, Alexander von Humboldt, Carl Ritter) are in the *International Encyclopedia of the Social Sciences* (entry 703). Living American geographers were included in the Social and Behavioral Sciences volume of *American Men and Women of Science* (entry 706) through its 12th edition. In the 13th edition, they were moved to the Physical and Biological volumes. But they seem not to be included at all in the current edition of *American Men and Women of Science* (entry 1269). Some are in *Who's Who in America* (entry 120) and other current who's whos. The best way to learn where an American geographer is listed is by checking *Biography and Genealogy Master Index* (entry 121). They are also listed with brief biographical data in the two following works.

1208.   Association of American Geographers. **Directory.** Washington, D.C.: The Association, 1956- . Irregular.

The 1982 directory, the latest available, lists some five thousand members with their address, birth date and place, education, employment, special geographical field of interest, and geographical area of interest.

1209.   **Orbis Geographicus. World Directory of Geography.** Compiled and edited by E. Meynen on behalf of the International Geographical Union. Wiesbaden: Steiner, 1974. 798p.

Geographers of the United States and other countries are listed by country with very brief information (birth date, degrees, positions, current address, and telephone number) in part 2 of this directory.

22

THE SCIENCES

In the final set of chapters we deal with the basic and applied sciences. The contrast here is between "know why" and "know how," between study of the sciences to understand natural phenomena and the application of this knowledge for practical purposes. Subdivisions of the basic sciences include the physical sciences (astronomy, physics, chemistry), earth sciences, and biological sciences. The major areas of application are agriculture, medicine, and engineering. To regard the several areas of scientific inquiry as separated by sharply definable boundaries is unrealistic. One finds researchers (and reference tools) in such boundary areas as biochemistry and astrophysics. In addition, scientific research no longer has a solely disciplinary focus. As problem areas, like the environment and energy, have emerged as important areas of study, reference tools combining several disciplinary perspectives have been published, which reflect patterns of research in these new multidisciplinary domains.

To be successful in reference work in the sciences, one should develop an understanding of the structure of the literature and the role played by each type of material. The primary literature contains original reports of scientific and technical investigations and appears in a variety of forms: journals, technical reports, conference proceedings, government publications, patents, standards, trade literature, theses and dissertations. Publishers of this primary literature include not only trade publishers, but also professional associations, government agencies, universities, and other research organizations. The sources which make up the secondary literature are derived from primary sources and arranged according to some definite plan. Three different processes can be distinguished.[1] Secondary sources derived through surrogation, such as bibliographies, catalogs, indexes, abstracts, and current awareness services, facilitate identification and selection of pertinent documents. Secondary sources derived through repackaging, such as dictionaries, directories, tables, and handbooks, provide rapid access to desired specific pieces of information. Finally, secondary sources derived through compaction, such as reviews, monographs, texts, treatises, and encyclopedias, represent the assimilation of scientific knowledge. Tertiary sources, such as guides to the literature, aid in the use of primary and secondary sources.

---

[1]Krishna Subramanyam, *Scientific and Technical Information Resources* (New York: Marcel Dekker, 1981), 9.

Because the primary literature continues to grow at a rapid rate, it is necessary for secondary sources to grow to keep pace. This is accomplished through various means: the regularly published issues of indexes and abstracts, new editions of reference books, and newly published titles. The rapidly changing nature of all scientific fields requires that librarians be aware of new reference sources and attempt to have reference collections keep pace with new developments and trends. Any published guide to science reference books is only a starting point because it will omit new editions or new titles which have appeared since its publication. It is necessary to keep in mind that scientific literature is worldwide in origin and international in language. Finally, many secondary sources and, to a lesser extent, primary sources now exist as databases. In many cases the databases have printed counterparts, but others exist only in machine-readable form. Directories of databases (e.g., entry 115) are helpful in keeping track of what is available. The description of reference sources covered in this book includes whether or not they are machine-searchable.

In outlining types of information needs common to scientists and engineers, it is convenient to make use of a categorization first proposed by Melvin Voigt.[2] He distinguishes three types of needs. The current approach is a need for information about current research and development in one's own field of specialization and peripheral fields. Current awareness services and scanning of primary journals are most often used to meet this need. The everyday approach is a need for a specific piece of information or data (e.g., formula, physical constant, definition, description of an organism, publication date, address) essential to day-to-day work. Reference books usually satisfy this need. Finally, in the exhaustive approach, the scientist wishes to find and check through all relevant information existing on a given subject to determine the state of the art. This approach is followed at the start of an investigation or at the point where the scientist is preparing to report on the results of his investigation in the form of a paper, patent application, technical report, or dissertation. In this case indexing and abstracting services, bibliographies, and databases can be used. To these three needs can be added the need for background information, when an introductory account sufficient to enable the scientist to understand a subject new to him is required. This need may be satisfied through consultation of encyclopedias, textbooks, or review articles. For the undergraduate, the everyday and background approaches are most common. The graduate student shares with the faculty member the need for current awareness, in-depth literature searching, and ready reference and background information. Other factors affecting the frequency with which these needs arise include the type of work (research vs. teaching) and the discipline.

Some differences among disciplines are discussed in the introductory sections of each subject chapter. It is also important to emphasize that libraries, librarians, and recorded information are only one channel used by the scientist in satisfying his information needs. Studies of information gathering in the sciences have demonstrated the importance of informal sources, particularly consultation with other scientists. On the other hand not all requests for scientific information in the university library come from specialists. For the student or faculty member from another discipline with a casual interest in science, it is necessary to identify materials written at a suitable level. Many of the general science sources described in this chapter can be used successfully by nonspecialists. Depending on the location of the university, reference questions may also be received from researchers in industry, particularly when no special library is available to the industrial researcher.

---

[2]Melvin J. Voigt, *Scientists' Approaches to Information*, ACRL Monograph no. 24 (Chicago: American Library Association, 1961), 21.

Sources described in this chapter cover more than one subject area in the sciences. In identifying sources to be consulted in response to a reference question, these general science sources should not be overlooked. General science materials are particularly helpful when the specific subject area which should be searched is not known. Once the most appropriate subject area has been identified, its sources can be used to supplement information located through use of more general tools. In addition, for the nonspecialist in science, the general science sources may provide the amount and level of information required, and it is not always necessary to extend the search to more specialized sources.

GUIDES, BIBLIOGRAPHIES, INDEXES

Guides, bibliographies, and indexes are essential tools in making effective use of the primary and secondary literature in the sciences. Those covering more than one area of science are described here. Because there is a growing interest in research questions that cross traditional disciplinary boundaries, these multidisciplinary sources are valuable supplements to the guides, bibliographies, and indexes of specific disciplines. Though necessarily more limited in the coverage of any given discipline, the guides are useful for orientation since they provide descriptions of the major sources in each discipline, and the general indexes may suffice when the objective is selective rather than comprehensive searching of the primary literature.

Guides

Guides may be classified into two types: inventory guides provide extensive lists of publications, and expository guides provide narrative descriptions of selected sources. The former are more useful in daily reference work; the latter are helpful in bibliographic instruction. In the expository type of guide, the emphasis is on description of various forms of literature and search procedures rather than on comprehensive listing of individual titles. Examples of both types can be found in this section. To be most useful, guides should be updated on a regular basis to keep pace with the rapid growth in the science reference literature, including the availability of databases. As none of the guides provides thorough coverage of available databases, directories of databases (e.g., entry 115) must also be consulted.

1210.   Malinowsky, H. Robert, and Jeanne M. Richardson. **Science and Engineering Literature: A Guide to Reference Sources.** 3d ed. Littleton, Colo.: Libraries Unlimited, 1980. 342p.

1211.   Chen, Ching-Chih. **Scientific and Technical Information Sources.** Cambridge, Mass.: MIT Press, 1977. 519p.

These two guides offer the most comprehensive coverage of the sciences in general. There are differences in coverage and arrangement. *Science and Engineering Literature* provides only limited coverage of agriculture, while *Scientific and Technical Information Sources* excludes medicine altogether. The former is arranged by subject and by type of material within subject; the latter is arranged by type of material and then by subject within type. *Science and Engineering Literature* is usually more helpful because it allows one to get an overview of the range of sources within a subject area. It has fourteen sections. The first two are tutorial, providing an introduction and discussion of forms of the literature. The next eleven sections, with detailed annotations describing reference sources in each subject area, are arranged as follows: multidiscipline sources of information, history of science, mathematics, astronomy, physics, chemistry, biological sciences, geoscience, energy and environment, engineering, and biomedical sciences. The last section is a bibliography of selected materials on various topics of special relevance to science librarians. An author/title/subject index is also provided. *Scientific and Technical Information Sources* is more comprehensive, listing 3,650 sources compared to the 1,273 described in *Science and Engineering Literature.* Some of these additional sources are very important primary sources, such as journals. Annotations are quite brief, but sources of reviews are identified. A bibliography of articles discussing the various forms of scientific literature is included. The index covers only author names. Because of its more recent publication date, detailed annotations, and subject arrangement, *Science and Engineering Literature* should be consulted first, and *Scientific and Technical Information Sources* can be used to identify additional reference titles should they be required.

1212.   Primack, Alice Lefler. **Finding Answers in Science and Technology.** New York: Van Nostrand, Reinhold, 1984. 364p.

1213.   Pritchard, Eileen, and Paula R. Scott. **Literature Searching in Science, Technology, and Agriculture.** Westport, Conn.: Greenwood, 1984. 175p.

These guides emphasize instruction in search strategy together with discussion of selected sources in the subject areas covered. *Finding Answers in Science and Technology* is intended for use by "hobby scientists," students at the advanced high school, community college, or undergraduate level, teachers, and librarians. Chapters are in essay form, emphasizing materials in print and likely to be widely available. The first three chapters discuss search strategy, computer searching, and general science sources. There are then 10 topical chapters: mathematics/computer science, astronomy, physics, chemistry, earth sciences, natural history, botany, zoology, medicine, and engineering/energy. Appendixes give directories of libraries, U.S. government depository libraries, NASA information centers, and U.S. patent depository libraries, and there is a detailed index. *Literature Searching in Science, Technology, and Agriculture* is intended to be an overview of important library tools and research techniques for students and librarians unfamiliar with science materials. Initial chapters provide an orientation to types of literature, search preparation, and finding books in libraries. Succeeding chapters present major publications, such as abstracting and indexing services, with detailed descriptions on how to use them. One chapter explains the basic logic of a computer search. Appendixes include lists of the major abstracting and indexing services, journals, databases, and sources for review articles. There is also a subject index.

1214.   Grogan, Denis. **Science and Technology: An Introduction to the Literature.** 4th ed. London: Bingley, 1982. 400p.

1215.   Subramanyam, Krishna. **Scientific and Technical Information Resources.** New York: Marcel Dekker, 1981. 416p. (Books in Library and Information Science, vol. 33).

These two guides are most useful as texts which can be read to develop an understanding of the characteristics of the various forms of literature in the sciences. Grogan's text begins with an introductory chapter, "The Literature," followed by chapters on various forms, such as encyclopedias, handbooks, standards, translations, and trade literature. There is no attempt to be comprehensive; specific sources are cited only as examples of what is available. English language sources, particularly British, are emphasized. Chapters include suggestions for further reading and there is a subject index. Subramanyam's text begins with chapters on scientific and technical communication and scientific societies, and concludes with a chapter on current trends and prospects. The intervening chapters provide detailed discussions of the major forms of primary and secondary literature. Although the emphasis is on describing the form, most of these chapters conclude with lists of notable examples of the form, arranged by subject (excluding medicine). There are author and subject indexes for titles discussed in the text, but items listed only at the ends of chapters do not appear in the index.

1216.   Herner, Saul, Gene P. Allen, and Nancy D. Wright. **A Brief Guide to Sources of Scientific and Technical Information.** 2d ed. Arlington, Va.: Information Resources Press, 1980. 160p. Paper.

1217.   Aluri, Rao, and Judith Schiek Robinson. **A Guide to U.S. Government Scientific & Technical Resources.** Littleton, Colo.: Libraries Unlimited, 1983. 259p.

1218.   Arny, Linda Ray. **The Search for Data in the Physical and Chemical Sciences.** New York: Special Libraries Association, 1984. 150p. Paper.

Because the more general guides to the scientific literature cannot treat particular titles or forms in great depth, there is a place for guides which provide more in-depth discussions of some portion of the literature. The three titles listed here are all valuable supplements to the more general guides. Herner's guide is intended for use by the engineer or scientist and emphasizes directories, guides, bibliographies, indexes, and databases. Quite detailed descriptions of sources are given in four chapters according to function: information directories and source guidance, information on ongoing research and development, current or recent research and development results, and past research and development results. In addition there is a section on American libraries with strong science collections and a discussion of organization of personal index files. An index provides access to authors, titles, and subjects. Recognizing the important role of the federal government as a producer and distributor of scientific and technical information, Aluri and Robinson describe different sorts of scientific and technical information provided by government agencies and how it can be acquired. Organization of the book reflects the pattern of scientific communication, in which information goes through a number of stages. Thus, following a chapter on grants, awards, fellowships, and scholarships, there are chapters on research in progress, technical reports, periodicals, patents, scientific translations, standards and specifications, audiovisual and nonbook resources, indexes and abstracts, databases, information analysis centers, and reference sources. Entries for titles, subjects, and agencies appear in the index. Arny's *The Search for Data in the Physical and Chemical Sciences* is a valuable aid in identifying and describing available data sources in the physical and chemical sciences, often a particularly difficult search problem. The first part of the guide discusses the creation, compilation, and retrieval of data in a series of 12 chapters including selection sources for handbooks and data compilations, data journals and related publications, and online access to data. The second part discusses data compilations of the National Bureau of Standards and there is an appendix on the National Standard Reference Data System.

1219.   Durbin, Paul T., ed. **A Guide to the Culture of Science, Technology, and Medicine.** New York: Free Press, 1980. 723p.

1220.   Corsi, Pietro, and Paul Weindling, eds. **Information Sources in the History of Science and Medicine.** London: Butterworths, 1983. 531p. (Butterworths Guides to Information Sources).

There is increasing interest in what might be termed the *culture* of science, the points of intersection between the sciences and the humanities or social sciences. *A Guide to the Culture of Science, Technology, and Medicine* offers state-of-the-field surveys including bibliographies for nine areas: history of science, technology, medicine; philosophy of science, technology, medicine; sociology of science and technology, medicine; and policy studies. Each chapter is written by an expert in the field and an index is provided. *Information Sources in the History of Science and Medicine* has 23 separately authored bibliographic essays providing discussion of the development of studies in particular areas, an evaluation of major works, and identification of problems requiring investigation. A bibliography of journals in the history of science and an index are included.

Indexes

Because of the importance of the primary literature in science, it is essential to have indexes providing effective access to this literature for literature searching and bibliographic verification. Titles included in this section cover more than one area of the sciences. They should always be considered when planning a literature search, particularly when only a few references to the primary literature are required. If dissertations are sought, sources described in chapter 2 (entries 40-41) should be consulted.

1221. **General Science Index.** New York: Wilson, 1978- . Monthly, except June and December, with quarterly and annual cumulations.

1222. **Applied Science and Technology Index.** New York: Wilson, 1958- . Monthly, except July, with quarterly and annual cumulations.

The scope of these two Wilson indexes is not completely described by their titles. *General Science Index* includes coverage of journals in medicine, as well as all areas of basic science from astronomy to zoology. It is a subject index to articles in 111 English-language journals and there is an author index to book reviews. Extensive use of cross-references facilitates identification of the appropriate subject heading corresponding to the topic sought. *Applied Science and Technology Index*, which was preceded by the *Industrial Arts Index* (1913-57), emphasizes journals in engineering and technology, but also includes some basic science journals in chemistry, geology, and physics. It is a subject index to articles in 336 English-language journals and has an author index to book reviews as a separate section. As with *General Science Index*, cross-references aid subject searching. Both *Applied Science and Technology Index* and *General Science Index* are machine-searchable through Wilsonline.

1223. **Science Citation Index.** Philadelphia: Institute for Scientific Information, 1961- . Bimonthly with annual and 5-year cumulations.

1224. **Index to Scientific Reviews.** Philadelphia: Institute for Scientific Information, 1974- . Semiannual.

Science Citation Index (SCI), the first citation index to be developed by the Institute for Scientific Information, is an important research tool. The two other citation indexes have already been described (entries 223, 699). *SCI* provides a number of unique approaches to searching the literature which are particularly valuable in the sciences. *SCI* covers about 3,100 major journals in the sciences as well as about two hundred multi-authored monographic series. It is international in scope, including many non-English-language publications. Indexing is quite complete, including coverage of such items as editorials, letters to the editor, and research papers. Coverage has recently been extended back to 1955, with cumulated indexes available for the periods 1955-64, 1965-69, 1970-74, and 1975-79. There are four major components: Source Index, Citation Index, Permuterm Subject Index, and Corporate Index. It is essential to understand their interrelationships in order to use *SCI* effectively. Although *SCI* has detailed and clearly written instructions to aid in its use, students may seek the help of librarians in mastering this tool. The unique design of *SCI* rests on the observation that papers citing a known relevant paper are also likely to be of interest. This is particularly true in the sciences where one is expected to include references to prior work related to the research being reported. The Citation Index shows which items previously published are being referred to in the current literature. In the Citation Index entries are arranged alphabetically by cited author, and within this chronologically by cited year. Each entry contains brief bibliographic information for the citing article, including author, journal name, volume, page, and year. There is a separate Patent Citation Index, arranged in numerical order by patent number, to identify current papers citing previously issued patents. Complete bibliographic information for citing articles, including author address information, is given in the Source Index, arranged alphabetically by author. The Permuterm Subject Index is created from significant terms appearing in the titles of citing articles. It is arranged alphabetically by keyword from titles, with entries indicating co-occurring keywords and the author of the article. The Source Index must be consulted to locate bibliographic information for the articles. The Corporate Index is in two parts. The geographic section lists for each location those organizations and individuals within those organizations who have published items listed in the Source Index. The organization section is an alphabetical list of source authors' organizations, giving the geographic location of each. The enumeration of indexes suggests the type of searches for which *SCI* is well suited: locating recent articles which cite a known author or prior article (Citation Index); locating articles on a specific topic, particularly when the term has been recently coined (Permuterm Subject Index); locating recent articles by a particular author (Source Index); and identifying recently published work written by scientists affiliated with a particular organization (Corporate Index). SCISEARCH, the database version of *SCI*, can be machine searched back to 1974 through DIALOG. Because review articles are often sought as a means of getting an evaluative overview of recent research on a particular topic, it is sometimes useful to limit a search to review articles. *Index to Scientific Reviews* (*ISR*), as an international interdisciplinary index to the review literature of science, medicine, agriculture, technology and behavioral science, is therefore a helpful companion to *SCI* when only review articles are wanted. Items are selected for inclusion in *ISR* using a number of criteria: appearance in a review publication (e.g., *Annual Review of ...*), inclusion of particular keywords (e.g., "review") in an article's title, or inclusion of an extensive bibliography as part of the article. The Source Index, Corporate Index, and Permuterm Subject Index in *ISR* play the same role as they do in *SCI*. Although a Citation Index used to appear in *ISR*, it has now been replaced by a Research Front Specialty Index. This enables one to identify related articles based on patterns of shared citations.

1225. **Government Reports Announcements & Index.** Springfield, Va.: National Technical Information Service, 1946- . Biweekly with annual cumulation of indexes.

Technical reports are indexed only selectively, if at all, in the major discipline-based indexes and abstracts. Because technical reports are often the initial, and sometimes the only, written report of a research project, it is helpful to have indexes provide access to them in a timely manner. The National Technical Information Service (NTIS) is the central source for the public sale of government-sponsored research and development reports prepared by government agencies, contractors, and grantees. NTIS issues *Government Reports Announcements & Index*, providing indexing and abstracting of unclassified reports together with indications of where they may be purchased. The publication was previously entitled *U.S. Government Research and Development Reports* and then *Government Reports Announcements*, taking its present title in 1975. The abstracts describing reports are divided into 22 broad subject fields, with more specific subdivisions, as defined by the COSATI classification. Subjects covered reflect the full range of funded research in the U.S., including all areas of science and technology. Indexes provide several means of access to the classified arrangement: subject keyword, personal author, corporate author, contract/grant number, and NTIS accession/report number. Annual cumulations of the indexes facilitate retrospective searching. NTIS, also the name of the database version of *Government Reports Announcements & Index*, can be machine searched back to 1964 through DIALOG and SDC and back to 1970 through BRS.

Bibliographies

1226. **Scientific and Technical Books and Serials in Print.** New York: Bowker, 1972- . Annual.

1227. **Pure and Applied Science Books, 1876-1982.** 6 vols. New York: Bowker, 1982.

Scientific and Technical Books and Serials in Print represents a repackaging of titles in science and technology from *Books in Print* (entry 6), *Ulrich's International Periodicals Directory* (entry 51), and *Irregular Serials and Annuals* (entry 52). It may thus be of use in the departmental library not holding the parent tools. Citations to books are arranged in three sections: author, title, and subject (using Library of Congress subject headings). Citations to serials are arranged by both title and subject. There is also a directory of publishers and distributors. The scope of *Pure and Applied Science Books, 1876-1982* includes books published or distributed in the U.S., both in and out of print, for the time period covered. Entries in the five main volumes are arranged by Library of Congress subject headings. The sixth volume includes author and title indexes. Entries provide basic cataloging data and thus are useful for bibliographic verification. Given the importance of scientific associations functioning as publishers of scientific information, *Associations' Publications in Print* (entry 31) is an essential supplement to the coverage of the two sources described here.

1228. **World List of Scientific Periodicals Published in the Years 1900-1960.** 4th ed. 3 vols. London: Butterworths, 1963-65.

For bibliographic verification of citations to older journals, the *World List of Scientific Periodicals* can be consulted as a supplement to the *Union List of Serials* (entry 48) and *New Serial Titles* (entry 49). It is a union list of scientific journals held by British libraries, giving full title, abbreviation, dates, and holding libraries.

1229. **ISIS Cumulative Bibliography: A Bibliography of the History of Science Formed from ISIS Critical Bibliographies 1-90, 1913-65.** Edited by Magda Whitrow. 6 vols. London: Mansell, 1971-84.

1230. **ISIS Cumulative Bibliography 1966-1975: A Bibliography of the History of Science Formed from ISIS Critical Bibliographies 91-100, Indexing Literature Published from 1965 through 1974.** Edited by John Neu. 2 vols. London: Mansell, 1980-85.

ISIS is a major journal in the history of science that has for many years included publication of bibliographies of work in the history of science. These two cumulative bibliographies make this literature more readily accessible; they are an essential tool for literature searching in the history of science. The cumulative bibliography derived from *ISIS* critical bibliographies 1-90 has six volumes: volumes 1 and 2 cover personalities and institutions, volume 3 covers subjects, volumes 4 and 5 cover civilizations and periods, and volume 6 covers authors. The cumulative bibliography for bibliographies 91-100 has two volumes: volume 1 covers personalities and institutions, and volume 2 covers subjects, periods and civilizations.

CONFERENCES AND CONFERENCE PROCEEDINGS

In the sciences there are two types of tools dealing with conferences: one identifies conferences scheduled to take place, and the other identifies publications resulting from conferences. Both are needed in science reference work. Patrons frequently ask what future meetings are planned and whether papers presented at a conference have been published.

1231. **Scientific Meetings; Describing Future Meetings of Technical, Scientific, Medical, and Management Organizations and Universities.** San Diego, Calif.: Scientific Meetings Publications, 1957- . Quarterly.

1232. **World Meetings: United States and Canada; A Two-Year Registry of Future Scientific, Technical, and Medical Meetings.** New York: Macmillan, 1963- . Quarterly.

1233. **World Meetings: Outside United States and Canada; A Two-Year Registry of Future Scientific, Technical, and Medical Meetings.** New York: Macmillan, 1968- . Quarterly.

Many types of questions are likely to be asked about upcoming conferences: Where is the next meeting of the American Chemical Society scheduled to take place? What is the deadline for papers? Are there any computer science conferences planned to take place in Sweden in 1986? Are there plans to publish the proceedings of a special symposium on acid rain? The last question is also of particular interest to the librarian planning acquisitions of conference proceedings. The three titles listed here may provide the answers to such questions. Their purpose is to give descriptive information about future scientific conferences. Each issue of *Scientific Meetings* has three parts: the main section, alphabetical by organization name, telling dates and place of future national, international, and regional meetings together with addresses from which to obtain additional information; a chronological listing of meetings; and a subject index. As indicated by their subtitles, the two sections of *World Meetings* differ in geographic scope. They offer more details on the meetings than *Scientific Meetings*, including an indication of plans for availability of proceedings. Each is a two-year registry, arranged by date, revised and updated each quarter. Indexes offer multiple access points to meeting descriptions: date of meeting, keyword, location, deadline for submission of papers, and sponsors. Descriptions include title, location, dates, sponsor, contact person, description of technical contents, deadlines, plans for availability of papers, and plans for exhibits.

1234. **Conference Papers Index: Life Sciences, Physical Sciences, Engineering.** Bethesda, Md.: Cambridge Scientific Abstracts, 1978- . Vol. 6- . Monthly with annual cumulation. (Earlier title: *Current Programs*.)

1235. **Directory of Published Proceedings: Series SEMT. Science/Engineering/Medicine/ Technology.** Harrison, N.Y.: InterDok, 1965- . Monthly, September-June, with annual cumulation.

1236. **Index to Scientific and Technical Proceedings.** Philadelphia: Institute for Scientific Information, 1978- . Monthly with annual cumulation.

Sources of information on conference proceedings have already been described in chapter 2 (entries 32-38), but the three titles emphasizing coverage of science and technology are briefly described again here to point out their unique features. *Conference Papers Index* covers conferences in science, technology, and medicine. It is an index to the papers presented at those conferences, which may or may not result in published proceedings. Information is gathered from final conference programs, and bibliographic data are given for the proceedings if they are available. Entries are arranged under broad subject headings. Each entry identifies the conference (title, dates, location, sponsoring organizations), followed by a list of papers presented together with author addresses. There are subject and author indexes. *Conference Papers Index* can be machine searched back to 1973 through DIALOG. Because it is derived from the final program of a meeting, it may be more timely than *Index to Scientific and Technical Proceedings* which also indexes individual conference papers. *Index to Scientific and Technical Proceedings* covers only published proceedings, but these can include proceedings published as books, reports, sets of preprints, and parts of journals in English and foreign languages and for all scientific subjects. Full bibliographic and order information is given for each proceedings covered. A complete table of contents for the conference follows its citation in the main part. Indexes include a category index of conference topics, a permuterm subject index (derived from keywords in conference paper titles), an author/editor index, sponsor index, meeting location index, and corporate index. Both *Conference Papers Index* and *Index to Scientific and Technical Proceedings* are quite useful for bibliographic verification and literature searching. *Directory of Published Proceedings* (commonly known as InterDok) does not index individual papers, but it is still useful in verifying the availability of conference proceedings in the sciences. Entries give bibliographic information and order information, and are arranged chronologically with indexes by editor, location, and subject/sponsor. There is a directory of publisher addresses.

TRANSLATIONS

Although much scientific literature appears in English, important work may also be originally reported in languages other than English. This can lead to requests for translations of various items from the primary literature. Because translation is an expensive process, it is important to be able to identify whether a translation has already been made, as in the case of the availability of a particular journal title in a cover-to-cover translation. Alternatively, the translation may be unpublished, but deposited with a center serving as a clearinghouse for translations. The two major centers of this kind are the National Translations Center in the United States and the International Translations Centre in the Netherlands. The tools described in this section provide access to both published and unpublished translations.

1237.   Himmelsbach, Carl J., and Grace E. Brociner. **A Guide to Scientific and Technical Journals in Translation.** 2d ed. New York: Special Libraries Association, 1972. Various paging.

1238.   **Journals in Translation.** New ed. Boston Spa, West Yorkshire, England: British Library Lending Division; Delft, Netherlands: International Translations Centre, 1978. 181p.

These two sources can be used to determine the availability of journals in translation, whether cover-to-cover or selective. Himmelsbach and Brociner include bibliographic and descriptive information for cover-to-cover translation journals (278 items) and selections and collections (53 items). It is arranged by original title and indexed by translated title. Publishers and distributors are identified. *Journals in Translation* emphasizes translations into English, but includes some journals translated into languages other than English. It is arranged by translated title with details of the translation. There is a keyword subject index, an index of original titles, and a list of publishing and distributing agencies.

1239.   National Translations Center. **Consolidated Index of Translations into English.** New York: Special Libraries Association, 1969. 948p.

1240.   **Translations Register-Index.** Chicago: National Translations Center, 1967- . Monthly with semiannual cumulation of indexes.

1241.   **World Transindex.** Delft, Netherlands: International Translations Centre, 1978- . 10 per year with annual cumulation of indexes.

Consolidated Index of Translations into English identifies English translations of journal articles, technical reports, standards, and patents. It is in two parts. The journal citation index is arranged alphabetically by title and chronologically under title, with an indication of the source for a translation. The patent citation index is arranged by number within country, again indicating the source for a translation. There is a directory of sources. Included are translations made prior to 1967. The index is a cumulation of several previously published lists. To update the *Consolidated Index, Translations Register-Index* has been issued monthly by the National Translations Center. The register section lists new acquisitions of the National Translations Center arranged by subject categories. The index is in two parts, a listing of journal citations arranged by title and a listing of patent citations arranged by country. There is also a directory of sources identifying institutions, including the National Translations Center, from which copies of materials listed in the index section may be obtained. The *World Transindex* replaces three publications: *World Index of Scientific Translations, Transatom Bulletin*, and *Bulletin des Traductions*. It cites translations from all languages into Western languages (but primarily English, French, and German), arranged in subject categories based on the COSATI classification. Entries include full bibliographic information and identification of an organization from which the translation can be obtained. There are also source and author indexes.

DICTIONARIES, ENCYCLOPEDIAS

Because each field of science has its own specialized terminology, there is a frequent need for sources such as dictionaries and encyclopedias which can provide definitions of terms, explanations of concepts, and illustrations not found in general dictionaries and encyclopedias. To keep pace with the growth of science and the emergence of new terms and concepts, these sources should be updated on a regular basis. Science dictionaries often provide only term definitions and an indication of the field to which the definition applies. Questions dealing with etymology or pronunciation may be answerable only in more general dictionaries. The dictionaries described in this section are all English-language dictionaries giving term definitions. It should be recognized that there are also a number of scientific and technical dictionaries suitable for use with foreign-language literature. These can provide definitions for foreign-language terms or identification of the corresponding term in English. No attempt has been made to discuss either foreign-language or multilingual dictionaries in this chapter or in chapters on specific areas of science. Descriptions of such dictionaries can be found in the various guides to the literature.

Science encyclopedias are particularly useful to undergraduates trying to better understand a concept which they have encountered in lectures or in reading. Librarians also make use of science encyclopedias to better understand topics so as to be able to assist library users in developing search strategies for manual and machine searches. Where bibliographies are included at the ends of articles, science encyclopedias present leads for locating additional information. The science dictionaries and encyclopedias described in this section should always be considered as supplements to the specific subject sources described in subsequent chapters, particularly if the disciplinary sources are somewhat dated.

1242.   **McGraw-Hill Dictionary of Scientific and Technical Terms.** 3d ed. Edited by Sybil P. Parker. New York: McGraw-Hill, 1984. 1781p. plus appendix, 65p.

1243.   **McGraw-Hill Dictionary of Science and Engineering.** New York: McGraw-Hill, 1984. 942p.

The *McGraw-Hill Dictionary of Scientific and Technical Terms* includes definitions for about one hundred thousand terms with some illustrations. Entries include an indication of the field to which the definition applies and a definition. Appendixes include tables of conversion between measurement systems, the periodic table, mathematical signs, constants, classification of living organisms, and brief biographical entries for about one thousand scientists. The *McGraw-Hill Dictionary of Science and Engineering*, intended primarily for personal rather than library collections, includes 36,000 terms from among those defined in the parent dictionary.

1244. **McGraw-Hill Encyclopedia of Science and Technology.** 5th ed. 15 vols. New York: McGraw-Hill, 1982.

1245. **McGraw-Hill Concise Encyclopedia of Science and Technology.** Edited by Sybil P. Parker. New York: McGraw-Hill, 1984. 2065p.

1246. **McGraw-Hill Yearbook of Science and Technology.** New York: McGraw-Hill, 1962- . Annual.

The *McGraw-Hill Encyclopedia of Science and Technology* is the leading multi-volume science encyclopedia. It is authoritative and kept up-to-date through regular revision. Topics covered include all areas of the basic and applied sciences, but exclude biography and history. Extensive use is made of illustrations. The 7,700 articles are arranged alphabetically and there are both a topical index, arranging article titles under 75 major subject areas of science and technology, and an analytical index with entries for text, illustrations, tables, and maps. Each article begins with a definition of the subject and most articles contain bibliographies. Cross-references are used to link related articles. The *Concise Encyclopedia* has 7,300 entries, extracting the essential text in one to two paragraphs from most articles in the parent set to meet the requirements of the one-volume encyclopedia user. Although most material is derived from the parent encyclopedia, some has also been extracted from other McGraw-Hill publications, including the *McGraw-Hill Dictionary of Scientific and Technical Terms* (entry 1242). In addition to an index, there is an appendix section including bibliographies of books and journals by subject area, a list of databases, and various scientific data. The *Yearbook* is published in years between editions of the encyclopedia. Each volume has two sections: a few feature articles on timely topics of special interest, and a comprehensive review of the past year in alphabetically arranged articles. There is an index, and references to the main encyclopedia are given for background.

1247. **Concise Encyclopedia of the Sciences.** Edited by John-David Yule. New York: Facts on File, 1980. 590p.

1248. **Van Nostrand's Scientific Encyclopedia.** 6th ed. Edited by Douglas M. Considine. New York: Van Nostrand, Reinhold, 1983. 3069p.

Two other recently published one-volume encyclopedias provide coverage of several areas of science and technology. The *Concise Encyclopedia* attempts to cover the most commonly used words of science and technology and background material in about 5,500 entries. The articles are written by specialists, and many are accompanied by illustrations and cross-references to related articles. Biographical sketches of prominent scientists are also included. *Van Nostrand's Scientific Encyclopedia* is more extensive with over 7,300 articles. Articles vary in length, with bibliographies for major entries and many illustrations. There is no index, but cross-references link related entries.

1249. **Chambers Dictionary of Science and Technology.** Rev. ed. Edited by T. C. Collocott and A. B. Dobson. Edinburgh: Chambers, 1974. 1328p.

1250. **Concise Science Dictionary.** Edited by Alan Isaacs, John Daintith, and Elizabeth Martin. New York: Oxford University Press, 1984. 762p.

1251.   Godman, Arthur, ed. **Longman Illustrated Science Dictionary: All Fields of Scientific Language Explained and Illustrated.** Harlow, Essex, England: Longman, 1981. 256p.

1252.   Daintith, John, ed. **A Dictionary of Physical Sciences.** New York: Pica Press, 1977. 333p.

These four dictionaries differ in scope, with only *Chambers* and the *Concise Science Dictionary* covering all areas of science. *Longman* has terms in three main sections: physics, chemistry (including geology), and biology. *A Dictionary of Physical Sciences* emphasizes terms from physics, chemistry, and astronomy. *Chambers* is the most comprehensive. The other three are intended primarily for student use. The *Concise Science Dictionary* has more than 7,000 definitions of the commoner scientific terms and includes illustrations and appendixes on units and fundamental constants. *Longman* covers about 1,500 terms, many with illustrations; since the main body has a categorized arrangement, it has an alphabetic index. *A Dictionary of Physical Sciences* has about 4,000 entries.

1253.   Ocran, Emanuel Benjamin. **Ocran's Acronyms: A Dictionary of Abbreviations and Acronyms Used in Scientific and Technical Writing.** London: Routledge & Kegan Paul, 1978. 262p.

1254.   **Dictionary of Report Series Codes.** 2d ed. Edited by Lois E. Godfrey and Helen F. Redman. New York: Special Libraries Association, 1973. 645p.

Although the science dictionaries described above include some entries for abbreviations, acronyms, and codes, there are reference tools which provide more complete coverage. A source for interpreting periodical title abbreviations has already been described (entry 47). *Ocran's Acronyms* has as its main part an alphabetical arrangement of abbreviations and acronyms with the meaning and subject field in which the abbreviation is used. The second part lists subject fields alphabetically, and under each it lists abbreviations and acronyms alphabetically with their meaning. Research reports issued in series are often identified by a report number beginning with an alphanumeric code. *Dictionary of Report Series Codes* is a guide to such codes. It consists of two main sections: a list of report series codes by letter with an identification of the corresponding agency, and a list of corporate entries with corresponding report series codes. A bibliography of articles on report series codes is also provided.

1255.   Jerrard, H. G., and D. B. McNeill. **A Dictionary of Scientific Units Including Dimensionless Numbers and Scales.** 4th ed. New York: Chapman and Hall, 1980. 212p.

1256.   Dresner, Stephen. **Units of Measurement: An Encyclopaedic Dictionary of Units Both Scientific and Popular and the Quantities They Measure.** New York: Hastings House, 1972. 287p.

1257.   Drazil, J. V. **Quantities and Units of Measurement: A Dictionary and Handbook.** London: Mansell, 1983. 313p.

Measurement is an essential aspect of scientific investigation, and definitions are often sought for the quantities to be measured and the units used. Although such terms are often included in general science dictionaries, the three titles listed here offer more in-depth treatment. They can answer such questions as, what is a coulomb? a rad? a parsec? Jerrard and McNeill include definitions of more than eight hundred units in a number of scientific fields, together with relevant historical facts and references to the literature. Dresner is more number oriented, with two main parts: units and quantities. Drazil is the most recent and comprehensive. Part 1 is an alphabetical listing of the names of all SI (International

System of Units) and other commonly used units and combinations of units giving usage, standard abbreviations, and conversion factors. Part 2 is a dictionary of quantities and constants used in all branches of science and technology. Each entry gives definition, standard symbol, French and German equivalents, dimensions, and SI units of measurement. Part 3 is a list of symbols used to denote quantities and constants. There is a bibliography and French and German indexes.

1258.   Ballentyne, D. W. G., and D. R. Lovett. **A Dictionary of Named Effects and Laws in Chemistry, Physics, and Mathematics.** 4th ed. New York: Chapman and Hall, 1980. 346p.

1259.   Carter, E. F., ed. **Dictionary of Inventions and Discoveries.** 2d rev. ed. New York: Crane, Russak, 1974. 208p.

Many scientific terms denoting equations, laws, theorems, effects, and constants include the name of the scientist noted for investigating the phenomenon. Ballentyne and Lovett's dictionary is devoted exclusively to such terms (e.g., Curies's law, Fourier's series, Maxwell's demon), providing a brief explanation of the term. There is no biographical information for the scientists, however. Carter's dictionary has entries of two kinds interfiled alphabetically: terms for inventions, discoveries, and developments; and names of the discoverers or inventors. Thus one has an entry for both *dynamite* and *Nobel, Alfred B.* Entries for the invention or discovery indicate to whom it is attributable and the year. Entries for people indicate the inventions and discoveries with which they were associated.

1260.   Bynum, W. F., E. J. Browne, and Roy Porter, eds. **Dictionary of the History of Science.** Princeton, N.J.: Princeton University Press, 1981. 494p.

This dictionary presents key ideas and theories in science, giving their origins, meaning, and significance, with emphasis on Western science over the last five hundred years. Entries differ in length, depending on the importance of the concept. There are cross-references linking related articles, and longer articles have short bibliographies. There are no separate entries for individuals, but a biographical index gives brief biographical notes, dates, and an indication of the concept(s) with which each individual is associated. There is an analytical table of contents, identifying concepts by subject area, such as astronomy, biology, chemistry, earth sciences, medicine, or physics.

DIRECTORIES

Directory questions in science may seek addresses and descriptive information for individuals, professional societies, organizations involved in research, or sources of supplies. Directories of associations described in chapter 3 (entries 100-104) are important sources of information in the sciences. *Thomas's Register* (entry 951) is an example of a product directory. Directories of research grants (entries 106-8) are also of considerable interest to faculty and graduate students in the sciences. This section describes one directory of directories and some directories of organizations involved in scientific research. Directories more limited in subject scope are described in the chapters on specific subjects.

1261.   **Directory of Scientific Directories: A World Guide to Scientific Directories Including Medicine, Agriculture, Engineering, Manufacturing, and Industrial Directories.** 3d ed. Compiled by J. Burkett. Harlow, Essex, England: Hodgson, 1979. 649p.

The *Directory of Scientific Directories* has briefly annotated entries divided geographically (by country within continent) and then by subject. There is an author index and a subject index based on title keywords. Entries cover both separately published books and directories published as part of periodicals. Because it is updated more frequently, the *Directory of Directories* (entry 119) should also be consulted to identify additional titles of available scientific directories.

1262. **Industrial Research Laboratories of the United States.** 19th ed. Edited by Jaques Cattell Press. New York: Bowker, 1985. 742p.

1263. **Government Research Centers Directory.** 3d ed. Edited by Kay Gill. Detroit: Gale, 1985. 675p.

1264. **Research Centers Directory.** 10th ed. Edited by Mary Michelle Watkins. 2 vols. Detroit: Gale, 1985.

These three directories are complementary in their coverage, describing organizations conducting research in the industrial, government, and nonprofit sectors. *Industrial Research Laboratories* contains information on research and development facilities belonging to industrial organizations in the United States. Entries are arranged alphabetically by name of the corporation, with indexes by place, personal name, and subject of research activities. Entries include laboratory addresses, key administrative and research personnel, staff size, and description of primary research and development activities. The scope of *Government Research Centers Directory* is described by its subtitle, *A Guide to U.S. Government Research and Development Centers, Institutes, Laboratories, Bureaus, Test Facilities, Experiment Stations, Data Collection and Analysis Centers, and Grants Management and Research Coordinating Offices in Agriculture, Art, Business, Education, Energy, Engineering, Environment, Medicine, Military Science, and Basic and Applied Sciences. Research Centers Directory* describes university-related and nonprofit research organizations in the United States and Canada. It is arranged by major subjects (e.g., astronomy and space sciences, life sciences, computers and mathematics) with detailed subject, center name, and parent organization name indexes. In addition to name and address information, entries include a description of research activities, publications, and services.

HANDBOOKS

Handbooks are essential tools for ready reference in the sciences. They can take a variety of forms, such as field guides, method books, and data compilations. Most are specific to a particular discipline and are described in the various subject chapters. Titles included here are relevant to more than one area of the sciences.

1265. Powell, Russell H., ed. **Handbooks and Tables in Science and Technology.** 2d ed. Phoenix: Oryx Press, 1983. 297p.

When trying to identify the availability of a handbook on a particular subject, this bibliography is a valuable tool. Complete bibliographic information is given for about 3,400 handbooks and tables in science, technology, and medicine. Most entries are annotated with a brief description of content. Entries are arranged alphabetically by title, and there are both an author/editor index and a subject index. A directory of publisher addresses is also provided.

1266. **Composite Index for CRC Handbooks.** 2d ed. Cleveland: CRC Press, 1977. 1111p.

One of the problems in making effective use of a collection of handbooks is the difficulty in easily identifying which of many specialized titles is most likely to contain the particular data sought. The *Composite Index* is designed to offer a solution to that problem by combining index entries from more than 50 handbook volumes published by CRC Press that cover specific topics in mathematics and in the physical, life, and engineering sciences. It is in two parts: subjects and chemical substances. Each entry indicates the location of information on the topic in one or more CRC handbooks. This principle has been extended in the SUPERINDEX database, which can be machine searched through BRS. It includes a merging of the back-of-the-book index data from reference volumes published by several publishers including CRC Press.

1267. **CRC Handbook of Laboratory Safety.** 2d ed. Edited by Norman V. Steere. Cleveland: CRC Press, 1971. 854p.

Laboratory safety is an issue arising in all of the experimental sciences, and this handbook is designed to serve as a comprehensive reference on types of hazards and ways to prevent them. Categories of hazards discussed include fire, toxicity, radiation, electrical and mechanical, biological, and chemical. There is a subject index.

1268. Moses, Alfred J. **The Practicing Scientist's Handbook: A Guide for Physical and Terrestrial Scientists and Engineers.** New York: Van Nostrand, Reinhold, 1978. 1292p.

This handbook gives property data for physics, chemistry, and engineering. Categories of materials covered include the elements, organic and inorganic compounds, alloys, glasses and ceramics, composites, polymers and adhesives, and semiconductors. An index allows quick location of data values reported in the compilation.

BIOGRAPHY

Locating biographical information on both contemporary researchers and scientists of historical interest is facilitated by the availability of several good biographical sources covering the sciences. As in other subject fields, the search for information about prominent scientists is usually quite straightforward, and multiple sources are likely to contain the requested information. Information about more obscure figures may require more extensive searching, but several of the sources described in this section include less well known scientists. Many sources described in chapter 4 also include scientists in their coverage. In particular, the *Current Contents Address Directory* (entry 124) is a useful source of address and recent publication information for many scientists in the United States and abroad because it includes those who publish in books and journals covered by the *Science Citation Index* (entry 1223) in any given year. Almost all professional societies provide annual or otherwise regular membership directories. These are essential sources of current information on address and organizational affiliations of working scientists. Many science dictionaries have brief biographical entries, and journals often have biographical notes about authors. Thus there are a number of alternative places to check if the biographical sources included in this section fail to cover the person sought.

1269. **American Men and Women of Science: Physical and Biological Sciences.** 15th ed. Edited by Jaques Cattell Press. 7 vols. New York: Bowker, 1982.

1270. **American Men and Women of Science, Editions 1-14 Cumulative Index.** Compiled by Jaques Cattell Press. New York: Bowker, 1983. 847p.

American Men and Women of Science provides biographical sketches for more than 130,000 active U.S. and Canadian scientists, arranged alphabetically by name. Inclusion is based on achievement, quality of research, and/or attainment of a position of responsibility in the scientific community. As the subtitle indicates, coverage includes all of the physical and biological sciences. Engineering, mathematics, and computer science are included as well. Sketches are prepared from information submitted by biographees and include birth date and place, education, areas of interest, positions held, professional memberships, research and development activities, and address. There are no indexes in this edition because it can be machine searched through BRS and DIALOG. Thus the online version must be used for subject, geographic or other such approaches. Since *American Men and Women of Science* is limited to scientists who are currently active, earlier editions must be consulted for scientists who were active in the early decades of the twentieth century. An aid to searching earlier editions is the *Cumulative Index* to editions 1-14, which lists over 270,000 scientists alphabetically by name, with an indication of the edition(s) in which a biographical entry appears. The time span covered is from 1906, when the first edition appeared, through 1979, the 14th edition.

1271. **McGraw-Hill Modern Scientists and Engineers.** 3 vols. New York: McGraw-Hill, 1980.

1272. **Who's Who in Frontier Science and Technology, 1984-1985.** Chicago: Marquis Who's Who, 1984. 846p.

Like *American Men and Women of Science*, these two sources also emphasize scientists active in the twentieth century. *McGraw-Hill Modern Scientists and Engineers* serves as a biographical supplement to the encyclopedia (entry 1244), which has no separate biographical articles. It provides in-depth biographies for 1,140 leading scientists who have been recipients of major awards and prizes given by leading societies, organizations, and institutions. It is international in scope and covers the 1920s through 1978. Entries are arranged alphabetically and most are autobiographical, with the scientist providing a detailed discussion of his or her work in addition to basic biographical data such as birthplace and date. Each entry is accompanied by a portrait; where appropriate, cross-references are made to related biographical articles in the set and to the encyclopedia for background on the subject of a scientist's investigations. Volume 3 has a two-part index: a field index for areas of activity, and an analytical index of persons and subjects. *Who's Who in Frontier Science and Technology* provides biographical information submitted by biographees in North America who are working on new research directions and advanced technologies such as fiber optics, laser medicine, and robotics. Personal and professional data are included for more than 16,500 individuals, including some who are in the early stages of their careers. There is an index by field of specialization. The contents can be machine searched as part of the MARQUIS WHO'S WHO database through DIALOG.

1273. **Dictionary of Scientific Biography.** Edited by Charles Coulston Gillispie. 16 vols. New York: Scribner's, 1970-80.

1274. **Concise Dictionary of Scientific Biography.** Edited by American Council of Learned Societies. New York: Scribner's, 1981. 773p.

The *Dictionary of Scientific Biography* is the major biographical source for prominent, deceased scientists, including mathematicians, astronomers, physicists, chemists, biologists, and earth scientists. More than 4,500 individuals of all periods and all regions are described in scholarly articles emphasizing significant contributions to the advancement of science. Articles are accompanied by bibliographies listing important original works of the biographee and secondary works about the biographee. There is a separate index volume with entries for inventions, instruments, subjects, and names. Another volume contains a series of essays on the scientific outlook and accomplishments of certain ancient civilizations, as well as some biographical entries supplementing those in the main work.

The *Concise Dictionary* is a one-volume publication derived from the original set, presenting essential information from each article, with the content corresponding to about 10 per cent of the original.

1275.   Ireland, Norma Olin. **Index to Scientists of the World, from Ancient to Modern Times: Biographies and Portraits.** Boston: Faxon, 1962. 662p.

1276.   Pelletier, Paul A., ed. **Prominent Scientists: An Index to Collective Biographies.** New York: Neal-Schuman, 1980. 311p.

1277.   Barr, E. Scott. **An Index to Biographical Fragments in Unspecialized Scientific Journals.** University, Ala.: University of Alabama Press, 1973. 294p.

These three indexes can assist in the location of biographical information that appears in monographs and journals in the library's collection. Ireland's index has entries for biographies and portraits (if included) for 7,500 scientists in 338 collections published prior to 1960. Entries give name, date, a brief description, and sources of biographical information. Pelletier's index is intended to update Ireland by indexing biographies appearing in books, most published between 1960 and 1979. There are entries for more than 10,000 scientists drawn from 159 collective biographies. Entries include name, dates, field of specialization, and an indication of the collective works in which biographies appear. Barr's index traces biographical information on about 8,000 scientists that appeared in any of seven English-language, general science journals (such as *Nature*), published between 1798 and 1933. Entries give name, specialization, dates, nationality, and citation of biographical fragments.

1278.   Asimov, Isaac. **Asimov's Biographical Encyclopedia of Science and Technology: The Lives and Achievements of 1510 Great Scientists from Ancient Times to the Present, Chronologically Arranged.** 2d rev. ed. Garden City, N.Y.: Doubleday, 1982. 941p.

1279.   **A Biographical Encyclopedia of Scientists.** Edited by John Daintith, Sarah Mitchell, and Elizabeth Tootill. 2 vols. New York: Facts on File, 1981.

1280.   Williams, Trevor I., ed. **A Biographical Dictionary of Scientists.** 3d ed. New York: Halsted, 1982. 674p.

1281.   **World Who's Who in Science: A Biographical Dictionary of Notable Scientists from Antiquity to the Present.** Chicago: Marquis Who's Who, 1968. 1855p.

These four sources are similar in scope, including scientists from ancient to modern times with no geographical limitations. Asimov's encyclopedia is arranged chronologically, with an alphabetical list of names at the front of the volume and a subject index at the back. It is a more popular treatment, with no bibliographical references. Entries include dates, birthplace, subject area, and a brief biographical sketch. Portraits are provided for many of the scientists profiled. The *Biographical Encyclopedia of Scientists* covers about two thousand scientists, emphasizing those in physics, chemistry, biology, astronomy, and earth sciences with about one-fourth of them contemporary scientists. Entries describe lives and contributions. There are indexes of names and subjects, and some supplementary material such as a chronology of scientific discoveries and publications. Williams includes only scientists who are deceased. Brief biographies are given for more than one thousand scientists. *World Who's Who in Science* is by far the most comprehensive, providing brief biographical sketches for about 30,000 scientists of all periods, about half historical. Basic biographical data are given together with a brief interpretation of the individual's contribution.

1282.   Elliott, Clark A. **Biographical Dictionary of American Science: The Seventeenth through the Nineteenth Centuries.** Westport, Conn.: Greenwood, 1979. 361p.

Elliott's *Biographical Dictionary of American Science*, designed as a retrospective companion to *American Men and Women of Science* (entry 1269), is a guide to about nine hundred Americans born between 1606 and 1867. Entries of from 300 to 400 words describe the lives and scientific contributions of scientists never included in *American Men and Women of Science*, and briefer entries describe those who were included in the other book but who reached a significant stage in their careers before 1900. Appendixes list biographees by year of birth, place of birth, education, occupation, and field of science. There is also an index.

23

MATHEMATICS

It is appropriate to begin the series of chapters on particular topic areas within the sciences with a chapter on mathematics because mathematics plays a part in research in all areas of science. The reference literature of mathematics is, therefore, of concern not only to students and faculty specializing in mathematics. Mathematics reference books are also often included in departmental collections devoted primarily to some other scientific subject, such as chemistry or engineering. Investigations within mathematics are sometimes divided into pure mathematics, involving the intrinsic study of mathematical structures, and applied mathematics, arising from the study of physical phenomena. This chapter also includes coverage of reference tools in statistics, which describes techniques for dealing with the collection, analysis, interpretation, and presentation of masses of numerical data.

In the field of mathematics the reference questions of undergraduates most often involve the definition of a term, the correct form of a formula, or the identification of tables of values for a particular mathematical function. The frequency of need for tables of values has diminished somewhat with the proliferation of pocket calculators, which provide such functions as taking the square root of a number. Graduate students have needs similar to those of undergraduates, but the topics are at a more advanced level. In addition, graduate students may require guidance in searching the primary literature and in verifying or interpreting bibliographic references. Faculty questions deal primarily with bibliographic verification and location of documents. Since the older mathematics literature continues to be consulted, bibliographic verification may involve identification of materials published many years ago as well as those published recently. Foreign language literature is sought more often in mathematics than in some other areas of science because important mathematical work is frequently reported in languages other than English. Although many graduate students and faculty are likely to have a knowledge of one or more foreign languages (French, German, Russian), translations may be sought occasionally. Sources cited in chapter 22 (entries 1237-41) can be used to identify whether translations are available.

GUIDES, BIBLIOGRAPHIES, INDEXES

1283. Dorling, A. R., ed. **Use of Mathematical Literature.** London: Butterworths, 1977. 260p. (Information Sources for Research and Development).

1284.   Schaefer, Barbara Kirsch. **Using the Mathematical Literature: A Practical Guide.** New York: Marcel Dekker, 1979. 141p. (Books in Library and Information Science, vol. 25).

The two most recently published guides to the mathematics literature offer complementary approaches. Schaefer's guide is not intended to be comprehensive; it describes types of publications and discusses selected titles. The introductory chapters provide useful background on the history of mathematics literature, the nature of mathematics and its literature, information needs in mathematics, and the organization of mathematical literature in libraries. This is followed by discussions of reference materials, books, and journals in pure mathematics, applied mathematics, statistics, and operations research. An index is included. Dorling's guide is at the graduate level, with separately authored chapters written in the form of bibliographic essays. The first five chapters cover general topics: the role of literature in mathematics, major organizations and journals, reference material, education, and history. These are followed by nine chapters on the literature of major branches of mathematics, such as logic, combinatorics, algebra, group theory, probability, complex analysis, and topology. Author and subject indexes are provided.

1285.   Dick, Elie M. **Current Information Sources in Mathematics: An Annotated Guide to Books and Periodicals, 1960-1972.** Littleton, Colo.: Libraries Unlimited, 1973. 281p.

1286.   Pemberton, John E. **How to Find Out in Mathematics: A Guide to Sources of Information.** 2d rev. ed. Oxford: Pergamon, 1969. 193p.

Although not as current as the guides by Schaefer and Dorling, these two guides are still useful. Dick includes more than 1,600 annotated entries in 37 chapters. Items cited were published in the period 1960-72, in English or English translation. Most of the 37 chapters describe books in a particular branch of mathematics, with entries arranged alphabetically by author. The final chapters are more general, covering bibliographies, dictionaries, tables, periodicals, guides and directories, professional organizations and government agencies, and publishers of mathematics materials. Both author and subject indexes are included. Pemberton's guide, written in narrative style, is intended as an introduction to the literature for use by librarians and students. Chapters on various types of materials in pure mathematics are supplemented by chapters on probability and statistics and operations research. An index to authors, titles, and subjects concludes the book.

1287.   **Mathematical Reviews.** Providence, R.I.: American Mathematical Society, 1940- . Monthly with semiannual and annual cumulation of indexes.

1288.   **Current Mathematical Publications.** Providence, R.I.: American Mathematical Society, 1969- . 17 per year.

The major abstracting publication in mathematics provides international coverage of all types of publications in both pure and applied mathematics. As the title *Mathematical Reviews* indicates, the entries are actually signed reviews evaluating the contents of the items covered. Although most reviews are in English, about one-third of the materials reviewed are in languages other than English. Given this type of treatment, there are often considerable time delays between publication of an item and its appearance in *Mathematical Reviews.* Entries are arranged according to a classification scheme developed by the American Mathematical Society. Because the classified arrangement is the only form of subject access to all items, *Mathematical Reviews* is most useful to graduate students and faculty members who have a detailed knowledge of the subject. The undergraduate may have more success using indexes, such as *General Science Index* (entry 1221), which include some mathematics periodicals in their coverage. *Mathematical Reviews* has an author index to the classified arrangement. The author indexes cumulate annually, and a cumulated classified subject index is issued annually as well. The database version, MATHFILE, can be machine searched back to 1973 through BRS and DIALOG, although only bibliographic citations are included for the period 1973-79. To compensate for the time delay in *Mathematical Reviews*, the American Mathematical Society also publishes *Current Mathematical Publications* (formerly *Contents of Contemporary Mathematical Journals*) for current awareness. Using the same classification scheme as *Mathematical Reviews*, it provides bibliographic information for items that will later be reviewed in *Mathematical Reviews*. An author index is also included in each issue.

1289.   **Zentralblatt für Mathematik und ihre Grenzgebiete.** Berlin: Springer, 1931- . 27 per year with periodic cumulation of indexes.

To insure greater completeness in searching the mathematics literature, this abstracting service should also be consulted. The *Mathematical Reviews* classification scheme is used to arrange abstracts, which are written in English, German, or French. Each issue has an author index and every 10th issue is a cumulated index for the preceding 9 issues, with author and classified subject sections.

1290.   **Statistical Theory and Method Abstracts.** Voorburg, Netherlands: International Statistical Institute, 1959- . Quarterly.

The literature of statistics has its own abstracting publication, with a classified arrangement of entries. The classification system currently used divides the abstracts into 16 sections, such as probability theory, hypothesis testing, regression analysis, analysis of variance, sampling, and design of experiments.

1291.   May, Kenneth O. **Bibliography and Research Manual of the History of Mathematics.** Toronto: University of Toronto Press, 1973. 818p.

For the student or faculty member interested in the history of mathematics, May has prepared both a research manual and a bibliography. The research manual includes sections on information retrieval, personal information storage, and historical analysis and writing. The bibliography is a classified list with about 30,000 entries arranged under specific subjects within five broad categories: biography, mathematical topics, epimathematical topics, historical classifications, and information retrieval. There is a list of serials to be used in providing complete bibliographic information for items cited in the bibliography.

DICTIONARIES, ENCYCLOPEDIAS

1292.   James, Glenn, and Robert C. James, eds. **Mathematics Dictionary.** 4th ed. New York: Van Nostrand, Reinhold, 1976. 509p.

1293.   **Facts on File Dictionary of Mathematics.** 2d ed. Edited by Carol Gibson. New York: Facts on File, 1981. 215p.

1294.   **McGraw-Hill Dictionary of Physics and Mathematics.** Edited by Daniel N. Lapedes. New York: McGraw-Hill, 1978. 1074p. plus appendix, 46p.

The *Mathematics Dictionary* covers about eight thousand terms which occur in the mathematics taught at the undergraduate level and before. Detailed definitions are given, including some biographical entries. Appendixes include lists of mathematical symbols and their interpretation, collections of differentiation formulas, and tables of integrals. Multilingual indexes in French, German, Russian, and Spanish are provided, allowing translation and definition of terms encountered in reading foreign literature. Also of use to the undergraduate is the *Facts on File Dictionary of Mathematics*, providing definitions of selected terms in mathematics and some areas of application (e.g., banking, accounting, physics), with cross-references linking related terms. The *McGraw-Hill Dictionary of Physics and Mathematics* is derived to a large extent from the second edition of its parent work (entry 1242) and contains brief definitions of over 20,000 terms in physics, mathematics, statistics, astronomy, and related fields. It can be used to supplement the other two mathematics dictionaries described here.

1295. **International Dictionary of Applied Mathematics.** Edited by W. F. Freiberger. Princeton, N.J.: Van Nostrand, 1960. 1173p.

When definitions of terms related to applied mathematics are sought, this dictionary, although now somewhat dated, can be consulted. It defines terms and describes methods in the application of mathematics to 31 fields of science and engineering. French, German, Russian, and Spanish term indexes are included.

1296. Mathematical Society of Japan. **Encyclopedic Dictionary of Mathematics.** Edited by Shôkichi Iyanaga and Yukiyosi Kawada. 2 vols. Cambridge, Mass.: MIT Press, 1977.

1297. Sneddon, I. N., ed. **Encyclopaedic Dictionary of Mathematics for Engineers and Applied Scientists.** Oxford: Pergamon, 1976. 800p.

When more than a definition is sought, these encyclopedic dictionaries are valuable for their detailed entries. The *Encyclopedic Dictionary of Mathematics* has been translated from the Japanese and includes coverage of advanced mathematical topics. Over four hundred articles, including some biographical entries, are alphabetically arranged. Articles give definitions of important terms in pure and applied mathematics, as well as discussions of historical background and the present state of research. Articles are supplemented by literature references which can provide additional sources of information. Both subject and name indexes are included for the set. A systematic list of articles can be found in the appendixes together with a bibliography of tables and some tables of formulas and numerical values. For topics in applied mathematics, the *Encyclopaedic Dictionary of Mathematics for Engineers and Applied Scientists* may give more adequate coverage. Articles discuss those mathematical concepts and techniques most widely and frequently used in engineering. Bibliographies follow the longer articles, and there is a detailed subject index.

1298. **Universal Encyclopedia of Mathematics.** London: Allen & Unwin, 1964. 715p.

1299. **The VNR Concise Encyclopedia of Mathematics.** New York: Van Nostrand, Reinhold, 1977. 760p.

These two one-volume encyclopedias will be most useful to the undergraduate. The *Universal Encyclopedia of Mathematics* has alphabetically arranged articles on subjects and concepts in mathematics from elementary arithmetic through calculus. Articles are followed by sections of mathematical formulas and mathematical tables. The *VNR Concise Encyclopedia of Mathematics* includes topics from higher mathematics as well. Color is used extensively to differentiate formulas and definitions from examples and theorems. Both tables and a subject index are also included.

1300. Kendall, Maurice G., and William R. Buckland. **A Dictionary of Statistical Terms.** 4th ed., rev. & enl. London: Longman, 1982. 213p.

1301. **International Encyclopedia of Statistics.** Edited by William H. Kruskal and Judith M. Tanur. 2 vols. New York: Free Press, 1978.

1302.   **Encyclopedia of Statistical Sciences.** Vol. 1- . New York: Wiley, 1982- . In progress.

Although some terms and concepts from statistics are included in the mathematics dictionaries and encyclopedias, sources devoted exclusively to statistics should be consulted for fuller treatment. *A Dictionary of Statistical Terms* presents detailed definitions, together with formulas where appropriate, for terms in current use. For more recently coined terms, a reference to the source introducing a term is given. For the advanced undergraduate or graduate student needing a more detailed discussion of statistical techniques, two encyclopedias are available. The *International Encyclopedia of Statistics* is based to a large extent on the statistical articles originally appearing in the *International Encyclopedia of the Social Sciences* (entry 703). Articles related to statistics were extracted and updated for the purpose of making them available to a wider audience. In addition, a few articles were prepared exclusively for the new encyclopedia. The *Encyclopedia of Statistical Sciences*, when complete, will provide an even more comprehensive treatment of statistical theory and applications, dealing with both methodology and historical background. Articles cover all principal subfields, including probability theory, statistical distribution theory, computer methods, sampling survey methods, decision theory, and multivariate analysis. Six volumes (through the entry for *Plackett and Burman designs*) have already appeared.

HANDBOOKS, TABLES

Although the information associated with handbooks (formulas, tables of values, etc.) can often be found in mathematics dictionaries and encyclopedias, it may be more easily located in available handbooks and tables, which usually have quite detailed subject indexes and complete compilations. As noted in the introduction to this chapter, the need to consult handbooks and tables has diminished with the availability of calculators and computers, but they are still needed to aid in computations which are not functions of the devices available to the student. Titles cited here are among the most commonly used. More specialized titles are described in the guides to the mathematics literature (entries 1283-86) and in the bibliography in Powell (entry 1265).

1303.   Burington, Richard Stevens. **Handbook of Mathematical Tables and Formulas.** 5th ed. New York: McGraw-Hill, 1973. 500p.

1304.   **CRC Handbook of Mathematical Sciences.** 5th ed. Edited by William H. Beyer. Boca Raton, Fla.: CRC Press, 1978. 982p.

1305.   **CRC Standard Mathematical Tables.** 27th ed. Edited by William H. Beyer. Boca Raton, Fla.: CRC Press, 1984. 615p.

Burington's handbook is in two parts. The first provides formulas, definitions, and theorems from such subjects as algebra, geometry, trigonometry, calculus, differential equations, and statistics. The second part provides tables such as logarithms, hyperbolic functions, and probability distributions. Indexes provide access to numerical tables and subjects. The *CRC Handbook of Mathematical Sciences* includes tables, formulas, and some explanatory text for several topic areas, covering elementary mathematics, higher mathematics, probability and statistics, and some applications. There is an appendix identifying mathematical symbols and abbreviations as well as an index. *CRC Standard Mathematical Tables* covers the same range of subjects as the *CRC Handbook*, but is more selective in the material presented, emphasizing tables.

1306.   Grazda, Edward E., Morris Brenner, and William R. Minrath. **Handbook of Applied Mathematics.** 4th ed. New York: Van Nostrand, Reinhold, 1966. 1119p.

1307.   Pearson, Carl E., ed. **Handbook of Applied Mathematics: Selected Results and Methods.** 2d ed. New York: Van Nostrand, Reinhold, 1983. 1307p.

1308.   Tuma, Jan J. **Engineering Mathematics Handbook: Definitions, Theorems, Formulas, Tables.** 2d ed. New York: McGraw-Hill, 1979. 394p.

For more complete treatment of formulas and tables useful in applied mathematics, these handbooks can be consulted. *Handbook of Applied Mathematics* begins with six chapters on subdivisions of mathematics (algebra, trigonometry, calculus), with the remaining chapters each covering the formulas and tables needed by particular trades (brickwork, carpentry, electronics). In contrast, both Pearson and Tuma have chapters arranged according to the type of mathematics covered, with detailed discussions of concepts, formulas, and examples. The mathematics covered in these two books goes considerably beyond that summarized in the first book.

1309.   Burington, Richard Stevens, and Donald Curtis May, Jr. **Handbook of Probability and Statistics with Tables.** 2d rev. ed. New York: McGraw-Hill, 1970. 462p.

1310.   **CRC Handbook of Tables for Probability and Statistics.** 2d ed. Edited by William H. Beyer. Cleveland: Chemical Rubber Company, 1968. 642p.

When formulas and tables of values to be used in statistical analysis are sought, these two sources should be checked first. Burington and May give a summary of the more important formulas, definitions, theorems, tests, and methods of elementary statistics and probability theory together with tables of distributions and other quantities used in statistical applications. The *CRC Handbook* begins with a brief survey of important definitions and functions in probability and statistics, and then has extensive sections of statistical tables and graphs, including such commonly used distributions as the normal, student's t, chi-square, and F. There is also a section on non-parametric statistics.

BIOGRAPHY

1311.   **Combined Membership List: American Mathematical Society, Mathematical Association of America, Society for Industrial and Applied Mathematics.** Providence, R.I.: American Mathematical Society, 1984. 340p.

1312.   **World Directory of Mathematicians.** 7th ed. Kyoto, Japan: Bureau of the World Directory of Mathematicians, International Mathematical Union, 1982. 725p.

These two directories can be used when the address of a mathematician is sought. The Mathematical Association of America, American Mathematical Society, and Society for Industrial and Applied Mathematics are the three major professional societies for mathematicians in the United States, so the *Combined Membership List* is a good source of addresses for Americans and those from other countries who happen to be a member of at least one of the three societies. The *World Directory of Mathematicians* provides name and address data for prominent mathematicians from all over the world. Both directories include geographic listings to supplement the alphabetical arrangement of entries.

24

ASTRONOMY, PHYSICS

Astronomy and physics are considered together in this chapter because they are closely related. Many of the ideas and techniques of astronomy derive from modern physical theory. Many physics reference tools include substantial coverage of astronomy. Reference work in astronomy is considered first, but it should be noted that many of the reference tools described in the second section under "Physics" are relevant to astronomy as well. There are some related topics covered in other chapters: astronautics is included in chapter 31, "Engineering," and nuclear energy is included in chapter 27, "Environmental Sciences, Energy."

Astronomy is concerned with all objects outside the earth and its atmosphere, including the moon, sun, planets, stars, galaxies, interplanetary and interstellar matter, and the universe as a whole. Research in astronomy has changed dramatically in the last few decades as a result of developments in instrumentation and the space program. Observations are no longer confined to the visible spectrum as viewed from the earth's surface. Astronomers now study the entire electromagnetic spectrum, not just that which is visible to the human eye. Much has been learned through studies made possible by instruments carried by satellites and space probes.

In the university there may be a separate astronomy department or some courses may be offered by the physics department. In addition to faculty and students involved in research and courses in astronomy, there are likely to be amateur astronomers who seek information to aid them in making observations. In astronomy familiar categories of reference works, such as encyclopedias and handbooks, must be supplemented with atlases and catalogs to support observation. Atlases contain maps and photographs of astronomical objects; catalogs list these objects with a variety of data for each. Although it is important to have current reference materials reflecting new concepts and discoveries, the older observational literature is also still consulted. Students at all levels are likely to need definitions of terms, explanations of formulas, and descriptions of observational techniques as well as the data provided by atlases and catalogs. Graduate students and faculty may also seek assistance in literature searching and verification of bibliographic references.

Physics is concerned with matter and energy and their interactions, those aspects of nature which can be understood in terms of principles and laws. Classical physics is based on certain general classes of natural phenomena, with major areas of study being mechanics, thermodynamics (heat), electricity and magnetism, acoustics (sound), and optics (light). Subdivisions of study in modern physics reflect types of structures in nature:

particle physics, nuclear physics, atomic physics, molecular physics, solid state physics, physics of liquids, physics of gases, and biophysics. Physics is characterized by precision of measurement and expression of results in mathematical terms. Both theoretical and experimental work are important.

Many undergraduates take basic physics courses and have a need for definitions of terms, explanations of concepts and formulas, or particular data values. More advanced students and faculty are likely to seek data and literature relevant to their work. Because research in physics advances very quickly, tools for current awareness are also important.

ASTRONOMY

GUIDES, BIBLIOGRAPHIES, INDEXES

1313.   Seal, Robert A. **A Guide to the Literature of Astronomy.** Littleton, Colo.: Libraries Unlimited, 1977. 306p.

1314.   Kemp, D. A. **Astronomy and Astrophysics: A Bibliographical Guide.** London: Macdonald Technical & Scientific, 1970. 584p.

1315.   Seal, Robert A., and Sarah S. Martin. **A Bibliography of Astronomy, 1970-1979.** Littleton, Colo.: Libraries Unlimited, 1982. 407p.

A Guide to the Literature of Astronomy is a valuable starting point for literature searching in astronomy, suitable for use by both students and laymen. Entries are arranged in four sections: reference sources, general materials (including texts and periodicals), descriptive astronomy, and special topics. Each entry includes full bibliographic data and a detailed annotation. Both author/title and subject indexes are provided, and a bibliography of basic reference materials is included as an appendix. The other two bibliographies are suitable for use by more advanced students and faculty members, and, taken together, span three decades. Kemp's bibliography has over three thousand entries in 75 subject categories, identifying important books and periodical articles published in the period 1950-68. Each entry includes full bibliographic information, the number of references cited, and a brief comment. There are author and subject indexes. As the title indicates, Seal and Martin's bibliography covers the period 1970-79 with about two thousand entries in a guide to bibliographic and review sources. Entries are annotated and in a topical arrangement. Indexes provide access to authors, subjects, and monograph titles, and conference proceedings.

1316.   **Astronomy and Astrophysics Abstracts.** Berlin: Springer, 1969- . Semiannual.

Astronomy and Astrophysics Abstracts is a comprehensive abstracting service for the literature of astronomy and astrophysics. Publications covered include books, journals, reports, conference proceedings, and series issued by observatories. It supersedes *Astronomischer Jahresbericht* (Berlin: de Gruyter, 1899-1968). Abstracts are arranged in over one hundred subject categories. There are author and subject indexes in each volume, which cumulate every five years (1969-73, 1974-78, 1979-83). *Physics Abstracts* (entry 1339) and *Physics Briefs* (entry 1340) also include coverage of astronomy. Although not as comprehensive as *Astronomy and Astrophysics Abstracts*, they appear more often and can therefore be used to search recently published literature. In addition, *Current Contents:*

Physical, Chemical & Earth Sciences (entry 1341) includes coverage of astronomy journals in its section on space sciences.

1317. Collins, Mike, comp. **Astronomical Catalogues, 1951-1975.** London: Institution of Electrical Engineers, 1977. 325p.

Catalogs are an important category of reference tool in astronomy. Supplementing listings of catalogs in the guides to the literature, this bibliography can be consulted. It cites nearly 2,500 catalogs and listings of stars, nebulae, galaxies, sources of radiation, and other astronomical phenomena and objects. It includes both separately published catalogs and those appearing as part of a journal or book. Arrangement is by subject with an author index. Entries contain bibliographic details and a summary of content.

DICTIONARIES, ENCYCLOPEDIAS

1318. **The Facts on File Dictionary of Astronomy.** Edited by Valerie Illingworth. New York: Facts on File, 1979. 378p.

1319. Hopkins, Jeanne. **Glossary of Astronomy and Astrophysics.** 2d ed. Chicago: University of Chicago Press, 1980. 196p.

1320. Moore, Patrick. **The A-Z of Astronomy.** Rev. ed. New York: Scribner's, 1976. 192p. Paper.

1321. Nicolson, Iain. **Dictionary of Astronomy: Terms and Concepts of Space and the Universe.** New York: Barnes & Noble, 1980. 250p. Paper.

1322. Tver, David F. **Dictionary of Astronomy, Space, and Atmospheric Phenomena.** New York: Van Nostrand, Reinhold, 1979. 281p.

Available astronomy dictionaries vary in comprehensiveness and level of difficulty. Two dictionaries are particularly suitable for use by faculty and more advanced students. *The Facts on File Dictionary of Astronomy* contains detailed definitions of theories and laws, phenomena, equipment, and celestial bodies and features as well as entries for organizations and observatories. Tables and line drawings appear throughout and there are numerous cross-references. Appendixes provide data on astronomical phenomena, famous astronomers, and major observatories. The *Glossary of Astronomy and Astrophysics* is a scholarly work, giving definitions of specific astronomical objects, techniques, and theories together with related terms from physics and chemistry. The dictionaries by Moore, Nicolson, and Tver are all accessible to the student and amateur astronomer. Moore is the most selective, providing simple but clear definitions for major astronomical terms, with occasional illustrations. Tver covers terms related to astronomy, space research, and meteorology in a brief manner with some illustrations. Appendixes provide data on planets and stars. Nicolson gives somewhat more detailed definitions, often with cross-references and illustrations. There is a guide to further reading.

1323. **McGraw-Hill Encyclopedia of Astronomy.** Edited by Sybil P. Parker. New York: McGraw-Hill, 1983. 450p.

1324. **Cambridge Encyclopaedia of Astronomy.** Edited by Simon Mitton. New York: Crown, 1977. 495p.

1325. Satterthwaite, Gilbert E. **Encyclopedia of Astronomy.** New York: St. Martin's, 1971. 537p.

1326. Weigert, A., and H. Zimmermann. **Concise Encyclopedia of Astronomy.** 2d ed. London: Adam Hilger, 1976. 532p.

One-volume encyclopedias in astronomy can be used to augment entries found in dictionaries and are suitable for use by undergraduates. The *McGraw-Hill Encyclopedia of Astronomy* reprints 230 articles from the fifth edition of the parent encyclopedia (entry 1244). It is well illustrated and has an index. The *Cambridge Encyclopaedia of Astronomy* differs from the others described here in that it has a topical rather than an alphabetical arrangement. Twenty-three well-illustrated chapters cover the universe, stars, solar system, galaxies, cosmology, life in the universe, ground-based astronomy, and astronomy in space. Appendixes provide a star atlas and an outline of physics. The index gives access to specific subjects. The encyclopedia by Satterthwaite is somewhat dated, but can be consulted for explanations of concepts and biographical sketches of outstanding astronomers. Translated from German, the *Concise Encyclopedia of Astronomy* provides more technical treatment in about 1,500 entries ranging from definitions to longer articles, many with illustrations.

HANDBOOKS

To aid in observation astronomers rely on various types of data books, including star catalogs and atlases. This section includes books which are compilations of data, formulas, and techniques as well as field guides. Citations to catalogs can be found in the bibliography by Collins (entry 1317), and the next section gives an example of an atlas.

1327. **Astronomical Almanac.** Washington, D.C.: Government Printing Office; London: Her Majesty's Stationery Office, 1981- . Annual.

1328. Robinson, J. Hedley, and James Muirden. **Astronomy Data Book.** 2d ed. New York: Wiley, 1979. 272p.

The *Astronomical Almanac* is a standard source of astronomical data, such as the position of celestial bodies, in tabular form. It also includes a list of observatories, a glossary, and an index. It replaces two titles that previously provided much of the same type of information (*American Ephemeris and Nautical Almanac* [Washington, D.C.: GPO, 1852-1980] and the *Astronomical Ephemeris* [London: H.M.S.O., 1767-1980]) and is a joint publication of Her Majesty's Nautical Almanac Office, Royal Greenwich Observatory, and the U.S. Naval Observatory Nautical Almanac Office. Another convenient data compilation is the *Astronomy Data Book*, each chapter of which gives a general introduction and then data on specific features. Topical chapters include telescopes, earth, sun, moon, each planet, comets, meteors, stars, and radio astronomy. There are a brief glossary and an index.

1329. Allen, C. W. **Astrophysical Quantities.** 3d ed. London: University of London, Athlone Press, 1973. 310p.

1330. Kitchin, C. R. **Astrophysical Techniques.** Bristol: Adam Hilger, 1984. 438p.

1331. Lang, Kenneth R. **Astrophysical Formulae: A Compendium for the Physicist and Astrophysicist.** 2d ed. Berlin: Springer, 1980. 783p.

These three handbooks provide complementary information useful to advanced students and faculty. *Astrophysical Quantities* consists entirely of tabular information for ready reference, with sections on atoms, spectra, radiation, earth, planets, interplanetary matter, sun, stars, nebulae, and galaxies. *Astrophysical Formulae* presents formulas in a categorized arrangement together with references to sources where their derivations are given. *Astrophysical Techniques* provides an account of instruments and techniques used in astronomy and astrophysics today. Sections cover detectors, imaging, photometry, and spectroscopy.

1332.   Burnham, Robert, Jr. **Burnham's Celestial Handbook: An Observer's Guide to the Universe beyond the Solar System.** 3 vols. New York: Dover, 1978.

1333.   Menzel, Donald H., and Jay M. Pasachoff. **A Field Guide to the Stars and Planets.** 2d ed. Boston: Houghton Mifflin, 1983. 473p. (Peterson Field Guide Series).

Both these books are intended for the observer. Following introductory chapters on observational techniques, *Burnham's Celestial Handbook* is arranged by constellation. Photographs, diagrams, and charts accompany the text describing stars which are visible in the vicinity of each constellation. The *Field Guide to the Stars and Planets* describes approaches to observing various objects such as the moon, planets, stars, and comets. Many maps are provided to aid in locating objects to be observed. Supplementary sections include a glossary, bibliography, index, and descriptions of telescopes.

1334.   Murdin, Paul, and David Allen. **Catalogue of the Universe.** New York: Crown, 1979. 256p.

This book differs from other tools for observers in that it is a selective guide to astronomical phenomena. Its three major sections (galaxies, stars and nebulae, solar system) contain detailed descriptions of selected objects with accompanying photographs. There are also a glossary and an index.

ATLASES

1335.   Moore, Patrick. **Rand McNally New Concise Atlas of the Universe.** New York: Rand McNally, 1978. 190p.

This atlas, suitable for use by both amateurs and professionals, has four sections: the earth from space, the moon, the solar system, and the stars. Each section has maps, photographs, diagrams, and descriptive text. In addition, there is a catalog of stellar objects, a glossary, and an index.

PHYSICS

GUIDES, BIBLIOGRAPHIES, INDEXES

1336.   Shaw, Dennis F., ed. **Information Sources in Physics.** 2d ed. London: Butterworths, 1985. 456p. (Butterworths Guides to Information Sources).

1337.   Whitford, Robert H. **Physics Literature: A Reference Manual.** 2d ed. Metuchen, N.J.: Scarecrow, 1968. 272p.

1338.   Yates, B. **How to Find Out about Physics: A Guide to Sources of Information Arranged by the Decimal Classification.** Oxford: Pergamon, 1965. 175p.

Each of these guides offers a somewhat different approach to the physics literature. The Shaw guide is the most current, with 6 chapters devoted to more general topics and 14 covering the literature of the various subdivisions of physics (e.g., atomic and molecular physics, mechanics and acoustics). Chapters are authored by experts, written in a narrative style, and include a brief introduction to each specialty and discussions of major sources. There is an appendix of publisher addresses, and both an author index and a subject and title index are provided. Whitford has organized his discussion around what he terms "approaches," aspects of physics information which an information seeker may have in mind. In addition to the topical approach, which covers literature in the various subdivisions of physics, the guide discusses bibliographical, historical, biographical, experimental, mathematical, educational, and terminological approaches. Most sources described are at the college level. Both author and subject indexes are included. Now somewhat dated, Yates is intended for student use, with questions at the end of each chapter to aid in self-study. Initial chapters cover types of materials (books, reference books, documents, periodicals, abstracts), and the remaining chapters cover major subdivisions of physics such as mechanics and optics. There is an index.

1339.   **Physics Abstracts.** Hitchin, Herts., England: INSPEC, Institution of Electrical Engineers, 1898- . Semimonthly with semiannual cumulation of indexes.

1340.   **Physics Briefs. Physikalische Berichte.** Weinheim: Physik-Verlag, 1979- . Semimonthly with semiannual cumulation of indexes.

The two major abstracting publications in physics are *Physics Abstracts*, one of three abstracting services published by INSPEC, and *Physics Briefs*, sponsored jointly by the American Institute of Physics, the Deutsche Physikalische Gesellschaft, and the Fachinformationszentrum Energie/Physik/Mathematik GmbH. They are arranged using the same classification scheme, which uses 10 major sections: general; physics of elementary particles and fields; nuclear physics; atomic and molecular physics; classical areas of phenomenology; fluids, plasmas and electric discharges; condensed matter (2 sections); cross-disciplinary physics; and geophysics, astronomy and astrophysics. Both are international in coverage and provide indexing and abstracting for journals, books, patents, dissertations, reports, and conference proceedings. *Physics Briefs* places special emphasis on nonconventional literature and literature in Eastern languages. In *Physics Abstracts* each issue carries an author index, bibliography index (to articles containing a significant list of references or a bibliography), a book index, a conference index (to conference papers which are abstracted), and a corporate author index. In addition, there is a subject guide to the classified arrangement. Issue indexes cumulate semiannually and a detailed subject index is also produced semiannually. Each issue of *Physics Briefs* has an author index, with semiannual author and subject indexes. Prior to *Physics Briefs*, the Deutsche Physikalische Gesellschaft published *Physikalische Berichte* from 1920-1978 with abstracts in German. *Physics Abstracts* can be machine searched online as part of the INSPEC database. Coverage goes back to 1969 on DIALOG, to 1970 on BRS, and to 1977 on SDC. Although the two abstracting services overlap in coverage, both should be consulted when doing a comprehensive literature search.

1341.   **Current Contents: Physical, Chemical & Earth Sciences.** Philadelphia: Institute for Scientific Information, 1961- . Weekly.

1342.   **Current Papers in Physics.** Hitchin, Herts., England: INSPEC, Institution of Electrical Engineers, 1966- . Semimonthly.

1343.   **Current Physics Index.** New York: American Institute of Physics, 1975- . Quarterly with annual cumulation of indexes.

Three publications are available to assist with current awareness in physics. *Current Contents* has the smallest time lag. It appears weekly, reproducing the tables of contents of major journals arranged by broad topic areas. Relevant topics include physics and applied physics/condensed matter. Each issue also covers a few multi-authored monographs. In addition, there is a keyword index, and an author index and address directory. Although used primarily by advanced students and faculty for current awareness, *Current Contents* can be used by reference librarians to verify recently published articles and to locate current addresses for authors known to have published articles recently. *Current Papers in Physics* is a companion publication to *Physics Abstracts* (entry 1339), with citations in the same classified arrangement. Publications cited here are later abstracted in *Physics Abstracts*, so *Current Papers in Physics* is useful for current awareness browsing in the interim. *Current Physics Index* is much more restricted in scope, covering research journals published by the American Institute of Physics and affiliated societies. Abstracts appear in a classified arrangement, with an author index in each issue and annual author and subject indexes. *Current Physics Index* can be machine searched online back to 1975 as part of the SPIN database through DIALOG.

DICTIONARIES, ENCYCLOPEDIAS

1344. **The Facts on File Dictionary of Physics.** Edited by John Daintith. New York: Facts on File, 1981. 217p.

1345. Gray, H. J., and Alan Isaacs. **A New Dictionary of Physics.** 2d ed. London: Longman, 1975. 619p.

1346. Thewlis, J. **Concise Dictionary of Physics and Related Subjects.** 2d ed., rev. & enl. Oxford: Pergamon, 1979. 370p.

Students seeking definitions of terms in all branches of physics should find all three of these dictionaries useful. *The Facts on File Dictionary of Physics* has about two thousand entries for the most commonly used terms in physics, and some illustrations. Appendixes include explanations of symbols and tables of conversion factors. The *New Dictionary of Physics* also emphasizes basic terminology, particularly that related to modern developments, and also provides some illustrations. Biographical entries are included and several tables, providing data such as the Nobel prize winners in physics, supplement the text. The *Concise Dictionary* is based in part on the *Encyclopaedic Dictionary of Physics* (entry 1350), but its usefulness is not confined to advanced students. Definitions are brief, with some cross-references and no illustrations. Appendixes include the periodic table, conversion tables for units, and values of physical constants.

1347. **Encyclopedia of Physics.** Edited by Rita G. Lerner and George L. Trigg. Reading, Mass.: Addison-Wesley, 1981. 1157p.

1348. Besançon, Robert M., ed. **Encyclopedia of Physics.** 3d ed. New York: Van Nostrand, Reinhold, 1985. 1378p.

1349. **McGraw-Hill Encyclopedia of Physics.** Edited by Sybil P. Parker. New York: McGraw-Hill, 1983. 1343p.

These three one-volume encyclopedias are intended for use both by students and by physicists seeking information outside their fields of specialization. The encyclopedia edited by Lerner and Trigg has broad coverage, including physics, astrophysics, and related topics. Experts have contributed survey articles of major areas and more specialized articles within each field. Both cross-references and an index aid in locating relevant material. Bibliographies accompany most articles, and many are coded to indicate the level of difficulty of the recommended sources. The encyclopedia edited by Besançon is similar in scope and intended audience, and the current edition includes recent research findings.

Articles are at three levels: main divisions of physics are described for the general reader; subdivisions of physics are explained for readers with a background in science; and specific topics are presented for readers with a background in physics and mathematics. There is a detailed index, and many articles include bibliographies and cross-references. The *McGraw-Hill Encyclopedia of Physics* has taken 760 physics-related articles from the fifth edition of the parent encyclopedia (entry 1244). It includes appendixes of conversion factors, symbols, mathematical notation, and fundamental constants, as well as an index.

1350.   **Encyclopaedic Dictionary of Physics: General, Nuclear, Solid State, Molecular, Chemical, Metal and Vacuum Physics, Astronomy, Geophysics, Biophysics and Related Subjects.** Edited by J. Thewlis. 9 vols. Oxford: Pergamon, 1961-1964. Supplements, 1966- .

1351.   **Handbuch der Physik. Encyclopedia of Physics.** Edited by S. Flügge. 54 sections. Berlin: Springer, 1955-1984.

These two multi-volume works are at a more advanced level than the one-volume encyclopedias and are most likely to be useful to graduate students and faculty. As the subtitle indicates, the *Encyclopaedic Dictionary of Physics* covers physics and related fields in articles ranging in length from a few sentences to several pages. All articles are signed and many include brief bibliographies. In the original set, volume 8 has subject and author indexes and volume 9 is a multilingual glossary, giving the English equivalent for terms in French, German, Spanish, Russian, and Japanese. Supplements are published irregularly. There have been five to date, dealing with new topics and new developments in topics covered in the original set. *Handbuch der Physik* is a treatise covering the entire field of physics. Each volume deals with a specific topic in scholarly and highly technical articles intended for the advanced researcher. Articles have extensive bibliographic references, and each volume is fully indexed in English and German. Languages of the texts of articles are predominantly English or German, with some in French. Neither of these sets can be used to locate explanations of recent discoveries, but they are a good starting point for retrospective searching by the advanced student.

1352.   **International Dictionary of Physics and Electronics.** 2d ed. Princeton, N.J.: Van Nostrand, 1961. 1355p.

1353.   **McGraw-Hill Dictionary of Physics and Mathematics.** Edited by Daniel N. Lapedes. New York: McGraw-Hill, 1978. 1074p. plus appendix, 46p.

As their titles indicate, physics is one of the main subjects, but not the exclusive subject, of both of these dictionaries. The *McGraw-Hill Dictionary of Physics and Mathematics* has been described in the chapter on mathematics (entry 1294). It also contains a number of appendixes useful in reference work in physics and astronomy, such as conversion tables for units and tables of elementary particles, planets and stars. In the *International Dictionary of Physics and Electronics* definitions reflect the likely background of users, with more technical definitions for more specialized terms. French, German, Russian, and Spanish term indexes are provided.

DIRECTORIES

1354.   **Graduate Programs in Physics, Astronomy and Related Fields, 1984-85.** New York: American Institute of Physics, 1984. 911p.

When information about graduate programs at other institutions is sought, this directory can be used to locate detailed descriptions of master's and doctoral level programs in the United States, Canada, and Mexico. Entries list graduate faculty, research specialties, admissions and financial aid data, and course requirements for each department. Arrangement of entries is by state and province and by institution within state. Appendixes provide tables with comparative data on the academic programs included in the directory.

HANDBOOKS

There are many handbooks and data books important for physics research and only a few are mentioned here. Both Arny's guide to data sources (entry 1218) and Powell's bibliography of handbooks (entry 1265) should be consulted for guidance in locating more specific titles.

1355.   **American Institute of Physics Handbook.** 3d ed. Edited by Dwight E. Gray. New York: McGraw-Hill, 1972. Various paging.

1356.   Condon, E. U., and Hugh Odishaw. **Handbook of Physics.** 2d ed. New York: McGraw-Hill, 1967. Various paging.

1357.   **CRC Handbook of Chemistry and Physics.** 66th ed. Edited by Robert C. Weast. Boca Raton, Fla.: CRC Press, 1985. Various paging.

The first two handbooks are comparable in scope, providing authoritative coverage of the major subdivisions of physics: mechanics, acoustics, heat, electricity and magnetism, optics, atomic and molecular physics, nuclear physics, and solid state physics. Each section includes definitions, tables, formulas, text, and bibliographic references with an emphasis on basic concepts and mathematical methods. Detailed indexes make it easy to locate specific terms and formulas. Students at all levels and even faculty may make use of these compilations for ready reference. Revised annually, the *CRC Handbook of Chemistry and Physics* is perhaps the most well known data book in physics and chemistry. Both the mathematical tables and the section on physical constants are likely to be frequently consulted by students in physics. The volume is well indexed.

BIOGRAPHY

1358.   **Directory of Physics and Astronomy Staff Members, 1984-1985.** New York: American Institute of Physics, 1984. 412p.

This directory provides current name and address information for faculty and staff associated with colleges and universities, federally funded research and development centers, government laboratories, and industrial laboratories doing research in physics or astronomy. Geographical coverage includes the United States, Canada, Mexico, and Central America. The major portion of the directory is an alphabetical listing of all staff members, their work addresses and telephone numbers. Parts 2 and 3 are alphabetical listings of academic institutions and research and development organizations, giving institution address and phone number together with a list of faculty or staff, with academic rank or job title. Part 4 provides a geographical list of academic institutions; part 5 lists research and development organizations by type (federally funded research and development centers, government laboratories, industrial and not-for-profit laboratories).

25

CHEMISTRY

This chapter covers both chemistry and chemical engineering. Chemistry is the scientific study of the nature, properties, and composition of substances, the reactions that occur between them, and laws governing chemical phenomena. Chemical engineering deals with the development and application of manufacturing processes which chemically convert raw materials into a variety of products, and with the design and operation of plants and equipment to perform such work. Major subdivisions of chemistry include analytical chemistry (determination of the composition of substances), inorganic chemistry, organic chemistry (carbon compounds), and physical chemistry (study of fundamental laws and theories). Biochemistry and geochemistry are areas of study where chemistry overlaps with biology and geology, respectively.

The reference literature of chemistry is extensive, and this chapter can only discuss some of the major reference tools. Fortunately there are several recent guides to the literature which can be used to explore the chemical literature in more depth. In one of these guides, Mellon identifies the types of questions which commonly arise in chemistry:

1. *Bibliography.* Partial or complete list of references, with or without annotations.

2. *History and biography.* Events in the life of an individual or in the development of an industry; the influences operating, and contributions made, during certain periods; the beginning and development of a theory or an industry.

3. *Existence, occurrence, and source.* The location of raw material; its form; compounds which are known.

4. *Composition.* Natural materials and artificial products; specifications and standards; formulas and workshop recipes.

5. *Methods of production, preparation, and manipulation.* Laboratory and commercial processes; details of procedure; materials required; apparatus employed.

6. *Properties.* Physical and chemical (including physiological action); general and specific reactions.

7. *Uses.* Laboratory and industrial; general and special applications.

8. *Identification, testing, and analysis.* Methods available; interpretation of results.

9. *Patents and trademarks.* Date of expiration; details of specifications; objects previously protected.

10. *Statistical data.* Production; consumption; cost; supply; price; market.[1]

Reference tools have been developed to aid in easier location of the information required to respond to these questions. *Chemical Abstracts* (entry 1367), for example, provides excellent coverage of the chemical literature. Numerous handbooks and data books have data culled from the primary literature, describing composition and properties of substances. Books on technique similarly describe methods of preparation and analysis. Chemistry is notable for the many multi-volume treatises which synthesize information in a particular subdivision of chemistry. Undergraduates are likely to need instruction to make effective use of the major reference tools, and graduate students and faculty may bring questions to the library that cannot be answered in the reference tools kept at hand in the chemical laboratory. Because information is so often sought on chemicals for which the formula is known, formula indexes appear in some of the major reference tools such as *Chemical Abstracts.* Instructions for using formula indexes and many of the reference tools in chemistry are included in the literature guides described below.

GUIDES, BIBLIOGRAPHIES, INDEXES

1359. Antony, Arthur. **Guide to Basic Information Sources in Chemistry.** New York: Wiley, 1979. 219p. (Information Resources Series).

1360. Bottle, R. T., ed. **Use of Chemical Literature.** 3d ed. London: Butterworths, 1979. 306p. (Butterworths Guides to Information Sources).

1361. Maizell, Robert E. **How to Find Chemical Information: A Guide for Practicing Chemists, Teachers, and Students.** New York: Wiley, 1979. 261p.

1362. Mellon, M. G. **Chemical Publications: Their Nature and Use.** 5th ed. New York: McGraw-Hill, 1982. 419p.

The importance of the literature to chemists is reflected in the number of guides to the literature which have been published. Some represent the contents of courses in chemical literature taught at particular universities and thus are especially well suited to the needs of the student. All four of these guides provide quite detailed surveys of available information sources in chemistry. Antony, Maizell, and Mellon are arranged by type of material; Bottle includes some chapters dealing with the literature of particular subdivisions within chemistry. Mellon, now in its fifth edition, has been brought up-to-date to reflect new developments, such as computer searching. Antony's guide, with an emphasis on pure chemistry, is primarily intended for the student of chemistry. Most chapters cover a type of material. A brief discussion of the type is followed by an annotated bibliography of the major sources of that type. There is a chapter on bibliographic searching by computer and a final chapter on chemical information search strategy with a series of cases. There are indexes for subject and for author and title. Bottle's guide stresses British chemical literature and has chapters by various authors. Several chapters cover types of material (e.g., patents,

---

[1]M. G. Mellon, *Chemical Publications: Their Nature and Use.* 5th ed. (New York: McGraw-Hill, 1982), 4-5.

government publications, tables), and there are a few topical chapters (inorganic chemistry, nuclear chemistry, organic chemistry, and polymer chemistry). The book includes some practical exercises and an index for the student. Maizell emphasizes the most important classical tools of chemical information, the more significant newer tools, and search strategies for their effective use. Chapters focusing on particular types of information needs include those on safety, physical property and related data, chemical marketing and business information sources, and process information. Other chapters cover different types of material, and there are separate chapters on Chemical Abstracts Service and computer-based services. An index is included. Mellon's guide is in two parts. He describes the principal sources for reference and research in part 1 (periodicals, technical reports, patents, indexes and abstracts, bibliographies, reference works, textbooks, guides and directories). Part 2 covers both manual and computer searching of the literature. There are author and subject indexes.

1363. Skolnik, Herman. **The Literature Matrix of Chemistry.** New York: Wiley, 1982. 297p.

1364. Wolman, Yecheskel. **Chemical Information: A Practical Guide to Utilization.** New York: Wiley, 1983. 191p.

1365. Woodburn, Henry M. **Using the Chemical Literature: A Practical Guide.** New York: Marcel Dekker, 1974. 302p. (Books in Library and Information Science, vol. 11).

These three guides can be used to supplement those described above to provide a more complete picture of chemical information sources and search strategies. Skolnik seeks to describe the scope and content of the "literature matrix" so that it can be used more effectively. Chapters cover books, encyclopedias and treatises, numerical data compilations, patents, journal literature, secondary services, Chemical Abstracts Service, other abstracting and indexing services, and computer-based information services. There are chapters on the history of the chemical literature and chemistry in America as well as name and subject indexes. Wolman's book is based on a course in chemical information taught to undergraduates and emphasizes search strategies, with several chapters describing sources and strategies relevant to particular information needs: obtaining numerical data, synthetic reaction search, structure and substructure searches, chemical marketing and process information, and gathering information about individuals and organizations. There are also a chapter on online searching and an index. Woodburn is aimed at the undergraduate and emphasizes those sources which may require some explanation to use effectively. Complete chapters are devoted to *Chemical Abstracts, Beilsteins Handbuch der Organischen Chemie*, and *Gmelins Handbuch der Anorganischen Chemie*. In addition, there are chapters on particular types of material such as government publications, collections of data, translations, patents, and computer-readable material. There is also an index.

1366. Peck, Theodore P. **Chemical Industries Information Sources.** Detroit: Gale, 1979. 595p. (Management Information Guide, no. 29).

This guide differs from those already described in its emphasis on chemical industries and its inclusion of organizations as well as printed information sources. There are eight major sections: "General Information on Chemical Engineering and Chemical Industries"; "Agricultural Engineering"; "Bioengineering"; "Food Engineering"; "Materials Including Plastics, Metals, Ceramics, Rubbers, and Textiles"; "Nuclear Engineering"; "Paper and Pulp Engineering"; and "Petroleum Engineering." Each section is divided into two parts, one describing organizations and associations (e.g., government agencies, professional societies, trade associations, research centers) and the other describing literature (subdivided by type). Some entries have brief annotations. There are organization and subject indexes, and a directory of publishers' names and addresses.

1367.   **Chemical Abstracts.** Columbus, Ohio: American Chemical Society, Chemical Abstracts Service, 1907- . Weekly with semiannual and 5-year cumulation of indexes.

Chemical Abstracts is the major abstracting service in chemistry and an essential tool in literature searching. Because of its extensive coverage, *Chemical Abstracts* will also be useful to students and faculty in disciplines overlapping chemistry. To use *Chemical Abstracts* effectively it is necessary to have a good understanding of its organization. It is international in scope and covers all types of documents: journals, monographs, conference proceedings, reports, dissertations, and patents. The abstracts are arranged in five broad sections with a total of 80 topical subdivisions. *Chemical Abstracts* is issued weekly. Sections on biochemistry and organic chemistry (covering subdivisions 1-34) appear in odd-numbered issues, and sections on macromolecular chemistry, applied chemistry and chemical engineering, and physical, inorganic and analytical chemistry (covering subdivisions 35-80) appear in even-numbered issues. Each issue has three indexes: keyword (uncontrolled terms drawn mostly from titles and abstracts of documents), author, and patent. Volume indexes appear every six months. In addition to indexes for author, patent, formula, and ring systems, there are two types of subject indexes: chemical substance and general subject. Both use controlled terms, and it is important to consult the *Index Guide* which accompanies *Chemical Abstracts* to determine the appropriate terms under which to search. The *Index Guide* contains index terms, cross-references, synonyms, and notes on indexing policy as well as some useful appendixes: hierarchies of general subject headings; explanations of the organization and use of indexes to *Chemical Abstracts*; selection of general subject headings; and selection of chemical substance index names. Volume indexes are merged and republished as collective indexes every five years (every 10 years prior to 1957). Abstracts of articles discussing a particular chemical include its registry number, a unique identifier which Chemical Abstracts Service creates for each substance mentioned in a paper covered by *Chemical Abstracts.* The *Chemical Abstracts Service Registry Handbook: Number Section* records registry numbers together with *Chemical Abstracts* names and molecular formulas. These registry numbers are particularly helpful when searching online since a unique number (rather than a list of alternative names) can be used to designate a chemical substance. The CA SEARCH database includes bibliographic and indexing information for items abstracted in *Chemical Abstracts.* It can be machine searched back to 1967 on DIALOG and SDC, and back to 1970 on BRS. In addition, Chemical Abstracts Service maintains its own online service, STN International, on which abstracts that supplement the bibliographic and indexing information in CA SEARCH are available back to 1975. For more detailed discussions of *Chemical Abstracts*, the various guides to the chemical literature (entries 1359-65) should be consulted. The reference librarian must be able both to use *Chemical Abstracts* and to explain its use to students who may initially find its sheer bulk rather overwhelming.

1368.   **Chemical Titles: Current Author and Keyword Indexes from Selected Chemical Journals.** Columbus, Ohio: American Chemical Society, Chemical Abstracts Service, 1960- . Biweekly.

1369.   **Current Contents: Physical, Chemical & Earth Sciences.** Philadelphia: Institute for Scientific Information, 1961- . Weekly.

Because there is a time lag of a few months before publications are covered in *Chemical Abstracts*, it is convenient to have sources for current awareness in the interim. As its subtitle indicates, *Chemical Titles* provides author and keyword indexes to articles which have recently appeared in any of more than seven hundred important chemical journals. Each issue has three parts: a keyword-in-context (KWIC) index derived from words in article titles, a bibliography section reproducing tables of contents of journals arranged by CODEN (a six-character notation to represent titles of periodicals), and an author index. *Current Contents* has already been described (entry 1341). Sections of each issue relating to chemistry include organic chemistry/polymer science, analytical, inorganic and nuclear chemistry, and physical chemistry/chemical physics.

1370.   **Chemical Abstracts Service Source Index: 1907-1984 Cumulative.** 2 vols. Columbus, Ohio: American Chemical Society, Chemical Abstracts Service, 1985. Quarterly supplement, 1985- .

Chemical Abstracts Service Source Index, commonly known as *CASSI*, is a valuable tool for bibliographic verification and interlibrary loan. Because the literature monitored for possible inclusion in *Chemical Abstracts* includes publications in many disciplines in addition to chemistry and chemical engineering, the publications listed here cover many areas of the sciences. *CASSI* includes citations for serials and conference proceedings that have been covered in *Chemical Abstracts* since 1907, in *Chemisches Zentralblatt* during the period 1830-1969, or in *Beilsteins Handbuch der Organischen Chemie.* Each entry includes full title, abbreviated title, translation for a foreign title, references to variant titles, CODEN, ISSN or ISBN, history of publication, frequency, publisher, language of publication, and holdings in over 350 major libraries worldwide. Titles are arranged by their abbreviated form, so *CASSI* is useful in identifying the full title of a journal when only the abbreviated form is known. It is updated quarterly, allowing verification of newly published titles as well as identification of changes in titles. The quarterly supplements cumulate annually. *CASSI* can be machine searched through SDC.

DICTIONARIES, ENCYCLOPEDIAS

1371.   **The Facts on File Dictionary of Chemistry.** Edited by John Daintith. New York: Facts on File, 1981. 233p.

1372.   Hampel, Clifford A., and Gessner G. Hawley. **Glossary of Chemical Terms.** 2d ed. New York: Van Nostrand, Reinhold, 1982. 306p.

1373.   **McGraw-Hill Dictionary of Chemistry.** Edited by Sybil P. Parker. New York: McGraw-Hill, 1984. 665p.

1374.   **Miall's Dictionary of Chemistry.** 5th ed. Edited by D. W. A. Sharp. Harlow, Essex, England: Longman, 1981. 501p.

These dictionaries all emphasize common chemical terms and are suitable for use by undergraduates. *Facts on File Dictionary of Chemistry* covers about 2,200 terms with occasional illustrations of chemical equations and structures where appropriate. Supplementary tables present data on chemical elements, physical constants, and elementary particles. The *Glossary of Chemical Terms* has about 2,000 entries, including chemical elements and compounds, basic phenomena and processes, and some biographical notes. *McGraw-Hill Dictionary of Chemistry* draws more than 9,000 terms from the third edition of the parent work (entry 1242), focusing on the vocabulary of theoretical and applied chemistry rather than on chemicals and materials. *Miall's Dictionary of Chemistry* is also good for basic definitions and has some biographical entries.

1375.   Flood, W. E. **Dictionary of Chemical Names.** Totowa, N.J.: Littlefield, Adams, 1967. 238p.

This dictionary is unique in its emphasis on the history and derivation of chemical names. Following an introductory section on the development of the main branches of chemistry and the evolution of systematic nomenclature, part 1 covers the chemical elements and part 2 covers chemical compounds, minerals, and other substances of chemical interest. Entries give etymology and the history of the substance's discovery or initial preparation. An appendix provides biographical notes on prominent chemists mentioned in the text.

1376.   Bennett, H. **Concise Chemical and Technical Dictionary.** 3d enl. ed. New York: Chemical Publishing, 1974. 1175p.

1377.   **Condensed Chemical Dictionary.** 10th ed. Revised by Gessner G. Hawley. New York: Van Nostrand, Reinhold, 1981. 1135p.

1378.   **Hackh's Chemical Dictionary.** 4th ed. Edited by Julius Grant. New York: McGraw-Hill, 1969. 738p.

These three dictionaries also perform a handbook function in that many of the entries detail the properties of specific chemicals. Bennett has entries for the most important manufacturing techniques and machinery, raw materials, and finished products. Data given for chemical substances include name, alternate names, formula, molecular weight, properties, and uses. Many trade names are identified and there is a guide to pronunciation of chemical terms. *Condensed Chemical Dictionary* has descriptions of chemicals, trademarked products, processes, and equipment and definitions of chemical terminology. Additional entries cover chemical abbreviations, short biographies of chemists of historical importance, and technical societies and trade associations. Data given for chemical substances are extensive, listing (where applicable) name, alternate names, formula, properties, source or occurrence, derivation, uses, grades, hazardous nature, and shipping regulations. An appendix gives the etymologies of some chemical terms. *Hackh's Chemical Dictionary* has over 50,000 entries, and is similar in scope to the *Condensed Chemical Dictionary.* Data given for chemical substances include formula, alternate names, properties, and uses.

1379.   **McGraw-Hill Encyclopedia of Chemistry.** Edited by Sybil P. Parker. New York: McGraw-Hill, 1983. 1195p.

1380.   **Van Nostrand Reinhold Encyclopedia of Chemistry.** 4th ed. Edited by Douglas M. Considine and Glenn D. Considine. New York: Van Nostrand, Reinhold, 1984. 1082p.

These two encyclopedias are intended for use both by students and by chemists seeking information outside their fields of specialization. Drawn from the fifth edition of the parent work (entry 1244), the *McGraw-Hill Encyclopedia of Chemistry* has 790 articles with entries for specific compounds, processes, and techniques. Articles are well illustrated and there is a detailed index. The *Van Nostrand Reinhold Encyclopedia of Chemistry* has been updated to reflect recent developments in chemistry. There are about 1,300 articles of varying lengths, with reference lists appended to longer articles. A detailed subject index and cross-references are provided.

1381.   Hampel, Clifford A., ed. **Encyclopedia of the Chemical Elements.** New York: Reinhold, 1968. 849p.

1382.   **Chemical and Process Technology Encyclopedia.** Edited by Douglas M. Considine. New York: McGraw-Hill, 1974. 1261p.

1383. **Kingzett's Chemical Encyclopaedia: A Digest of Chemistry and Its Industrial Applications.** 9th ed. London: Baillière, Tindall and Cassell, 1966. 1092p.

These one-volume encyclopedias are narrower in scope than the two described above (entries 1379 and 1380). *Encyclopedia of the Chemical Elements* is a good source of information on individual chemical elements; it has a detailed article on each element (e.g., carbon, hydrogen) and a few more general articles, such as one on the periodic law and periodic table. The scope of *Chemical and Process Technology Encyclopedia* is indicated by the categories of articles identified in its classified index: chemical elements, organic compounds, major raw materials, physical operations and energy systems, chemical processes, chemical and engineering terms, atomic and nuclear chemical technology, biochemical technology, plastics, and functional and end-products. Most articles in *Kingzett's Chemical Encyclopaedia* are brief and would be of use primarily to students seeking clarification of a concept or information about a class of substances. All three encyclopedias have subject indexes.

1384. **Kirk-Othmer Encyclopedia of Chemical Technology.** 3d ed. 24 vols. plus supplement and index vols. New York: Wiley, 1978-84.

1385. **Kirk-Othmer Concise Encyclopedia of Chemical Technology.** New York: Wiley, 1985. 1318p.

1386. **Encyclopedia of Industrial Chemical Analysis.** Edited by Foster Dee Snell, Clifford L. Hilton, and Leslie S. Ettre. 20 vols. New York: Interscience, 1966-74.

1387. **Chemical Technology: An Encyclopedic Treatment; The Economic Application of Modern Technological Developments.** 8 vols. New York: Barnes & Noble, 1968-75.

When a more detailed treatment of a topic is sought, multi-volume encyclopedias can be consulted. *Kirk-Othmer Encyclopedia of Chemical Technology* is a resource for the advanced student and faculty member, containing long, well-documented and well-illustrated articles authored by specialists. Approximately half of the articles deal with chemical substances, their properties, manufacture, and use. Others cover fundamental principles, unit operations, and methods of analysis. Cross-references link related articles, and there is a detailed subject index. In addition, *Kirk-Othmer* can be machine searched through BRS. The *Kirk-Othmer Concise Encyclopedia of Chemical Technology* is a one-volume condensation of the parent work, which can be consulted when only brief treatments of topics are required. The *Encyclopedia of Industrial Chemical Analysis*, with an emphasis on analytical chemistry, complements *Kirk-Othmer.* The first three volumes describe general techniques common to the analysis of many industrial products, while volumes 4 through 19 discuss the analysis of specific substances or classes. Articles are long and detailed, with tables, illustrations, and bibliographies. The final volume is the index. Unlike the other two multi-volume encyclopedias, *Chemical Technology* was prepared primarily for the nonspecialist interested in learning more about materials. Arrangement is systematic with coverage subdivided as follows: air, water, inorganic chemicals, and nucleonics; nonmetallic ores, silicate industries, and solid mineral fuels; metals and ores; petroleum and organic chemicals; natural organic materials and related synthetic products; wood, paper, textiles, plastics and photographic materials; vegetable food products and luxuries; and edible oils, fats, animal food products. The final volume includes an index for the set.

DIRECTORIES

1388.   **Chem Sources — U.S.A.** Ormond Beach, Fla.: Directories Publishing, 1958- . Annual.

This is one example of a directory identifying sources of chemicals which may be needed in the academic chemical laboratory. In the chemicals section, chemicals are listed by name together with codes for companies from which they are available. A trade name section is arranged similarly. The company by code section is used to identify the full company name, and the company directory section gives name, address, and telephone number for companies whose products are listed in the directory.

HANDBOOKS

Chemistry has a wide range of handbooks and data books, from the small, one-volume compilations of commonly used data to the large, multi-volume treatises that are much more comprehensive. This section emphasizes some of the more widely used one-volume handbooks. For discussions of multi-volume sets, such as *Gmelins Handbuch der Anorganischen Chemie* and *Beilsteins Handbuch der Organischen Chemie*, the guides to the chemical literature (entries 1359-65) should be consulted. In addition, both Arny's guide to data sources (entry 1218) and Powell's bibliography of handbooks (entry 1265) can be used to identify many more specialized titles.

1389.   **CRC Handbook of Chemistry and Physics.** 66th ed. Edited by Robert C. Weast. Boca Raton, Fla.: CRC Press, 1985. Various paging.

1390.   **Lange's Handbook of Chemistry.** 13th ed. Edited by John A. Dean. New York: McGraw-Hill, 1985. Various paging.

1391.   Gordon, Arnold J., and Richard A. Ford. **The Chemist's Companion: A Handbook of Practical Data, Techniques, and References.** New York: Wiley, 1972. 537p.

The contents of *CRC Handbook of Chemistry and Physics* and *Lange's Handbook* overlap, but each covers some substances not found in the other. Both contain much data useful to the chemist. *CRC* has already been discussed in the chapter on physics (entry 1357). For the chemist it offers long sections of tables of property values for the elements and inorganic compounds, the organic compounds, and general chemical information. *Lange's* also subdivides the tables with sections including atomic and molecular structure, inorganic chemistry, analytical chemistry, electrochemistry, organic chemistry, spectroscopy, thermodynamic properties, and physical properties. Both handbooks have detailed indexes. *The Chemist's Companion* is a more selective compilation of data, a practical tool for use by both students and faculty. It includes what the compilers believe to be the most useful and often needed data. In addition to a subject index, there is a suppliers index which lists all suppliers and manufacturers mentioned in the book and cites the page on which an address appears.

1392.   **Merck Index: An Encyclopedia of Chemicals, Drugs and Biologicals.** 10th ed. Rahway, N.J.: Merck, 1983. 1463p. plus appendixes.

1393.   Brady, George S., and Henry R. Clauser. **Materials Handbook.** 11th ed. New York: McGraw-Hill, 1977. 1011p.

These handbooks can be used as sources of data on chemicals and materials of commercial importance. *Merck Index* has entries called *monographs* which contain name, *Chemical Abstracts* name (if different), alternate names, molecular formula, molecular weight, composition, literature references, structural diagram, physical data, derivatives, use, and therapeutic category. A name index and formula index are provided, and there are several appendixes including a dictionary of name reactions, a company register, and tables. *Merck Index* can be machine searched through BRS. *Materials Handbook* has technical and trade information for materials of commercial importance, such as minerals, crops, and chemicals. There are general sections on the elements of materials economics and the nature and properties of materials; it also has an index.

1394.   **Encyclopedia of Chemical Trademarks and Synonyms.** Edited by H. Bennett. 3 vols. New York: Chemical Publishing, 1981-83.

1395.   Gardner, William, Edward I. Cooke, and Richard W. I. Cooke. **Handbook of Chemical Synonyms and Trade Names: A Dictionary and Commercial Handbook Containing Over 35,000 Definitions.** 8th ed. Cleveland: CRC Press, 1978. 769p.

Both of these tools have entries for chemicals and can be used to identify certain characteristics of a product and its manufacturer when only a trade name is known. They provide more entries for chemicals than the *Trade Names Dictionary* (entry 940). The *Encyclopedia of Chemical Trademarks and Synonyms* gives the composition of each product or its end use and the producer. The *Handbook of Chemical Synonyms and Trade Names* also provides data on uses and chemical composition. All entries known to be proprietary trade names are distinguished by a reference number linked to the index of manufacturers at the end of the volume.

1396.   Bennett, H. **The Chemical Formulary.** New York: Chemical Publishing, 1933- . Irregular.

This publication is of interest to both the student and the amateur chemist, providing recipes and formulas for making domestic and industrial products, such as adhesives, cosmetics, and coatings. An appendix identifies suppliers of chemicals. Over 20 volumes have appeared to date, each containing a different set of formulas.

1397.   Manufacturing Chemists Association. **Guide for Safety in the Chemical Laboratory.** 2d ed. New York: Van Nostrand, Reinhold, 1972. 505p.

1398.   Sax, N. Irving. **Dangerous Properties of Industrial Materials.** 6th ed. New York: Van Nostrand, Reinhold, 1984. 3124p.

1399.   Bretherick, L. **Handbook of Reactive Chemical Hazards.** 2d ed. London: Butterworths, 1979. 1281p.

Both students and faculty members share a concern for safety in the chemical laboratory, and a number of handbooks can be consulted for guidance in safe handling of potentially hazardous materials. *Guide for Safety in the Chemical Laboratory* discusses methods and equipment for laboratory safety in chapters on various topics, such as evaluating hazards of unstable substances. Appendixes include a bibliography and a chart arranged by substance name, giving waste disposal procedures and other data. The handbooks by Sax and Bretherick represent convenient compilations of data originally reported in many different sources. Sax begins with five survey articles related to hazards and hazard control: "Toxicology," "Industrial Air Contaminant Control," "Industrial and Environmental Cancer Risks," "Occupational Biohazards," and "Nuclear Medicine Applications, Benefits, and Risks." The main part of the book is a listing of about 20,000 hazardous materials, providing for each material a name, registry number, molecular weight and formula, alternate names, a hazard analysis, standards and regulations, and references to relevant literature. A synonym index allows the correct entry to be located when only an alternate name is known. Bretherick is designed to allow the chemist to assess the likely reaction hazard potential of existing or proposed chemical compounds or reaction systems. A general discussion of hazards is followed by listings for chemicals or classes of chemicals, giving detailed information on fire or explosion hazards. Entries provide references to the primary literature where hazards have been reported, and there is an index.

1400.   **Perry's Chemical Engineers' Handbook.** 6th ed. Edited by Don W. Green and James O. Maloney. New York: McGraw-Hill, 1984. Various paging.

1401.   **Handbook of Chemical Engineering Calculations.** Edited by Nicholas P. Chopey and Tyler G. Hicks. New York: McGraw-Hill, 1984. Various paging.

1402.   **Riegel's Handbook of Industrial Chemistry.** 8th ed. Edited by James A. Kent. New York: Van Nostrand, Reinhold, 1983. 979p.

Chemical engineering has some of its own handbooks, useful to both students and faculty. *Perry's* is the major handbook in chemical engineering. Each of the 27 sections is authored by specialists, with many references to the primary literature. A detailed index is included. As the title suggests, *Handbook of Chemical Engineering Calculations* shows how to solve the main process-related problems that arise in chemical engineering practice. It consists of solved, numerical illustrative examples in topical sections such as "Heat Transfer" and "Phase Equilibrium." Specific formulas can be located by using the index. *Riegel's Handbook of Industrial Chemistry* is not strictly a handbook, but a collection of state-of-the-art reviews in industrial chemistry. Each chapter is authored by an expert on a particular industry, such as coal technology, synthetic plastics, pharmaceuticals, and pesticides. Students interested in learning more about a particular branch of the chemical industry should find this useful for its up-to-date accounts.

BIOGRAPHY

1403.   **American Chemists and Chemical Engineers.** Edited by Wyndham D. Miles. Washington, D.C.: American Chemical Society, 1976. 544p.

This biographical source is limited in scope by country and date, with biographical sketches for about five hundred deceased American chemists and chemical engineers. Biographies cover the period from colonial times to 1976 and include bibliographies. An index has entries for names mentioned in the biographies.

1404.   **College Chemistry Faculties.** 6th ed. Edited by Marjory A. Grant. Washington, D.C.: American Chemical Society, 1983. 205p.

1405.   **Chemical Engineering Faculties, 1985-1986.** Edited by John G. Ekerdt. New York: American Institute of Chemical Engineers, 1985. 255p.

These directories can be used to identify affiliation and address when a faculty member's name is known. *College Chemistry Faculties* covers departments of chemistry, chemical engineering, medicinal/pharmaceutical chemistry, and biochemistry at two- and four-year colleges and universities in the United States and Canada. Arrangement is by state or province with indexes of institutions and names. For each institution, the department's name and address are given, together with notes on degrees awarded and a roster of faculty with rank and field of specialization indicated. *Chemical Engineering Faculties* provides similar information for departments of chemical engineering worldwide.

1406.   **Directory of Graduate Research.** Washington, D.C.: American Chemical Society, 1983. 1207p. plus appendix, 23p.

1407. **Chemical Research Faculties: An International Directory.** Edited by Gisella Linder
       Pollock. Washington, D.C.: American Chemical Society, 1984. 407p. plus indexes.

These two directories are complementary, with the *Directory of Graduate Research* covering
universities in the United States and Canada, and *Chemical Research Faculties* covering
universities in other countries with departments that offer graduate degrees in chemistry,
chemical engineering, biochemistry, and pharmaceutical or medicinal chemistry. In addition
Directory of Graduate Research includes clinical chemistry and polymer science. Entries for
each department give address, phone number, degrees offered, fields of specialization, and
biographical information for faculty members (name, rank, year of birth, education, field of
research, recent publications). The *Directory of Graduate Research* also lists doctoral
candidates and thesis titles. There are statistical summaries of data from the departments
surveyed and an index of instructional staff. *Chemical Research Faculties* also includes
indexes for research subjects and institutions, as well as a section on chemical societies
detailing address, principal officer, publications, purpose, and number of members. The
Directory of Graduate Research can be machine searched through BRS.

26

EARTH SCIENCES

This chapter is concerned with the earth sciences, which encompass the geological sciences, atmospheric sciences, oceanography, and hydrology (study of continental water); physical geography is included here but other aspects of geography are dealt with in chapter 21. The geological sciences can be further subdivided. The subjects concerned with the composition of the earth include mineralogy, petrology (study of rocks), economic geology, and geochemistry. Those investigating the structure of the earth include geodesy, geophysics, structural geology, and volcanology. Those dealing with surface features and processes include geomorphology, glaciology, and environmental geology. Finally, those studying the earth's history include paleontology, sedimentology, and stratigraphy (study of rock strata). The atmospheric sciences include meteorology and climatology. Physical geography is the study of the distribution and spatial patterns of various earth features. The earth sciences are closely related to the environmental sciences and energy, both covered in chapter 27.

Some of the earth sciences interest the public at large. Thus, those seeking information include nonspecialists as well as students and faculty in the various areas of study which make up the earth sciences. Both the amateur and the scientist are interested in reference books on weather and in handbooks describing rocks, minerals, and fossils and providing aids to their identification. When assisting advanced students and faculty with literature searching, a number of characteristics of geological literature become important. The literature retains its value for long periods of time, so bibliographies and abstracting and indexing services providing access to the older literature will continue to be needed for searching and bibliographic verification. Because region is often an important aspect of the search topic, sources providing a geographic approach are especially helpful. For studies dealing with regions in other parts of the world, foreign-language literature may be required. In addition to books and journals, maps are heavily used because they are a method of recording geological information and discoveries. Multidisciplinary studies are becoming more common. For example, geologists often apply physics and chemistry to geological problems and need access to information in these fields. Thus, many of the types of questions already identified in the chapters on physics and chemistry will also be asked by students and faculty in the earth sciences.

GUIDES, BIBLIOGRAPHIES, INDEXES

1408. Ward, Dederick C., Marjorie W. Wheeler, and Robert A. Bier, Jr. **Geologic Reference Sources: A Subject and Regional Bibliography of Publications and Maps in the Geological Sciences.** 2d ed. Metuchen, N.J.: Scarecrow, 1981. 560p.

1409. Wood, D. N., ed. **Use of Earth Sciences Literature.** Hamden, Conn.: Archon, 1973. 459p. (Information Sources for Research and Development).

These two guides are complementary in their approaches to the literature. *Use of Earth Sciences Literature* is selective, treating the major sources of information in narrative chapters by different authors. *Geologic Reference Sources* is primarily a bibliography, with only a few descriptive notes, but it is much more comprehensive. *Use of Earth Sciences Literature* has 17 chapters. The first 8 chapters cover earth sciences literature in general (e.g., primary literature, secondary literature, translations) with separate chapters on geological maps and literature searching. The remaining 9 chapters are topical: stratigraphy (historical geology), including regional geology; palaeontology; mineralogy, petrology, geochemistry and crystallography; structural geology and tectonics; applied geology; geophysics; hydrology, glaciology, meteorology, oceanography and geomorphology; soil science; and history of geology. The book concludes with a set of exercises for the student and a subject index. *Geologic Reference Sources* provides a bibliography of about 4,300 titles, including maps. There are three sections: general, subject, regional. The general section is divided into general information sources, general bibliographic sources, and special subjects (e.g., history and philosophy of the geological sciences, map and cartographic literature). The subject section cites reference books, texts, and treatises in 20 different subject categories (e.g., oceanography, mineralogy, geomorphology). The regional section lists reference works and maps for regions and countries. The volume has subject and geographic indexes.

1410. **Bibliography and Index of Geology.** Alexandria, Va.: American Geological Institute, 1969- . Monthly with annual cumulation.

This is the major indexing service in the earth sciences. It continues two publications, *Bibliography and Index of Geology Exclusive of North America* (Washington, D.C.: Geological Society of America, 1934-1968) and *Bibliography of North American Geology* (Washington, D.C.: U.S. Geological Survey, 1923-1973). It is international in coverage and includes citations to books, journals, conferences, reports, maps, and theses. Each monthly issue groups citations under 29 broad subject categories (e.g., mineralogy and crystallography, paleontology), subdivided by type of material. Each issue has an author index and a detailed subject index. Citations are cumulated annually into a bibliography arranged by author; the subject indexes for the year's issues are also cumulated. Only a few entries have abstracts in addition to bibliographic citations. The contents can be machine searched as part of the GEOREF database back to 1969 through DIALOG and SDC. Citations from several related publications covering earlier literature are also included in GEOREF.

1411. **Geo Abstracts.** Norwich, England: Geo Abstracts, 1966- . 6 issues per year.

1412. **Meteorological and Geoastrophysical Abstracts.** Boston: American Meteorological Society, 1950- . Monthly with annual cumulation of indexes.

1413. **Mineralogical Abstracts.** London: Mineralogical Society of Great Britain and Mineralogical Society of America, 1920- . Quarterly with annual indexes.

1414. **Oceanic Abstracts.** Bethesda, Md.: Cambridge Scientific Abstracts, 1964- . Bimonthly with annual cumulation of indexes.

Because *Bibliography and Index of Geology* carries almost no abstracts, the advanced student or faculty member undertaking a literature search may also wish to consult one or more of the special abstracting services covering a particular facet of the earth sciences. *Geo Abstracts* has already been described in chapter 21 (entry 1184), where three series related to geography were cited. There are four series related to the earth sciences: A. *Landforms and the Quaternary* (1966-); B. *Climatology and Hydrology* (1966-); E. *Sedimentology* (1972-); and G. *Remote Sensing, Photogrammetry and Cartography* (1974-). Each has abstracts in a classified arrangement, reflecting subdivisions of the subject covered by that series. Combined author and subject indexes to series A, B, E, and G are issued annually. There are also annual author and regional indexes for each series. *Meteorological and Geoastrophysical Abstracts* provides international coverage of several types of publications. It has abstracts in six sections: environmental sciences, meteorology, astrophysics, hydrosphere/hydrology, glaciology, and physical oceanography. There are author, subject and geographic indexes which cumulate annually. *Meteorological and Geoastrophysical Abstracts* can be machine searched back to 1972 through DIALOG. Each issue of *Mineralogical Abstracts* arranges abstracts of journal articles and reports in about 20 categories, such as "Physical Properties of Rocks and Minerals," "Geochemistry," and "Petrology." There is a separate book notices section. Each issue also has an author index, and there are annual author and subject indexes. Each issue of *Oceanic Abstracts* has abstracts of journal articles, books, conferences, reports, and trade publications arranged in eight sections with further subdivisions: "Marine Biology, Biological Oceanography, Ecology"; "Physical and Chemical Oceanography and Meteorology"; "Marine Geology, Geophysics, Geochemistry"; "Marine Pollution, Environmental Pollution"; "Marine Resources — Living"; "Marine Resources — Nonliving"; "Ships and Shipping"; "Books and Conferences." There are subject, organism, geographic, and author indexes in each issue, which cumulate annually. *Oceanic Abstracts* can be machine searched back to 1964 through DIALOG.

1415. **Geotitles Weekly.** London: Geosystems, 1969- . Weekly with annual cumulation of indexes.

1416. **Current Contents: Physical, Chemical & Earth Sciences.** Philadelphia: Institute for Scientific Information, 1961- . Weekly.

Since *Bibliography and Index of Geology* (1410) appears only monthly and the specialized abstracting services are even less frequent, it is convenient to have some more frequent publications for current awareness. *Geotitles Weekly* presents citations for all types of publications from many countries in a classified arrangement with an author index, subject index, geographic index, and stratigraphic index. Indexes cumulate annually. *Geotitles Weekly* can be machine searched as part of the GEOARCHIVE database back to 1969 through DIALOG. *Current Contents* has already been described in the chapter on physics (entry 1341). The section of *Current Contents* dealing with the earth sciences is simply titled "Earth Sciences."

DICTIONARIES, ENCYCLOPEDIAS

1417. **Glossary of Geology.** 2d ed. Edited by Robert L. Bates and Julia A. Jackson. Falls Church, Va.: American Geological Institute, 1980. 751p.

1418. **Dictionary of Geological Terms.** 3d rev. ed. Edited by Robert L. Bates and Julia A. Jackson. Garden City, N.Y.: Anchor Press/Doubleday, 1984. 571p.

1419.   Challinor, John. **A Dictionary of Geology.** 5th ed. New York: Oxford University Press, 1978. 365p.

The *Glossary of Geology* is the most comprehensive dictionary, printing definitions for about 36,000 terms and with an emphasis on preferred current meanings. Definitions are quite detailed and many include references to the literature. It is useful to both the advanced student and faculty member. The *Dictionary of Geological Terms* is an abridged version of the *Glossary*, covering the more commonly used terms in geology and related earth sciences. It may therefore suffice for use by the beginning student or nonspecialist. The *Dictionary of Geology* is also more selective than the *Glossary*, but it has quite detailed entries, many with selected quotations illustrating usage and references. To supplement the alphabetical arrangement of terms, there is a classified index grouping related terms so that one can identify the entries relevant to a particular subfield of geology.

1420.   Watt, Alec. **Longman Illustrated Dictionary of Geology: The Principles of Geology Explained and Illustrated.** Harlow, Essex, England: Longman, 1982. 192p.

1421.   **A Dictionary of Earth Sciences.** Edited by Stella E. Stiegeler. New York: Pica Press, 1977. 301p.

1422.   **McGraw-Hill Dictionary of Earth Sciences.** Edited by Sybil P. Parker. New York: McGraw-Hill, 1984. 837p.

If the dictionaries described above fail to adequately define a term, three other dictionaries can be consulted. The *Longman Illustrated Dictionary of Geology* has about 1,500 terms in a categorized arrangement, with terms grouped under headings such as "Palaeontology," "Plate Tectonics," and "Geomorphology and Land Forms." There are some appendixes, such as explanations of common abbreviations and prefixes and suffixes used to build scientific words. There are numerous illustrations in color, which should be helpful to the beginning student. An index of terms provides access to the categorized arrangement. The *Dictionary of Earth Sciences* has detailed definitions for about 3,000 terms, but only a few illustrations. The *McGraw-Hill Dictionary of Earth Sciences* has over 15,000 terms, most drawn from the third edition of the parent work (entry 1242), but no illustrations are included. Terms are from the earth sciences or related fields, such as mapping and mining engineering.

1423.   **The Planet We Live On: An Illustrated Encyclopedia of the Earth Sciences.** Edited by Cornelius S. Hurlbut, Jr. New York: Abrams, 1976. 528p.

1424.   **The Cambridge Encyclopedia of Earth Sciences.** Edited by David G. Smith. New York: Crown/Cambridge University Press, 1981. 496p.

These two one-volume encyclopedias are suitable for use by the nonspecialist and the undergraduate in the earth sciences. *The Planet We Live On* provides an overview of the entire range of earth sciences, covering 21 subject areas ranging from crystallography to volcanology. There are about 1,800 brief articles. Illustrations are numerous but there are no bibliographies. Appendixes include tables of mineral properties and principal geological features, as well as a guide to entries by subject categories (e.g., geomorphology, meteorology, mineralogy, paleontology, volcanology). *The Cambridge Encyclopedia of Earth Sciences* has a topical rather than an alphabetical arrangement with 27 chapters grouped in six parts: "The Earth Sciences in Perspective"; "Physics and Chemistry of the Earth"; "Crustal Processes and Evolution"; "Surface Processes and Environments"; "Evaluation of Earth Resources and Hazards"; and "Extraterrestrial Geology." The text is well illustrated and emphasizes recent developments. There is a glossary, a bibliography for further reading, and an index.

1425.   **Encyclopedia of Oceanography.** Edited by Rhodes W. Fairbridge. New York: Reinhold, 1966. 1021p. (Encyclopedia of Earth Sciences Series, vol. 1).

1426.   **Encyclopedia of Atmospheric Sciences and Astrogeology.** Edited by Rhodes W. Fairbridge. New York: Reinhold, 1967. 1200p. (Encyclopedia of Earth Sciences Series, vol. 2).

1427.   **Encyclopedia of Geomorphology.** Edited by Rhodes W. Fairbridge. New York: Reinhold, 1968. 1295p. (Encyclopedia of Earth Sciences Series, vol. 3).

1428.   **Encyclopedia of Geochemistry and Environmental Sciences.** Edited by Rhodes W. Fairbridge. New York: Van Nostrand, Reinhold, 1972. 1321p. (Encyclopedia of Earth Sciences Series, vol. 4A).

1429.   **Encyclopedia of Mineralogy.** Edited by Keith Frye. Stroudsburg, Pa.: Hutchinson Ross, 1981. 794p. (Encyclopedia of Earth Sciences Series, vol. 4B).

1430.   **Encyclopedia of Sedimentology.** Edited by Rhodes W. Fairbridge and Joanne Bourgeois. Stroudsburg, Pa.: Dowden, Hutchinson & Ross, 1978. 901p. (Encyclopedia of Earth Sciences Series, vol. 6).

1431.   **Encyclopedia of Paleontology.** Edited by Rhodes W. Fairbridge and David Jablonski. Stroudsburg, Pa.: Dowden, Hutchinson & Ross, 1979. 886p. (Encyclopedia of Earth Sciences Series, vol. 7).

1432.   **Encyclopedia of World Regional Geology, Part 1: Western Hemisphere (Including Antarctica and Australia).** Edited by Rhodes W. Fairbridge. Stroudsburg, Pa.: Dowden, Hutchinson & Ross, 1975. 704p. (Encyclopedia of Earth Sciences Series, vol. 8).

1433.   **Encyclopedia of Soil Science. Part 1. Physics, Chemistry, Biology, Fertility, and Technology.** Edited by Rhodes W. Fairbridge and Charles W. Finkl, Jr. Stroudsburg, Pa.: Dowden, Hutchinson & Ross, 1979. 646p. (Encyclopedia of Earth Sciences Series, vol. 12).

1434.   **Encyclopedia of Applied Geology.** Edited by Charles W. Finkl, Jr. New York: Van Nostrand, Reinhold, 1984. 644p. (Encyclopedia of Earth Sciences Series, vol. 13).

1435.   **Encyclopedia of Beaches and Coastal Environments.** Edited by Maurice L. Schwartz. Stroudsburg, Pa.: Hutchinson Ross, 1982. 940p. (Encyclopedia of Earth Sciences Series, vol. 15).

Although several volumes have already appeared, the Encyclopedia of Earth Sciences series is not yet complete. These volumes are suitable for use by advanced students and faculty. Each covers some aspect of the earth sciences in great detail. Signed articles are authored by experts and are well illustrated. Both cross-references and detailed subject indexes in each volume assist in locating discussion of specific subjects. Many of the volumes begin with a guide to the literature of the field which is the subject of that volume. The contents of the older volumes are now somewhat dated, so discussions of new discoveries and theories must be sought elsewhere.

1436.   **McGraw-Hill Encyclopedia of the Geological Sciences.** Edited by Daniel N. Lapedes. New York: McGraw-Hill, 1978. 915p.

1437.   **International Dictionary of Geophysics, Seismology, Geomagnetism, Aeronomy, Oceanography, Geodesy, Gravity, Marine Geophysics, Meteorology, the Earth as a Planet and Its Evolution.** Edited by S. K. Runcorn. 2 vols. Oxford: Pergamon, 1967.

When technical but less-detailed treatment of topics is sought, these two sources can be consulted. *McGraw-Hill Encyclopedia of the Geological Sciences* draws most of its 560 articles dealing with aspects of geology, geochemistry, and geophysics from the fourth edition of the parent work (entry 1244). There is an appendix listing properties of 1,500 mineral species and an index. The *International Dictionary of Geophysics* is actually an encyclopedic dictionary with entries ranging from definitions to lengthy articles with bibliographies. It is well illustrated and there are cross-references and an index.

1438.   **Encyclopedia of Prehistoric Life.** Edited by Rodney Steel and Anthony P. Harvey. New York: McGraw-Hill, 1979. 218p.

1439.   Glut, Donald F. **The New Dinosaur Dictionary.** Secaucus, N.J.: Citadel Press, 1982. 288p.

When discussions of topics in paleontology are sought, these two sources can be consulted by both the researcher and nonspecialist. The *Encyclopedia of Prehistoric Life* has entries for prehistoric orders and species, periods, and terms in paleontology. In addition, there are some biographical entries and descriptions of organizations. Illustrations include a series of charts depicting evolution. There is a bibliography, a glossary, and an index. *The New Dinosaur Dictionary* is narrower in scope, with an entry for every dinosaur genus known to paleontologists. Following an introductory discussion, the main body of the dictionary has entries describing the information known about each genus; there are numerous illustrations. A bibliography and an index are also provided.

1440.   **McGraw-Hill Encyclopedia of Ocean and Atmospheric Sciences.** Edited by Sybil P. Parker. New York: McGraw-Hill, 1980. 580p.

1441.   Tver, David F. **Ocean and Marine Dictionary.** Centreville, Md.: Cornell Maritime Press, 1979. 358p.

The *McGraw-Hill Encyclopedia of Ocean and Atmospheric Sciences* draws most of its 236 articles from the fourth edition of the parent work (entry 1244), with illustrations, cross-references, and an analytical index. The *Ocean and Marine Dictionary* is broader in scope since the terminology covered is not confined to marine science and oceanography. It includes concise definitions for terms describing all aspects of the marine and ocean environment and the activities, such as sailing, associated with oceans and seas.

1442.   Mitchell, Richard Scott. **Mineral Names: What Do They Mean?** New York: Van Nostrand, Reinhold, 1979. 229p.

This book brings together the derivations of mineral names currently used, and is thus helpful to the student or faculty member seeking to know more about terminology in mineralogy. The first part discusses categories of mineral names, such as those associated with persons, places, or properties. It also introduces commonly used prefixes and suffixes. The main body of the book is an alphabetical list of mineral names with etymological notes. Biographical notes are provided for persons after whom minerals are named.

1443.   Whittow, John B. **The Penguin Dictionary of Physical Geography.** London: Penguin, 1984. 591p. Paper.

The dictionary has over five thousand entries, including new terminology in the field of physical geography. Definitions are detailed, and there are some illustrations and cross-references.

DIRECTORIES

1444.   **A Directory of Information Resources in the United States: Geosciences and Oceanography.** Washington, D.C.: Library of Congress, National Referral Center, 1981. 375p.

One of a series of directories prepared from files maintained by the National Referral Center at the Library of Congress, this directory has entries for organizations such as museums, research institutes, professional societies, universities, government agencies, and companies which offer earth sciences information of some kind. The entry describing each organization gives an address, areas of interest, holdings, publications, and information services. A subject index is also included.

1445.   Cleevely, R. J. **World Palaeontological Collections.** London: British Museum and Mansell, 1983. 365p.

1446.   International Mineralogical Association. Commission on Museums. **World Directory of Mineral Collections.** 2d ed. Copenhagen: International Mineralogical Association, 1977. 474p.

Because specimens (fossils, minerals, rock samples) are essential objects of study in branches of geology such as mineralogy or paleontology, it is helpful to have directories of major collections. The two described here are complementary in that the former emphasizes fossils, and the latter covers minerals. They also differ in their organization. *World Palaeontological Collections* is arranged by the name of the British or European collector, and includes short biographical and bibliographical notes as well as descriptions of their collections and identification of the institutions where they are currently housed. There is an institution index to collection holdings. *World Directory of Mineral Collections* is arranged by organization name within country, covering 455 collections in 32 countries. Each entry contains name and address, person in charge, number of specimens (minerals, rocks, ores, gems, meteorites), uses, and specialties.

HANDBOOKS

Handbooks in the earth sciences include both aids to identification of specimens and compilations of data. Examples of both are given in this section. Citations for others can be found in the guides to the literature (entries 1408-9) and in Powell's bibliography of handbooks (entry 1265).

1447.   Chesterman, Charles W. **The Audubon Society Field Guide to North American Rocks and Minerals.** New York: Knopf, 1978. 850p.

1448.   Thompson, Ida. **The Audubon Society Field Guide to North American Fossils.** New York: Knopf, 1982. 846p.

These two field guides are representative of handbooks intended to aid in identification of specimens and can be used by both amateurs and professional scientists. Chesterman's guide presents color photographs and descriptions of 232 mineral species and 40 types of rocks. Other features of the book include a list of rock-forming minerals, a glossary, a bibliography, and indexes by name and locality. Following descriptions of geological time and fossil-bearing rocks, Thompson's guide has sections of color photographs arranged by shapes of specimens and the main text following a systematic arrangement. Descriptions of fossils include information on age and distribution as well as comments on habits and ecology. There are a number of helpful appendixes, including a discussion of how to collect and preserve fossils, a glossary, a list of major fossil displays, and a directory of geological surveys. There is also an index.

1449.   **Handbook of Physical Properties of Rocks.** Edited by Robert S. Carmichael. 3 vols. Boca Raton, Fla.: CRC Press, 1982-84.

1450.   Roberts, Willard Lincoln, George Robert Rapp, Jr., and Julius Weber. **Encyclopedia of Minerals.** New York: Van Nostrand, Reinhold, 1974. 693p.

These two sources provide extensive data on rocks and minerals useful to the advanced student and faculty member. The *Handbook of Physical Properties of Rocks* presents data on various properties of rocks, minerals, and other related materials in a largely tabular format. Each volume covers a different set of properties: volume 1 addresses mineral composition, electrical properties, spectroscopic properties; volume 2, seismic velocities, magnetic properties, engineering properties; and volume 3, density of rocks and minerals, elastic constants of minerals, inelastic properties, radioactivity, seismic attenuation. The *Encyclopedia of Minerals* has entries for 2,200 minerals arranged alphabetically by name, with data including chemical formula, crystal system, hardness, density, cleavage, habit, color-luster, mode of occurrence, and best reference in English. Color photomicrographs are used as illustrations, and a glossary is included.

1451.   Schaefer, Vincent J., and John A. Day. **A Field Guide to the Atmosphere.** Boston: Houghton Mifflin, 1981. 359p. (Peterson Field Guide Series no. 26).

1452.   **The Weather Almanac.** 4th ed. Edited by James A. Ruffner and Frank E. Bair. Detroit: Gale, 1984. 812p.

These two handbooks will be of interest to the nonspecialist as well as the student of meteorology. The *Field Guide to the Atmosphere* is a guide to observing atmospheric phenomena, with photographs and other illustrations and explanatory text. There are instructions for some simple experiments, a glossary, a bibliography, an index, and several appendixes of tabular and graphical information as well as safety rules for severe storms. The *Weather Almanac* is a reference guide to weather, climate, and air quality in the United States and its key cities; it also gives world climatological highlights. There are sections on weather in relation to health and listings of safety rules for environmental hazards associated with storms, weather extremes, earthquakes, and volcanoes. Basic meteorological information includes a glossary of weather terms and a section on weather fundamentals. An index provides access to the varied contents.

1453.   **Climates of the States: National Oceanic and Atmospheric Administration Narrative Summaries, Tables, and Maps for Each State with Overview of State Climatologist Programs.** 2d ed. Edited by James A. Ruffner. 2 vols. Detroit: Gale, 1980.

1454.   **Weather of U.S. Cities: A Guide to the Weather History of 293 Key Cities and Weather Observation Stations in the United States and Its Island Territories.** 2 vols. Detroit: Gale, 1981.

1455.   Pearce, E. A., and C. G. Smith. **The World Weather Guide.** London: Hutchinson, 1984. 480p.

Although *The Weather Almanac* (entry 1452) conveniently presents the most commonly sought weather-related data, these three data compilations are available as supplements. The titles are indicative of their scope. *Climates of the States* is arranged alphabetically by state. Each entry begins with a narrative essay followed by tables of data and maps showing temperature, precipitation, and other climatic events, noting normals, means, and extremes. *Weather of U.S. Cities* provides similar data for 293 cities arranged by city within state. Each has a narrative summary of the location's year-round weather as well as tables of weather statistics. *World Weather Guide* is arranged by country within continent or geographic area (Africa, North America, Central and South America, Asia, Australasia, Caribbean Islands, Europe, Oceanic Islands). Each country has descriptive text and tables giving data on temperature, humidity, and precipitation for major cities. Some maps are also included, and there is an index.

ATLASES

1456.   Snead, Rodman E. **World Atlas of Geomorphic Features.** New York: Van Nostrand, Reinhold, 1980. 301p.

1457.   **The Rand McNally Atlas of the Oceans.** New York: Rand McNally, 1977. 208p.

1458.   U.S. Environmental Data Service. **Weather Atlas of the United States.** Detroit: Gale, 1975. 262p.

Maps are an important tool in research in the earth sciences. Both *Geologic Reference Sources* (entry 1408) and *Bibliography and Index of Geology* (entry 1410) include coverage of maps, and *Use of Earth Sciences Literature* (entry 1409) has a chapter discussing the history and types of geological maps. The three atlases listed here are an illustrative sampling of the types of maps useful in reference work in the earth sciences. *World Atlas of Geomorphic Features* is an introductory level work, covering landforms grouped in categories such as oceanographic and hydrographic features, coastal features, glaciation, wind-created landforms, and water-created landforms. The accompanying text defines the landform, indicating major characteristics and the reasons for its occurrence and distribution. Maps and satellite photographs are used to illustrate the landforms. There are a bibliography and a subject index. *The Rand McNally Atlas of the Oceans* has written material, photographs, drawings, and maps arranged in sections: "Ocean Realm," "Man's Oceanic Quest," "Life in the Oceans," "The Great Resource," and "The Face of the Deep." There is also an encyclopedia of marine life, a glossary, and an index. Maps in the *Weather Atlas of the United States* are used to depict patterns of climatic elements. They show national distributions of mean, normal, and/or extreme values of such elements as temperature, precipitation, wind, sunshine, barometric pressure, and humidity.

BIOGRAPHY

1459.   American Geological Institute. **Directory of Geoscience Departments: United States and Canada.** 23d ed. Alexandria, Va.: American Geological Institute, 1984. 212p.

This directory lists faculty in geoscience departments located in universities in the United States and Canada. Arranged by university within state, the faculty listings include name, highest degree, institution awarding the degree and date awarded, and a specialty code indicating subject expertise. There are specialty and name indexes.

1460.   Sarjeant, William A. S. **Geologists and the History of Geology: An International Bibliography from the Origins to 1978.** 5 vols. New York: Arno, 1980.

This bibliography has been placed in this section of the chapter because it is a good source of biographical information on geologists from many periods and countries. The bibliography's entries for books, journal and newspaper articles, and pamphlets are in three parts. Volume 1 includes general histories of science, of geology and its subdivisions, and of allied sciences; historical accounts of institutions concerned with geology; histories of the petroleum industry; and accounts of geological events. Entries for individual geologists, with last names beginning with the letters *A* through *K* appear in volume 2; such persons with last names beginning with the letters *L* through *Z* appear in volume 3. A few entries for prospectors, diviners, and mining engineers also appear in volume 3. In these two volumes, biographical notes about an individual are followed by citations to autobiographical works, biographical works, and descriptions of their work. Volumes 4 and 5 are indexes to the bibliography. Volume 4 has geologists indexed by country and specialty; volume 5 is an index of authors, editors, and translators.

27

ENVIRONMENTAL SCIENCES, ENERGY

Into the Information Age describes three information transfer eras with different approaches to scientific and technical information. Era 1 is the discipline-oriented era, focusing on individual fields, such as physics; era 2 is the mission-oriented era, organizing to do a job, such as put a man on the moon; and era 3 is the problem-oriented era, confronting problems like environmental protection and energy resources.[1] Because publishers are responding to the need for problem-oriented materials, this chapter covers sources in environmental sciences and energy, two problem areas which emerged as focal points for research and public interest in the last two decades. Although the other chapters in this book reflect disciplinary and university departmental divisions, this chapter deals with problem areas which are inherently multidisciplinary. Thus, while a university may well have an environmental sciences or energy research institute, no single department within the university is likely to have energy or environmental sciences as its exclusive domain. As a result, the potential users of materials on such subjects will come from many different departments and must be alerted to the availability of resources which cross traditional disciplinary boundaries. Although much of the information in the sources covered here is repackaged from various discipline-based sources, it is often easier to use when it is assembled in one place. In addition, particularly in the environmental sciences, information from the social sciences is often included.

One important aspect of environmental studies is the process of environmental impact assessment, the systematic examination of the environmental consequences of proposed projects, policies, and programs. Such an assessment requires the use of techniques and data both from many scientific disciplines, such as chemistry and biology, and from the social sciences. An environmental impact statement is a document presenting the results of an environmental impact assessment. A number of the sources in this chapter deal with this process.

With respect to the study of energy, interest has grown in "alternative" energy sources as traditional resources have become less available and more expensive. Titles in this chapter all consider many forms of energy. The guides to the literature (entries 1482-84) can be used to identify materials on specific types of energy, such as those devoted to solar or wind energy.

---

[1]Arthur D. Little, Inc., *Into the Information Age: A Perspective for Federal Action on Information* (Chicago: American Library Association, 1978), 19-25.

Because there is such widespread interest in environmental and energy issues, there is likely to be a demand by undergraduates for nontechnical information. A number of the sources described in this chapter are intended for use by a wide audience. For the advanced student and the faculty member, there are several indexes and abstracts to aid in literature searching; there are also handbooks providing convenient compilations of data. Depending on the topic, the appropriate discipline-based sources (e.g., chemistry, biology, earth sciences) can be used to supplement the material in sources described in this chapter.

ENVIRONMENTAL SCIENCES

GUIDES, BIBLIOGRAPHIES, INDEXES

1461.   Morris, Jacquelyn M., and Elizabeth A. Elkins. **Library Searching: Resources and Strategies with Examples from the Environmental Sciences.** New York: Jeffrey Norton, 1978. 129p.

1462.   **Sourcebook on the Environment: A Guide to the Literature.** Edited by Kenneth A. Hammond, George Macinko, and Wilma B. Fairchild. Chicago: University of Chicago Press, 1978. 614p.

Because the environmental sciences draw on many subject areas, guides to the literature of specific disciplines, such as chemistry, will prove useful. The two guides cited here have environmental sciences as their domain; each offers a different approach to the literature. Based on course materials used at the SUNY College of Environmental Science and Forestry, *Library Searching* is intended for student use, either for self-study or as part of formal bibliographic instruction. It emphasizes types of sources and development of search strategy. There is an annotated bibliography of indexing and abstracting services in the appendix, but other reference materials are simply cited without annotation. Most of the *Sourcebook* is made up of reviews of the literature written by subject specialists and grouped into three sections: "Environmental Perspectives and Prospects," "Environmental Modification: Case Studies," and "Major Elements of the Environment" (air and air quality, water and water quality, landforms and soils, vegetation, animals in the biosphere, coastal zone, human population and the environment, and energy and environment). Each section reviews the basic literature and gives directions for examination of more advanced work. The final section of the guide includes a list of environmental periodicals, a review of U.S. environmental legislation, and a list of environmental organizations. There are author and subject indexes.

1463.   **Environment Abstracts.** New York: EIC/Intelligence, 1971- . Ten issues per year with annual cumulation.

1464.   **Environment Index.** New York: EIC/Intelligence, 1971- . Annual.

Both popular and technical literature on the environment is covered by *Environment Abstracts*, so it is a useful tool for both students and faculty carrying out literature searches on environmental topics. The 21 section headings used to arrange abstracts define its subject scope: "Air Pollution," "Chemical and Biological Contamination," "Energy," "Environmental Education," "Environmental Design and Urban Ecology," "Food and Drugs," "General," "International," "Land Use and Misuse," "Noise Pollution," "Nonrenewable Resources," "Oceans and Estuaries," "Population Planning and Control," "Radiological Contamination," "Renewable Resources – Terrestrial," "Renewable Resources – Water,"

"Solid Waste," "Transportation," "Water Pollution," "Weather Modification and Geophysical Change," and "Wildlife." Types of publications abstracted include journals, reports, government documents, conferences, books, newsletters, and newspapers. Each issue has four indexes: subject, author, source, and industry (Standard Industrial Classification codes). There is also a list of forthcoming conferences and a bibliography of new books on environmental topics in each issue. Abstracts cumulate annually in a bound volume. *Environment Index* is the annual cumulative index volume with five different indexes: subject, author, source, industry, and geographic. The volume also has a review of the year's events related to environmental issues as well as sections for a list of periodicals indexed, new films, new books, conferences, and a directory of environmental organizations. *Environment Abstracts* and *Environment Index* can be machine searched as the ENVIROLINE database back to 1971 through DIALOG and SDC.

1465. **Pollution Abstracts.** Bethesda, Md.: Cambridge Scientific Abstracts, 1970- Bimonthly with annual cumulation of indexes.

When some aspect of pollution is the topic being investigated, this abstracting service is an appropriate place to begin a literature search. It provides international coverage of the technical literature on environmental pollution, including journals, conference proceedings, books, and reports. Abstracts are arranged in topical sections: air pollution, marine pollution, freshwater pollution, sewage and wastewater treatment, waste management, land pollution, toxicology and health, noise, radiation, and environmental action. There are subject and author indexes which cumulate annually. *Pollution Abstracts* can be machine searched back to 1970 through BRS and DIALOG.

1466. **Environmental Periodicals Bibliography.** Santa Barbara, Calif.: Environmental Studies Institute, International Academy at Santa Barbara, 1972- . Bimonthly with annual cumulation of indexes.

1467. **EIS: Digests of Environmental Impact Statements.** Arlington, Va.: Information Resources Press, 1977- . Monthly with annual cumulation.

These two services are narrower in scope than *Environment Abstracts* because each is limited to a particular type of material. *Environmental Periodicals Bibliography* covers about three hundred periodicals, with tables of contents of recent issues arranged in six categories: "General/Human Ecology," "Air," "Energy," "Land Resources/Agriculture," "Marine and Freshwater Resources/Water Pollution," and "Nutrition and Health." There are author and subject indexes in each issue, which cumulate annually. *Environmental Periodicals Bibliography* can be machine searched back to 1973 through DIALOG. As the title indicates, *EIS* provides digests of environmental impact statements issued by or through the federal government. The digests are arranged in subject categories: air transportation, defense programs, energy, hazardous substances, land use, manufacturing, parks, refuges and forests, research and development, roads and railroads, urban and social programs, wastes, and water. There are several indexes in each issue: subject, originating agency/organization, legal mandate, geography/site, and EIS number. Digests and indexes cumulate annually. The annotation for each environmental impact statement summarizes purpose, positive impacts, negative impacts, legal mandates, and prior references.

1468. **Current Contents: Agriculture, Biology & Environmental Sciences.** Philadelphia: Institute for Scientific Information, 1970- . Weekly.

Although *Environmental Periodicals Bibliography* (entry 1466) has a table of contents format, it only appears bimonthly. To provide current awareness for recently published journals, *Current Contents* can be consulted. Journals relevant to the environmental sciences are in the "Environment/Ecology" section of each issue. The organization and possible uses of this section parallel those already described for *Current Contents: Physical, Chemical & Earth Sciences* (entry 1341).

1469.   **EPA Index: A Key to U.S. Environmental Protection Agency Reports and Superintendent of Documents and NTIS Numbers.** Edited by Cynthia E. Bower and Mary L. Rhoads. Phoenix: Oryx Press, 1983. 385p.

Because the Environmental Protection Agency (EPA) is the major federal agency concerned with the environment, EPA documents are often sought in conjunction with studies in the environmental sciences. This index is intended to provide better access to EPA documents issued between 1970 and 1981 and housed in documents collections which are often arranged by Superintendent of Documents classification number. Part 1 of the index arranges in alphanumeric order all EPA report numbers or NTIS accession numbers, giving the citation for the document and the appropriate Superintendent of Documents classification number. Part 2 arranges entries in alphabetical order by title, giving the Superintendent of Documents classification number and the NTIS accession number as part of the citation. Regional federal depository libraries are listed in an appendix.

1470.   Clark, Brian D., Ronald Bisset, and Peter Wathern. **Environmental Impact Assessment: A Bibliography with Abstracts.** New York: Bowker, 1980. 516p.

The literature dealing with environmental impact assessment becomes more accessible with the aid of this annotated bibliography. There are five main subject areas, further subdivided into 18 sections, each preceded by a short introduction providing a synopsis of the main themes of the literature. The five main divisions are: "Aids to Impact Assessment"; "Critiques and Reviews of Environmental Impact Assessment"; "Environmental Impact Assessment and Other Aspects of Planning"; "Environmental Impact Assessment in Selected Countries"; and "Information Sources" (bibliographies and periodicals). There are author and subject indexes.

DICTIONARIES, ENCYCLOPEDIAS

1471.   **McGraw-Hill Encyclopedia of Environmental Science.** 2d ed. Edited by Sybil P. Parker. New York: McGraw-Hill, 1980. 858p.

This encyclopedia is in two parts. It begins with five survey articles on topics of general interest: "Environmental Protection," "Precedents for Weather Extremes," "Environmental Satellites," "Urban Planning," and "Environmental Analysis." These are followed by more than 250 articles on various topics in the environmental sciences and engineering, many of which are drawn from the fourth edition of the parent encyclopedia (entry 1244). Articles are illustrated and there is an index.

1472.   Allaby, Michael. **A Dictionary of the Environment.** 2d ed. New York: New York University Press, 1983. 529p.

1473.   Durrenberger, Robert W. **Dictionary of the Environmental Sciences.** Palo Alto, Calif.: National Press Books, 1973. 282p.

1474.   Monkhouse, F. J., and John Small. **Dictionary of the Natural Environment.** New York: Wiley, 1978. 320p.

These three dictionaries all draw terms from a number of disciplines in an effort to encompass topics relevant to the environmental sciences. Because the boundaries of the environmental sciences are not well defined, it may be necessary to consult more than one dictionary to find the definition for a term. All are suitable for use by students. *A Dictionary of the Environment* covers about 6,000 terms for basic physical, chemical, biological, and geographical phenomena of environmental interest. The *Dictionary of the Environmental Sciences* includes appendixes on the geological time scale and systems of measurement. *Dictionary of the Natural Environment* has nearly 4,500 terms, with an emphasis on physical geography.

1475.   Tver, David F. **Dictionary of Dangerous Pollutants, Ecology, and Environment.** New York: Industrial Press, 1981. 347p.

This dictionary offers the student detailed definitions and some illustrations of terms relevant to pollution and energy. Specifically, topic areas encompassed include noise pollution, air pollution, water pollution, nuclear energy, geothermal energy, solar energy, coal, waste control, biomass conversion, recycling, ecology, meteorology, and climatology. The work thus can supplement other dictionaries both in the environmental sciences and in energy.

1476.   **Environmental Impact Statement Glossary: A Reference Source for EIS Writers, Reviewers, and Citizens.** Edited by Marc Landy. New York: IFI/Plenum, 1979. 537p.

This glossary is intended for those interested in the environmental impact assessment process, as it tries to clarify the amalgam of professional languages which frequently make up an environmental impact statement. It is composed of 16 thematic glossaries, grouping terms from a particular perspective (e.g., earth, air, water, noise). There are also a bibliography and an index.

DIRECTORIES

1477.   **Conservation Directory: A List of Organizations, Agencies and Officials Concerned with Natural Resource Use and Management.** 30th ed. Washington, D.C.: National Wildlife Federation, 1985. 302p.

1478.   **World Environmental Directory.** 4th ed. Silver Spring, Md.: Business Publishers, 1980. 965p.

Revised annually, the *Conservation Directory* lists governmental and nongovernmental personnel and organizations engaged in conservation work at state, national, and international levels. The main portion of the directory covers first U.S. and then Canadian organizations in three categories: federal departments, agencies, and offices; international, national, interstate organizations and commissions; state and territorial agencies and citizens groups. Additional listings identify such things as national wildlife refuges, national parks, national forests, and national seashores in the United States. There are bibliographies of periodicals and directories relevant to conservation and a personnel name index to the work. Although the *Conservation Directory* emphasizes the United States and Canada, the *World Environmental Directory* is international in scope. It consists of listings in several categories in part 1, which covers the United States, and in part 2, which covers foreign organizations in more than 150 countries arranged by continent and country. The United States portion includes product manufacturers, professional services, government agencies (legislative branch, independent agencies, and commissions), attorneys with environmental interests, state government agencies, professional/scientific/trade/labor and public interest organizations, universities, environmental libraries, corporate environment officials, and periodicals. The foreign portion covers government agencies, product manufacturers, consultants, professional/scientific/trade and public interest organizations, and universities. There is an index of personnel and an index of companies, agencies, and organizations.

HANDBOOKS

1479.	Holum, John R. **Topics and Terms in Environmental Problems.** New York: Wiley, 1977. 729p.

This is a particularly helpful source for the student beginning research on an environmental topic. The text is at an introductory level and there are references to other publications for additional information. The 239 main entries provide definitions, discussions, and data for environmental issues that emphasize energy, air pollution, water pollution, wastes, and pesticides. There are cross-references and a detailed index.

1480.	**Environmental Impact Analysis Handbook.** Edited by John G. Rau and David C. Wooten. New York: McGraw-Hill, 1980. Various paging.

1481.	**Environmental Impact Data Book.** Edited by Jack Golden, Robert P. Ouellette, Sharon Saari, and Paul N. Cheremisinoff. Ann Arbor, Mich.: Ann Arbor Science Publishers, 1979. 864p.

Both of these handbooks should prove useful to students and faculty interested in environmental impact assessment. The *Environmental Impact Analysis Handbook* describes techniques and tools. The first chapter is a good introduction to concepts, discussing the legislative and legal background, the topics which make up an environmental impact statement, and the kinds of impacts associated with particular types of projects. Subsequent chapters go into more detail on types of assessments, such as air quality, noise, water quality, vegetation, and wildlife. The *Environmental Impact Data Book* brings together data needed for assessing impacts in areas such as noise, water resources, air quality, ecosystems, and toxic chemicals. Data are presented mostly in tabular form, with references to the original sources. There is an index so that specific data can be located easily.

ENERGY

GUIDES, BIBLIOGRAPHIES, INDEXES

1482.	Weber, R. David. **Energy Information Guide.** 3 vols. Santa Barbara, Calif.: ABC-Clio, 1982-84.

The reference literature dealing with energy is thoroughly covered in this three-volume set. The division of the subject is clearly indicated by the title of each volume: Volume 1. *General and Alternative Energy Sources;* Volume 2. *Nuclear and Electric Power;* Volume 3. *Fossil Fuels.* Within each volume, sources are further subdivided by topic and then by type of material (e.g., dictionaries, encyclopedias, handbooks). Sources are annotated and there are author, title, subject, and document number indexes.

1483.	**World Directory of Energy Information.** Compiled by Cambridge Information and Research Services. 3 vols. New York: Facts on File, 1981-84.

These volumes treat energy information from a geographic perspective: volume 1 covers Western Europe; volume 2 covers the Middle East, Africa, and Asia/Pacific; and volume 3 covers the Americas including the Caribbean. A variety of types of reference questions can be answered using these sources, but they are included in this section because they provide a guide to sources of information on energy. Each volume has the same arrangement. The first section gives a general overview of the region's energy production and consumption. The second section has more detailed discussion on the situation in the most important countries in the geographic area covered by that volume. The country summaries include key energy indicators, energy market trends, energy supply industries, energy trade, and energy policies. The third section is a directory of organizations in the energy sector (government departments, companies, professional and trade associations), and the fourth section is a bibliography of publications (statistics, journals, books) relating to energy arranged by country.

1484.   Crowley, Maureen, ed. **Energy: Sources of Print and Nonprint Materials.** New York: Neal-Schuman, 1980. 341p.

Rather than a bibliography of sources, Crowley provides a guide to organizations which can be expected to be continuing sources of energy information. Descriptions of 777 organizations are divided by type: governmental and quasigovernmental, activist/ civic/public education, professional/labor/trade associations, universities, independent research organizations, corporations, publishers and distributors, and international. Each entry notes name, address, phone number, purpose or major activity, special energy programs or information services, and the scope of the publishing program together with citations to representative titles. Coverage includes sources of books, pamphlets, periodicals, and nonprint media. There are source, title, and subject indexes.

1485.   **Energy Information Abstracts.** New York: EIC/Intelligence, 1976- . Ten issues per year with annual cumulation.

1486.   **Energy Index.** New York: EIC/Intelligence, 1973- . Annual.

For the student seeking material on an energy-related topic, these are a good starting point because they encompass both popular and more technical material and they are straight-forward to use. In *Energy Information Abstracts* abstracts are arranged in 21 categories dealing with various types of energy resources, fuel processing and transport, energy conversion and transmission, consumption, and environmental impact. Publications abstracted include journal and newspaper articles, books, conference proceedings, reports, and government documents. Each issue has author, subject, source, and industry (Standard Industrial Classification codes) indexes. There are also lists of forthcoming conferences and new books. Abstracts cumulate annually in a bound volume. *Energy Index* is the companion annual volume which has cumulative indexes for the year: source, author, geographic, subject, and industry. In addition, there is a review section covering the main energy-related events of the previous year, a statistics section, a list of periodicals indexed, a list of energy conferences, and a bibliography of new books on energy. *Energy Information Abstracts* and *Energy Index* form the ENERGYLINE database which can be machine searched back to 1971 through DIALOG and SDC.

1487.   **Energy Research Abstracts**. Oak Ridge, Tenn.: U.S. Department of Energy, Office of Scientific and Technical Information, 1976- . Semimonthly with annual cumulation of indexes.

1488.   **Energy Abstracts for Policy Analysis.** Oak Ridge, Tenn.: U.S. Department of Energy, Office of Scientific and Technical Information, 1975- . Monthly with annual cumulation of indexes.

1489.   **INIS Atomindex.** Vienna: International Atomic Energy Agency, 1970- . Semimonthly with semiannual and annual cumulation of indexes.

For the advanced student and faculty member doing a literature search on an energy topic, these abstracting services provide very thorough coverage, particularly for the report literature. Both published by the Office of Scientific and Technical Information of the U.S. Department of Energy, *Energy Research Abstracts* and *Energy Abstracts for Policy Analysis* provide complementary coverage, with the former emphasizing the scientific and technical literature and the latter focusing on the nontechnological literature that discusses analysis and evaluation of energy research, conservation, and policy. Both have abstracts in a categorized arrangement with personal author, corporate author, subject, and report number indexes. *Energy Research Abstracts* also has a contract number index. *Energy Abstracts for Policy Analysis* covers government documents, periodicals, reports, conference proceedings, and books emphasizing legislative and regulatory issues as well as social, economic, and environmental impacts. *Energy Research Abstracts* covers all scientific and technical reports, journal articles, conference proceedings, books, patents, theses, and monographs originated by Department of Energy laboratories, energy centers, and contractors. In addition, it covers energy information in report form from federal and state governments, foreign governments, domestic and foreign universities, and research organizations. Subject coverage includes all types of energy resources, and considers production, storage, conversion, and conservation. Environmental and health issues are also covered. *Energy Abstracts for Policy Analysis* and *Energy Research Abstracts* are both part of the DOE ENERGY database which can be machine searched back to 1974 through DIALOG. *INIS Atomindex* covers nuclear science and its peaceful applications. It is produced by the International Nuclear Information System, a cooperative, decentralized effort set up by the International Atomic Energy Agency through which an agency in each participating country indexes and abstracts the relevant literature from that country for inclusion in a centralized database. Abstracts in each issue are in a categorized arrangement. Books, journal articles, technical reports, conferences, patents, and theses are all covered. There are numerous indexes: personal author, corporate author, conference (in two parts: chronological and geographic), report/standard/patent number, and subject.

1490.   Balachandran, Sarojini. **Energy Statistics: A Guide to Information Sources.** Detroit: Gale, 1980. 272p.

This is a useful guide to be used in answering reference questions requiring statistical data in the energy field. The main body of the work is an annotated bibliography of 40 serials providing statistical data, and an index providing subject and geographic access to these serials. Another section, arranged by subject, lists additional statistical sources, some with annotations. There is a directory of publishers and both author and subject indexes.

1491.   Viola, John, Newell B. Mack, and Thomas R. Stauffer. **Energy Research Guide: Journals, Indexes, and Abstracts.** Cambridge, Mass.: Ballinger, 1983. 285p.

This guide can be used to identify periodicals, indexes, and abstracts covering energy or related fields. More than five hundred English-language sources are listed, including trade and academic journals, statistical bulletins, newsletters, and some annuals. The description of each publication includes a contents note and an indication of frequency and price, together with the address and phone number of the publisher. Subject lists categorize the sources according to emphasis: energy use and conservation, renewable and alternative energy sources, oil and gas, coal, electric and nuclear power, environment, and world energy.

DICTIONARIES, ENCYCLOPEDIAS

1492. **McGraw-Hill Encyclopedia of Energy.** 2d ed. Edited by Sybil P. Parker. New York: McGraw-Hill, 1981. 838p.

The encyclopedia begins with six survey articles, giving overviews of energy conservation, energy choices, risk of energy production, energy consumption, outlook for fuel reserves, and protection of the environment. The main body of the encyclopedia is made up of three hundred articles concerning technologies for energy discovery, development, and distribution. Many are drawn from the fourth edition of the parent encyclopedia (entry 1244). Appendixes include measurement systems, conversion factors, an outline of federal energy legislation and organizations, and a bibliography of energy-related publications. There is also an index.

1493. Counihan, Martin. **A Dictionary of Energy.** London: Routledge & Kegan Paul, 1981. 157p.

1494. Hunt, V. Daniel. **Energy Dictionary.** New York: Van Nostrand, Reinhold, 1979. 518p.

1495. Slesser, Malcolm, ed. **Dictionary of Energy.** New York: Schocken Books, 1983. 299p.

Each of these dictionaries can be used by both the student and the specialist. All provide definitions and some illustrations of energy-related terms with some supplementary material. In addition to its 550 entries, Counihan includes some statistical data and a bibliography. Terms are drawn from the sciences, engineering, and economics to cover the nature, forms, conversion, and use of fossil fuels and other sources. Hunt begins with an energy overview and also has a list of conversion factors, a glossary of acronyms, and a bibliography subdivided by type of energy source. The main body of the dictionary has over 4,000 entries for terms on all types of energy and related topics, emphasizing production, conservation, and environmental aspects. Slesser also draws terms from a number of disciplines and includes some entries for organizations. There is a list of acronyms.

1496. Kut, David, ed. **Dictionary of Applied Energy Conservation.** New York: Nichols, 1982. 214p.

This dictionary is somewhat more specialized, defining more than 1,500 terms employed in energy conservation practice together with some illustrations. Appendixes cover conversion factors and units of measurement.

DIRECTORIES

1497. **Energy Directory.** New York: EIC/Intelligence, 1983. 393p.

When name, address, and descriptive information are sought for an energy-related organization in the United States, this is an appropriate directory to check first. Entries are divided by type of organization: the Congressional energy establishment, the federal executive establishment, state energy officials, energy associations (trade, professional, public interest, research centers), energy companies, and information/publishing companies. An organization index, subject index, and personnel index provide alternative access points to the content of each entry. *Energy Directory* can be machine searched as the ENERGYNET database through DIALOG.

1498. **World Energy Directory: A Guide to Organizations and Research Activities in Non-Atomic Energy.** Edited by J. A. Bauly and C. B. Bauly. Harlow, Essex, England: Longman, 1981. 567p.

1499. **World Nuclear Directory: A Guide to Organizations and Research Activities in Atomic Energy.** 7th ed. Edited by C. W. J. Wilson. Harlow, Essex, England: Longman, 1985. 387p.

As the titles of these two directories suggest, their contents are complementary. The *World Energy Directory* lists and describes institutes, research centers, companies, and university departments in more than 80 countries which are involved in a broad range of non-atomic energy research. Arrangement is by name of the institution within country, and both organization name and subject indexes are provided. The *World Nuclear Directory* provides a guide to organizations in over 70 countries that conduct or promote research and development in pure and applied atomic energy. Included are nuclear research institutes, government departments, public corporations, industrial firms, professional societies, and academic institutions. Arrangement and indexing are like that of the *World Energy Directory*.

1500. **Energy Research Programs.** Edited by Jaques Cattell Press. New York: Bowker, 1980. 444p.

1501. **International Directory of New and Renewable Energy Information Sources and Research Centres.** Paris: UNESCO and SERI, 1982. 469p.

These two directories can be used to supplement the two described above. Geographic coverage of *Energy Research Programs* is confined to the United States, Canada, and Mexico. Included are industries, nonprofit organizations, universities, and government facilities involved in research on various aspects of energy production and application. Information given includes name, address, telephone number, principal staff, and research activities. Arrangement of entries is by name of the parent organization; a geographic index, a personnel index, and a subject index are provided. The *International Directory* has entries representing 139 countries, providing names and addresses of organizations, institutions and publications in some areas of new and renewable energy. Entries are arranged by country, with an organization index, a subject index, and a publications index. Sources profiled are governmental organizations, research centers, information resources, professional and trade associations, and publications (journals, directories, or databases). Alternative energy sources considered include alcohol fuels, biomass, wood, geothermal energy, hydropower, ocean energy, oil shale, peat, solar energy, and wind.

HANDBOOKS

1502. Dorf, Richard. **The Energy Factbook.** New York: McGraw-Hill, 1981. 227p.

1503. Loftness, Robert L. **Energy Handbook.** 2d ed. New York: Van Nostrand, Reinhold, 1984. 763p.

1504. **The World Energy Book: An A-Z, Atlas and Statistical Source Book.** Edited by David Crabbe and Richard McBride. New York: Nichols, 1978. 259p.

These three handbooks assemble data from numerous sources for convenient access and are suitable for use by both students and faculty. The *Energy Factbook* has 21 topical chapters with text and data compilations providing information about uses of energy, supplies of fossil fuels, alternative energy sources, and policy alternatives for the United States and the world. There is a glossary and an index. *Energy Handbook* has text, illustrations, and tables in 16 topical chapters covering energy resources, energy consumption trends and projections, extraction and utilization, conversion and storage, conservation, transport, environmental aspects of use, costs, and futures. A glossary, conversion tables, and an index are also provided. *World Energy Book* has a different format. The "A-Z" is an encyclopedic dictionary with definitions of terms related to the search for, extraction of, production and utilization of major and alternative energy sources. The atlas graphically illustrates patterns of production and consumption with maps displaying the geographic distribution and movement of fuel sources. The statistical section provides statistical background relating to both widely used and alternative energy sources. Cross-references link related data in the various sections.

1505.   **Energy Technology Handbook.** Edited by Douglas M. Considine. New York: McGraw-Hill, 1977. Various paging.

This handbook is intended for the advanced student and specialist, with chapters discussing technology relevant to production and utilization of the major forms of energy. Chapters authored by different experts cover coal, gas, petroleum, chemical fuels, nuclear energy, solar energy, geothermal energy, and hydropower, with a final chapter on trends in energy technology. There is a detailed index.

ATLASES

1506.   Cuff, David J., and William J. Young. **The United States Energy Atlas.** New York: Free Press, 1980. 416p.

This atlas provides maps, graphs, and charts depicting present and potential availability of each type of energy source. Both nonrenewable (coal, oil and natural gas, oil shale and tar sands, nuclear fuels, geothermal heat) and renewable (solar radiation, wind power, hydroelectric power, ocean thermal gradients, biomass) resources are covered. Other features of the atlas include a glossary, a list of readings, references used in gathering data presented in the atlas, an appendix of tables, and an index.

BIOGRAPHY

1507.   **International Who's Who in Energy and Nuclear Sciences.** Harlow, Essex, England: Longman, 1983. 531p.

Although international in scope, this biographical source is necessarily selective, with entries for fewer than four thousand scientists, engineers, and others engaged in energy and nuclear science research. Personal and career data are provided. There is a country index subdivided by topic that identifies individuals by country and specialization.

28

BIOLOGICAL SCIENCES, AGRICULTURE

Biological sciences and agriculture are treated together in this chapter because the two are closely linked. The formal separation between the study of pure sciences such as botany and genetics and applied sciences such as horticulture and plant breeding may be maintained in universities, but boundaries are becoming increasingly blurred with the emergence of biotechnology. This involves the programming of living cells to generate products ranging from simple molecules to complex proteins. In this chapter reference work in the biological sciences is considered first, but many of the reference tools discussed in that context are relevant to agriculture as well. There is also a close link between the biological sciences and the medical sciences, which are covered in chapter 29. Veterinary medicine is included within agriculture.

Biology is the science of living organisms. It has many areas of specialization, reflecting two major principles of division. The division may be according to the type of organism studied, effecting botany (the study of plants) and zoology (the study of animals). Each of these may be further subdivided, effecting, among many others, mycology (the study of fungi) and entomology (the study of insects). Alternatively, biology can be divided by levels of investigation. Molecular biology seeks to interpret biological phenomena in terms of molecules within the cell, with special attention to biochemistry, biophysics, and genetics. Cell biology is the study of the structure and function of cells, including microbiology. Organismic biology is the study of the whole organism in relation to its constituent parts, encompassing such fields as embryology, morphology, and physiology. Population biology is the study of organisms that inhabit a given area, involving such fields as biogeography and ecology. And finally, in using some reference tools dealing with organisms, it is necessary to understand the principles of biological classification and nomenclature which result in taxonomic groups arranged in a hierarchy of levels from most general to most specific: kingdom, phylum, class, order, family, genus, and species.

Depending on the size of the university, there may be a single biological sciences department or separate departments for each of the major areas of study (e.g., botany, entomology, genetics). In addition to faculty and students involved in research and courses in the biological sciences, there are likely to be amateur naturalists who seek information to aid them in identifying plants and animal species. Faculty and students may seek definitions of terms, interpretations of biological nomenclature, identifications of specimens, or descriptions of experimental methods. Although the need for current awareness in many areas of the biological sciences and biotechnology is great, the older literature is also of interest, particularly for taxonomic studies. Thus both current abstracting and indexing services and retrospective bibliographies are needed for literature searching. The literature of the biological sciences is extensive, reflecting the numerous specialized areas of study.

Paralleling the division between botany and zoology in the biological sciences, major subdivisions in agriculture include the plant sciences (e.g., horticulture, plant breeding, plant pathology, forestry) and animal sciences (e.g., animal husbandry, veterinary medicine, fisheries). Crop protection, including studies of pesticides and pest control, is a related area. There is also the study of animal and plant products as food, so food science and technology and nutrition are within the scope of this chapter.

The university with a college of agriculture must support research, teaching, and agricultural extension activities. In addition to handling questions related to research work of faculty and graduate students and to the course work of undergraduates, the library may have to support those interested in agriculture-related business and in agricultural extension activities, explaining to farmers and the general public the agricultural methods improved by scientific research. For the university without an instructional and research program in agriculture, only a small number of reference questions are likely to deal with agricultural topics, and a small collection of reference books in this area will suffice. Topics of interest to the nonspecialist include gardening and nutrition information. Gardening is outside the scope of this chapter. Emphasis has been placed on guides, bibliographies, and indexes which can be used to identify both specialized literature and materials suitable for use by the nonspecialist.

BIOLOGICAL SCIENCES

GUIDES, BIBLIOGRAPHIES, INDEXES

1508.   Bottle, R. T., and H. V. Wyatt, eds. **The Use of Biological Literature.** 2d ed. Hamden, Conn.: Archon, 1971. 379p. (Information Sources for Research and Development).

1509.   Davis, Elisabeth B. **Using the Biological Literature: A Practical Guide.** New York: Marcel Dekker, 1981. 286p. (Books in Library and Information Science, vol. 35).

These two guides provide the most detailed coverage of the biological literature. *The Use of Biological Literature* is made up of 20 bibliographic essays by different authors. Following an introduction and a chapter on libraries and their use, there are chapters dealing with primary sources, keys to information, specific subjects, and general subjects (e.g., history and biography). The specific subjects include both the basic biological sciences (taxonomy, botany, zoology, ecology, genetics, biochemistry and biophysics, microbiology) and some more applied aspects (biomedicine, food and agriculture). Since the guide is intended for use by students, exercises are included. There is a subject and title index. *Using the Biological Literature* is based on literature guides prepared by the author for users of the Biology Library at the University of Illinois at Urbana-Champaign, so it provides good coverage of the literature likely to be found in larger academic libraries in the United States. It begins with a chapter on the history of biology and its literature, followed by a chapter on subject headings. The remaining nine chapters deal with various areas of study: general biology; biochemistry, biophysics, and molecular biology; botany; ecology; entomology; genetics; microbiology and immunology; physiology; zoology. Sources within chapters are subdivided by form, with entries for both primary and secondary sources. The emphasis is on current English-language materials and almost all entries are annotated. There is an index covering authors, titles, and subjects.

1510. Smith, Roger C., W. Malcolm Reid, and Arlene E. Luchsinger. **Smith's Guide to the Literature of the Life Sciences.** 9th ed. Minneapolis: Burgess, 1980. 223p. Paper.

1511. Kirk, Thomas G., Jr. **Library Research Guide to Biology: Illustrated Search Strategy and Sources.** Ann Arbor, Mich.: Pierian Press, 1978. 79p. (Library Research Guide Series, no. 2).

More selective than the above guides, these two titles are particularly well suited for use by students. In addition to covering major reference sources, *Smith's Guide* emphasizes strategies for searching the literature and preparing scientific papers. Chapters discussing sources cover certain forms: textbooks and reviews, bibliographies and indexes, abstracting journals, ready reference works, serials, and taxonomic literature. There are library assignments at the end of chapters and an index. Kirk emphasizes the strategy for carrying out a literature search and provides detailed information on using some major abstracting and indexing services such as *Biological Abstracts* (entry 1513) and *Science Citation Index* (entry 1223). The appendixes include lists of review serials, guides to the literature, and basic reference sources.

1512. Crafts-Lighty, A. **Information Sources in Biotechnology.** New York: Nature Press, 1983. 306p.

With the increasing interest in biotechnology, Crafts-Lighty's guide is a valuable aid to understanding its scope and identifying its information sources. There are 13 chapters, beginning with "What is Biotechnology?" The second chapter, on information sources in biotechnology, is followed by chapters covering: monographs, book series and texts; conferences and their proceedings; trade periodicals and newsletters; research and review periodicals; abstracting and secondary sources; computer databases; patents and patenting; market surveys; directories of company, product, and research project information; organizations. The final chapter discusses provision of library and information services in biotechnology. The chapters on sources describe the category and review the most important titles in some depth. There is a directory of publishers' addresses and a subject index.

1513. **Biological Abstracts.** Philadelphia: BioSciences Information Service, 1926- . Semimonthly with semiannual cumulation of indexes.

1514. **Biological Abstracts/RRM: Reports, Reviews and Meetings.** Philadelphia: BioSciences Information Service, 1980- . Semimonthly with semiannual cumulation of indexes.

Taken together, *Biological Abstracts* and *Biological Abstracts/RRM* provide quite thorough coverage of the biological sciences literature. As the title of the latter suggests, they differ in the types of materials covered. *Biological Abstracts* provides citations and abstracts for journal articles. *Biological Abstracts/RRM* provides citations and content summaries (subject terms, subject concepts, taxonomic names) for reports and reviews. Entries in both follow a categorized arrangement under 84 broad subject headings (e.g., behavioral biology, phytopathology). In addition, *Biological Abstracts/RRM* has a book section with synopses of books and a meetings section with entries for proceedings in which individual papers are cited. Four indexes provide additional approaches to the entries. There is an author index, a biosystematic index (taxonomic categories at the phylum, class, order, and family levels subdivided by major concept), a generic index (genus-species names subdivided by major concept), and a subject index (a keyword-in-context arrangement of every significant word in titles and significant words extracted from articles to expand or clarify titles). In searching, it is necessary to identify as many synonyms as possible for subject terms since the vocabulary in the subject index is uncontrolled. Indexes cumulate semiannually. The predecessor of *Biological Abstracts/RRM* was titled *Bioresearch Index* (1965-79). *Biological*

Abstracts, Biological Abstracts/RRM, and *Bioresearch Index* can be machine searched as the BIOSIS PREVIEWS database back to 1969 through DIALOG and back to 1970 through BRS. Abstracts are available online only back to 1976. Descriptions of several more specialized abstracting publications in the biological sciences, such as *Genetics Abstracts* and *Entomology Abstracts,* can be found in the guides to the literature (entries 1508-11). Several published by Cambridge Scientific Abstracts can be searched as the *Life Sciences Collection* back to 1978 through DIALOG. They may be useful to the advanced student and faculty member as a supplement to *Biological Abstracts* and *Biological Abstracts/RRM.*

1515. **Biological and Agricultural Index.** New York: Wilson, 1964- . Monthly, except August, with quarterly and annual cumulations.

1516. **Biology Digest.** Medford, N.J.: Plexus, 1974- . Nine issues per year, September-May, with annual cumulation of indexes.

For the student who does not require the extensive coverage of *Biological Abstracts* and *Biological Abstracts/RRM,* two other sources are likely to be easier to use. *Biological and Agricultural Index,* which was preceded by the *Agricultural Index* (New York: Wilson, 1916-64), is one of the Wilson indexes. It covers about two hundred English-language journals dealing with various aspects of biology and agriculture. The main portion is a subject index with numerous cross-references, and in a separate section there is an author index to book reviews. *Biological and Agricultural Index* can now be machine searched through Wilsonline. *Biology Digest* is an abstracting publication intended for use at the undergraduate level. Detailed abstracts of articles from two hundred journals are arranged under eight broad categories: "Viruses, Microflora and Plants"; "Animal Kingdom"; "The Human Organism"; "Infectious Diseases"; "Population and Health"; "Cell Biology and Biogenesis"; "Environmental Quality"; and "General Topics." There is a separate section of book reviews and author and subject indexes which cumulate annually. Each issue also carries a feature article on some topic of current interest in biology.

1517. **Current Contents: Life Sciences.** Philadelphia: Institute for Scientific Information, 1958- . Weekly.

Current Contents: Life Sciences is a valuable publication for current awareness in the biological sciences. It appears weekly, reproducing the tables of contents of major journals arranged by broad topic areas (e.g., biochemistry, molecular biology and genetics, microbiology and cell biology, animal and plant science). The organization and possible uses of this section of *Current Contents* parallel those already described for *Current Contents: Physical, Chemical & Earth Sciences* (entry 1341). The section *Current Contents: Agriculture, Biology & Environmental Sciences* (entry 1570) is also relevant for the biological sciences, particularly botany.

1518. **Serial Sources for the BIOSIS Data Base.** Philadelphia: BioSciences Information Service, 1938- . Annual.

Serial Sources is a helpful supplementary publication to be used in conjunction with *Biological Abstracts* (entry 1513) and *Biological Abstracts/RRM* (entry 1514). It includes titles of serials presently covered in BioSciences Information Service products as well as archival entries for those no longer active. Entries include both the full and abbreviated titles, CODEN, frequency, and a number which leads to the directory section of publisher names and addresses. This publication can be used both to determine the full title of a serial cited in *Biological Abstracts* or *Biological Abstracts/RRM* in abbreviated form and to get publisher information for placing orders.

1519. Roe, Keith E., and Richard G. Frederick. **Dictionary of Theoretical Concepts in Biology.** Metuchen, N.J.: Scarecrow, 1981. 267p.

Although titled a "dictionary," this source actually functions as an index to more than 1,100 theories, laws, and ideas related to biology. Entries are arranged alphabetically, giving the biological field in which the term occurs and identifying a number of sources that explain the topic, including original sources and reviews in which concepts are elucidated. Entries cover both plant and animal biology, identifying literature discussing such terms as *complexity, coevolution,* and *neoteny.*

1520. Thompson, John W., comp. **Index to Illustrations of the Natural World: Where to Find Pictures of the Living Things of North America.** Syracuse, N.Y.: Gaylord Professional Publications, 1977. 265p.

1521. Munz, Lucile Thompson, and Nedra G. Slauson. **Index to Illustrations of Living Things Outside North America: Where to Find Pictures of Flora and Fauna.** Hamden, Conn.: Archon, 1981. 441p.

When an illustration of a plant or animal is sought, these two indexes are particularly helpful in locating pictures that have appeared in books such as field guides. As the titles indicate, they are complementary in coverage. Thompson covers plants and animals found on the North American continent and the Hawaiian and Caribbean islands, while Munz and Slauson cover those outside North America. Entries in Thompson are drawn from 178 books; Munz and Slauson cover 206 books. In each case the books are authoritative, likely to be available in medium-size or larger libraries and containing quality illustrations. In both indexes the main index is arranged alphabetically by common name, with a separate index by scientific name and a bibliography of source books by title.

DICTIONARIES, ENCYCLOPEDIAS

1522. Gray, Peter. **The Dictionary of the Biological Sciences.** New York: Reinhold, 1967. 602p.

1523. **Henderson's Dictionary of Biological Terms.** 9th ed. Edited by Sandra Holmes. New York: Van Nostrand, Reinhold, 1979. 510p.

These two dictionaries provide extensive listings of terminology from the biological sciences. Gray's dictionary has definitions for 40,000 terms, including some entries for taxa, word roots, and personal names. There is a bibliography of works consulted in compiling the dictionary. The most recent edition of *Henderson's Dictionary of Biological Terms* provides definitions and etymology for more than 22,500 terms. In addition, there are appendixes that classify plants and animals to the order level.

1524. **Facts on File Dictionary of Biology.** Edited by Elizabeth Tootill. New York: Facts on File, 1981. 282p.

1525. **Dictionary of Life Sciences.** 2d ed. Edited by E. A. Martin. New York: Pica Press, 1984. 396p.

1526. **McGraw-Hill Dictionary of Biology.** Edited by Sybil P. Parker. New York: McGraw-Hill, 1984. 384p. Paper.

These three dictionaries are more selective than the two described above, but they may prove to be adequate for the needs of the undergraduate student. Each defines a few thousand of the most commonly encountered terms in the biological sciences. *Facts on File Dictionary of Biology* has clear, detailed definitions with some illustrations. *Dictionary of*

Life Sciences has been updated to reflect recent developments in genetics, molecular biology, microbiology, and immunology. It has variable length definitions with some illustrations. *McGraw-Hill Dictionary of Biology* has definitions drawn from the third edition of the parent work (entry 1242).

1527. Gray, Peter, ed. **The Encyclopedia of the Biological Sciences.** 2d ed. New York: Van Nostrand, Reinhold, 1970. 1027p.

Although the publication date of 1970 means that Gray is of no use for locating discussions of biological concepts which have emerged in the past fifteen years, this encyclopedia is still useful to students seeking information on many topics in the biological sciences. There are about eight hundred signed articles written by specialists, with illustrations and bibliographies. There are some biographical entries, but terms for applications in such areas as medicine and agriculture are excluded. The volume concludes with an index.

1528. Grzimek, Bernhard, ed. **Grzimek's Animal Life Encyclopedia.** 13 vols. New York: Van Nostrand, Reinhold, 1972-75.

1529. **Macmillan Illustrated Animal Encyclopedia.** Edited by Philip Whitfield. New York: Macmillan, 1984. 600p.

1530. Leftwich, A. W. **A Dictionary of Zoology.** 3d ed. New York: Crane, Russak, 1973. 478p.

1531. Pennak, Robert W. **Collegiate Dictionary of Zoology.** New York: Ronald Press, 1964. 583p.

For the student and faculty member in zoology, these sources assemble much descriptive detail and terminology on the animal kingdom. *Grzimek's Animal Life Encyclopedia* has four volumes on mammals, three on birds, two on fishes and amphibians, and one each on reptiles, insects, mollusks and echinoderms, and lower animals. Entries are arranged in taxonomic sequence. Chapters cover orders or families and provide readable descriptions of such characteristics as appearance, evolution, range and habitat, and feeding and mating habits. Articles are illustrated, and each volume has both a classified index and an alphabetical index of the organisms discussed. There is also a polyglot dictionary of animal names in English, German, French, and Russian, and a bibliography in each volume. The *Macmillan Illustrated Animal Encyclopedia* treats only vertebrates, with sections on mammals, birds, reptiles, amphibians, and fishes. Each section is organized at the family level except for fishes, which is at the order level. Brief descriptions giving name, range, habitat, size, and other characteristics are accompanied by good color illustrations. There is an index. The two dictionaries have numerous definitions of zoological terms. Leftwich's *Dictionary of Zoology* has a number of sections: definitions of 6,700 technical terms in zoology and related branches of biology; a list of eight hundred English names of animals, giving brief descriptions and cross-references to families and other groups; and a discussion of the principles of classification and nomenclature in zoology. There is also a bibliography. Pennak's dictionary has definitions of about 19,000 terms including 8,600 names. A taxonomic outline is provided as an appendix.

1532. **The Facts on File Dictionary of Botany.** Edited by Stephen Blackmore and Elizabeth Tootill. New York: Facts on File, 1984. 391p.

1533. Little, R. John, and C. Eugene Jones. **A Dictionary of Botany.** New York: Van Nostrand, Reinhold, 1980. 400p.

1534. Swartz, Delbert. **Collegiate Dictionary of Botany.** New York: Ronald Press, 1971. 520p.

1535. **Longman Illustrated Dictionary of Botany: The Elements of Plant Science Illustrated and Defined.** Edited by Andrew Sugden. Harlow, Essex, England: Longman, 1984. 192p.

In these four dictionaries the emphasis is on botanical terminology rather than plant names. *Facts on File Dictionary of Botany* has over 3,000 detailed definitions of terms from the pure and applied plant sciences, including the designations of the higher ranks of plant groups. There are also a few illustrations. Little and Jones briefly define about 5,500 terms drawn from more than 100 sources. There are illustrations and a bibliography of sources. Swartz has brief definitions of about 24,000 terms drawn from more than 170 sources. There is an outline of the plant kingdom as an appendix. The *Longman Illustrated Dictionary of Botany* is more elementary, with many color illustrations. Terms are grouped into 24 subject sections (e.g., fruits and seeds, phytochemistry) with an index. An appendix explains Greek and Latin prefixes.

1536. **Grzimek's Encyclopedia of Ecology.** Edited by Bernhard Grzimek, Joachim Illies, and Wolfgang Klausewitz. New York: Van Nostrand, Reinhold, 1976. 705p.

1537. **Grzimek's Encyclopedia of Evolution.** Edited by Bernhard Heberer and Herbert Wendt. New York: Van Nostrand, Reinhold, 1976. 560p.

1538. Lewis, Walter H. **Ecology Field Glossary: A Naturalist's Vocabulary.** Westport, Conn.: Greenwood, 1977. 153p.

1539. Lincoln, R. J., G. A. Boxshall, and P. F. Clark. **A Dictionary of Ecology, Evolution and Systematics.** Cambridge: Cambridge University Press, 1982. 298p.

The two Grzimek encyclopedias complement coverage in *Grzimek's Animal Life Encyclopedia* (entry 1528) by providing a series of well-illustrated articles on major areas of study within ecology and evolution. The 35 chapters in *Grzimek's Encyclopedia of Ecology* treat the interrelationships of animals and man to the environment. There are two major sections: environment of animals (24 chapters) and environment of man (11 chapters). *Grzimek's Encyclopedia of Evolution* has 23 chapters dealing with the forces that have influenced the evolution of various plant and animal species including man. There is a systematic classification in an appendix. Articles in both volumes are written by experts but are not too technical, so they are suitable for use by undergraduates. Each volume has a detailed index and a list of supplementary readings. For students seeking definitions of terms in the fields of ecology and evolution, two other dictionaries should be useful. The *Ecology Field Glossary* has brief definitions arranged alphabetically, but also provides an outline of the terms arranged under broad subject headings: terrestrial ecosystems, aquatic ecosystems, soil ecosystem, and man's impact on ecosystems. There is a bibliography and appendixes giving measurements, equivalents, and conversions. *A Dictionary of Ecology, Evolution and Systematics* is a much more comprehensive dictionary with brief definitions of about 10,000 terms. There are several appendixes, including the geological time scale, taxonomic hierarchy, and acronyms.

1540. **Grzimek's Encyclopedia of Ethology.** Edited by Klaus Immelmann. New York: Van Nostrand, Reinhold, 1977. 705p.

1541. Heymer, Armin. **Ethological Dictionary: German-English-French.** New York: Garland, 1977. 238p.

Like the volumes on ecology and evolution (entries 1536, 1537), *Grzimek's Encyclopedia of Ethology* consists of chapters written by experts. The 43 chapters cover various topics in ethology, the study of animal behavior, and are well illustrated. The volume includes a supplementary reading list, a glossary, and an index. A more comprehensive listing of terminology in ethology can be found in the *Ethological Dictionary*, which provides full definitions in German, English, and French for about one thousand terms. Arrangement is alphabetical by the German term, with English and French indexes. Some illustrations are included and there is a bibliography.

1542.   Gray, Peter, ed. **The Encyclopedia of Microscopy and Microtechnique.** New York: Van Nostrand, Reinhold, 1973. 638p.

1543.   Singleton, Paul, and Diana Sainsbury. **Dictionary of Microbiology.** New York: Wiley, 1978. 481p.

The microscope is an important instrument in biological research, and the student should find entries in *The Encyclopedia of Microscopy and Microtechnique* helpful in understanding the operation of microscopes and the preparation of materials intended for examination. Although not exclusively concerned with biology, the emphasis of many of the articles is microscopy in the biological sciences. Articles are illustrated and have reference lists. There is an index for the volume. The *Dictionary of Microbiology* has definitions of concepts, techniques, tests, and microbial taxa. There is also an appendix of microbial metabolic pathways.

1544.   Evans, A. **Glossary of Molecular Biology.** New York: Wiley, 1974. 55p.

1545.   Rieger, R., A. Michaelis, and M. M. Green. **Glossary of Genetics and Cytogenetics: Classical and Molecular.** 4th ed. Berlin: Springer, 1976. 647p. Paper.

1546.   King, Robert C., and William D. Stansfield. **A Dictionary of Genetics.** 3d ed. New York: Oxford University Press, 1985. 480p.

For the student of molecular biology, Evans's glossary provides detailed definitions of selected terms likely to be encountered in reading the literature. There is also a bibliography. The two dictionaries of genetics are more extensive. *Glossary of Genetics and Cytogenetics* has about 2,500 entries with detailed definitions and citations to the literature, supplemented by a bibliography of sources cited. *A Dictionary of Genetics* covers about 6,000 terms from all fields related to genetics, including species and genera used in genetic research. It has been updated to cover recent developments and there are several useful appendixes: a classification of organisms, a list of scientific names for domestic species, a chronology of genetic research and discoveries with a bibliography, and a list of periodicals frequently cited in the literature of genetics, cytology, and molecular biology. Both dictionaries are suitable for use by students and researchers.

1547.   **Concise Encyclopedia of Biochemistry.** Edited by Thomas Scott and Mary Brewer. Berlin: De Gruyter, 1983. 519p.

1548.   Stenesh, J. **Dictionary of Biochemistry.** New York: Wiley, 1975. 344p.

The *Concise Encyclopedia of Biochemistry* is a translation and updating of the second German edition of *Brockhaus ABC Biochemie.* Entries vary in length from one paragraph to several pages and cover compounds, groups of substances, pathways, processes, and techniques. The articles provide current information and some illustrations and references to other sources. The text can be understood by advanced undergraduates as well as graduate students and faculty. The *Dictionary of Biochemistry,* with 12,000 entries from reference books, texts, and the research literature in biochemistry, can supplement the encyclopedia and may suffice when only a definition is sought.

1549.   Jaeger, Edmund C. **The Biologist's Handbook of Pronunciations.** Springfield, Ill.: Thomas, 1960. 317p.

1550.   Jaeger, Edmund C. **A Source-book of Biological Names and Terms.** 3d ed. Springfield, Ill.: Thomas, 1955. 323p.

These two dictionaries are aids to using and understanding biological terminology. The guide to pronunciation includes more than nine thousand technical terms and generic names of plants and animals. It is helpful because most biological dictionaries fail to include guides to pronunciation of terms defined therein. The *Source-book* is a dictionary of elements used to make up genus and species names and technical terms. It includes adjectival and noun stems, prefixes and suffixes, geographic place name stems, and short biographies of persons commemorated in names. Entries provide information on origin, meaning, and examples of use.

DIRECTORIES

1551.   Coombs, J. **The Biotechnology Directory 1985: Products, Companies, Research, and Organizations.** New York: Nature Press, 1985. 494p.

1552.   **A Directory of Information Resources in the United States: Biological Sciences.** Washington, D.C.: Library of Congress, National Referral Center, 1972. 577p

Coombs's directory encompasses both the established biotechnologies (e.g., food processing, pharmaceuticals) and the new, advanced genetic engineering technologies which permit manipulation of biological organisms in such a way that they may be induced to make useful products, such as the production of synthetic insulin by genetically engineered bacteria. Entries are in three parts. The first section describes international organizations and information services (databases, journals, newsletters). The second section presents national profiles, government departments, and professional societies for several countries active in biotechnology. The final section covers products and areas of research, listing noncommercial organizations and companies by country, with a products, research, and services buyers' guide. Organizations in Western Europe, North America, Brazil, and Japan are described. Indexing is quite thorough, making access to the contents of entries convenient. For more traditional sources of biological information, *A Directory of Information Resources in the United States* can be consulted. It is one of a series of directories prepared from files maintained by the National Referral Center at the Library of Congress, with entries for organizations such as museums, research institutes, professional societies, universities, government agencies, and companies that offer biological sciences information of some kind. The entry describing each organization gives an address, telephone number, areas of interest, holdings, publications, and information services. There is a subject index.

HANDBOOKS

The handbook literature of the biological sciences is extensive and only a few titles can be covered here. In particular, both books describing animals and plants (such as field guides) and books describing experimental methods are important parts of reference collections in the biological sciences. Powell's bibliography of handbooks (entry 1265) and the guides to the literature in biology (entries 1508-11) can be consulted for guidance in locating additional specific titles.

1553.   **Synopsis and Classification of Living Organisms.** Edited by Sybil P. Parker. 2 vols. New York: McGraw-Hill, 1982.

1554.   **A Synoptic Classification of Living Organisms.** Edited by R. S. K. Barnes. Oxford: Blackwell Scientific, 1984. 273p.

When there is a question regarding the appropriate taxonomic class of living organisms or the need for information on their characteristics, the *Synopsis and Classification of Living Organisms* provides a wealth of detail. It provides a classification down to the family level of all living organisms from viruses to primates with descriptions including such characteristics as geographic distribution and life cycles. Each section is written by an authority, and major references are given for each family. For smaller families all genera are listed; for larger families representative forms are listed. There are illustrations and an index to common and scientific names. Appendixes in volume 2 discuss nomenclature and biological classification and present a taxonomy. Barnes's *Synoptic Classification* is more selective, treating the taxa to the level of orders. Only groups with some living representatives are discussed, and a single illustration is provided for each phylum. There is a brief bibliography and an index to taxa.

1555.   Altman, Philip L., and Dorothy S. Dittmer, eds. **Biology Data Book.** 2d ed. 3 vols. Bethesda, Md.: Federation of American Societies for Experimental Biology, 1972-74.

The three volumes of the *Biology Data Book* bring together much data needed for biological research, organizing it into tables, charts, and diagrams with many citations to sources of the data. Data relate to man and to the more important laboratory, domestic, commercial, and field organisms. Volume 1 covers genetics and cytology, reproduction, development and growth, properties of biological substances, and materials and methods. Volume 2 deals with biological regulators and toxins, environment and survival, parasitism, and sensory and neurobiology. Volume 3 includes nutrition, digestion and excretion, metabolism, respiration and circulation, and blood and other body fluids. Each volume is indexed independently, and has a listing of scientific with associated common names and the reverse. Volume 1 also contains a classification outline.

1556.   King, Robert C., ed. **Handbook of Genetics.** 5 vols. New York: Plenum, 1974-76.

1557.   **CRC Handbook of Microbiology**. 2d ed. Edited by Allen I. Laskin and Hubert A. Lechevalier. Boca Raton, Fla.: CRC Press, 1977- . To be completed in 9 volumes; 7 volumes published to date.

1558.   **CRC Handbook of Biochemistry and Molecular Biology.** 3d ed. Edited by Gerald D. Fasman. 9 vols. Cleveland: CRC Press, 1975-77.

These three more specialized handbooks are useful to graduate students and faculty. Authored by different specialists, *Handbook of Genetics* has well-documented essays and annotated compilations of data on species of interest for genetic investigation. Each of four volumes treats particular groups of organisms: bacteria, bacteriophages and fungi; plants, plant viruses, and protists; invertebrates; and vertebrates. A fifth volume covers molecular genetics. Each has author and subject indexes. *CRC Handbook of Microbiology* covers microorganisms (bacteria, fungi, algae, protozoa, viruses), including properties, composition, products, and activities. Both taxonomic and topical indexes are provided. Data in the *CRC Handbook of Biochemistry and Molecular Biology* cover proteins, nucleic acids, lipids, carbohydrates, and steroids. There is an index volume for the set.

1559.   Atkinson, Bernard, and Ferda Mavituna. **Biochemical Engineering and Biotechnology Handbook.** New York: Nature Press, 1983. 1119p.

This handbook is intended to assist in the development of both large and small biotechnological processes by discussing their scientific and engineering basis, factors influencing performance, and their integration into complete processes. Information is presented as text, tables, and figures; there is an index of topics. With the growth of interest in biotechnology, this handbook should be useful to both the student and faculty member in the applied biological sciences.

BIOGRAPHY

1560.   American Institute of Biological Sciences. **AIBS Directory of Bioscience Departments and Faculties in the United States and Canada.** 2d ed. Edited by Peter Gray. Stroudsburg, Pa.: Dowden, Hutchinson & Ross, 1975. 660p.

This directory includes information on more than two thousand bioscience departments in colleges and universities in the United States and Canada. Arrangement is by state or province, subdivided by institution. Entries include name and address of the institution, name and telephone number of the department, chairman and faculty names, degree programs, and undergraduate and graduate courses. Institution and faculty indexes are provided. Although there are no biographical entries for faculty, the directory can be used to locate the institution with which a faculty member was affiliated in 1975.

AGRICULTURE

GUIDES, BIBLIOGRAPHIES, INDEXES

1561.   **Guide to Sources for Agricultural and Biological Research.** Edited by J. Richard Blanchard and Lois Farrell. Berkeley, Calif.: University of California Press, 1981. 735p.

1562.   **Information Sources in Agriculture and Food Science.** Edited by G. P. Lilley. London: Butterworths, 1981. 603p. (Butterworths Guides to Information Sources).

These two guides offer detailed treatment of the literature of agriculture and related areas. *Guide to Sources for Agricultural and Biological Research* has nine subject chapters covering agriculture, plant sciences, crop protection, animal sciences, physical sciences, food science and nutrition, environmental sciences, social sciences, and computerized databases. Each chapter begins with a brief introduction, followed by an annotated list of sources. Some chapters are further divided into subtopics. There are author, subject, and title indexes and an appendix of acronyms and abbreviations. *Information Sources in Agriculture and Food Science* is a series of 20 bibliographic essays authored by different specialists. There is a series of general chapters (e.g., secondary literature, maps and atlases, statistical sources), followed by 13 chapters dealing with resources in particular subject areas: soils and fertilizers; agricultural engineering; weed biology, weed control, and herbicides; crop protection; field crops and grasslands; temperate horticulture; tropical agriculture; animal production; veterinary science; forestry; food science; agricultural economics; and agrarian and food history. The volume has an index and an appendix listing abbreviations.

1563. **Comparative and Veterinary Medicine: A Guide to the Resource Literature.** Compiled by Ann E. Kerker and Henry T. Murphy. Madison, Wis.: University of Wisconsin Press, 1973. 308p.

This guide to the literature of comparative and veterinary medicine is intended for use by the veterinarian, the research scientist, and the graduate student. Emphasis is on recent, English-language publications. General materials appear in part 1, which has discussions of indexes and abstracts, bibliographies, periodicals, review serials, reference works, and handbooks and manuals of laboratory technique. Part 2 has 14 chapters covering traditional subject disciplines of the biomedical sciences, such as anatomy, physiology, and neurology. Part 3 has 15 chapters on veterinary medicine, arranged by the types of animals normally encountered in practice (e.g., cattle, horses, dogs, cats). Part 4 covers laboratory animals of various types. Some entries are annotated, and there are thorough author and subject indexes.

1564. **Bibliography of Agriculture.** Phoenix: Oryx Press, 1942- . Monthly with annual cumulation of indexes.

1565. **Agrindex.** Rome: AGRIS, Food and Agriculture Organization, 1975- . Monthly.

These two publications are the two most comprehensive indexing services in agriculture. *Bibliography of Agriculture* primarily covers additions to the collections of the U.S. National Agricultural Library, while *Agrindex,* sponsored by AGRIS (the International Information System for the Agricultural Sciences and Technology of the Food and Agriculture Organization of the United Nations), is the product of a cooperative effort among participants in more than one hundred countries. Coverage in the *Bibliography of Agriculture* is international and includes journal articles, pamphlets, government documents, reports, and conference proceedings. Each monthly issue is divided into eight sections: a main entry section with citations in a categorized arrangement; five main entry subsections for certain types of publications (U.S. Department of Agriculture publications, state agricultural experiment station publications, state agricultural extension service publications, Food and Agriculture Organization publications, and translations); and three indexes (corporate author, personal author, subject). Indexes are cumulated annually. *Bibliography of Agriculture* can be machine searched as part of the AGRICOLA database back to 1970 through BRS and DIALOG. *Agrindex* has international coverage of journal and other literature relevant to research and development in the food and agricultural sector. Entries are arranged alphabetically by author within subject categories (subdivided by commodity code if applicable). There are several indexes in each issue: personal author, corporate author, report and patent number, commodities, geographical — political geography and marine areas, and geographical — physical geography.

1566. **Food Science and Technology Abstracts.** Reading, Berkshire, England: International Food Information Service, 1969- . Monthly with annual cumulation of indexes.

1567. **Nutrition Abstracts and Reviews.** Farnham Royal, Slough, England: Commonwealth Agricultural Bureaux, 1931- . Monthly with annual cumulation of indexes.

There are a number of specialized abstracting publications relevant to agriculture which can be used to supplement coverage of *Bibliography of Agriculture* (entry 1564) and *Agrindex* (entry 1565). *Food Science and Technology Abstracts* covers journal articles, patents, standards, and other materials on the scientific and technical aspects of foods and food processing. Abstracts are arranged in 19 subject categories (e.g., food microbiology, food packaging, milk and dairy products), and there are author and subject indexes which cumulate annually. It can be machine searched back to 1969 through DIALOG and SDC. *Nutrition Abstracts and Reviews* is typical of the more than 40 abstracting publications that the Commonwealth Agricultural Bureaux in England issue. Since 1977 each issue of this publication has appeared in two parts: A. *Human and Experimental* and B. *Livestock Feeds and Feeding.* Each has a categorized arrangement of abstracts of journal articles with separate sections for reports, conferences, and books. Author and subject indexes appear in each issue and cumulate annually. *Nutrition Abstracts and Reviews* can be machine searched as part of the CAB ABSTRACTS database back to 1972 through DIALOG.

1568.   **Dictionary Catalog of the National Agricultural Library, 1862-1965.** 73 vols. New York: Rowman & Littlefield, 1967-70.

1569.   **National Agricultural Library Catalog.** Totowa, N.J.: Rowman & Littlefield, 1966- Monthly with semiannual cumulation of indexes.

Given the size of the National Agricultural Library's collection, these two catalogs are valuable aids to searching the monographic literature in agriculture. The *Dictionary Catalog* reproduces the author, title, and subject listings for monographs, serials, and analytics cataloged by the National Agricultural Library up to 1965. The final volume of the set lists translations of articles in the Library's collection. The *National Agricultural Library Catalog* is a continuing publication, reflecting new monographs and serial titles added to the Library's collection. Monthly issues contain a list of main entries with complete cataloging data arranged by broad subject categories (e.g., human nutrition, plant science, animal science), indexes (subject, personal author, corporate author, title), and an alphabetical list of translations added to the collection during the previous month. Indexes cumulate semiannually. Five-year cumulations have been issued for the periods 1966-1970 and 1971-1975. *National Agricultural Library Catalog* can be machine searched as part of the AGRICOLA database back to 1970 through BRS and DIALOG.

1570.   **Current Contents: Agriculture, Biology & Environmental Sciences.** Philadelphia: Institute for Scientific Information, 1970- . Weekly.

To provide current awareness for recently published journals, this section of *Current Contents* can be consulted. Journals relevant to agriculture appear in several sections: agriculture/agronomy, agricultural chemistry, plant sciences, entomology/pest control, animal sciences, and food/nutrition. The organization and possible uses of this section parallel those already described for *Current Contents: Physical, Chemical & Earth Sciences* (entry 1341).

1571.   **Agricultural Journal Titles and Abbreviations.** 2d ed. Phoenix: Oryx Press, 1983. 136p.

This list covers journals scanned for articles to be included in the *Bibliography of Agriculture* (entry 1564). There are two parts: journal title followed by journal title abbreviation; and journal title abbreviation followed by journal title. The list can be used to verify the full journal title for items cited in the *Bibliography of Agriculture* and to determine whether a particular journal is included in its coverage.

DICTIONARIES, ENCYCLOPEDIAS

1572.   **A Dictionary of Agricultural and Allied Terminology.** Edited by John N. Winburne. East Lansing, Mich.: Michigan State University Press, 1962. 905p.

1573.   **Black's Agricultural Dictionary.** Edited by D. B. Dalal-Clayton. London: Adam & Charles Black, 1981. 499p.

Both of these dictionaries are suitable for use by students and faculty. *A Dictionary of Agricultural and Allied Terminology* defines words and idioms taken from books, magazines, and pamphlets which are listed in an appendix. Definitions reflect American usage. *Black's Agricultural Dictionary,* because it is published in the United Kingdom, has a British emphasis, but it can be used as a supplement to *A Dictionary of Agricultural and Allied Terminology*. It is particularly useful for recent terminology. *Black's* also has some illustrations and a list of abbreviations and acronyms.

1574.   **McGraw-Hill Encyclopedia of Food, Agriculture & Nutrition.** Edited by Daniel N. Lapedes. New York: McGraw-Hill, 1977. 732p.

This encyclopedia begins with five feature articles on topics of general interest: "Feeding the World," "Climate and Crops," "Energy in the Food System," "Food from the Sea," and "The Green Revolution." These are followed by four hundred articles on various aspects of food, agriculture, and nutrition. Much of this material is drawn from the fourth edition of the parent work (entry 1244). There is an appendix, giving composition of foods, and a detailed index.

1575.   Everett, Thomas H. **The New York Botanical Garden Illustrated Encyclopedia of Horticulture.** 10 vols. New York: Garland, 1981-82.

1576.   Bailey, Liberty Hyde, and Ethel Zoe Bailey. **Hortus Third: A Concise Dictionary of Plants Cultivated in the United States and Canada.** 3d ed. New York: Macmillan, 1976. 1290p.

Both of these sources provide much authoritative information suitable for professional and popular use. The *New York Botanical Garden Illustrated Encyclopedia of Horticulture* is an encyclopedic dictionary covering practice in the United States and Canada. Entries are in alphabetical order by names of taxonomic groups of plants, giving characteristics, garden and landscaping uses, cultivation, pests, and diseases. There are also longer articles on such topics as plant propagation, gardening methods, fertilizers, pests, and diseases. Most genera are illustrated with photographs, some of which are in color. The final volume contains an index to the color plates. *Hortus Third* presents brief information for 281 families, 3,301 genera, and 20,397 species found in the United States, Canada, Puerto Rico, and Hawaii. Entries give the correct botanical name, botanical synonyms, common names, notes on uses, and methods of propagation and culture. Illustrations accompany family descriptions. There are also some general articles describing groups of plants and methods of cultivation. Appendixes include a glossary of botanical terms, a list of authors cited in the text, and an index to common names.

1577.   **Foods and Food Production Encyclopedia.** Edited by Douglas M. Considine and Glenn D. Considine. New York: Van Nostrand, Reinhold, 1982. 2305p.

This encyclopedia can be used by students at all levels to locate information on all aspects of food. Its 1,201 entries cover food commodities, food processing, diseases and pests of animals and plants, agricultural chemicals, land and soil-related topics, food ingredients, biochemistry and nutrition, and scientific fundamentals. Articles are well illustrated and often have cross-references and bibliographies. Appendixes give the principal characteristics of food chemicals and daily dietary information and there is an index to aid in locating discussions of particular topics.

1578.   **Black's Veterinary Dictionary.** 14th ed. Edited by Gregory P. West. London: Adam & Charles Black, 1982. 902p.

This encyclopedic dictionary, with entries ranging from brief definitions to descriptions several pages in length, provides reliable and current information on diseases and conditions of various animals. Entries for diseases include discussions of causes, symptoms, treatment, and prevention. There are cross-references to lead to related entries and numerous illustrations. As is true of *Black's Agricultural Dictionary* (entry 1573), some entries in this volume have a British emphasis.

DIRECTORIES

1579. **Agricultural Research Centres: A World Directory of Organizations and Programmes.** 7th ed. Edited by Nigel Harvey. 2 vols. Harlow, Essex, England: Longman, 1983.

This directory identifies more than 11,000 laboratories engaged in agricultural research worldwide. The subject scope includes agriculture, fisheries, food, forestry, horticulture, and veterinary sciences. Entries are arranged alphabetically within country and contain organization name, address, telephone, senior staff, activities and projects, and publications. There are two indexes: titles of establishments and subjects.

1580. **North American Horticulture: A Reference Guide.** Compiled by the American Horticultural Society. New York: Scribner's, 1982. 367p.

This directory has chapters covering many aspects of horticulture: organizations (national horticultural organizations, plant societies, scholarly organizations, national garden club associations, garden centers, conservation organizations), nomenclature and international registration authorities, U.S. government programs, pesticide and herbicide regulations, sources of education, botanical and horticultural libraries, displays and collections (herbaria, public gardens and arboreta, museums and historic gardens, community gardens, test and demonstration gardens), major horticultural awards, major flower shows, and books and periodicals. Within chapters, where applicable, entries are arranged alphabetically by state or province. The index for the volume covers subjects, organizations, and botanical names.

1581. **Directory of Food and Nutrition Information Services and Resources.** Edited by Robyn C. Frank. Phoenix: Oryx Press, 1984. 288p. Paper.

Intended to assist professionals in identifying sources of food and nutrition information, this directory is organized into nine chapters: organizations; databases; microcomputer software; journals and newsletters; abstracts, indexes, and current awareness; producers of books, audiovisuals, and microcomputer software; key reference materials; regional, state, and area agencies; and nutrient tables. Four indexes (subject, geographic, organization type, and American Dietetic Association Approved Training programs) provide access to the contents. Each chapter lists and describes the sources within its scope.

HANDBOOKS

The guides to the literature (entries 1561-63) can be used to identify handbooks in agriculture and related areas. Only a few examples are given here.

1582. **Westcott's Plant Disease Handbook.** 4th ed. Revised by R. Kenneth Horst. New York: Van Nostrand, Reinhold, 1979. 803p.

This handbook provides a useful compilation of data on plant pathogens and methods of control. The main body of the book is a description of plant diseases, their pathogens (e.g., rusts, nematodes), and remedies. This is followed by a chapter listing host plants and their diseases. Supplementary material includes a list of land grant institutions and agricultural experiment stations, a glossary, a bibliography, and an index.

1583. **The Pesticide Manual: A World Compendium.** 7th ed. Edited by Charles R. Worthing and S. Barrie Walker. Croydon, England: British Crop Protection Council, 1983. 695p.

As one of the more comprehensive guides to agricultural chemicals, this manual can be used to respond to questions regarding the characteristics of particular pesticides. Entries are alphabetical by name, giving structure, nomenclature, chemical properties, uses, toxicology, formulations, and citations to literature describing methods of analysis. The appendixes give names and addresses of companies manufacturing chemicals, scientific and common names of organisms, and a brief bibliography. The index includes formulas and common names for chemicals.

1584.   Crabbe, David, and Simon Lawson. **The World Food Book: An A-Z, Atlas and Statistical Source Book.** New York: Nichols, 1981. 240p.

This is a useful compendium suitable for use by both specialists and nonspecialists. It treats production, processing, distribution, and consumption of food in a global context. As the title suggests, it is organized into sections with different types of information. The "A-Z" defines more than eight hundred terms related to agriculture, food, and nutrition with some illustrations and tables. The food resources atlas presents 18 maps illustrating the geographic distribution of food production and consumption. The statistical appendix provides data on production and consumption of various foodstuffs. There is also a brief bibliography.

1585.   **Merck Veterinary Manual: A Handbook of Diagnosis and Therapy for the Veterinarian.** 5th ed. Rahway, N.J.: Merck, 1979. 1680p.

As the subtitle indicates, this manual is to be used in diagnosing and treating animal diseases. It contains authoritative information in brief format. The major section on diseases is subdivided by body systems (e.g., digestive system, nervous system) and types of diseases (e.g., infectious diseases, parasitic diseases). Discussions include etiology and occurrence, clinical findings, diagnosis, treatment, and control. The remaining sections of text discuss toxicology, poultry, special categories of animals (fur, laboratory, and zoo), nutrition, behavior, and prescriptions. There is an index.

BIOGRAPHY

1586.   **Who's Who in World Agriculture: A Biographical Guide in the Agricultural and Veterinary Sciences.** 2d ed. 2 vols. Harlow, Essex, England: Longman, 1985.

This volume has about 12,000 entries giving biographical information for individuals from about one hundred countries. Entries are arranged in alphabetical order and include name, year of birth, education, work experience, society memberships, major publications, research interests, telephone, and address. The country and subject index lists experts in particular subject areas in each of the countries represented by one or more biographees.

29

MEDICAL SCIENCES

The medical sciences encompass not only clinical medicine and its numerous areas of specialization, but also nursing, dentistry, pharmacy, and health services administration. Although some reference sources cover the medical sciences in general, many others deal with particular clinical specialties (e.g., ophthalmology, pediatrics, psychiatry). In addition to sources intended primarily for use by physicians, there are many titles prepared specifically for nurses or various categories of allied health professionals (e.g., occupational therapists, physical therapists, medical technologists). With the growing emphasis on consumer health information, there are now many reference sources suitable for use by the consumer of health care who has no formal medical training. In the United States the National Library of Medicine has played an important role in improving access to medical literature through its publication of bibliographies and indexes and its creation of databases suitable for machine searching.

The extent and arrangement of a university's medical sciences collections will depend on the types of academic programs offered in the medical sciences. If there are schools of medicine, nursing, dentistry, and pharmacy and schools for the allied health professions, there may be separate collections supporting each program or an integrated medical sciences library. Where there are few or no academic programs in the medical sciences, there will still be a demand for some medical reference materials from students and faculty in related fields, such as the biological sciences. In all cases there will be a need for some medical reference materials suitable for any library user seeking answers to such questions as the symptoms of a disease, the purpose and possible side effects of a drug, the qualifications of a physician, or the definition of a medical term. Students and faculty in the medical sciences will have questions related to their research, teaching, and clinical work. Because of the large size of the reference literature in the medical sciences, this chapter emphasizes guides, bibliographies, and indexes that describe and provide access to this literature. Some of the major tools that form the core of medical sciences reference collections are described, but many more titles can be identified using the available guides. Consumer health reference titles are not described separately, but a guide to this literature has been included. In addition to sources in the medical sciences, two titles covering bioethics are described, reflecting the growing concern for the systematic study of value questions that arise in the biomedical and behavioral fields.

GUIDES, BIBLIOGRAPHIES, INDEXES

1587.   Roper, Fred W., and Jo Anne Boorkman. **Introduction to Reference Sources in the Health Sciences.** 2d ed. Chicago: Medical Library Association, 1984. 302p.

1588.   Chen, Ching-Chih. **Health Sciences Information Sources.** Cambridge, Mass.: MIT Press, 1981. 767p.

1589.   Morton, L. T., and S. Godbolt, eds. **Information Sources in the Medical Sciences.** 3d ed. London: Butterworths, 1984. 534p. (Butterworths Guides to Information Sources).

These guides are complementary in their approaches to the literature of the medical sciences. All three cover the core reference literature, but *Health Sciences Information Sources* and *Information Sources in the Medical Sciences* also include the literature of numerous specialties. Both *Introduction to Reference Sources in the Health Sciences* and *Information Sources in the Medical Sciences* have narrative presentations, while *Health Sciences Information Sources* is organized for ready reference. *Introduction to Reference Sources in the Health Sciences* is intended for use primarily by librarians and library science students. It discusses various types of reference sources and their use. There are three sections: "The Reference Collection" has a chapter on the organization and management of the reference collection; "Bibliographic Sources" has six chapters on sources covering various types of materials (monographs, periodicals, indexing and abstracting services, databases, government documents and technical reports, conferences, reviews, and translations); and "Information Sources" has nine chapters on categories of reference tools useful in the medical sciences (terminology, handbooks and manuals, drug information sources, audiovisual reference sources, medical and health statistics, directories and biographical sources, history sources, grant sources, health legislation sources). Each chapter begins with a discussion of the general characteristics of the type of source, followed by examples of the most important tools with emphasis on their effective use. There is a detailed index to authors, titles, and subjects. *Health Sciences Information Sources* has 24 chapters, each covering a certain type of material. Within each chapter subdivisions are by subject area, with entries giving complete bibliographic information, brief annotations, and citations to published reviews. There are author and title indexes. *Information Sources in the Medical Sciences* has 24 chapters prepared by different authors. Some cover general medical sources (e.g., primary sources of information, standard reference sources), but 15 chapters consider the literature of particular clinical specialties (e.g., pediatrics, tropical medicine, psychiatry). One chapter deals specifically with information for patients and the general public. This edition has been revised to include the recent medical literature and the development of mechanized sources of information. The volume has an index.

1590.   Lunin, Lois F. **Health Sciences and Services: A Guide to Information Sources.** Detroit: Gale, 1979. 614p. (Management Information Guide, no. 36)

This guide encompasses databases and organizations in addition to publications. The scope is quite wide ranging with chapters on health sciences and services, basic health sciences, clinical sciences, dentistry, nursing, public health, veterinary medicine, allied health, hospitals, health insurance, pharmacy, and communication of health information. In each subject area the publications, databases, and organizations are identified and many are described. There are indexes to authors, titles, databases, and organizations.

1591.   Rees, Alan M., and Jodith Janes. **The Consumer Health Information Source Book.** 2d ed. New York: Bowker, 1984. 530p.

This guide is unique in its emphasis on medical sciences materials suitable for use by the general public; it will therefore be particularly useful both to nonspecialists seeking information on medical topics and to medical sciences personnel planning consumer health education programs. Following an introductory chapter on new trends in medical consumerism, sources are described in two sections: "Reference and Research Aids" has four chapters covering particular types of information sources (bibliographies and selection guides; health magazines, newsletters, and consumer publications; professional literature; and health information clearinghouses and hotlines); "Literature" has 14 chapters describing and evaluating books and pamphlets suitable for the nonspecialist interested in various subject areas within the medical sciences (e.g., health of children, health of women, health of the elderly, cancer, heart disease, mental health). Two appendixes present directories of pamphlet suppliers and of publishers. Author, title, and subject indexes provide access to the many titles listed.

1592.   **Index Medicus.** Bethesda, Md.: National Library of Medicine, 1960- . Monthly with annual cumulation.

1593.   **Excerpta Medica.** Amsterdam: Excerpta Medica Foundation, 1947- . 46 sections.

Index Medicus is the major indexing service for the medical journal literature. Its predecessors cover the period back to 1879 and are described in *Introduction to Reference Sources in the Health Sciences* (entry 1587). Each issue of *Index Medicus* has a subject index, an author index, and a bibliography of medical reviews. Subject headings are drawn from *Medical Subject Headings,* a controlled vocabulary that is revised annually and issued as part 2 of the January issue of *Index Medicus.* Monthly issues cumulate annually to form *Cumulated Index Medicus. Index Medicus* can be machine searched as part of the MEDLINE database back to 1966 through BRS, DIALOG, and the National Library of Medicine. *Excerpta Medica* is the major abstracting service covering the journal and book literature in the basic medical sciences and clinical medicine. In printed form it appears in many sections (e.g., physiology, pharmacology, ophthalmology, surgery, nuclear medicine). The section titles have varied over the years as new titles have been added and others have split. The frequency of sections varies, but each has abstracts in a classified arrangement with author and subject indexes that cumulate annually. All parts of *Excerpta Medica* can be machine searched as the EMBASE database back to 1974 through DIALOG, and back to 1980 through BRS. Both *Index Medicus* and *Excerpta Medica* are important tools for students and faculty in the medical sciences who are conducting literature searches. For nonspecialists, more general tools, such as *General Science Index* (entry 1221), may prove to be more manageable.

1594.   **Current Contents: Clinical Practice.** Philadelphia: Institute for Scientific Information, 1973- . Weekly.

For current awareness in clinical medicine, *Current Contents: Clinical Practice* can be consulted. It appears weekly, reproducing the tables of contents of journals arranged by specialties within medicine, such as pediatrics, neurology, orthopedics, oncology, and dermatology. The organization and possible uses of this section of *Current Contents* parallel those already described for *Current Contents: Physical, Chemical & Earth Sciences* (entry 1341). *Current Contents: Life Sciences* (entry 1517) is also of interest to graduate students and faculty researchers in the basic medical sciences.

1595.   **Health Science Books, 1876-1982.** 4 vols. New York: Bowker, 1982.

1596.   **Medical and Health Care Books and Serials in Print: An Index to Literature in the Health Sciences.** New York: Bowker, 1972- . Annual.

The scope of *Health Science Books, 1876-1982* includes books published or distributed in the United States, in and out of print, for the time period covered. Entries in the three main volumes are arranged by Library of Congress subject headings. The fourth volume includes author and title indexes. Entries provide basic cataloging data and thus are useful for bibliographic verification. For the user more familiar with *Medical Subject Headings,* there is a guide to equivalents with Library of Congress subject headings. *Medical and Health Care Books and Serials in Print* represents a repackaging of titles in the medical sciences from *Books in Print* (entry 6), *Ulrich's International Periodicals Directory* (entry 51), and *Irregular Serials and Annuals* (entry 52). It may thus be of use in the departmental library not holding the parent tools. Citations to books are arranged in three sections: author, title, subject. Citations to serials are arranged by both title and subject. There is also a publishers and distributors directory.

1597.   **National Library of Medicine Current Catalog.** Bethesda, Md.: National Library of Medicine, 1966- . Quarterly with annual and 5-year cumulations.

1598.   **National Library of Medicine Audiovisuals Catalog.** Bethesda, Md.: National Library of Medicine, 1977- . Quarterly with annual cumulation.

National Library of Medicine Current Catalog provides complete cataloging data for monographs and serials cataloged by the National Library of Medicine. Entries are arranged in both a name/title section and a subject section for monographs, followed by the same two sections for serials. Medical reference works are listed in a separate section. The *National Library of Medicine Audiovisuals Catalog* provides complete cataloging data for audiovisual materials cataloged by the National Library of Medicine, again with entries in both a name/title section and a subject section. *Medical Subject Headings* are used for subject access in both catalogs. The *National Library of Medicine Current Catalog* and the *National Library of Medicine Audiovisuals Catalog* can be searched as the CATLINE and AVLINE databases, respectively, through the National Library of Medicine. They complement *Index Medicus* (entry 1592), which covers only the journal literature.

1599.   **Index of NLM Serial Titles.** 5th ed. 2 vols. Bethesda, Md.: National Library of Medicine, 1984.

1600.   **List of Journals Indexed in Index Medicus.** Bethesda, Md.: National Library of Medicine, 1960- . Annual.

These two lists of journal titles are helpful for bibliographic verification. The *Index of NLM Serial Titles* lists over 40,000 serials for which the National Library of Medicine has holdings. It is arranged by keyword from serial title, giving the full title, the National Library of Medicine call number, and the International Standard Serial Number. The *List of Journals Indexed in Index Medicus* is much more limited since it covers only those approximately 2700 journals that have been selected for coverage in *Index Medicus*. These titles appear in four lists: full title, abbreviated title, subject, and country of origin. Entries give abbreviated title, full title, place of publication, National Library of Medicine call number, and International Standard Serial Number.

1601.   Blake, John B., and Charles Roos, eds. **Medical Reference Works, 1679-1966: A Selected Bibliography.** Chicago: Medical Library Association, 1967. Three supplements, 1970-75.

This guide can be consulted for descriptions of older reference works in the medical sciences. It has three sections: general medicine, the history of medicine, and special subjects. Entries give complete bibliographic information and brief annotations. There is an index to authors, titles, and subjects. The supplements provide coverage for the period

1967-74. Thereafter, the *National Library of Medicine Current Catalog* (entry 1597) must be consulted for more recently published reference books.

1602.   Binger, Jane L., and Lydia M. Jensen. **Lippincott's Guide to Nursing Literature: A Handbook for Students, Writers and Researchers.** Philadelphia: Lippincott, 1980. 303p.

1603.   Strauch, Katina P., and Dorothy J. Brundage. **Guide to Library Resources for Nursing.** New York: Appleton-Century-Crofts, 1980. 509p. Paper.

Because the field of nursing has its own literature, it is helpful to have guides written specifically for nursing students and faculty. *Lippincott's Guide to Nursing Literature* emphasizes methods of literature searching and preparation of papers for publication. Part 1 describes how to use a library and how to do literature searching; part 2 is an annotated bibliography of nursing journals; part 3 covers indexing and abstracting services, reference tools, and computer searches. There is an index. *Guide to Library Resources for Nursing* also has a section on how to use a library, but the major portion is an annotated bibliography of sources arranged by broad subjects (e.g., fundamentals of nursing, women's health, child health). There is an appendix giving addresses of selected medical and nursing publishers as well as author, title, and subject indexes.

1604.   **International Nursing Index.** New York: American Journal of Nursing Company, in cooperation with the National Library of Medicine, 1966- . Quarterly with annual cumulation.

1605.   **Cumulative Index to Nursing and Allied Health Literature.** Glendale, Calif.: Glendale Adventist Medical Center, 1956- . Bimonthly with annual cumulation.

Both of these publications provide author and subject indexing of the core nursing journal literature. In addition, *International Nursing Index* covers foreign-language material and nursing articles appearing in non-nursing journals while *Cumulative Index to Nursing and Allied Health Literature* covers some more popular literature of interest to nurses. Each issue of *International Nursing Index* includes lists of nursing books and publications of organizations and agencies. Each issue of *Cumulative Index to Nursing and Allied Health Literature* has a separate section covering books. *International Nursing Index* can be machine searched as part of the MEDLINE database back to 1966 through BRS, DIALOG, and the National Library of Medicine. *Cumulative Index to Nursing and Allied Health Literature* can be machine searched back to 1983 through BRS and DIALOG.

1606.   **Index to Dental Literature.** Chicago: American Dental Association and National Library of Medicine, 1962- . Quarterly with annual cumulation.

Index to Dental Literature provides author and subject indexing of the journal literature in dentistry. Each issue also contains lists of dental books and of dissertations and theses. *Index to Dental Literature* can be machine searched as part of the MEDLINE database back to 1966 through BRS, DIALOG, and the National Library of Medicine.

1607.   **Hospital Literature Index.** Chicago: American Hospital Association, in cooperation with the National Library of Medicine, 1945- . Quarterly with annual cumulation.

Hospital Literature Index covers the nonclinical aspects of health care delivery, such as the administration, financing, and staffing of hospitals and related health care institutions. Journal articles are indexed by author and subject. There are also lists of books, audiovisuals, and journals recently received by the library of the American Hospital Association. *Hospital Literature Index* can be machine searched as the HEALTH PLANNING AND ADMINISTRATION database back to 1975 through BRS, DIALOG, and the National Library of Medicine.

1608.   Brunn, Alice Lefler. **How to Find Out in Pharmacy: A Guide to Sources of Pharma-ceutical Information.** Oxford: Pergamon, 1969. 130p.

1609.   Sewell, Winifred. **Guide to Drug Information.** Hamilton, Ill.: Drug Intelligence Publications, 1976. 218p.

As drug information sources form an important subcategory of the medical literature, these guides will be useful to many students and faculty in the medical sciences in addition to those specializing in pharmacy. Although the guide by Brunn is somewhat dated and has a British emphasis, it is still useful for its descriptions of some of the major drug information sources. Discussions are divided into six chapters: overview of the field; periodicals and indexing and abstracting services; bibliographies, guides to use of libraries; law, welfare, marketing, physical pharmacy, drug adulteration controls; pharmacology and drug compendia; crude drugs, practical pharmacy, pharmacodynamics, toxicology. Appendixes list libraries with strong pharmacy collections in the United States, Canada, Great Britain, and Ireland. There is also an index. *Guide to Drug Information* is in four parts. The first part describes handbooks and compendia of drug information, with tables to aid in comparing their characteristics. Part 2 emphasizes primary sources such as periodicals, and part 3 describes aids to literature searching such as indexing and abstracting services. The final part identifies trends in information handling. The book concludes with an index.

1610.   Wexler, Philip. **Information Resources in Toxicology.** New York: Elsevier/North-Holland, 1982. 333p.

Wexler's guide provides thorough coverage of sources of information on chemical, physical, and biological hazards to man, with an emphasis on health effects. Annotated entries are arranged in seven parts: reference sources, organizations, legislation and regulations, international activities, education, information handling, and journal articles. Appendixes include a directory of poison control centers, a list of selected abbreviations, and additional reference sources. There are indexes to subjects and journal articles.

1611.   Greenberg, Bette. **How to Find Out in Psychiatry: A Guide to Sources of Mental Health Information.** New York: Pergamon, 1978. 113p.

This is a guide to reference works in psychiatry and related fields, emphasizing English-language materials. It has a narrative style, treating various categories of reference tools in separate chapters: introduction to the literature of psychiatry; guides to libraries and the psychiatric literature; primary sources of information: periodicals and books; secondary sources of information: bibliographies, indexes, abstracts and reviews; dictionaries, glossaries, encyclopedias and handbooks; directories; nomenclature and classification; education; mental health statistics; drugs and drug therapy; tests and measurements; and nonprint materials. There is an appendix, listing classics in psychiatric literature, and an index.

1612.   Self, Phyllis. C., ed. **Physical Disability: An Annotated Literature Guide.** New York: Marcel Dekker, 1984. 474p. (Books in Library and Information Science, vol. 44).

This guide to rehabilitation literature is intended for professionals who work with physically disabled individuals and students who are preparing for such work. Chapter authors provide detailed annotations. The first three chapters give overviews of three types of physical disability: mobility, visual, and hearing impairment. The next eight chapters discuss social, psychological, medical, and legal considerations. There is also a chapter on the disabled child. The last three chapters treat specific types of materials: government publications, journals, and audiovisual materials. There are author and title indexes.

1613.	Weise, Frieda O. **Health Statistics: A Guide to Information Sources.** Detroit: Gale, 1980. 137p. (Health Affairs Information Guide Series, vol. 4).

Strategies for dealing with statistical questions have been discussed in chapter 5. Because statistical questions make up an important part of reference questions in the medical sciences, it is helpful to have a guide describing available information sources. Weise has compiled an annotated bibliography of basic sources of vital and health statistics in the United States. Separate chapters deal with vital statistics, morbidity, health care resources (facilities, manpower, education), health services utilization, health care costs and expenditures, and population characteristics. Appendixes cover newsletters and journals, government agencies, associations, regional depository libraries, and suppliers of bibliographic data files. There is a glossary as well as author, title, and subject indexes.

1614.	Cordasco, Francesco, and David N. Alloway. **Medical Education in the United States: A Guide to Information Sources.** Detroit: Gale, 1980. 393p. (Education Information Guide Series, vol. 8).

This guide gives citations and some annotations for sources on various aspects of medical education. Following a chapter that identifies bibliographies, dictionaries, and directories, there are topical chapters on the history of medicine, medical school admissions, medical education, health policy, women's medical education, hospitals, and biographical sources. Appendixes list professional health organizations and medical schools. There are author, title, and subject indexes.

1615.	Goldstein, Doris Mueller. **Bioethics: A Guide to Information Sources.** Detroit: Gale, 1982. 366p. (Health Affairs Information Guide Series, vol. 8).

1616.	**Bibliography of Bioethics.** Washington, D.C.: Georgetown University, Kennedy Institute of Ethics, 1975- . Annual.

These two sources provide guidance in locating information on the moral, ethical, and legal aspects of the medical and biological sciences. Topics such as euthanasia, abortion, genetic intervention, and human experimentation are of considerable interest to both specialists and nonspecialists. Many types of users, from the freshman doing a rhetoric paper on euthanasia to the researcher seeking scholarly discussions of newly emerging issues, will find these sources helpful. Goldstein's guide emphasizes publications appearing during the 1970s. It is in three parts: organizations, programs, collections; general sources of information (e.g., periodicals, dictionaries); and topical sources (e.g., abortion, genetic intervention). Entries are annotated and there is an index. The *Bibliography of Bioethics* can be used to update Goldstein's guide. Its coverage includes journals, books, legal documents, reports, conference proceedings, newspapers, and audiovisual materials. Entries are arranged by subject, with author and title indexes. There is also a list of journals cited. *Bibliography of Bioethics* can be machine searched as the BIOETHICSLINE database back to 1975 through the National Library of Medicine.

1617.	**Bibliography of the History of Medicine.** Bethesda, Md.: National Library of Medicine, 1965- . Annual with 5-year cumulations.

1618.	**Current Work in the History of Medicine.** London: Wellcome Institute for the History of Medicine, 1954- . Quarterly.

Both these bibliographies cover the international journal and monographic literature on the history of medicine. The *Bibliography of the History of Medicine* has both a biographical and a subject section, and an author index. It can be machine searched as the HISTLINE database back to 1970 through the National Library of Medicine. *Current Work in the History of Medicine* has a topical arrangement with an author index. It does not cumulate, but its quarterly issues can provide more timely indexing than the *Bibliography of the History of Medicine,* which appears annually.

DICTIONARIES, ENCYCLOPEDIAS

Sources explaining terminology are essential for reference work in the medical sciences. This chapter emphasizes general medical dictionaries, but a few topical dictionaries are also cited. Many other dictionaries can be identified by using the guides to the literature (e.g., entries 1587-89). Medical encyclopedias are produced for the nonspecialist; they are not an important category of reference tool for the specialist.

1619.   **Blakiston's Gould Medical Dictionary.** 4th ed. New York: McGraw-Hill, 1979. 1632p.

1620.   **Dorland's Illustrated Medical Dictionary.** 26th ed. Philadelphia: Saunders, 1981. 1485p.

1621.   **Stedman's Medical Dictionary.** 24th ed. Baltimore: Williams & Wilkins, 1982. 1678p.

These three dictionaries are all authoritative and comprehensive. Although many terms are common to all three, each contains some terms not defined in the others. Unlike many scientific and technical dictionaries, these dictionaries do give pronunciation and derivation in addition to definition of terms. Each has some special features. *Blakiston's Gould Medical Dictionary* has anatomical plates and an appendix of anatomical tables of arteries, bones, muscles, nerves, joints and ligaments, and veins. *Dorland's Illustrated Medical Dictionary* also has plates and tables, which can be located through an index. It provides a thorough discussion of the fundamentals of medical etymology. *Stedman's Medical Dictionary* includes a number of appendixes such as information on blood groups, weights and measures, laboratory analyses, and terms used in writing prescriptions. There is a root word list explaining the meaning of Greek and Latin roots commonly used in the formation of medical terms. Both *Dorland's* and *Stedman's* group related terms under a main entry. In *Stedman's* these subentries can be located through an index, which is included as one of the appendixes.

1622.   Dox, Ida, Biagio John Melloni, and Gilbert M. Eisner. **Melloni's Illustrated Medical Dictionary.** 2d ed. Baltimore: Williams & Wilkins, 1985. 533p.

1623.   **Taber's Cyclopedic Medical Dictionary.** 15th ed. Edited by Clayton L. Thomas. Philadelphia: F. A. Davis, 1985. 2170p.

1624.   **Urdang Dictionary of Current Medical Terms for Health Science Professionals.** New York: Wiley, 1981. 455p.

Although not as comprehensive as the three dictionaries described above, these three medical dictionaries are likely to prove especially useful to students and nonspecialists for the terms which they do include. Those with limited training in the medical sciences may find the definitions given in these sources to be more understandable. *Melloni's Illustrated Medical Dictionary* is notable for its extensive use of illustrations. It also has tables of anatomic terms and explanations of prefixes and suffixes used in forming medical terms. The appendixes in *Taber's Cyclopedic Medical Dictionary* contain information like that found in handbooks (e.g., units of measurement, normal reference laboratory values, tables of anatomical parts, drug interactions, and medical emergencies). It includes directories of burn centers and poison control centers, and a section translating patient examination questions and statements into Spanish, Italian, French, and German. The *Urdang Dictionary of Current Medical Terms for Health Science Professionals* gives basic definitions supplemented by detailed explanations if required. Illustrations include line drawings and color transparencies of the human body.

1625. Hamilton, Betty, and Barbara Guidos. **MASA: Medical Acronyms, Symbols, and Abbreviations.** New York: Neal-Schuman, 1984. 186p.

Although standard medical dictionaries do include some entries for abbreviations and acronyms, there is a need for supplementary dictionaries to interpret the acronyms, symbols, and abbreviations that readers of medical literature encounter. This source has more than 20,000 entries explaining acronyms, symbols, and abbreviations drawn from medicine and related fields.

1626. **Mosby's Medical & Nursing Dictionary.** Edited by Laurence Urdang and Helen Harding Swallow. St. Louis: Mosby, 1983. 1476p.

1627. **McGraw-Hill Nursing Dictionary.** New York: McGraw-Hill, 1979. 1008p. plus appendixes, 203p.

Both of these dictionaries are intended for use by nurses and nursing students. *Mosby's Medical & Nursing Dictionary* has detailed definitions, many illustrations and tables, a color atlas of human anatomy, and numerous appendixes (e.g., units of measurement, prefixes and suffixes, laboratory values, nutritional information, and directories of associations, burn centers, and poison control centers). *McGraw-Hill Nursing Dictionary* also has several appendixes, including anatomic tables, communicable and infectious diseases, laboratory values, dietary tables, lists of nursing organizations and poison control centers, and a language interpreter.

1628. Jablonski, Stanley. **Illustrated Dictionary of Dentistry.** Philadelphia: Saunders, 1982. 919p.

This dictionary can be consulted for definition, pronunciation, and etymology of terms in dentistry. It has illustrations and tables, as well as appendices describing the American Dental Association and the Canadian Dental Association and listing dental schools, dental hygiene programs, and dental assisting programs in the United States and Canada.

1629. Campbell, Robert J. **Psychiatric Dictionary.** 5th ed. New York: Oxford University Press, 1981. 693p.

This dictionary gives pronunciation and definition of terms in psychiatry and psychoanalysis, including some biographical entries. Many definitions are quite detailed, with quotations illustrating usage and references to sources of terms.

1630. Miller, Benjamin F., and Claire Brackman Keane. **Encyclopedia and Dictionary of Medicine, Nursing, and Allied Health.** 3d ed. Philadelphia: Saunders, 1983. 1270p.

Because it is an encyclopedic dictionary, this source may be more useful to the nonspecialist than those medical dictionaries which give briefer definitions. Entries include pronunciation and there are illustrations, tables, and plates. The appendixes cover weights and measures, symbols, sources of patient education materials, laboratory reference values, and addresses of voluntary health and welfare agencies.

1631. **Encyclopedia of Bioethics.** Edited by Warren T. Reich. 4 vols. New York: Free Press, 1978.

Intended for both general readers and professionals, this encyclopedia has 315 articles on various ethical and legal problems in the medical and biological sciences (e.g., abortion, organ transplantation, gene therapy). Articles deal with basic concepts and principles, ethical theories, religious traditions, and historical perspectives. A systematic classification of the articles provides an overview of the encyclopedia's contents. Articles present balanced discussions and include bibliographies to lead the reader to additional treatments of the topics. The appendix gives the text of various medical-ethical codes, and the set has an index.

DIRECTORIES

1632. **Medical and Health Information Directory.** 2d ed. Edited by Anthony T. Kruzas. Detroit: Gale, 1980. 835p.

This directory brings together diverse types of information sources, with listings for state, national, and international associations, state and federal government agencies, U.S. and foreign medical schools, hospitals, health care delivery agencies, grant-award sources, libraries and information centers, and consulting organizations, as well as journals, newsletters, review serials, abstracting services, computerized databases, audiovisual services, and publishers. Entries are arranged in 36 sections, some of which have their own indexes, but there is no overall index for the entire volume.

1633. **Encyclopedia of Medical Organizations and Agencies.** Edited by Anthony T. Kruzas. Detroit: Gale, 1983. 768p.

1634. **Health Services Directory.** Edited by Anthony T. Kruzas. Detroit: Gale, 1981. 620p.

1635. **Health Organizations of the United States, Canada, and the World: A Directory of Voluntary Associations, Professional Societies and Other Groups Concerned with Health and Related Fields.** 5th ed. Edited by Paul Wasserman and Marek Kaszubski. Detroit: Gale, 1981. 411p.

These three directories all provide at least name and address data for organizations concerned with various aspects of the medical sciences. *Encyclopedia of Medical Organizations and Agencies* has organizations in 78 categories dealing with disease conditions, medical specialties, social health problems, and special aspects of general medicine. Within a subject chapter (e.g., aging, arthritis, surgery, vision), organizations are listed by type: national and international associations, foundations and funding agencies, state government, federal government, information and database services, research centers and institutes, and education and training. Indexes list organization names and subjects. *Health Services Directory* identifies clinics, centers, programs, and services in the United States for the treatment of major health and social problems such as alcoholism, burns, cancer, and sports injuries. The topical chapters begin with an explanation of arrangement and scope. Appendixes supplement the listings in the main body of the directory by identifying related medical and social service organizations as well as community information and referral services. The index includes both organization names and keywords. As the subtitle indicates, *Health Organizations of the United States, Canada, and the World* describes voluntary associations, professional societies, and other nongovernmental organizations. Entries include name, address, founding date, membership, purpose, finances, meetings, and publications. Entries are alphabetical by organization name with both keyword and subject indexes.

1636. **American Hospital Association Guide to the Health Care Field.** Chicago: American Hospital Association, 1972- . Annual.

This directory is a convenient source of names, addresses, and descriptive data for hospitals in the United States. The main section lists hospitals geographically by state and city, giving address, telephone, chief administrator, and codes denoting facilities, services, and governing structure. Brief statistical information, such as percent of occupancy and size of staff is also given. Additional sections list accredited long-term care facilities, headquarters of multihospital systems, American Hospital Association members, and health organizations and agencies. There is a detailed index.

1637.   **Research Programs in the Medical Sciences.** Edited by Jaques Cattell Press. New York: Bowker, 1980. 578p.

1638.   **Medical Research Centres: A World Directory of Organizations and Programmes.** 6th ed. Edited by Leslie T. Morton and Jean F. Hall. 2 vols. Harlow, Essex, England: Longman, 1983.

These two directories can be consulted for profiles of organizations conducting research in the medical sciences. *Research Programs in the Medical Sciences* covers all types of organizations in the United States and Canada (companies, government agencies, universities, nonprofit organizations) with research programs in medicine, dentistry, nursing, pharmacy, veterinary medicine, and health care. Arrangement is by organization name with address, telephone, staffing information, and a description of current research. There are three indexes: geographic, personnel, and subject. *Medical Research Centres* also covers all types of organizations in about one hundred countries. Organization is by country, with entries giving organization name, address, telephone, director of research, staff, scope of activities, and publications. Indexes list titles of establishments and subjects.

HANDBOOKS

The handbook literature of the medical sciences is extensive. Important categories include handbooks related to classification and diagnosis of diseases, drug information sources, and manuals for dealing with medical emergencies. The guides to the literature of the medical sciences should be consulted for descriptions of the many handbooks available. In particular, two guides to drug information (entries 1608-09) are available. in addition, Powell's bibliography of handbooks (entry 1265) includes many medical titles. This chapter includes two examples of handbooks, one for physicians and one for nurses.

1639.   **Merck Manual of Diagnosis and Therapy.** 14th ed. Edited by Robert Berkow. Rahway, N.J.: Merck, 1982. 2578p.

This manual has 24 chapters describing approaches to diagnosing and treating particular categories of disease (e.g., cardiovascular disorders, pulmonary disorders). For each disease the entry includes a description, etiology, symptoms, diagnosis, and treatment. There is also a section on drugs and an index.

1640.   **The Handbook of Nursing.** Edited by Jeanne Howe, Elizabeth J. Dickason, Dorothy A. Jones, Martha J. Snider, and Margaret E. Armstrong. New York: Wiley, 1984. 1756p.

The 50 chapters in this source cover six broad areas of nursing: parents and infants, children and adolescents, adults, mental health problems, the elderly, and emergencies. The discussions are structured in terms of the nursing process, considering prevention, assessment, actual or potential nursing diagnoses, expected outcomes, interventions, and evaluation. Each chapter has an annotated bibliography. Appendixes provide data for ready reference, such as conversion tables, laboratory values, nutritional information, and growth charts. There is also an index.

BIOGRAPHY

1641. **American Medical Directory.** 29th ed. 4 vols. Chicago: American Medical Association, 1985.

1642. **Directory of Medical Specialists.** 22d ed. 3 vols. Chicago: Marquis Who's Who, 1985.

1643. **American Dental Directory.** Chicago: American Dental Association, 1985. 1532p.

For the library user seeking information on physicians and dentists in the United States, these directories provide the most comprehensive coverage. *American Medical Directory* has entries for all physicians in the United States and its possessions. An alphabetical listing of physicians indicates their city and state of residence. The geographic section must then be consulted to find address, year of license, and coded information on education, specialty board, and type of practice. *Directory of Medical Specialists* is more limited as it covers only those physicians who are certified by at least 1 of 23 specialty boards (e.g., allergy and immunology, dermatology, family practice). Profiles are arranged geographically within specialty board and include date of birth, education, career history, date of certification, memberships, teaching positions, hospital affiliations, type of practice, office address, and telephone. There is a name index. *American Dental Directory* attempts to list all U.S. dentists. Like the *American Medical Directory*, an alphabetical listing of dentists gives city and state, which provides access to the geographical listing where full address and brief biographical information (year of birth, dental school and year of graduation, type of practice) are given. Supplementary sections describe the American Dental Association and list national dental organizations, dental meetings, and dental boards.

1644. **Who's Who in Health Care.** 2d ed. Rockville, Md.: Aspen Systems, 1981. 612p.

1645. **International Medical Who's Who: A Biographical Guide in the Biomedical Sciences.** 2d ed. 2 vols. Harlow, Essex, England: Longman, 1985.

Who's Who in Health Care includes more than 7,000 people who have positions of responsibility and have made contributions in professional schools, voluntary associations, corporations, research institutes, or hospitals. Entries include date and place of birth, occupation, personal data, education, career, memberships, awards, publications, and address. There are professional and geographic indexes. *International Medical Who's Who* includes about 12,000 individuals in about 100 countries working in research centers, university departments, institutes, industry, or medical associations. Entries are arranged in alphabetical order and include name, year of birth, education, work experience, society memberships, major publications, research interests, telephone, and address. The second part lists experts in particular subject areas in each of the countries represented by one or more biographees.

1646. **Dictionary of American Medical Biography.** Edited by Martin Kaufman, Stuart Galishoff, and Todd L. Savitt. 2 vols. Westport, Conn.: Greenwood, 1984.

This biographical dictionary covers more than five hundred individuals who have had an impact on health care in the United States from the colonial period through 1976. Both physicians and related specialties (e.g., biochemists, medical educators, hospital administrators) are included. Each entry gives dates, parentage, education, career, and contributions. Both major writings and biographical works are identified. The appendix provides several helpful lists, arranging biographees by date and place of birth, specialty or occupation, state in which prominent, medical college or graduate-level college. There is a separate list of female biographees, and the volumes have an index.

30

COMPUTER SCIENCE

The widespread availability of personal computers on many campuses has transformed computer science from a specialized field of study to one which interests, at least in part, many students and faculty. The user of computers is concerned with both hardware and software as tools for specific applications. Students and faculty in computer science may share this interest in applications, but they also investigate more specialized topics such as the mathematics of computing, the theory of computing, and the methods and techniques of the discipline. In addition, they may emphasize computer engineering, i.e., the design of hardware. Because computers and other devices are frequently interconnected by tele-communications lines to form networks, this chapter encompasses telecommunications as well as computer science and engineering.

The explosion of interest in computers and computing has led to a proliferation of publications. New reference sources are appearing at a rapid rate, and only some representative titles can be cited here. They reflect the types of information commonly sought by users of computers: definitions of terms, interpretations of acronyms, descriptions of available hardware and software, addresses of producers and distributors of hardware and software, and citations to books and journals on a topic of interest. If the university library maintains a good reference collection in computer science, it is likely to attract users from the community as well. In addition to asking questions common to other computer users, faculty and graduate students in computer science are likely to seek help in searching the technical literature, tracking down specialized reports and conference proceedings, and locating explanations of technical concepts. Because the computer science literature obsolesces rapidly, it is important to acquire bibliographic and other reference tools that attempt to keep up-to-date. Thus, most of the titles described in this chapter have quite recent imprint dates.

GUIDES, BIBLIOGRAPHIES, INDEXES

1647.   Hildebrandt, Darlene Myers. **Computing Information Directory.** Federal Way, Wash.:
        Pedaro, 1985. 557p.

1648.   Carter, Ciel. **Guide to Reference Sources in the Computer Sciences.** New York:
        Macmillan, 1974. 237p.

Each chapter in *Computing Information Directory* is devoted to a particular type of
information source: computer journals; university computer center newsletters; computer
books; technical reports; indexing and abstracting serials; software resources; review
resources; hardware resources; dictionaries, directories, and handbooks; and programming
languages. Each chapter contains an introductory discussion and subject index as well as
complete bibliographic data for all entries listed. The final chapter contains names and
addresses of the more than 1,200 publishers cited in the book. Appendixes provide a list of
medical users' groups and a master index. Although much of the information in *Guide to
Reference Sources in the Computer Sciences* is dated, it is still useful for its detailed
descriptions of organizations and their publishing programs. Coverage is international and
arrangement is by type of source. Chapters cover professional organizations, research and
information centers, bibliographies and bibliographic aids, conference literature,
encyclopedias, vocabulary, directories and catalogs, handbooks and manuals, journals, and
the computer industry. There is a list of acronyms of organizations, a directory of publishers,
and an index of titles and organizations.

1649.   **Computer Publishers & Publications: An International Directory and Yearbook.** New
        Rochelle, N.Y.: Communications Trends, 1984. 379p.

1650.   **Computers and Information Processing World Index.** Edited by Suzan Deighton, John
        Gurnsey, and Janet Tomlinson. Phoenix: Oryx Press, 1984. 616p.

1651.   **Computer Books and Serials in Print.** New York: Bowker, 1984. 551p.

These three guides all cover the current book and journal literature in computer science, but
each has somewhat different features. *Computer Publishers & Publications* provides a
directory of computer book publishers with examples of representative book titles which
each has issued. This section has an index to book publishers by type, an index to book
publishers by specific machines covered, and a geographical index. There is a section with
information on over six hundred English-language computer periodicals with several
indexes: group publishers, periodicals by type (consumer, educational, scholarly,
trade/professional), looseleaf services and newsletters, periodicals by specific machines
covered, geographical, and periodicals by frequency. Additional sections include
introductory material giving statistics on computer publishing, a bookseller's guide to
computer book selection, and a librarian's guide to computer book and periodical selection.
There is a title index for books listed in the section on computer book publishers and a
personnel index to publishers, editors, marketing managers, and advertising sales managers
mentioned in entries for book publishers and periodicals. *Computers and Information
Processing World Index* identifies both organizations and publications concerned with
computing. The first section arranges organizations by country, giving name, address,
telephone, and brief descriptive information for research centers, libraries, user groups,
trade associations, manufacturers, and professional associations. The next three sections
cover publications: reference works, texts and major journals devoted to particular
applications areas, and journals arranged by country of publication. The last two sections
list standards bodies and publisher addresses. There is an index for the volume. *Computer
Books and Serials in Print* gives bibliographic data for the books and serials listed. Book
citations appear in subject, author, and title sections, while serials are arranged by both

subject and title. There is a subject area directory providing a topical outline of the subject headings used. A directory of publishers and distributors is also included.

1652. **Computer and Control Abstracts.** Hitchin, Hertfordshire, England: INSPEC, Institution of Electrical Engineers, 1966- . Monthly with semiannual cumulation of indexes.

1653. **Computer and Information Systems Abstracts Journal.** Bethesda, Md.: Cambridge Scientific Abstracts, 1962- . Monthly with semiannual cumulation of indexes.

1654. **Computing Reviews.** New York: Association for Computing Machinery, 1960- . Monthly with annual cumulation of index.

Computer and Control Abstracts is the most comprehensive abstracting service in computer science, covering the journal, book, conference, and report literature. Each issue has an author index, a bibliography index (to articles containing a significant list of references or a bibliography), a book index, a conference index (to conference papers which are abstracted), and a corporate author index. In addition, there is a subject guide to the classified arrangement in which abstracts appear. Issue indexes cumulate semiannually, and a detailed subject index is also produced semiannually. All aspects of hardware, software, and applications are covered. *Computer and Control Abstracts* can be machine searched as part of the INSPEC database. Coverage goes back to 1969 on DIALOG, to 1970 on BRS, and to 1977 on SDC. When doing a comprehensive literature search, *Computer and Information Systems Abstracts Journal* can also be consulted. It covers all types of publications and arranges abstracts in five broad subject sections: computer software, computer applications, computer mathematics, computer electronics, and general. There are author, subject, and acronym indexes that cumulate semiannually. Although *Computing Reviews* has more limited coverage than the two abstracting services already described, it is of interest for its critical reviews of books, journal articles, and conference papers. Reviews vary in length from a paragraph to more than a page and are divided into two sections: books and proceedings, and nonbook literature. Within each section there is a topical arrangement covering general literature, hardware, computer systems organization, software, data, theory of computation, mathematics of computing, information systems, computing methodologies, computer applications, and computing milieux. The author indexes from each issue are cumulated annually.

1655. **Current Papers on Computers and Control.** Hitchin, Hertfordshire, England: INSPEC, Institution of Electrical Engineers, 1966- . Monthly.

Current Papers on Computers and Control is a companion publication to *Computer and Control Abstracts* (entry 1652) with citations in the same classified arrangement. Publications cited here are later abstracted in *Computer and Control Abstracts,* so this publication is useful for current awareness browsing in the interim.

1656. **ABI/SELECTS: The Annotated Bibliography of Computer Periodicals.** Louisville, Ky.: Data Courier, 1983. 576p. Paper.

This bibliography provides detailed descriptions of 533 periodicals arranged in six sections: "Personal Computing," "Systems and Software Specific," "Data Processing," "Data Communications & Teletext," "Office Automation," and "Trade and Application Specific." *ABI/SELECTS* is helpful in answering questions about the target audience, content, and special features of many computer science periodicals. It has an index to titles and publishers.

DICTIONARIES, ENCYCLOPEDIAS

1657.   Rosenberg, Jerry M. **Dictionary of Computers, Data Processing, and Telecommunications.** New York: Wiley, 1984. 614p.

1658.   Edmunds, Robert A. **The Prentice-Hall Standard Glossary of Computer Terminology.** Englewood Cliffs, N.J.: Prentice-Hall, 1985. 489p.

1659.   **McGraw-Hill Dictionary of Electronics and Computer Technology.** Edited by Sybil P. Parker. New York: McGraw-Hill, 1984. 582p.

These three are among the newest and most comprehensive dictionaries covering computer science terminology. As the title indicates, *Dictionary of Computers, Data Processing, and Telecommunications* includes coverage of both computer science and telecommunications. It has more than 10,000 entries for both general and more specialized terms to meet the needs of a range of users. Where definitions are drawn from other sources, the sources are identified. An appendix gives French and Spanish equivalents for terms defined. *The Prentice-Hall Standard Glossary of Computer Terminology* has a nontechnical orientation. Definitions include detailed explanations where required, and hierarchical relationships between terms are indicated. There are some entries for product names, abbreviations, and acronyms. The *McGraw-Hill Dictionary of Electronics and Computer Technology* has definitions for 10,000 terms drawn from the third edition of the parent work (entry 1242). Coverage includes computer science, electronics, and related disciplines.

1660.   Burton, Philip E. **A Dictionary of Minicomputing and Microcomputing.** New York: Garland STPM Press, 1982. 347p.

1661.   Maynard, Jeff. **Dictionary of Data Processing.** 2d ed. London: Butterworths, 1981. 275p.

1662.   Sippl, Charles J., and Roger J. Sippl. **Computer Dictionary.** 3d ed. Indianapolis, Ind.: Howard W. Sams, 1980. 624p. Paper.

All three of these dictionaries are well suited for use by students and other computer users who lack a technical background. *A Dictionary of Minicomputing and Microcomputing* supplements the major alphabetical list of terms and definitions with a number of topical glossaries covering the terminology of structured programming, Pascal, magnetic bubble memory technology, printers, automatic control, multiprocessing, data communications, and magnetic recording and storage technology. There are some illustrations and a list of references. *Dictionary of Data Processing* has brief definitions for the terms included as well as several appendixes (a list of common acronyms and abbreviations, codes, flowchart symbols, standards relating to data processing, and logic symbols). *Computer Dictionary* includes illustrations for some terms and emphasizes terms likely to be sought by the student and computer hobbyist.

1663.   **Encyclopedia of Computer Science and Engineering.** 2d ed. Edited by Anthony Ralston and Edwin D. Reilly, Jr. New York: Van Nostrand, Reinhold, 1983. 1664p.

1664.   **Encyclopedia of Computer Science and Technology.** 16 vols. New York: Marcel Dekker, 1975-80.

1665.   **McGraw-Hill Encyclopedia of Electronics and Computers.** Edited by Sybil P. Parker. New York: McGraw-Hill, 1984. 964p.

When more than a definition is required, one or more of these encyclopedias can be consulted for explanations of many topics in computer science. The *Encyclopedia of Computer Science and Engineering* is intended for use by nonspecialists as well as specialists outside their areas of expertise. It has 550 signed articles, many with illustrations and bibliographies. The volume begins with a classified listing of articles in the following categories: hardware, computer systems, information and data, software, mathematics of computing, theory of computing, methodologies, applications, and computing milieux. Related entries are connected by cross-references and there is a detailed index. There are a number of useful appendixes, e.g., abbreviations and acronyms, a list of computer science and engineering research journals, a list of computer science departments offering the Ph.D. in the United States and Canada, identification of key high level languages, and a glossary of computer terms in five languages (English, French, German, Russian, Spanish). If a more extended discussion is required, the *Encyclopedia of Computer Science and Technology* can be consulted. It has lengthy, well-documented articles on computer technology and its applications. The index volume for the set has author and subject entries. Given its publication date, the set can provide background information but more recent sources must be consulted for current developments. The *McGraw-Hill Encyclopedia of Electronics and Computers* is drawn to a large extent from the fifth edition of the parent work (entry 1244), but it does include some new material as well as some revisions of articles. Its 477 articles cover electronics and applications of electronic devices with particular emphasis on computer science and engineering. Articles have bibliographies and illustrations, and the volume has a detailed index.

1666.   Longley, Dennis, and Michael Shain. **Dictionary of Information Technology.** 2d ed. London: Macmillan, 1985. 382p.

1667.   Meadows, A. J., M. Gordon, and A. Singleton. **Dictionary of Computing and New Information Technology.** 2d ed. London: Kogan Page, 1984. 229p.

1668.   Stokes, Adrian V. **Concise Encyclopedia of Information Technology.** Englewood Cliffs, N.J.: Prentice-Hall, 1983. 271p.

Computers are one form of information technology, but there are others such as videotex, cable television, satellite communications, and word processing. Each has its own terminology, with new words being coined at a rapid rate. The three dictionaries noted here go beyond the scope of dictionaries emphasizing only computer terminology, and include terms for other forms of information technology as well. *Dictionary of Information Technology* emphasizes terminology associated with new technologies and includes 11 essays on major concepts, such as videotex and word processing. There are illustrations and cross-references. The new edition of the *Dictionary of Computing and New Information Technology* includes more computing terms, but also covers the many related technologies which make up information technology. It has extended discussions of a few important terms and some terms are illustrated. The *Concise Encyclopedia of Information Technology* is actually a dictionary, similar in scope to *Dictionary of Computing and New Information Technology.* In appendixes there are a list of acronyms and abbreviations and illustrations of the ASCII and EBCDIC character sets.

1669.   Aries, S. J. **Dictionary of Telecommunications.** London: Butterworths, 1983. 329p.

1670.   Graham, John. **Facts on File Dictionary of Telecommunications.** New York: Facts on File, 1983. 199p.

1671.   Weik, Martin H. **Communications Standard Dictionary.** New York: Van Nostrand, Reinhold, 1983. 1045p.

When the term sought is more closely associated with telecommunications than computer science, any of these dictionaries can be consulted. They are similar in scope, providing definitions and explanations of terms included. *Dictionary of Telecommunications* has an appendix of common abbreviations and *Facts on File Dictionary of Telecommunications* has appendixes with illustrations of various network configurations, the electromagnetic spectrum, and other information similar to that found in handbooks. As the title suggests, definitions given in *Communications Standard Dictionary* are drawn from standards when possible.

1672.   Gordon, M., A. Singleton, and C. Rickards. **Dictionary of New Information Technology Acronyms.** London: Kogan Page, 1984. 217p.

1673.   Wrathall, Claude P. **Computer Acronyms, Abbreviations, Etc.** New York: Petrocelli Books, 1981. 483p.

Although many of the computer science dictionaries include several entries for acronyms and abbreviations, it is convenient to have dictionaries devoted exclusively to interpreting this type of term. *Dictionary of New Information Technology Acronyms* is an alphabetical listing of more than eight thousand abbreviations covering all areas of information technology. Each term is expanded, with an annotation where necessary. *Computer Acronyms, Abbreviations, Etc.* has more than 10,000 entries including many commonly used acronyms, abbreviations, and names from the computer and communication fields. There is an appendix listing additional sources of information such as dictionaries and encyclopedias, directories, and standards.

DIRECTORIES

1674.   **Bowker's 1985 Complete Sourcebook of Personal Computing.** New York: Bowker, 1984. 1050p. Paper.

1675.   **Microcomputer Marketplace.** New York: Bowker, 1985. 820p. Paper.

Both of these directories will be heavily used to identify available hardware and software products and their producers. *Bowker's 1985 Complete Sourcebook of Personal Computing* has major sections describing hardware and software as well as sections on books, magazines, consumer databases, clubs and user groups, wholesalers and distributors, and mail order houses. The section on hardware has a number of subdivisions: IBM compatible computers, portable computers, hardware review citations, hardware producers, peripheral hardware products, peripheral hardware review citations, and peripheral hardware producers. The software section includes lists of software review citations and software producers, and the book section lists book review citations and book publishers. In addition, there is an introductory discussion of personal computing, a glossary, and an index. *Microcomputer Marketplace* identifies the many firms which produce products to be used with microcomputers as well as the microcomputers themselves. A section on software publishers gives profiles of companies who publish software. Indexes for this section provide many different approaches: microcomputer systems, operating systems, business/ professional applications, utility applications, educational applications, and consumer applications. There are also directories of distributors, wholesalers and mail order houses, manufacturers of microcomputer systems, peripheral manufacturers, and manufacturers of supplies. The remaining sections cover periodicals, associations, special services, and a calendar of meetings and exhibits. The book includes a telephone directory with entries for the organizations and personnel profiled in the various sections.

1676. **The Software Catalog: Science and Engineering.** 2d ed. New York: Elsevier, 1985. 540p. Paper.

1677. Webster, Tony. **Microcomputer Buyer's Guide.** 3d ed. New York: McGraw-Hill, 1984. 343p. Paper.

Some directories deal only with hardware or with software. The two titles given here are examples of the many available. *The Software Catalog: Science and Engineering* describes software suitable for various science and engineering applications and available for purchase. Entries are arranged by International Standard Program Number and describe key characteristics of the software package (e.g., the vendor, specific configuration requirements, distribution medium, minimum memory, purchase price, date of release). There are six indexes to the entries: computer system, operating system, programming language, microprocessor, subject and application, and keyword and program name. The entries are included in *Menu*™ – *The International Software Database* which can be machine searched through DIALOG. Although *Microcomputer Buyer's Guide* identifies a few microcomputer software packages (popular operating systems and applications), the emphasis is on microcomputers. Arrangement is by company, with descriptions of about five hundred systems available from more than 180 companies. An appendix gives name, address, and telephone of the manufacturers together with pricing information for their systems.

1678. **Telecommunications Systems and Services Directory.** 2d ed. Edited by John Schmittroth, Jr. and Martin Connors. Detroit: Gale, 1985. 975p.

This directory covers both new and established telecommunications systems and services, including voice and data communications, teleconferencing, electronic mail, cable television, transactional services, telegram, telex, facsimile, satellite services, and videotex and teletext. Each entry provides detailed information about the system or service, noting name, address, telephone, date founded, head, related organizations, function or service type, number of staff, specific applications, means of access, geographic area served, rate structure, documentation, availability, key features, planned new services, and a contact point. The master index for names, acronyms, and keywords is supplemented by indexes for function/service, geographic region, and personal name.

HANDBOOKS

1679. **McGraw-Hill Computer Handbook.** Edited by Harry Helms. New York: McGraw-Hill, 1983. Various paging.

This handbook has 30 chapters covering the workings of computers, peripherals, and software. Many of the chapters are drawn from other texts published by McGraw-Hill. They can be read by users with little prior knowledge of computer science to learn the basics of such topics as computer graphics, voice recognition, timesharing, and high-level programming languages. There is also a glossary and an index for specific subject access.

31

ENGINEERING

Engineering may be viewed as the application of science toward useful ends. There are a number of major divisions within engineering. Chemical engineering has already been considered together with chemistry in chapter 25. Aerospace englneering pertains to the design and construction of aircraft and space vehicles. Civil engineering deals with the design, construction and maintenance of structures and facilities, as, for example, in industry, transportation, and control of water. Industrial engineering seeks to apply engineering principles to insure maintenance of high productivity at optimum cost in industrial enterprises. Mechanical engineering is concerned with the generation, transport, and utilization of heat and mechanical power. Electrical engineering includes electrical power and communications. Other subdivisions, such as mining engineering, agricultural engineering, and ceramic engineering, may also be represented as separate academic departments within a college of engineering.

Each field of engineering has its own core literature, but all share an emphasis on certain types of materials. Numerous handbooks attempt to assemble data and techniques relevant to particular specialties. These usually have multiple authors, with detailed indexes to allow quick location of specific facts, and need to be updated regularly to keep pace with new developments and practices. Dictionaries of technical terms are also widely used, as are directories of sources of products and materials. Specialized indexing and abstracting services facilitate searching of the periodical and conference literature.

In addition to the types of information sources already identified in this book, patents and standards make up an important part of the engineering literature. A patent protects the inventor's right to prohibit others from making, using, or selling his invention for a fixed period of time. The patent document is the official record of the invention as registered in a particular country; it includes both a drawing (the graphic description of the invention) and a specification (its written description). Patent searching is undertaken to determine whether an idea can be patented, to obtain state-of-the-art information in a specific subject area, to find particular specifications and drawings, or to prepare a list of prior developments. Standards state how materials and products should be manufactured, measured, tested, or defined. There are dimensional standards, standards of performance or quality, materials standards, standards of testing, terminological standards, and codes of practice. Sources issuing standards include individual companies, trade associations and technical societies, government departments, national standardizing bodies, and international standards organizations. Standards will often be sought when engineers are involved in design projects. This chapter includes some guides to patents and standards, but does not treat the reference literature related to patents and standards in depth. Only large university libraries are likely to maintain extensive collections of patents and standards, but smaller libraries may have finding tools such as indexes and directories.

Reference needs of engineering students and faculty will vary depending on their area of specialization and their type of work. The research engineer may need information from mathematics and the physical sciences to support theoretical work, while the design engineer needs to have information about materials and devices so as to design solutions to practical engineering problems. In addition to relying on basic scientific knowledge, research and teaching in engineering draw on sources of physical data, product characteristics, computational formulas, design methods, and standards. A reference department serving a college of engineering needs a wide range of handbooks, dictionaries, directories, and indexing and abstracting services. Bibliographic verification is often required to identify complete and accurate citations for technical reports, conference papers, journal articles, and standards and patents. This chapter describes some general engineering sources together with representative titles from major divisions such as civil engineering and mechanical engineering.

GUIDES, BIBLIOGRAPHIES, INDEXES

1680. Mildren, K. W., ed. **Use of Engineering Literature.** London: Butterworths, 1976. 621p. (Information Sources for Research and Development).

1681. Mount, Ellis. **Guide to Basic Information Sources in Engineering.** New York: Wiley, 1976. 196p. (Information Resources Series).

These two guides differ in their arrangement, with *Use of Engineering Literature* including several chapters on specific subject divisions of engineering and *Guide to Basic Information Sources in Engineering* emphasizing types of materials. *Use of Engineering Literature* has chapters on the structure of the literature, classification and indexing in engineering, literature searching, and personal indexes as well as 9 chapters covering types of materials (e.g., patents, standards, product information, reports, standard reference sources) and 22 chapters on the literature of particular specialties (e.g., electronics, aeronautical and astronautical engineering, automotive engineering, highway traffic and transport engineering, structural engineering). Chapters have been prepared by different authors and are narrative in style, providing background and describing selected titles. There is an index for the volume. *Guide to Basic Information Sources in Engineering*, intended for use by engineering students and researchers, describes the features of each type of literature and gives selected examples. Its 28 chapters are divided into four parts: technical literature (what it is, where to find it), books (including reference books), periodicals and technical reports (including abstracting and indexing services), and other sources (such as conferences, patents and trademarks, dissertations, newspapers, translations). There is an index to authors, titles, and subjects.

1682. Schenk, Margaret T., and James K. Webster. **What Every Engineer Should Know About Engineering Information Resources.** New York: Marcel Dekker, 1984. 216p.

Although more selective than the guides described above, *What Every Engineer Should Know About Engineering Information Resources* is valuable for its inclusion of databases and recently published sources. As the title suggests, it is intended for the practicing engineer and engineering student. It has 25 chapters, 24 giving descriptions and examples of materials (e.g., tables, standards and specifications, patents, dictionaries) and the final chapter identifying libraries, information centers, and information brokers. There are an appendix of publishers' addresses and an index.

1683.   Carr, Fred K. **Searching Patent Documents, for Patentability and Information.** Chapel Hill, N.C.: Patent Information, 1982. 258p.

1684.   Kase, Francis J. **Foreign Patents: A Guide to Official Patent Literature.** Dobbs Ferry, N.Y.: Oceana, 1972. 358p.

1685.   Struglia, Erasmus J. **Standards and Specifications Information Sources: A Guide to Literature and to Public and Private Agencies Concerned with Technological Uniformities.** Detroit: Gale, 1965. 187p. (Management Information Guide, no. 6).

Although the general guides to the engineering literature include discussion of patents and standards as information sources, it is useful to have guides which treat these specialized sources in more depth. Carr's book on patents explains the patent document as an information source and describes procedures for obtaining information about U.S and foreign patents. Patent classification systems are also outlined. Kase's book on the foreign patent literature is arranged alphabetically by country. Each entry gives the name and address of the country's patent office and descriptions of official patent documents, such as patent specifications and patent journals. Struglia's book on standards has seven sections: general sources and directories, bibliographies and indexes to periodicals, catalogs and indexes, government sources, associations and societies, international standardization, and periodicals. Entries are annotated, and there are author-title and subject indexes.

1686.   **Engineering Index.** New York: Engineering Information, 1884- . Monthly with annual cumulation.

1687.   **Current Technology Index.** London: Library Association, 1962- . Monthly with annual cumulation.

Although *Applied Science and Technology Index* (entry 1222) may provide adequate coverage for searches of the literature by undergraduates, more comprehensive indexes are necessary for graduate students and faculty. *Engineering Index* is actually an abstracting service covering all aspects of engineering. It is international in scope and includes citations for reports, monographs, conference proceedings, and standards as well as journal articles. Each abstract appears under a single subject heading, with cross-references to subject headings covering related material. Each issue also has an author index. Both the subject section and author index are cumulated annually. The annual cumulation also includes an author affiliation index, leading to publications by individuals associated with particular organizations. *Engineering Index* can be machine searched as the COMPENDEX database back to 1970 through DIALOG and SDC, and back to 1976 through BRS. Engineering Information also publishes the EI ENGINEERING MEETINGS database, covering individual conference papers. It can be machine searched back to 1979 through DIALOG and SDC. *Current Technology Index,* titled *British Technology Index* until 1981, is much more limited in its coverage as it indexes only British technical periodicals. Citations are arranged under subject headings and there is an author index. The monthly issues cumulate annually.

1688.   **Current Contents: Engineering, Technology & Applied Sciences.** Philadelphia: Institute for Scientific Information, 1970- . Weekly.

Current Contents: Engineering, Technology & Applied Sciences can be used for current awareness in engineering. It appears weekly, reproducing the tables of contents of major journals arranged by broad topic areas such as aerospace, electric & electronic, environmental/civil, mechanics, and nuclear. The organization and possible uses of this section of *Current Contents* parallel those already described for *Current Contents: Physical, Chemical & Earth Sciences* (entry 1341).

1689. **International Aerospace Abstracts.** New York: American Institute of Aeronautics and Astronautics, 1961- . Semimonthly with annual cumulation of indexes.

1690. **Scientific and Technical Aerospace Reports.** Washington, D.C.: National Aeronautics and Space Administration, 1963- . Semimonthly with annual cumulation of indexes.

These two abstracting publications are similar in arrangement and complementary in coverage. Taken together, they give quite complete coverage of the aerospace literature. Both have abstracts arranged under the same broad subject categories. In addition to aeronautics and astronautics, subject coverage includes related topics in chemistry and materials, geosciences, life sciences, mathematics and computer sciences, physical sciences, and social sciences. *International Aerospace Abstracts* covers the published literature, such as journals, books, meeting papers, and translations. *Scientific and Technical Aerospace Reports* emphasizes report literature and also includes some patents, dissertations, and theses. Both have subject, personal author, and contract number indexes. *International Aerospace Abstracts* also has indexes for accession number and for meeting paper and report number, while *Scientific and Technical Aerospace Reports* has corporate author and report/accession number indexes. In both cases the indexes cumulate annually. *International Aerospace Abstracts* and *Scientific and Technical Aerospace Reports* can be machine searched as the AEROSPACE database back to 1984 through DIALOG.

1691. **Applied Mechanics Reviews.** New York: American Society of Mechanical Engineers, 1948- . Monthly with annual indexes.

1692. **International Civil Engineering Abstracts.** Dublin: CITIS, 1974- . Ten issues per year with annual cumulation of index.

As the titles suggest, *Applied Mechanics Reviews* and *International Civil Engineering Abstracts* cover the fields of mechanical engineering and civil engineering, respectively. *Applied Mechanics Reviews* provides coverage of the book and journal literature. The book review section is followed by abstracts of journal articles arranged under broad subject headings (e.g., foundations and basic methods, dynamics and vibration). Author and subject indexes appear annually. *International Civil Engineering Abstracts* covers more than three hundred journals. Abstracts are arranged in broad topic areas (e.g., bridges, buildings-materials-construction), and the subject index cumulates annually.

1693. **Electrical and Electronics Abstracts.** Hitchin, Hertfordshire, England: INSPEC, Institution of Electrical Engineers, 1898- . Monthly with semiannual cumulation of indexes.

1694. **Current Papers in Electrical and Electronics Engineering.** Hitchin, Hertfordshire, England: INSPEC, Institution of Electrical Engineers, 1964- . Monthly.

Electrical and Electronics Abstracts provides international coverage of the literature in electrical and electronics engineering, including journals, books, dissertations, reports, and conference proceedings. Abstracts appear in a classified arrangement and each issue has an author index, a bibliography index (to articles containing a significant list of references or a bibliography), a book index, a conference index (to conference papers which are abstracted), and a corporate author index. In addition, there is a subject guide to the classified arrangement. Issue indexes cumulate semiannually, and a detailed subject index is also produced semiannually. *Electrical and Electronics Abstracts* can be machine searched as part of the INSPEC database. Coverage goes back to 1969 on DIALOG, to 1970 on BRS, and to 1977 on SDC. *Current Papers in Electrical and Electronics Engineering* is a companion publication to *Electrical and Electronics Abstracts* with citations in the same classified arrangement. Publications cited here are later abstracted in *Electrical and Electronics Abstracts,* so *Current Papers in Electrical and Electronics Engineering* is useful for current awareness in the interim.

1695.   Balachandran, Sarojin. **Directory of Publishing Sources: The Researcher's Guide to Journals in Engineering and Technology.** New York: Wiley, 1982. 343p.

This guide is intended to help researchers identify the most appropriate journal in which to publish research results. Entries cover nearly three hundred journals published by professional associations and commercial firms. Each entry gives the publisher, scope and content, type of acceptable contribution, manuscript submission procedure, style guide, and data on how papers are handled for review (number of referees, review time, and acceptance rate). There is a subject index.

DICTIONARIES, ENCYCLOPEDIAS

1696.   **McGraw-Hill Dictionary of Engineering.** Edited by Sybil P. Parker. New York: McGraw-Hill, 1984. 659p.

1697.   **McGraw-Hill Encyclopedia of Engineering.** Edited by Sybil P. Parker. New York: McGraw-Hill, 1983. 1264p.

These two publications are a selection of engineering terms and articles from the parent works (entries 1242, 1244). The *McGraw-Hill Dictionary of Engineering* excludes electrical and chemical engineering but has definitions for 16,000 terms in aerospace engineering, civil engineering, design engineering, industrial engineering, materials science, mechanical engineering, metallurgy and mining, petroleum engineering, and systems engineering. The *McGraw-Hill Encyclopedia of Engineering* has more than 690 articles covering topics in civil engineering, design engineering, electrical engineering, industrial engineering, mechanical engineering, metallurgy and mining, nuclear engineering, petroleum engineering, and production. It also includes some articles on the mechanical, electrical, and thermodynamic principles basic to all fields of engineering. Articles are well illustrated and have cross-references and bibliographies. There is also a detailed index.

1698.   Tver, David F., and Roger W. Bolz. **Encyclopedic Dictionary of Industrial Technology: Materials, Processes, and Equipment.** New York: Chapman and Hall, 1984. 353p.

As an encyclopedic dictionary, this source has definitions and explanations of terms dealing with industrial materials (e.g., brass, plastics), production equipment (e.g., furnaces, riveting machines), and manufacturing processes (e.g., steel processing, extrusion). In addition to illustrations, there are some tables summarizing characteristics of materials. A bibliography is also included.

1699.   Gunston, Bill. **Jane's Aerospace Dictionary.** London: Jane's, 1980. 493p.

1700.   **IEEE Standard Dictionary of Electrical and Electronics Terms.** 3d ed. New York: Institute of Electrical and Electronics Engineers, 1984. 1173p.

1701.   **Industrial Engineering Terminology.** Norcross, Ga.: Institute of Industrial Engineers, 1983. 398p.

These three dictionaries are representative of those covering particular subfields within engineering. In each case they provide more comprehensive coverage of the subfield's terminology than is possible with a more general technical dictionary. In addition, they sometimes emphasize terminology as established through standards developed by professional associations. *IEEE Standard Dictionary of Electrical and Electronics Terms* and *Industrial Engineering Terminology* are both of this type. *Jane's Aerospace Dictionary* provides definitions of many terms and acronyms in the aerospace field. *IEEE Standard Dictionary of Electrical and Electronics Terms* defines terms and gives an indication of the source of the definition. There is a separate bibliography of sources and a section interpreting acronyms. *Industrial Engineering Terminology* follows a topical rather than a strictly alphabetical arrangement. Terms are arranged alphabetically within 17 topical areas: e.g., biomechanics, cost engineering, production planning and control, human factors, safety. There is an index to all keywords occurring in terms.

DIRECTORIES

1702. **Directory of Engineering Societies and Related Organizations.** New York: American Association of Engineering Societies, 1984. 286p.

In response to questions about engineering societies in the United States or abroad, this directory provides descriptions of 485 organizations which are primarily engineering-oriented or which have activities related to engineering. The description of each organization includes name, address, telephone, officers, founding date, budget, publications, membership requirements, and objectives. There are geographic and keyword indexes to aid in identification of organizations in a particular region or those concerned with a particular topic.

1703. **Engineering Research Centres: A World Directory of Organizations and Programmes.** Edited by T. Archbold, J. C. Laidlaw, and J. McKechnie. Harlow, Essex, England: Longman, 1984. 1031p.

This directory has profiles of organizations which are funding, carrying out, or promoting research and development work in engineering. Government, industrial, and academic units are all included, as are consulting firms employing a substantial number of engineers. Coverage is not confined to a particular area of engineering, as aerospace, electrical, civil, industrial, and mechanical engineering are all included. Arrangement is by country with indexes for titles of establishments and for subjects. Each entry includes name, address, telephone, products, major personnel, research activities, publications, and links with other organizations.

HANDBOOKS

This chapter can describe only a small sample of the many handbooks dealing with engineering and its subdivisions. Other titles are identified in the guides to the literature (entries 1680-82) and in Powell's bibliography (entry 1265).

1704. Eshbach, Ovid W., and Mott Souders, eds. **Handbook of Engineering Fundamentals.** 3d ed. New York: Wiley, 1975. 1562p.

1705. **Kempe's Engineers Year-book.** 90th ed. Edited by J. P. Quayle. London: Morgan-Grampian, 1985. Various paging.

These two handbooks are both general in scope, but they differ in emphasis. *Handbook of Engineering Fundamentals* emphasizes the sciences underlying engineering with 16 sections on such topics as mechanics of rigid bodies, mechanics of incompressible fluids, electromagnetics and circuits, heat transfer, and properties of materials. There is a detailed index. Although a few of the 79 chapters of *Kempe's Engineers Year-book* cover the physical sciences underlying engineering practice, many deal with topics in the various subfields of engineering, such as civil engineering. There are also chapters on materials (e.g., plastics), processes (e.g., welding and cutting) and components (e.g., springs). The index is essential to exploiting its contents.

1706. Hicks, Tyler G., ed. **Standard Handbook of Engineering Calculations.** 2d ed. New York: McGraw-Hill, 1985. Various paging.

Although the engineering student and faculty member can find treatments of computational techniques by using mathematical reference tools, it is helpful to have a handbook which compiles and explains techniques commonly used in engineering. *Standard Handbook of Engineering Calculations* groups discussions of procedures for carrying out engineering calculations in 12 chapters, reflecting formulas commonly used in 12 engineering subfields: civil engineering, architectural engineering, mechanical engineering, electrical engineering, electronics engineering, chemical and process plant engineering, control engineering, aeronautical and astronautical engineering, marine engineering, nuclear engineering, sanitary engineering, and engineering economics. There is an index.

1707. **CRC Handbook of Tables for Applied Engineering Science.** 2d ed. Edited by Ray E. Bolz and George L. Tuve. Cleveland: CRC Press, 1973. 1166p.

This collection of tables is designed to provide the practicing engineer and student with a wide spectrum of data covering many subfields of engineering, with references to more complete sources. The 11 chapters deal with engineering materials and their properties: electrical science and radiation; chemistry and applications; nuclides and nuclear engineering; energy engineering and transport; mechanics, structures, and machines; environmental and bioengineering; environmental protection and human safety; communication and computation; measurement and instrumentation; and processes and control. There is an appendix, listing engineering organizations and publishers, and an index.

1708. **Marks' Standard Handbook for Mechanical Engineers.** 8th ed. Edited by Theodore Baumeister, Eugene A. Avallone, and Theodore Baumeister, III. New York: McGraw-Hill, 1978. Various paging.

1709. **Standard Handbook for Civil Engineers.** 3d ed. Edited by Frederick S. Merritt. New York: McGraw-Hill, 1983. Various paging.

1710. **Standard Handbook for Electrical Engineers.** 11th ed. Edited by Donald G. Fink and H. Wayne Beaty. New York: McGraw-Hill, 1978. Various paging.

1711. **Electronics Engineers' Handbook.** 2d ed. Edited by Donald G. Fink and Donald Christiansen. New York: McGraw-Hill, 1982. Various paging.

1712. **Handbook of Industrial Engineering.** Edited by Gavriel Salvendy. New York: Wiley, 1982.

These handbooks share common features: treatment of specialized topics by different authors, illustrations and tables to supplement the text, bibliographic references to lead to more detailed discussions in the primary literature, and indexes to allow quick location of specific facts. In addition, as is evident from the citations, these handbooks are updated regularly to reflect new developments in each field. *Marks' Standard Handbook for Mechanical Engineers* has 19 sections on such topics as fuels and furnaces, power generation, and pumps and compressors. *Standard Handbook for Civil Engineers* has 23 sections covering all domains of civil engineering (e.g., highway engineering, bridge engineering, airport engineering, water engineering). Some sections describe particular materials, such as wood design and construction or concrete design and construction. *Standard Handbook for Electrical Engineers* and *Electronics Engineers' Handbook* are complementary, with the former emphasizing power generation, transmission, and distribution and the latter covering electronics systems and applications such as broadcasting and data processing. *Handbook of Industrial Engineering* has 14 chapters discussing topics of special concern to industrial engineers (e.g., ergonomics/human factors, quality assurance, optimization).

BIOGRAPHY

1713.   Carvill, James. **Famous Names in Engineering.** London: Butterworths, 1981. 93p.

Famous Names in Engineering presents brief biographies of 83 famous individuals whose laws, theories, and inventions form the basis of advanced courses in engineering. It should be of particular interest to engineering students. In addition to giving a brief biographical sketch for each person, there is a portrait and an illustration, formula, or diagram depicting the contribution. There is a list of bibliographic references and a chronological table. Individuals covered include James Watt, Anders Celsius, and Nikola Tesla.

1714.   **Who's Who in Engineering.** 5th ed. New York: American Association of Engineering Societies, 1982. 889p.

1715.   **Who's Who in Technology Today.** 4th ed. Edited by Barbara A. Tinucci and Louann Chaudier. 5 vols. Woodbridge, Conn.: Research Publications, 1984.

When biographical information on prominent engineers is sought, these two sources can be consulted. *Who's Who in Engineering* includes members of the National Academy of Engineering and individuals with senior positions in professional societies, universities, industry, government, or consulting firms. The biographical sketch includes name, address, date of birth, education, career history, and society affiliations. Both geographic and area of specialization indexes are provided. In addition, there is a section noting facts about major engineering societies (officers, members of governing bodies, national awards with recipients). The five volumes of *Who's Who in Technology Today* are arranged as follows: volume 1. *Electronics and Computer Science*; volume 2. *Physics and Optics*; volume 3. *Chemistry and Biotechnology*; volume 4. *Mechanical, Civil, Energy and Earth Science*; and volume 5. *Index*. The index includes sections of names and of principal expertise. Coverage is selective, recognizing contributions made through patents, publications, or positions of leadership in research and development. Biographical sketches include name, address, positions held, education, publications, patents, principal area of expertise, organization memberships, major technical achievements, and personal data.

AUTHOR/TITLE INDEX

References are to entry numbers, except in a few cases where a page reference, preceded by "p." or "pp.," has been given. Names of databases are printed in capitals. This index includes references for each book and periodical to which an entry number has been assigned. Books and periodicals which are mentioned in the descriptive note for a numbered entry are designated with the entry number followed by "n." Titles mentioned in a descriptive note are not indexed if they are given only as examples of the kind of books useful for reference questions of a certain type. A reference is given for each author, editor, and others who have had a significant role in compiling a book. Subtitles have usually not been given unless they are necessary for clarification. Articles at the beginning of titles have been omitted. Entries are arranged in accordance with the word-by-word principle of filing. An author's name beginning with "De" or "La" is filed under that prefix. Names beginning with "Mc" are interfiled with those beginning with "M'" and "Mac." Numerals are filed as though spelled out. Acronyms are filed as words. Works by a single author are filed before works by that author with one or more joint authors.

ABC POL SCI, 1004
ABI/SELECTS: The Annotated Bibliography of Computer Periodicals, 1656
Abingdon Dictionary of Living Religions, K. Crim, 265
Abramovitz, M., Journal of Economic Literature, 931
Abrams, M. H., Glossary of Literary Terms, 367
Abramson, H. J., Index to Sociology Readers, 813
Abstracts in Anthropology, 868
Access: The Supplementary Index to Periodicals, 692
Accountants' Handbook, L. J. Seidler and D. R. Carmichael, 956
Actor Guide to the Talkies, A. A. Aros, 656
Actor Guide to the Talkies, R. B. Dimmitt, 655
Adams, C. J., Reader's Guide to the Great Religions, 254
Advances in Experimental Social Psychology, 798
AEROSPACE, 1689n

AGRICOLA, 1564n, 1569n
Agricultural Index, 1515n
Agricultural Journal Titles and Abbreviations, 1571
Agricultural Research Centres, N. Harvey, 1579
Agrindex, 1565
Aharoni, Y., and M. Avi-Yonah, Macmillan Bible Atlas, 316
Aherne, Sister C. M., P. K. Meagher, and T. C. O'Brien, Encyclopedic Dictionary of Religion, 270
AIBS Directory of Bioscience Departments and Faculties in the United States and Canada, American Institute of Biological Sciences, 1560
Aids to Geographical Research, J. K. Wright and E. T. Platt, 1179n
Alcoholism and Drug Abuse Treatment Centers Directory, 840
Alderson, M., International Mortality Statistics, 172n

Alexander, G. L., and J. N. Kane, Nicknames
and Sobriquets of U.S. Cities, States,
and Counties, 1198
Alexander, R. J., Political Parties of the
Americas, 1077
Alkire, L. G., Periodical Title Abbreviations, 47
Allaby, M., Dictionary of the Environment, 1472
Allen, C. W., Astrophysical Quantities, 1329
Allen, D., and P. Murdin, Catalogue of the
Universe, 1334
Allen, G. P., S. Herner, and N. D. Wright, Brief
Guide to Sources of Scientific and Tech-
nical Information, 1216
Allen, R. R., The Eighteenth Century, 346
Allgemeine deutsche Biographie, 150
Allgemeines Lexikon der bildenden Künstler,
U. Thieme and F. Becker, 554; p. 7
Allgemeines Lexikon der bildenden Künstler
dex XX. Jahrhunderts, H. Vollmer, 555
Alloway, D. N., and F. Cordasco, Medical Edu-
cation in the United States, 1614
Almanac of American Politics, M. Barone,
B. Ujifusa, and D. Matthews, 1024
Altman, E. I., and M. J. McKinney, Financial
Handbook, 957
Altman, P. L., and D. S. Dittmer, Biology Data
Book, 1555
Aluri, R., and J. S. Robinson, Guide to U.S.
Government Scientific and Technical
Resources, 1217
America: History and Life, 1163
America Votes, R. M. Scammon, 1052
American and British Literature, 1945-1975,
J. L. Somer and B. E. Cooper, 358
American and British Theatrical Biography,
J. P. Wearing, 644
American Anthropological Association, Guide
to Departments of Anthropology, 903
American Architects Directory, J. F. Gane, 564
American Art Directory, 541
American Association of Engineering Societ-
ies, Directory of Engineering Societies
and Related Organizations, 1702
American Authors and Books, 1640 to the
Present Day, W. J. Burke and W. D.
Howe, 400
American Authors, 1600-1900, S. S. Kunitz and
H. Haycraft, 394
American Bibliography, C. Evans, 24
American Bibliography, R. Shaw and R. Shoe-
maker, 23
American Book Publishing Record, 5, 18, 19
American Catalogue, 17
American Catalogue of Books, J. Kelly, 20
American Catholic Who's Who, J. Anderson,
292
American Chemists and Chemical Engineers,
W. D. Miles, 1403

American Council of Learned Societies, Con-
cise Dictionary of Scientific Biography,
1274
American Counties, J. N. Kane, 1199
American Dental Directory, 1643
American Drama Criticism, F. E. Eddleman,
428
American Economic Association, Directory of
Members, 980
American Ephemeris and Nautical Almanac,
1327n
American Film Institute Catalog of Motion Pic-
tures Produced in the United States, 647
American Folklore, C. C. Flanagan and J. T.
Flanagan, 882
American Foundation for the Blind, Directory
of Agencies Serving the Visually Handi-
capped in the United States, 837
American Geographical Society, Research
Catalogue, 1181
American Geological Institute, Directory of
Geoscience Departments, 1459
American Governors and Gubernatorial Elec-
tions, 1775-1978, R. R. Glashan, 1037
American Heritage Pictorial Atlas of United
States History, 1175
American Historical Association, Guide to
Historical Literature, 1111
American Horticultural Society, North Ameri-
can Horticulture, 1580
American Hospital Association, Hospital
Literature Index, 1607
American Hospital Association Guide to the
Health Care Field, 1636
American Humanities Index, 220
American Institute of Biological Sciences,
AIBS Directory of Bioscience Depart-
ments and Faculties in the United
States and Canada, P. Gray, 1560
American Institute of Physics Handbook, D. E.
Gray, 1355
American Jewish Yearbook, M. Himmelfarb
and D. Singer, 288
American Library Association, Association of
College and Research Libraries, Biblio-
graphic Instruction Section, Research
Committee Subcommittee on Evalua-
tion, Evaluating Bibliographic Instruc-
tion, 195
American Library Directory, 111
American Literary Manuscripts, Modern Lan-
guage Association of America, Ameri-
can Literature Section, 362
American Literary Scholarship, J. A. Robbins
and W. G. French, 360
American Literature, English Literature, and
World Literature in English Information
Guide Series, T. Grieder, 347

American Mathematical Society, Mathematical Association of America, Society for Industrial and Applied Mathematics, Combined Membership List, 1311

American Medical Directory, 1641

American Men and Women of Science, Editions 1-14 Cumulative Index, 1270

American Men and Women of Science: Physical and Biological Sciences, 1269

American Men and Women of Science: Social and Behavioral Sciences, 706; p. 204

American Movies Reference Book, P. Michael, 614

American Musical Theatre, G. Bordman, 662

American Newspapers, 1821-1936, W. Gregory, 53

American Novel since 1789, D. Gerstenberger and G. Hendrick, 423

American Political Dictionary, J. Plano and M. Greenberg, 1008

American Political Process, D. A. Smith and L. W. Garrison, 1044

American Political Science Association, Membership Directory, 1015

American Political Terms, H. Sperber and T. Trittschuh, 1011

American Psychological Association, APA Membership Register, 800

American Religion and Philosophy, E. R. Sandeen and F. Hale, 256

American Social Attitudes Data Handbook, P. E. Converse, 855

American Society of Composers, Authors, and Publishers, ASCAP Biographical Dictionary, 462

American Sociological Association, Directory, 862

American Statistics Index, 174; p. 45

American Theatre Annual, C. Hughes, 623n

American Theatrical Arts, W. C. Young, 592

American Universities and Colleges, 717

American Writers, L. Unger and G. T. Wright, 399

America's Corporate Families: The Billion Dollar Directory, 948

America's Corporate Families and International Affiliates, 949

Ames, J. G., Comprehensive Index to the Publications of the United States Government, 1881-1893, 62

Analytical Bibliography of Universal Collected Biography, M. Riches, 142

Analytical Concordance to the Bible, R. Young, 311n

Analytical Concordance to the Revised Standard Version of the New Testament, C. Morrison, 311

Anderberg, M. M., C. L. Thompson, and J. B. Antell, Current History Encyclopedia of Developing Nations, 1082

Andersen, C. J., and K. D. Roose, Rating of Graduate Programs, 761n

Anderson, I. G., Directory of European Associations, 102

Anderson, J., American Catholic Who's Who, 292

Annals of English Drama, 975-1700, A. Harbage, 385

Annals of English Literature, 1475-1950, 384n

Annals of Opera, 1597-1940, A. Loewenberg, 477

Annals of the New York Stage, G. C. D. Odell, 668

Année philologique, 1121

Annuaire de statistique internationale des grandes villes, 173

Annual Bibliography of English Language and Literature, Modern Humanities Research Association, 337

Annual Index to Popular Music Record Reviews, D. Tudor and L. Biesenthal, 488

Annual Register of Grant Support, 106

Annual Review of Anthropology, 918

Annual Review of Psychology, 799

Annual Review of Sociology, 812

Annual Review of United Nations Affairs, 1084

Antell, J. B., C. L. Thompson, and M. M. Anderberg, Current History Encyclopedia of Developing Nations, 1082

Anthropological Bibliography of South Asia, E. von Fürer-Haimendorf, 870

Anthropological Index to Current Periodicals, Museum of Mankind Library, 867

Anthropological Literature, 866

Antony, A., Guide to Basic Information Sources in Chemistry, 1359

APA Membership Register, American Psychological Association, 800

Apel, W., Harvard Dictionary of Music, 449

Applied and Decorative Arts, D. L. Ehresmann, 516

Applied Mechanics Reviews, 1691

Applied Science and Technology Index, 1222

Aptakin, K., Good Works: A Guide to Social Change Careers, 844

Archaeological Atlas of the World, D. Whitehouse and R. Whitehouse, 914

Archaeology, R. F. Heizer, T. R. Hester, and C. Graves, 877

Archbold, T., J. C. Laidlaw, and J. McKechnie, Engineering Research Centres, 1703

Architecture, D. L. Ehresmann, 515

Archives of American Art, Card Catalog of the Manuscript Collection of the Archives of American Art, 530

Aries, S. J., Dictionary of Telecommunications, 1669

Armour, R. A., Film, 579

Armstrong, M. E., and others, Handbook of Nursing, 1640

Arnim, M., Internationale Personalbibliographie, 84, 158

Arnold, D., New Oxford Companion to Music, 455

Arntzen, E., and R. Rainwater, Guide to the Literature of Art History, 510

Arny, L. R., Search for Data in the Physical and Chemical Sciences, 1218

Aronson, E., and G. Lindzey, Handbook of Social Psychology, 797

Aros, A. A., Actor Guide to the Talkies, 656

Aros, A. A., Title Guide to the Talkies, 654

Art Books, E. Lucas, 512

Art Index, 518

ARTbibliographies Modern, 517

Arthur D. Little, Inc., Into the Information Age, p. 316

Articles on American Literature, L. G. Leary, 338-40

Arts and Humanities Citation Index, 223

Arts in America, B. Karpel, 513

ASCAP Biographical Dictionary, 462

Ash, L., Subject Collections, 114

Asimov, I., Asimov's Biographical Encyclopedia of Science and Technology, 1278

Aslib, Index to Theses Accepted for Higher Degrees in the Universities of Great Britain and Ireland, 45

Assessment of Quality in Graduate Education, A. M. Cartter, 761n

Assessment of Research-Doctorate Programs in the United States, Conference Board of Associated Research Councils, 761

Association of American Geographers, Directory, 1208

Association of American Geographers, Guide to Graduate Departments of Geography in the United States and Canada, 1196

Associations' Publications in Print, 31, 1226n

Astronomical Almanac, 1327

Astronomical Catalogues, 1951-1975, M. Collins, 1317

Astronomical Ephemeris, 1327n

Astronomischer Jahresbericht, 1316n

Astronomy and Astrophysics, D. A. Kemp, 1314

Astronomy and Astrophysics Abstracts, 1316

Astrophysical Formulae, K. R. Lang, 1331

Astrophysical Quantities, C. W. Allen, 1329

Astrophysical Techniques, C. R. Kitchin, 1330

Atkinson, B., and F. Mavituna, Biochemical Engineering and Biotechnology Handbook, 1559

Atkinson, F., Dictionary of Literary Pseudonyms, 404

Atlante internazionale, 1204n

Atlas Mira, 1204n

Atlas of American History, K. T. Jackson, 1176

Atlas of Ancient Archaeology, J. Hawkes, 915

Atlas of Classical Archaeology, M. I. Finley, 916

Atlas of Early Man, J. Hawkes, 1143

Atlas of Economic Development, N. S. Ginsburg, 977

Atlas of Medieval Man, C. Platt, 1144

Atlas of World History, S. de Vries, 1150

Atlas of World Population History, C. McEvedy and R. Jones, 850

Attwater, D., and H. Thurston, Butler's Lives of the Saints, 296

Auchard, J., and L. G. Leary, Articles on American Literature, 338-40

Audubon Society Field Guide to North American Fossils, I. Thompson, 1448

Audubon Society Field Guide to North American Rocks and Minerals, C. W. Chesterman, 1447

Aufricht, H., Guide to League of Nations Publications, 81

Author Biographies Master Index, B. McNeil and M. C. Herbert, 392

Author-Title Index to Joseph Sabin's Dictionary of Books Relating to America, J. E. Molnar, 27

Avallone, E. A., T. Baumeister, and T. Baumeister, III, Marks' Standard Handbook for Mechanical Engineers, 1708

Avato, R. M., and F. A. Foy, Catholic Almanac, 287

Avery Architectural Library, Catalog, 519

Avery Index to Architectural Periodicals, Columbia University, Avery Architectural Library, 529

Avery Obituary Index of Architects, Columbia University, Avery Architectural Library, 566

Avi-Yonah, M., and Y. Aharoni, Macmillan Bible Atlas, 316

AVLINE, 1598n

Awards, Honors, and Prizes, P. Wasserman and G. Siegman, 109

Ayer Directory of Publications, 56

A-Z of Astronomy, P. Moore, 1320

Babchuk, N., and A. J. Schmidt, Fraternal Organizations, 831

Bahm, A., Directory of American Philosophers, 248

Bailey, E. Z., and L. H. Bailey, Hortus Third, 1576

Bailey, L. H., and E. Z. Bailey, Hortus Third, 1576

Bair, F. E., and J. A. Ruffner, Weather Almanac, 1452

Baird, D., and I. F. Bell, The English Novel, 1578-1956, 419

Baker, B. M., Theatre and Allied Arts, 588

Baker's Biographical Dictionary of Musicians, 460

Balachandran, M., Subject Approach to Business Reference Sources, p. 219

Balachandran, S., Directory of Publishing Sources, 1695

Balachandran, S., Energy Statistics, 1490

Baldensperger, F., and W. P. Friederich, Bibliography of Comparative Literature, 334

Ballentine, J. A., Law Dictionary with Pronunciations, 1094

Ballentyne, D. W. G., and D. R. Lovett, Dictionary of Named Effects and Laws in Chemistry, Physics, and Mathematics, 1258

Bank and Finance Manual, Moody's Manuals, 985n

Banks, A. S., Economic Handbook of the World, 961

Bantly, H. A., and J. L. Freedman, Information Searching, 194

Barkas, J. L., The Help Book, 832

Barlow, H., and S. Morgenstern, Dictionary of Musical Themes, 470

Barlow, H., and S. Morgenstern, Dictionary of Opera and Song Themes, 471

Barlow, H., and S. Morgenstern, Dictionary of Vocal Themes, 471n

Barnes, C., Men of the Supreme Court, 1034

Barnes, R. S. K., Synoptic Classification of Living Organisms, 1554

Barnhart, C. L., New Century Cyclopedia of Names, 162

Barone, M., B. Ujifusa, and D. Matthews, Almanac of American Politics, 1024

Barr, E. S., Index to Biographical Fragments in Unspecialized Scientific Journals, 1277

Barraclough, G., Times Concise Atlas of World History, 1149

Barron's Guide to the Best, Most Popular, and Most Exciting Colleges, 732

Barron's Guide to the Most Prestigious Colleges, 733

Barron's Guide to the Two-Year Colleges, 737

Barron's Profiles of American Colleges, 730

Bart, P., and L. Frankel, Student Sociologist's Handbook, 801

Basics of Online Searching, C. T. Meadow and P. A. Cochrane, 209

Bates, R. L., and J. A. Jackson, Dictionary of Geological Terms, 1418

Bates, R. L., and J. A. Jackson, Glossary of Geology, 1417

Batty, L., Retrospective Index to Film Periodicals, 585

Baugh, A. C., Literary History of England, 390n

Baughman, E. W., Type and Motif-Index of the Folktales of England and North America, 886

Bauly, C. B., and J. A. Bauly, World Energy Directory, 1498

Bauly, J. A., and C. B. Bauly, World Energy Directory, 1498

Baumeister, T., E. A. Avallone, and T. Baumeister, III, Marks' Standard Handbook for Mechanical Engineers, 1708

Baumeister, T., III, T. Baumeister, and E. A. Avallone, Marks' Standard Handbook for Mechanical Engineers, 1708

Bawden, L., Oxford Companion to Film, 612

Baxter, C., I. Herbert, and R. E. Finley, Who's Who in the Theatre, 642

Baxter, P. M., and J. G. Reed, Library Use: A Handbook for Psychology, 786

BCD. See Business Conditions Digest

Beacham, W., and F. N. Magill, Critical Survey of Short Fiction, 373

Beal, P., Index of English Literary Manuscripts, 363

Beaty, H. W., and D. G. Fink, Standard Handbook for Electrical Engineers, 1710

Beaubien, A. K., S. A. Hogan, and M. W. George, Learning the Library, 196

Bechtle, T. C., and M. F. Riley, Dissertations in Philosophy Accepted at American Universities, 234

Becker, F., and U. Thieme, Allgemeines Lexikon der bildenden Künstler, 554; p. 7

Beckson, K., and A. Ganz, Literary Terms, 364

Bédé, J. A., and W. B. Edgerton, Columbia Dictionary of Modern European Literature, 369

Beers, H. P., Bibliographies in American History, 1942-1978, 1160

Beilsteins Handbuch der Organischen Chemie, p. 302

Bell, D. L., Contemporary Art Trends, 1960-1980, 514

Bell, I. F., and D. Baird, The English Novel, 1578-1956, 419

Bell, R. E., Dictionary of Classical Mythology, 323

Belli, D., and G. A. Schlachter, Minorities and Women, 806

Bemis, S. F., and G. Griffin, Guide to the Diplomatic History of the United States, 1775-1921, 1060n

Benet, W. R., Reader's Encyclopedia, 377; p. 92

Benezit, E., Dictionnaire critique et documentaire des peintres, sculpteurs, dessinateurs, et graveurs, 556

Bennett, H., Chemical Formulary, 1396

Bennett, H., Concise Chemical and Technical Dictionary, 1376

Bennett, H., Encyclopedia of Chemical Trademarks and Synonyms, 1394

Berkow, R., Merck Manual of Diagnosis and Therapy, 1639

Bernhardt, W. F., and W. J. Smith, Granger's Index to Poetry, 352

Bernier, B. A., K. F. Gould, and P. Humphrey, Popular Names of U.S. Government Reports, 64

Berring, R. C., and M. Cohen, How to Find the Law, 1087

Berry, D. M., Bibliographic Guide to Educational Research, 707n

Besançon, R. M., Encyclopedia of Physics, 1348

Best Plays of [year], O. L. Guernsey, Jr., 625

Besterman, T., World Bibliography of Bibliographies, 29, 216

Beyer, W. H., CRC Handbook of Mathematical Sciences, 1304

Beyer, W. H., CRC Handbook of Tables for Probability and Statistics, 1310

Beyer, W. H., CRC Standard Mathematical Tables, 1305

Bibliographic Guide to Art and Architecture, 524

Bibliographic Guide to Conference Publications, 32

Bibliographic Guide to Educational Research, D. M. Berry, 707n

Bibliographic Index, 217

Bibliographic Instruction, B. Renford and L. Hendrickson, 193

Bibliographie de la philosophie, 235

Bibliographie géographique internationale, 1185

Bibliographie linguistique de l'année, Permanent International Committee of Linguists, 879

Bibliographies in American History, 1942-1978, H. P. Beers, 1160

Bibliography and Index of Geology, 1410, 1456n

Bibliography and Index of Geology Exclusive of North America, 1410n

Bibliography and Research Manual of the History of Mathematics, K. O. May, 1291

Bibliography of Agriculture, 1564, 1571n

Bibliography of American Literature, J. N. Blanck, 331

Bibliography of Astronomy, 1970-1979, R. A. Seal and S. S. Martin, 1315

Bibliography of Bibliographies in American Literature, C. H. Nilon, 333

Bibliography of Bioethics, 1616

Bibliography of British Bibliography and Textual Criticism, T. H. Howard-Hill, 332

Bibliography of British Literary Bibliographies, T. H. Howard-Hill, 332

Bibliography of Comparative Literature, F. Baldensperger and W. P. Friederich, 334

Bibliography of Contemporary North American Indians, W. Hodge, 876

Bibliography of Ethnicity and Ethnic Groups, R. Kolm, 808

Bibliography of Geography, C. D. Harris, 1179

Bibliography of Modern History, J. Roach, 1113

Bibliography of North American Folklore and Folksong, C. Haywood, 883

Bibliography of North American Geology, 1410n

Bibliography of Philosophical Bibliographies, H. Guerry, 231

Bibliography of Philosophy, 235

Bibliography of Publications on Old English Literature, S. B. Greenfield and F. C. Robinson, 344

Bibliography of the American Theatre, Excluding New York City, C. J. Stratman, 591

Bibliography of the History of Medicine, 1617

Bibliotheca Americana, O. Roorbach, 21

Bier, R. A., Jr., D. C. Ward, and M. W. Wheeler, Geologic Reference Sources, 1408, 1456n

Biesenthal, L., and D. Tudor, Annual Index to Popular Music Record Reviews, 488

Billion Dollar Directory, 948

Binger, J. L., and L. M. Jensen, Lippincott's Guide to Nursing Literature, 1602

Biochemical Engineering and Biotechnology Handbook, B. Atkinson and F. Mavituna, 1559

Bioethics, D. M. Goldstein, 1615

BIOETHICSLINE, 1616n

Biographical Dictionaries and Related Works, R. B. Slocum, 153

Biographical Dictionary of American Educators, J. F. Ohles, 757

Biographical Dictionary of American Music, C. E. Claghorn, 461

Biographical Dictionary of American Science, C. A. Elliott, 1282

Biographical Dictionary of British Architects, 1600-1840, H. M. Colvin, 567

Biographical Dictionary of Dance, B. N. Cohen-Stratyner, 646

Biographical Dictionary of Jazz, C. E. Claghorn, 495

Biographical Dictionary of Scientists, T. I. Williams, 1280

Biographical Directory of the American Congress, 1774-1971, U.S. Congress, 1026

Biographical Directory of the Governors of the United States, 1789-1978, R. Sobel and J. Raimo, 1038

Biographical Directory of the United States Executive Branch, 1774-1977, R. Sobel, 1030

Biographical Encyclopedia and Who's Who of the American Theatre, W. Rigdon, 621n

Biographical Encyclopedia of Scientists, J. Daintith, S. Mitchell, and E. Tootill, 1279

Biographie universelle, ancienne et moderne, J. F. Michaud, 159

Biography and Genealogy Master Index, 121

Biography Index, 126

BIOGRAPHY MASTER INDEX, 121n

Biological Abstracts, 1513, 1518n

Biological Abstracts/RRM, 1514, 1518n

Biological and Agricultural Index, 1515

Biologist's Handbook of Pronunciations, E. C. Jaeger, 1549

Biology Data Book, P. L. Altman and D. S. Dittmer, 1555

Biology Digest, 1516

Bioresearch Index, 1514n

BIOSIS PREVIEWS, 1513n

Biotechnology Directory, 1985, J. Coombs, 1551

Birnbaum, M., and J. Cass, Comparative Guide to American Colleges for Students, Parents, and Counselors, 726

Bishko, C. J., E. U. Crosby, and R. L. Kellogg, Medieval Studies, 1118

Bisset, R., B. D. Clark, and P. Wathern, Environmental Impact Assessment, 1470

Bitner, H., M. O. Price, and S. R. Bysiewicz, Effective Legal Research, 1089

Black, H. C., Black's Law Dictionary, 1093

Black American Reference Book, M. M. Smythe, 911

Blackey, R., Revolutions and Revolutionists, 1051

Blackmore, S., and E. Tootill, Facts on File Dictionary of Botany, 1532

Black's Agricultural Dictionary, D. B. Dalal-Clayton, 1573, 1578n

Black's Veterinary Dictionary, G. P. West, 1578

Blake, J. B., and C. Roos, Medical Reference Works, 1679-1966, 1601

Blakiston's Gould Medical Dictionary, 1619

Blanchard, J. R., and L. Farrell, Guide to Sources for Agricultural and Biological Research, 1561

Blanck, J. N., Bibliography of American Literature, 331

Blaug, M., and P. Sturges, Who's Who in Economics, 979

Blaustein, A. P., and G. H. Flanz, Constitutions of the Countries of the World, 1075

BLL Conference Index, British Library Lending Division, 38

Blume, F., Musik in Geschichte und Gegenwart, 452

Boast, C., and L. Foster, Subject Compilations of State Laws, 1092

Bolz, R. E., and G. L. Tuve, CRC Handbook of Tables for Applied Engineering Science, 1707

Bolz, R. W., and D. F. Tver, Encyclopedic Dictionary of Industrial Technology, 1698

Bond Guide, Standard and Poor, 990

Bondanella, J., and P. Bondanella, Dictionary of Italian Literature, 368n

Bondanella, P., and J. Bondanella, Dictionary of Italian Literature, 368n

Book of the Dance, J. Martin, 632

Book of the States, 93, 94, 94n, 1035

Book Review Digest, 179

Book Review Index, 181

Books in Print, 6, 1226n, 1596n

Boorkman, J. A., and F. W. Roper, Introduction to Reference Sources in the Health Sciences, 1587

Bordman, G., American Musical Theatre, 662

Bordman, G., Oxford Companion to American Theatre, 620

Borgman, C. L., D. Moghdam, and P. K. Corbett, Effective Online Searching, 208

Borich, G. D., and S. K. Madden, Evaluating Classroom Instruction, 765

Boston Public Library, Dictionary Catalog of the Music Collection, 442

Bottle, R. T., Use of Chemical Literature, 1360

Bottle, R. T., and H. V. Wyatt, Use of Biological Literature, 1508

Bourgeois, J., and R. W. Fairbridge, Encyclopedia of Sedimentology, 1430

Bowden, H. W., Dictionary of American Religious Biography, 294

Bower, C. E., and M. L. Rhoads, EPA Index, 1469

Bowker, R. R., State Publications, 71

Bowker's 1985 Complete Sourcebook of Personal Computing, 1674

Bowles, S. E., Index to Critical Film Reviews, 687

Boxshall, G. A., R. J. Lincoln, and P. F. Clark, Dictionary of Ecology, Evolution and Systematics, 1539

Boyce, G. C., Literature of Medieval History, 1930-1975, 1117

Brady, G. S., and H. R. Clauser, Materials Handbook, 1393

Brady, J., and P. J. Schemenaur, Writer's Market, 376

Brandon, S. G. F., Dictionary of Comparative Religion, 266

Breed, P. F., and D. De Charms, Songs in Collections, 506

Breed, P. F., and F. M. Sniderman, Dramatic Criticism Index, 427

Brehier, E., History of Philosophy, 252

Breivik, P. S., Planning the Library Instruction Program, 197

Brenner, M., E. E. Grazda, and W. R. Minrath, Handbook of Applied Mathematics, 1306

Bretherick, L., Handbook of Reactive Chemical Hazards, 1399

Brewer, J. G., Literature of Geography, 1178

Brewer, M., and T. Scott, Concise Encyclopedia of Biochemistry, 1547

Brief Guide to Sources of Scientific and Technical Information, S. Herner, G. P. Allen, and N. D. Wright, 1216

Briggs, K. M., Dictionary of British Folk-Tales in the English Language, 899

Brigham, C. S., History and Bibliography of American Newspapers, 1690-1820, 54

Britannica Encyclopedia of American Art, 533

British Authors before 1800, S. S. Kunitz and H. Haycraft, 394

British Authors of the Nineteenth Century, S. S. Kunitz and H. Haycraft, 394

British Bibliography to 1890, T. H. Howard-Hill, 332

British Broadcasting Corporation, Central Music Library, Song Catalogue, 509

British Humanities Index, 221

British Library, General Catalogue of Printed Books to 1975, 14

British Library Lending Division, BLL Conference Index, 38

British Library Lending Division, Index of Conference Proceedings Received, 38

British Literary Bibliography and Textual Criticism, 1890-1969, T. H. Howard-Hill, 332

British Literary Bibliography, 1970-1979, T. H. Howard-Hill, 332

British Museum, General Catalogue of Printed Books, 13

British Technology Index, 1687n

British Writers, 398

Broadway Bound, W. T. Leonard, 626

Brociner, G. E., and C. J. Himmelsbach, Guide to Scientific and Technical Journals in Translation, 1237

Brock, C., Literature of Political Science, 997

Brockhaus ABC Biochemie, 1548n

Brogan, T. V. F., English Versification, 1570-1980, 348

Bromiley, G. W., International Standard Bible Encyclopedia, 304

Bronner, E., Encyclopedia of the American Theatre, 1900-1975, 660

Brook, B. S., Thematic Catalogues in Music, 472

Brown, L., Les Brown's Encyclopedia of Television, 606

Brown, R. E., J. A. Fitzmyer, and R. E. Murphy, Jerome Bible Commentary, 314

Browne, E. J., W. F. Bynum, and R. Porter, Dictionary of the History of Science, 1260

Brownson, C. W., Congressional Staff Directory, 87, 1018

Brownstone, D. M., and G. Carruth, Where to Find Business Information, p. 206

Bruccoli, M. J., Dictionary of Literary Biography, 395

Brugger, W., Philosophical Dictionary, 243

Brundage, D. J., and K. P. Strauch, Guide to Library Resources for Nursing, 1603

Brunn, A. L., How to Find Out in Pharmacy, 1608

Brunnings, F. E., Folk Song Index, 507

Brunvand, J. H., Folklore, 881

Buchanan, R. O., Illustrated Dictionary of Geography, 1187

Buchanan, W. W., and E. M. Kanely, Cumulative Subject Index to the Monthly Catalog of U.S. Government Publications, 1900-1971, 61

Buchanan-Brown, J., Cassell's Encyclopedia of World Literature, 368; p. 92

Buckland, W. R., and M. G. Kendall, Dictionary of Statistical Terms, 1300

Budget of the United States Government, U.S. Executive Office of the President, Office of Management and Budget, 992

Buenker, J. D., and N. C. Burckel, Immigration and Ethnicity, 807

Bugelski, B. R., and A. M. Graziano, Handbook of Practical Psychology, 795

Bull, S., Index to Biographies of Contemporary Composers, 463

Bulletin analytique de documentation politique, économique, et sociale contemporaine, 1064

Bulletin des Traductions, 1241n

Bulletin signalétique. 519: Philosophie, 237

Bulletin signalétique. 527: Sciences religieuses, 263

Burckel, N. C., and J. D. Buenker, Immigration and Ethnicity, 807

Burdick, E. B., and J. Merin, International Directory of Theatre, Dance, and Folklore Festivals, 609

Burington, R. S., Handbook of Mathematical Tables and Formulas, 1303

Burington, R. S., and D. C. May, Jr., Handbook of Probability and Statistics with Tables, 1309

Burke, A. J., and M. A. Burke, Documentation in Education, 707n

Burke, W. J., and W. D. Howe, American Authors and Books, 1640 to the Present Day, 400

Burkett, J., Directory of Scientific Directories, 1261

Burks, M. P., Requirements for Certification for Elementary Schools, Secondary Schools, Junior Colleges, 770

Burnham, R., Jr., Burnham's Celestial Handbook, 1332

Burns, R. D., Guide to American Foreign Relations since 1700, 1060

Buros, O. K., English Tests and Reviews, 762n

Buros, O. K., Foreign Language Tests and Reviews, 762n

Buros, O. K., Intelligence Tests and Reviews, 762n

Buros, O. K., Mathematics Tests and Reviews, 762n

Buros, O. K., Mental Measurements Yearbook, 762n

Buros, O. K., Personality Tests and Reviews, 762n

Buros, O. K., Reading Tests and Reviews, 762n

Buros, O. K., Science Tests and Reviews, 762n

Buros, O. K., Social Studies Tests and Reviews, 762n

Buros, O. K., Vocational Tests and Reviews, 762n

Burr, J. R., Handbook of World Philosophy, 251

Burr, N. R., Critical Bibliography of Religion in America, 256n

Burrows, R. M., and B. C. Redmond, Concerto Themes, 471n

Burrows, R. M., and B. C. Redmond, Symphony Themes, 471n

Burton, P. E., Dictionary of Minicomputing and Microcomputing, 1660

Business Conditions Digest, U.S. Dept. of Commerce, Bureau of Economic Analysis, 968

Business Index, 926

Business Information Sources, L. M. Daniells, 919

Business Organizations and Agencies Directory, A. Kurzas and K. Gill, 953

Business Periodicals Index, 925

Business Publications Index and Abstracts, 930

Business Reference Sources, Harvard University, Graduate School of Business Administration, 922

Business Statistics, U.S. Dept. of Commerce, Bureau of Economic Analysis, 967

Butler, A., Lives of the Saints, 296

Byerly, G., Online Searching, 202

Byler, M. G., A. B. Hirschfelder, and M. A. Dorris, Guide to Research on North American Indians, 874

Bynum, W. F., E. J. Browne, and R. Porter, Dictionary of the History of Science, 1260

Bysiewicz, S. R., M. O. Price, and H. Bitner, Effective Legal Research, 1089

C.R.I.S., Combined Retrospective Index Set to Journals in History, 1838-1974, 1114

C.R.I.S., Combined Retrospective Index Set to Journals in Political Science, 1005

C.R.I.S., Combined Retrospective Index Set to Journals in Sociology, 804

CA SEARCH, 1367n

CAB ABSTRACTS, 1567n

Calvert, S. J., and O. S. Weber, Literary and Library Prizes, 389

Cambridge Ancient History, I. E. S. Edwards, 1154

Cambridge Encyclopaedia of Astronomy, S. Mitton, 1324

Cambridge Encyclopedia of Archaeology, A. S. Sherratt, 895

Cambridge Encyclopedia of Earth Sciences, D. G. Smith, 1424

Cambridge Guide to English Literature, M. Stapleton, 380

Cambridge History of English Literature, 390n

Cambridge Information and Research Services, World Directory of Energy Information, 1483

Cambridge Medieval History, J. B. Bury, 1155

Cambridge Modern History, A. W. Ward, 1157

Campbell, R. J., Psychiatric Dictionary, 1629

Caponigri, A. R., F. N. Magill, and T. P. Neill, Masterpieces of Catholic Literature in Summary Form, 290

Carlyon, R., Guide to the Gods, 320

Carmichael, D. R., and L. J. Seidler, Accountants' Handbook, 956

Carmichael, R. S., Handbook of Physical Properties of Rocks, 1449

Carnell, H., and D. Eagle, Oxford Illustrated Guide to Great Britain and Ireland, 386

Carr, F. K., Searching Patent Documents for Patentability and Information, 1683

Carroll, M. J., Key to League of Nations Documents Placed on Public Sale, 82

Carruth, G., Encyclopedia of American Facts and Dates, 1174

Carruth, G., and D. M. Brownstone, Where to Find Business Information, p. 206

Carter, C., Guide to Reference Sources in the Computer Sciences, 1648

Carter, E., Records in Review, 487

Carter, E. F., Dictionary of Inventions and Discoveries, 1259

Cartter, A. M., Assessment of Quality in Graduate Education, 761n

Carvill, J., Famous Names in Engineering, 1713

Casebook Series, 434

Cass, J., and M. Birnbaum, Comparative Guide to American Colleges for Students, Parents, and Counselors, 726

Cassell's Encyclopedia of World Literature, J. Buchanan-Brown, 368; p. 92

Cassetta, A., W. D. Hand, and S. Thiederman, Popular Beliefs and Superstitions, 887

CASSI, 1370n

Cassis, A. F., Twentieth Century English Novel, 422

Catalog of Folklore and Folk Songs, Cleveland Public Library, John G. White Department, 884

Catalog of Sound Recordings, Sibley Music Library, University of Rochester, 484

Catalog of the Public Documents of Congress and of All Departments of the Government of the United States, 60

Catalogue des thèses de doctorat soutenue devant les universités françaises, 42

Catalogue générale des livres imprimés. Bibliothèque Nationale, 15

Catalogue of Reproductions of Paintings, 1860-1979, UNESCO, 568n

Catalogue of Reproductions of Paintings prior to 1860, UNESCO, 568n

Catalogue of the Universe, P. Murdin and D. Allen, 1334

Catholic Almanac, F. A. Foy and R. M. Avato, 287

Catholic Periodical and Literature Index, 262

CATLINE, 1597n

Cawkwell, T., and J. M. Smith, World Encyclopedia of the Film, 638

Census, U.S. Dept. of Commerce, Bureau of the Census, 169

Census of Governments, U.S. Dept. of Commerce, Bureau of the Census, 994

Center for the American Woman in Politics, Women in Public Office, 1042

CFR Index and Finding Aids, 1104

Challinor, J., Dictionary of Geology, 1419

Chamberlin, M., Guide to Art Reference Books,, 511n

Chambers, C. A., and P. Romanovsky, Social Service Organizations, 830

Chambers Directory of Science and Technology, T. C. Collocott and A. B. Dobson, 1249

Chambers's Biographical Dictionary, 139

Champion, S., Dictionary of Terms and Techniques in Archaeology, 892

Charles, S. R., Handbook of Music and Music Literature in Sets and Series, 447n

Charles-Picard, G., Larousse Encyclopedia of Archaeology, 896

Chase's Calendar of Annual Events, p. 146

Chaudier, L., and B. A. Tinucci, Who's Who in Technology Today, 1715

Checklist of American Imprints, R. A. Shoemaker, 22

Checklist of United Nations Documents, 1946-49, 80

Checklist of United States Public Documents, 1789-1975, 68

Chem Sources – U.S.A., 1388

Chemical Abstracts, 1367

Chemical Abstracts Service Registry Handbook: Number Section, 1367n

Chemical Abstracts Service Source Index, 1370

Chemical and Process Technology Encyclopedia, D. M. Considine, 1382

Chemical Engineering Faculties, J. G. Ekerdt, 1405

Chemical Formulary, H. Bennett, 1396

Chemical Industries Information Sources, T. P. Peck, 1366

Chemical Information, Y. Wolman, 1364

Chemical Publications, M. G. Mellon, 1362; p. 296

Chemical Research Faculties, G. L. Pollock, 1407

Chemical Technology, 1387

Chemical Titles, 1368

Chemist's Companion, A. J. Gordon and R. A. Ford, 1391

Chen, C.-C., Health Sciences Information Sources, 1588

Chen, C.-C., Scientific and Technical Information Sources, 1211

Chen, C.-C., and S. Schweizer, Online Bibliographic Searching, 210

Cheney, S., The Theatre, 631n

Cheremisinoff, P. N., J. Golden, R. P. Ouellette, S. Saari, Environmental Impact Data Book, 1481

Chester, E. W., Guide to Political Platforms, 1046

Chesterman, C. W., Audubon Society Field Guide to North American Rocks and Minerals, 1447

Chevalier, C. U. J., Répertoire des sources historiques du moyen âge: Bio-bibliographie, 161

Chicago Art Institute, Ryerson Library, Index
    to Art Periodicals, 528
Chicorel, M., Chicorel Index to Abstracting and
    Indexing Services, 224
Chicorel, M., Chicorel Index to Short Stories
    in Anthologies and Collections, 353
Chicorel, M., Chicorel Theater Index to Drama
    Literature, 589
Chicorel, M., Chicorel Theater Index to Plays,
    671
Chicorel Index to Abstracting and Indexing
    Services, M. Chicorel, 224
Chicorel Index to Short Stories in Anthologies
    and Collections, M. Chicorel, 353
Chicorel Theater Index to Drama Literature,
    M. Chicorel, 589
Chicorel Theater Index to Plays, M. Chicorel,
    671
Children's Authors and Illustrators, A.
    Sarkissian, 403
Chopey, N. P., and T. G. Hicks, Handbook
    of Chemical Engineering Calculations,
    1401
Christiansen, D., and D. G. Fink, Electronics
    Engineers' Handbook, 1711
Chronological Outline of British Literature,
    S. J. Rogal, 384
Chronology of the Ancient World, 10,000 B.C.
    to A.D. 799, H. E. L. Mellersh, 1139
Chronology of the Expanding World, 1492
    to 1762, N. Williams, 1141
Chronology of the Medieval World, 800 to 1491,
    R. L. Storey, 1140
Chronology of the Modern World, 1763 to
    1965, N. Williams, 1142
Chujoy, A., and P. W. Manchester, Dance
    Encyclopedia, 603
Chun, K., Measures for Psychological Assess-
    ment, 766
CIS/Index, 59
CIS: U.S. Congressional Committee Hearings
    Index, 66
CIS: U.S. Congressional Committee Prints
    Index, 67
CIS: U.S. Serial Set Index, 65
CIS Federal Register Index, 1102
Cities of the World, M. W. Young, 1193
Claghorn, C. E., Biographical Dictionary of
    American Music, 461
Claghorn, C. E., Biographical Dictionary of
    Jazz, 495
Clapp, J., Sculpture Index, 575
Clark, A. N., and L. D. Stamp, Glossary
    of Geographical Terms, 1189
Clark, B. D., R. Bissett, and P. Wathern,
    Environmental Impact Assessment, 1470
Clark, P. F., R. J. Lincoln, and G. A.
    Boxshall, Dictionary of Ecology, Evo-
    lution and Systematics, 1539

Clarke, M., and D. Vaughan, Encyclopedia of
    Dance and Ballet, 604
Clauser, H. R., and G. S. Brady, Materials
    Handbook, 1393
Cleevely, R. J., World Palaeontological
    Collections, 1445
Cleveland Public Library, John G. White
    Department, Catalog of Folklore and
    Folk Songs, 884
Climates of the States, J. A. Ruffner, 1453
Close, A. C., and C. Colgate, Jr., Washington
    Representatives, 1025
Cochrane, P. A., and C. T. Meadow, Basics of
    Online Searching, 209
Coco, A., Finding the Law, 1086
Code of Federal Regulations, 1103
Cohen, G. A., U.S. College-Sponsored Programs
    Abroad: Academic Year, 778
Cohen, G. A., Vacation Study Abroad, 779
Cohen, M., Legal Research in a Nutshell, 1085
Cohen, M., and R. C. Berring, How to Find
    the Law, 1087
Cohen-Stratyner, B. N., Biographical Dictionary
    of Dance, 646
Colby, V., and S. S. Kunitz, European Authors,
    1000-1900, 394
Cole, K., Minority Organizations, 834
Coleman, A., and G. R. Taylor, Drama
    Criticism, 426
Coleman, E. E., Bibliography of American
    Literature, 331n
Coleman, W. E., Grants in the Humanities,
    227
Colgate, C. Jr., and A. C. Close, Washington
    Representatives, 1025
Collector's Guide to the American Musical
    Theatre, D. Hummel, 627
College Blue Book, 729, 769
College Chemistry Faculties, M. A. Grant,
    1404
Collegiate Dictionary of Botany, D. Swartz,
    1534
Collegiate Dictionary of Zoology, R. W. Pennak,
    1531
Collins, M., Astronomical Catalogues, 1951-
    1975, 1317
Collison, R., Dictionary of Dates, 1135
Collocott, T. C., and A. B. Dobson, Chambers
    Dictionary of Science and Technology,
    1249
Colubmia Dictionary of Modern European
    Literature, J. A. Bédé and W. B.
    Edgerton, 369
Columbia University, Avery Architectural
    Library, Avery Index to Architectural
    Periodicals, 529
Columbia University, Avery Architectural
    Library, Avery Obituary Index of
    Architects, 566

Columbia University, Avery Architectural
    Library, Catalog, 519
Columbia University, Columbia College, Guide
    to Oriental Classics, 437
Columbia-Lippincott Gazetteer of the World,
    L. Seltzer, 1205
Colvin, H. M., Biographical Dictionary of British
    Architects, 1600-1840, 567
Combined Membership List: American Mathe-
    matical Society, Mathematical Associa-
    tion of America, Society for Industrial
    and Applied Mathematics, 1311
Combined Retrospective Index Set to Journals
    in History, C.R.I.S., 1114
Combined Retrospective Index Set to Journals
    in Political Science, C.R.I.S., 1005
Combined Retrospective Index Set to Journals
    in Sociology, C.R.I.S., 804
Combined Retrospective Index to Book
    Reviews in Humanities Journals, 1802-
    1974, E. Farber, S. Hannah, and S.
    Schindler, 186
Combined Retrospective Index to Book
    Reviews in Scholarly Journals, 1886-
    1974, E. Farber, 185
Commager, H. S., Documents of American
    History, 1173
Commodity Yearbook, 963
Commonwealth Political Facts, C. Cook and
    J. Paxton, 1080
Commonwealth Universities Yearbook, 721
Communications Standard Dictionary, M. H.
    Weik, 1671
Comparative and Veterinary Medicine, A. E.
    Kerker and H. T. Murphy, 1563
Comparative Guide to Colleges for Students,
    Parents, and Counselors, J. Cass and
    M. Birnbaum, 726
COMPENDEX, 1686n
Compendium of Housing Statistics, United
    Nations, Statistical Office, 851
Compendium of Social Statistics, United
    Nations, Statistical Office, 845
Complete Concordance to the Bible (Douay
    Version), N. W. Thompson and R. Stock,
    310
Complete Encyclopedia of Popular Music and
    Jazz, 1900-1950, R. D. Kinkle, 490
Complete Encyclopedia of Television
    Programs, V. Terrace, 678
Complete Guide to Nontraditional Education,
    W. J. Halterman, 734
Composers of Tomorrow's Music, D. Ewen, 465
Composers since 1900, D. Ewen, 464
Composite Index for CRC Handbooks, 1266
Comprehensive Bibliography for the Study
    of American Minorities, W. C. Miller,
    809

Comprehensive Dictionary of Psychological
    and Psychoanalytical Terms, H. B.
    English and A. C. English, 790
Comprehensive Dissertation Index, 1861-1972,
    40
Comprehensive Index to the Publications of
    the United States Government, J. G.
    Ames, 62
Computer Acronyms, Abbreviations, Etc.,
    C. P. Wrathall, 1673
Computer and Control Abstracts, 1652, 1655n
Computer and Information Systems Abstracts
    Journal, 1653
Computer Books and Serials in Print, 1651
Computer Dictionary, C. J. Sippl and R. J.
    Sippl, 1662
Computer Publishers and Publications, 1649
Computerized Literature Searching, C. L.
    Gilreath, 213
Computers and Information Processing World
    Index, S. Deighton, J. Gurnsey, and J.
    Tomlinson, 1650
Computing Information Directory, D. M. Hilde-
    brandt, 1647
Computing Reviews, 1654
Concerto Themes, R. M. Burrows and B. C.
    Redmond, 471n
Concise Cambridge Bibliography of English
    Literature, G. Watson, 363n
Concise Chemical and Technical Dictionary,
    H. Bennett, 1376
Concise Dictionary of American History, D. W.
    Voorhees, 1166n
Concise Dictionary of Indian Tribes of North
    America, B. A. Leitch, 890
Concise Dictionary of Physics and Related
    Subjects, J. Thewlis, 1346
Concise Dictionary of Scientific Biography,
    American Council of Learned Societies,
    1274
Concise Encyclopedia of Astronomy, A.
    Weigert and H. Zimmerman, 1326
Concise Encyclopedia of Biochemistry, T.
    Scott and M. Brewer, 1547
Concise Encyclopedia of Information Tech-
    nology, A. V. Stokes, 1668
Concise Encyclopedia of the Italian
    Renaissance, J. R. Hale, 1127
Concise Encyclopedia of the Sciences,
    J.-D. Yule, 1247
Concise Encyclopedia of Western Philosophy
    and Philosophers, J. O. Urmson, 246
Concise Oxford Dictionary of Ballet, H.
    Koegler, 602
Concise Oxford Dictionary of Opera, H.
    Rosenthal and J. Warrack, 474
Concise Science Dictionary, A. Isaacs,
    J. Daintith, and E. Martin, 1250

Concordance to the Apocrypha/Deuterocanonical Books of the Revised Standard Version, 308

Condensed Chemical Dictionary, G. G. Hawley, 1377

Condition of Education, National Center for Education Statistics, 744

Condon, E. U., and H. Odishaw, Handbook of Physics, 1356

Conference Board of Associated Research Councils, Assessment of Research-Doctorate Programs in the United States, 761

Conference Papers Index: Life Sciences, Physical Sciences, Engineering, 35, 1234

Congdon, K., Contemporary Poets in American Anthologies, 1960-1977, 350

Congressional Index, 1021

Congressional Quarterly Almanac, 1020

Congressional Quarterly's Guide to the Congress of the United States, 1022

Congressional Quarterly's Guide to the U.S. Supreme Court, 1033

Congressional Staff Directory, C. W. Brownson, 87, 1018

Connor, B. M., and J. M. Connor, Ottemiller's Index to Plays in Collections, 673

Connor, J. M., and B. M. Connor, Ottemiller's Index to Plays in Collections, 673

Connors, M., and J. Schmittroth, Jr., Telecommunications Systems and Services Directory, 1678

Conotillo, B. C., Teaching Abroad, 780

Conrad, J. H., Reference Sources in Social Work, 802

Conservation Directory, 1477

Considine, D. M., Chemical and Process Technology Encyclopedia, 1382

Considine, D. M., Energy Technology Handbook, 1505

Considine, D. M., Van Nostrand's Scientific Encyclopedia, 1248

Considine, D. M., and G. D. Considine, Foods and Food Production Encyclopedia, 1577

Considine, D. M., and G. D. Considine, Van Nostrand Reinhold Encyclopedia of Chemistry, 1380

Considine, G. D., and D. M. Considine, Foods and Food Production Encyclopedia, 1577

Considine, G. D., and D. M. Considine, Van Nostrand Reinhold Encyclopedia of Chemistry, 1380

Consolidated Index of Translations into English, National Translations Center, 1239

Constitution of the United States of America, 1097

Constitutions of Nations, A. J. Peaslee, 1074

Constitutions of the Countries of the World, A. P. Blaustein and G. H. Flanz, 1075

Consumer Health Information Source Book, A. M. Rees and J. Janes, 1591

Contemporary American Poetry, L. Davis and R. Irwin, 349

Contemporary Architects, M. Emanuel, 565

Contemporary Art and Artists: An Index to Reproductions, P. J. Parry, 574

Contemporary Art Trends, 1960-1980, D. L. Bell, 514

Contemporary Artists, M. Emanuel, 563

Contemporary Literary Criticism, J. C. Stine, 432

Contemporary Poets in American Anthologies, 1960-1977, K. Congdon, 350

Contemporary Psychology, 787

Contemporary Sociology, 805

Contents of Contemporary Mathematical Journals, 1288n

Continental Novel, E. L. Kearney and L. S. Fitzgerald, 424-25

Converse, P. E., American Social Attitudes Data Handbook, 855

Cook, C., and J. Paxton, Commonwealth Political Facts, 1080

Cook, C., and J. Paxton, European Political Facts, 1789-1973, 1079

Cooke, E. I., W. Gardner, and R. W. I. Cooke, Handbook of Chemical Synonyms and Trade Names, 1395

Cooke, R. W. I., W. Gardner, and E. I. Cooke, Handbook of Chemical Synonyms and Trade Names, 1395

Coombs, J., Biotechnology Directory 1985, 1551

Cooper, B. E., and J. L. Somer, American and British Literature, 1945-1975 358

Cooper, W. W., and Y. Ijiri, Kohler's Dictionary for Accountants, 938

Copleston, F. C., History of Philosophy, 253

Corbett, P. K., C. L. Borgman, and D. Moghdam, Effective Online Searching, 208

Cordasco, F., and D. N. Alloway, Medical Education in the United States, 1614

Cormier, R., International Directory of Philosophy and Philosophers, 249

Corsi, P., and P. Weindling, Information Sources in the History of Science and Medicine, 1220

Cote, N., and M. M. Grant, Directory of Business and Financial Services, p. 206

Cotterell, A., Dictionary of World Mythology, 319

Cotterell, A., Encyclopedia of Ancient Civilization, 1131

Council on Foreign Relations, Foreign Affairs Bibliography, 1062
Counihan, M., Dictionary of Energy, 1493
Countries of the World and their Leaders Yearbook, 1073
County and City Data Book, U.S. Dept. of Commerce, Bureau of the Census, 166
County Yearbook, 97, 1040
CQ Weekly Report, 1019
Crabbe, D., and S. Lawson, World Food Book, 1584
Crabbe, D., and R. McBride, World Energy Book, 1504
Crafts-Lighty, A., Information Sources in Biotechnology, 1512
Craig, T. L., Directory of Historical Societies and Agencies in the United States and Canada, 1134
Craig, W., Sweet and Lowdown, 491
Crawford, P., and M. Sears, Song Index, 506n
CRC Handbook of Biochemistry and Molecular Biology, G. D. Fasman, 1558
CRC Handbook of Chemistry and Physics, R. C. Weast, 1357, 1389
CRC Handbook of Laboratory Safety, N. V. Steere, 1267
CRC Handbook of Mathematical Sciences, W. H. Beyer, 1304
CRC Handbook of Microbiology, A. I. Laskin and H. A. Lechevalier, 1557
CRC Handbook of Tables for Applied Engineering Science, R. E. Bolz and G. L. Tuve, 1707
CRC Handbook of Tables for Probability and Statistics, W. H. Beyer, 1310
CRC Standard Mathematical Tables, W. H. Beyer, 1305
Crim, K., Abingdon Dictionary of Living Religions, 265
Crisis Bulletin — Emergency After-Hours Facilities, 843
Critical Bibliography of Religion in America, N. R. Burr, 256n
Critical Heritage Series, 434
Critical Index, J. Gerlach and L. Gerlach, 586
Critical Survey of Long Fiction, F. N. Magill, 374
Critical Survey of Short Fiction, F. N. Magill and W. Beacham, 373
Critical Temper, M. Tucker, 413
Croner, H. B., National Directory of Private Social Agencies, 828
Crosby, E. U., C. J. Bishko, and R. L. Kellogg, Medieval Studies, 1118
Cross, F. L., and E. A. Livingstone, Oxford Dictionary of the Christian Church, 268

Cross, L. R., and W. F. Owen, Guide to Graduate Study in Economics and Agricultural Economics in the United States of America and Canada, 955
Crowell's Handbook of Classical Mythology, E. Tripp, 322
Crowley, M., Energy: Sources of Print and Nonprint Materials, 1484
Cuddon, J. A., Dictionary of Literary Terms, 365
Cuff, D. J., and W. J. Young, United States Energy Atlas, 1506
Cummings, P., Dictionary of Contemporary American Artists, 559
Cummings, P., Fine Arts Market Place, 542
Cumulated Dramatic Index, 1909-1949, 590
Cumulative Book Index, 3, 16
Cumulative Index to Nursing and Allied Health Literature, 1605
Cumulative Subject Index to the Monthly Catalog of U.S. Government Publications, 1900-1971, W. W. Buchanan and E. M. Kanely, 61
Cumulative Title Index to U.S. Government Publications, 1789-1975, D. W. Lester and S. Faull, 68
Curley, A., and D. N. Curley, Modern Romance Literature, 418
Curley, D. N., and A. Curley, Modern Romance Literature, 418
Curley, D. N., M. Kramer, and E. F. Kramer, Modern American Literature, 416
Current Book Review Citations, 180
Current Career and Occupational Literature, L. H. Goodman, 772-73
Current Contents: Agriculture, Biology & Environmental Sciences, 1468, 1517n, 1570
Current Contents: Clinical Practice, 1594
Current Contents: Engineering, Technology & Applied Sciences, 1688
Current Contents: Life Sciences, 1517
Current Contents: Physical, Chemical & Earth Sciences, 1316n, 1341, 1369, 1416
Current Contents Address Directory, 124; p. 276
Current Geographical Publications, 1182
Current History Encyclopedia of Developing Nations, C. L. Thompson, M. M. Anderberg, and J. B. Antell, 1082
Current Index to Journals in Education, 708
Current Information Sources in Mathematics, E. M. Dick, 1285
Current Law Index, 1091
Current Mathematical Publications, 1288
Current Papers in Electrical and Electronics Engineering, 1694
Current Papers in Physics, 1342

Current Papers on Computers and Control, 1655

Current Physics Index, 1343

Current Programs, 1234n

Current Technology Index, 1687

Current Work in the History of Medicine, 1618

Cyclopedia of Literary Characters, F. N. Magill, 382

Daintith, J., Dictionary of Physical Sciences, 1252

Daintith, J., Facts on File Dictionary of Chemistry, 1371

Daintith, J., Facts on File Dictionary of Physics, 1344

Daintith, J., A. Isaacs, and E. Martin, Concise Science Dictionary, 1250

Daintith, J., S. Mitchell, and E. Tootill, Biographical Encyclopedia of Scientists, 1279

Dalal-Clayton, D. B., Black's Agricultural Dictionary, 1573, 1578n

Dance Encyclopedia, A. Chujoy and P. W. Manchester, 603

Dance World, J. Willis, 624

Dangerous Properties of Industrial Materials, N. I. Sax, 1398

Daniel, G., Illustrated Encyclopedia of Archaeology, 894

Daniells, L. M., Business Information Sources, 919

Daniells, L. M., Business Reference Sources, 922

Darnay, B. T., Directory of Special Libraries and Information Centers, 112

Darnay, B. T., Subject Directory of Special Libraries and Information Centers, 113

Database, 206

David, N., TV Season, 683

Davis, E. B., Using the Biological Literature, 1509

Davis, L., and R. Irwin, Contemporary American Poetry, 349

Day, J. A., and V. J. Schaefer, Field Guide to the Atmosphere, 1451

Dean, J. A., Lange's Handbook of Chemistry, 1390

DeBary, W. T., and A. T. Embree, Guide to Oriental Classics, 437

Decennial Census, U.S. Dept. of Commerce, Bureau of the Census, 169

De Charms, D., and P. F. Breed, Songs in Collections, 506

De Conde, A., Encyclopedia of American Foreign Policy, 1066

Deffontaines, P., Larousse Encyclopedia of World Geography, 1191

DeGeorge, R. T., Philosopher's Guide to Sources, Research Tools, Professional Life, and Related Fields, 229

Deighton, L. C., Encyclopedia of Education, 712

Deighton, S., J. Gurnsey, and J. Tomlinson, Computers and Information Processing World Index, 1650

De la Croix, H., and R. G. Tansey, Gardner's Art through the Ages, 550

Delaney, J. J., and J. E. Tobin, Dictionary of Catholic Biography, 295

Dell, D. J., Guide to Hindu Religion, 258

Delury, G. E., World Encyclopedia of Political Systems and Parties, 1076

Demographic Estimates for Countries with Populations of 10 Million or More, U.S. Dept. of Commerce, Bureau of the Census, 848

Demographic Yearbook, United Nations, Statistical Office, 847

Derry, C., J. C. Ellis, and S. Kern, Film Book Bibliography, 582

Descriptive Catalogue of the Government Publications of the United States, B. P. Poore, 63

Deutsche Bibliographie: Hochschulschriften-Verzeichnis, 44

Developing Labor Law, C. J. Morris, 960

Dewe, A., and J. L. Hall, Online Information Retrieval, 200

Dexter, B., Foreign Affairs 50-Year Bibliography, 1063

Diamond, H. J., Music Criticism, 446

Dick, E. M., Current Information Sources in Mathematics, 1285

Dickason, E. J., and others, Handbook of Nursing, 1640

Dickerson, G. F., and E. Rubinstein, Religion Index Two: Multi-author Works, 1970-1975, 261n

Dictionary Catalog of the National Agricultural Library, 1568

Dictionary Catalog of the Research Libraries of the New York Public Library, 12, 15n

Dictionary of Agricultural and Allied Terminology, J. N. Winburne, 1572

Dictionary of American Biography, 144

Dictionary of American Communal and Utopian History, R. S. Fogarty, 1169

Dictionary of American Diplomatic History, J. E. Findling, 1065

Dictionary of American History, 1166

Dictionary of American Library Biography, 758

Dictionary of American Medical Biography, M. Kaufman, S. Galishoff, and T. L. Savitt, 1646

Dictionary of American Penology, V. L.
    Williams, 823
Dictionary of American Politics, E. C. Smith
    and A. J. Zucher, 1007
Dictionary of American Proverbs and
    Proverbial Phrases, A. Taylor and
    B. J. Whiting, 901
Dictionary of American Religious Biography,
    H. W. Bowden, 294
Dictionary of Anonymous and Pseudonymous
    English Literature, S. Halkett and
    J. Laing, 357
Dictionary of Anonymous and Pseudonymous
    Publications in the English Language,
    J. Holden, 357n
Dictionary of Anthropology, C. Winick, 888
Dictionary of Applied Energy Conservation,
    D. Kut, 1496
Dictionary of Architecture, N. Pevsner, J.
    Fleming, and H. Honour, 535
Dictionary of Architecture and Construction,
    C. M. Harris, 538
Dictionary of Astronomy, I. Nicolson, 1321
Dictionary of Astronomy, Space and
    Atmospheric Phenomena, D. F. Tver,
    1322
Dictionary of Banking and Finance, J. M.
    Rosenberg, 936
Dictionary of Basic Geography, A. A.
    Schmieder, 1188
Dictionary of Biochemistry, J. Stenesh, 1548
Dictionary of Books Relating to America
    from its Discovery to the Present
    Time, J. Sabin, 26
Dictionary of Botany, R. J. Little and C. E.
    Jones, 1533
Dictionary of British Folk-Tales in the English
    Language, K. M. Briggs, 899
Dictionary of Business and Management, J. M.
    Rosenberg, 933
Dictionary of Catholic Biography, J. J. Delaney
    and J. E. Tobin, 295
Dictionary of Chemical Names, W. E. Flood,
    1375
Dictionary of Christian Theology, A. Richard-
    son, 273
Dictionary of Classical Mythology, R. E. Bell,
    323
Dictionary of Comparative Religion, S. G. F.
    Brandon, 266
Dictonary of Computers, Data Processing, and
    Telecommunications, J. M. Rosenberg,
    1657
Dictionary of Computing and New Information
    Technology, A. J. Meadows, M. Gordon,
    and A. Singleton, 1667
Dictionary of Concepts on American Politics,
    J. B. Whisker, 1009n

Dictionary of Contemporary American Artists,
    P. Cummings, 559
Dictionary of Contemporary Artists, V. B.
    Smith, 560
Dictionary of Contemporary Music, J. Vinton,
    453
Dictionary of Dangerous Pollutants, Ecology
    and Environment, D. F. Tver, 1475
Dictionary of Data Processing, J. Maynard,
    1661
Dictionary of Dates, R. Collison, 1135
Dictionary of Earth Sciences, S. E. Stiegeler,
    1421
Dictionary of Ecology, Evolution and
    Systematics, R. J. Lincoln, G. A.
    Boxshall, and P. F. Clark, 1539
Dictionary of Economics and Business,
    E. E. Nemmers, 943
Dictionary of Education, C. V. Good, 710
Dictionary of Energy, M. Counihan, 1493
Dictionary of Energy, M. Slesser, 1495
Dictionary of Fictional Characters, W.
    Freeman, 383
Dictionary of Genetics, R. C. King and
    W. D. Stansfield, 1546
Dictionary of Geological Terms, R. L. Bates
    and J. A. Jackson, 1418
Dictionary of Geology, J. Challinor, 1419
Dictionary of Human Behavior, D. Statt, 789
Dictionary of Imaginary Places, A. Manguel
    and G. Guadalupi, 388
Dictionary of Information Technology, D.
    Longley and M. Shain, 1666
Dictionary of International Biography, 134
Dictionary of Inventions and Discoveries, E. F.
    Carter, 1259
Dictionary of Irish Literature, R. Hogan, 368n
Dictionary of Italian Literature, P. Bondanella
    and J. Bondanella, 368n
Dictionary of Life Sciences, E. A. Martin,
    1525
Dictionary of Literary Biography, M. J.
    Bruccoli, 395-97
Dictionary of Literary Pseudonyms, F.
    Atkinson, 404
Dictionary of Literary Terms, J. A. Cuddon, 365
Dictionary of Microbiology, P. Singleton and
    D. Sainsbury, 1543
Dictionary of Minicomputing and Micro-
    computing, P. E. Burton,
    1660
Dictionary of Modern Economics, D. W.
    Pearce, 944
Dictionary of Modern Sociology, T. F. Hoult,
    820
Dictionary of Musical Themes, H. Barlow and
    S. Morgenstern, 470

Dictionary of Named Effects and Laws in Chemistry, Physics, and Mathematics, D. W. G. Ballentyne and D. R. Lovett, 1258

Dictionary of National Biography, L. Stephen and S. Lee, 147

Dictionary of New Information Technology Acronyms, M. Gordon, A. Singleton, and C. Rickards, 1672

Dictionary of Non-Christian Religions, E. G. Parrinder, 278

Dictionary of Opera and Song Themes, H. Barlow and S. Morgenstern, 471

Dictionary of Personnel Managment and Labor Relations, M. J. Shafritz, 935

Dictionary of Philosophy, A. Flew, 242

Dictionary of Philosophy, A. R. Lacey, 241

Dictionary of Physical Sciences, J. Daintith, 1252

Dictionary of Political Analysis, J. Plano, R. E. Riggs, and H. S. Robin, 1009

Dictionary of Political Analysis, G. K. Roberts, 1009n

Dictionary of Politics, W. Lacquer, 1006

Dictionary of Report Series Codes, L. E. Godfrey and H. F. Redman, 1254

Dictionary of Scientific Biography, C. C. Gillispie, 1273

Dictionary of Scientific Units including Dimensionless Numbers and Scales, H. G. Jerrard and D. B. McNeill, 1255

Dictionary of Social Science Methods, P. M. Miller and M. J. Wilson, 702

Dictionary of Sociology, G. D. Mitchell, 822

Dictionary of Statistical Terms, M. G. Kendall and W. R. Buckland, 1300

Dictionary of Subjects and Symbols in Art, J. Hall, 540

Dictionary of Telecommunciations, S. J. Aries, 1669

Dictionary of Terms and Techniques in Archaeology, S. Champion, 892

Dictionary of the Bible, J. Hastings, 302

Dictionary of the Bible, J. L. McKenzie, 305

Dictionary of the Biological Sciences, P. Gray, 1522

Dictionary of the Environment, M. Allaby, 1472

Dictionary of the Environmental Sciences, R. W. Durrenberger, 1473

Dictionary of the History of Science, W. F. Bynum, E. J. Browne, and R. Porter, 1260

Dictionary of the Middle Ages, J. R. Strayer, 1129

Dictionary of the Natural Environment, F. J. Monkhouse and J. Small, 1474

Dictionary of the Social Sciences, J. Gould and W. L. Kolb, 701

Dictionary of the Social Sciences, H. F. Reading, 700

Dictionary of Theoretical Concepts in Biology, K. E. Roe and R. G. Frederick, 1519

Dictionary of Universal Biography of All Ages and All People, M. Hyamson, 141

Dictionary of Vocal Themes, H. Barlow and S. Morgenstern, 471n

Dictionary of World Mythology, A. Cotterell, 319

Dictionary of Zoology, A. W. Leftwich, 1530

Dictionnaire critique et documentaire des peintres, sculpteurs, dessinateurs, et graveurs, E. Benezit, 556

Dictionnaire de biographie française, 149

Digest of Educational Statistics, National Center for Educational Statistics, 743

Dimmitt, R. B., Actor Guide to the Talkies, 655

Dimmitt, R. B., Title Guide to the Talkies, 653

Directory for Exceptional Children, 839

Directory of Agencies, National Association of Social Workers, 829

Directory of Agencies Serving the Visually Handicapped in the United States, American Foundation for the Blind, 837

Directory of American Philosophers, A. Bahm, 248

Directory of American Scholars, 228

Directory of Archives and Manuscript Repositories in the United States, U.S. General Services Administration, National Archives and Records Service, National Historical Publications and Record Commission, 1133

Directory of British Associations and Associations in Ireland, G. P. Henderson and S. P. A. Henderson, 101

Directory of Business and Financial Services, M. M. Grant and N. Cote, p. 206

Directory of Corporate Affiliations: Who Owns Whom, 950

Directory of Directories, J. M. Ethridge, 119, 1261n

Directory of Engineering Societies and Related Organizations, 1702

Directory of European Associations, I. G. Anderson, 102

Directory of European Political Scientists, European Consortium for Political Research, 1016

Directory of Food and Nutrition Information Services and Resources, R. C. Frank, 1581

Directory of Geoscience Departments, American Geological Institute, 1459

Directory of Graduate Research, American Chemical Society, 1406

Directory of Historical Societies and
    Agencies in the United States and
    Canada, T. L. Craig, 1134
Directory of Industry Data Sources, 924
Directory of Information Resources in the
    United States: Biological Sciences, 1552
Directory of Information Sources in the United
    States: Geosciences and Oceanography,
    1444
Directory of Medical Specialists, 1642
Directory of National Unions and Employee
    Associations, 954
Directory of Online Databases, 115
Directory of Physics and Astronomy Staff
    Members, 1358
Directory of Published Proceedings: Series
    SEMT, 33, 1235
Directory of Published Proceedings: Series
    SSH, 33, 225, 704
Directory of Published Sources, S.
    Balachandran, 1695
Directory of Religious Bodies in the United
    States, J. G. Melton, 284
Directory of Religious Organizations in the
    United States, 283
Directory of Research Grants, 107
Directory of Resources for Cultural and
    Educational Exchanges and
    International Communication, 781
Directory of Scientific Directories, J. Burkett,
    1261
Directory of Social and Health Agencies of
    New York City, N. Lecyn and W. P.
    Germano, 841
Directory of Special Libraries and Information
    Centers, B. T. Darnay, 112
Directory of Special Programs for Minority
    Group Members, W. L. Johnson, 833
Directory of World Museums, K. Hudson and
    A. Nichols, 544
Dissertation Abstracts International, 41
DISSERTATION ABSTRACTS ONLINE, 41n
Dissertations in American Literature, J. L.
    Woodress, 343
Dissertations in English and American Litera-
    ture, L. F. D. McNamee, 342
Dissertations in Philosophy Accepted at
    American Universities, T. C. Bechtle and
    M. F. Riley, 234
Dittmer, D. S., and P. L. Altman, Biology
    Data Book, 1555
Dizionario Biografico degli Italiani, 152
Dobrée, B., and F. P. Wilson, Oxford History
    of English Literature, 390
Dobson, A. B., and T. C. Collocott, Chambers
    Dictionary of Science and Technology,
    1249
Document Catalog, U.S. Superintendent of
    Documents, 60n

Documentation in Education, A. J. Burke and
    M. A. Burke, 707n
Documents of American History, H. S.
    Commager, 1173
DOE ENERGY, 1487n
Dorf, R., Energy Factbook, 1502
Dorland's Illustrated Medical Dictionary,
    1620
Dorling, A. R., Use of Mathematical Literature,
    1283
Dorris, M. A., A. B. Hirschfelder, and M. G.
    Byler, Guide to Research on North
    American Indians, 874
Dougherty, J. J., Writings on American
    History, 1162n
Douglas, J. D., New International Dictionary
    of the Christian Church, 269
Dow Jones-Irwin Business and Investment
    Almanac, 958
Downes, E., Guide to Symphonic Music, 456
Dox, I., B. J. Melloni, and G. M. Eisner,
    Melloni's Illustrated Medical Dictionary,
    1622
Drama Criticism, A. Coleman and G. R.
    Tyler, 426
Drama Scholar's Index to Plays and Film-
    strips, G. Samples, 674
Dramatic Criticism Index, P. F. Breed and
    F. M. Sniderman, 427
Drazil, J. V., Quantities and Units of
    Measurement, 1257
Dresner, S., Units of Measurement, 1256
DRG: Directory of Research Grants, 107
Drone, J. M., Index to Opera, Operetta, and
    Musical Comedy Synopses in
    Collections and Periodicals, 479
Drury's Guide to Best Plays, J. M. Salem,
    676
Duckles, V., Music Reference and Research
    Materials, 438
Duncan, E. E., and P. J. Klingensmith, Easy
    Access to DIALOG, ORBIT, and BRS,
    212
Dunn, R. J., English Novel, 421
Dunning, J., Tune in Yesterday, 677
Dun's Business Rankings, 984
Dupuy, R. E., and T. N. Dupuy, Encyclopedia
    of Military History from 3500 B.C.
    to the Present, 1125
Dupuy, T. N., and R. E. Dupuy, Encyclopedia
    of Military History from 3500 B.C. to
    the Present, 1125
Durbin, P. T., Guide to the Culture of Science,
    Technology, and Medicine, 1219
Durrenberger, R. W., Dictionary of the
    Environmental Sciences, 1473
Dyson, A. J., and H. H. Palmer, English
    Novel Explication, 420

Eagle, D., Oxford Companion to English Literature, 379

Eagle, D., and H. Carnell, Oxford Illustrated Literary Guide to Great Britain and Ireland, 386

Eastern Definitions, E. Rice, 279

Easy Access to DIALOG, ORBIT, and BRS, P. J. Klingensmith and E. E. Duncan, 212

Ecology Field Glossary, W. H. Lewis, 1538

Economic Handbook of the World, A. S. Banks, 961

Economic Indicators, U.S. Council of Economic Advisors, 969; p. 45

Economic Report of the President to the Congress, 970

Economics, P. Melnyk, 921

Economics Dictionary, D. W. Moffat, 942

Eddleman, F. E., American Drama Criticism, 428

Ede, D., Guide to Islam, 259

Edgerton, W. B., and J. A. Bédé, Columbia Dictionary of Modern European Literature, 369

Editor and Publisher Market Guide, 964

Edmunds, R. A., Prentice-Hall Standard Glossary of Computer Terminology, 1658

Education Directory, U.S. Dept. of Education, National Center for Education Statistics, 715

Education Index, 709

Educational Testing Service, ETS Test Collection, 764

Edwards, I. E. S., Cambridge Ancient History, 1154

Edwards, P., Encyclopedia of Philosophy, 245

Effective Legal Research, M. O. Price, H. Bitner, and S. R. Bysiewicz, 1089

Effective Online Searching, C. L. Borgman, D. Moghdam, and P. K. Corbett, 208

Egan, E. W., Kings, Rulers, and Statesmen, 1145n

Ehrenhalt, A., and M. Glennon, Politics in America, 1023

Ehresmann, D. L., Applied and Decorative Arts, 516

Ehresmann, D. L., Architecture, 515

Ehresmann, D. L., Fine Arts, 511

EI ENGINEERING MEETINGS, 1686n

Eighteenth Century, R. R. Allen, 346

EIS: Digests of Environmental Impact Statements, 1467

Eisenberg, G. G., Learning Vacations, 782

Eisler, E., N. Hatch, and E. Eisler, World Chronology of Music History, 458

Eisler, P. E., N. Hatch, and E. Eisler, World Chronology of Music History, 458

Eisler, R. Wörterbuch der philosophischen Begriffe, 244n

Eisner, G. M., I. Dox, and B. J. Melloni, Melloni's Illustrated Medical Dictionary, 1622

Ekerdt, J. G., Chemical Engineering Faculties, 1405

Ekwurzel, D., and N. Perlman, Index of Economic Articles in Journals and Collective Volumes, 932

Electrical and Electronics Abstracts, 1693

ELECTRONIC YELLOW PAGES, p. 29, p. 59

Electronics Engineers' Handbook, D. G. Fink and D. Christiansen, 1711

Elkins, E. A., and J. M. Morris, Library Searching: Resources and Strategies with Examples from the Environmental Sciences, 1461

Elliott, C. A., Biographical Dictionary of American Science, 1282

Ellis, J. C., C. Derry, and S. Kern, Film Book Bibliography, 582

Ellison, J. W., Nelson's Complete Concordance of the Revised Standard Version Bible, 307

Ellwood, R. S., Religious and Spiritual Groups in Modern America, 300

Emanuel, M., Contemporary Architects, 565

Emanuel, M., Contemporary Artists, 563

EMBASE, 1593n

Embree, A. T., and W. T. DeBary, Guide to Oriental Classics, 437

Emmens, C. A., Famous People on Film, 659

Enciclopedia dello Spettacolo, 595; p. 7

Enciclopedia filosofica, 247

Encyclopaedia Judaica, 276

Encyclopaedia of Religion and Ethics, J. Hastings, 267

Encyclopaedic Dictionary of Mathematics for Engineers and Applied Scientists, I. N. Sneddon, 1297

Encyclopaedic Dictionary of Physics, J. Thewlis, 1346n, 1350

Encyclopedia and Dictionary of Medicine, Nursing, and Allied Health, B. F. Miller and C. B. Keane, 1630

Encyclopedia of American Architecture, W. D. Hunt, 536

Encyclopedia of American Facts and Dates, G. Carruth, 1174

Encyclopedia of American Foreign Policy, A. De Conde, 1066

Encyclopedia of American History, R. B. Morris and J. B. Morris, 1171

Encyclopedia of American Religions, J. G. Melton, 298

Encyclopedia of Ancient Civilization, A. Cotterell, 1131

Encyclopedia of Anthropology, D. E. Hunter and P. Whitten, 889

Encyclopedia of Applied Geology, C. W. Finkl, Jr., 1434

Encyclopedia of Associations, 100; p. 28
Encyclopedia of Astronomy, G. E.
    Satterthwaite, 1325
Encyclopedia of Atmospheric Sciences and
    Astrogeology, R. W. Fairbridge, 1426
Encyclopedia of Banking and Finance, G. G.
    Munn, 937
Encyclopedia of Beaches and Coastal Environ-
    ments, M. L. Schwartz, 1435
Encyclopedia of Bioethics, W. T. Reich, 1631
Encyclopedia of Business Information Sources,
    P. Wasserman, C. Georgi, and J. Woy,
    920
Encyclopedia of Chemical Trademarks and
    Synonyms, H. Bennett, 1394
Encyclopedia of Computer Science and
    Engineering, A. Ralston and E. D.
    Reilly, Jr., 1663
Encyclopedia of Computer Science and Tech-
    nology, 1664
Encyclopedia of Crime and Justice, S. H.
    Kadish, 825
Encyclopedia of Dance and Ballet, M. Clarke
    and D. Vaughan, 604
Encyclopedia of Economics, D. Greenwald, 945
Encyclopedia of Education, L. C. Deighton,
    712
Encyclopedia of Educational Research, H. E.
    Mitzel, 748
Encyclopedia of Folk, Country, and Western
    Music, I. Stambler and G. Landon,
    496
Encyclopedia of Geochemistry and Environ-
    mental Sciences, R. W. Fairbridge, 1428
Encyclopedia of Geomorphology, R. W. Fair-
    bridge, 1427
Encyclopedia of Human Behavior, R. M.
    Goldenson, 794
Encyclopedia of Industrial Chemical Analysis,
    F. D. Snell, C. L. Hilton, and L. S.
    Ettre, 1386
Encyclopedia of Information Systems and
    Services, J. Schmittroth, 116
Encyclopedia of Islam, H. A. R. Gibb, 280
Encyclopedia of Jazz, L. Feather, 492
Encyclopedia of Jazz in the Seventies,
    L. Feather, 494
Encyclopedia of Jazz in the Sixties, L. Feather,
    493
Encyclopedia of Management, C. Heyel, 934
Encyclopedia of Medical Organizations and
    Agencies, A. T. Kruzas, 1633
Encyclopedia of Microscopy and Microtech-
    nique, P. Gray, 1542
Encyclopedia of Military History from 3500 B.C.
    to the Present, R. E. Dupuy and T. N.
    Dupuy, 1125
Encyclopedia of Mineraology, K. Frye, 1429
Encyclopedia of Minerals, W. L. Roberts,
    G. R. Rapp, Jr., and J. Weber, 1450

Encyclopedia of Modern Architecture,
    W. Pehnt, 537
Encyclopedia of Oceanography, R. W. Fair-
    bridge, 1425
Encyclopedia of Paleontology, R. W. Fair-
    bridge and D. Jablonski, 1431
Encyclopedia of Philosophy, P. Edwards, 245
Encyclopedia of Physics, R. M. Besançon,
    1348
Encyclopedia of Physics, R. G. Lerner and
    G. L. Trigg, 1347
Encyclopedia of Pop, Rock, and Soul,
    I. Stambler, 497
Encyclopedia of Prehistoric Life, R. Steel
    and A. P. Harvey, 1438
Encyclopedia of Psychology, H. J. Eysenck,
    793
Encyclopedia of Sedimentololgy, R. W. Fair-
    bridge and J. Bourgeois, 1430
Encyclopedia of Social Work, J. B. Turner,
    824
Encyclopedia of Soil Science, R. W. Fair-
    bridge and C. W. Finkl, Jr., 1433
Encyclopedia of Statistical Sciences, 1302
Encyclopedia of the American Theatre, 1900-
    1975, E. Bronner, 660
Encyclopedia of the Biological Sciences,
    P. Gray, 1527
Encyclopedia of the Chemical Elements,
    C. A. Hampel, 1381
Encyclopedia of the Musical Film, S. Green,
    599
Encyclopedia of the Musical Theatre, S. Green,
    605
Encyclopedia of the Opera, L. Orrey, 475
Encyclopedia of the Third World, G. Kurian,
    1081
Encyclopedia of World Art, 532
Encyclopedia of World Geography, 1190
Encyclopedia of World History, W. L. Langer,
    1123
Encyclopedia of World Literature in the 20th
    Century, L. S. Klein, 370; p. 92
Encyclopedia of World Regional Geology,
    R. W. Fairbridge, 1432
Encyclopedia of World Theater, M. Esslin, 600
Encyclopedic Dictionary of Industrial Tech-
    nology, D. F. Tver and R. W. Bolz,
    1698
Encyclopedic Dictionary of Mathematics,
    S. Iyanaga and Y. Kawada, 1296
Encyclopedic Dictionary of Psychology,
    R. Harré and R. Lamb, 791
Encyclopedic Dictionary of Religion,
    P. K. Meagher, T. C. O'Brien, and
    Sister C. M. Aherne, 270
Energy: Sources of Print and Nonprint Mate-
    rials, M. Crowley, 1484
Energy Abstracts for Policy Analysis, 1488

Energy Dictionary, V. D. Hunt, 1494
Energy Directory, 1497
Energy Factbook, R. Dorf, 1502
Energy Handbook, R. L. Loftness, 1503
Energy Index, 1486
Energy Information Abstracts, 1485
Energy Information Guide, R. D. Weber,
    1482
Energy Research Abstracts, 1487
Energy Research Guide, J. Viola, N. B. Mack,
    and T. R. Stauffer, 1491
Energy Research Programs, 1500
Energy Statistics, S. Balachandran, 1490
Energy Technology Handbook, D. M.
    Considine, 1505
ENERGYLINE, 1485n
ENERGYNET, 1497n
Engineering Index, 1686
Engineering Mathematics Handbook, J. J.
    Tuma, 1308
Engineering Research Centres, T. Archbold,
    J. C. Laidlaw, and J. McKechnie, 1703
English, A. C., and H. B. English, Compre-
    hensive Dictionary of Psychological and
    Psychoanalytical Terms, 790
English, H. B., and A. C. English, Compre-
    hensive Dictionary of Psychological and
    Psychoanalytical Terms, 790
English Association, Year's Work in English
    Studies, 359
English Novel, R. J. Dunn, 421
English Novel Explication, H. H. Palmer and
    A. J. Dyson, 420
English Novel, 1578-1956, I. F. Bell and
    D. Baird, 419
English Tests and Reviews, 762n
English Versification, 1570-1980, T. V. F.
    Brogan, 348
Entomology Abstracts, 1513n
ENVIROLINE, 1464n
Environment Abstracts 1463
Environment Index, 1464
Environmental Impact Analysis Handbook,
    J. G. Rau and D. C. Wooten, 1480
Environmental Impact Assessment, B. D. Clark,
    R. Bisset, and P. Wathern, 1470
Environmental Impact Data Book, J. Golden,
    R. P. Ouellette, S. Saari, and P. N.
    Cheremisinoff, 1481
Environmental Impact Statement Glossary,
    M. Landy, 1476
Environmental Periodicals Bibliography, 1466
EPA Index, C. E. Bower and M. L. Rhoads,
    1469
Eshbach, O. W., and M. Souders, Handbook
    of Engineering Fundamentals, 1704
Espina, N., Repertoire for the Solo Voice,
    467

Esslin, M., Encyclopedia of World Theater,
    600
Ethnographic Atlas, G. P. Murdock, 904
Ethnographic Bibliography of North America,
    G. P. Murdock and T. J. O'Leary,
    871
Ethnographic Bibliography of South America,
    T. J. O'Leary, 872
Ethological Dictionary, A. Heymer, 1541
Ethridge, J. M., Directory of Directories,
    119
ETS Test Collection, 764
Ettre, L. S., F. D. Snell, and C. L. Hilton,
    Encyclopedia of Industrial Chemical
    Analysis, 1386
Europa Year Book, 98, 1071; p. 45
Europe, R. J. Theodoratus, 873
European Authors, 1000-1900, S. S. Kunitz and
    V. Colby, 394
European Consortium for Political Research,
    Directory of European Political
    Scientists, 1016
European Drama Criticism, 1900-1975, H. H.
    Palmer, 429
European Historical Statistics, 1750-1975, B. R.
    Mitchell, 172, 1151
European Political Facts, 1789-1973, C. Cook
    and J. Paxton, 1079
Evaluating Bibliographic Instruction, American
    Library Association, Association of
    College and Research Libraries, Biblio-
    graphic Instruction Section, Research
    Committee Subcommittee on
    Evaluation, 195
Evaluating Classroom Instruction, G. D. Borich
    and S. K. Madden, 765
Evans, A., Glossary of Molecular Biology,
    1544
Evans, C., American Bibliography, 24
Everett, T. H., New York Botanical Garden
    Illustrated Encyclopedia of Horticulture,
    1575
Everyman's Dictionary of Non-Classical
    Mythology, E. Sykes, 321
Ewen, D., Composers of Tomorrow's Music,
    465
Ewen, D., Composers since 1900, 464
Ewen, D., Musicians since 1900, 466
Ewen, D., New Complete Book of the American
    Musical Theater, 661
Excerpta Medica, 1593
Exhaustive Concordance of the Bible,
    J. Strong, 309
Eysenck, H. J., Encyclopedia of Psychology,
    793
Eysenck, H. J., Handbook of Abnormal Psy-
    chology, 796

Facts about the Presidents, J. N. Kane, 1029

Facts and Figures on Government Finance, 995

Facts on File Dictionary of Archaeology, R. D. Whitehouse, 893

Facts on File Dictionary of Astronomy, V. Illingworth, 1318

Facts on File Dictionary of Biology, E. Tootill, 1524

Facts on File Dictionary of Botany, S. Blackmore and E. Tootill, 1532

Facts on File Dictionary of Chemistry, J. Daintith, 1371

Facts on File Dictionary of European History, 1485-1789, E. N. Williams, 1126

Facts on File Dictionary of Mathematics, C. Gibson, 1293

Facts on File Dictionary of Physics, J. Daintith, 1344

Facts on File Dictionary of Telecommunications, J. Graham, 1670

Faculty Alert Bulletin, 107n

Fairbridge, R. W., Encyclopedia of Atmospheric Sciences and Astrogeology, 1426

Fairbridge, R. W., Encyclopedia of Geochemistry and Environmental Sciences, 1428

Fairbridge, R. W., Encyclopedia of Geomorphology, 1427

Fairbridge, R. W., Encyclopedia of Oceanography, 1425

Fairbridge, R. W., Encyclopedia of World Regional Geology, 1432

Fairbridge, R. W., and J. Bourgeois, Encyclopedia of Sedimentology, 1430

Fairbridge, R. W., and C. W. Finkl, Jr., Encyclopedia of Soil Science, 1433

Fairbridge, R. W., and D. Jablonski, Encyclopedia of Paleontology, 1431

Fairchild, W. B., K. A. Hammond, and G. Macinko, Sourcebook on the Environment, 1462

Falk, B. A., and V. R. Falk, Personal Name Index to "The New York Times Index," 1851-1974, 140

Falk, V. R., and B. A. Falk, Personal Name Index to "The New York Times index," 1851-1974, 140

Famous Actors and Actresses on the American Stage, W. C. Young, 645

Famous Names in Engineering, J. Carvill, 1713

Famous People on Film, C. A. Emmens, 659

Farber, E., Combined Retrospective Index to Book Reviews in Scholarly Journals, 1886-1974, 185

Farber, E., S. Hannah, and S. Schindler, Combined Retrospective Index to Book Reviews in Humanities Journals, 1802-1974, 186

Farish, M., String Music in Print, 468

Farmer, D. H., Oxford Dictionary of Saints, 297

Farrell, L., and J. R. Blanchard, Guide to Sources for Agricultural and Biological Research, 1561

Fasman, G. D., CRC Handbook of Biochemistry and Molecular Biology, 1558

Faull, S., and D. W. Lester, Cumulative Title Index to U.S. Government Publications, 1789-1975, 68

Feather, L., Encyclopedia of Jazz, 492

Feather, L., Encyclopedia of Jazz in the Seventies, 494

Feather, L., Encyclopedia of Jazz in the Sixties, 493

Federal Executive Directory, 89

Federal Register, 1101

Federal Regulatory Directory, 90, 1028

Federal Tax Guide, 996

Feingold, M., and S. N. Feingold, Scholarships, Fellowships, and Loans, 767

Feingold, S. N., and M. Feingold, Scholarships, Fellowships, and Loans, 767

Fenichel, C. H., and T. H. Hogan, Online Searching, 207

Fenster, C. K., Guide to American Literature, 327

Ferres, J. H., and M. Tucker, Modern Commonwealth Literature, 417

Field Guide to the Atmosphere, V. J. Schaefer and J. A. Day, 1451

Field Guide to the Stars and Planets, D. H. Menzel and J. M. Pasachoff, 1333

Fifth International Directory of Anthropologists, 902; p. 204

Film, R. A. Armour, 579

Film Book Bibliography, J. C. Ellis, C. Derry, and S. Kern, 582

Film Criticism, R. Heinzkill, 686

Film Encyclopedia, E. Katz, 597

Film Facts, C. S. Steinberg, 618

Film Literature Index, 583

Filmarama, J. Stewart, 640

Filmgoer's Companion, L. Halliwell, 613

Financial Aids for Higher Education, O. Keeslar, 768

Financial Handbook, E. I. Altman and M. J. McKinney, 957

Finding Answers in Science and Technology, A. L. Primack, 1212

Finding the Law, A. Coco, 1086

Findling, J. E., Dictionary of American Diplomatic History, 1065

Fine Art Reproductions of Old and Modern Masters, New York Graphic Society, 568

Fine Arts, D. L. Ehresmann, 511

Fine Arts Market Place, P. Cummings, 542

Fink, D. G., and H. W. Beaty, Standard Handbook for Electrical Engineers, 1710

Fink, D. G., and D. Christiansen, Electronics Engineers' Handbook, 1711

Finkl, C. W., Jr., Encyclopedia of Applied Geology, 1434

Finkl, C. W., Jr., and R. W. Fairbridge, Encyclopedia of Soil Science, 1433

Finely, M. I., Atlas of Classical Archaeology, 916

Finley, R. E., I. Herbert, and C. Baxter, Who's Who in the Theatre, 642

Fisher, J., and D. L. Nortman, Population and Family Planning Programs, 849

Fisher, L. H., Literary Gazetteer of England, 387

Fiske, E. B., Selective Guide to Colleges, 727

Fitzgerald, L. S., and E. L. Kearney, Continental Novel, 424-25

Fitzgerald, S., and L. L. Harris, Nineteenth Century Literature Criticism, 432

Fitzmyer, J. A., R. E. Brown, and R. E. Murphy, Jerome Bible Commentary, 314

Flanagan, C. C., and J. T. Flanagan, American Folklore, 882

Flanagan, J. T., and C. C. Flanagan, American Folklore, 882

Flanz, G. H., and A. P. Blaustein, Constitutions of the Countries of the World, 1075

Fleming, J., Penguin Dictionary of Architecture, 538n

Fleming, J., N. Pevsner, and H. Honour, Dictionary of Architecture, 535

Fletcher, B. F., History of Architecture, 552

Flew, A., Dictionary of Philosophy, 242

Flood, W. E., Dictionary of Chemical Names, 1375

Flügge, S., Handbuch der Physik/Encyclopedia of Physics, 1351

Fogarty, R. S., Dictionary of American Communal and Utopian History, 1169

Fogg Art Museum, Catalogue of the Harvard University of Fine Arts Library, the Fogg Art Museum, 521

Folio-Dex, 508

Folk Song Index, F. E. Brunnings, 507

Folklore, J. H. Brunvand, 881

Folksingers and Folksongs of America, R. M. Lawless, 502

Food Science and Technology Abstracts, 1566

Foods and Food Production Encyclopedia, D. M. Considine and G. D. Considine, 1577

Ford, R. A., and A. J. Gordon, Chemist's Companion, 1391

Foreign Affairs Bibliography, 1062

Foreign Affairs 50-Year Bibliography, B. Dexter, 1063

Foreign Language Tests and Reviews, 762n

Foreign Patents, F. J. Kase, 1684

Forthcoming Books, 9

Foster, L., and C. Boast, Subject Compilations of State Laws, 1092

Foundation Directory, 108

Fox, H. N., and D. Messerlia, Index to Periodical Fiction in English, 1965-1969, 355

Foy, F. A., and Avato, R. M., Catholic Almanac, 287

Frank, R. C., Directory of Food and Nutrition Information Services and Resources, 1581

Frankel, L., and P. Bart, Student Sociologist's Handbook, 801

Fraternal Organizations, A. J. Schmidt and N. Babchuk, 831

Frederick, R. G., and K. E. Roe, Dictionary of Theoretical Concepts in Biology, 1519

Freedley, G., and J. A. Reeves, History of the Theatre, 631

Freedman, J. L., and H. A. Bantly, Information Searching, 194

Freeman, W., Dictionary of Fictional Characters, 383

Freer Gallery of Art, Dictionary Catalog, 520

Freiberger, W. F., International Dictionary of Applied Mathematics, 1295

Freidel, F., and R. K. Showman, Harvard Guide to American History, 1161

French, W. G., and J. A. Robbins, American Literary Scholarship, 360

Fried, J., and M. Lech, Funk & Wagnalls Standard Dictionary of Folklore, Mythology, and Legend, 898

Friederich, W. P., and F. Baldensperger, Bibliography of Comparative Literature, 334

Friedrichs Theaterlexikon, K. Gröning and W. Kliess, 600n

Frye, K., Encyclopedia of Mineralogy, 1429

Fullard, H., and R. F. Treherne, Muir's Historical Atlas, 1146

Fuller, E., and H. Haydn, Thesaurus of Book Digests, 409n

Fuller, G., and A. Lloyd, Illustrated Who's Who of the Cinema, 636

Fundamentals of Legal Research, J. M. Jacobstein and R. M. Mersky, 1088

Funk & Wagnalls Standard Dictionary of Folklore, Mythology, and Legend, M. Leach and J. Fried, 898

Fürer-Haimendorf, E. Von, Anthropological Bibliography of South Asia, 870

Gale Literary Criticism Series, 432

Galishoff, S., M. Kaufman, and T. L. Savitt Dictionary of American Medical Biography, 1646

Gallup, George H., Gallup International Public Opinion Polls, 859-60, 1057-58

Gallup, George H., Gallup Poll, 856-58, 1054-56

Gane, J. F., American Architects Directory, 564

Ganz, A., and K. Beckson, Literary Terms, 364

Garcia, F. L., Encyclopedia of Banking and Finance, 937

Gardner, H., Art through the Ages, 550

Gardner, W., E. I. Cooke, and R. W. I. Cooke, Handbook of Chemical Synonyms and Trade Names, 1395

Garling, M., Human Rights Handbook, 1048

Garraty, J. A., L. von Klemperer, and C. J. H. Taylor, New Guide to Study Abroad, 776

Garrison, L. W., and D. A. Smith, American Political Process, 1044

Gassner, J., and E. Quinn, Reader's Encyclopedia of World Drama, 371

Gehman, H. S., New Westminster Dictionary of the Bible, 301

Geisinger, M., Plays, Players, and Playwrights, 631n

General Science Index, 1221

General World Atlases in Print, S. P. Walsh, 1201

Genetics Abstracts, 1513n

Geo Abstracts, 1184, 1411

GEOARCHIVE, 1415n

Geographical Bibliography for American College Libraries, G. R. Lewthwaite, 1183

Geologic Reference Sources, D. C. Ward, M. W. Wheeler, and R. A. Bier, Jr., 1408, 1456n

Geologists and the History of Geology, W. A. S. Sarjeant, 1460

GEOREF, 1410n

George, M. W., A. K. Beaubien, and S. A. Hogan, Learning the Library, 196

Georgi, C., P. Wasserman, and J. Woy, Encyclopedia of Business Information Sources, 920

Geotitles Weekly, 1415

Gerlach, J., and L. Gerlach, Critical Index, 586

Gerlach, L., and J. Gerlach, Critical Index, 586

German Literature in English Translation, P. O'Neill, 436

Germano, W. P., and N. Lecyn, Directory of Social and Health Agencies of New York City, 841

Gerstenberger, D., and G. Hendrick, American Novel since 1789, 423

Gianakos, L. J., Television Drama Series Programming, 680-82a

Gibb, H. A. R., Encyclopedia of Islam, 280

Gibson, C., Facts on File Dictionary of Mathematics, 1293

Giedion, S., Space, Time and Architecture, 553

Gill, K., Government Research Centers Directory, 1263

Gill, K., and A. Kruzas, Business Organizations and Agencies Directory, 953

Gillispie, C. C., Dictionary of Scientific Biography, 1273

Gilmartin, K. J., Social Indicators, 811

Gilreath, C. L., Computerized Literature Searching, 213

Ginsburg, N. S., Atlas of Economic Development, 977

Glashan, R. R., American Governors and Gubernatorial Elections, 1775-1978, 1037

Glennon, M., and A. Ehrenhalt, Politics in America, 1023

Glossary of Art, Architecture, and Design since 1945, J. A. Walker, 534

Glossary of Astronomy and Astrophysics, J. Hopkins, 1319

Glossary of Behavioral Terminology, O. R. White, 792

Glossary of Chemical Terms, C. A. Hampel and G. G. Hawley, 1372

Glossary of Genetics and Cytogenetics, R. Rieger, A. Michaelis, and M. M. Green, 1545

Glossary of Geographical Terms, L. D. Stamp and A. N. Clark, 1189

Glossary of Geology, R. L. Bates and J. A. Jackson, 1417

Glossary of Literary Terms, M. H. Abrams, 367

Glossary of Molecular Biology, A. Evans, 1544

Glut, D. F., New Dinosaur Dictionary, 1439

Gmelins Handbuch der Anorganischen Chemie, p. 302

Godbolt, S., and L. T. Morton, Information Sources in the Medical Sciences, 1589

Goddard, S., Guide to Information Sources in the Geographical Sciences, 1180

Godfrey, L. E., and H. F. Redman, Dictionary of Report Series Codes, 1254

Godman, A., Longman Illustrated Science Dictionary, 1251

Golden, J., R. P. Ouellette, S. Saari, and P. N. Cheremisinoff, Environmental Impact Data Book, 1481

Goldenson, R. M., Encyclopedia of Human Behavior, 794

Goldenstein, D. M., Bioethics, 1615

Good, C. V., Dictionary of Education, 710

Good Works: A Guide to Social Change
Careers, K. Aptakin, 844
Goodman, L. H., Current Career and Occupa-
tional Literature, 772-73
Goodman, S. E., Handbook on Contemporary
Education, 714
Gordon, A. J., and R. A. Ford, Chemist's
Companion, 1391
Gordon, M., A. J. Meadows, and A. Singleton,
Dictionary of Computing and New Infor-
mation Technology, 1667
Gordon, M., A Singleton, and C. Rickards,
Dictionary of New Information Tech-
nology Acronyms, 1672
Gould, J., and W. L. Kolb, Dictionary of
the Social Sciences, 701
Gould, K. F., B. A. Bernier, and P. Humphrey,
Popular Names of U.S. Government
Reports, 64
Gourman, J., Gourman Reports, 759-60
Government Publications, V. M. Palic, 57
Government Reports Announcements, 1225n
Government Reports Announcements and
Index, 1225
Government Research Centers Directory,
K. Gill, 1263
Grabois, A., Illustrated Encyclopedia of
Medieval Civilization, 1130
Graduate Programs in Physics, Astronomy,
and Related Fields, 1354
Graham, J., Facts on File Dictionary of
Telecommunications, 1670
Granger's Index to Poetry, W. J. Smith, 351
Granger's Index to Poetry, W. J. Smith and
W. F. Bernhardt, 352
Grant, F. C., and H. H. Rowley, Hasting's
Dictionary of the Bible, 302
Grant, J., Hackh's Chemical Dictionary, 1378
Grant, M., Greek and Latin Authors, 800
B.C. - A.D. 1000, 394
Grant, M. A., College and Chemistry Faculties,
1404
Grant, M. M., and N. Cote, Directory of Busi-
ness and Financial Services, p. 206
Grant Information System Quarterly, B. L.
Wilson and W. K. Wilson, 107n
Grants in the Humanities, W. E. Coleman, 227
Graves, C., R. F. Heizer, and T. R. Hester,
Archaeology, 877
Gray, D. E., American Institute of Physics
Handbook, 1355
Gray, H. J., and A. Isaacs, New Dictionary
of Physics, 1345
Gray, L. H., Mythology of All Races, 324
Gray, P., AIBS Directory of Bioscience
Departments and Faculties in the
United States and Canada, 1560
Gray, P., Dictionary of the Biological Sciences,
1522

Gray, P., Encyclopedia of Microscopy and
Microtechnique, 1542
Gray, P., Encyclopedia of the Biological
Sciences, 1527
Gray, R. A., Guide to Book Review Citations,
188
Gray, R. A., Serial Bibliographies in the
Humanities and Social Sciences, 218
Grazda, E. E., M. Brenner, and W. R. Minrath,
Handbook of Applied Mathematics, 1306
Graziano, A. M., and B. R. Bugelski, Hand-
book of Practical Psychology, 795
Great Spy Pictures, J. R. Parish and M. R.
Pitts, 657
Greek and Latin Authors, 800 B.C. - A.D. 1000,
M. Grant, 394
Greek and Latin Literatures, G. B. Parks,
435n
Green, D. W., and J. O. Maloney, Perry's
Chemical Engineers' Handbook, 1400
Green, M. M., R. Rieger, and A. Michaelis,
Glossary of Genetics and Cytogenetics,
1545
Green, S., Encyclopedia of the Musical Film,
599
Green, S., Encyclopedia of the Musical
Theatre, 605
Greenberg, B., How to Find Out in Psychiatry,
1611
Greenberg, M., and J. Plano, American Political
Dictionary, 1008
Greenfield, S. B., and F. C. Robinson, Bibliog-
raphy of Publications on Old English
Literature to the End of 1972, 344
Greenwald, D., Encyclopedia of Economics,
945
Greenwald, D., McGraw-Hill Dictionary of
Modern Economics, 941
Gregory, W., American Newspapers, 1821-1936,
53
Gregory, W., International Congresses and
Conferences, 39
Gregory, W., List of the Serial Publications
of Foreign Governments, 1815-1931, 72
Gresswell, R. K., and A. Huxley, Standard
Encyclopedia of the World's Rivers and
Lakes, 1194
Grieder, T., American Literature, English
Literature, and World Literature in
English Information Guide Series, 347
Griffin, G., and S. F. Bemis, Guide to the
Diplomatic History of the United States,
1775-1921, 1060n
Gröning, K., and W. Kliess, Friedrichs Theater-
lexikon, 600n
Grogan, D., Science and Technology, 1214
Grun, B., Timetables of History, 1137
Grzimek, B., Grzimek's Animal Life Encyclo-
pedia, 1528

Grzimek, B., Grzimek's Encyclopedia of
    Ecology, 1536
Grzimek's Animal Life Encyclopedia,
    B. Grzimek, 1528
Grzimek's Encyclopedia of Ecology,
    B. Grzimek, J. Illies, and
    W. Klausewitz, 1536
Grzimek's Encyclopedia of Ethology,
    K. Immelmann, 1540
Grzimek's Encyclopedia of Evolution,
    B. Heberer and H. Wendt, 1537
Guadalupi, G., and A. Manguel, Dictionary
    of Imaginary Places, 388
Guernsey, O. L., Best Plays of [year], 625
Guerry, H., Bibliography of Philosophical
    Bibliographies, 231
Guide for Safety in the Chemical Laboratory,
    Manufacturing Chemists Association, 1397
Guide to American Foreign Relations since
    1700, R. D. Burns, 1060
Guide to American Law, 1095
Guide to American Literature, V. K. Fenster,
    327
Guide to Archives and Manuscripts in the
    United States, P. A. Hamer, 1133n
Guide to Art Reference Books, M. Chamberlin,
    511n
Guide to Basic Information Sources in
    Chemistry, A. Antony, 1359
Guide to Basic Information Sources in
    Engineering, E. Mount, 1681
Guide to Book Review Citations, R. A. Gray,
    188
Guide to Buddhist Religion, F. E. Reynolds,
    J. Holt, and J. Strong, 257
Guide to Catholic Literature, 262n
Guide to Critical Reviews, J. M. Salem,
    685
Guide to Departments of Anthropology, Amer-
    ican Anthropological Association, 903
Guide to Drug Information, W. Sewell, 1609
Guide to Graduate Departments of Geography
    in the United States and Canada,
    Association of American Geographers,
    1196
Guide to Graduate Study in Economics and
    Agricultural Economics in the United
    States and Canada, W. F. Owen and
    L. R. Cross, 955
Guide to Great Plays, J. T. Shipley, 669
Guide to Hindu Religion, D. J. Dell, 258
Guide to Historical Literature, American
    Historical Association, 1111
Guide to Information Sources in the Geo-
    graphical Sciences, S. Goddard, 1180
Guide to Islam, D. Ede, 259
Guide to Jewish Religious Practice,
    I. Klein, 277
Guide to League of Nations Publications,
    H. Aufricht, 81

Guide to Library Resources for Nursing, K. P.
    Strauch and D. J. Brundage, 1603
Guide to Oriental Classics, Columbia Univer-
    sity, Columbia College, 437
Guide to Political Platforms, E. W. Chester,
    1046
Guide to Published Library Catalogs, B. R.
    Nelson, 30
Guide to Reference Books, E. P. Sheehy,
    R. G. Keckeissen, and E. McIlvaine,
    811n; pp. 14-16, 39, 41, 44, 74, 255
Guide to Reference Sources in the Computer
    Sciences, C. Carter, 1648
Guide to Research on North American Indians,
    A. B. Hirschfelder, M. G. Byler, and
    M. A. Dorris, 874
Guide to Scientific and Technical Journals
    in Translation, C. J. Himmelsbach and
    G. E. Brociner, 1237
Guide to Serial Bibliographies for Modern
    Literatures, W. A. Wortman, 341
Guide to Sources for Agricultural and
    Biological Research, J. R. Blanchard
    and L. Farrell, 1561
Guide to Sources of Educational Information,
    M. Woodbury, 707
Guide to Symphonic Music, E. Downes, 456
Guide to the Culture of Science, Technology,
    and Medicine, P. T. Durbin, 1219
Guide to the Diplomatic History of the United
    States, 1775-1921, S. F. Bemis and
    G. Griffin, 1060n
Guide to the Gods, R. Carlyon, 320
Guide to the Literature of Art History,
    E. Arntzen and R. Rainwater, 510
Guide to the Literature of Astronomy,
    R. A. Seal, 1313
Guide to the Pianist's Repertoire, M. Hinson,
    469
Guide to the Study of Medieval History,
    L. J. Paetow, 1116
Guide to Theses and Dissertations, M. M.
    Reynolds, 46
Guide to U.S. Government Scientific and Tech-
    nical Resources, R. Aluri and J. S.
    Robinson, 1217
Guidos, B., and B. Hamilton, MASA: Medical
    Acronyms, Symbols, and Abbreviations,
    1625
Gunston, B., Jane's Aerospace Dictionary, 1699
Gurnsey, J., S. Deighton, and J. Tomlinson,
    Computers and Information Processing
    World Index, 1650
Guss, A., and F. A. Rice, Information Sources
    in Linguistics, 878
Guthrie, D., and J. A. Motyer, New Bible
    Commentary, 315
Gwatkin, H. M., Cambridge Medieval History,
    1155

Haas, M. L., Indians of North America, 875

Hackh's Chemical Dictionary, J. Grant, 1378

Hale, F., and E. R. Sandeen, American Religion and Philosophy, 256

Hale, J. R., Concise Encyclopedia of the Italian Renaissance, 1127

Halkett, S., and J. Laing, Dictionary of Anonymous and Pseudonymous English Literature, 357

Hall, J., Dictionary of Subjects and Symbols in Art, 540

Hall, J. F., and L. T. Morton, Medical Research Centres, 1638

Hall, J. L., and A. Dewe, Online Information Retrieval, 200

Halliwell, L., Filmgoer's Companion, 613

Halliwell, L., Halliwell's Film Guide, 648

Halterman, W. J., Complete Guide to Non-traditional Education, 734

Hamer, P. A., Guide to Archives and Manuscripts in the United States, 1133n

Hamilton, B., and B. Guidos, MASA: Medical Acronyms, Symbols, and Abbreviations, 1625

Hammond, K. A., G. Macinko, and W. B. Fairchild, Sourcebook on the Environment, 1462

Hammond, N. G. L., and H. H. Scullard, Oxford Classical Dictionary, 1132

Hampel, C. A., Encyclopedia of the Chemical Elements, 1381

Hampel, C. A., and G. G. Hawley, Glossary of Chemical Terms, 1372

Hand, W. D., A Cassetta, and S. Thiederman, Popular Beliefs and Superstitions, 887

Handbook of Abnormal Psychology, H. J. Eysenck, 796

Handbook of American Indians North of Mexico, F. W. Hodge, 907

Handbook of American Popular Culture, M. T. Inge, 913

Handbook of Applied Mathematics, E. E. Grazda, M. Brenner, and W. R. Minrath, 1306

Handbook of Applied Mathematics, C. E. Pearson, 1307

Handbook of Chemical Engineering Calculations, N. P. Chopey and T. G. Hicks, 1401

Handbook of Chemical Synonyms and Trade Names, W. Gardner, E. I. Cooke, and R. W. I. Cooke, 1395

Handbook of Engineering Fundamentals, O. W. Eshbach and M. Souders, 1704

Handbook of Genetics, R. C. King, 1556

Handbook of Geographic Nicknames, H. S. Sharp, 1197

Handbook of Industrial Engineering, G. Salvendy, 1712

Handbook of Labor Statistics, U.S. Dept. of Labor, Bureau of Labor Statistics, 971

Handbook of Mathematical Tables and Formulas, R. S. Burington, 1303

Handbook of Middle American Indians, R. Wauchope, 909

Handbook of Music and Music Literature in Sets and Series, S. R. Charles, 447n

Handbook of North American Indians, W. C. Sturtevant, 908

Handbook of Nursing, J. Howe and others, 1640

Handbook of Physical Properties of Rocks, R. S. Carmichael, 1449

Handbook of Physics, E. U. Condon and H. Odishaw, 1356

Handbook of Practical Psychology, B. R. Bugelski and A. M. Graziano, 795

Handbook of Private Schools, 739

Handbook of Probability and Statistics with Tables, R. S. Burington and D. C. May, Jr., 1309

Handbook of Pseudonyms and Personal Nicknames, H. S. Sharp, 164

Handbook of Reactive Chemical Hazards, L. Bretherick, 1399

Handbook of Research on Teaching, Second, R. M. Travers, 751

Handbook of Social Psychology, G. Lindzey and E. Aronson, 797

Handbook of South American Indians, J. H. Steward, 910

Handbook of World Philosophy, J. R. Burr, 251

Handbook on Contemporary Education, S. E. Goodman, 714

Handbook to Literature, C. H. Holman, 366

Handbooks and Tables in Science and Technology, R. H. Powell, 1265

Handbuch der Geschichte der Philosophie, W. Totok and others, 232

Handbuch der Physik/Encyclopedia of Physics, S. Flügge, 1351

Handel, B., National Directory for the Performing Arts and Civic Centers, 607

Handel, B., National Directory for the Performing Arts/Educational, 608

Handlin, O., S. Thernstrom, and A. Orlov, Harvard Encyclopedia of American Ethnic Groups, 826

Hannah, S., E. Farber, and S. Schindler, Combined Retrospective Index to Book Reviews in Humanities Journals, 1802-1974, 186

Hanson, S. L., P. K. Hanson, and F. N. Magill, Magill's Survey of Cinema, 649-51

Harbage, A., Annals of English Drama, 975-1700, 385

Hardon, J. A., Modern Catholic Directory, 271

Harewood, Earl of, New Kobbé's Opera Book, 473

Harmon, R. B., Political Science, 999

Harper Encyclopedia of the Modern World, R. B. Morris and G. W. Irwin, 1124

Harper's Bible Dictionary, M. S. Miller, and J. L. Miller, 306

Harper's Dictionary of Classical Literature and Antiquities, H. T. Peck, 1132n

Harper's Dictionary of Hinduism, M. Stutley and J. Stutley, 281

Harré, R., and R. Lamb, Encyclopedic Dictionary of Psychology, 791

Harris, C. D., Bibliography of Geography, 1179

Harris, C. M., Dictionary of Architecture and Construction, 538

Harris, L. L., Shakespearean Criticism, 432

Harris, L. L., and S. Fitzgerald, Nineteenth Century Literature Criticism, 432

Hart, J. D., Oxford Companion to American Literature, 378

Hartnoll, P., Oxford Companion to the Theatre, 619

Hartung, A. E., and J. B. Severs, Manual of the Writings in Middle English, 1050-1500, 345

Harvard Dictionary of Music, W. Apel, 449

Harvard Encyclopedia of American Ethnic Groups, S. Thernstrom, A. Orlov, and O. Handlin, 826

Harvard Guide to American History, F. Friedel and R. K. Showman, 1161

Harvard University, Fine Arts Library, Catalogue of the Harvard University Fine Arts Library, the Fogg Art Museum, 521

Harvard University, Graduate School of Business Administration, Baker Library, Business Reference Sources, 922

Harvard University, Peabody Museum of Archaeology and Ethnology, Library, Catalogue, 864

Harvey, A. P., and R. Steel, Encyclopedia of Prehistoric Life, 1438

Harvey, N., Agricultural Research Centres, 1579

Harvey, P., Oxford Companion to English Literature, 379

Harzfeld, L. A., Periodical Indexes in the Social Sciences and Humanities, 222

Hastings, E. H., and P. K. Hastings, Index to International Public Opinion, 861, 1059

Hastings, J., Dictionary of the Bible, 302

Hastings, J., Encyclopedia of Religion and Ethics, 267

Hastings, P. K., and E. H. Hastings, Index to International Public Opinion, 861, 1059

Hatch, N., P. E. Eisler, and E. Eisler, World Chronology of Music History, 458

Havlice, P., Index to Artistic Biography, 558

Havlice, P., Index to Literary Biography, 393

Havlice, P., Popular Song Index, 505

Havlice, P., World Painting Index, 569

Hawkes, J., Atlas of Ancient Archaeology, 915

Hawkes, J., Atlas of Early Man, 1143

Hawkins, D. T., Online Information Retrieval Bibliography, 201

Hawley, G. G., Condensed Chemical Dictionary, 1377

Hawley, G. G., and C. A. Hampel, Glossary of Chemical Terms, 1372

Haycraft, H., and S. S. Kunitz, American Authors, 1600-1900, 394

Haycraft, H., and S. S. Kunitz, British Authors before 1800, 394

Haycraft, H., and S. S. Kunitz, British Authors of the Nineteenth Century, 394

Haydn, H., and E. Fuller, Thesaurus of Book Digests, 409n

Haywood, C., Bibliography of North American Folklore and Folksong, 883

Health Organizations of the United States, Canada, and the World, P. Wasserman and M. Kaszubski, 1635

HEALTH PLANNING AND ADMINISTRATION, 1607n

Health Science Books, 1876-1982, 1595

Health Sciences and Services, L. F. Lunin, 1590

Health Sciences Information Sources, C.-C. Chen, 1588

Health Services Directory, A. T. Kruzas, 1634

Health Statistics, F. O. Weise, 1613

Heberer, B., and H. Wendt, Grzimek's Encyclopedia of Evolution, 1537

Hegener, K. C., National College Data-bank, 731

Hegener, K. C., and J. Hunter, Peterson's Annual Guide to Undergraduate Study, 725

Heinzkill, R., Film Criticism, 686

Heizer, R. F., T. R. Hester, and C. Graves, Archaeology, 877

Helms, H., McGraw-Hill Computer Handbook, 1679

Help Book, J. L. Barkas, 832

Henderson, G. P., and S. P. A. Henderson, Directory of British Associations and Associations in Ireland, 101

Henderson, S. P. A., and G. P. Henderson, Directory of British Associations and Associations in Ireland, 101

Henderson's Dictionary of Biological Terms, S. Holmes, 1523

Hendrick, G., and D. Gerstenberger, American Novel since 1789, 423

Hendrickson, L., and B. Renford, Bibliographic Instruction, 193

Herbert, I., C. Baxter, and R. E. Finely, Who's Who in the Theatre, 642

Herbert, M. C., and B. McNeil, Author Biographies Master Index, 392

Herbert, M. C., and B. McNeil, Historical Biographical Dictionaries Master Index, 1159

Herbert, M. C., and B. McNeil, Performing Arts Biography Master Index, 634

Herner, S., G. P. Allen, and N. D. Wright, Brief Guide to Sources of Scientific and Technical Information, 1216

Hernon, P., Municipal Government Reference Sources, 1041

Hester, T. R., R. F. Heizer, and C. Graves, Archaeology, 877

Heyel, C., Encyclopedia of Management, 934

Heyer, A. H., Historical Sets, Collected Editions, and Monuments of Music, 447

Heymer, A., Ethological Dictionary, 1541

Hicks, T. G., Standard Handbook of Engineering Calculations, 1706

Hicks, T. G., and N. P. Chopey, Handbook of Chemical Engineering Calculations, 1401

Higher Education Exchange 78/79, J. A. Mitchell, 719

Hildebrandt, D. M., Computing Information Directory, 1647

Hilton, C. L., F. D. Snell, and L. S. Ettre, Encyclopedia of Industrial Chemical Analysis, 1386

Himmelfarb, M., and D. Singer, American Jewish Yearbook, 288

Himmelsbach, C. J., and G. E. Brociner, Guide to Scientific and Technical Journals in Translation, 1237

Hindu World, B. Walker, 282

Hinson, M., Guide to the Pianist's Repertoire, 469

Hirschfelder, A. B., M. G. Byler, and M. A. Dorris, Guide to Research on North American Indians, 874

HISTLINE, 1617n

Historian's Handbook, H. J. Poulton and M. S. Howland, 1110

Historic Documents of [year], 1032

Historical Abstracts, 1115

Historical Biographical Dictionaries Master Index, B. McNeil and M. C. Herbert, 1159

Historical Sets, Collected Editions, and Monuments of Music, A. H. Heyer, 447

Historical Statistics of the United States, U.S. Dept. of Commerce, Bureau of the Census, 168, 1177; p. 45

Historisches Wörterbuch der Philosophie, J. Ritter, 244

History and Bibliography of American Newspapers, 1690-1820, C. S. Brigham, 54

History of Architecture, B. F. Fletcher, 552

History of Art, H. W. Janson and D. J. Janson, 551

History of Philosophy, E. Brehier, 252

History of Philosophy, F. C. Copleston, 253

History of the Theatre, G. Freedley and J. A. Reeves, 631

Hochman, S., McGraw-Hill Encyclopedia of World Drama, 601

Hochman, S., Yesterday and Today, 1167

Hodge, F. W., Handbook of American Indians North of Mexico, 907

Hodge, W., Bibliography of Contemporary North American Indians, 876

Hoefer, J. Ch. F., Nouvelle biographie générale, 160

Hoffman, F., Literature of Rock, 1954-1978, 498

Hogan, R., Dictionary of Irish Literature, 368n

Hogan, S. A., A. K. Beaubien, and M. W. George, Learning the Library, 196

Hogan, T. H., and C. H. Fenichel, Online Searching, 207

Holden, J., Dictionary of Anonymous and Pseudonymous Publications in the English Language, 357n

Holler, F. L., Information Sources of Political Science, 998

Holman, C. H., Handbook to Literature, 366

Holmes, S., Henderson's Dictionary of Biological Terms, 1523

Holt, J., F. E. Reynolds, and J. Strong, Guide to Buddhist Religion, 257

Holum, J. R., Topics and Terms in Environmental Problems, 1479

Home Book of Bible Quotations, B. E. Stevenson, 312

Honour, H., N. Pevsner, and J. Fleming, Dictionary of Architecture, 535

Hoover, R. E., Online Search Strategies, 214

Hopkins, J., Glossary of Astronomy and Astrophysics, 1319

Horn, D., Literature of American Music in Books and Folk Music Collections, 440

Horror and Science Fiction Films II, D. C. Willis, 658

Horst, R. K., Westcott's Plant Disease Handbook, 1582

Hortus Third, L. H. Bailey and E. Z. Bailey, 1576

Hospital Literature Index, American Hospital Association, 1607

Hoult, T. F., Dictionary of Modern Sociology, 820

How to Find Chemical Information, R. E. Maizell, 1361

How to Find Out about Physics, B. Yates, 1338

How to Find Out in Mathematics, J. E. Pemberton, 1286

How to Find Out in Pharmacy, A. L. Brunn, 1608

How to Find Out in Psychiatry, B. Greenberg, 1611

How to Find the Law, M. Cohen and R. C. Berring, 1087

How to Locate Reviews of Plays and Films, G. Samples, 684

Howard-Hill, T. H., Index to British Literary Biographies, 332

Howe, J., and others, Handbook of Nursing, 1640

Howe, W. D., and W. J. Burke, American Authors and Books, 1640 to the Present Day, 400

Howland, M. S., and H. J. Poulton, Historian's Handbook, 1110

HRAF. See Human Relations Area Files

Hudson, K., and A. Nichols, Directory of World Museums, 544

Hughes, C., American Theatre Annual, 623n

Human Relations Area Files, 906

Human Resources Abstracts, 816

Human Rights Directory, L. S. Wiseberg and H. M. Scoble, 1050

Human Rights Handbook, M. Garling, 1048

Humanities, A. R. Rogers, 215; p. xvi

Humanities Index, 219

Hummel, D., Collector's Guide to the American Musical Theatre, 627

Humphrey, P., B. A. Bernier, and K. F. Gould, Popular Names of U.S. Government Reports, 64

Hunt, V. D., Energy Dictionary, 1494

Hunt, W. D., Jr., Encyclopedia of American Architecture, 536

Hunter, D. E., and P. Whitten, Encyclopedia of Anthropology, 889

Hunter, J., and K. C. Hegener, Peterson's Annual Guide to Undergraduate Study, 725

Hunter, J., R. A. Shepherd, and P. S. Mast, Peterson's Annual Guide to Independent Secondary Schools, 741

Hurd, A. E., Religion Index Two, 261

Hurlbut, C. S., Jr., Planet We Live On, 1423

Huxley, A., and R. K. Gresswell, Standard Encyclopedia of the World's Rivers and Lakes, 1194

Hyamson, A. M., Dictionary of Universal Biography of All Ages and All People, 141

IBN: Index bio-bibliographicus notorum hominum, J. P. Lobies, 154

IEEE Standard Dictionary of Electrical and Electronics Terms, 1700

Ijiri, Y., and W. W. Cooper, Kohler's Dictionary for Accountants, 938

Illies, J., B. Grzimek, and W. Klausewitz, Grzimek's Encyclopedia of Ecology, 1536

Illingworth, V., Facts on File Dictionary of Astronomy, 1318

Illustrated Dictionary of Dentistry, S. Jablonski, 1628

Illustrated Dictionary of Geography, R. O. Buchanan, 1187

Illustrated Directory of Film Stars, D. Quinlan, 637

Illustrated Encyclopedia of Archaeology, G. Daniel, 894

Illustrated Encyclopedia of Medieval Civilization, A. Grabois, 1130

Illustrated Who's Who of the Cinema, A. Lloyd and G. Fuller, 636

Immelmann, K., Grzimek's Encyclopedia of Ethology, 1540

Immigration and Ethnicity, J. D. Buenker and N. C. Burckel, 807

Index bio-bibliographicus notorum hominum, J. P. Lobies, 154

Index Medicus, 1592, 1597n

Index of Conference Proceedings Received, British Library Lending Division, 38

Index of Economic Articles in Journals and Collective Volumes, N. Perlman and D. Ekwurzel, 932

Index of English Literary Manuscripts, P. Beal, 363

Index of NLM Serial Titles, 1599

Index to America: Life and Customs, N. Ireland, 1165

Index to Art Periodicals, Chicago Art Institute, Ryerson Library, 528

Index to Artistic Biography, P. Havlice, 558

Index to Biographical Fragments in Unspecialized Scientific Journals, E. S. Barr, 1277

Index to Biographies of Contemporary Composers, S. Bull, 463

Index to Book Reviews in the Humanities, 182

Index to British Literary Bibliographies, T. H. Howard-Hill, 332

Index to Characters in the Performing Arts, H. S. Sharp and M. Z. Sharp, 611

Index to Critical Film Reviews, S. E. Bowles, 687

Index to Dental Literature, 1606

Index to Foreign Legal Periodicals and Collections of Essays, 1091n

Index to Illustrations of Living Things Outside North America, L. T. Munz and N. G. Slauson, 1521

Index to Illustrations of the Natural World, J. W. Thompson, 1520

Index to International Public Opinion, E. H. Hastings and P. K. Hastings, 861, 1059

Index to International Statistics, 176

Index to Legal Periodicals, 1090

Index to Literary Biography, P. Havlice, 393

Index to Opera, Operetta, and Musical Comedy Synopses in Collections and Periodicals, 479

Index to Periodical Fiction in English, 1965-1969, D. Messerli and H. N. Fox, 355

Index to Plays in Periodicals, D. H. Keller, 672

Index to Record and Tape Reviews, A. Maleady, 489

Index to Record Reviews, K. Myers, 486

Index to Reproductions of American Paintings, I. S. Monro and K. M. Monro, 572

Index to Reproductions of American Paintings, L. W. Smith and N. D. W. Moure, 571

Index to Reproductions of European Paintings, I. S. Monro and K. M. Monro, 573

Index to Scientific and Technical Proceedings, 36, 1236

Index to Scientific Reviews, 1224

Index to Scientists of the World, from Ancient to Modern Times, N. O. Ireland, 1275

Index to Social Sciences and Humanities Proceedings, 37, 226, 705

Index to Sociology Readers, H. J. Abramson, 813

Index to the Code of Federal Regulations, 1106

Index to "The London Stage, 1660-1800," B. R. Schneider, 664

Index to the Portraits in Odell's "Annals of the New York Stage," 668n

Index to Theses Accepted for Higher Degrees in the Universities of Great Britain and Ireland, Aslib, 45

Index to Two-dimensional Art Works, Y. H. Korwin, 570

Indians of North America, M. L. Haas, 875

Industrial Arts Index, 1222n

Industrial Engineering Terminology, 1701

Industrial Manual, Moody's Manuals, 985n

Industrial Outlook, U.S. Dept. of Commerce, Bureau of Industrial Economics, 982

Industrial Research Laboratories of the United States, 1262

Industry Surveys, 981

Information Market Place, 117

Information on Music, G. Marco, 439

Information Please Almanac, 1029n; p. 45

Information Resources in Toxicology, P. Wexler, 1610

Information Searching, J. L. Freedman and H. A. Bantly, 194

Information Sources in Agriculture and Food Science, G. P. Lilley, 1562

Information Sources in Biotechnology, A. Crafts-Lighty, 1512

Information Sources in Linguistics, F. A. Rice and A. Guss, 878

Information Sources in Physics, D. F. Shaw, 1336

Information Sources in the History of Science and Medicine, P. Corsi and P. Weindling, 1220

Information Sources of Political Science, F. L. Holler, 998

Inge, M. T., Handbook of American Popular Culture, 913

INIS Atomindex, 1489

INSPEC, 1339n, 1652n, 1693n

Institute of Electrical and Electronics Engineers, IEEE Standard Dictionary of Electrical and Electronics Terms, 1700

Intelligence Tests and Reviews, 762n

International Aerospace Abstracts, 1689

International Almanac of Electoral History, T. T. Mackie and R. Rose, 1053

International Bank for Reconstruction and Development, World Tables, 973

International Bibliography of Economics, 923

International Bibliography of Political Science, 1002

International Bibliography of Social and Cultural Anthropology, 865

International Bibliography of Sociology, 803

International Biblliography of the Historical Sciences, International Committee of Historical Sciences, 1112

International Bibliography of the History of Religions, 264

International City Management Association, County Yearbook, 1040

International City Management Association, Municipal Yearbook, 1039

International Civil Engineering Abstracts, 1692

International Committee of Historical Sciences, International Bibliography of the Historical Sciences, 1112

International Congresses and Conferences, W. Gregory, 39

International Cyclopedia of Music and Musicians, O. Thompson, 451

International Dictionary of Applied Mathematics, W. F. Freiberger, 1295

International Directory of Education, T. G. Page, J. B. Thomas, and A. R. Marshall, 711

International Dictionary of Geophysics, Seismology, Geomagnetism . . ., S. K. Runcorn, 1437

International Dictionary of Physics and Electronics, 1352

International Directory of Anthropologists, Fifth, 902; p. 204

International Directory of New and Renewable Energy Information Sources and Research Centres, 1501

International Directory of Philosophy and Philosophers, R. Cormier, 249

International Directory of Services for the Deaf, S. L. Mathis, III, 838

International Directory of Theatre, Dance, and Folklore Festivals, J. Merin and E. B. Burdick, 609

International Encyclopedia of Film, 598

International Encyclopedia of Higher Education, A. S. Knowles, 713

International Encyclopedia of Statistics, W. H. Kruskal and J. M. Tanur, 1301

International Encyclopedia of the Social Sciences, D. L. Sills, 703, 1012, 1301n; p. 204

International Financial Statistics, 972

International Geographical Bibliography, 1185

International Handbook of Universities and Other Institutions of Higher Education, 722

International Historical Statistics, B. R. Mitchell, 1152-53

International Index to Film Periodicals, M. Moulds, 584

International Maps and Atlases in Print, K. L. Winch, 1186

International Mathematical Union, World Directory of Mathematics, 1312

International Medical Who's Who, 1645

International Medieval Bibliography, R. J. Walsh, 1119

International Mineralogical Association, Commission on Museums, World Directory of Mineral Collections, 1446

International Mortality Statistics, M. Alderson, 172n

International Motion Picture Almanac, 616

International Nursing Index, 1604

International Political Science Abstracts, 1003

International Relations Information Guide Series, 1061

International Repertory of the Literature of Art (RILA), 526

International Scholar's Directory, 135

International Schools Services, ISS Directory of Overseas Schools, 783

International Standard Bible Encyclopedia, G. W. Bromiley, 304

International Statistical Yearbook of Large Towns, 173

International Television Almanac, 628

International Who's Who, 136

International Who's Who in Energy and Nuclear Sciences, 1507

Internationale Bibliographie der Rezensionen wissenschaftlicher Literatur, 187

Internationale Personalbibliographie, M. Arnim, 84, 158

Interpreter's Bible, 313

Interpreter's Dictionary of the Bible, 303

Into the Information Age, Arthur D. Little, Inc., p. 316

Introduction to Reference Sources in the Health Sciences, F. W. Roper and J. A. Boorkman, 1587

Introduction to United States Public Documents, J. Morehead, 1106n

Investment Companies, Wiesenberger, 991

Ireland, N., Index to America: Life and Customs, 1165

Ireland, N. O., Index to Scientists of the World, from Ancient to Modern Times, 1275

Irregular Serials and Annuals, 52, 1226n, 1596n

Irwin, G. W., and R. B. Morris, Harper Encyclopedia of the Modern World, 1124

Irwin, R., and L. Davis, Contemporary American Poetry, 349

Isaacs, A., and H. J. Gray, New Dictionary of Physics, 1345

Isaacs, A., J. Daintith, and E. Martin, Concise Science Dictionary, 1250

ISIS Cumulative Bibliography, 1229, 1230

Israel, F. L., Major Peace Treaties of Modern History, 1070

ISS Directory of Overseas Schools, 783

Iyanaga, S., and Y. Kawada, Encyclopedic Dictionary of Mathematics, 1296

Jablonski, D., and R. W. Fairbridge, Encyclopedia of Paleontology, 1431

Jablonski, S., Illustrated Dictionary of Dentistry, 1628

Jackson, E., Subject Guide to Major United States Government Publications, p. 21

Jackson, J. A., and R. L. Bates, Dictionary of Geological Terms, 1418

Jackson, J. A., and R. L. Bates, Glossary of Geology, 1417

Jackson, K. T., Atlas of American History, 1176

Jackson, S. M., New Schaff-Herzog Encyclopedia of Religious Knowledge, 275

Jacobs, D. M., P. G. Schuman, and S. A. Rodriguez, Materials for Occupational Education, 775

Jacobstein, J. M., and R. M. Mersky, Fundamentals of Legal Research, 1088

Jacquet, C. H., Jr., Yearbook of American and Canadian Churches, 286

Jaeger, E. C., Biologist's Handbook of Pronunciations, 1549

Jaeger, E. C., Source-book of Biological Names and Terms, 1550

Jahresverzeichnis der deutschen Hochschulschriften, 43

James, G., and R. C. James, Mathematics Dictionary, 1292

James, R. C., and G. James, Mathematics Dictionary, 1292

Janes, J., and A. M. Rees, Consumer Health Information Source Book, 1591

Jane's Aerospace Dictionary, B. Gunston, 1699

Janson, D. J., and H. W. Janson, History of Art, 551

Janson, H. W., and D. J. Janson, History of Art, 551

Jensen, L. M., and J. L. Binger, Lippincott's Guide to Nursing Literature, 1602

Jerome Bible Commentary, R. E. Brown, J. A. Fitzmyer, and R. E. Murphy, 314

Jerrard, H. G., and D. B. McNeill, Dictionary of Scientific Units Including Dimensionless Numbers and Scales, 1255

John Willis' Dance World, 624

Johnson, D. B., National Party Platforms, 1840-1976, 1045

Johnson, T. H., Oxford Companion to American History, 1170

Johnson, W. L., Directory of Special Programs for Minority Group Members, 833

Jones, C. E., and R. J. Little, Dictionary of Botany, 1533

Jones, D. A., and others, Handbook of Nursing, 1640

Jones, R., and C. McEvedy, Atlans of World Population History, 850

Journal of Economic Literature, M. Abramovitz, 931

Journals in Translation, 1238

Kadish, S. H., Encyclopedia of Crime and Justice, 825

Kane, J. N., American Counties, 1199

Kane, J. N., Facts about the Presidents, 1029

Kane, J. N., and G. L. Alexander, Nicknames and Sobriquets of U.S. Cities, States, and Counties, 1198

Kanely, E. M., and W. W. Buchanan, Cumulative Subject Index to Monthly Catalog of U.S. Government Publications, 1900-1971, 61

Kaplan, M., Variety Who's Who in Show Business, 641

Karpel, B., Arts in America, 513

Karpman, I. J. C., Who's Who in World Jewry, 293

Kase, F. J., Foreign Patents, 1684

Kaszubski, M., and P. Wasserman, Health Organizations of the United States, Canada, and the World, 1635

Katz, E., Film Encyclopedia, 597

Kaufman, M., S. Galishoff, and T. L. Savitt, Dictionary of American Medical Biography, 1646

Kawada, Y., and S. Iyanaga, Encyclopedic Dictionary of Mathematics, 1296

Keane, C. B., and B. F. Miller, Encyclopedia and Dictionary of Medicine, Nursing, and Allied Health, 1630

Kearney, E. L., and L. S. Fitzgerald, Continental Novel, 424-25

Keckeissen, R. G., E. P. Sheehy, and E. McIlvaine, Guide to Reference Books, 811n; pp. 14-16, 39, 41, 44, 74, 255

Keeslar, O., Financial Aids for Higher Education, 768

Keller, D. H., Index to Plays in Periodicals, 672

Keller, H., Reader's Digest of Books, 405n

Kellogg, R. L., E. U. Crosby, and C. J. Bishko, Medieval Studies, 1118

Kelly, J., American Catalogue of Books, 20

Kelly's Manufacturers and Merchants Directory, 952

Kemp, D. A., Astronomy and Astrophysics, 1314

Kempe's Engineers Year-book, J. P. Quayle, 1705

Kendall, M. G., and W. R. Buckland, Dictionary of Statistical Terms, 1300

Kent, J. A., Riegel's Handbook of Industrial Chemistry, 1402

Kerker, A. E., and H. T. Murphy, Comparative and Veterinary Medicine, 1563

Kern, S., J. C. Ellis, and C. Derry, Film Book Bibliography, 582

Key Sources in Comparative and World Literature, G. A. Thompson, Jr., 328

Key to League of Nations Documents Placed on Public Sale, 1920-29, World Peace Foundation, 82

King, R. C., Handbook of Genetics, 1556

King, R. C., and W. D. Stansfield, Dictionary of Genetics, 1546

Kings, Rulers, and Statesmen, E. W. Egan, 1145n

Kingzett's Chemical Encyclopedia, 1383

Kinkle, R. D., Complete Encyclopedia of Popular Music and Jazz, 1900-1950, 490

Kirk, T. G., Jr., Library Research Guide to Biology, 1511

Kirk-Othmer Concise Encyclopedia of Chemical Technology, 1385

Kirk-Othmer Encyclopedia of Chemical Technology, 1384

Kirkpatrick, D. L., Twentieth Century Children's Writers, 401

Kister, K. F., Kister's Atlas Buying Guide, 1200

Kister's Atlas Buying Guide, K. F. Kister, 1200

Kitchin, C. R., Astrophysical Techniques, 1330

Klausewitz, W., B. Grzimek, and J. Illies, Grzimek's Encyclopedia of Ecology, 1536

Klein, I., Guide to Jewish Religious Practice, 277

Klein, L. S., Encyclopedia of World Literature in the 20th Century, 370; p. 92

Klemperer, L. von, J. A. Garraty, and C. J. H. Taylor, New Guide to Study Abroad, 776

Kliess, W., and K. Gröning, Friedrichs Theaterlexikon, 600n

Kline, P., Urban Needs, 810

Klingensmith, P. J., and E. E. Duncan, Easy Access to DIALOG, ORBIT, and BRS, 212

Knowles, A. S., International Encyclopedia of Higher Education, 713

Kobbé, G., New Kobbé's Opera Book, 473

Koegler, H., Concise Oxford Dictionary of Ballet, 602

Kohler's Dictionary for Accountants, W. W. Cooper and Y. Ijiri, 938

Kolar, C. K., Plot Summary Index, 412

Kolb, W. L., and J. Gould, Dictionary of the Social Sciences, 701

Kolm, R., Bibliography of Ethnicity and Ethnic Groups, 808

Korwin, Y. H., Index to Two-dimensional Art Works, 570

Kramer, E. F., D. N. Curley, and M. Kramer, Modern American Literature, 416

Kramer, M., D. N. Curley, and E. F. Kramer, Modern American Literature, 416

Krause, G., and G. Müller, Theologische Realenzyklopädie, 275n; p. 7

Krummel, D. W., Resources of American Music History, 448

Kruskal, W. H., and J. M. Tanur, International Encyclopedia of Statistics, 1301

Kruzas, A. T., Encyclopedia of Medical Organizations and Agencies, 1633

Kruzas, A. T., Health Services Directory, 1634

Kruzas, A. T., Medical and Health Information Directory, 1632

Kruzas, A. T., Social Service Organizations and Agencies Directory, 827

Kruzas, A. T., and K. Gill, Business Organizations and Agencies Directory, 953

Kunitz, S. S., and V. Colby, European Authors, 1000-1900, 394

Kunitz, S. S., and H. Haycraft, American Authors, 1600-1900, 394

Kunitz, S. S., and H. Haycraft, British Authors before 1800, 394

Kunitz, S. S., and H. Haycraft, British Authors of the Nineteenth Century, 394

Kunitz, S. S., and H. Haycraft, Twentieth Century Authors, 394

Kuntz, J. M., and N. C. Martinez, Poetry Explication, 431

Kurian, G., Encyclopedia of the Third World, 1081

Kut, D., Dictionary of Applied Energy Conservation, 1496

Labor Almanac, A. A. Paradis and G. D. Paradis, 959

Lacey, A. R., Dictionary of Philosophy, 241

Lacquer, W., Dictionary of Politics, 1006

Laidlaw, J. C., T. Archbold, and J. McKechnie, Engineering Research Centres, 1703

Laing, J., and S. Halkett, Dictionary of Anonymous and Pseudonymous English Literature, 357

Lalande, A., Vocabulaire technique et critique de la philosophie, 244n

Lamar, H., Reader's Encyclopedia of the American West, 1168

Lamb, R., and R. Harré, Encyclopedic Dictionary of Psychology, 791

Landon, G., and I. Stambler, Encyclopedia of Folk, Country, and Western Music, 496

Landy, M., Environmental Impact Statement Glossary, 1476

Lang, K. R., Astrophysical Formulae, 1331

Langer, W. L., Encyclopedia of World History, 1123

Lange's Handbook of Chemistry, J. A. Dean, 1390

Language and Language Behavior Abstracts, LLBA, 880

Language of American Popular Entertainment, D. B. Wilmeth, 596

Lapedes, D. N., McGraw-Hill Dictionary of Physics and Mathematics, 1294, 1353

Lapedes, D. N., McGraw-Hill Encyclopedia of Food, Agriculture and Nutrition, 1574

Lapedes, D. N., McGraw-Hill Encyclopedia of the Geological Sciences, 1436

Larousse Dictionary of Painters, 557

Larousse Encyclopedia of Archaeology, G. Charles-Picard, 896

Larousse Encyclopedia of Mythology, 325

Larousse Encyclopedia of World Geography, P. Deffontaines, 1191

Laskin, A. I., and H. A. Lechevalier, CRC Handbook of Microbiology, 1557

Law Dictionary with Pronunciations, J. A. Ballentine, 1094

Lawless, R. M., Folksingers and Folksongs of America, 502

Lawson, S., and D. Crabbe, World Food Book, 1584

Leach, M., and J. Fried, Funk & Wagnalls Standard Dictionary of Folklore, Mythology, and Legend, 898

League of Nations Documents, 1919-1946, E. A. Reno, 83

Learning the Library, A. K. Beaubien, S. A. Hogan, and M. W. George, 196

Learning Vacations, G. G. Eisenberg, 782

Leary, L. G., Articles on American Literature, 338-40

Lechevalier, H. A., and A. I. Laskin, CRC Handbook of Microbiology, 1557

Lecyn, N., and W. P. Germano, Directory of Social and Health Agencies of New York City, 841

Lee, J. M., Who's Who in Library and Information Services, 756

Lee, S., and L. Stephen, Dictionary of National Biography, 147

Leftwich, A. W., Dictionary of Zoology, 1530

Legal Research in a Nutshell, M. Cohen, 1085

Legal Resource Index, 1091n

Leidy, W. P., Popular Guide to Government Publications, p. 21

Leitch, B. A., Concise Dictionary of Indian Tribes of North America, 890

Leonard, W. T., Broadway Bound, 626

Leonard, W. T., Theatre, Stage to Screen to Television, 670

Lerner, R. G., and G. L. Trigg, Encyclopedia of Physics, 1347

Les Brown's Encyclopedia of Television, 606

Lester, D. W., and S. Faull, Cumulative Title Index to U.S. Government Publications, 1789-1975, 68

Levy, F., Obituaries on File, 156

Lewanski, R. C., Slavic Literatures, 435n

Lewis, W. H., Ecology Field Glossary, 1538

Lewthwaite, G. R., Geographical Bibliography for American College Libraries, 1183

Li, T., Social Science Reference Sources, 697; p. 194

Library HiTech, 203

Library Instruction, D. L. Lockwood, 189

Library Instruction for Librarians, A. F. Roberts, 199

Library Orientation and Instruction, H. B. Rader, 190

Library Research Guide to Biology, T. G. Kirk, Jr., 1511

Library Searching: Resources and Strategies with Examples from the Environmental Sciences, J. M. Morris and E. A. Elkins, 1461

Library Use: A Handbook for Psychology, J. G. Reed and P. M. Baxter, 786

Lichtenstein, N., and E. N. Schoenebaum, Political Profiles, 1031

LIFE SCIENCES COLLECTION, 1513n

Lilley, G. P., Information Sources in Agriculture and Food Science, 1562

Lincoln, R. J., G. A. Boxshall, and P. F. Clark, Dictionary of Ecology, Evolution and Systematics, 1539

Lindzey, G., and E. Aronson, Handbook of Social Psychology, 797

Linguistic Bibliography for the Year, Permanent International Committee of Linguists, 879

Lippincott's Guide to Nursing Literature, J. L. Binger and L. M. Jensen, 1602

List-O-Tapes "All in One" Tape Catalog, 482

Lists of Journals Indexed in Index Medicus, 1600

List of the Serial Publications of Foreign Governments, 1815-1931, W. Gregory, 72

Literary and Library Prizes, O. S. Weber and S. J. Calvert, 389

Literary Criticism from 1400 to 1800 (excluding Shakespeare), D. Poupard, 432

Literary Gazetteer of England, L. H. Fisher, 387

Literary History of England, A. C. Baugh, 390n

Literary History of the United States, R. E. Spiller, 330, 391

Literary Market Place (LMP), 118, 375; p. 28

Literary Research Guide, M. C. Patterson, 326; p. xvi

Literary Terms, K. Beckson and A. Ganz, 364

Literature Matrix of Chemistry, H. Skolnik, 1363

Literature of American Music in Books and Folk Music Collections, D. Horn, 440

Literature of Geography, J. G. Brewer, 1178

Literature of Medieval History, 1930-1975, G. C. Boyce, 1117

Literature of Political Science, C. Brock, 997

Literature of Rock, 1954-1978, F. Hoffman, 498

Literature Searching in Science, Technology, and Agriculture, E. Pritchard and P. R. Scott, 1213

Literatures of the World in English Translation, 435

Little, R. J., and C. E. Jones, Dictionary of Botany, 1533

Lives of the Saints, A. Butler, 296

Livingstone, E. A., and F. L. Cross, Oxford Dictionary of the Christian Church, 268

LLBA: Language and Language Behavior Abstracts, 880

Lloyd, A., and G. Fuller, Illustrated Who's Who of the Cinema, 636

LMP: Literary Market Place, 118, 375; p. 28

Lobies, J. P., IBN: Index bio-bibliographicus notorum hominum, 154

Lockwood, D. L., Library Instruction, 189

Loetscher, L. A., Twentieth Century Encyclo-pedia of Religious Knowledge, 275n

Loewenberg, A., Annals of Opera, 477

Loftness, R. L., Energy Handbook, 1503

London Stage, 1660-1800, 663

London Stage, 1890-1929, J. P. Wearing, 665-67a

Longley, D., and M. Shain, Dictionary of Information Technology, 1666

Longman Illustrated Dictionary of Botany, A. Sugden, 1535

Longman Illustrated Dictionary of Geology, A. Watt, 1420

Longman Illustrated Science Dictionary, A. Godman, 1251

Lovejoy's Career and Vocational School Guide, C. T. Straughn and B. L. Straughn, 738

Lovejoy's Prep and Private School Guide, C. T. Straughn and B. L. Straughn, 740

Lovett, D. R., and D. W. G. Ballentyne, Dictionary of Named Effects and Laws in Chemistry, Physics, and Mathematics, 1258

LSA-List of CFR Sections Affected, 1105

Lucas, E., Art Books, 512

Luchsinger, A. E., R. C. Smith, and W. M. Reid, Smith's Guide to the Literature of the Life Sciences, 1510

Lunin, L. F., Health Sciences and Services, 1590

McAllister, M. H., R. Stillwell, and W. L. McDonald, Princeton Encyclopedia of Classical Sites, 897

McBride, R., and D. Crabbe, World Energy Book, 1504

MacCann, R. D., and E. S. Perry, New Film Index, 587

McCavitt, W. E., Radio and Television, 593

McDonald, W. L., R. Stillwell, and M. H. McAllister, Princeton Encyclopedia of Classical Sites, 897

McEvedy, C., and R. Jones, Atlas of World Population History, 850

McGill, R. D., Notable Names in the American Theatre, 621

McGraw-Hill Computer Handbook, H. Helms, 1679

McGraw-Hill Concise Encyclopedia of Science and Technology, S. P. Parker, 1245

McGraw-Hill Dictionary of Art, B. S. Myers, 531

McGraw-Hill Dictionary of Biology, S. P. Parker, 1526

McGraw-Hill Dictionary of Chemistry, S. P. Parker, 1373

McGraw-Hill Dictionary of Earth Sciences, S. P. Parker, 1422

McGraw-Hill Dictionary of Electronics and Computer Technology, S. P. Parker, 1659

McGraw-Hill Dictionary of Engineering, S. P. Parker, 1696

McGraw-Hill Dictionary of Modern Economics, D. Greenwald, 941

McGraw-Hill Dictionary of Physics and Mathe-matics, D. N. Lapedes, 1294, 1353

McGraw-Hill Dictionary of Science and Engineering, 1243

McGraw-Hill Dictionary of Scientific and Technical Terms, S. P. Parker, 1242, 1245n

McGraw-Hill Encyclopedia of Astronomy, S. P. Parker, 1323

McGraw-Hill Encyclopedia of Chemistry, S. P. Parker, 1379

McGraw-Hill Encyclopedia of Electronics and Computers, S. P. Parker, 1665

McGraw-Hill Encyclopedia of Energy, S. P. Parker, 1492

McGraw-Hill Encyclopedia of Engineering, S. P. Parker, 1697

McGraw-Hill Encyclopedia of Environmental Science, S. P. Parker, 1471

McGraw-Hill Encyclopedia of Food, Agriculture, and Nutrition, D. N. Lapedes, 1574

McGraw-Hill Encyclopedia of Ocean and Atmospheric Sciences, S. P. Parker, 1440

McGraw-Hill Encyclopedia of Physics, S. P. Parker, 1349

McGraw-Hill Encyclopedia of Science and Technology, 1244

McGraw-Hill Encyclopedia of the Geological Sciences, D. N. Lapedes, 1436

McGraw-Hill Encyclopedia of World Biography, 143

McGraw-Hill Encyclopedia of World Drama, S. Hochman, 601

McGraw-Hill Modern Scientists and Engineers, 1271

McGraw-Hill Nursing Dictionary, 1627

McGraw-Hill Yearbook of Science and Technology, 1246

McGreal, I. P., and F. N. Magill, Masterpieces of Christian Literature in Summary Form, 289

McGreal, I. P., and F. N. Magill, World Philosophy, 250

McHale, V. E., and S. Skowronski, Political Parties of Europe, 1078

McIlvaine, E., E. P. Sheehy, and R. G. Keckeissen, Guide to Reference Books, 811n; pp. 14-16, 39, 41, 44, 74, 255

Macinko, G., K. A. Hammond, and W. B. Fairchild, Sourcebook on the Environment, 1462

McInnis, R. G., Research Guide for Psychology, 785

McInnis, R. G., and J. W. Scott, Social Science Research Handbook, 696

Mack, N. B., J. Viola, and T. R. Stauffer, Energy Research Guide, 1491

McKechnie, J., T. Archbold, and J. C. Laidlaw, Engineering Research Centres, 1703

McKenzie, J. L., Dictionary of the Bible, 305

Mackesy, E. M., K. Mateyak, and D. Siegel, MLA Directory of Periodicals, 336

Mackie, T. T., and R. Rose, International Almanac of Electoral History, 1053

McKinney, M. J., and E. I. Altman, Financial Handbook, 957

Macmillan Bible Atlas, Y. Aharoni and M. Avi-Yonah, 316

Macmillan Concise Dictionary of World History, B. Wetterau, 1122

Macmillan Dictionary of Archaeology, R. D. Whitehouse, 893n

Macmillan Film Bibliography, G. Rehrauer, 581

Macmillan Illustrated Animal Encyclopedia, P. Whitfield, 1529

McMurtry, J., Victorian Life and Victorian Fiction, 381

McNamee, L. F. D., Dissertations in English and American Literature, 342

McNeil, A., Total Television, 679

McNeil, B., and M. C. Herbert, Author Biographies Master Index, 392

McNeil, B., and M. C. Herbert, Historical Biographical Dictionaries Master Index, 1159

McNeil, B., and M. C. Herbert, Performing Arts Biography Master Index, 634

McNeill, D. B., and H. G. Jerrard, Dictionary of Scientific Units Including Dimensionless Numbers and Scales, 1255

Madden, S. K., and G. D. Borich, Evaluating Classroom Instruction, 765

Magazine Index, 926n

Magill, F. N., Critical Survey of Long Fiction, 374

Magill, F. N., Cyclopedia of Literary Characters, 382

Magill, F. N., Masterplots, 405

Magill, F. N., Survey of Contemporary Literature, 406

Magill, F. N., Survey of Science Fiction Literature, 408

Magill, F. N., and W. Beacham, Critical Survey of Short Fiction, 373

Magill, F. N., A. R. Caponigri, and T. P. Neill, Masterpieces of Catholic Literature in Summary Form, 290

Magill, F. N., and I. P. McGreal, Masterpieces of Christian Literature in Summary Form, 289

Magill, F. N., and I. P. McGreal, World Philosophy, 250

Magill Books Index, 411

Magill's Bibliography of Literary Criticism, F. N. Magill, 433

Magill's Cinema Annual, 652

Magill's Literary Annual, 407

Magill's Survey of Cinema, 649-51

Maizell, R. E., How to Find Chemical Information, 1361

Major Peace Treaties of Modern History, F. L. Israel, 1070

Maleady, A., Index to Record and Tape Reviews, 489

Malinowsky, H. R., and J. M. Richardson, Science and Engineering Literature, 1210; p. xvi

Maloney, J. O., and D. W. Green, Perry's Chemical Engineers' Handbook, 1400

MANAGEMENT CONTENTS, 930n

Manchester, P. W., and A. Chujoy, Dance Encyclopedia, 603

Manguel, A., and G. Guadalupi, Dictionary of Imaginary Places, 388

Manual of the Writings in Middle English, 1050-1500, J. B. Severs and A. E. Hartung, 345

Manuel de bibliographie philosophique, G. Varet, 233

Manufacturing Chemists Association, Guide for Safety in the Chemical Laboratory, 1397

Marco, G., Information on Music, 439

Marks, P., Plays, Players, and Playwrights, 631n

Marks' Standard Handbook for Mechanical Engineers, T. Baumeister, E. A. Avallone, and T. Baumeister, III, 1708

MARQUIS WHO'S WHO, 120n, 1272n

Marshall, A. R., T. G. Page, and J. B. Thomas, International Dictionary of Education, 711

Martin, E., A. Isaacs, and J. Daintith, Concise Science Dictionary, 1250

Martin, E. A., Dictionary of Life Sciences, 1525

Martin, G., Opera Companion to Twentieth Century Opera, 476

Martin, J., Book of the Dance, 632

Martin, S. S., and R. A. Seal, Bibliography of Astronomy, 1970-1979, 1315

Martindale-Hubbell Law Directory, 1096

Martinez, N. C., and J. M. Kuntz, Poetry Explication, 431

Maryknoll Catholic Dictionary, A. J. Nevins, 272

MASA: Medical Acronyms, Symbols, and Abbreviations, B. Hamilton and B. Guidos, 1625

Mast, P. S., R. A. Shepherd, and J. Hunter, Peterson's Annual Guide to Independent Secondary Schools, 741

Masterpieces of Catholic Literature in Summary Form, F. N. Magill, A. R. Caponigri, and T. P. Neill, 290

Masterpieces of Christian Literature in Summary Form, F. N. Magill and I. P. McGreal, 289

Masterplots, F. N. Magill, 405

Masterplots: Cyclopedia of Fictional Characters, 382n

Masterplots Annuals, 406n

Materials for Occupational Education, P. G. Schuman, S. A. Rodriguez, and D. M. Jacobs, 775

Materials Handbook, G. S. Brady and H. R. Clauser, 1393

Mateyak, K., E. M. Mackesy, and D. Siegel, MLA Directory of Periodicals, 336

Mathematical Association of America, American Mathematical Society, Society for Industrial and Applied Mathematics, Combined Membership List, 1311

Mathematical Reviews, 1287

Mathematical Society of Japan, Encyclopedic Dictionary of Mathematics, 1296

Mathematics Dictionary, G. James and R. C. James, 1292

Mathematics Tests and Reviews, 762n

MATHFILE, 1287n

Mathis, S. L., III, International Directory of Services for the Deaf, 838

Mattfeld, J., Variety Music Cavalcade, 1620-1961, 504

Matthews, D., M. Barone, and B. Ujifusa, Almanac of American Politics, 1024

Maurer, D. J., U.S. Politics and Elections, 1043

Mavituna, F., and B. Atkinson, Biochemical Engineering and Biotechnology Handbook, 1559

May, D. C., Jr., and R. S. Burington, Handbook of Probability and Statistics with Tables, 1309

May, H. G., Oxford Bible Atlas, 317

May, K. O., Bibliography and Research Manual of the History of Mathematics, 1291

Maynard, J., Dictionary of Data Processing, 1661

Meadow, C. T., and P. A. Cochrane, Basics of Online Searching, 209

Meadows, A. J., M. Gordon, and A. Singleton, Dictionary of Computing and New Information Technology, 1667

Meagher, P. K., T. C. O'Brien, and Sister C. M. Aherne, Encyclopedic Dictionary of Religion, 270

Measures for Psychological Assessment, K. Chun, 766

Medical and Health Care Books and Serials in Print, 1596

Medical and Health Information Directory, A. T. Kruzas, 1632

Medical Education in the United States, F. Cordasco and D. N. Alloway, 1614

Medical Reference Works, 1679-1966, J. B. Blake and C. Roos, 1601

Medical Research Centres, L. T. Morton and J. F. Hall, 1638

Medieval Studies, E. U. Crosby, C. J. Bishko, and R. L. Kellogg, 1118

MEDLINE, 1592n, 1604n, 1606n

Mellersh, H. E. L., Chronology of the Ancient World, 10,000 B.C. to A.D. 799, 1139

Mellon, M. G., Chemical Publications, 1362; p. 296

Melloni, B. J., I. Dox, and G. M. Eisner, Melloni's Illustrated Medical Dictionary, 1622

Melloni's Illustrated Medical Dictionary, B. J. Melloni, I. Dox, and G. M. Eisner, 1622

Melnyk, P., Economics, 921

Melton, J. G., Directory of Religious Bodies in the United States, 284

Melton, J. G., Encyclopedia of American Religions, 298

Men of the Supreme Court, C. Barnes, 1034

Mental Measurements Yearbook, O. Buros, 762

MENU™ — THE INTERNATIONAL SOFTWARE DATABASE, 1676n

Menzel, D. H., and J. M. Pasachoff, Field Guide to the Stars and Planets, 1333

Merck Index, 1392

Merck Manual of Diagnosis and Therapy, R. Berkow, 1639

Merck Veterinary Manual, 1585

Merin, J., and E. B. Burdick, International Directory of Theatre, Dance, and Folklore Festivals, 609

Merritt, F. S., Standard Handbook for Civil Engineers, 1709

Mersky, R. M., and J. M. Jacobstein, Fundamentals of Legal Research, 1088

Messerli, D., and H. N. Fox, Index to Periodical Fiction in English, 1965-1969, 355

Meterological and Geoastrophysical Abstracts, 1412

Metropolitan Opera Annals, W. H. Seltsam, 478

Meynen, E., Orbis Geographicus, 1195, 1209

Miall's Dictionary of Chemistry, D. W. A. Sharp, 1374

Michael, P., American Movies Reference Book, 614

Michaelis, A., R. Rieger, and M. M. Green, Glossary of Genetics and Cytogenetics, 1545

Michaud, J. F., Biographie universelle ancienne et moderne, 159

Microcomputer Buyer's Guide, T. Webster, 1677

Microcomputer Marketplace, 1675

Mildren, K. W., Use of Engineering Literature, 1680

Miles, W. D., American Chemists and Chemical Engineers, 1403

Miller, B. F., and C. B. Keane, Encyclopedia and Dictionary of Medicine, Nursing, and Allied Health, 1630

Miller, J., Rolling Stone Illustrated History of Rock & Roll, 499

Miller, J. L., and M. S. Miller, Harper's Bible Dictionary, 306

Miller, M. S., and J. L. Miller, Harper's Bible Dictionary, 306

Miller, P. M., and M. J. Wilson, Dictionary of Social Science Methods, 702

Miller, W. C., Comprehensive Bibliography for the Study of American Minorities, 809

Million Dollar Directory, 947

Mineral Names, R. S. Mitchell, 1442

Mineralogical Abstracts, 1413

Minorities and Women, G. A. Schlachter D. Belli, 806

Minority Organizations, K. Cole, 834

Minrath, W. R., E. E. Grazda, and M. Brenner, Handbook of Applied Mathematics, 1306

Mirkin, S. M., What Happened When, 1136

Mitchell, B. R., European Historical Statistics, 1750-1975, 172, 1151

Mitchell, B. R., International Historical Statistics, 1152-53

Mitchell, G. D., Dictionary of Sociology, 822

Mitchell, J. A., Higher Education Exchange, 78/79, 719

Mitchell, J. E., Jr., Tests in Print III, 763

Mitchell, R. S., Mineral Names, 1442

Mitchell, S., J. Daintith, and E. Tootill, Biographical Encyclopedia of Scientists, 1279

Mitton, S., Cambridge Encyclopaedia of Astronomy, 1324

Mitzel, H. E., Encylopedia of Educational Research, 748

MLA Directory of Periodicals, E. M. Mackesy, K. Mateyak, and D. Siegel, 336

MLA International Bibliography of Books and Articles on the Modern Languages and Literatures, 335

Modern American Literature, D. N. Curley, M. Kramer, and E. F. Kramer, 416

Modern British Literature, R. Z. Temple and M. Tucker, 414

Modern Catholic Dictionary, J. A. Hardon, 271

Modern Commonwealth Literature, J. H. Ferres and M. Tucker, 417

Modern Dictionary of Sociology, G. A. Theodorson and A. G. Theodorson, 821

Modern Humanities Research Association, Annual Bibliography of English Language and Literature, 337

Modern Language Association of America, MLA International Bibliography of Books and Articles on the Modern Languages and Literatures, 335

Modern Language Association of America, American Literature Section, American Literary Manuscripts, 362

Modern Romance Literature, D. N. Curley and A. Curley, 418

Moffat, D. W., Economics Dictionary, 942

Moghdam, D., C. L. Borgman, and P. K. Corbett, Effective Online Searching, 208

Molnar, J. E., Author-Title Index to Joseph Sabin's Dictionary of Books Relating to America, 27

Money Business, 545

Monkhouse, F. J., and J. Small, Dictionary of the Natural Environment, 1474

Monro, I. S., and K. M. Monro, Index to Reproductions of American Paintings, 572

Monro, I. S., and K. M. Monro, Index to Reproductions of European Paintings, 573

Monro, K. M., and I. S. Monro, Index to Reproductions of American Paintings, 572

Monro, K. M., and I. S. Monro, Index to Reproductions of European Paintings, 573

Monthly Bulletin of Statistics, 171

Monthly Catalog of United States Government Publications, U.S. Superintendent of Documents, 58; p. 21

Monthly Checklist of State Publications, U.S. Library of Congress, Exchange and Gift Division, 69

Moody's Handbook of Common Stocks, 989

Moody's Manuals, 985

Moore, P., A-Z of Astronomy, 1320

Moore, P. Rand McNally New Concise Atlas of the Universe, 1335

Moore, R. I., Rand McNally Historical Atlas of the World, 1147

Morehead, J., Introduction to United States Public Documents, 1106n

Morgenstern, S., and H. Barlow, Dictionary of Musical Themes, 470

Morgenstern, S., and H. Barlow, Dictionary of Opera and Song Themes, 471

Morgenstern, S., and H. Barlow, Dictionary of Vocal Themes, 471n

Morris, C. J., Developing Labor Law, 960

Morris, J. B., and R. B. Morris, Encyclopedia of American History, 1171

Morris, J. M., and E. A. Elkins, Library Searching: Resources and Strategies with Examples from the Environmental Sciences, 1461

Morris, R. B., and G. W. Irwin, Harper Encyclopedia of the Modern World, 1124

Morris, R. B., and J. B. Morris, Encyclopedia of Ameican History, 1171

Morrison, C., Analytical Concordance to the Revised Standard Version of the New Testament, 311

Morton, L. T., and S. Godbolt, Information Sources in the Medical Sciences, 1589

Morton, L. T., and J. F. Hall, Medical Research Centres, 1638

Mosby's Medical and Nursing Dictionary, L. Urdang and H. H. Swallow, 1626

Moses, A. J., Practicing Scientist's Handbook, 1268

Mossman, J., Pseudonyms and Nicknames Dictionary, 163

Motif-Index of Folk Literature, S. Thompson, 885

Motyer, J. A., and D. Guthrie, New Bible Commentary, 315

Moulds, M., International Index to Film Periodicals, 584

Mount, E., Guide to Basic Information Sources in Engineering, 1681

Moure, N. D. W., and L. W. Smith, Index to Reproductions of American Paintings, 571

Moving Pictures, E. Sheahan, 580

Muirden, J., and J. H. Robinson, Astronomy Data Book, 1328

Muir's Historical Atlas, R. F. Treherne and H. Fullard, 1146

Müller, G., and G. Krause, Theologische Realenzyklopädie, 275n; p. 7

Municipal and Government Manual, Moody's Manuals, 985n

Municipal Government Reference Sources, P. Hernon, 1041

Municipal Yearbook, 96, 1039

Munn, G. G., Encyclopedia of Banking and Finance, 937

Munz, L. T., and N. G. Slauson, Index to Illustrations of Living Things Outside North America, 1521

Murdin, P., and D. Allen, Catalogue of the Universe, 1334

Murdock, G. P., Ethnographic Atlas, 904

Murdock, G. P., and T. J. O'Leary, Ethnographic Bibliography of North America, 871

Murphy, H. T., and A. E. Kerker, Comparative and Veterinary Medicine, 1563

Murphy, R. E., R. E. Brown, and J. A. Fitzmyer, Jerome Bible Commentary, 314

Museum of Mankind Library, Anthropological Index to Current Periodicals, 867

Music, Books on Music, and Sound Recordings, U.S. Library of Congress, 443

Music Criticism, H. J. Diamond, 446

Music Index, 444

Music Reference and Research Materials, V. Duckles, 438

Music since 1900, N. Slonimsky, 459

Musician's Guide, 454

Musicians since 1900, D. Ewen, 466

Musik in Geschichte und Gegenwart, F. Blume, 452

Muslim Peoples, R. V. Weekes, 891

Myers, B. S., McGraw-Hill Dictionary of Art, 531

Myers, K., Index to Record Reviews, 486

Mythology of All Races, L. H. Gray, 324

NASW. See National Association of Social Workers

National Agricultural Library Catalog, 1569

National Association of Counties, County Yearbook, 1040

National Association of Social Workers,
    Directory of Agencies, 829
National Association of Social Workers, NASW
    Directory of Professional Social
    Workers, 863
National Association of Social Workers,
    NASW Register of Clinical Social
    Workers, 863n
National Center for Education Statistics,
    Condition of Education, 744
National Center for Education Statistics,
    Digest of Educational Statistics, 743
National Center for Education Statistics,
    Education Directory, 715
National Center for Education Statistics,
    Projections of Educational Statistics,
    745
National College Data-bank, K. C. Hegener, 731
National Criminal Justice Information and
    Statistics Service, Sourcebook of
    Criminal Justice Statistics, 852
National Cyclopedia of American Biography,
    145
National Directory for the Performing Arts
    and Civic Centers, B. Handel, 607
National Directory for the Performing Arts/
    Educational, B. Handel, 608
National Directory of Private Social Agencies,
    H. B. Croner, 828
National Faculty Directory, 125, 753
National Index of American Imprints
    through 1800, C. Shipton, 25
National Library of Medicine Audiovisuals
    Catalog, 1598
National Library of Medicine Current Catalog,
    1597, 1601n
National Library Service Cumulative Book
    Review Index, 1905-1974, 184
National Party Platforms, 1840-1976,
    D. B. Johnson, 1045
National Technical Information Service,
    (NTIS), 1225n
National Translations Center, Consolidated
    Index of Translations into English, 1239
National Union Catalog: A Cumulative Author
    List, 2, 122
National Union Catalog: Pre-1966 Imprints, 1,
    15n, 123
National Vocational Guidance Association,
    NVGA Bibliography of Current Career
    Information, 774
Negro Almanac, H. A. Ploski and J. Williams,
    912
Neill, T. P., F. N. Magill, and A. R. Caponigri,
    Masterpieces of Catholic Literature in
    Summary Form, 290
Nelson, B. R., Guide to Published Library
    Catalogs, 30

Nelson's Complete Concordance of the
    Revised Standard Version Bible, J. W.
    Ellison, 307
Nemmers, E. E., Dictionary of Economics and
    Business, 943
Neue deutsche Biographie, 151
Nevins, A. J., Maryknoll Catholic
    Dictionary, 272
New Bible Commentary, D. Guthrie and J. A.
    Motyer, 315
New Cambridge Bibliography of English Litera-
    ture, G. Watson, 329
New Cambridge Modern History, G. R. Potter,
    1158
New Catholic Encyclopedia, 274
New Century Cyclopedia of Names, C. L. Barn-
    hart, 162
New Century Italian Renaissance
    Encyclopedia, 1128
New Complete Book of the American Musical
    Theater, D. Ewen, 661
New Dictionary of Physics, H. J. Gray and A.
    Isaacs, 1345
New Dinosaur Dictionary, D. F. Glut, 1439
New Encyclopedic Dictionary of Business
    Law—with Forms, M. J. Ross and J. S.
    Ross, 939
New Film Index, R. D. MacCann and E. S.
    Perry, 587
New Grove Dictionary of Music and Musicians,
    S. Sadie, 450
New Guide to Study Abroad, J. A. Garraty,
    L. von Klemperer, and C. J. H. Taylor,
    776
New International Atlas, 1203
New International Dictionary of the Christian
    Church, J. D. Douglas, 269
New Kobbé's Opera Book, G. Kobbé, 473
New Oxford Companion to Music, D. Arnold,
    455
New Oxford History of Music, 457
New Sabin, L. S. Thompson, 28
New Schaff-Herzog Encyclopedia of Religious
    Knowledge, S. M. Jackson, 275
New Schwann Record and Tape Guide, 480
New Serial Titles, 49, 1228n
New Westminster Dictionary of the Bible,
    H. S. Gehman, 301
New York Botanical Garden Illustrated
    Encyclopedia of Horticulture,
    T. H. Everett, 1575
New York Graphic Society, Fine Art
    Reproductions of Old and Modern
    Masters, 568
New York, Metropolitan Museum of Art,
    Library, Catalog, 522
New York, Museum of Modern Art, Library,
    Catalog, 523

New York Philharmonic Guide to the
      Symphony, E. Downes, 456n
New York Public Library, Dictionary Catalog
      of the Research Libraries, 12, 15n
New York Public Library, Performing Arts
   '   Research Center, Rodgers and Hammer-
      stein Archives of Recorded Sound, 483
New York Public Library, Research Libraries,
      Dictionary Catalog of the Art and
      Architecture Division, 524
New York Public Library, Research Libraries,
      Dictionary Catalog of the Music Collec-
      tion, 441
New York Theatre Annual, 623n
New York Theatre Critics' Reviews, 691
New York Times Atlas of the World, 1204
New York Times Directory of the Film, 615
New York Times Directory of the Theater, 622
New York Times Encyclopedia of Television,
      L. Brown, 606n
New York Times Film Reviews, 688
New York Times Obituaries Index, 1858-1968,
      155
New York Times Theater Reviews, 690
Newspapers in Microform, 55
Nichols, A., and K. Hudson, Directory of World
      Museums, 544
Nicknames and Sobriquets of U.S. Cities,
      States, and Counties, J. N. Kane and
      G. L. Alexander, 1198
Nicolson, I., Dictionary of Astronomy, 1321
Nilon, C. H., Bibliography of Bibliographies
      in American Literature, 333
Nineteenth Century Literature Criticism, L. L.
      Harris and S. Fitzgerald, 432
Nite, N. N., Rock On, 500
Norback, C. T., and P. G. Norback, Older
      American's Handbook, 836
Norback, C. T., and P. G. Norback, TV Guide
      Almanac, 630
Norback, P. G., and C. T. Norback, Older
      American's Handbook, 836
Norback, P. G., and C. T. Norback, TV Guide
      Almanac, 630
North American Horticulture, American Horti-
      cultural Society, 1580
North American Human Rights Directory, L. S.
      Wiseberg and H. M. Scoble, 1049
Nortman, D. L., and J. Fisher, Population
      and Family Planning Programs, 849
Norton History of Music, 457n
Notable Names in the American Theatre, R. D.
      McGill, 621
Notes, Music Library Association, 485
Nouvelle biographie générale, J. Ch. F.
      Hoefer, 160
NTIS, National Technical Information Service,
      1225n

Nutrition Abstracts and Reviews, 1567
NVGA Bibliography of Current Career
      Information, E. Weinstein, 774

Obituaries from The Times, 1951-1975, F. C.
      Roberts, 157
Obituaries on File, F. Levy, 156
O'Brien, B. A., and E. J. O'Brien, Religion
      Index Two: Festschriften, 1960-1969,
      261n
O'Brien, E. J., and B. A. O'Brien, Religion
      Index Two: Festschriften, 1960-1969,
      261n
O'Brien, J., and P. Wasserman, Statistics
      Sources, 177
O'Brien, T. C., Sister C. M. Aherne, and
      P. K. Meagher, Encyclopedic Dictionary
      of Religion, 270
Occupational Outlook Handbook, U.S. Dept.
      of Labor, Bureau of Labor Statistics,
      771
Ocean and Marine Dictionary, D. F. Tver,
      1441
Oceanic Abstracts, 1414
Ocran, E. B., Ocran's Anonyms, 1253
Odell, G. C. D., Annals of the New York
      Stage, 668
Odishaw, H., and E. U. Condon, Handbook
      of Physics, 1356
Office of Population Research, School of
      Public Affairs, Princeton University,
      Population Index, 819
Official Congressional Directory, U.S.
      Congress, 86, 1017
Official Museum Directory, 543
Ohles, J. F., Biographical Dictionary of
      American Educators, 757
Older American's Handbook, C. T. Norback
      and P. G. Norback, 836
O'Leary, T. J., Ethnographic Bibliography of
      South America, 872
O'Leary, T. J., and G. P. Murdock, Ethno-
      graphic Bibliography of North America,
      871
O'Neill, P., German Literature in English
      Translation, 436
Online, 205
Online Bibliographic Searching, C. Chen and
      S. Schweizer, 210
Online Information Retrieval, J. L. Hall and
      A. Dewe, 200
Online Information Retrieval Bibliography, D. T.
      Hawkins, 201
Online Reference and Information Retrieval,
      R. C. Palmer, 211
Online Review, 204
Online Search Strategies, R. E. Hoover, 214

Online Searching, G. Byerly, 202

Online Searching, C. H. Fenichel and T. H. Hogan, 207

Opera Companion to Twentieth Century Opera, G. Martin, 476

Opitz, H., and B. Verrel, World Guide to Scientific Associations and Learned Societies, 724

Obris Geographicus, E. Meynen, 1195, 1209

Orlov, A., S. Thernstrom, and O. Handlin, Harvard Encyclopedia of American Ethnic Groups, 826

Orrey, L., Encyclopedia of the Opera, 475

Osborne, H., Oxford Companion to Art, 547

Osborne, H., Oxford Companion to the Decorative Arts, 549

Osborne, H., Oxford Companion to Twentieth Century Art, 548

OTC Industrial Manual, Moody's Manuals, 985n

Ottemiller's Index to Plays in Collections, J. M. Connor and B. M. Connor, 673

Ouellette, R. P., J. Golden, S. Saari, and P. N. Cheremisinoff, Environmental Impact Data Book, 1481

Owen, W. F., and L. R. Cross, Guide to Graduate Study in Economics and Agricultural Economics in the United States and Canada, 955

Oxford Bible Atlas, H. G. May, 317

Oxford Classical Dictionary, N. G. L. Hammond and H. H. Scullard, 1132

Oxford Companion to American History, T. H. Johnson, 1170

Oxford Companion to American Literature, J. D. Hart, 378

Oxford Companion to American Theatre, G. Bordman, 620

Oxford Companion to Art, H. Osborne, 547

Oxford Companion to English Literature, P. Harvey, 379

Oxford Companion to Film, L. Bawden, 612

Oxford Companion to the Decorative Arts, H. Osborne, 549

Oxford Companion to the Theatre, P. Hartnoll, 619

Oxford Companion to Twentieth Century Art, H. Osborne, 548

Oxford Dictionary of English Proverbs, F. P. Wilson, 900

Oxford Dictionary of Saints, D. H. Farmer, 297

Oxford Dictionary of the Christian Church, F. L. Cross and E. A. Livingstone, 268

Oxford Economic Atlas of the World, 976

Oxford History of English Literature, F. P. Wilson and B. Dobrée, 390

Oxford Illustrated Guide to Great Britain and Ireland, D. Eagle and H. Carnell, 386

Paetow, L. J., Guide to the Study of Medieval History, 1116

Page, T. G., J. B. Thomas, and A. R. Marshall, International Dictionary of Education, 711

PAIS. See Public Affairs Information Service

PAIS INTERNATIONAL, 70n, 73n

Palic, V. M., Government Publications, 57

Palmer, H. H., European Drama Criticism, 1900-1975, 429

Palmer, H. H., and A. J. Dyson, English Novel Explication, 420

Palmer, R. C., Online Reference and Information Retrieval, 211

Palmes, J. C., Fletcher's History of Architecture, 552

Paperbound Books in Print, 8

Paradis, A. A., and G. D. Paradis, Labor Almanac, 959

Paradis, G. D., and A. A. Paradis, Labor Almanac, 959

Paris. Bibliothèque Nationale, Catalogue générale des livres imprimés, 15

Parish, D. W., State Government Reference Publications, 1036

Parish, J. R., and M. R. Pitts, Great Spy Pictures, 657

Parker, S. P., McGraw-Hill Concise Encyclopedia of Science and Technology, 1245

Parker, S. P., McGraw-Hill Dictionary of Biology, 1526

Parker, S. P., McGraw-Hill Dictionary of Chemistry, 1373

Parker, S. P., McGraw-Hill Dictionary of Earth Sciences, 1422

Parker, S. P., McGraw-Hill Dictionary of Electronics and Computer Technology, 1659

Parker, S. P., McGraw-Hill Dictionary of Engineering, 1696

Parker, S. P., McGraw-Hill Dictionary of Scientific and Technical Terms, 1242, 1245n

Parker, S. P., McGraw-Hill Encyclopedia of Astronomy, 1323

Parker, S. P., McGraw-Hill Encyclopedia of Chemistry, 1379

Parker, S. P., McGraw-Hill Encyclopedia of Electronics and Computers, 1665

Parker, S. P., McGraw-Hill Encyclopedia of Energy, 1492

Parker, S. P., McGraw-Hill Encyclopedia of Engineering, 1697

Parker, S. P., McGraw-Hill Encyclopedia of Environmental Science, 1471

Parker, S. P., McGraw-Hill Encyclopedia of Ocean and Atmospheric Sciences, 1440

Parker, S. P., McGraw-Hill Encyclopedia of Physics, 1349

Parker, S. P., Synopsis and Classification of Living Organisms, 1533

Parks, G. B., Greek and Latin Literatures, 435n

Parrinder, E. G., Dictionary of Non-Christian Religions, 278

Parry, P. M., Contemporary Art and Artists: An Index to Reproductions, 574

Pasachoff, J. M., and D. H. Menzel, Field Guide to the Stars and Planets, 1333

Passionate Amateur's Guide to Archaeology in the United States, J. Wilson, 917

Patterson, M. C., Literary Research Guide, 326; p. xvi

Patterson's American Education, 716

Pauly's Realencyclopädie der klassischen Altertumswissenschaft, 1132n

Paxton, J., Statesman's Year-Book, 99, 1072

Paxton, J., and C. Cook, Commonwealth Political Facts, 1080

Paxton, J., and C. Cook, European Political Facts, 1789-1973, 1079

Pearce, D. W., Dictionary of Modern Economics, 944

Pearce, E. A., and C. G. Smith, World Weather Guide, 1455

Pearson, C. E., Handbook of Applied Mathematics, 1307

Peaslee, A. J., Constitutions of Nations, 1074

Peck, H. T., Harper's Dictionary of Classical Literature and Antiquities, 1132n

Peck, T. P., Chemical Industries Information Sources, 1366

Pehnt, W., Encyclopedia of Modern Architecture, 537

Pelletier, P. A., Prominent Scientists, 1276

Pemberton, J. E., How to Find Out in Mathematics, 1286

Penguin Dictionary of Architecture, J. Fleming, 538n

Penguin Dictionary of Physical Geography, J. B. Whittow, 1443

Pennak, R. W., Collegiate Dictionary of Zoology, 1531

People's Chronology, J. Trager, 1138

Performing Arts Biography Master Index, B. McNeil and M. C. Herbert, 634

Performing Arts Books, 1876-1981, 577

Performing Arts Information Guide Series, 578

Performing Arts Research, M. K. Whalon, 576

Periodical Indexes in the Social Sciences and Humanities, L. A. Herzfeld, 222

Periodical Title Abbreviations, L. G. Alkire, 47

Perlman, N., and D. Ekwurzel, Index of Economic Articles in Journals and Collective Volumes, 932

Permanent International Committee of Linguists, Bibliographie linguistique de l'année, 879

Perry, E. S., and R. D. MacCann, New Film Index, 587

Perry, J. H., Variety Obits, 635

Perry's Chemical Engineers' Handbook, D. W. Green and J. O. Maloney, 1400

Personal Name Index to "The New York Times Index," 1851-1974, B. A. Falk and V. R. Falk, 140

Personality Tests and Reviews, 762n

Pesticide Manual, C. R. Worthing and S. B. Walker, 1583

Peterson, P. D., Religion Index One, 260

Peterson's Annual Guide to Graduate Study, 736

Peterson's Annual Guide to Independent Secondary Schools, R. A. Shepherd, J. Hunter, and P. S. Mast, 741

Peterson's Annual Guide to Undergraduate Study, K. C. Hegener and J. Hunter, 725

PETERSON'S COLLEGE DATABANK, 730n

Pevsner, N., J. Fleming, and H. Honour, Dictionary of Architecture, 535

Philosopher's Guide to Sources, Research Tools, Professional Life, and Related Fields, R. T. DeGeorge, 229

Philosopher's Index, 238-40

Philosophical Dictionary, W. Brugger, 243

Phonolog, 481

Physical Disability, P. C. Self, 1612

Physics Abstracts, 1316n, 1339, 1342n

Physics Briefs/Physikalische Berichte, 1316n, 1340

Physics Literature, R. H. Whitford, 1337

Pieper, F. C., SISCIS: Subject Index to Sources of Comparative International Statistics, 178

Piepkorn, A. C., Profiles in Belief, 299

Pitts, M. R., and J. R. Parish, Great Spy Pictures, 657

Planet We Live On, C. S. Hurlbut, Jr., 1423

Planning the Library Instruction Program, P. A. Breivik, 197

Plano, J., and M. Greenberg, American Political Dictionary, 1008

Plano, J., R. E. Riggs, and H. S. Robin, Dictionary of Political Analysis, 1009

Platt, C., Atlas of Medieval Man, 1144

Platt, E. T., and J. K. Wright, Aids to Geographical Research, 1179n

Play Index, 675

Plays, Players, and Playwrights, M. Geisinger, 631n

Ploski, H. A., and J. Williams, Negro Almanac, 912

Plot Summary Index, C. K. Kolar, 412

Plots and Characters Series, 410

Poetry Explication, J. M. Kuntz and N. C. Martinez, 431

Political Parties and Civic Action Groups, E. L. Schlapsmeier and F. H. Schlapsmeier, 1047

Political Parties of Europe, V. E. McHale and S. Skowronski, 1078

Political Parties of the Americas, R. J. Alexander, 1077

Political Profiles, N. Lichtenstein and E. N. Schoenebaum, 1031

Political Science, R. B. Harmon, 999

Politics in America, A. Ehrenhalt and M. Glennon, 1023

Pollock, G. L., Chemical Research Faculties, 1407

Pollution Abstracts, 1465

Poore, B. P., Descriptive Catalogue of the Government Publications of the United States, 63

Popular Beliefs and Superstitions, W. D. Hand, A. Cassetta, and S. Thiederman, 887

Popular Guide to Government Publications, W. P. Leidy, p. 21

Popular Music, N. Shapiro, 503

Popular Names of U.S. Government Reports, B. A. Bernier, K. F. Gould, and P. Humphrey, 64

Popular Song Index, P. Havlice, 505

Population and Family Planning Programs, D. L. Nortman and J. Fisher, 849

Population Index, 819

Porter, R., W. F. Bynum, and E. J. Browne, Dictionary of the History of Science, 1260

Poteet, G. H., Published Radio, Television, and Film Scripts, 594

Potter, G. R., New Cambridge Modern History, 1158

Poulton, H. J., and M. S. Howland, Historian's Handbook, 1110

Poupard, D., Literary Criticism from 1400 to 1800 (excluding Shakespeare), 432

Poupard, D., Twentieth Century Literary Criticism, 432

Powell, R. H., Handbooks and Tables in Science and Technology, 1265

Practicing Scientist's Handbook, A. J. Moses, 1268

Predicasts F & S Index, 927-29, 950n

Preminger, A., Princeton Encyclopedia of Poetry and Poetics, 372

Prentice-Hall Standard Glossary of Computer Terminology, R. A. Edmunds, 1658

Previte-Orton, C. W., Shorter Cambridge Medieval History, 1156

Price, M. O., H. Bitner, and S. R. Bysiewicz, Effective Legal Research, 1089

Primack, A. L., Finding Answers in Science and Technology, 1212

Princeton Encyclopedia of Classical Sites, R. Stillwell, W. L. McDonald, and M. H. McAllister, 897

Princeton Encyclopedia of Poetry and Poetics, A. Preminger, 372

Pritchard, E., and P. R. Scott, Literature Searching in Science, Technology, and Agriculture, 1213

Private Independent Schools, 742

Proceedings in Print, 34

ProFile: The Official Directory of the American Institute of Architects, H. W. Schirmer, 546

Profiles in Belief, A. C. Piepkorn, 299

Projections of Educational Statistics, National Centers for Education Statistics, 745

Prominent Scientists, P. A. Pelletier, 1276

Pseudonyms and Nicknames Dictionary, J. Mossman, 163

Psychiatric Dictionary, R. J. Campbell, 1629

Psychological Abstracts, 788

PSYCINFO, 788n

PTS F&S INDEXES, 929n

Public Affairs Information Service, Bulletin, 70

Public Affairs Information Service, Foreign Language Index, 73

Public Utility Manual, Moody's Manuals, 985n

Published Radio, Television, and Film Scripts, G. H. Poteet, 594

Publishers' Trade List Annual, 11

Pure and Applied Science Books, 1876-1982, 1227

Quantities and Units of Measurement, J. V. Drazil, 1257

Quayle, J. P., Kempe's Engineers Year-book, 1705

Quinlan, D., Illustrated Directory of Film Stars, 637

Quinn, E., and J. Gassner, Reader's Encyclopedia of World Drama, 371

Rader, H. B., Library Orientation and Instruction, 190

Radio and Television, W. E. McCavitt, 593

Raimo, J., and R. Sobel, Biographical Directory of the Governors of the United States, 1789-1978, 1038

Rainwater, R., and E. Arntzen, Guide to the Literature of Art History, 510

Ralston, A., and E. D. Reilly, Jr., Encyclopedia of Computer Science and Engineering, 1663

Rand McNally Atlas of Mankind, 905

Rand McNally Atlas of the Oceans, 1457

Rand McNally Commercial Atlas and Marketing Guide, 975

Rand McNally Historical Atlas of the World, R. I. Moore, 1147

Rand McNally New Concise Atlas of the Universe, P. Moore, 1335

Rapp, G. R., Jr., W. L. Roberts, and J. Weber, Encyclopedia of Minerals, 1450

Rating of Graduate Programs, K. D. Roose and C. J. Andersen, 761n

Rau, J. G., and D. C. Wooten, Environmental Impact Analysis Handbook, 1480

Reader's Digest Atlas of the Bible, 318

Reader's Digest of Books, H. Keller, 405n

Reader's Encyclopedia, W. R. Benet, 377; p. 92

Reader's Encyclopedia of the American West, H. R. Lamar, 1168

Reader's Encyclopedia of World Drama, J. Gassner and E. Quinn, 371

Reader's Guide to the Great Religions, C. J. Adams, 254

Reading, H. F., Dictionary of the Social Sciences, 700

Reading Tests and Reviews, 762n

Realencyclopädie der klassischen Alterumswissenschaft, 1132n

Realencyclopädie für protestantische Theologie und Kirche, 275n

Records in Review, E. Carter, 487

Redman, H. F., and L. E. Godfrey, Dictionary of Report Series Codes, 1254

Redmond, B. C., and R. M. Burrows, Concerto Themes, 471n

Redmond, B. C., and R. M. Burrows, Symphony Themes, 471n

Reed, J. G., and P. M. Baxter, Library Use: A Handbook for Psychology, 786

Rees, A. M., and J. Janes, Consumer Health Information Source Book, 1591

Reeves, J. A., and G. Freedley, History of the Theatre, 631

Reference Sources in Social Work, J. H. Conrad, 802

Reginald, R., Science Fiction and Fantasy Literature, 356

Rehabilitation Literature, 817

Rehrauer, G., Macmillan Film Bibliography, 581

Reich, W. T., Encyclopedia of Bioethics, 1631

Reid, W. M., R. C. Smith, and A. E. Luchsinger, Smith's Guide to the Literature of the Life Sciences, 1510

Reilly, E. D., Jr., and A. Ralston, Encyclopedia of Computer Science and Engineering, 1663

Religion Index One, 260

Religion Index Two, A. E. Hurd, 261

Religion Index Two: Festschriften, 1960-1969, B. A. O'Brien and E. J. O'Brien, 261n

Religion Index Two: Multi-Author Works, 1970-1975, G. F. Dickerson and E. Rubinstein, 261n

Religious and Spiritual Groups in Modern America, R. S. Ellwood, 300

Renford, B., and L. Hendrickson, Bibliographic Instruction, 193

Reno, E. A., League of Nations Documents, 1919-1946, 83

Répertoire bibliographique de la philosophie, 236

Répertoire d'art et d'archéologie, 527

Répertoire des sources historiques du moyen âge: Bio-bibliographie, C. U. J. Chevalier, 161

Repertoire for the Solo Voice, N. Espina, 467

Répertoire internationale de la Littérature Musicale (RILM), 445

Requirements for Certification for Elementary Schools, Secondary Schools, Junior Colleges, M. P. Burks, 770

Research Centers Directory, M. M. Watkins, 1264

Research Guide for Psychology, R. G. McInnis, 785

Research Guide to Philosophy, T. N. Tice and T. P. Slavens, 230

Research Guide to Religious Studies, J. F. Wilson and T. P. Slavens, 255

Research Programs in the Medical Sciences, 1637

Research Strategies, 191

Resources in Education, 752

Resources of American Music History, D. W. Krummel, 448

Retrospective Index to Film Periodicals, L. Batty, 585

Review of Educational Research, 750

Review of Research in Education, 749

Review of the Arts: Film and Television, 693

Review of the Arts: Performing Arts, 694

Reviews in Anthropology, 869

Revolutions and Revolutionists, R. Blackey, 1051

Reynolds, F. E., J. Holt, and J. Strong, Guide to Buddhist Religion, 257

Reynolds, M. M., Guide to Theses and Dissertations, 46

Rhoads, M. L., and C. E. Bower, EPA Index, 1469

Rhodes, D. E., and A. E. C. Simoni, Dictionary of Anonymous and Pseudonymous English Literature, 357n

Rice, E., Eastern Definitions, 279

Rice, F. A., and A. Guss, Information Sources in Linguistics, 878

Rice, J., Jr., Teaching Library Use, 198

Richardson, A., Dictionary of Christian Theology, 273

Richardson, J. M., and H. R. Malinowsky, Science and Engineering Literature, 1210; p. xvi

Riches, P. M., Analytical Bibliography of Universal Collected Biography, 142

Rickards, C., M. Gordon, and A. Singleton, Dictionary of New Information Technology Acronyms, 1672

Riegel's Handbook of Industrial Chemistry, J. A. Kent, 1402

Rieger, R., A. Michaelis, and M. M. Green, Glossary of Genetics and Cytogenetics, 1545

Rigdon, W., Biographical Encyclopedia and Who's Who of the American Theatre, 621n

Riggs, R. E., J. Plano, and H. S. Robin, Dictionary of Political Analysis, 1009

RILA: International Repertory of the Literature of Art, 526

Riley, M. F., and T. C. Bechtle, Dissertations in Philosophy Accepted at American Universities, 234

RILM: Abstracts of Music Literature, 445

Rischbieter, H., Friedrichs Theaterlexikon, 600n

Ritter, J., Historisches Wörterbuch der Philosophie, 244

Roach, J., Bibliography of Modern History, 1113

Robbins, J. A., American Literary Manuscripts, 362

Robbins, J. A., and W. G. French, American Literary Scholarship, 360

Roberts, A. F., Library Instruction for Librarians, 199

Roberts, F. C., Obituaries from The Times, 1951-1975, 157

Roberts, G. K., Dictionary of Political Analysis, 1009n

Roberts, W. L., G. R. Rapp, Jr., and J. Weber, Encyclopedia of Minerals, 1450

Robin, H. S., J. Plano, and R. E. Riggs, Dictionary of Political Analysis, 1009

Robinson, F. C., and S. B. Greenfield, Bibliography of Publications on Old English Literature to the End of 1972, 344

Robinson, J. H., and J. Muirden, Astronomy Data Book, 1328

Robinson, J. S., and R. Aluri, Guide to U.S. Government Scientific and Technical Resources, 1217

Rock On, N. N. Nite, 500

Rodgers and Hammerstein Archives of Recorded Sound, 483

Rodriguez, S. A., P. G. Schuman, and D. M. Jacobs, Materials for Occupational Education, 775

Roe, K. E., and R. G. Frederick, Dictionary of Theoretical Concepts in Biology, 1519

Rogal, S. J., Chronological Outline of British Literature, 384

Rogers, A. R., Humanities, 215; p. xvi

Rolling Stone Illustrated History of Rock & Roll, J. Miller, 499

Romanovsky, P., and C. A. Chambers, Social Service Organizations, 830

Roorbach, O., Bibliotheca Americana, 21

Roos, C., and J. B. Blake, Medical Reference Works, 1679-1966, 1601

Roose, K. D., and C. J. Andersen, Rating of Graduate Programs, 761n

Roper, F. W., and J. A. Boorkman, Introduction to Reference Sources in the Health Sciences, 1587

Rose, R., and T. T. Mackie, International Almanac of Electoral History, 1053

Rosenberg, J. M., Dictionary of Banking and Finance, 936

Rosenberg, J. M., Dictionary of Business and Management, 933

Rosenberg, J. M., Dictionary of Computers, Data Processing, and Telecommunications, 1657

Rosenthal, H., and J. Warrack, Concise Oxford Dictionary of Opera, 474

Ross, J. S., and M. J. Ross, New Encyclopedic Dictionary of Business Law — with Forms, 939

Ross, M., and B. Spuler, Rulers and Governments of the World, 1145

Ross, M. J., and J. S. Ross, New Encyclopedic Dictionary of Business Law — with Forms, 939

Roth, C., Standard Jewish Encyclopedia, 276n

Rouse, R. H., Serial Bibliographies for Medieval Studies, 1120

Rowley, H. H., and F. C. Grant, Hastings's Dictionary of the Bible, 302

Royal Anthropological Institute of Great Britain and Ireland Library. See Museum of Mankind Library

Rubinstein, E., and G. F. Dickerson, Religion Index Two: Multi-author Works, 1970-1975, 261n

Ruffner, J. A., Climates of the States, 1453

Ruffner, J. A., and F. E. Blair, Weather Almanac, 1452

Rulers and Governments of the World, M. Ross and B. Spuler, 1145

Runcorn, S. K., International Dictionary of Geophysics, Seismology, Geomagnetism . . ., 1437

Ryerson Library, Chicago Art Institute, Index to Art Periodicals, 528

Saari, S., J. Golden, R. P. Ouellette, and P. N. Cheremisinoff, Environmental Impact Data Book, 1481

Sabin, J., Dictionary of Books Relating to America from Its Discovery to the Present Time, 26

Sachs, C., World History of the Dance, 633

Sachs, M. Y., Worldmark Encyclopedia of the Nations, 1192

Sadie, S., New Grove Dictionary of Music and Musicians, 450

Safire, W., Safire's Political Dictionary, 1010

Sainsbury, D., and P. Singleton, Dictionary of Microbiology, 1543

Salem, J. M., Drury's Guide to Best Plays, 676

Salem, J. M., Guide to Critical Reviews, 685

Salvendy, G., Handbook of Industrial Engineering, 1712

Samples, G., Drama Scholar's Index to Plays and Filmstrips, 674

Samples, G., How to Locate Reviews of Plays and Films, 684

Sandeen, E. R., and F. Hale, American Religion and Philosophy, 256

Sarjeant, W. A. S., Geologists and the History of Geology, 1460

Sarkissian, A., Children's Authors and Illustrators, 403

Sarkissian, A., Writers for Young Adults Biography Master Index, 402

Satterthwaite, G. E., Encyclopedia of Astronomy, 1325

Savitt, T. L., M. Kaufman, and S. Galishoff, Dictionary of American Medical Biography, 1646

Sax, N. I., Dangerous Properties of Industrial Materials, 1398

Scammon, R. M., America Votes, 1052

Schaefer, B. K., Using the Mathematical Literature, 1284

Schaefer, V. J., and J. A. Day, Field Guide to the Atmosphere, 1451

Schemenaur, P. J., and J. Brady, Writer's Market, 376

Schenk, M. T., and J. K. Webster, What Every Engineer Should Know about Engineering and Information Resources, 1682

Schindler, S., E. Farber, and S. Hannah, Combined Retrospective Index to Book Reviews in Humanities Journals, 1802-1974, 186

Schirmer, H. W., ProFile: The Official Directory of the American Institute of Architects, 546

Schlachter, G. A., and D. Belli, Minorities and Women, 806

Schlapsmeier, E. L., and F. H. Schlapsmeier, Political Parties and Civic Action Groups, 1047

Schlapsmeier, F. H., and E. L. Schlapsmeier, Political Parties and Civic Action Groups, 1047

Schlueter, J., and P. Schlueter, Twentieth Century Novelists, 421

Schlueter, P., and J. Schlueter, Twentieth Century Novelists, 421

Schmidt, A. J., and N. Babchuk, Fraternal Organizations, 831

Schmieder, A. A., Dictionary of Basic Geography, 1188

Schmittroth, J., Jr., Encyclopedia of Information Systems and Services, 116

Schmittroth, J., Jr., and M. Connors, Telecommunications Systems and Services Directory, 1678

Schneider, B. R., Index to "The London Stage, 1600-1800," 664

Schoenebaum, E. N., and N. Lichtenstein, Political Profiles, 1031

Scholarships, Fellowships, and Loans, S. N. Feingold and M. Feingold, 767

Schonberg, B., World History of the Dance, 633

Schools Abroad of Interest to Americans, 784

Schuman, P. G., S. A. Rodriguez, and D. M. Jacobs, Materials for Occupational Education, 775

Schwann-1 Record and Tape Guide, 480n

Schwann-2, 480n

Schwartz, M. L., Encyclopedia of Beaches and Coastal Environments, 1435

Schweizer, S., and C. Chen, Online Bibliographic Searching, 210

Science and Engineering Literature, H. R. Malinowsky and J. M. Richardson, 1210; p. xvi

Science and Technology, D. Grogan, 1214

Science Citation Index, 1223; p. 276

Science Fiction and Fantasy Literature, R. Reginald, 356

Science Tests and Reviews, 762n
Scientific and Technical Aerospace Reports, 1690
Scientific and Technical Books and Serials in Print, 1226
Scientific and Technical Information Resources, K. Subramanyam, 1215; p. 261
Scientific and Technical Information Sources, C.-C. Chen, 1211
Scientific Meetings, 1231
Scientists' Approaches to Information, M. J. Voigt, p. 262
SCISEARCH, 1223n
Scoble, H. M., and L. S. Wiseberg, Human Rights Directory, 1050
Scoble, H. M., and L. S. Wiseberg, North American Human Rights Directory, 1049
Scott, J. W., and R. G. McInnis, Social Sciences Research Handbook, 696
Scott, P. R., and E. Pritchard, Literature Searching in Science, Technology, and Agriculture, 1213
Scott, T., and M. Brewer, Concise Encyclopedia of Biochemistry, 1547
Scott-Kilvert, I., British Writers, 398
Screen World, 617
Scullard, H. H., and N. G. L. Hammond, Oxford Classical Dictionary, 1132
Sculpture Index, J. Clapp, 575
Seal, R. A., Guide to the Literature of Astronomy, 1313
Seal, R. A., and S. S. Martin, Bibliography of Astronomy, 1970-1979, 1315
Search for Data in the Physical and Chemical Sciences, L. R. Arny, 1218
Searching Patent Documents for Patentability and Information, F. K. Carr, 1683
Sears, M., and P. Crawford, Song Index, 506n
Second Handbook of Research on Teaching, R. M. Travers, 751
Security Owner's Stock Guide, 988
Seidler, L. J., and D. R. Carmichael, Accountants' Handbook, 956
Selective Guide to Colleges, E. B. Fiske, 727
Self, P. C., Physical Disability, 1612
Seltsam, W. H., Metropolitan Opera Annals, 478
Seltzer, L., Columbia-Lippincott Gazetteer of the World, 1205
Serial Bibliographies for Medieval Studies, R. H. Rouse, 1120
Serial Bibliographies in the Humanities and Social Sciences, R. A. Gray, 218
Serial Sources for the BIOSIS Data Base, 1518

Severs, J. B., and A. E. Hartung, Manual of the Writings in Middle English, 1050-1500, 345
Sewell, W., Guide to Drug Information, 1609
Shafritz, J. M., Dictionary of Personnel Management and Labor Relations, 935
Shain, M., and D. Longley, Dictionary of Information Technology, 1666
Shakespearean Criticism, L. L. Harris, 432
Shakespearean Bibliography and Textual Criticism, T. H. Howard-Hill, 332
Shapiro, N., Popular Music, 503
Sharp, D. W. A., Miall's Dictionary of Chemistry, 1374
Sharp, H. S., Handbook of Geographic Nicknames, 1197
Sharp, H. S., Handbook of Pseudonyms and Personal Nicknames, 164
Sharp, H. S., and M. Z. Sharp, Index to Characters in the Performing Arts, 611
Sharp, M. Z., and H. S. Sharp, Index to Characters in the Performing Arts, 611
Shaw, D. F., Information Sources in Physics, 1336
Shaw, R., and R. Shoemaker, American Bibliography, 23
Sheahan, E., Moving Pictures, 580
Sheehy, E. P., R. G. Keckeissen, and E. McIlvaine, Guide to Reference Books, 811n; pp. 14-16, 39, 41, 44, 74, 255
Shepard's Acts and Cases by Popular Names, 1108
Shepherd, R. A., J. Hunter, and P. S. Mast, Peterson's Annual Guide to Independent Secondary Schools, 741
Shepherd, W. R., Shepherd's Historical Atlas, 1148
Sherratt, A. S., Cambridge Encyclopedia of Archaeology, 895
Shipley, J. T., Guide to Great Plays, 669
Shipton, C., National Index of American Imprints through 1800, 25
Shoemaker, R. A., Checklist of American Imprints, 22
Shoemaker, R., and R. Shaw, American Bibliography, 23
Short Story Index, 354
Shorter Cambridge Medieval History, C. W. Previté-Orton, 1156
Shorter New Cambridge Bibliography of English Literature, 329n
Showman, R. K., and F. Freidel, Harvard Guide to American History, 1161
Sibley Music Library, University of Rochester, Catalog of Sound Recordings, 484

Siegel, D., E. M. Mackesy, and K. Mateyak, MLA Directory of Periodicals, 336

Siegman, G., and P. Wasserman, Awards, Honors, and Prizes, 109

Sills, D. L., International Encyclopedia of the Social Sciences, 703, 1012; p. 204

Simoni, A. E. C., and D. E. Rhodes, Dictionary of Anonymous and Pseudonymous English Literature, 357n

Singer, D., and M. Himmelfarb, American Jewish Yearbook, 288

Singleton, A., M. Gordon, and C. Rickards, Dictionary of New Information Technology Acronyms, 1672

Singleton, A., A. J. Meadows, and M. Gordon, Dictionary of Computing and New Information Technology, 1667

Singleton, P., and D. Sainsbury, Dictionary of Microbiology, 1543

Sippl, C. J., and R. J. Sippl, Computer Dictionary, 1662

Sippl, R. J., and C. J. Sippl, Computer Dictionary, 1662

SISCIS: Subject Index to Sources of Comparative International Statistics, F. C. Pieper, 178

Skolnik, H., Literature Matrix of Chemistry, 1363

Skowronski, S., and V. E. McHale, Political Parties of Europe, 1078

Slauson, N. G., and L. T. Munz, Index to Illustrations of Living Things Outside of North America, 1521

Slavens, T. P., and T. N. Tice, Research Guide to Philosophy, 230

Slavens, T. P. and J. F. Wilson, Research Guide to Religious Studies, 255

Slavic Literatures, R. C. Lewanski, 435n

Slesser, M., Dictionary of Energy, 1495

Slocum, R. B., Biographical Dictionaries and Related Works, 153

Slonimsky, N., Music since 1900, 459

Small, J., and F. J. Monkhouse, Dictionary of the Natural Environment, 1474

Smith, C. G., and E. A. Pearce, World Weather Guide, 1455

Smith, D. A., and L. W. Garrison, American Political Process, 1044

Smith, D. G., Cambridge Encyclopedia of Earth Sciences, 1424

Smith, E. C., and A. J. Zurcher, Dictionary of American Politics, 1007

Smith, J. M., and T. Cawkwell, World Encyclopedia of the Film, 638

Smith, L. W., and M. D. W. Moure, Index to Reproductions of American Paintings, 571

Smith, R. C., W. M. Reid, and A. E. Luchsinger, Smith's Guide to the Literature of the Life Sciences, 1510

Smith, V. B., Dictionary of Contemporary Artists, 560

Smith, W. J., Granger's Index to Poetry, 351

Smith, W. J., and W. F. Bernhardt, Granger's Index to Poetry, 352

Smyers, V. L., and M. Winship, Bibliography of American Literature, 331n

Smythe, M. M., Black American Reference Book, 911

Snead, R. E., World Atlas of Geomorphic Features, 1456

Sneddon, I. N., Encyclopaedic Dictionary of Mathematics for Engineers and Applied Scientists, 1297

Snell, F. D., C. L. Hilton, and L. S. Ettre, Encyclopedia of Industrial Chemical Analysis, 1386

Snider, M. J., and others, Handbook of Nursing, 1640

Sniderman, F. M., and P. F. Breed, Dramatic Criticism Index, 427

Sobel, R., Biographical Directory of the United States Executive Branch, 1774-1977, 1030

Sobel, R., and J. Raimo, Biographical Directory of the Governors of the United States, 1789-1978, 1038

Social History of the United States, D. F. Tingley, 1164

Social Indicators, K. J. Gilmartin, 811

Social Indicators and Societal Monitoring, L. D. Wilcox, 811n

Social Indicators III, U.S. Dept. of Commerce, Bureau of the Census, 846

Social Science Reference Sources, T. Li, 697; p. 194

Social Sciences Citation Index, 699

Social Sciences Index, 698

Social Sciences Research Handbook, R. G. McInnis and J. W. Scott, 696

Social Service Directory, Metropolitan Chicago, 842

Social Service Organizations, P. Romanovsky and C. A. Chambers, 830

Social Service Organizations and Agencies Directory, A. T. Kruzas, 827

Social Studies Tests and Reviews, 762n

Social Work Research and Abstracts, 815

Society for Historians of American Foreign Relations, Guide to American Foreign Relations since 1700, 1060

Society for Industrial and Applied Mathe-
matics, American Mathematical Society,
Mathematical Association of America,
Combined Membership List, 1311

Sociological Abstracts, 814

Software Catalog: Science and Engineering,
1676

Somer, J. L., and B. E. Cooper, American
and British Literature, 1945-1975, 358

Song Catalogue, British Broadcasting Corporation, Central Music Library, 509

Song Index, M. Sears and P. Crawford, 506n

Songs in Collections, D. De Charms and P. F.
Breed, 506

Souders, M., and O. W. Eshbach, Handbook of
Engineering Fundamentals, 1704

Source-book of Biological Names and Terms,
E. C. Jaeger, 1550

Sourcebook of Criminal Justice Statistics,
National Criminal Justice Information
and Statistics Service, 852

Sourcebook on Aging, 854

Sourcebook on the Environment, K. A.
Hammond, G. Macinko, and W. B.
Fairchild, 1462

Sources of Information in the Social Sciences,
C. M. White, 695; p. xvi, p. 194

Space, Time and Architecture, S. Giedion, 553

Sperber, H., and T. Trittschuh, American
Political Terms, 1011

Spiller, R. E., Literary History of the United
States, 330, 391

SPIN, 1343n

Spuler, B., and M. Ross, Rulers and Governments of the World, 1145

Stambler, I., Encyclopedia of Pop, Rock, and
Soul, 497

Stambler, I., and G. Landon, Encyclopedia of
Folk, Country, and Western Music, 496

Stamp, L. D., and A. N. Clark, Glossary of
Geographical Terms, 1189

STANDARD AND POOR'S CORPORATE
DESCRIPTIONS, 986n

Standard and Poor's Register of Corporations, Directors, and Executives, 946

Standard Corporation Records, 986

Standard Education Almanac, 746

Standard Encyclopedia of the World's Rivers
and Lakes, R. K. Gresswell and A.
Huxley, 1194

Standard Handbook for Civil Engineers, F. S.
Merritt, 1709

Standard Handbook for Electrical Engineers,
D. G. Fink and H. W. Beaty, 1710

Standard Handbook of Engineering Calculations, T. G. Hicks, 1706

Standard Jewish Encyclopedia, C. Roth, 276n

Standard Periodical Directory, 50

Standards and Specifications Information
Sources, E. J. Struglia, 1685

Stansfield, W. D., and R. C. King, Dictionary of Genetics, 1546

Stapleton, Michael, Cambridge Guide to
English Literature, 380

State Administrative Officials Classified
by Function, 93

State and Metropolitan Area Data Book, U.S.
Dept. of Commerce, Bureau of the
Census, 167

State Elective Officials and the Legislatures,
94

State Government Reference Publications,
D. W. Parish, 1036

State Publications, R. R. Bowker, 71

Statesman's Year-Book, J. Paxton, 99, 1072

Statistical Abstract of the United States,
U.S. Dept. of Commerce, Bureau of the
Census, 165; p. 45

Statistical Reference Index, 175; p. 45

Statistical Theory and Method Abstracts, 1290

Statistical Yearbook, United Nations, Statistical Office, 170

Statistics Sources, P. Wasserman and
J. O'Brien, 177; p. 45

Statt, D., Dictionary of Human Behavior,
789

Stauffer, T. R., J. Viola, and N. B. Mack,
Energy Research Guide, 1491

Stedman's Medical Dictionary, 1621

Steel, R., and A. P. Harvey, Encyclopedia
of Prehistoric Life, 1438

Steere, N. V., CRC Handbook of Laboratory
Safety, 1267

Steinberg, C. S., Film Facts, 618

Steinberg, C. S., TV Facts, 629

Stenesh, J., Dictionary of Biochemistry,
1548

Stephen, L., and S. Lee, Dictionary of
National Biography, 147

Stevenson, B. E., Home Book of Bible
Quotations, 312

Steward, J. H., Handbook of South American
Indians, 910

Stewart, J., Filmarama, 640

Stiegeler, S. E., Dictionary of Earth Sciences,
1421

Stillwell, R., W. L. McDonald, and M. H.
McAllister, Princeton Encyclopedia of
Classical Sites, 897

Stine, J. C., Contemporary Literary Criticism,
432

Stock, R., and N. W. Thompson, Complete
Concordance to the Bible (Douay
version), 310

Stokes, A. V., Concise Encyclopedia of
Information Technology, 1668

Storey, R. L., Chronology of the Medieval World, 800 to 1491, 1140

Stratman, C. J., Bibliography of the American Theatre, Excluding New York City, 591

Strauch, K. P., and D. J. Brundage, Guide to Library Resources for Nursing, 1603

Straughn, B. L., and C. T. Straughn, Lovejoy's Career and Vocational School Guide, 738

Straughn, B. L., and C. T. Straughn, Lovejoy's Prep and Private School Guide, 740

Straughn, C. T., and B. L. Straughn, Lovejoy's Career and Vocational School Guide, 738

Straughn, C. T., and B. L. Straughn, Lovejoy's Prep and Private School Guide, 740

Strayer, J. R., Dictionary of the Middle Ages, 1129

String Music in Print, M. Farish, 468

Strong, J., Exhaustive Concordance of the Bible, 309

Strong, J., F. E. Reynolds, and J. Holt, Guide to Buddhist Religion, 257

Struglia, E. J., Standards and Specifications Information Sources, 1685

Student Sociologist's Handbook, P. Bart and L. Frankel, 801

Studies in English Literature, 434

Studio Dictionary of Design and Decoration, 539

Study Abroad, 777

Sturges, P., and M. Blaug, Who's Who in Economics, 979

Sturtevant, W. C., Handbook of North American Indians, 908

Stutley, J., and M. Stutley, Harper's Dictionary of Hinduism, 281

Stutley, M., and J. Stutley, Harper's Dictionary of Hinduism, 281

Subject Collections, L. Ash, 114

Subject Compilations of State Laws, C. Boast and L. Foster, 1092

Subject Directory of Special Libraries and Information Centers, B. T. Darnay, 113

Subject Guide to Books in Print, 7

Subject Guide to Forthcoming Books, 10

Subject Guide to Major United States Government Publications, E. Jackson, p. 21

Subject Index to Sources of Comparative International Statistics (SISCIS), F. C. Pieper, 178

Subramanyam, K., Scientific and Technical Information Resources, 1215; p. 261

Sugden, A., Longman Illustrated Dictionary of Botany, 1535

SUPERINDEX, 1266n

Survey of Buying Power, 965

Survey of Contemporary Literature, F. N. Magill, 406

Survey of Current Business, U.S. Dept. of Commerce, Bureau of Economic Analysis, 966; p. 45

Survey of Science Fiction Literature, F. N. Magill, 408

Survey Research Consultants International, Index to International Public Opinion, 861

Swallow, H. H., and L. Urdang, Mosby's Medical and Nursing Dictionary, 1626

Swartz, D., Collegiate Dictionary of Botany, 1534

Sweet and Lowdown, W. Craig, 491

Sykes, E., Everyman's Dictionary of Non-Classical Mythology, 321

Symphony Themes, R. M. Burrows and B. C. Redmond, 471n

Synopsis and Classification of Living Organisms, S. P. Parker, 1533

Synoptic Classification of Living Organisms, R. S. K. Barnes, 1554

Taber's Cyclopedic Medical Dictionary, C. L. Thomas, 1623

Tansey, R. G., and H. de la Croix, Gardner's Art through the Ages, 550

Tanur, J. M., and W. H. Kruskal, International Encyclopedia of Statistics, 1301

Tarbert, G. C., Book Review Index, 181

Taylor, A., and B. J. Whiting, Dictionary of American Proverbs and Proverbial Phrases, 901

Taylor, C. J. H., J. A. Garraty, and L. von Klemperer, New Guide to Study Abroad, 776

Teaching Abroad, B. C. Conotillo, 780

Teaching Library Use, J. Rice, Jr., 198

Technical Book Review Index, 183

Telecommunications Systems and Services Directory, J. Schmittroth, Jr., and M. Connors, 1678

Television Drama Series Programming, L. J. Gianakos, 680-82a

Temple, R. Z., and M. Tucker, Modern British Literature, 414

Temple, R. Z., and M. Tucker, Twentieth Century British Literature, 415

Terrace, V., Complete Encyclopedia of Television Programs, 678

Tests in Microfiche, Annotated Index, 764n
Tests in Print III, J. E. Mitchell, Jr., 763
Theatre, S. Cheney, 631n
Theatre: Stage to Screen to Television, W. T. Leonard, 670
Theatre and Allied Arts, B. M. Baker, 588
Theatre World, 623
Thematic Catalogues in Music, B. S. Brook, 472
Theodoratus, R. J., Europe, 873
Theodorson, A. G., and G. A. Theodorson, Modern Dictionary of Sociology, 821
Theodorson, G. A., and A. G. Theodorson, Modern Dictionary of Sociology, 821
Theologische Realenzyklopädie, G. Krause and G. Müller, 275n; p. 7
Thernstrom, S., A. Orlov, and O. Handlin, Harvard Encyclopedia of American Ethnic Groups, 826
Thesaurus of Book Digests, H. Haydn and E. Fuller, 409n
Thesaurus of Book Digests, 1950-1980, I. Weiss and A. de la Verne Weiss, 409
Thesaurus of ERIC Descriptors, 708n
Thewlis, J., Concise Dictionary of Physics and Related Subjects, 1346
Thewlis, J., Encyclopaedic Dictionary of Physics, 1346n, 1350
Thiederman, S., A. Cassetta, and W. D. Hand, Popular Beliefs and Superstitions, 887
Thieme, U., and F. Becker, Allgemeines Lexikon der bildenden Künstler, 554; p. 7
Thomas, C. L., Taber's Cyclopedic Medical Dictionary, 1623
Thomas, J. B., T. G. Page, and A. R. Marshall, International Dictionary of Education, 711
Thomas's Register of American Manufacturers, 951; p. 274
Thompson, C. L., M. M. Anderberg, and J. B. Antrell, Current History Encyclopedia of Developing Nations, 1082
Thompson, G. A., Jr., Key Sources in Comparative World Literature, 328
Thompson, I., Audubon Society Field Guide to North American Fossils, 1448
Thompson, J. W., Index to Illustrations of the Natural World, 1520
Thompson, L. S., The New Sabin, 28
Thompson, N. W., and R. Stock, Complete Concordance to the Bible (Douay version), 310
Thompson, O., International Cyclopedia of Music and Musicians, 451
Thompson, S., Motif-Index of Folk Literature, 885
Thurston, H., and D. Attwater, Butler's Lives of the Saints, 296
TIAS, Treaties and Other International Acts Series, U.S. Dept. of State, 1068
Tice, T. N., and T. P. Slavens, Research Guide to Philosophy, 230
Tietjen, J. A., Profiles in Belief, 299
Time Atlas of the World, 1202
Times Concise Atlas of the World, 1204
Times Concise Atlas of World History, R. Barraclough, 1149
Times Index-Gazetteer of the World, 1207
Timetables of History, B. Grun, 1137
Tingley, D. F., Social History of the United States, 1164
Tinucci, B. A., and L. Chaudier, Who's Who in Technology Today, 1715
Title Guide to the Talkies, A. A. Aros, 654
Title Guide to the Talkies, R. B. Dimmitt, 653
Titus, E. B., Union List of Serials in Libraries of the United States and Canada, 48
Tobin, J. E., and J. J. Delaney, Dictionary of Catholic Biography, 295
Tomlinson, J., S. Deighton, and J. Gurnsey, Computers and Information Processing World Index, 1650
Toomey, A. F., World Bibliography of Bibliographies, Supplement, 1964-74, 29, 216
Tootill, E., Facts on File Dictionary of Biology, 1524
Tootill, E., and S. Blackmore, Facts on File Dictionary of Botany, 1532
Tootill, E., J. Daintith, and S. Mitchell, Biographical Encyclopedia of Scientists, 1279
Topics and Terms in Environmental Problems, J. R. Holum, 1479
Total Television, A. McNeil, 679
Totok, W., and others, Handbuch der Geschichte der Philosophie, 232
Trade Names Directory, D. Wood, 940, 1394n
Trager, J., People's Chronology, 1138
Transatom Bulletin, 1241n
Translations Register-Index, 1240
Transportation Manual, Moody's Manuals, 985n
Travers, R. M., Second Handbook of Research on Teaching, 751
Treaties and Other International Acts Series (TIAS), U.S. Dept. of State, 1068
Treaties in Force, U.S. Dept. of State, 1069
Treherne, R. F., and H. Fullard, Muir's Historical Atlas, 1146

Trigg, G. L., and R. G. Lerner, Encyclopedia
of Physics, 1347
Tripp, E., Crowell's Handbook of Classical
Mythology, 322
Trittschuh, T., and H. Sperber, American
Political Terms, 1011
Truitt, E. M., Who Was Who on the Screen,
639
Tucker, M., Critical Temper, 413
Tucker, M., and J. H. Ferres, Modern Common-
wealth Literature, 417
Tucker M., and R. Z. Temple, Modern British
Literature, 414
Tucker, M., and R. Z. Temple, Twentieth
Century British Literature, 415
Tudor, D., and L. Beisenthal, Annual Index
to Popular Music Record Reviews, 488
Tuma, J. J., Engineering Mathematics Hand-
book, 1308
Tune in Yesterday, J. Dunning, 677
Turner, J. B., Encyclopedia of Social
Work, 824
Tuve, G. L., and R. E. Bolz, CRC Hand-
book of Tables for Applied Engineering
Science, 1707
TV Facts, C. S. Steinberg, 629
TV Guide Almanac, C. T. Norback and P. G.
Norback, 630
TV Season, N. David, 683
Tver, D. F., Dictionary of Astronomy, Space
and Atmospheric Phenomena, 1322
Tver, D. F., Dictionary of Dangerous
Pollutants, Ecology and Environment,
1475
Tver, D. F., Ocean and Marine Dictionary,
1441
Tver, D. F., and R. W. Bolz, Encyclopedic
Dictionary of Industrial Technology,
1698
Twentieth Century Authors, S. S. Kunitz and
H. Haycraft, 394
Twentieth Century British Literature, R. Z.
Temple and M. Tucker, 415
Twentieth Century Children's Writers, D. L.
Kirkpatrick, 401
Twentieth Century Encyclopedia of Religious
Knowledge, L. A. Loetscher, 275n
Twentieth Century English Novel, A. F. Cassis,
422
Twentieth Century Interpretations, 434
Twentieth Century Literary Criticism,
D. Poupard, 432
Twentieth Century Novelists, P. Schlueter and
J. Schlueter, 421
Twentieth Century Short Story Explication,
W. S. Walker, 430
Twentieth Century Views, 434

Tyler, G. R., and A. Coleman, Drama Criticism,
426
Type and Motif-Index of the Folktales of
England and North America, E. W.
Baughman, 886

Ujifusa, B., M. Barone, and D. Matthews,
Almanac of American Politics, 1024
Ulrich's International Periodicals
Directory, 51, 1226n, 1596n
ULRICH'S INTERNATIONAL PERIODICALS
DIRECTORY, 52n
UNDEX: United Nations Documents Index,
75-77
UNDOC: Current Index, United Nations
Documents Index, 74
UNESCO, Catalogue of Reproductions of
Paintings, 1860-1979, 568n
UNESCO, Catalogue of Reproductions of
Paintings prior to 1860, 568n
UNESCO Statistical Yearbook, 747
Unger, L., and G. T. Wright, American Writers,
399
Uniform Crime Reports, Federal Bureau of
Investigation, 853
Union List of Serials in Libraries of the
United States and Canada, E. B. Titus,
48, 1228n
United Nations, Yearbook, 1083
United Nations Documents Index, 74-79
United Nations Educational, Scientific and
Cultural Organization, Catalogue of
Reproductions of Paintings, 1860-1979,
568n
United Nations Educational, Scientific and
Cultural Organization, Catalogue of
Reproductions of Paintings prior to
1860, 568n
United Nations, Statistical Office, Com-
pendium of Housing Statistics, 851
United Nations, Statistical Office,
Compendium of Social Statistics,
845
United Nations, Statistical Office,
Demographic Yearbook, 847
United Nations, Statistical Office,
Statistical Yearbook, 170; p. 45
United States Budget in Brief, 992n
United States Code, 1098
United States Code Congressional and
Administrative News, 1100
U.S. College-Sponsored Programs Abroad:
Academic Year, G. A. Cohen, 778
U.S. Congress, Biographical Directory of
the American Congress, 1774-1971,
1026

U.S. Congress, Official Congressional Directory, 86, 1017

U.S. Congressional Committee Hearings Index, CIS, 66

U.S. Congressional Committee Prints Index, CIS, 67

U.S. Council of Economic Advisors, Economic Indicators, 969

U.S. Dept. of Commerce, Bureau of the Census, Census, 169

U.S. Dept. of Commerce, Bureau of the Census, Census of Governments, 994

U.S. Dept. of Commerce, Bureau of the Census, County and City Data Book, 166

U.S. Dept. of Commerce, Bureau of the Census, Demographic Estimates for Counties with Population of 10 Million or More, 848

U.S. Dept. of Commerce, Bureau of the Census, Historical Statistics of the United States, 168, 1177

U.S. Dept. of Commerce, Bureau of the Census, Social Indicators III, 846

U.S. Dept. of Commerce, Bureau of the Census, State and Metropolitan Area Data Book, 167

U.S. Dept. of Commerce, Bureau of the Census, Statistical Abstract of the United States, 165

U.S. Dept. of Commerce, Bureau of Economic Analysis, Business Conditions Digest, 968

U.S. Dept. of Commerce, Bureau of Economic Analysis, Business Statistics, 967

U.S. Dept. of Commerce, Bureau of Economic Analysis, Survey of Current Business, 966

U.S. Dept. of Commerce, Buearu of Industrial Economics, Industrial Outlook, 982

U.S. Dept. of Education, National Center for Education Statistics. See National Center for Education Statistics

U.S. Dept. of Labor, Bureau of Labor Statistics, Handbook of Labor Statistics, 971

U.S. Dept. of Labor, Bureau of Labor Statistics, Occupational Outlook Handbook, 771

U.S. Dept. of State, Treaties and Other International Acts Series (TIAS), 1068

U.S. Dept. of State, Treaties in Force, 1069

United States Energy Atlas, D. J. Cuff and W. J. Young, 1506

U.S. Environmental Data Service, Weather Atlas of the United States, 1458

U.S. Executive Office of the President, Office of Management and Budget, Budget of the United States Government, 992

U.S. Federal Bureau of Investigation, Uniform Crime Reports, 853

U.S. General Services Administration, National Archives and Records Service, National Historical Publications and Record Commission, Directory of Archives and Manuscript Repositories in the United States, 1133

U.S. General Services Administration, National Archives and Records Service, Office of the Federal Register, United States Government Manual, 85, 1027

United States Government Manual, U.S. General Services Administration, National Archives and Records Service, Office of the Federal Register, 85, 1027

U.S. Government Research and Development Reports, 1225n

U.S. International Communication Agency, Directory of Resources for Cultural and Educational Exchanges and International Communication, 781

U.S. Library of Congress, Music, Books on Music, and Sound Recordings, 443

U.S. Library of Congress, Exchange and Gift Division, Monthly Checklist of State Publications, 69

United States Political Science Documents, 1001

U.S. Politics and Elections, D. J. Maurer, 1043

U.S. President, Economic Report of the President to the Congress, 970

U.S. Serial Set Index, CIS, 65

United States Statutes at Large, 1099

U.S. Superintendent of Documents, Catalog of the Public Documents of Congress and of All Departments of the Government of the United States, 60

U.S. Superintendent of Documents, Monthly Catalog of United States Government Publications, 58; p. 21

United States Treaties and Other International Agreements, 1067

Units of Measurement, S. Dresner, 1256

Universal Encyclopedia of Mathematics, 1298

Universal Reference System: Political Science, Government, and Public Policy Series, 1000

Urban Needs, P. Kline, 810

Urdang, L., and H. H. Swallow, Mosby's Medical and Nursing Dictionary, 1626

Urdang Dictionary of Current Medical Terms for Health Science Professionals, 1624

Urmson, J. O., Concise Encyclopedia of Western Philosophy and Philosophers, 246

Urquhart, F., Dictionary of Fictional Characters, 383

Use of Biological Literature, R. T. Bottle and H. V. Wyatt, 1508

Use of Chemical Literature, R. T. Bottle, 1360

Use of Earth Sciences Literature, D. N. Wood, 1409, 1456n

Use of Engineering Literature, K. W. Mildren, 1680

Use of Mathematical Literature, A. R. Dorling, 1283

Using the Biological Literature, E. B. Davis, 1509

Using the Chemical Literature, H. M. Woodburn, 1365

Using the Mathematical Literature, B. K. Schaefer, 1284

Vacation Study Abroad, G. A. Cohen, 779

Value Line Investment Survey, 983, 987

Van Antwerp, M. A., Dictionary of Literary Biography: Documentary Series, 397

Van Nostrand Reinhold Encyclopedia of Chemistry, D. M. Considine and G. D. Considine, 1380

Van Nostrand's Scientific Encyclopedia, D. M. Considine, 1248

Varet, G., Manuel de bibliographie philosophique, 233

Variety: International Showbusiness Reference, 610

Variety Film Reviews, 689

Variety Music Cavalcade, 1620-1961, J. Mattfeld, 504

Variety Obits, J. H. Perry, 635

Variety Who's Who in Show Business, M. Kaplan, 641

Vaughan, D., and M. Clarke, Encyclopedia of Dance and Ballet, 604

Verrel, B., and H. Opitz, World Guide to Scientific Associations and Learned Societies, 724

Victorian Life and Victorian Fiction, J. McMurty, 381

Vinton, J., Dictionary of Contemporary Music, 453

Viola, J., N. B. Mack, and T. R. Stauffer, Energy Research Guide, 1491

VNR Concise Encyclopedia of Mathematics, 1299

Vocabulaire technique et critique de la philosophie, A. Lalande, 244n

Vocational Tests and Reviews, 762n

Voight, M. J., Scientists' Approaches to Information, p. 262

Vollmer, H., Allgemeines Lexikon der bildenden Künstler des XX. Jahrhunderts, 555

Voorhees, D. W., Concise Dictionary of American History, 1166n

Vries, S., Atlas of World History, 1150

Wakeman, J., World Authors, 1950-1970, 394

Wakeman, J., World Authors, 1970-1975, 394

Walford, A. J., Walford's Guide to Reference Material, pp. 14-16, 39, 41, 74, 255

Walker, B., Hindu World, 282

Walker, J. A., Glossary of Art, Architecture, and Design since 1945, 534

Walker, S. B., and C. R. Worthing, Pesticide Manual, 1583

Walker, W. S., Twentieth Century Short Story Explication, 430

Walsh, R. J., International Medieval Bibliography, 1119

Walsh, S. P., General World Atlases in Print, 1201

Ward, A., Larousse Encyclopedia of Archaeology, 896

Ward, A. W., Cambridge Modern History, 1157

Ward, D. C., M. W. Wheeler, and R. A. Bier, Jr., Geologic Reference Sources, 1408, 1456n

Warrack, J., and H. Rosenthal, Concise Oxford Dictionary of Opera, 474

Washington Information Directory, 88

Washington Representatives, A. C. Close and C. Colgate, Jr., 1025

Wasserman, P., C. Georgi, and J. Woy, Encyclopedia of Business Information Sources, 920

Wasserman, P., and M. Kaszubski, Health Organizations of the United States, Canada, and the World, 1635

Wasserman, P., and J. O'Brien, Statistics Sources, 177

Wasserman, P., and G. Siegman, Awards, Honors, and Prizes, 109

Wathern, P., B. D. Clark, and R. Bisset, Environmental Impact Assessment, 1470

Watkins, M. M., Research Centers Directory, 1264

Watson, G., Concise Cambridge Bibliography of English Literature, 363n

Watson, G., New Cambridge Bibliography of English Literature, 329

Watt, A., Longman Illustrated Dictionary of Geology, 1420

Wauchope, R., Handbook of Middle American Indians, 909

Wearing, J. P., American and British Theatrical Biography, 644

Wearing, J. P., London Stage, 1890-1929, 665-67a

Weast, R. C., CRC Handbook of Chemistry and Physics, 1357, 1389

Weather Almanac, J. A. Ruffner and F. E. Bair, 1452

Weather Atlas of the United States, U.S. Environmental Data Service, 1458

Weather of U.S. Cities, 1454

Weber, J., W. L. Roberts, and G. R. Rapp, Jr., Encyclopedia of Minerals, 1450

Weber, O. S., and S. J. Calvert, Literary and Library Prizes, 389

Weber, R. D., Energy Information Guide, 1482

Webster, J. K., and M. T. Schenk, What Every Engineer Should Know about Engineering Information Resources, 1682

Webster, T., Microcomputer Buyer's Guide, 1677

Webster's Biographic Dictionary, 138

Webster's Geographical Dictionary, 1206

Webster's Guide to American History, 1172

Weekes, R. V., Muslim Peoples, 891

Weekly Record, 4

Weigert, A., and H. Zimmerman, Concise Encyclopedia of Astronomy, 1326

Weik, M. H., Communications Standard Dictionary, 1671

Weindling, P., and P. Corsi, Information Sources in the History of Science and Medicine, 1220

Weinstein, E., NVGA Bibliography of Current Career Information, 774

Weise, F. O., Health Statistics, 1613

Weiss, A. de la Vergne, and I. Weiss, Thesaurus of Book Digests, 1950-1980, 409

Weiss, I., and A. de la Vergne Weiss, Thesaurus of Book Digests, 1950-1980, 409

Wells, J. E., Manual of the Writings in Middle English, 1050-1500, 345n

Wendt, H., and B. Heberer, Grzimek's Encyclopedia of Evolution, 1537

Wer ist wer, 129

West, G. P., Black's Veterinary Dictionary, 1578

Westcott's Plant Disease Handbook, R. K. Horst, 1582

Wetterau, B., Macmillan Concise Dictionary of World History, 1122

Wexler, P., Information Resources in Toxicology, 1610

Whalon, M. K., Performing Arts Research, 576

What Every Engineer Should Know about Engineering Information Resources, M. T. Schenk and J. K. Webster, 1682

What Happened When, S. M. Mirkin, 1136

Wheeler, M. W., D. C. Ward, and R. A. Bier, Jr., Geologic Reference Sources, 1408 1456n

Where to Find Business Information, D. M. Brownstone and G. Carruth, p. 206

Whisker, J. B., Dictionary of Concepts on American Politics, 1009n

White, C. M., Sources of Information in the Social Sciences, 695; pp. xvi, 194, 255

White, O. R., Glossary of Behavioral Terminology, 792

Whitehouse, D., and R. Whitehouse, Archaeological Atlas of the World, 914

Whitehouse, R., and D. Whitehouse, Archaeological Atlas of the World, 914

Whitehouse, R. D., Facts on File Dictionary of Archaeology, 893

Whitehouse, R. D., Macmillan Dictionary of Archaeology, 893n

Whitfield, P., Macmillan Illustrated Animal Encyclopedia, 1529

Whitford, R. H., Physics Literature, 1337

Whiting, B. J., and A. Taylor, Dictionary of American Proverbs and Proverbial Phrases, 901

Whitten, P., and D. E. Hunter, Encyclopedia of Anthropology, 889

Whittow, J. B., Penguin Dictionary of Physical Geography, 1443

Who Offers Part-Time Degree Programs?, 735

Who Owns Whom, 950

Who Was Who, 148

Who Was Who in America, 146

Who Was Who in the Theatre, 1912-1976, 643

Who Was Who on the Screen, E. M. Truitt, 639

Who's Who, 127

Who's Who Biographical Record: Child Development Professionals, 755

Who's Who Biographical Record: School District Officials, 754

Who's Who in America, 120
Who's Who in American Art, 561
Who's Who in American Law, 1109
Who's Who in American Politics, 1013;
    p. 22
Who's Who in Art, 562
Who's Who in Economics, M. Blaug and P.
    Sturges, 979
Who's Who in Engineering, 1714
Who's Who in Europe, 133
Who's Who in Finance and Industry, 978
Who's Who in France, qui est qui en
    France, 128
Who's Who in Frontier Science and Tech-
    nology, 1272
Who's Who in Germany, 130
Who's Who in Government, 1014; p. 22
Who's Who in Health Care, 1644
Who's Who in Italy, 131
Who's Who in Library and Information
    Services, J. M. Lee, 756
Who's Who in Religion, 291
Who's Who in Rock Music, W. York, 501
Who's Who in Technology Today, B. A.
    Tinucci and L. Chaudier, 1715
Who's Who in the Arab World, 132
Who's Who in the Theatre, I. Herbert,
    C. Baxter, and R. E. Finley, 642
Who's Who in the World, 137
Who's Who in World Agriculture, 1586
Who's Who in World Jewry, I. J. C.
    Karpman, 293
Wilcox, L. D., Social Indicators and
    Societal Monitoring, 811n
Williams, E. N., Facts on File Dic-
    tionary of European History,
    1485-1789, 1126
Williams, J., and H. A. Ploski, Negro
    Almanac, 912
Williams, N., Chronology of the Expanding
    World, 1492 to 1762, 1141
Williams, N., Chronology of the Modern
    World, 1763 to 1965, 1142
Williams, T. I., Biographical Dictionary
    of Scientists, 1280
Williams, V. L., Dictionary of American
    Penology, 823
Willis, D. C., Horror and Science Fiction
    Films II, 658
Wilmeth, D. B., Language of American
    Popular Entertainment, 596
Wilson, B. L., and W. K. Wilson, Grant
    Information System Quarterly, 107n
Wilson, C. W. J., World Nuclear Directory,
    1499
Wilson, F. P., Oxford Dictionary of English
    Proverbs, 900

Wilson, F. P., and B. Dobrée, Oxford History
    of English Literature, 390
Wilson, J., Passionate Amateur's Guide to
    Archaeology in the United States, 917
Wilson, J. F., and T. P. Slavens, Research
    Guide to Religious Studies, 255
Wilson, M. J., and P. M. Miller, Dictionary
    of Social Science Methods, 702
Wilson, W. K., and B. L. Wilson, Grant
    Information System Quarterly, 107n
Wilson Authors Series, 394
Winburne, J. N., Dictionary of Agricultural
    and Allied Terminology, 1572
Winch, K. L., International Maps and Atlases
    in Print, 1186
Winick, C., Dictionary of Anthropology, 888
Winship, M., and V. L. Smyers, Bibliography
    of American Literature, 331n
Winterthur Museum Libraries, Collection of
    Printed Books and Periodicals, 525
Wiseberg, L. S., and H. M. Scoble, Human
    Rights Directory, 1050
Wiseberg, L. S., and H. M. Scoble, North
    American Human Rights Directory, 1049
Woellner, E. H., Requirements for Certifi-
    cation for Elementary Schools,
    Secondary Schools, Junior Colleges,
    770
Wolman, Y., Chemical Information, 1364
Women Helping Women, Women's Action
    Alliance, 835
Women in Public Office, Center for the
    American Woman in Politics, 1042
Women Studies Abstracts, 818
Wood, D., Trade Names Dictionary, 940
Wood, D. N., Use of Earth Sciences Literature,
    1409, 1456n
Woodburn, H. M., Using the Chemical
    Literature, 1365
Woodbury, M., Guide to Sources of Educa-
    tional Information, 707
Woodress, J. L., Dissertations in American
    Literature, 343
Wooten, D. C., and J. G. Rau, Environmental
    Impact Analysis Handbook, 1480
World Almanac and Book of Facts, 1029n;
    p. 45
World Atlas of Geomorphic Features, R. E.
    Snead, 1456
World Authors, 1950-1970, J. Wakeman, 394
World Authors, 1970-1975, J. Wakeman, 394
World Bibliography of Bibliographies, T.
    Besterman, 29, 216
World Chronology of Music History, P. E.
    Eisler, N. Hatch, and E. Eisler, 458
World Development Report, 962
World Dictionary of Awards and Prizes, 110

World Directory of Energy Information, Cambridge Information and Research Services, 1483

World Directory of Mathematicians, International Mathematical Union, 1312

World Directory of Mineral Collections, International Mineralogical Association, Commission on Museums, 1446

World Encyclopedia of Political Systems and Parties, G. E. Delury, 1076

World Encyclopedia of the Film, J. M. Smith and T. Cawkwell, 638

World Energy Book, D. Crabbe and R. McBride, 1504

World Energy Directory, J. A. Bauly and C. B. Bauly, 1498

World Environmental Directory, 1478

World Food Book, D. Crabbe and S. Lawson, 1584

World Guide to Higher Education, 723

World Guide to Scientific Associations and Learned Societies, B. Verrel and H. Opitz, 724

World History of the Dance, C. Sachs, 633

World Index of Scientific Translations, 1241n

World List of Scientific Periodicals Published in the Years 1900-1960, 1228

World Meetings: Outside United States and Canada, 1233

World Meetings: United States and Canada, 1232

World Nuclear Directory, C. W. J. Wilson, 1499

World of Learning, 104, 720

World Painting Index, P. Havlice, 569

World Palaeontological Collections, R. J. Cleevely, 1445

World Peace Foundation, Key to League of Nations Documents Placed on Public Sale, 1920-29, 82

World Philosophy, F. N. Magill and I. P. McGreal, 250

World Tables, International Bank for Reconstruction and Development, 973

World Transindex, 1241

World Weather Guide, E. A. Pearce and C. G. Smith, 1455

World Who's Who in Science, 1281

Worldmark Encyclopedia of the Nations, M. Y. Sachs, 1192

Wörterbuch der philosophischen Begriffe, R. Eisler, 244n

Worthing, C. R., and S. B. Walker, Pesticide Manual, 1583

Wortman, W. A., Guide to Serial Bibliographies for Modern Literatures, 341

Woy, J., P. Wasserman, and C. Georgi, Encyclopedia of Business Information Sources, 920

Wrathall, C. P., Computer Acronyms, Abbreviations, Etc., 1673

Wright, G. T., and L. Unger, American Writers, 399

Wright, J. K., and E. T. Platt, Aids to Geographical Research, 1179n

Wright, N. D., S. Herner, and G. P. Allen, Brief Guide to Sources of Scientific and Technical Information, 1216

Writers for Young Adults Biography Master Index, A. Sarkissian, 402

Writer's Market, J. Brady and P. J. Schemenaur, 376

Writings on American History, 1162

Wyatt, H. V., and R. T. Bottle, Use of Biological Literature, 1508

Wynar, B. S., Dictionary of American Library Biography, 758

Yates, B., How to Find Out about Physics, 1338

Yearbook of American and Canadian Churches, C. H. Jacquet, Jr., 286

Yearbook of Higher Education, 718

Yearbook of International Organizations, 103

Yearbook of International Trade Statistics, 974

Year's Work in English Studies, English Association, 359

Year's Work in Modern Language Studies, 361

Yesterday and Today, S. Hochman, 1167

York, W., Who's Who in Rock Music, 501

Young, M. W., Cities of the World, 1193

Young, R., Analytical Concordance to the Bible, 311n

Young, W. C., American Theatrical Arts, 592

Young, W. C., Famous Actors and Actresses on the American Stage, 645

Young, W. J., and D. J. Cuff, United States Energy Atlas, 1506

Yule, J.-D., Concise Encyclopedia of the Sciences, 1247

Zentralblatt für Mathematik und ihre Grenzgebiete, 1289

Zimmermann, H., and A. Weigert, Concise Encyclopedia of Astronomy, 1326

Zurcher, A. J., and E. C. Smith, Dictionary of American Politics, 1007

SUBJECT INDEX

Access is provided here to those subjects which the librarian may need for answering reference questions which are not readily identified through the table of contents. Most references are to entry number; a few references to page number are preceded by "p." or "pp."

Accountants, 938, 956
Acronyms, 1253, 1625, 1672-73
Actors and actresses, 598-601, 605, 610, 612-21, 634-45
Aerospace engineering, 1689-90, 1699
Agricultural economics, 955
Agricultural researchers, 1586
Agriculture, 1213, 1515, 1561-62, 1564-65, 1568-74
Alcoholism and drug abuse, 840
Animals. See Zoology
Anonyms, 357
Anthropologists, 703, 706; p. 204
Applied mathematics. See Mathematics, applied
Archaeology, 877, 892-97, 914-17
Architects, 564-67
Architecture, 515, 519, 529, 534-38
Architecture, history of, 552-53
Archives, 397, 530, 1133
Art, history of, 510, 550-51
Artists, 554-63
Associations, publications of, 31; pp. 16-17
Astronomers, 1358
Astronomical catalogs, 1317
Astronomy, 1252, 1313-16, 1318-28, 1332-35, 1339-41, 1354
Astrophysics, 1314, 1316, 1319, 1329-31

Atlases
    astronomical, 1335
    Bible, 316-18
    economic, 975-77
    energy, 1504, 1506
    food, 1584
    geographical, 1200-1204
    geomorphological, 1456
    historical, 1146-50, 1175-76
    oceanographic, 1457
    weather, 1458
Atmospheric sciences. See Metereology
Atomic energy, 1489, 1499
Audiovisual materials, 1598
Authors, 392-404
Awards and prizes, 109-10, 389, 545, 610, 615-18, 622-23

Ballet, 602-4, 624
BALLOTS, p. 12
Banking, 936-37
Bibliographic instruction
    bibliographies, 189-90
    guidelines, p. 54
    handbooks, 193-95
    materials, p. 53
    methods, pp. 52-53

Bibliographic instruction (*continued*)
  periodicals, 191-92
  textbooks, 196-99
Bibliographic Retrieval Services. *See* BRS
Bibliographic utilities, pp. 11-12, p. 14, p.
  57
Biochemistry, 1547-48, 1558
Bioethics, 1615-16, 1631
Biographical dictionaries, credibility of,
  pp. 43-44
Biologists, 1560
Biology, 1508-11, 1513-19, 1522-27, 1549-50,
  1555, 1561, 1570
Biotechnology, 1512, 1551, 1559
Blacks, 806, 808-9, 911-12
Botany, 1532-35. *See also* Horticulture
BRS, 209, 211-12; p. 57
Buddhism, 254, 257
Business executives, 706, 946, 978
Business law, 939

Career counseling, 771-75
Certification of teachers, librarians, school
  administrators, 770
Characters, fictional, 382-83, 611
Chemical engineering, 1366, 1382-87, 1400-1402
Chemical engineers, 1403, 1405-7
Chemical names, 1375, 1394-95
Chemical technology. *See* Chemical
  engineering
Chemicals, 1388, 1392
  hazards of, 1399
Chemistry, 1218, 1252, 1268, 1359-65,
  1367-81, 1389-91, 1396
Chemists, 1403-4, 1406-7
Child development professionals, 755
Cheoreographers, 610
Chronologies, 1137-42
Cinema. *See* Film
Cities, 1193
Civic centers, 607
Civil engineering, 1692, 1709
Classification of organisms, 1553-54
Climatology. *See* Meteorology
Commodities, 963, 974
Composers, 450-53, 460-66, 610
Computer science, 1647-65, 1673, 1679
Computer searching. *See* Online searching
Conference proceedings, 32-39, 225-26,
  704-5, 1234-36
Conferences. *See* Scientific meetings
Congress, members of, 1017-18, 1023-24,
  1026
Conservation, 1477
Consumer health information, 1591
Correspondence schools, 716, 734
Crime, 825, 852-53

Cultural exchange, 781
Current awareness, 1288, 1341-42, 1368-69,
  1416, 1468, 1517, 1570, 1594, 1655,
  1688, 1694; p. 262

Dance, 603-4
Dance, history of, 632-33
Dancers, 610, 646
Data books. *See* Handbooks
Data processing. *See* Computer science
Database searching. *See* Online searching
Databases, 115, 206, 213; pp. 57-59
Decorative arts, 516, 539, 549
Demography. *See* Population
Dentistry, 1606, 1628. *See also* Health
  sciences
Dentists, 1643
Design, 539
DIALOG, 209-12; p. 57
DIALOG Information Services. *See* DIALOG
Dinosaurs, 1439
Discoveries, 1259
Dissertations
  English and American literature, 342-43
  indexes, 40-46
Drugs. *See* Pharmacy

Earth sciences, 1408-9, 1411, 1415-16, 1421-24,
  1437
Ecology, 1536, 1538-39
Economic indicators, 969
Economists, 706, 979-80
Education associations, 715
Educational tests. *See* Tests
Elections, 1043-46, 1052-53
Electrical engineering, 1693-94,
  1700, 1710
Electronic engineering, 1352, 1659, 1665, 1693-
  94, 1700, 1711
Energy, 1482-88, 1491-97, 1502-6
Energy researchers, 1507
Engineering, 1210-17, 1222, 1225-27,
  1242-46, 1249, 1268, 1680-82, 1686-88,
  1695-98, 1704-7
Engineers, 1713-15. *See also* Scientists
Environmental impact assessment, 1467, 1470,
  1476, 1480-81
Environmental sciences, 1428, 1461-64, 1466,
  1468-69, 1471-74, 1478-79
Ephemeral publications, pp. 16-17
Eponyms, scientific. *See* Scientific eponyms
Ethics. *See* Bioethics
Ethnic groups, 806-9, 826
Ethnography, 870-73, 904-10
Ethology, 1540-41
Evolution, 1537, 1539

Federal regulations, 1100-1106
Fellowships. *See* Scholarships
Festivals, 609
Fictional characters. *See* Characters, fictional
Fictional places. *See* Places, fictional
Film, 579-87, 597-99, 612-18, 647-59; pp. 139-40
Finance, 936-37, 958, 972
Folklore, 881-87, 898-901
Folksong, 496, 502, 505-7, 882-84
Food, 1562, 1566, 1574, 1577, 1581, 1584
Foreign language reference books, use of, pp. 7-8
Foreign relations, 1060-66
Formularies, 1396
Fossils. *See* Paleontology
Fugitive publications. *See* Ephermal publications

Gazetteers, 1205-7
Genetics, 1545-46, 1556
Geochemistry, 1428
Geographers, 1208-9
Geologists, 1459-60
Geology, 1410, 1417-20, 1432, 1434, 1436. *See also* Earth sciences
Geology, history of, 1460
Geomorphology, 1427, 1456
Government finance, 992-96
Government officials, 1014, 1030-31
Government publications, 57-68, 1217
Governors, 1037-38
Graduate schools, 736
  ratings of, 760-61
Grants. *See* Research grants

Handbooks, 1218, 1265-66
Handicapped, 837-39
Health organizations, 1632-35
Health sciences, 1587-88, 1590, 1595-99, 1601.
  See also Dentistry; Medicine; Nursing; Pharmacy; Psychiatry
Hinduism, 254, 258, 281-82
Historians, 228, 703, 1159
Historical societies, 1134
Horticulture, 1575-76, 1580
Hospitals, 1607, 1636
Human rights, 1048-50

Illustrations
  of living things, 1520-21
Immigration, 806-9, 826
Indians, American, 874-76, 883, 890, 907-10

Industrial chemistry. *See* Chemical engineering
Industrial engineering, 1701, 1712
Industry, 924, 927-29, 981-82
Information centers, 111-17, 1444, 1552
Information technology, 1666-68, 1672
Inventions, 1259
Investment, 958, 987-91
Islam, 254, 259, 280

Jazz, 490, 492-95
Journals. *See* Scientific serials
Judaism, 254, 276-77

Labor, 935, 954, 959-60
Laboratories. *See* Research centers
Lakes, 1194
Law, 939, 1085-96, 1109
Lawyers, 228, 1096, 1109
League of Nations documents, 81-83
Learned societies, 720, 724
Librarians, 756, 758
Libraries, 111-14, 720
Library catalogs, 1-2, 12-15, 30, 441-43, 519-25, 530, 864, 884, 1568-69, 1597
Library instruction. *See* Bibliographic instruction
Life sciences. *See* Biology
Linguistics, 878-80
Literacy, 747
Literature, history of, 390-91
Location of reference service, p. 6

Machine searching. *See* Online searching
Management, 933-34
Manufacturers, 951-52
Manuscripts, 362-63, 397, 530, 592, 1133
Maps, p. 314. *See also* Atlases
Marketing guides, 964-65
Materials, 1393, 1698
  hazards of, 1398
Mathematicians, 1311-12
Mathematics, 1283-89, 1292-94, 1296, 1298-99, 1303-5
Mathematics, applied, 1295, 1297, 1306-8
Mathematics, history of, 1291
Mechanical engineering, 1691, 1708
Medical education, 1614
Medical organizations. *See* Health organizations
Medicine, 1589, 1592-94, 1600, 1619-26, 1630, 1639. *See also* Health sciences
Medicine, history of, 1219-20, 1617-18
Meetings. *See* Scientific meetings

Meteorology, 1322, 1412, 1426, 1440,
    1451-55, 1458
Microbiology, 1543, 1557
Microcomputing, 1660, 1674-75, 1677
Microscopy, 1542
Mineralogy, 1413, 1429, 1442, 1446-47, 1450
Minorities, 806-9, 826, 833-34
Molecular biology, 1544, 1558
Moving pictures. *See* Film
Municipal government, 96, 1039-41
Museums, 543-44
Music, history of, 457-59
Musical film, 599
Musical theater, 605, 661-62
Musicians, 450-53, 460-66

National Agricultural Library, 1564, 1568-69
National Library of Medicine, 1592, 1597-
    1600, 1604, 1606-7, 1616-17; p. 343
Nicknames, geographical, 1197-98
Nuclear energy. *See* Atomic energy
Nursing, 1602-5, 1626-27, 1630, 1640. *See also*
    Health sciences
Nutrition, 1567, 1574, 1581

Oceanography, 1414, 1425, 1435, 1440-41,
    1457
OCLC, pp. 11-12, p. 14, p. 57
Online Computer Library Center (OCLC).
    See OCLC
Online searching
    bibliographies, 200-202
    dictionary, 202
    management, p. 60
    periodicals, 203-5
    reference use, p. 58
    search strategy, 213-14; p. 59
    textbooks, 207-12
Opera, 473-79
ORBIT, 209, 211-12; p. 57
Organization of reference service, pp. 6-7

Paleontology, 1431, 1438-39, 1445, 1448
Party platforms, 1045-46
Patents, 1683-84; p. 362
Penology. *See* Crime
Periodicals. *See* Scientific serials
Personal computing. *See* Microcomputing
Personnel management, 935
Pesticides, 1583
Pharmacy, 1608-9. *See also* Health sciences
Philosophers, 228, 245-46, 248-49
Philosophy, history of, 252-53
Physical geography, 1443

Physicians, 1641-42, 1644-46
Physicists, 1358
Physics, 1218, 1252, 1268, 1336-57. *See also*
    Astrophysics
Places, fictional, 388
Plant diseases, 1582
Plants. *See* Botany
Plot summaries, 405-12
Poetry, 348-52, 372
Political parties, 1043-47, 1076-78
Political scientists, 706-1013, 1015-16
Pollution, 1465, 1475
Popular culture, 913
Population, 819, 847-50
Primary sources, p. 261
Prisons, 823
Private schools, 739-42
Prizes. *See* Awards and prizes
Probability. *See* Statistical sciences
Proceedings of conferences. *See*
    Conference proceedings
Professors, 228, 706
Programs, radio and television, 677-83
Proverbs, 900-901
Pseudonyms, 357, 404
Psychiatry, 1611, 1629. *See also*
    Health sciences
Psychological tests. *See* Tests
Psychologists, 706, 800
Public opinion polls, 856-61, 1054-59
Publishers, 118

Radio, 593-94, 677; pp. 139-40
Ready reference, p. 7, p. 58
Recordings and tapes, 480-89
Reference collection, p. 4
Reference needs of users, pp. 4-5,
    p. 7
Reference staff, p. 4
Reference users, pp. 4-5
Rehabilitation, 817, 1612
Religion, history of, 264, 267
Religious denominations, history
    of, 298-99
Religious leaders, 270-71, 274-76, 280,
    291-95
Report series codes, 1254
Reports. *See* Research reports
Reproductions
    paintings, 568-74
    sculpture, 574-75
Research centers, 1262-64, 1498-1501, 1579,
    1637-38, 1703
Research grants, 106-8, 227, 545
Research Libraries Information Network (RLIN).
    See RLIN

Research reports, 1225, 1469, 1487, 1690.
        See also Report series codes
Review articles. *See* Scientific reviews
Reviews
    books, 178-87
    films, 684-89, 692-93
    plays, 684-85, 690-92, 694
Rivers, 1194
RLIN, p. 11, p. 14, p. 57
Rocks, 1447, 1449

Safety, 1267, 1397
Saints' lives, 296-97
Scholarships, 767-69
School administrators, 754
School systems, 715-16
Science, 1210-17, 1221-28, 1242-51
Science, history of, 1219-20, 1229-30,
        1260
Scientific associations, 720, 724, 1702
Scientific directories, 1261
Scientific discoveries. *See* Discoveries
Scientific eponyms, 1258
Scientific meetings, 1231-33
Scientific reviews, 1224
Scientific serials, 1226, 1228, 1237-38,
        1370, 1518, 1571, 1596, 1599-1600,
        1651, 1656, 1695
Scientific units. *See* Units of measurement
Scientists, 1269-82
SDC, p. 57. *See also* ORBIT
SDC Information Services. *See* SDC
Secondary sources, p. 261
Sedimentology, 1430
Senators, 1017-18, 1023-24, 1026
Senior citizens, 836
Serials. *See* Scientific serials
Short stories, 353-55, 373
Social indicators, 811, 846
Social services, 827-43
Sociologists and social workers, 703, 706,
        824, 862-63
Software, 1676
Soil science, 1433
Song writers, 462, 490, 502
Space science. *See* Astronomy
Standards, 1685; pp. 362-63
Stars. *See* Astronomy
State government, 91-94, 1035-38
State government officials, 91-94
State publications, 69-71
Statistical sciences, 1290, 1300-1302, 1309-10
Statistics
    business, 964-68
    church membership, 285-86
    commodities, 963, 974

economic, 969-74
educational, 743-47
energy, 1490, 1504
film industry, 616, 618
financial, 969-73
food, 1584
health, 1613
historical, 168, 172, 1151-53, 1177
housing, 845-46, 851
labor, 971
labor union membership, 954, 959
social, 845-54
television industry, 628-30
theater, 610, 621, 663-67a
voting, 1052-53
Supreme Court justices, 1034
Symbols in art, 540

Taxes, 995-96
Teachers, 757
Technical reports. *See* Research reports
Technology. *See* Engineering
Technology, history of, 1219
Telecommunications, 1657, 1669-71, 1678; p. 57
Telephone directories, 95; p. 35
Television, 593-94, 606, 628-30, 678-83; pp.
        139-40
Tests, 762-66
Theater, 588-92, 600-601, 619-23, 625-27, 660-
        70; pp. 139-40
Theater, history of, 63
Theaters, 607, 621
Thematic dictionaries (music), 470-72
Third World, 1081-82
Toxicology, 1610
Trade names, 940, 951, 1394-95
Translations, 1237-41
Treaties, 1067-70

United Nations documents, 74-80
United States Congress, 86-87, 1017-26
United States executive branch, 88-90,
        1027-31
United States government offices, 85-90
United States Supreme Court, 1033-34
Units of measurement, 1255-57
User education. *See* Bibliographic instruction

Veterinarians, 1586
Veterinary medicine, 1563, 1578, 1585
Vocational counseling, 771-75
Vocational tests. *See* Tests

Weather. *See* Meteorology
Weeding, p. 7
Western Library Network (WLN). *See* WLN
Wilsonline, p. 57
WLN, p. 11
Women studies, 806, 818, 835, 1042

Zoology, 1528-31

123350